THE GNOSTIC SCRIPTURES

THE ANCHOR BIBLE REFERENCE LIBRARY is designed to be a third major component of the Anchor Bible group, which includes the Anchor Bible commentaries on the books of the Old Testament, the New Testament, and the Apocrypha, and the Anchor Bible Dictionary. While the Anchor Bible commentaries and the Anchor Bible Dictionary are structurally defined by their subject matter, the Anchor Bible Reference Library will serve as a supplement on the cutting edge of the most recent scholarship. The series is open-ended; its scope and reach are nothing less than the biblical world in its totality, and its methods and techniques the most up-to-date available or devisable. Separate volumes will deal with one or more of the following topics relating to the Bible: anthropology, archaeology, ecology, economy, geography, history, languages and literatures, philosophy, religion(s), theology.

As with the Anchor Bible commentaries and the Anchor Bible Dictionary, the philosophy underlying the Anchor Bible Reference Library finds expression in the following: the approach is scholarly, the perspective is balanced and fair-minded, the methods are scientific, and the goal is to inform and enlighten. Contributors are chosen on the basis of their scholarly skills and achievements, and they come from a variety of religious backgrounds and communities. The books in the Anchor Bible Reference Library are intended for the broadest possible readership, ranging from world-class scholars, whose qualifications match those of the authors, to general readers, who may not have special training or skill in studying the Bible but are as enthusiastic as any dedicated professional in expanding their knowledge of the Bible and its world.

David Noel Freedman
GENERAL EDITOR

THE ANCHOR BIBLE REFERENCE LIBRARY

THE GNOSTIC
SCRIPTURES

A NEW TRANSLATION
WITH ANNOTATIONS
AND INTRODUCTIONS
BY

BENTLEY LAYTON

DOUBLEDAY

NEW YORK   LONDON   TORONTO   SYDNEY   AUCKLAND

THE ANCHOR BIBLE REFERENCE LIBRARY

PUBLISHED BY DOUBLEDAY
a division of Bantam Doubleday Dell Publishing Group, Inc.
1540 Broadway, New York, New York 10036

THE ANCHOR BIBLE REFERENCE LIBRARY, DOUBLEDAY, and the portrayal
of an anchor with the letters ABRL are trademarks of Doubleday, a division of
Bantam Doubleday Dell Publishing Group, Inc.

The Gnostic Scriptures was originally published by Doubleday in 1987.
This edition published by arrangement with Doubleday.

ISBN 0-385-47843-7

First Paperback Edition: August 1995

1 3 5 7 9 10 8 6 4 2

To
Scott Maloney

CONTENTS

THE GNOSTIC SCRIPTURES

I

CLASSIC GNOSTIC SCRIPTURE

II

THE WRITINGS OF VALENTINUS

III
THE SCHOOL OF VALENTINUS

Related Writings

IV
THE SCHOOL OF ST. THOMAS

V
OTHER EARLY CURRENTS

CONTENTS

PREFACE

In this book I have tried to make a readable, coherent collection of the scriptures of ancient gnostic religion and its relatives. The works in this collection are heretical—a heretical counterpart of the holy scripture of Christianity and Judaism (which gnostics also read). But despite their highly unorthodox character these works shed great light on the theology, atmosphere, and literary traditions of ancient Christianity and Hellenistic Judaism. The gnostic movement did not simply share in the culture to which early Christianity belonged. Gnostics in fact made up one of the earliest and most long-lived branches of the ancient Christian religion, as Map 2 makes abundantly clear; it was only after centuries of struggle that they could be eradicated by the established church. After the official Christianization of the late Roman empire (A.D. 313–81), theological objections to the gnostic scriptures were given the force of law, and most copies of these scriptures were banned and eventually perished. By a lucky accident of preservation and the careful efforts of modern scholars, the gnostic scriptures have now begun to be known again.

Orthodox Christian doctrine of the ancient world—and thus of the modern church—was partly conceived of as being what gnostic scripture was *not*. For this reason, a knowledge of gnostic scripture is indispensable for anyone who hopes to understand the historical roots of Christian theology and belief. Moreover, the gnostic myth grew up in an intimate dialogue—though often a hostile one—with Jewish learning of the Greek-speaking synagogue. Thus the gnostic scriptures cannot fail to increase, however obliquely, our knowledge of the foundations of classical Judaism.

Gnostics did not have a fixed bible, as church and synagogue do today: the selection of what to include in this book has had to be my own, based on principles set forth in the "General Introduction" that follows. Accordingly, a number of works sometimes labeled "gnostic," though only in a vague and looser sense, have been deliberately omitted.

All English translations in this book are my own, made from revised editions of the original texts. My aim has been to translate all important terms in a similar way, so that readers can confidently compare the wording of one work with another. I have also tried, so far as possible, to avoid theological jargon or mere transcription of Greek terms in these translations. Except for a few deliberate obscurities, gnostic scripture was coherent in antiquity; there is no reason why it should not be so today.

At the publisher's suggestion I have written this book for the general public as well as students and scholars, without the usual network of references to primary and secondary sources. Instead, the annotations are simply meant to help the reader understand the immediate sense of the text; such annotations are especially needed with gnostic literature. Although they lay a foundation for close study of the text, these annotations do not try to decide what gnostic scripture ultimately meant: readers must make that important decision for themselves.

The historical introductions to the five parts of this book and the introductions to individual works are meant to help interpreters, but not to impose any particular theological or philosophical point of view. Interpreters will also find help in the many select bibliographies, scattered throughout the book, which list scholarly studies that are accessible, broadly relevant, and sound in their manner of approach. But the general reader and the student must be cautioned that in a field as controversial as this one, where much of the evidence was published only in recent years, there are no standard or accepted lines of interpretation.

In particular, three famous questions about the works translated in this book still remain to be answered: (1) In which religious milieu (Jewish? Christian? other?) was classic gnostic myth and religion born? (2) Did such a thing as the gnostic myth exist in the day of St. Paul or St. John, and if so can it be seen reflected in their writings? (3) In what sense is a historian justified in speaking of a general pattern, whether psychological or philosophical, called gnostic*ism*? These ultimate questions have troubled scholarship for more than two hundred years. Because the third question has never gotten a satisfactory answer I prefer *not* to start from a philosophical description of something called "gnosticism." Rather, I begin my exploration of this theme concretely, with the first coherent sect that actually called itself "gnostic," then trace its historical and ideological evolution into a later form. I believe that this essentially historical method of description takes the reader to the real heart of the gnostic phenomenon and that it sheds considerable light on the broader concepts of "gnosticism," "gnostic religion," and *"gnōsis."*

ACKNOWLEDGMENTS

Because this book contains no footnote references to the scholarly literature, I must emphasize my great indebtedness to the colleagues and predecessors who laid its foundations by their own research. Most are mentioned by name in one or another of the select bibliographies, but their contribution to my understanding of the gnostic scriptures goes beyond the books and articles listed there. When biblical texts are quoted in the ancient scriptures in this book, I have conformed my translation to the Revised Standard Version insofar as the context allows. The fundamental historical thesis of this book—that Valentinus was a Christian reformer of the classic gnostic tradition—was enunciated sketchily in antiquity by St. Irenaeus (about A.D. 180) and in the twentieth century by Gilles Quispel and others; it was the organizing principle of an International Conference on Gnosticism, at Yale University, which I directed in 1978. The coherence and identity of the classic gnostic sect are defended in essays by Hans-Martin Schenke, which should be read in combination with a recent article by Morton Smith. I have also been inspired by a Yale Ph.D. dissertation by Anne McGuire, in which these issues were explored in considerable detail.

My firsthand study of the ancient Coptic manuscripts was made possible by the generosity and cooperation of Egyptian and American colleagues over the seven years that I was able to work in Cairo. James M. Robinson and other members of the Institute for Antiquity and Christianity, H.-M. Schenke, and the Berlin (GDR) *Arbeitskreis* were always generous with information, support, and prepublication copies. Stephen Emmel cast a careful eye over all the material translated from Coptic and saved me from many slips. Professors Jonas Greenfield, Wayne A. Meeks, Hans-Martin Schenke, Mark Smith, and John Strugnell preserved me from error or ignorance at many points, as did Martin Bloomer and Alan Scott; various other friends have also made valuable suggestions here and there. Jane Greenfield gave me advice on the graphic planning of the illustrations. The extremely useful indexes to this book are the work of David Dawson. The maps were compiled and designed by myself and then drafted by Mr. Rafael D. Palacios. John A. Miles, Jr., formerly of Doubleday, is responsible for the original concept of the book; my New York editors, Theresa D'Orsogna, Viera Morse, and Glenn Rounds, have also contributed style and learning to this work. To all these people I express sincere gratitude.

Finally, it was the persistence of my students—including beginners without a specialist's training—that led me to see how gnostic scripture is in its own way coherent, beautiful, and possessed of an extraordinary kind of sense. May this book repay the debt I owe to them.

GENERAL INTRODUCTION

THE CONTENTS OF THIS COLLECTION

Five collections of scripture are included in this book: the classic gnostic (Sethian) scripture, the writings of Valentinus, the works by his followers, the scripture of the school of St. Thomas, and a selection of other, related writings. Each collection is preceded by a historical introduction that explains the circumstances of its composition and the nature of its contents. So far as possible, complete works have been chosen for inclusion. They are supplemented, where necessary, by fragments and summaries of important lost works, preserved for us by one or another writer of antiquity.

Part One is classic gnostic scripture, authoritative works read by an ancient group that called themselves "gnostics"—"people fit to have acquaintance (*gnōsis*) with god." The name "gnostic" most properly applies to members of this group. In modern scholarship they are sometimes called "Sethians," "Barbeloites," "Barbelognostics," "Ophians," or "Ophites." Most of their scripture comes down to us in an obviously Christian or Christianized form. The received Christian form is what is translated here. Some scholars consider the Christian elements to be foreign to the original text.

Part Two consists of writings by Valentinus (A.D. ca. 100–ca. 175), the great Christian reformer of gnostic theology. *The Gospel of Truth* is included here, and its attribution to Valentinus is accepted, following B. Standaert. Valentinus revised classic gnostic tradition in the light of another, quite different form of Christianity (represented in Part Four, The School of St. Thomas), consciously adopting some of the language of the New Testament and stamping the result with his own rhetorical genius (see Table 1).

Part Three illustrates at some length the various kinds of literature written by the followers of Valentinus. It is not feasible in a book such as this to make a complete survey of the Valentinian school in its Eastern and Western branches, since much of the evidence consists of fragments or excerpts whose significance is best conveyed by a detailed discussion of the original Greek. Instead, complete works (in one case a long ancient summary) have been selected, to demonstrate the brilliance of Valentinian scholasticism and the character of Valentinian Christianity. The select bibliographies in Part Three provide the means for interested readers to pursue the history of Valentinian theology in even greater detail.

Part Four presents traditional Christian scripture from Northern Meso-

Table 1

Historical Relationships of the Writings in This Book

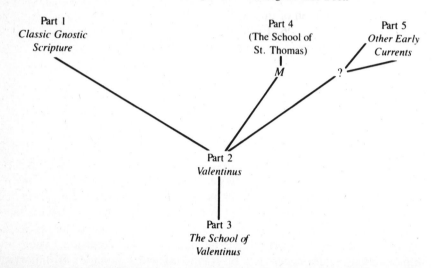

NOTE: *M* = the doctrine of mystical salvation through acquaintance with the self and Jesus, now exemplified by the Thomas Scripture and probably known to Valentinus by reading works of that school.

potamia, whose patron saint was St. Thomas (Didymus Jude Thomas). Despite their Mesopotamian origin, the works included here enjoyed a wide international circulation in several languages, starting in the second century A.D. In itself the Thomas scripture shows no influence of the gnostic sect. But it expresses a mystical concept of salvation through self-acquaintance, which is identical with one of the main Christian components in Valentinus's revisionism. In modern discussion, this mystical component seems to be what some scholars mean by "gnostic*ism*"; but in any case it has no direct connection with the gnostics of Part One. *The Hymn of the Pearl* has been included in this part because it comes down to us as part of the Thomas scripture and because its story and language correspond to the myth presupposed by *The Gospel According to Thomas* and *The Book of Thomas*.

Part Five illustrates two other early currents that probably had an influence on the young Valentinus: the system of Basilides (according to St. Irenaeus's summary) and the Hermetic writings, a non-Christian esoteric philosophy somewhat resembling gnostic myth and imagery. Unlike the Hermetic writings, Basilides' Christian philosophy is very different from the other scripture translated in this book; its historical relevance lies in a very shadowy connection with Valentinus. It was during his education in Alexandria, A.D. ca. 120, that Valentinus could have encountered these two currents. Further components of his education, including the exegesis of the Jewish Platonist Philo Judaeus and other aspects of Middle Platonic philosophy, are referred to in the appropriate bibliographies.

The five parts thus fit together in a hypothetical family tree (see Table 1) whose focal point is the great reformer Valentinus.

GNOSTIC SCRIPTURE AND THE CHRISTIAN BIBLE

One of the major watersheds in the vast terrain of ancient Christian history is the accession of the pro-Christian emperor Constantine the Great to the throne in A.D. 306. From this time on, Christianity was more and more clearly adopted as the religion of the Roman imperial government. In the course of these events the idea and reality of a single, unified, and orthodox church gradually became more established. But in the three centuries before the reign of Constantine it is harder to find anything resembling one mainstream church or one central tradition: instead of a mainstream one finds many tributaries.

The scriptures translated in this book were written before the time of Constantine or the establishment of an orthodox Christianity. Thus in order to understand their original place in the ancient churches we must begin by putting ourselves back into Christianity of the second and third centuries A.D., without the illumination of orthodox hindsight. Our exploration can usefully begin with the concept of "scripture."

Scripture, canon, and diversity

Scripture ("writing")—in the general sense of the word—means a body of written religious literature that members of a religion or group consider authoritative in matters such as belief, conduct, rhetoric, or the running of practical affairs. Scripture often contains a system of symbols within which readers can orient themselves and make sense of their relationship to the world, the divine, and other people. Such a system is sometimes expressed in story form and is then technically called *myth*. Sometimes it also tells where the religion and its members came from and explains why they are distinct and special.

When Christianity was born it had little or no scripture that was uniquely its own. The new religion was an offshoot of the Judaism of its day, and many of the earliest Christians had once been Jews. Like Jesus, they read, accepted, and interpreted scriptural works of Judaism—books of the Jewish Bible, which they would later come to call "the Old Testament," along with various other books.[1] But after Jesus' death and with the beginning of faith in his resurrection, Christians changed the way in which they read those books, now interpreting them in particularly Christian ways to bring out the meaning of Jesus' coming and death.

Early Christians lived in urban, and sometimes economically comfortable, settings; a proportionally high number of them must have been able to read and write. Thus small collections of Christian writings quickly accumulated in one place or another; and it was in these writings that the inspired insights of interpreters and leaders of the religion were often set forth. These works

---

[1] Some of these "other" books are readily available in *The Old Testament Pseudepigrapha* (2 vols.; J. H. Charlesworth, ed.; Garden City, N.Y.: Doubleday & Company, 1983–85). Still others can be found in *The Dead Sea Scrolls in English* (G. Vermes, ed.; Harmondsworth, Middlesex, England: Penguin Books, 1963).

served many different purposes and so were written in many literary forms, appropriate to their functions within the churches that used them.

A vast quantity of this early Christian "scripture" (in the general sense) from the first, second, and third centuries still survives today, though sometimes only in fragmentary form—not only the twenty-seven books of the New Testament but many other books as well: epistles, wisdom books, revelations, biographies and journey literature, accounts of Jesus' passion, rules for Christian congregational life, polemics, and theological treatises.

When a group of early Christians agreed in recognizing the presence of inspired authority in a particular writing or collection of writings, the work in question effectively rose to the status of scripture, sometimes equaling or even surpassing the authority of Jewish scripture. In some cases works written for very specific purposes—e.g. St. Paul's letter to Philemon about a runaway slave—later acquired scriptural status. In other cases, new books were deliberately composed as scripture. In a few instances these works were even meant to attack or replace parts of the already accepted body of scripture ("It is not . . . as Moses wrote . . ." says the author of the gnostic *Secret Book According to John,* 22:22f).

Early Christian scriptures, then, sometimes presented messages or points of view that conflicted with one another. This is not surprising, for in the first three centuries there was only sporadic coordination among the various Christian groups and certainly no centralized uniformity. It was therefore only natural that in one group a particular book might be shown the respect due authoritative scripture, while another group elsewhere might accept it with less respect or even reject it.

In fact, the lack of uniformity in ancient Christian scripture during the early period is very striking, and it points to a substantial diversity within the early Christian religion, probably going back to a time just after Jesus' death in about the year 30. Although it is historically correct to speak of early Christianity as one religion, it can also be described as a complex network of individual parties, groups, sects, or denominations. To some extent the diversity of scripture resulted from accidental differences in cultural, social, and linguistic milieus—between, say, the usual forms of religious expression in Mesopotamia and those in the city of Rome. It also came from the coexistence of essentially different theological opinions and traditions about the significance of Jesus, some of which seem to be as old as Christianity itself—traditions about Jesus as miracle worker, wisdom incarnate, revealer, Messiah of Israel, prophet, emanation from another world, etc. Furthermore, it reflected the different philosophies and symbolic systems on which the writers might base their religious thought (Platonism, Jewish apocalyptic, etc.). In the range of possibilities that ancient Christian theologians actually hit upon, some of the results will now seem familiar to the modern reader, while others seem bizarre.

Gnostic scripture belongs to this second category, the bizarre. Most readers will find it takes them into a breathtaking world of fantastic symbols, beautifully intricate myths, weird heavenly denizens, and extraordinary poetry—a world that resembles neither modern Christianity and Judaism nor today's secular culture. Of course, the unfamiliarity of the gnostic world is partly a function of our distance from all the conventions of ancient literature. But even more it is due to the audacity of ancient gnostic theologians, who attempted nothing less than to chart the whole mind of god (see Fig. 1, pp. 12–13) and from that chart to show the origin both of the world's beauty and of its imperfection. The unfamiliarity is due also to the ambitious mystical agenda that gnostic writers, and especially Valentinians, set for themselves: about this, more is said below.

Finally, gnostic scripture now seems strange because it rebels against important beliefs shared by many early Christians and their Jewish predecessors, beliefs which even now belong to the core of ordinary Western Judaism and Christianity—especially belief in the goodness and omnipotence of the Creator: gnostics believed that Satan made the world. From the ordinary modern perspective, then, gnostic scripture may seem both Christian and anti-Christian, both Jewish and anti-Jewish: the strength of this paradoxical ambiguity eventually made it the classic example of heretical scripture.

The diversity of ancient Christian scripture, then, covered a very broad spectrum, which included the Christian works translated in this book; the viewpoints it expressed were often in conflict with one another. Because a person could travel quickly and easily along the major international roads and sea lanes of the Roman empire, Christians in one city or social setting could quickly learn of Christians elsewhere who held quite different views. As Christian scripture of diverse kinds circulated throughout the empire, it multiplied the options open to those who could read or listen and gave rise to tensions as very different groups began to communicate. This is confirmed by all that historians can learn about the ancient spread of Christian literature, the places where manuscripts have been found, and the languages into which scriptures were eventually translated.

Some Christian leaders therefore began to shield the members of their groups from exposure to unwelcome outside ideas and literature by drawing up authoritative lists of the scriptural books that should be accepted and those that should be rejected. The original motivation for such lists had been constructively theological. But an important implication of their formal acceptance was that nothing else should be added, at least to the collection of works with full scriptural authority. Thus *a closed list of fully authoritative scripture* could also be a powerful weapon in the conflict between rival factions within early Christianity. It should be noted that a great many works of Christian scripture ended up in a third category—neither authoritative nor rejected, but merely edifying. Today the neutral term "early Christian literature" is often applied to such edifying works.

In modern parlance, a list of the fully authoritative scripture read by a particular group or religion is called its *canon* ("yardstick") of scripture. Modern Roman Catholic and Protestant churches, for example, officially accept the books of the Old Testament, taken from Judaism, and twenty-seven books of Christian scripture (the New Testament) as their canon of scripture. Although there is still no full agreement on the exact contents (Catholics and Protestants politely disagree over some fifteen books and parts of books in the Old Testament), the outlines of the main modern

Western Christian canon were already being drawn in at least some churches by the end of the second century. From today's vantage point, such churches of the second century can be seen as *proto-orthodox* (anticipating later orthodoxy) in their canon of scripture.

It is hard to know what number of second- and third-century Christian congregations shared in this proto-orthodoxy, but probably not very many (the evidence is slim; the canons of a few individual churches can be pieced together from circumstantial evidence and passing remarks). If a traveler had set out to visit Christian churches throughout the Roman empire in A.D. 200 or thereabouts, he or she would have been struck mainly by the great variety of canons then in use—some quite self-conscious; others informal, fluid, and simply reflecting local customs. Let us imagine a female traveler, since women played an active and mobile role in ancient Christian affairs. In Rome, and almost everywhere else, our traveler would find churches affiliated with a famous movement that read a fixed canon consisting of a very short bible (constructed about A.D. 145 by Marcion), which contained an abridgment of the Gospel of Luke, a modified version of the letters of Paul, *no* Old Testament—and nothing else. Also in Rome she would find yet other canons in use by other Christian groups. On reaching Alexandria in Egypt, she would discover several factions of Christianity, one of them being a wealthy, aristocratic, and well-educated community that read as scripture not only the Old Testament and most books of today's New Testament canon, but also (with the same authority) the *Gospel According to the Hebrews, Revelation of Peter, Preaching of Peter, Epistle of Barnabas, Epistle of Clement, Traditions of Matthew, Teaching of the Twelve Apostles, Gospel of Peter, Acts of Pilate, Clementine Recognitions, Epistles of Ignatius, Acts of Paul,* and *The Shepherd* (about the last two works more is said below). When she got to northern Mesopotamia she would meet Syrian Christians who venerated St. Thomas as their founding apostle and saw in his life a model for wandering ascetics. She would find them reading about Jesus' teachings in an authoritative *Gospel According to Thomas* (translated in Part Four of this book). However, for stories about Jesus' life they would be reading a single *Harmony* (*Diatessaron*) of the gospels made by skillfully combining Matthew, Mark, Luke, and John, together with *The Gospel According to Thomas*. Published in two languages, it would seem, about A.D. 170 by the bilingual theologian Tatian, the *Diatessaron,* along with separate gospels, was to remain in canonical use by Syriac-speaking churches until the fifth century. Other scriptural books in this region recorded the "acts" or exploits of St. Jude Thomas as an archetypal wandering missionary, as well as his conversations with Jesus (cf. *The Book of Thomas,* translated in Part Four).

These three geographical samples give us a glimpse of the great variety of canons that were in simultaneous use about A.D. 200. Some of the works being read as scripture had been written before the idea of a limited Christian canon emerged, and had simply survived in the usage of particular groups. But even after the idea of a closed canon emerged, Christian authors continued to claim the inspiration to produce new works meant to have canonical authority and thus to be added to Christian scripture (indeed, as can be seen in certain modern branches of Christianity, this process has never ceased). Sometimes these texts were titled as though they were the work of some respected authority of the past. Others reported the contents of a vision granted to a seer by god.

Thus, for example, about A.D. 150, a certain Greek-speaking freedman at Rome named Hermas—according to tradition, the brother of Pope Pius I—recorded five allegorical visions in a work called *The Shepherd,* which was rounded out by chapters of moral instruction. *The Shepherd* was widely accepted as fully canonical scripture by important Greek-speaking churches down to the fourth century and is found in bible manuscripts of that time. So also a second-century presbyter living near Ephesus (now in Turkey) composed what he claimed was a firsthand biography of Paul, even incorporating a pseudo-Pauline "Third Epistle to the Corinthians," and passed it off as genuine. The theology of this work has been described as anti-gnostic. As it happened, after their publication these *Acts of Paul According to the Apostle Himself* were unmasked, and the presbyter punished. Yet many users seem to have been unaware of this embarrassing fact, or refused to accept it, among them being Saints Hippolytus and Cyprian and the learned Origen. Although the *Acts* were eventually rejected as spurious in Greek-speaking churches, they were translated into Coptic for use by Egyptian Christians; and even today, *Third Corinthians* is found in old printed bibles of the Armenian church.

Gnostic scripture

Such is the context in which gnostic scripture—as a kind of Christian scripture—must be evaluated. There is no evidence, either direct or circumstantial, for the exact contents of a canon read in gnostic churches, nor is it known how formal or informal that canon was. But the gnostic scriptures themselves provide a partial answer, because they are held together by a distinctive type of scriptural myth, a coherent symbol system that enabled gnostics to orient themselves and make sense of their relationship to the world, the divine, and other people. Like the book of Genesis, this symbol system was meant to tell where the gnostics and their religion had come from and to explain why they were distinct and special. The details of the myth were parallel to the system of Genesis but quite incompatible with it. Thus the scriptures in Part One of this book form a loose cycle that tells a distinctive gnostic myth of origins. From a few passing remarks (IrSat 1.24.2 [end], IrUnid 1.30.11f [note 1 Co 15:50 at 1.30.13], RR 86:20f) one can also gather that gnostics read many books now belonging to the Old and the New Testament and accepted them as a necessary—or perhaps unavoidable—basis for interpretation.

Any modern evaluation of gnostic scripture therefore ought to take account of the following facts.

1. None of the works composed by gnostics is today in the authoritative canon of any Christian group. Hostility to them began in proto-orthodox quarters as soon as they were written, and to some degree

proto-orthodox theology was conceived of as being what gnostic theology was *not*.

2. When originally written, gnostic scripture was one of many competing bodies of Christian scripture, corresponding to one of the options or denominations open to ancient Christians everywhere.

3. The fact that gnostic scripture was being written as late as the second and third centuries, in traditional styles and meant to be added to authoritative scripture, is not unusual within the ancient context.

4. Likewise, the attribution of gnostic scripture to authoritative figures of the past or metaphysical beings and its claim to record authoritative visions are not unusual within the broad context of ancient Christian literature.

5. What *is* first and foremost in gnostic scripture is its doctrines and its interpretation of Old and New Testament books—especially its open hostility to the god of Israel and its views on resurrection, the reality of Jesus' incarnation and suffering, and the universality of Christian salvation. But also, gnostic scripture is distinctive because the gnostic myth competes strongly with the book of Genesis, thus rivaling the basic system used by other Christians to orient themselves to the world, the divine, and other people. On these points, the gap between gnostic religion and proto-orthodox Christianity was vast.

Valentinian writings

Valentinus, though essentially a gnostic, tried to bridge this gap. He and his followers consciously limited themselves to a proto-orthodox Christian canon, taking care not to invoke classic gnostic scripture in their theological writings. For example, *The Gospel of Truth,* though Valentinian, is also one of the earliest witnesses to the contents of the proto-orthodox canon—in it Valentinus takes pains to express himself by paraphrasing and alluding to New Testament passages, sometimes almost gratuitously. Thus in *The Gospel of Truth* the books of Mt, Jn, Ro, 1 Co, 2 Co, Ep, Col, Hb, 1 Jn, and Rv are used in this way; very significantly, Valentinus boldly paraphrases Genesis as well, as though signaling the abandonment of works hostile to Genesis such as BJn and RAd. Seen as a work of gnostic literature, *The Gospel of Truth* is a testimony to Valentinus's power as a writer, for in it he manages almost completely to obliterate the characteristic rhetoric, imagery, and atmosphere of gnostic style in favor of a tone that is distinctly proto-orthodox but unmistakably his own. Yet Valentinus and his school in fact used a version of the gnostic myth of origins as their main system of orientation (it even shows through in a few passages of GTr). By the process of allegorical interpretation (whose principles are discussed in the Historical Introduction to Part Three), they claimed to find their version of gnostic myth hidden in the authoritative canon of scripture that was being read by the proto-orthodox church and would later become the New Testament. Allegory seems to have provided heavy armor against the weapon of the canon list: opponents found it infuriatingly difficult to destroy Valentinian cells within the proto-orthodox and orthodox churches, and complaints about their presence continued to be made for centuries (see Map 1).

From this it follows that Valentinian canonical scripture in the proper sense was simply the proto-orthodox canon. Thus the works collected in Parts Two and Three of this book were probably edifying scripture, not canon.

Conclusions

It is clear that the five parts of this book contain bodies of scripture whose formal authority differed from case to case. Classic gnostic scripture (Part One) was a supplementary body that constituted a challenge to the proto-orthodox canon. The writings of Valentinus and his school (Parts Two and Three) were ostensibly just edifying scriptural works. The Thomas literature (Part Four) was probably authoritative scripture for the ordinary church of northern Mesopotamia, along with other works such as the *Harmony* (*Diatessaron*), *The Odes of Solomon,* and possibly separate gospels as well. These works would have been treated as normal canonical scripture and would have presented no sectarian challenge to the early Mesopotamian church. Finally, the Hermetic writings in Part Five are non-Christian, and therefore not Christian scripture at all, while the summary of Basilides' myth (also in Part Five) has an unknown relationship to Christian authoritative scripture.

THE NATURE OF THE PRIMARY SOURCES

All the works translated in this book were composed in Greek, a language used to some extent all over the Mediterranean world (*The Hymn of the Pearl* may be an exception, since it may have been written first in Syriac). The textual evidence or *primary source material* for these works survives partly in the original Greek and partly in the form of ancient translations done in two other languages of the Roman empire, Latin and Coptic. To these, Syriac must be added if the Syriac text of *The Hymn of the Pearl* is translated from a Greek original.

SOURCES IN GREEK

The evidence in Greek is of three types:

1. scripture manuscripts
2. verbatim citations in ancient Greek authors
3. summaries and descriptions by ancient Greek authors

1. Almost no Greek *scripture manuscripts* of the works in this book now survive, indicating that by some crucial moment in the transmission of Greek literature Greek-speaking copyists no longer had any incentive to copy them. Official pressure to cease copying such manuscripts began as

early as the fourth century A.D., when gnostics, Valentinians, readers of the Thomas literature, etc., began to be officially condemned at the instigation of the established orthodox church, and exclusive canon lists began to be promulgated more universally. The Hermetic writings (cf. Poim, CH7) were able to escape extinction owing to the respect in which "Hermes Trismegistus" was universally held. The Hermetic corpus continued to be copied down to the time of the Italian Renaissance, when its publication was enthusiastically patronized by Lorenzo de' Medici. As can be seen from the two tractates included in this book, the Hermetica are by no means as starkly heretical as classic gnostic scripture. Apart from the Hermetica, no Greek scripture manuscripts of the other complete works in this book have been found, save for scraps of three papyrus manuscripts that contained *The Gospel According to Thomas,* and a single Greek manuscript of *The Acts of Thomas* that includes *The Hymn of the Pearl* (as against seventy-four others that omit it!). The massive loss of these writings in the language of their composition is striking evidence of the dominating power of orthodoxy in Western history.

2. *Verbatim citations* in ancient Greek authors have preserved in their entirety two short but extremely precious works—Valentinus's *Summer Harvest* and Ptolemy's *Epistle to Flora.* In addition, short fragments of lost works by Valentinus (VFrA–H) and Basilides (BasFrA–H) are also preserved in this manner, as is a passage of a Ptolemaean commentary on the Gospel of John (IrPt 1.8.5). Other fragmentary citations of related types, especially Valentinian, have also been preserved but are not translated here.

3. The *summaries and descriptions* of gnostic, Valentinian, and Basilidian teachers and descriptions of their doctrines by ancient Greek authors are much more extensive than the citations listed above; they account for nearly a dozen substantial items translated in this book. Six such authors have been drawn upon:

1. St. Irenaeus of Lyon (A.D. ca. 130–ca. 200)
2. St. Clement of Alexandria (A.D. ca. 150–ca. 215)
3. St. Hippolytus of Rome (A.D. ca. 170–236)
4. Origen of Alexandria (A.D. ca. 185–ca. 254)
5. Porphyry of Tyre, the pagan Neoplatonist (A.D. 232/3–ca. 305)
6. St. Epiphanius of Salamis (A.D. ca. 315–403)

In addition, a passing remark is excerpted (VFrB) from a treatise by the Christian theologian Marcellus of Ancyra (died A.D. ca. 374).

Three of the saints—Irenaeus, Hippolytus, and Epiphanius—stand in the same literary tradition, as polemical writers of the history of ideas. They set out to define Christian orthodoxy by writing a genealogical history of error, as they understood it, in a literary genre often called the "catalogue of heresies" and are for this reason known as "heresiologists."

The three heresiologists' attitude to all the material they describe is openly and consistently hostile. Often their style is ironic or mocking (a traditional tone still found in some modern treatments of the gnostics), for their ultimate goal is not to describe but to destroy. Needless to say, the historian has to assess very cautiously the precision and truth of such sources. Porphyry of

Tyre, a pagan openly hostile to all that is Christian, also belongs in the polemical camp, though he marches under a different flag.

SOURCES IN OTHER LANGUAGES

(a) Irenaeus

The text of St. Irenaeus's catalogue of heresies presents a special problem. It was composed in Greek, in the European West, at a time when Christians of Irenaeus's diocese in Gaul (southern France) still used Greek as a language of learning and religion. But within a hundred years or so, Latin had virtually replaced Greek in the Christian churches of the western Mediterranean. Then, not surprisingly, the Greek text of Irenaeus ceased to be transmitted by Western copyists; while in the eastern Mediterranean it eventually was replaced by more up-to-date heresy catalogues in Greek, which to some extent were based on Irenaeus. As a result, what comes down to us of St. Irenaeus's catalogue is mainly an ancient Latin version made very early for use by West European (and North African) Christians who spoke Latin. The original Greek text can sometimes be found in Irenaeus's Greek successors of the East, who to some extent plagiarized or cited his text. Except where such citations exist, the ancient Latin version has to be used.

(b) Ancient translations of scripture manuscripts

The replacement of Greek by Latin in the Western churches and the eventual translation of Irenaeus into Latin were part of a much larger, international pattern in which the spoken languages of various peoples began to be used instead of Greek for the transmission of Christian literature— e.g. Coptic, the native Egyptian language (used by Christian writers since A.D. ca. 250); and Syriac, an important dialect of Aramaic centering in Edessa (Urfa, Turkey, east of Gaziantep) and western Mesopotamia (since before 200). On the periphery of the empire other native languages were eventually put to the same use: Gothic (since ca. 350), Armenian (406), Georgian (ca. 425), Ethiopic (ca. 500), and Old Nubian (ca. 550). Not only books of the Old and the New Testament were translated into these languages, but also liturgies, prayers, and a great deal of the rest of Christian literature, including many other works of scripture that were not to become part of the official canon of established orthodox Christianity.

Among these other works were the scriptures of the gnostics and Valentinians, Hermetic writings, Thomas literature, and similar or related works. The translations of such works must surely have been made to meet the demand of native congregations or for missionary purposes.

Generally speaking, after the fourth century A.D. the official suppression or nonpublication of unorthodox Christian literature extended to all regions and languages of the Roman empire. The result for our times is that, just as unorthodox scripture manuscripts in Greek have now disappeared almost without a trace, so too have the translations of these same scriptures made in parts of the empire that used Latin or regional languages.

Table 2
Published Manuscripts of the Coptic Gnostic Library

Present Location	Designation	Date of Discovery or Acquisition	Number of Codices	Number of Works Attested	Date of Copying (A.D)
Berlin GDR (Staatsbibliothek)	P. Berol. 8502 ("Berlin Codex")	1896	1	4	400–500?
Cairo (Coptic Museum)	Nag Hammadi Codices I–XIII	December 1945	13	Ca. 51	Just before 350
New Haven, Conn. (Yale Beinecke Library)	P. Yale inv. 1784	1964	(Fragment of Nag Hammadi Codex III)	Fragment	Just before 350
London (British Library)	MS Add.5114 ("Askew Codex")	1773	1	3	Ca. 350–400
London (British Library)	MS Or.4926(1) ("Oeyen Fragments")	1895	1 (Fragmentary)	1	Before ca. 350
Oxford (Bodleian Library)	Bruce MS 96 ("Bruce Codex," actually two codices)	Ca. 1769	2	6	300–500?
Summary:		1769–1964	18 codices	Ca. 64 works	Just before 350 to 400/500

NOTE: Statistics based on published data as of 1986.

The outstanding exception to this rule was southern, Coptic-speaking Egypt: there, for reasons of climate and settlement pattern, ancient manuscripts have been able to survive virtually forever if buried in the dry soil (the annual rainfall in well-inhabited parts of Egypt a bit south of Cairo is about zero).

For these reasons unorthodox scripture manuscripts hidden or abandoned in southern Egypt at or before the time of official suppression are still being discovered today. Some of the discoveries are in the original Greek (and these, unfortunately, are merely fragments); but no less than eighteen unorthodox scripture manuscripts containing works in Coptic translation have been found and published. There is reason to believe that other such manuscripts will soon come to light. Thus far, almost all that have been found contain one or more works of the gnostic sect or the school of Valentinus, and many of them are quite well preserved.

All eighteen of the published manuscripts and manuscript fragments can be loosely called "gnostic," and in fact in modern discussion they are designated the "Coptic Gnostic Library" (see Table 2). Copied in them together with gnostic and Valentinian works are other, more or less related ones—Thomas literature, Hermetic writings, etc. All are in the format of codices—that is, books gathered and bound like the printed book of today rather than scrolls, which were the older form of books.

These published manuscripts are all now in famous museums or libraries. Several were purchased from dealers and middlemen who gave no hint as to their original source. But the most spectacular are a hoard of thirteen early codices discovered all together by an Egyptian peasant in 1945, close to the site of ancient Pbou on the east bank of the Nile opposite the town of Nag Hammadi (see Map 1). The Nag Hammadi codices, as they are often called, were manufactured just before A.D. 350 and buried in a sealed pot in the low desert sometime thereafter by unknown persons. The reason for their burial is not specifically known. An archeological survey of the region has provided no context with which the hoard can be definitely associated; nothing in the manuscripts or in their construction materials suggests their exact source or identifies their users (despite occasional reports to the contrary). The variety of handwritings, codex sizes, writing materials, and even dialects in the codices suggests that they had come from several places along the Nile Valley and had been collected (at no small cost) by an interested person or group. It is mainly thanks to the Nag Hammadi codices that the works translated in this book can now be known (see the list of "Ancient Sources and Manuscripts of Works in This Collection").

It must be stressed that the works themselves were not composed in Coptic and that their date of composition in Greek is earlier—in some cases considerably earlier—than the Coptic manuscript witnesses; the possible date of composition is discussed in the introduction to each work. The fact that the manuscripts were preserved in Egypt is largely an accident of climate and human geography; the individual works themselves may have been composed anywhere in or near the Roman empire, subsequently transported to Egypt, and translated there into Coptic. There is no way to ascertain the exact date of the translation of each of them into Coptic.

EDITORIAL METHOD

The translations in this book are based on fresh revision of the ancient texts. Before translating any text I have critically reviewed the variants reported in the best modern edition. In the case of texts preserved in Coptic, I have also compared them with the manuscript or manuscripts in photographic facsimile. If a text has survived in two ancient languages, I have examined both versions, though the Syriac version of HPrl has not been restudied in detail. Any textual revisions that seemed necessary have been adopted silently, since the plan of this book does not permit philological notes. Colleagues in textual criticism can easily spot these changes by comparing my translation with the critical edition cited in the introduction to the work.

As editor-translator I viewed my task as being threefold:

1. where the manuscript was physically damaged, to ascertain whether or not the missing text could be restored with certainty;

2. to discover any ancient copyist's errors in the manuscript (there are always some) and if possible to correct them, or to accept a correction already proposed by some modern critic;

3. to insure that Greek literary, rhetorical, and philosophical traditions were taken into account in translating the text into English.

My aims as I performed these three tasks were the following:

1. to adopt a factual approach to the restoration of lacunae, rejecting mere speculation and admitting only restorations that are certain (always enclosed in square brackets [ ]);

2. to recompare carefully the details and systems of related gnostic myths—which has sometimes led me to reject modern critics' emendations in favor of the received reading of one of the manuscripts;

3. to be flexible in translating from the ancient Coptic, taking account of the text's original composition in Greek as a product of Hellenistic-Roman culture.

Needless to say, I am deeply dependent on the editorial research of my predecessors, who for the most part established the original text of these works.

I have used square brackets [ ] conservatively; often a word enclosed in brackets is significantly intact in the manuscript and so is virtually a preserved reading.

EXPLANATION OF TYPOGRAPHICAL AND REFERENCE SYSTEMS

The ancient manuscripts contain no headings, detailed numbering systems, or (in most cases) other marks to indicate divisions of text. The Coptic manuscripts also contain no punctuation corresponding to the kind that is used in English and Byzantine Greek.

Boldface numbers in the text

Boldface numbers which appear within the text indicate

(a) *in works translated from the Coptic (Nag Hammadi MSS)*, manuscript page numbers according to the standard Leiden facsimile edition (e.g. **1** = MS page 1);

(b) *in works translated from the Greek or Latin,* book, chapter, and section numbers (e.g. **1.24.1** = book 1, chapter 24, section 1) or, in Porphyry, chapter and section numbers.

Marginal numbers

Marginal numbers, set in small ordinary type, are the manuscript line numbers of the Coptic (Nag Hammadi) MS or, in Porph, the line numbers of the critical edition.

Dots • in the text are coordinated with these marginal numbers.

Line numbers are given only at the beginning of important sentences or phrases. Not every line of the Coptic manuscript is indicated in the text and margin.

The important sentences and phrases numbered in the English translation usually begin in the middle of a manuscript line of Coptic.

Boldface headings in the text

Boldface headings in the text have been added by the modern translator, as an aid to readers. They are not a part of the original text, and should be omitted when any part of this translation is quoted.

Italics

Italics, to indicate reliance on a parallel manuscript source, are used only in the text of BJn and EgG. Their use is explained in the introductions to those two works, under "Text."

Use of parentheses ( )

Words in parentheses ( ) have been added by the modern translator, as an interpretive supplement implied by the text but not literally present within it. They may be retained whenever the translation is being quoted.

Vertical lists in the text

When a vertical list of items appears in the text (e.g. BJn 6:5f) this typographical arrangement has been added by the modern translator. Such vertical lists do not appear in the ancient manuscripts.

Footnotes

In each division of a text, footnotes are lettered serially. Footnotes for each page of text are printed on the bottom of the page.

Marginal references

Marginal references direct the reader's attention to other passages that can contribute immediately to an understanding of the text—sources of quotations and allusions; use of special terms, phrases, and images in related scriptures collected in the same part of *The Gnostic Scriptures*; and, rarely, comparable use of such a term, phrase, or image in an *earlier* body of scripture (see Table 1). Biblical parallels of mere terminology and imagery have almost never been noted. The references often occur in groups, all relating to one text line; in such cases, the position of the first reference indicates the line to which the whole group applies. If two groups of references have to be run together in one place, they are separated by a boldface reference to the new verse number. The symbol f ("and following line or lines") is omitted in marginal references.

Within a group of references, the order of items is:

1. Cross-references within the same work, in the appropriate order (these are *not* preceded by the abbreviated name of the work)

2. References to books of the Old and the New Testament

3. References to other works in *The Gnostic Scriptures*

Reference to works translated from the Coptic (Nag Hammadi MSS) takes the form of "50:3," i.e. "page 50, line 3 of the manuscript."

Symbols in marginal references

f   "and following line (section) or lines (sections)." Either one or many lines (sections) may be represented by this symbol.

par.   "and parallels in the other gospel(s)"

+   "principal reference." A marginal reference followed by this symbol (e.g. 9:9+) indicates a passage in whose margin further references to the same item are listed. References carrying this symbol may be especially useful to the interpreter.

How to cite passages of this translation

Full titles of works should be preferred to the abbreviations used in this book. Note the list of "Other Accepted Names for the Works in This Collection"; these names may be used if desired.

(a) *For works translated from the Coptic (Nag Hammadi MSS)*, cite the MS page number (boldface, in the text) and the line number preceding the citation (ordinary type, in the margin) joined by the symbol : (colon) and written solid. Unless the Coptic text has been consulted it is safest to write the symbol f ("and following line or lines") after the line number; the Coptic lines of text are short. E.g. "*Revelation of Adam* 64:6f"; "*Revelation of Adam* 64:6–16f." It is unnecessary to specify the Nag Hammadi codex numbers except with *The Secret Book According to John* (Codex II) and *The Egyptian Gospel* (mostly Codex IV, but sometimes Codex III). E.g. "*The Secret Book According to John* (Codex II) 1:5f"; "*The Egyptian Gospel* (Codex IV) 50:1–21f"; "*The Egyptian Gospel* (Codex III) 55:22f."

The Gospel According to Thomas should be cited by saying (logion) number, but *The Gospel According to Philip* by page and line.

(b) *For works translated from the Greek or Latin,* cite the full boldface number or numbers found in the text. E.g. "St. Irenaeus of Lyon, *Against Heresies* 1.24.1"; "St. Epiphanius of Salamis, *Against Heresies* 39.1.4— 39.3.5." Citations of the *Hymn of the Pearl* should specify "Greek," and for precision the traditional (Syriac) verse numbers printed in the margin may be added to the Greek paragraph numbers: "*Hymn of the Pearl* (Greek) 108–109, verses 11–19."

Editorial symbols representing the state of the ancient text

[of the]   Missing because of physical damage (text conjecturally supplied by the modern editor)

[. . .]   One or more words missing because of physical damage

⟨not⟩   Inadvertently omitted by the ancient copyist (text conjecturally supplied by the modern editor)

⟨ . . . ⟩   One or more words inadvertently omitted by the ancient copyist

* * *   Passage omitted by the modern translator

OTHER ACCEPTED NAMES FOR
THE WORKS IN THIS COLLECTION

Logia Iēsou, The	GTh
Nature of the Archons, The	RR
Philip, The Gospel of	GPh
Phibionites, The	EpG
Pimander	Poim
Prayer of the Apostle Paul, The	PPl
Rheginus, The Epistle (or *Letter*) *to*	TRs
Rulers, The Nature of the	RR
Satornilos (or Satornil)	IrSat
Seth, The Three Steles of	3Tb
Stratiōtics, The	EpG
Thomas, The Gospel of	GTh
Thomas the Contender (*Athlete*), *The Book of*	BTh
Three Steles of Seth, The	3Tb
Thunder, Perfect Mind	Th
Trimorphic Protennoia, The	FTh
Triple Protennoia, The	FTh
Valentinus. *Harvest.*	VHr
—————. Frag. 1, ed. Völker	VFrC
—————. Frag. 2 Vö.	VFrH
—————. Frag. 3 Vö.	VFrE
—————. Frag. 4 Vö.	VFrF
—————. Frag. 5 Vö.	VFrD
—————. Frag. 6 Vö.	VFrG
—————. Frag. 7 Vö.	VFrA
—————. Frag. 8 Vö.	VHr
—————. Frag. 9 Vö.	VFrB

ANCIENT SOURCES AND
MANUSCRIPTS OF WORKS
IN THIS COLLECTION

Acts of Thomas (= *Acta Thomae*), 108–13 L.–B.	HPrl
Anthimus of Nicomedia, Pseudo-. *On the Holy Church*	
(= *De Sancta Ecclesia*) 9	VFrB
Berlin Gnostic Codex, pp. 19–77	BJn
Berol. 8502, pap. (or p.), pp. 19–77	BJn
BG, pp. 19–77	BJn
CG (Codex Cairensis Gnosticus). *See* Nag Hammadi Codices	
Clement of Alexandria, Saint (Titus Flavius Clemens),	
Miscellanies (= *Stromateis* = *Stromata*)	
2.36.2–4	VFrC
2.114.3–6	VFrH
3.59.3	VFrE
4.81.2–4.83.2	BasFrG
4.86.1	BasFrD
4.89.1–3	VFrF
4.89.6–4.90.1	VFrD
4.153.3	BasFrH
4.162.1	BasFrA
4.165.3	BasFrE
5.3.2–3	BasFrC
5.74.3	BasFrB
6.52.3–4	VFrG
Corpus Hermeticum. *See* Hermetic Writings	
Epiphanius of Salamis (Constantia), Saint, *Against Heresies*	
(= *Panarion* = *Adversus Haereses*)	
25.2.1–26.17.9	EpG
33.3.1–33.7.10	PtF
39.1.1–39.5.3	EpS
40.1.1–40.8.2	EpA
Hermetic Writings (Corpus Hermeticum)	
Tractate 1 (*Poimandrēs*)	Poim
Tractate 7	CH7

Hippolytus of Rome, Saint, *Against Heresies*
  (= *Refutatio* = *Elenchos*)
  6.37.7–8   VHr
  6.42.2   VFrA
Irenaeus of Lyon (Lugdunum), Saint, *Against Heresies*
  (= *Adversus Haereses* = *Elenchos* = *Detectio*)
  1.1.1–1.8.5   IrPt
  1.11.1   IrV
  1.24.1–2   IrSat
  1.24.3–7   IrBas
  1.29   IrG
  1.30–31   IrUnid
Marcellus of Ancyra. *On the Holy Church* (= *De Sancta*
  Ecclesia) 9   VFrB
Nag Hammadi Codices (NHC or CG)
  Cod. I, pp. A–B   PPl
  Cod. I, pp. 16–43   GTr
  Cod. I, pp. 43–50   TRs
  Cod. II, pp. 1–32   BJn
  Cod. II, pp. 32–51   GTh
  Cod. II, pp. 51–86   GPh
  Cod. II, pp. 86–97   RR
  Cod. II, pp. 138–45   BTh
  Cod. III, pp. 1–40   BJn
  Cod. III, pp. 40–69   EgG
  Cod. IV, pp. 1–49   BJn
  Cod. IV, pp. 50–81   EgG
  Cod. V, pp. 64–85   RAd
  Cod. VI, pp. 13–21   Th
  Cod. VII, pp. 118–27   3Tb
  Cod. VIII, pp. 1–132 (excerpts)   Zs
  Cod. XI, pp. 57–68   Fr
  Cod. XIII, pp. 35–50   FTh
NHC. *See* Nag Hammadi Codices
Origen of Alexandria, *Commentary on Romans,* Migne *PG*
  14.1015A–B   BasFrF
pap(yrus) Berol(inensis) 8502, pp. 19–77   BJn
pap(yrus) Oxyrhynchus 1, 654, and 655   GTh
Porphyry (or Porphyrius) of Tyre, *Life of Plotinus* (= *Vita*
  Plotini) 16   Porph

ILLUSTRATIONS

TABLES

FIGURE

MAPS

LIST OF ABBREVIATIONS

Biblical books of both the Old and the New Testament are abbreviated as in *The New Jerusalem Bible* and *The Jerusalem Bible Reader's Edition.* Other common abbreviations:

ca.	circa
f	and following line (section) or lines (sections)
lit.	literally
MS	manuscript
MSS	manuscripts
NHC	Nag Hammadi Codex (Cairo Coptic Museum)
plur.	plural
sing.	singular
+	principal reference

ABBREVIATIONS OF TITLES (ALPHABETICAL)
WITH PAGE NUMBERS

THE GNOSTIC SCRIPTURES

PART ONE

CLASSIC GNOSTIC SCRIPTURE

HISTORICAL INTRODUCTION

Classic gnostic scripture

The word "gnostic" has two meanings. One is a broad meaning, denoting all the religious movements represented in this book, and many more besides. The elusive category ("gnosti*cism*") that corresponds to this broad meaning has always been hard to define.

The other meaning of "gnostic" is narrow and more strictly historical: it is the self-given name of an ancient Christian sect, the *gnōstikoi*, or "gnostics." Because the ancient sect of the gnostics is relatively early, indisputably gnostic—even lending its name to the broader category—and a historical source of other important movements, it deserves a primary place in any general study of gnostic religion. In this book the word "gnostic" is mainly restricted to the narrow, historical meaning, and Part One is devoted to gnostic works in this classic sense of the word.

The date of the gnostic sect

The gnostics were active in the mid-second century A.D. (see Map 1) and beyond. Greek was the basic language of the sect, as it was of non-gnostic Christianity and Hellenistic Judaism of that period. The earliest surviving reference to the sect is by St. Irenaeus, writing in Lugdunum (modern Lyon, France) about A.D. 180; cf. IrG 1.29.1. According to Irenaeus the gnostics were a major influence on the Christian theologian Valentinus. This may have been before Valentinus arrived in Rome to begin his career of teaching, between A.D. 136 and 140 (cf. "Historical Introduction" to Part Two), or not long thereafter.

How much older might the sect actually be? There seems to be no direct answer to this question. However, an indirect answer might be obtained by considering the philosophical character of classic gnostic scripture within the context of Greek philosophy. In such a context, the characteristic gnostic myth of creation turns out to resemble philosophical mythic speculation already current in the time of Jesus. The formulation of the gnostic myth ultimately drew on Platonist interpretations of the myth of creation in

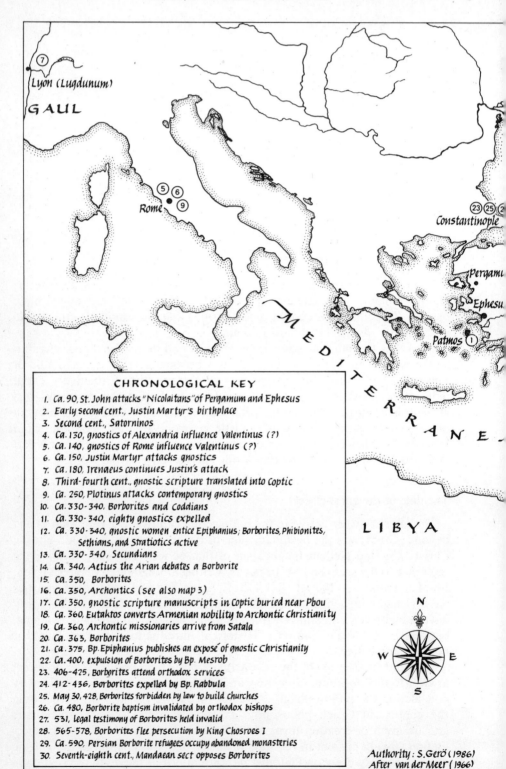

GAUL

Lyon (Lugdunum)

⑦

Rome ⑤ ⑥ ⑨

MEDITERRANEAN

Constantinople ㉓㉕②

Pergamu

Ephesu

Patmos ①

LIBYA

CHRONOLOGICAL KEY

1. Ca. 90, St. John attacks "Nicolaitans" of Pergamum and Ephesus
2. Early second cent., Justin Martyr's birthplace
3. Second cent., Satorninos
4. Ca. 130, gnostics of Alexandria influence Valentinus (?)
5. Ca. 140, gnostics of Rome influence Valentinus (?)
6. Ca. 150, Justin Martyr attacks gnostics
7. Ca. 180, Irenaeus continues Justin's attack
8. Third-fourth cent., gnostic scripture translated into Coptic
9. Ca. 250, Plotinus attacks contemporary gnostics
10. Ca. 330-340, Borborites and Coddians
11. Ca. 330-340, eighty gnostics expelled
12. Ca. 330-340, gnostic women entice Epiphanius; Borborites, Phibionites, Sethians, and Stratiotics active
13. Ca. 330-340, Secundians
14. Ca. 340, Aetius the Arian debates a Borborite
15. Ca. 350, Borborites
16. Ca. 350, Archontics (see also map 3)
17. Ca. 350, gnostic scripture manuscripts in Coptic buried near Pbou
18. Ca. 360, Eutaktos converts Armenian nobility to Archontic Christianity
19. Ca. 360, Archontic missionaries arrive from Satala
20. Ca. 363, Borborites
21. Ca. 375, Bp. Epiphanius publishes an exposé of gnostic Christianity
22. Ca. 400, expulsion of Borborites by Bp. Mesrob
23. 406-425, Borborites attend orthodox services
24. 412-436, Borborites expelled by Bp. Rabbula
25. May 30, 428, Borborites forbidden by law to build churches
26. Ca. 480, Borborite baptism invalidated by orthodox bishops
27. 531, legal testimony of Borborites held invalid
28. 565-578, Borborites flee persecution by King Chosroes I
29. Ca. 590, Persian Borborite refugees occupy abandoned monasteries
30. Seventh-eighth cent., Mandaean sect opposes Borborites

N
W E
S

Authority: S. Gerö (1986)
After van der Meer (1966)

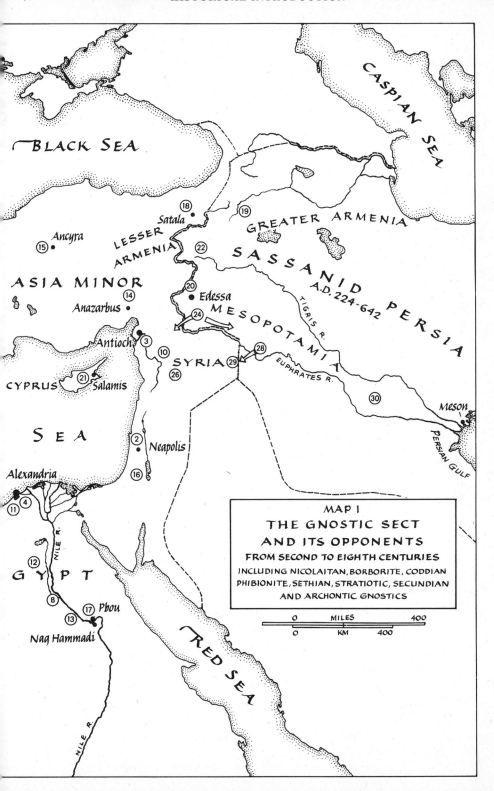

MAP I
THE GNOSTIC SECT
AND ITS OPPONENTS
FROM SECOND TO EIGHTH CENTURIES
INCLUDING NICOLAITAN, BORBORITE, CODDIAN
PHIBIONITE, SETHIAN, STRATIOTIC, SECUNDIAN
AND ARCHONTIC GNOSTICS

Plato's *Timaeus,* as combined with the book of Genesis. Speculation of this kind—from the period of "Middle Platonism"—was popular with learned Greek-speaking Jews of Alexandria at the time of Philo Judaeus (ca. 30 B.C.—ca. A.D. 45). Such speculation was also fashionable in pagan philosophical circles of the first and second centuries A.D., and beyond. Since the gnostic myth seems to presuppose this speculative tradition, it *might* be as old as Philo Judaeus. Yet nothing proves that it *must* be so old. Scholars are therefore unable to say exactly how much older than Irenaeus (A.D. ca. 180) the gnostic sect actually must be.

Gnostics continued to flourish in the third and fourth centuries A.D. (cf. Porph, EpS, EpA, EpG). But in A.D. 381, legislation of the emperor Theodosius I officially recognized a single branch of Christianity as catholic orthodoxy in the Roman empire and opened the way for sanctions and violence against the "heretics," who then included gnostics. Thereafter, gnostics are mainly heard of in Armenia, Syria, Mesopotamia, and Persia, with references to them continuing to crop up in medieval sources (see Map 2). Whether all such medieval sources are based on actual encounters with living members of the sect is not entirely clear. To a great extent, gnostic Christianity may have already been absorbed by the Valentinian church (see Parts Two and Three), and after A.D. 250 by the Manichaean world religion, which showed certain resemblances to the Gnostics (cf. EpG).

By the middle of the fourth century, gnostic Christianity (apart from its Valentinian branch) was known by several different names, perhaps indicating that it had split into denominations: "Archontics" (from *arkhōn,* "heavenly ruler"), "Sethians," "Barbēlites," etc.; see EpG 25.2.1, 26.3.7. In recent scholarship gnostic Christianity is often called "Sethian Gnosticism" because of its particular interest in Seth, son of Adam, as ancestor and prototype of the individual gnostic. Indeed, there is no point in arguing too much over which name should be used today.

The name "gnostic"

The original self-designation of the sect—*gnōstikos,* "gnostic"—was a very striking name; it must have sounded new and slightly odd to Greek speakers of the second century A.D. As a mere word, the Greek term *gnōstikos* goes back as far as the time of Plato. It was a rare technical word with philosophical overtones; it meant something like "leading to knowledge" or "capable of attaining knowledge." In normal usage the term was never applied to human beings; that is to say, normally a *person* would not be called "gnostic." Rather, the word "gnostic" regularly referred to disciplines of study, human faculties, capacities, and the like. Thus, for example, the Platonist philosopher Plutarch could write, "Human souls have a faculty that is *gnōstikos* (leads to knowledge) of visible things."

So when a social group in the early second century A.D. began to call itself *gnōstikoi,* or "gnostics," this usage would have sounded like odd sectarian jargon—as though a modern club began to call itself the Perceptives or the Epistemologicals.

The meaning of "gnōsis"

Gnostic scripture describes the salvation of the individual by the Greek word *gnōsis*, and the self-given name of the "gnostic" sect refers to their ability to attain *gnōsis*. The meaning of *gnōsis* is easy to grasp. Unlike its odd derivative *gnōstikos*, the word *gnōsis* was an ordinary part of Greek, both in daily life and in religion (including Judaism and Christianity). The basic translation of *gnōsis* is "knowledge" or "(act of) knowing." But the ancient Greek language could easily differentiate between two kinds of knowledge (a distinction that French, for example, also makes with ease).

One kind is propositional knowing—the knowledge *that* something is the case ("I know that Athens is in Greece"). Greek has several words for this kind of knowing—for example, *eidenai* (French *savoir*).

The other kind of knowing is personal acquaintance with an object, often a person ("I know Athens well"; "I have known Susan for many years"). In Greek the word for this is *gignōskein* (French *connaître*),[1] and in English one can call this kind of knowledge "acquaintance." The corresponding Greek noun is *gnōsis*. If, for example, two people have been introduced to one another, each one can claim to have *gnōsis* or acquaintance of the other. If one is introduced to god, one has *gnōsis* of god. The ancient gnostics described salvation as a kind of *gnōsis* or acquaintance, and the ultimate object of that acquaintance was nothing less than god.

Readers should note that in this book the English word "acquaintance" always translates *gnōsis* or its equivalent in Coptic or Latin.

Sectarian features in gnostic literature

Social information about the gnostics is very hard to come by. Most of the ancient gnostic literature consists of "pseudepigrapha"—that is, works attributed to the authority of a respected figure of the past such as Adam, Seth, or John the apostle; this literary convention does not leave much room for direct description of sectarian activities. The other records are brief and biased descriptions of gnostic teaching and practice left by Christian opponents; these give much less data than a historian and sociologist needs.

Nevertheless, an observer can find in gnostic scripture certain features that are typically sectarian, thus helping to confirm the cohesiveness of the gnostics as a group. First, a *complex and distinctive myth of origins* runs throughout the surviving records. It is the distinguishing mark of gnostic literature; without it, classic gnostic scripture could not be recognized. Second, this myth expresses a *strong sense of group identity,* which is backed up both by genealogies and by psychological analysis of humanity, with the conclusion that there are two essential types of human being, gnostic and non-gnostic. Along with this goes overt hostility to the non-gnostic population, and the prediction of their ultimate damnation and destruction. Third, the records often use a *special jargon or in-group*

---

[1] Ordinary language is not a rigid system, of course, and thus in natural usage the distinction between the two kinds of knowledge is sometimes blurred.

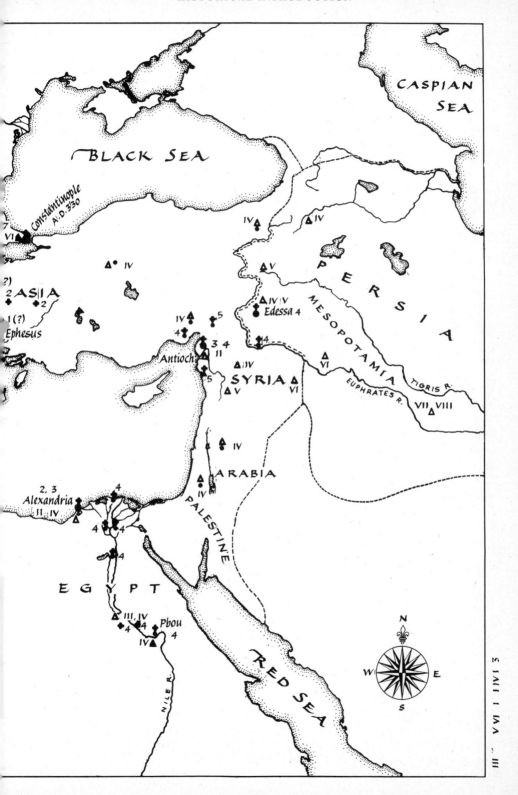

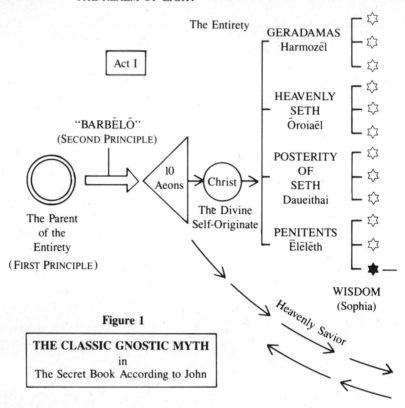

Figure 1

THE CLASSIC GNOSTIC MYTH
in
The Secret Book According to John

language, much of it not found in other branches of ancient Christianity. Fourth, there are references to a *ritual* of baptism. For non-gnostic Christians, baptism marked induction into the religion; the gnostic meaning of baptism may have been the same. Somehow associated are the sacramental "five seals" and their heavenly prototype (EgG); their use is never described.

What is normally excluded by the pseudepigraphic convention of gnostic scripture is information about the organization or daily life of the sect.

It must also be stressed that, despite the distinctive sectarian features mentioned above, gnostics had a great deal in common with non-gnostic Christians, including some of the same scripture, use of broadly Christian in-group language, certain shared theological traditions, and an ascetic life style (though here EpG presents evidence to the contrary). Both the gnostic sect and other branches of early Christianity created new scriptures and attributed them to respected religious figures of the past.

The gnostic myth

Gnostic myth is the literary creation of theological poets—an elaborate theological symbolic poem, and not the spontaneous product of a tribe or culture. "Philosophical myth" of this kind was generally fashionable in the second century A.D., following a revival of interest in Plato's mythic tale of creation, the *Timaeus,* in the previous two centuries.

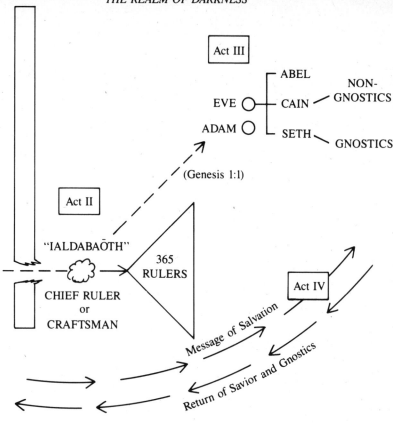

The mythic drama unfolds in four acts (see Fig. 1):

Act I. The expansion of a solitary first principle (god) into a full nonphysical (spiritual) universe

Act II. Creation of the material universe, including stars, planets, earth, and hell

Act III. Creation of Adam, Eve, and their children

Act IV. Subsequent history of the human race

Running throughout this drama (sometimes just below the surface) is a subplot of theft, loss, and ultimate recovery of a part of the divine. The subplot also expresses itself in the four acts, as follows:

Act I. Expansion of divine power ("the parent of the entirety") to fill the spiritual universe

Act II. Theft and loss of some of that power into the hands of a nonspiritual being ("Ialdabaōth")

Act III. Deception of the thief, leading to transfer of the power to a part of humanity (the "gnostics")

Act IV. Gradual recovery by the divine of the missing power as gnostic souls are summoned by a savior and return to god

From the divine perspective, therefore, the evolution of this subplot entails

(i) fullness or "entirety," (ii) lack (of the stolen power), and (iii) eventual fulfillment of the lack.

No single complete telling of the gnostic myth seems to have survived, though one may be reflected in *The Secret Book According to John* (BJn) and *The Egyptian Gospel,* and by St. Irenaeus's account of Satorninos (IrSat). But the surviving forms of the myth all show great variation in detail and structure.

Act I: The emanation of the spiritual universe

At the beginning of the myth is the perfect, ultimate, and omnipotent divine source, or "first principle," of all further existence; it is ineffable and beyond description. The characterization of this divine source in gnostic myth corresponds to philosophical talk about god found in Platonism of the second century A.D. (and before).[2]

For unfathomable reasons, according to the myth, this perfect omnipotent divine source emits a hypostasis, or second being, and through successive phases of emission produces a carefully structured series of other beings. These emanations are called in Greek *aiones* ("aeons"), meaning "realms," "eternities," "ages," or "eternal realms"; the aeons are at once places, extents of time, and abstractions (with names such as "forethought," "incorruptibility," "eternal life," etc.). The last of the aeons is "wisdom" (Sophia).

In such a story of creation the classic problem is why, from a perfect original source (a "first principle"), there should ever need to emanate a second, less perfect being (a "second principle") and thence a plenitude of forms. No gnostic text attempts a solution of this problem, although *The Secret Book According to John* provides three symbolic models showing how (though not why) such an evolution came about; these, too, are typical of second-century Platonism.

First, it is claimed, the first principle is a solitary *intellect,* whose only

---

[2] One need only compare the discourse about the "parent of the entirety" in BJn 2:26–4:24f with an excerpt from a second-century textbook of Platonist philosophy by a certain Albinus, also known as Alcinous:

"Since the ultimate intellect [that is, the divine source] is supremely beautiful, it must necessarily have a supremely beautiful object of intellection. But there is nothing more beautiful than the ultimate intellect itself. Therefore it will eternally think about itself and its own thoughts, and this activity constitutes its ideal form.

"Now, the first god is everlasting, ineffable, self-perfect, i.e. without need, eterno-perfect, i.e. ever perfect, complete, i.e. in every way perfect; deity, essentiality, truth, proportion, goodness. I do not speak as though distinguishing these things (as aspects of it), but rather as of one being conceived of in all kinds of ways. And it is "good," because it acts beneficently toward all things to the full extent, acting as cause of all goodness; "beautiful," because by its very nature it is perfect and proportional; "truth," because it is the source of all truth, just as the sun is the source of all light; "parent," in being the cause of all things and because it orients the celestial intellect and the soul of the universe in an orderly relationship to itself and to its own intellections. . . .

"It is ineffable and comprehensible by intellect alone, as stated, since it is neither a genus nor a species nor a variety. Indeed, it does not have any attributes: it is neither evil (it is impious to say so), nor good (for this would be by participation in something, namely, goodness), nor indifferent (for this does not accord with our thought of it); neither something with a quality . . . , nor something without any quality . . . ; neither a part of something, nor a whole having various parts . . . ; it neither moves nor is moved. . . . Just as the sun stands in relation to seeing and to the things seen—not itself being vision, but rather providing the seeing for the former and the being-seen for the latter—just so, the ultimate intellect stands in relation to intellection within the soul and to the things thought about. . . ."

function is to think and whose only possible object of thought is itself, since it alone exists. But its act of thinking is objectified, and this thinking is the second principle.

Again, the first principle is a solitary *eye,* floating in a luminous reflective medium. Its only function is to look, and all it has to see is itself. The reflection that it sees, however, is the second principle.

Finally, the first principle is a *spring of water* that flows perpetually. Its only function is to overflow, and that overflow is the second principle.

The second principle is called by the non-Greek name Barbēlō or occasionally (EpG 26.10.10) Barbērō. In antiquity, obscure mythic names like Barbēlō were sometimes invented ad hoc by theological writers rather than being produced by natural language; in some cases, therefore, ancient theological readers were expected to guess their meaning. Such a process is of course difficult to trace without precise identification of the linguistic milieu in which the text was first published. But if that milieu was Egyptian, the name "Barbērō" or "Barbēlō" might have called to mind the native words for "emission, projectile" and "great,"[3] yielding a pseudo-word meaning "the great emission"—an apt description of the Barbēlō's relation to the first principle.

Barbēlō is a stock character who occurs in various versions of the gnostic myth. There are other stock characters as well: especially important among these are *the anointed* ("Christ"), a metaphysical being that in some versions descends to unite with Jesus of Nazareth; and *the four luminaries* Harmozēl, Ōroiaēl, Daueithai, and Ēlēlēth. Since they are aeons, the luminaries are both eternal realms and actors. As realms, they are the dwelling places of four archetypes: *Geradamas* (or *Adamas*), the heavenly Adam; *Seth,* heavenly prototype of Adam's son; the heavenly *posterity of Seth,* prototypes of the gnostic church on earth; and a *fourth group,* whose identity varies from tale to tale. Some scholars also hold that the gnostic myth divides human history into four great epochs, corresponding to the four luminaries and their resident archetypes. According to one formulation of this theory, the first three epochs are antediluvian (the first, the second, and the third to ninth generations of humankind), while the fourth (the epoch of Ēlēlēth) begins with the time of Noah (cf. RR 92:3f) and extends to the end of the material universe. A parallel conception of history has been proposed in the Zoroastrian religion of Persia.

Act II: The creation of the material universe

After the emission of the spiritual universe has been completed, in order for creation to continue beyond the limit of spiritual existence the activity of a "craftsman"[4] or "maker" of the world is introduced; his name is

---

[3] Cf. Coptic *berbir,* "projectile, lance" (a grammatically feminine noun, surviving only in the northern, or Bohairic, dialect), presumably from Egyptian *brbr* or *b3b3;* and -*ō,* "great." The name might also have recalled Coptic *berber,* "boiling over, overflow" (a masculine noun).

[4] "Craftsman," "demiurge" (Greek *dēmiourgos*), is Plato's metaphorical term for the maker of the universe in his mythic account of the world's creation entitled *Timaeus.* Educated readers of gnostic scripture in the second and third centuries A.D. would surely have compared Ialdabaōth with the craftsman of the *Timaeus.*

Ialdabaōth. This part of the myth is clearly modeled on Plato's myth of creation, found in the *Timaeus*. Ialdabaōth the craftsman makes a universe out of matter, copying patterns provided by the spiritual universe. It is an elaborate structure of material aeons (realms), i.e. planets, stars, and heavenly spheres, populated by the craftsman's offspring, which are called "rulers," "authorities," "powers," "demons," "angels," etc.

Plato's *Timaeus* had already exerted an influence on Hellenistic Jewish philosophy when Philo Judaeus of Alexandria (ca. 30 B.C.–ca. A.D. 45) and his colleagues tried to show that the *Timaeus* said substantially the same thing as the opening chapters of Genesis; this can be seen in Philo's treatise *On the Creation of the World*. Such accomplishments may have paved the way for gnostic Christian theologians, since early Christianity took many of its cues from Hellenistic Judaism. The concept of an intermediate "craftsman" can also be seen, at some remove from Plato, in the Christian theology of the Logos, or Word: "The Word . . . was in the beginning with god; all things were made through it" (Jn 1:1–3).

In Plato's *Timaeus*, each of the cosmic craftsman's creations is a copy of some perfect pattern that exists in the spiritual realm. All the copies are as good as they possibly can be, given the resistance of the working material, for the craftsman works to the very best of his ability. But in contrast, Ialdabaōth, the gnostic craftsman of the world—though not exactly a principle of pure evil—is morally ambivalent, for though he loves the good he is fatally flawed by ignorance and self-centeredness. Thus, for example, he recognizes the goodness of the patterns in the spiritual realm and feels a natural attraction toward them; but this attraction is also experienced as an ignorant, selfish, erotic lust to possess the divine, even to rape it (cf. RR 89:18f). Ialdabaōth and his fellow heavenly "rulers" are possessive and arrogant and try to dominate all human affairs; their desire for domination leads them to create human sexual lust and the bond of destiny (control by the stars), by which they intend to enslave humanity.

Why should Ialdabaōth, the creator of our world, be so fatally imperfect? The cause of his imperfection in the myth was a point of continuing speculation and difficulty, and the gnostics explained it in various ways. In most accounts this imperfection is paralleled by a previous lustful act or emotion on the part of the creator's mother, wisdom, the lowest aeon in the spiritual universe. At the very least, then, Ialdabaōth's lustful selfishness is a family trait, inherited from his mother.

The gnostics' craftsman or cosmic creator is thus distinct from god the ultimate first principle, just as Plato's craftsman is an intermediate being between the highest principle and our world. Such a distinction had already been made both by Philo Judaeus and in the Gospel of John, where "god the father" (the first principle), the god of Israel, is distinguished from his offspring the "only begotten son," or Logos, or Word, on the one hand, and from ourselves on the other. But, unlike the author of the Gospel of John, the gnostics did not identify the god of Israel with the first principle. Rather, the god of Israel was equated either with Ialdabaōth the imperfect craftsman, or with Ialdabaōth's first-born offspring Sabaōth.

Act III: The creation of Adam, Eve, and their children

The rest of the myth concerns the efforts of wisdom, aided by higher aeons of the spiritual universe, to regain the stolen power. Although Ialdabaōth is lured into surrendering it, in the process Adam and then a human race are created; and the stolen power becomes dispersed in successive generations, whom Ialdabaōth's offspring enslave by creating destiny and a malevolent spirit of deception. The plot of this act of the drama closely follows Genesis 1–4, but with the extensive reinterpretations necessary to make the acts of the creator into actions of an imperfect craftsman. From Seth springs a race of people in whom the dispersed power resides to this day: these are the gnostics, and to the extent that the myth concerns these people it is a myth of their origins.

Act IV: The subsequent history of the human race

In gnostic eyes the final act of the drama is still in progress. A heavenly savior has been sent to "awaken" gnostic humanity, to give them acquaintance (*gnōsis*) with themselves and god, to free their souls from destiny and from bondage to the material body, and to teach them how to escape the influence of the malevolent rulers. To counteract the evil spirit of these rulers, a good spirit has been bestowed upon the gnostics. According as each soul responds and gains acquaintance, it either escapes and returns to god or becomes reincarnate in another body; a special "eternal punishment" is reserved for apostates from the sect.

Some versions of this final act of the myth are restricted to general theological issues and speak of the final advent of a savior without historical details. Others dwell on a futuristic description of the final destruction of the evil rulers and of death, thus emphasizing the result of the savior's advent. Still other versions refer to events in biblical history that non-gnostic Christianity saw as parts of the background of the incarnation (Noah and the flood, genealogies of humankind, the prophets of Israel, John the Baptist) and go on to speak of Jesus of Nazareth, his crucifixion, his resurrection, and his post-resurrection teachings, or his ascension. Jesus' special role in these versions results from his being the incarnation of a preexistent Christ, a preexistent Word, a preexistent Seth, or Barbēlō.

Gnostic in-group language (religious jargon)

Any modern reader, no matter how well informed, will be struck by the obscurity of many names and phrases that occur in the gnostic myth. For the most part, this obscurity is not a mark of our distance from classical antiquity but rather a function of the esoteric character of gnostic life in a closed, and sometimes persecuted, religious sect that was defiantly sure of its superiority to the rest of humanity.

In their mythic tales *the gnostics* do not refer to themselves, their ancestors, or their spiritual prototypes as "gnostics." Instead they are "the offspring (seed, posterity, race) of Seth" or "the offspring of the light";

"the perfect race," "the undominated race," or "the immovable race"; or, even more obscurely, "Those People."

Their true home, *the spiritual universe,* is "the light," "the fullness," their "root." It is populated by "aeons," also known as "eternals," "great eternals," "great eternal aeons," "incorruptible beings," or "immortals" (all of which are equivalent terms). The entire system of the aeons that are lower than the second principle is "the entirety," or, more obscurely, "all these," i.e. "all these spiritual beings." This system is a graded hierarchy of beings, each step of which is a "shadow" or image of the one above it.

Entities in the spiritual universe are identified by the epithets "eternal," "great," "living," "luminous," "male," "masculine," or, more obscurely, by the words "That" (plural "Those") and "other." The epithet "other" ("foreign," "alien") is based on Gn 4:25 (in Greek) describing the birth of Seth, "God has raised up to me some *other* seed," while the mystifying "That" had already been used by esoteric circles (Pythagoreans) in Greek philosophy.

There is no fixed terminology for describing *non-gnostic humanity,* but the *demonic heavenly enemies* of the gnostics are called by traditional names—"rulers," "powers," "authorities," "brigands"—most of which, incidentally, are also known from the letters in the New Testament written by Paul or attributed to Paul. The *material universe* is "the darkness," just as the spiritual universe is "the light." In the language of one gnostic text (RR 94:8), the two domains are divided from one another by a "veil."

Gnostic description of the components of the human being is simple and depends on common Platonizing clichés. The body is a "bond," "bondage," "fetter," or "prison" of the soul. The true person is the soul, and the body is merely a "garment" that we must "put on" and "wear"; compared to the vitality of the soul, the body is a "corpse." The realm of matter, to which the body belongs and to which it will return, is "shadow," a "cave," a realm of "sleep." It is "female" and "femininity"—for, according to a philosophical cliché, shape-giving form is called in Greek "male," while passive constituent matter is "female." What distinguishes the saved human being from the non-saved is the presence and activity of the good spirit ("holy spirit," "spirit of life") and the saved person's renunciation of deceptions held out by the rulers' "counterfeit spirit." The mark of this renunciation is a life of asceticism and contemplation. The capacity for *gnōsis* and salvation within a gnostic is a function of the inherited "power" or "glory" transmitted by the gnostic "race"—nothing less than a fragment of the "power" that the craftsman Ialdabaōth stole from his mother, wisdom, at the moment of his birth. It is not by accident that "power" and "glory" are also descriptions of Barbēlō, the second principle, for they are epithets that characterize the entire spiritual universe so far as it can be known or described.

Names of characters in the gnostic myth

Apart from this web of sectarian language, gnostic scripture is shot through with the obscure names of stock mythic characters—Barbēlō, Geradamas or Adamas, "luminaries," Ialdabaōth, etc. In the introduction to each individual work, such of these names as occur are catalogued; they are also commented on in the annotations.

The spelling of these mythic names in ancient manuscripts shows considerable variation—not only from work to work, but even from place to place within one work. This variation has been retained in the English translation. However, it has no obvious significance.

Thus: "Adamas," "Adama," "Geradamas"; "Daueithai," "Daueithe"; "Elōaios," "Elōaiō"; "Ialdabaōth," "Ialtabaōth," "Aldabaōth"; "Iōēl," "Iouēl"; "Norea," "Noria"; "Oroiaēl," "Ōroiaēl"; etc. Instances of such variation will be obvious to the reader who knows to expect them.

Gnostic baptism

Like other Christians, the gnostics laid great stress on the importance of baptism and made strong use of baptismal rhetoric when speaking of salvation. To judge from the texts, gnostic baptism marked a decisive step in the spiritual life of the gnostic, involving renunciation, instruction, learning, and initiation into a new "kinship" and a new state of life. Reception of gnostic baptism was closely associated with reception of *gnōsis* and was believed to enable the gnostic to overcome death.

Various stages of a gnostic baptismal ceremony are enumerated in FTh: the candidate strips off "darkness," puts on a robe of light, is washed in the waters of life, receives a throne of glory and is glorified with glory of "the kinship," and finally is raised to "the luminous place of . . . kinship." The baptized is also said in EgG to put on the name of Jesus, and according to BJn *gnōsis* is received when the savior seals the candidate with "the light of the water of the five seals." These five seals are mentioned in many passages of gnostic scripture as having a very intimate connection with *gnōsis,* but what they consist of is never clearly explained. EgG concludes with a lengthy, ecstatic baptismal invocation presumably spoken by a recipient of gnostic baptism.

Yet despite the insistence on baptism in gnostic scripture, the references to it are phrased in exaggerated poetic language, always giving the impression that the ceremony takes place not on earth, but only in the spiritual realm. For example, various aeons known from gnostic myth take a leading role in the ceremony; the spiritual baptismal water is even mythically personified, as are "the five seals." It may seriously be asked, then, whether such references to baptism are not mere metaphor, a mystical description of salvation by acquaintance (such an equation is explicitly made at the end of RAd). Was there also a physical gnostic rite of baptism, and if so was it a once-for-all initiation into the new kinship of the gnostic church or a repeatable act of mystical enlightenment? What was its relation, if any, to that baptism already received by members of the non-gnostic church who then converted to gnostic Christianity? No answer to these questions is given by the scriptures themselves, apart from silence. But St. Epiphanius, a hostile—and not fully reliable—fourth-century observer (EpA), reports that the Archontics, a subdivision of the gnostics, "curse and reject [non-gnostic] baptism, even though there are some among them who have already been baptized [as orthodox Christians]" because baptism is "alien and has been established in the name of Sabaōth," i.e. the god of Israel, who according to the Archontics is the son of Satan. Furthermore, according to St. Epiphanius, the Archontics believe that when the soul is saved it "gets *gnōsis* and flees baptism of the [non-gnostic] church."

The chronology of gnostic scripture

In the absence of any historical information about the authors of the various works of gnostic scripture and of any mention of historical facts in the texts themselves, nothing very precise can be said about the date of their composition.

The *latest possible dates* are as follows. A version of *The Secret Book According to John* seems to be already known and summarized by St. Irenaeus (IrG), writing about A.D. 180. *Zōstrianos* and *The Foreigner* are mentioned by Porphyry (Porph) as being among the works brought to Plotinus's attention about A.D. 250. It is worth noting that four other works show a striking similarity to these two in philosophical and mythic content: EgG, RAd, 3Tb, and FTh. The remaining works cannot in any case be later than the date of the Coptic manuscripts in which they are copied, roughly A.D. 350, and time must also be subtracted to allow for their prior translation from the original Greek into Coptic.

The *earliest possible dates* of any of the gnostic works, at least in their present form, are limited only by two factors. First, none of them (except possibly RAd and Th) can be earlier than the first serious efforts of Christian theologians to come to grips with Platonic philosophical myth, assuming that the gnostic myth emerged from Christianity. Second, none of them (except RAd and Th, which are not philosophical in character) seems to presuppose philosophical speculation more advanced than Plotinus or less advanced than Philo Judaeus, so they probably fall not too far outside the chronological framework of those two Platonists' careers, ca. 10 B.C. to A.D. 270. But it would be a mistake to suppose that the chronological sequence of these texts must correspond to their degree of philosophical elaboration in a spectrum from Philo to Plotinus.

In fact, it is reasonable to guess that the dates of composition of the gnostic works in Part One extend over a long period of time. Some of them probably date from before the evolution of Valentinianism (A.D. ca. 140), described in Parts Two and Three of *The Gnostic Scriptures,* and others from after that time. Later gnostic works might even be influenced by Valentinian ideas.

Gnostic scripture without distinctive Christian features

Distinctively Christian features appear both in classic gnostic scripture and in the ancient summaries about the gnostics, making it undeniable that the gnostics were a sect or movement of Christianity; and in the discussion above they have been considered only in this aspect.

In a fair number of gnostic works, however, distinctive Christian features are completely absent (see Table 3). Their absence has caused many scholars to raise the question whether the gnostics might have first, or also, existed as a non-Christian movement or sect.

Table 3
Distinctive Christian and Platonist Features in the
Gnostic Scriptures

	Distinctly Christian	Distinctly Platonist		Distinctly Christian	Distinctly Platonist
BJn	×	×	3Tb		×
RAd	× (?)		IrSat	×	×
RR	×	×	IrG	×	×
Th			IrUnid	×	
FTh	×	×	Porph	×	(×)
EgG	×	×	EpS	×	
Zs		×	EpA	×	
Fr		×	EpG	×	

How significant is the absence of Christian features in these works? In answering this question, it is important to remember that a sect or religion is a social group, and that its members are people, not texts or ideas. In this primary sense, it is not a written work that is "Christian" or "gnostic," but rather the people who produce and use it. Ancient Christians certainly made use of writings that contained no explicit reference to Jesus Christ or to other distinctive marks of their own religion; such writings even formed a central part of Christian scripture—for example, the book of Genesis and other Old Testament books. Throughout their history, Christians have not thought it strange to create and use literature that lacked such features. The question is whether early Christians would have written such literary works with the intention of adding them to Christian scripture. If the answer is yes for certain gnostic works, these would be very unusual cases in the history of ancient Christian literature. Yet the possibility seems hard to exclude, especially since one item on the gnostic agenda was the deliberate balancing of Genesis by a rival body of myth (cf. BJn 13:18f, 22:23f, etc.). Scholarship has therefore been hesitant to regard these works as conclusive evidence of an extra-Christian, or even pre-Christian, branch of the gnostic movement.

SELECT BIBLIOGRAPHY

Bousset, W. "Gnostiker." In *Paulys Real-Encyclopädie der classischen Altertums-wissenschaften,* edited by G. Wissowa et al. Vol. 7 (1912), cols. 1534–47.

Klijn, A. F. J. *Seth in Jewish, Christian, and Gnostic Literature.* Supplements to Novum Testamentum, vol. 46. Leiden: E. J. Brill, 1977.

Layton, B., ed. *The Rediscovery of Gnosticism: Proceedings of the International Conference on Gnosticism at Yale, New Haven, Connecticut, March 28–31, 1978.* Vol. 2, *Sethian Gnosticism.* Studies in the History of Religions, no. 41, vol. 2. Leiden: E. J. Brill, 1981. Note especially the following essays:

Colpe, C. "Sethian and Zoroastrian Ages of the World," pp. 540–52 (and discussion, 552–62).

Pearson, B. "The Figure of Seth in Gnostic Literature," pp. 472–504 (and discussion, 504–14).

Rudolph, K. "Die 'sethianische' Gnosis—Eine häresiologische Fiktion?" pp. 577–78 (and discussion, 578–87).

Schenke, H.-M. "The Phenomenon and Significance of Gnostic Sethianism," pp. 588–616 (and discussion, 634–40, 683–85).

Smith, M. "The History of the Term Gnostikos," pp. 796–807.

Wisse, F. "Stalking Those Elusive Sethians," pp. 563–76 (and discussion, 578–87).

McGuire, A. "Valentinus and the Gnōstikē Hairesis: An Investigation of Valentinus's Position in the History of Gnosticism." Ph.D. diss., Yale University, 1983.

MacRae, G. W. "Seth in Gnostic Texts and Traditions." In Society of Biblical Literature, 1977 Seminar Papers (113th Annual Meeting, 28–31 December 1977), edited by P. Achtemeier, pp. 17–24. Seminar Paper Series, no. 11. Missoula, Mont.: Scholars Press, 1977.

Pearson, B. "Egyptian Seth and Gnostic Seth." 1977 Seminar Papers (see preceding entry), pp. 25–43.

Philo Judaeus. "On the Account of the World's Creation Given by Moses (De Opificio Mundi)." In vol. 1 of Philo, translated by F. H. Colson and G. H. Whitaker, 1–137, 475–76. Loeb Classical Library. New York: G. P. Putnam's Sons, 1929.

Plato. "Timaeus." In vol. 7 of Plato with an English Translation, by R. G. Bury, 1–253. Loeb Classical Library. New York: G. P. Putnam's Sons, 1929.

Poirier, P.-H., and M. Tardieu. "Catégories du temps dans les écrits gnostiques non-valentiniens." Laval Théologique et Philosophique 37 (1981): 3–13.

Schenke, H.-M. "The Problem of Gnosis." The Second Century: A Journal of Early Christian Studies 3 (1983): 73–87.

—————. "Das sethianische System nach Nag-Hammadi-Handschriften." In Studia Coptica, edited by P. Nagel, 165–73. Berliner byzantinistischer Arbeiten, vol. 45. Berlin: Akademie, 1974.

Sevrin, J.-M. Le Dossier baptismal séthien: études sur la sacramentaire gnostique. Bibliothèque copte de Nag Hammadi, Section "Études," no. 2. Québec: Les Presses de l'Université Laval, 1986.

Stroumsa, G. Another Seed: Studies in Gnostic Mythology. Nag Hammadi Studies, vol. 24. Leiden: E. J. Brill, 1984.

Tardieu, M. "Les livres mis sous le nom de Seth et les sethiens de l'hérésiologie." In Gnosis and Gnosticism: Papers Read at the Seventh International Conference on Patristic Studies, Oxford (September 8th–13th 1975), edited by M. Krause, 204–10. Nag Hammadi Studies, vol. 8. Leiden: E. J. Brill, 1977.

Williams, M. The Immovable Race, A Gnostic Designation and the Theme of Stability in Late Antiquity. Nag Hammadi Studies, vol. 29. Leiden: E. J. Brill, 1985.

Classic gnostic works not in this volume

"Marsanes." Translated with notes and introduction by B. Pearson, in Nag Hammadi Codices IX and X, edited by B. Pearson, 229–347. Nag Hammadi Studies, vol. 15. Leiden: E. J. Brill, 1981. (Very fragmentary.)

"Melchizedek." Translated by S. Giversen and B. Pearson, with introduction and notes by Pearson, in the same volume, 19–85. (Very fragmentary.)

"The Thought of Nōrea." Translated by S. Giversen and B. Pearson, with introduction and notes by Pearson, in the same volume, 87–99.

"The Untitled Text in the Bruce Codex." Translated by V. Macdermot, in C. Schmidt and V. Macdermot, The Books of Jeu and the Untitled Text in the Bruce Codex, xviii–xxi, 225–345. Nag Hammadi Studies, vol. 13. Leiden: E. J. Brill, 1978. (Too long to be included in this volume.)

THE SECRET BOOK
ACCORDING TO JOHN

IN THE LONG VERSION
(BJn)

Contents

The Secret Book According to John ("Apocryphon of John") contains one of the most classic narrations of the gnostic myth.[1] After starting out with a philosophical description of god as the source of all being (2:26f), the gnostic author proceeds to describe the structure of the divine world in its glorious complexity (4:26–9:24f) telling, as it were, "what happened *before* Genesis 1:1." After this weighty prelude, the events of the Genesis story are retold from a gnostic perspective (starting at BJn 12:33f). The story finally ends with the gnostic savior's exhortation of the human race to "awaken" and be saved (30:11f).

Any reader who came upon BJn unprepared would surely have been puzzled by many of its obscurities. The web of highly structured emanations, for instance, that enfold the godhead (Fig. 1 and "Mythic Characters" below) forms a thick and almost inscrutable barrier between the human world and god, shutting off god from humanity by alienating human beings from the knowledge of the divine. The creator of the material world, though clearly identified with the figure called "god" in Gn 1:1, turns out to be not true god but Satan (here called "Ialdabaōth" and "Saklas," 10:19f, 11:15f). Furthermore, the creation of Adam is made out to be more complicated than Genesis says, for following Alexandrian Jewish teaching the gnostic author tells of a twofold creation of Adam—first an "animate" Adam made only of soul, though having all the anatomical parts (15:1f–20:27f); and second, a material shell to encase him (20:28f).

The detailed retelling of Genesis stops with the birth of Seth (cf. Gn 4:25); after this, the subsequent history of the human race is discussed only in general terms, within the context of a theological discourse on the activity of the holy spirit. Nothing is said about the history of Israel, nor about Jesus as an incarnation of the preexistent Christ (except in the last sentence of the work and by implication in the opening). Nevertheless, Christ ("the anointed") is an important character of the myth, making BJn an example of a Christian work that discusses the preexistent Christ but not the incarnation.

The narration of the gnostic myth in BJn is encapsulated within a frame story

---

[1] For a more detailed discussion of the gnostic myth, see the "Historical Introduction" to Part One and cf. Fig. 1.

which seems to imply that the content of the work is a post-resurrection teaching of Jesus. This would agree with the gnostic belief that after his resurrection Jesus remained on earth for eighteen months and taught "the plain truth" (IrUnid 1.30.14). Yet in terms of the gnostic myth the identity of the revealer is not Jesus but Barbēlō, the second principle, perhaps here manifested as the afterthought of the light.

Literary background

The author and place of composition of BJn are unknown. The date of its composition is probably sometime before A.D. ca. 180, the date of St. Irenaeus's summary of the work (cf. IrG, but the resemblance is not perfect, suggesting that Irenaeus knew a different version of the text); and in any case before A.D. 350, the approximate date of the MSS. The work is attributed to John the son of Zebedee, one of Jesus' twelve original disciples (Mt 4:21, Mk 1:19, Lk 5:10), recording words spoken by the savior; it is thus an example of pseudepigraphy. The language of composition was Greek.

BJn has a complex mixture of genres in which various traditional materials are subordinated to others:

    I. Romance (apocryphal acts of apostles)
       A. Angelic revelation and revelation dialogue
          1. Treatise
          2. Cosmogony and uranography
          3. "True history" of humankind
          4. Wisdom monologue

The narrative frame story is a typical episode from the literature called "apocryphal acts of the apostles," a Christianized version of the Greek *romance* or novel. Within the narrative of the romance, an *angelic revelation monologue* occurs, but after some pages it develops into an *angelic revelation dialogue*. In this genre a human interlocutor woodenly intervenes to provide excuses for the continuation of the angel's revelation; the genre has been traced back to the Greek school catechism (the so-called "erotapokriseis"), in which dry facts are presented in question-and-answer form.

The revelatory monologue comprises two kinds of material: a typical philosophical *treatise on theology,* and a *cosmogony* accompanied by "*uranographic details*" (details describing the structure of the universe). The revelation dialogue comprises a revisionistic "*true history*"—that is, an alternative, "corrected" version—of the events of Gn 1:2f. The dialogue eventually lapses back into monologue and ends by assuming the form of poetry (parallel strophes). The concluding poem is a *wisdom monologue* (for this genre, see the introduction to Th) and closely resembles FTh.

Mythic characters

I. The Immortals

The PARENT OF THE ENTIRETY. The perfect invisible virgin spirit.
An ANDROGYNOUS QUINTET OF AEONS, constituents of the parent:
    1. The PERFECT FORETHOUGHT OF THE ENTIRETY. The Barbēlō, a product of the parent's thinking, the image of the parent. Also known as:
        mother-father;
        first human being;
        holy spirit;
        thrice-male;
        the three powers;
        the triple androgynous name;
        eternal aeon.
    2. PRIOR ACQUAINTANCE

3. INCORRUPTIBILITY
4. ETERNAL LIFE
5. TRUTH

The DIVINE SELF-ORIGINATE. The anointed (Christ), a luminous spark, the only-begotten, maker of the entirety.

Its coactors: INTELLECT, WILL, WORD (or verbal expression)

FOUR LUMINARIES that stand before the divine self-originate, and TWELVE AEONS that are with them:

HARMOZĒL
    LOVELINESS, TRUTH, FORM
ŌROIAĒL
    AFTERTHOUGHT, PERCEPTION, MEMORY
DAUEITHAI
    INTELLIGENCE, LOVE, IDEAL FORM
ĒLĒLĒTH
    PERFECTION, PEACE, and
    WISDOM (Sophia) belonging to afterthought. Mother of Ialdabaōth, mother of the living, a holy spirit, sibling of the posterity of Seth. Also called life (Zōē), and referred to as "an afterthought."

FOUR BEINGS that dwell with the four luminaries:

The GERADAMAS, also called ADAMAS. The perfect human being. With Harmozēl.
SETH, his son. The "child of the human being" (son of man). With Ōroiaēl.
POSTERITY OF SETH. Souls of the holy persons, the immovable race or perfect race. With Daueithai.
SOULS who were not acquainted with the fullness and repented tardily. With Ēlēlēth.

II. The Rulers

IALDABAŌTH or IALTABAŌTH or ALTABAŌTH. The first and chief ruler, first begetter of the other rulers, an offspring of wisdom. Called SAKLAS and SAMAĒL.
Ialdabaōth's AUTHORITIES, KINGS, RULERS, POWERS, ANGELS, SERAPHIM, DEMONS, etc., amounting to 365 in number and having various names
DESTINY, child of wisdom and Ialdabaōth

III. Humankind

ADAM. The first material human being, created (as an animate body) in the image of the Geradamas, then fitted with a material body.
EVE. The first female human being, created in the image of the luminous afterthought.
ABEL. A just son of Ialdabaōth and Eve.
CAIN. An unjust son of Ialdabaōth and Eve.
SETH. A son of Adam and Eve/afterthought, created as a likeness of the heavenly Seth.
POSTERITY OF SETH on earth. The immovable or perfect race, including Noah, John the brother of James (a son of Zebedee), and John's fellow disciples.
OTHERS, including Arimanios, a Pharisee

IV. Spirits Active in Humankind

The SPIRIT OF LIFE. The mother's (wisdom's) spirit.
The COUNTERFEIT SPIRIT. A creature of the rulers, originating in matter.

Text

The original Greek apparently does not survive. The text is known mainly in Coptic translation, attested by four manuscripts: MSS NHC II (pp. 1–32), NHC III (pp. 1–40), NHC IV (pp. 1–49), which were copied just before A.D. 350 and are now in the Cairo Coptic Museum; and MS BG (Berolinensis gnosticus), that is, p. Berol. 8502 (pp. 19–77), which was copied ca. fifth century A.D. and is now in the papyrus collection of the East Berlin Museum. In addition, a summary of what appears to be the first part of the work, by St. Irenaeus, survives; it is translated elsewhere in this volume (see IrG).

The manuscripts and summary attest the circulation of no less than four distinct editions of the Greek text in antiquity. Such a series of editions must have resulted from continual study and revision of BJn by gnostic teachers; it is a measure of the importance and timeliness of the work for ancient gnostic Christianity. These four ancient editions, usually called "versions," comprise the following.

1. The *long version*, which is represented by two virtually identical Coptic manuscripts, MSS NHC II and NHC IV, is the text translated here. When one of its two manuscripts is defective, its original reading can often be restored from the other. The most obvious difference between the long version and the short version is that the former contains a lengthy excerpt from a certain *Book of Zoroaster* (cf. 15:29–19:8f).

2. A *short version*, which is represented by Coptic MS NHC III, differs from the others in certain details of phraseology and systematic theology; as a Coptic translation it differs in style and vocabulary from all the other Coptic versions.

3. Another *short version*, which is represented by Coptic MS p. Berol. 8502, also differs in certain details of phraseology and systematic theology; as a Coptic translation it differs in style and vocabulary from all the other Coptic versions.

4. The *summary* of BJn in St. Irenaeus (IrG) is too brief and compressed to classify as long or short, but in any case it shows certain minor differences that distinguish it from each of the three other versions.

The long version has been chosen for translation here because of its apparent coherence; however, scholars have not determined which version is the original.

In passages where the three texts of the Coptic versions run in parallel, they differ considerably in vocabulary and style. As in the case of EgG, careful comparison of such parallels has made it possible to gain a systematic understanding of the different ways in which the three ancient Coptic translators did their work; thus, in many places where both manuscripts of the long version are defective or erroneous, the original reading of the long version can be conjecturally restored by comparison and stylistic adjustment of a reading found in the other manuscripts. Such restorations, which are supported by the parallel versions, are *printed in italics*. Comparison of the versions has also clarified the meaning of certain Coptic expressions in the long version and has thus been an aid in translation. In a few instances all pertinent manuscripts are defective in a given passage, but the original text can nevertheless be conjectured with certainty: these totally conjectural restorations are enclosed within square brackets [ ].

No adequate critical edition of BJn has been published. The translation below is based on my own unpublished synopsis of the manuscripts, constructed from collation of photographic facsimiles and from Till's critical edition of the Berlin manuscript (see "Select Bibliography").

SELECT BIBLIOGRAPHY

Arai, S. "Zur Christologie des Apokryphons des Johannes." *New Testament Studies* 15 (1968): 302–18.

Barc, B. "Samaèl-Saklas-Yaldabaôth: Recherche sur la genèse d'un mythe gnostique." In *Colloque international sur les textes de Nag Hammadi (Québec 22–25 août 1978)*, edited by B. Barc, 123–50. Bibliothèque copte de Nag Hammadi, Section "Études," no. 1. Québec: Les Presses de l'Université Laval, 1981.

Dillon, J. *The Middle Platonists*. Ithaca, N.Y.: Cornell University Press, 1977.

Dörrie, H., and H. Dörries. "Erotapokriseis." In *Reallexikon für Antike und Christentum*, vol. 6 (1966), cols. 342–70.

Lovejoy, A. O. *The Great Chain of Being: A Study of the History of an Idea*. New York: Harper & Row, 1960.

Pearson, B. "Biblical Exegesis in Gnostic Literature." In *Armenian and Biblical Studies*, edited by M. E. Stone, 70–80. Supplementary Vol. 1 to *Sion*. Jerusalem: St. James Press, 1975.

Philo Judaeus. "On the Account of the World's Creation Given by Moses (De Opificio Mundi)." In vol. 1 of *Philo*, translated by F. H. Colson and G. H. Whitaker, 1–137, 475–76. Loeb Classical Library. New York: G. P. Putnam's Sons, 1929.

Plato. "Timaeus." In vol. 7 of *Plato with an English Translation*, by R. G. Bury, 1–253. Loeb Classical Library. New York: G. P. Putnam's Sons, 1929.

Quispel, G. "Valentinian Gnosis and the *Apocryphon of John*." In *The Rediscovery of Gnosticism: Proceedings of the International Conference on Gnosticism at Yale, New Haven, Connecticut, March 28–31, 1978*, edited by B. Layton. Vol. 1, *The School of Valentinus*, 118–27 (and discussion, 119–32). Leiden: E. J. Brill, 1980.

Rudolph, K. "Der gnostische 'Dialog' als literarisches Genus." In *Probleme der koptischen Literatur*, 85–107. Wissenschaftliche Beiträge der Martin-Luther-Universität Halle-Wittenberg, no. 1 [K2]. Halle: n.p., 1968.

Tardieu, M. *Écrits gnostiques: Codex de Berlin*, 26–47, 83–166, 239–345, 414–16, 421–518. Sources gnostiques et manichéennes 1. Paris: Le Cerf, 1984. (Synoptic translation of the different versions with a commentary.)

Till, W. "The Gnostic Apocryphon of John." *Journal of Ecclesiastical History* 3 (1952): 14–22.

Till, W., and H.-M. Schenke. *Die gnostischen Schriften des koptischen Papyrus Berolinensis 8502*. 2d ed. Texte und Untersuchungen, no. 60. Berlin: Akademie, 1972.

Tobin, T. H. *The Creation of Man: Philo and the History of Interpretation*. Catholic Biblical Quarterly Monograph Series, no. 14. Washington, D.C.: Catholic Biblical Association of America, 1983. (Jewish-Platonist predecessors of the author of BJn.)

van den Broek, R. "The Creation of Adam's Psychic Body in the *Apocryphon of John*." In *Studies in Gnosticism . . . Presented to Gilles Quispel*, edited by R. van den Broek and M. J. Vermaseren, 38–57. Études préliminaires aux religions orientales dans l'empire romain, no. 91. Leiden: E. J. Brill, 1981.

Welburn, A. J. "The Identity of the Archons in the 'Apocryphon Johannis.'" *Vigiliae Christianae* 32 (1978): 241–54.

Wintermute, O. "A Study of Gnostic Exegesis of the Old Testament." In *The Use of the Old Testament in the New and Other Essays: Studies in Honor of William Franklin Stinespring*, edited by J. M. Efird, 241–70. Durham, N.C.: Duke University Press, 1972.

THE SECRET BOOK[a]
ACCORDING TO JOHN[b]

Contents

1 **1** The teaching [of the] savior and [the revelation] of the mysteries, [which] are hidden in silence [and which] it (the savior) taught to John [its] disciple.

I. FRAME STORY (INTRODUCTION)

Dialogue of John and a Pharisee

5 *Once*[c] upon a time when John *the brother* of James, one of the *sons* 8 *of* Zebedee, was going up to the temple[d] •a Pharisee named Arimanios encountered him and said to him, *Where* is your teacher, the man *that* you *used* to follow?

11 And *he (John) said to him,* He has *returned to* the *place* from which he came.

12,13 The Pharisee *said to him,* •*That Nazarene*[e] *has greatly* misled you, 16 *filled your ears with lies,* closed [your hearts], •*and turned you* away [from] the traditions *of your* [ancestors].

II. JOHN'S NARRATION

John's distress

17 *When I*[f] heard these words, I *turned* away from the temple *towards* 20,21 *the barren mountain,*[g] •*and I was very* distressed, *saying,* •*How indeed* 22 *was* the savior *chosen?* •And *why was he sent into the world* by *his* 23,24 *parent who sent him?* •*And who is his parent who* [sent him]? •*And* 26 *what* is *that* realm *like, to which we shall go?* •For what [. . .] *he told us* that this realm [. . .] *has been stamped in the mold of that incorruptible realm, and did not tell* us *what that other one is like.*

Appearance of the savior

30 At the moment *that I was thinking these thoughts,* lo, the *heavens* 31 *opened,* •*and all creation shone with* light *that* [. . .] *below heaven.*

Title 1 a. Greek *apokryphon,* lit. "concealed (thing)."

b. In the manuscripts, the title is found after the text (at 32:7f).

c. For the meaning of *italics,* see the introduction to BJn, "Text."

d. The Jewish temple of god in Jerusalem. Ancient Christian tradition (cf. Acts 2:46f) held that the earliest Christians in Jerusalem continued to take part in the Jewish religious cult of the temple.

e. "Nazarene": Gk. *nasōraios,* "person

from Nazareth." Traditionally the term was also held to mean "one who is observant," and sometimes referred to members of a Jewish-Christian sect of that name or to Christians in general.

f. From here until 31:31f the narrator is John. But starting at 2:9f, John's narration quotes a long speech of the savior.

g. Or "toward the desert." The Judaean Desert begins at the back of the Mount of Olives, which on the other side overlooks the site of the temple.

33,1 *And the* [. . .] *world* moved. 2 •*For my part, I was afraid,* [. . .] saw
3 within the light *a child* standing before me. •When I saw [. . .] like an
4 elderly person. •And it changed (?) [its] manner of appearance to be like
5,6 a young person. •[. . .] in my presence. •And within the light there was
7 a multiform image (?). •And the [manners of appearance] were appearing
8 through one another. •[And] the [manner of appearance] had three forms.
9 [It][a] said to me, John, John, why do you have doubts, and why [are
11,12 you] afraid? •Are you alien to this kind of thing? •This is to say, do *not*
12,13 *be* timid. •It is I who *am with* [*you* (plur.)] always. •*It is I who am* [the   9:9+
15 father]; *it is I who am* the mother; it is I who am the son.[b] •It is I who
16 am *the* undefiled and the unpolluted. •[Now I have come] *to teach* you
(sing.) what exists, *and what* [has come to be], and what must *come to*
18 *be,* •*so that you might* [know about] *the invisible realm* [and the] *visible*
19 *realm*; •*and to* [teach you] *about the perfect* [human being].
20 Now, *then, lift up* your [face] *to hear and* [learn about] what I *shall say*
22 *to you* today, •*so that you too might convey it* [to those who are] *like*
23 [you] *in* spirit, •and who are [from] *the immovable* race of the perfect
human being [. . .], so that [they] *might understand* [. . .].

III. THE SAVIOR'S TEACHING

The parent of the entirety

26,26   *It said* to me: •The unit (monad), *since it is a unitary principle of rule,*   EgG 50:3
28 has nothing that presides over it. •[. . .] *god* and parent of the entirety   Fr 61:32
IrSat 1.24.1
30 [. . .] presides over [. . .] incorruptibility,[c] •existing [in] uncontaminated   IrG 1.29.1
IrUnid 1.30.1?
32 light, toward which no *vision* can gaze. •*This* [is] *the invisible spirit.*   EpA 40.5.2;
3Tb 121:33
33   It is not fitting[d] *to think* of it as divine or as something of the sort,   v.32
35,36 for it is superior to deity; •*nothing* presides over it, for nothing 3 has   FTh 35:7
v.33
1 mastery *over it*; •[it does] not [exist (?)] in any state of inferiority, [. . .]   Fr 62:27
4 exists in it alone.[a] [. . .] because it lacks *nothing*. •For *it* is utter fullness,
without having *become defective in* anything so that it might be completed
6,7 by [it]: •*rather,* it is always utterly perfect in [. . .]. •It is *unlimited*
because nothing [exists] *prior to it* so as to bestow limit upon it;
9 unfathomable, *because nothing* exists prior to it so as to *fathom* (?) *it*;
10,12 *immeasurable,* because nothing *else* has *measured* it; •*invisible, because*
13 nothing else *has* seen *it*; •*eternal,* since it [exists] unto eternity;
14 *ineffable, since* nothing has been able to reach it so as to *speak of it*;
15 unnameable, since *there is nothing that exists prior to it* so as to give a
17 name *to it*. •*It is immeasurable light,* which is uncontaminated, holy,
18,20 and *pure*; •it is ineffable *and perfect* in incorruptibility: •not in *perfection,*
22 nor in blessedness nor in divinity; •rather as being *far* superior *to these*.[b]
22,24   It is not corporeal, it is not *incorporeal,* •it is not large, it is not small,   Fr 63:5
24,26 it is *not* quantifiable, nor *is it* a *creature.* •Indeed, no one can *think of*
26 it. •It is not something among *the existents; rather it is something* far   3Tb 121:30
28 *superior to these:* •(yet) *it is not as though it were "superior"*; rather,
its proper characteristic is not *to share* in eternal realms (aeons), or in

---

2 a. As is explicitly stated in 30:11f, the
speaker of the teaching is forethought, or the
Barbēlō. Forethought is genderless because
it is simultaneously male and female (cf.
5:6f).

b. "[father] . . . mother . . . son": one of
the basic structures of the Barbēlō aeon (cf.
FTh, EgG, IrG). A similar triadic structure,
but without this terminology, is present in
Zs, Fr, 3Tb.

c. MS BG instead has "the [. . .] god,
parent of the entirety, the holy [spirit (?)],

the invisible, [which] presides over the entirety, which [exists in] its incorruptibility."

d. The description of god that follows
resembles some accounts in second-century
Platonist philosophy; see "Historical Introduction" to Part One.

3 a. MS BG instead has "For, it is eternal."

b. MSS BG and NHC III next have "It is
neither infinite, nor has it been limited; rather,
it is something superior to these."

30 spans of time. •For whatever shares in *an eternal realm* has been
31 prepared *beforehand.*[c] •*And it* [has not been] *divided* by time [. . .] any
33,34 other, *for* it does not receive anything. •For [. . .][d] •For [. . .] it, so that
36 it might receive from [. . .]. •For it gazes upon itself [alone (?)] within
1 **4** its *perfect* light. •For it is majesty;[a] it is an immeasurable [. . .].[b]
3,3 [It is] eternity, [as] bestowing[c] eternity.[d] •It is life, as bestowing *life*.
4,5 It is blessed, as bestowing blessedness. •It is acquaintance, as bestowing
6,7 acquaintance. •[It is] good, as bestowing goodness.[e] •[It is] *mercy*, [as
7,8 bestowing] mercy and ransom. •It is grace,[f] *as bestowing* grace. •(It is
all these things) [not] as possessing (attributes); rather, as bestowing
(them).
9 [It is] immeasurable, incorruptible *light*,[g] [in so far as I can speak]
10 with you (sing.) about it. •Its [eternal realm] is incorruptible, at peace
13 and dwelling in *silence, at repose, utterly* (?) *preceding*. •[It] is the head
of *all* the aeons, *since* it is this which in its goodness bestows strength
upon them.
15,16   Indeed, we [are] not *acquainted* with [. . .]; •we do not (?) know [. . .]   Zs 128:27 ?
except [for] *what* has been shown forth out of it,[h] that is, [the] parent: Fr 67:24
19 for it is the parent that *spoke* to us. •For it is this that gazes at its own   Fr 64:30
21,22 self in its light *around it*, •that is, the wellspring of living water;[i] •gives   FTh 46:16 +
22 unto *all* the *aeons*; •and in every way [thinks of (?)] its image, beholding   EgG 62:9
24 it in the wellspring of the [spirit][j] *and* •exercising will[k] in its [watery]   Zs 17:11
light, [that is,] the wellspring of the *pure, luminous* water around it.

Production of forethought

26   And *its thinking produced* something, and the thinking was disclosed,   FTh 35:1 +
29 *standing* [plainly] in its presence in *the brilliance of* its light. •This is   EgG 51:22
the first *power, which exists* prior to all (others), *and which was shown*   IrG 1.29.1
forth (?) out of its thinking, that *is, the perfect forethought of the*   EpG 25.2.2
32 *entirety*. •The light of this (thought) [. . .] light, the power of the [. . .],   v.29
10:20

---

c. MS NHC III instead has "prepared by others."

d. MS BG instead has "And it is not in need, (for) nothing at all exists prior to it."

4 a. Or "magnitude."

b. Instead of these two sentences, MSS BG and NHC III have simply "(It is) the immeasurable majesty."

c. Because it "bestows eternity," it might itself be termed "eternity." The savior qualifies these epithets at 4:8f.

d. MS BG next has "It is light, which bestows light."

e. MS BG next has "and doing goodness—not as though possessing (something); rather, as bestowing."

f. Or "loveliness": Greek *kharis*.

g. MSS BG and NHC III next have "What shall I say to you concerning it? The incomprehensible is the image of the light, in terms of what I can think about. Indeed, who can ever think about it?"

h. "Indeed . . . of it" (4:15f): MSS BG and NHC III instead have "For none of us has become acquainted with the properties of the immeasurable except for what has been shown forth by it."

i. MS BG next has "the light full of sanctification. The wellspring of the spirit streamed down from the living water of the light."

j. Three metaphors in this passage (4:19–36f) gloss over the difficult traditional problem of why a second principle (here called forethought, Barbēlō) would come to be "produced" from a perfect first principle (the parent). (1) The parent is a detached eye whose function is simply to look. It is surrounded by reflective "luminous water" so that it must "gaze at its own self"; its own "image" that it sees becomes objectified as a second principle, "the image of the perfect invisible virgin spirit." (2) The parent is an abstract intellect whose function is simply to think. It initially has no other object of thought than its own self; the act of "thinking" or thought becomes objectified as a second principle, "the perfect forethought." (3) The parent is a "spring of living (running) water" whose function is simply to overflow endlessly. The overflow becomes objectified as a second principle, the Barbēlō ("great overflow": see "Historical Introduction" in Part One). Note that the first metaphor implies that in the beginning there might have been something together with the parent ("its light"). Metaphors like these are used in a similar context by Platonist philosophers roughly contemporary with the author of BJn.

k. Or "desire."

34,36 that *is, the* image of the perfect invisible virgin spirit.[1] •*This is the* power, the glory of *the* Barbēlō,[m] the (most) perfect glory 5 among the aeons, the glory of the manifestation, which glorifies the virgin spirit and praises

3,4 it, •for because of the latter it was shown forth.[a] •It is the first thinking of the spirit's image.[b]

5,6   It (the Barbēlō) became a womb for the entirety,[c] •for it was prior to all (others), (being) the mother-father, the first human being, the holy spirit, the thrice-male,[d] the three powers; the thrice-androgynous name; and (was) the (most) eternal aeon among the invisible.

14:18
FTh 38:11
v.36
Th 13:2
RAd 64:6
EgG 52:2
IrG 1.29.1
EpG 26.10.4+

FTh 38:14+

Its request for more eternal realms: prior acquaintance

10   And the emanation, that is, *the* Barbēlō, made a request of the invisible virgin spirit, that it be given prior acquaintance (*prognōsis*).

14,14 And the spirit consented.[e] •And *when* it had *consented,* prior acquain-
15 tance became disclosed. •*And* prior acquaintance stood at rest[f] along with forethought, which derived from the thinking of the invisible virgin spirit;
18 and it glorified the spirit *and the* Barbēlō, the spirit's perfect power,
19 for prior acquaintance had come to exist *because of the Barbēlō.*

EgG 51:22
IrG 1.29.1

Incorruptibility

20   *And furthermore,* the Barbēlō made a request that it be given
21,22 *incorruptibility.* •And the spirit consented. •While *it was consenting,*
23 *incorruptibility became disclosed.* •And [they][g] *stood at rest* along with
24 thinking[h] and *prior acquaintance*; •*and they* glorified the invisible[i] and the Barbēlō because of which they had come to exist.

RR 86:32
EgG 51:22
IrG 1.29.1

Eternal life

26,27   And the Barbēlō made a request that it be given eternal *life*. •And the
28 invisible spirit consented. •And while it was consenting, eternal life
30,30 became disclosed. •And *they stood at rest,* •and they glorified the invisible spirit and the Barbēlō because of which they had come to exist.

EgG 51:22
IrG 1.29.1

Truth

32,33   And furthermore it made a request that it be given truth. •And the
34 invisible spirit consented. •And truth became disclosed.

35,35   And they stood at rest, •and they glorified the 6 acceptable (?), invisible spirit and its Barbēlō, because of which they had come to exist.

2   This is the quintet of aeons belonging to the parent, which is the first human being,[a] the image of the invisible spirit, namely:

IrG 1.29.2

3Tb 120:19

---

l. "the perfect invisible virgin spirit": the parent.

   m. For the meaning of this name, see "Historical Introduction" in Part One and note 4j.

5 a. MS BG next has "and thinks about it."
   b. MS BG instead has "the first thinking, the spirit's image."
   c. "entirety": the sum total of spiritual reality deriving from the Barbēlō.
   d. "thrice-male": cf. EgG, note 51f.
   e. "consented": here and throughout this passage, the Coptic word can be translated also "gazed out."
   f. To "stand at rest" is philosophical jargon for the state of permanence, non-change,

and real being, as opposed to what exists in instability, change, and becoming.
   g. I.e. prior acquaintance and incorruptibility.
   h. I.e. forethought, the Barbēlō.
   i. The "perfect invisible virgin spirit," the parent.

6 a. Forethought (cf. 5:6f). The quintet is made up of "forethought" and its four emanations. The four emanations are here considered to be mere aspects of their source, so that also the quintet as a whole can be spoken of as "the image of the invisible spirit," i.e. as being forethought, the Barbēlō.

5 forethought, which is *the* Barbēlō and thinking;
prior acquaintance;
incorruptibility;
eternal life;
truth.[b]

8 This is the androgynous quintet of aeons, that is, the group of *ten* aeons,[c] which constitutes the parent.[d]

Begetting of the self-originate

10 And it[e] gazed at the Barbēlō, (who was) in the uncontaminated light[f]   IrG 1.29.1
12 around the invisible spirit and (in) its radiation. •And the Barbēlō
13 conceived by it, •and it begot a luminous spark consisting of light in an image that was blessed, though *not* equal to its parent's magnitude.
15 This was the only-begotten offspring of the mother-father[g] which ap-
16 peared, •and the mother-father's only begetting; (it was) the only-begotten of the parent, the uncontaminated light.

Its anointment

18 And the invisible virgin spirit rejoiced at the light that had come to exist and that had been shown forth out of the first power of the spirit's
23 forethought, *who* is the Barbēlō. •And the spirit anointed it (the spark)   FTh 37:31
24 with its own kindness[h] until it became perfect, •needing no further   EgG 55:11
   IrG 1.29.1
kindness since it had been anointed with the *kindness* of the invisible   IrUnid 1.30.1
   EpS 39.3.5
26 spirit. •And it stood at rest in the presence of the spirit, which was   Zs 131:14
28 pouring upon it. •And the moment that it received from the spirit it glorified the holy spirit[i] and perfect forethought, because of which it had become disclosed.

Its request for coactors

33 And it made a request that it be given a coactor, namely intellect.   IrG 1.29.1
34,34 And the spirit consented [. . .]. •And while the invisible spirit was
1 consenting, 7 intellect was disclosed. •And it stood at rest along with   EgG 51:22
3 the anointed (Christ),[a] glorifying the spirit and the Barbēlō. •And all these beings came into existence within silence.[b]
4 And thinking[c] wished to make something by the Word (or verbal

---

b. MSS BG and NHC III omit "truth" from this list, counting "the Barbēlō" and "thought" as the first two members.

c. "forethought, . . . prior acquaintance, incorruptibility, . . . life, truth" are all grammatically feminine words in Greek (*pronoia, prognōsis, aphtharsia, zōē, alētheia*), and are here perhaps said to have grammatically masculine consorts, thus adding up to ten. Such an arrangement is hinted at in 7:11f and is explicit in IrG.

d. Lit. "which is the parent" (MS NHC III, "which belongs to the parent"). The parent "is" its emanations even while being distinguishable from them, just as forethought "is" its emanations but is also distinguishable from them (cf. note 6a).

e. The parent, the invisible spirit.

f. MS BG instead has "The Barbēlō, the uncontaminated light, gazed intently at it"; NHC III, "the Barbēlō gazed intently at the uncontaminated light."

g. "the mother-father": forethought (the Barbēlō); cf. 5:6f. Forethought's four emanations in the quintet (6:5f) merely "appeared"; they were not "begotten offspring" of forethought and the parent.

h. "kindness": Greek *khrēstotēs*. Once "anointed," the only-begotten will be both *khrēstos*, "kind," and *khristos* "the anointed." The two Greek words were pronounced identically at the time that BJn was written.

i. "spirit . . . holy spirit . . .": the parent.

7 a. "anointed" (cf. note 6h) and "Christ" are the same word in Greek.

b. In some gnostic systems (e.g. IrV) "silence" is distinguished as an entity that coexisted with the ineffable parent in the beginning.

c. MSS BG and NHC III instead have "and thinking. The invisible spirit wished to make something."

6,7 expression)[d] of the invisible spirit. •And its will became deed, •and was   EgG 51:22
disclosed along with intellect and the light, and glorified it.[e]

9,10 And Word (or verbal expression) followed after will. •For by the   FTh 37:3 +
Word, the anointed (Christ) divine self-originate made the entirety (or   EgG 51:22
all things).

11,12 Now, eternal life is with its will. •And intellect is with prior acquaintance.[f]

Its establishment as god of the entirety

13 They stood at rest and glorified the invisible spirit and the Barbēlō,
15 for because of the Barbēlō they had come to exist. •And the holy spirit[g]
perfected the divine self-originate,[h] the offspring of itself and the Barbēlō,
18 so as to make the offspring stand at rest before the great invisible virgin
19 spirit.[i] •The divine self-originate, the anointed (Christ), who glorified the
22 spirit with a great voice, was shown forth by forethought. •And the invisible virgin spirit established the self-originate as true god over the en-
25 tirety, •and subordinated to it (the self-originate) all authority and the
27 truth that was in it (the spirit), •so that it might know about the entirety:
27,29 which is called by a name that is superior to every name, •for that name
will be uttered to those who are worthy of it.

Appearance of four luminaries and twelve eternal realms

30 For by the gift of the spirit, out of the light that is the anointed (Christ)   FTh 38:33 +
and out of incorruptibility,[j] the four luminaries from the divine self-   EgG 62:11
originate gazed out[k] so as to stand **8** before it.   Zs 29:1
   IrG 1.29.2

1 And the three: will, thinking, and life.

2 And the four powers: IrG 1.29.2

> intelligence;
> loveliness;
> perception;
> prudence.[a]

Harmozēl

4 Now, loveliness dwells at the eternal realm (aeon) of the luminary
6 Harmozēl, and is the first angel. •And with this eternal realm (aeon) are
three additional aeons:

7 > loveliness;
> truth;
> form.[b]

---

d. "Word (or verbal expression)": the divine *Logos*.

e. The parent (?).

f. See note 6c.

g. MS NHC III instead has "the great invisible spirit."

h. "self-originate" (Greek *autogenēs*): the anointed (Christ).

i. MSS NHC II and IV here erroneously insert "of."

j. MS NHC II here erroneously inserts "of."

k. MSS BG and NHC III instead have "appeared."

8 a. "And the three ... prudence": the Coptic text of MS NHC II may be slightly garbled here. MSS BG and NHC III here list "loveliness; intelligence; perception; prudence." The parallel in IrG has "loveliness; perception; intelligence; prudence."

b. Greek *morphē*.

Ōroiaēl

8 Now, it is the second luminary Ōroiaēl that has been established in
10 charge of the second eternal realm, •and with it are three additional
aeons:

11　　　afterthought;[c]
　　　　perception;
　　　　memory.

Daueithai

12 Now, the third luminary is Daueithai, which has been established in
14 charge of the third eternal realm, •and with it are three additional aeons:

15　　　intelligence;
　　　　love;
　　　　ideal form.[d]

Ēlēlēth

16 Now, the fourth luminary Ēlēlēth was established in charge of the　　RR 93:8
18 fourth eternal realm, •and with it are three additional aeons:　　　　FTh 39:13

19　　　perfection;
　　　　peace;
　　　　wisdom (Sophia).　　　　　　　　　　　　　　　　　　　　　3Tb 123:16
　　　　　　　　　　　　　　　　　　　　　　　　　　　　　　　　EgG 68:9
20 Those are the four luminaries that stand before the divine self-originate,　IrG 1.29.4
22 and those are the twelve aeons that stand before the offspring of the
great self-originate anointed (Christ),[e] through the desire and the gift of
25 the invisible spirit. •The twelve aeons belong to the offspring of the self-
26 originate. •And it was by the will of the holy spirit that the entirety
became strong through the self-originate.

Appearance of four archetypes

28 Then—(deriving) from *prior acquaintance and* perfect intellect through　15:9
[disclosure] of the desire of the invisible spirit and the desire of the self-　RR 88:13
originate—the perfect human being, the first manifestation and true　EgG 61:5
　　　　　　　　　　　　　　　　　　　　　　　　　　　　　　Zs 6:21+
34 (person), was named •"the Geradamas (Ger-Adamas)"[f] by the virgin　3Tb 118:25
35 spirit. •And that being was established upon the first **9** eternal realm　IrG 1.29.3
(aeon) with the great self-originate and anointed (Christ), at the first
3,4 luminary Harmozēl, •and its powers[a] dwell with it. •And the invisible
gave to it an invincible intellectual faculty.
5 And it (the Geradamas) spoke, glorifying and praising the invisible
spirit, and said,

7　　　"Because of you the entirety has come to exist;
8　　　And it is unto you that the entirety will return.
9　　　And for my part I shall praise and glorify you and the self-
　　　　originate along with the *triple* aeon[b]—the father, mother, son,　2:13
　　　　the perfect power."　　　　　　　　　　　　　　　　　　　EgG 50:23+

c. Greek *epinoia*.　　　　　　　　　　　The prefix "Ger-" has been explained as Gk.
d. Greek *idea*.　　　　　　　　　　　　*hier-* from *hieros*, "holy"; in any case the
e. "offspring of the . . . anointed": the　name is a neologism in gnostic myth. MS
Geradamas (8:34f).　　　　　　　　　　BG instead has "Adam," NHC III "Ada-
　f. "Geradamas (Ger-Adamas)," known in　mas."
some works as "Adamas"; the name recalls
both "Adam," the first human being, and　**9** a. Cf. 8:2f.
Greek *adamas*, "steel, hard, unyielding."　　b. Forethought, the Barbēlō; cf. 2:13f,

11 And it established Geradamas's son Seth upon the second eternal
realm, before the second luminary Ōroiaēl.

14 And in the third *eternal realm,* upon the third luminary Daueithai, the
17 posterity of Seth was established, •and also the souls of the holy persons.

18 And in the fourth eternal realm were established the souls of those
who were not acquainted with the fullness and did not repent at once,
22 but rather held out for a while and then repented. •They came to exist
23,24 at the fourth luminary Ēlēlēth. •These were engendered beings,c •and
they glorified the invisible spirit.

24:34
RAd 65:5
EgG 62:30
Zs 6:21+
3Tb 118:10
v.14
EgG III 56:3
Zs 7:6+
3Tb 120:9
v.18
Zs 27:27?

Production of wisdom's offspring: Ialtabaōth

25 Now, the wisdom belonging to afterthought,d which is an aeon, thought
a thought derived from herself, (from) the thinking of the invisible spirit,
and (from) prior acquaintance.

28 She wanted to show forth within herselfe an image, without the spirit's
30,31 [will]; •and her consort did not consent. •And (she wished to do so)
31 without his pondering: •for the person of her malenessf did not join in
33 the consent; •for she had not discovered that being which was in harmony
34 with her.g •Rather, she ponderedh without the will of the spirit and
without acquaintance withi that being which was in harmony with her.

35 And she brought forth. **10**

1 And because of the invincible power within her,a her thinking did not
2 remain unrealized. •And out of her was shown forth an imperfect
5 product, that was different from her manner of appearance, •for she had
6 made it without her consort. •And compared to the image of its mother
it was misshapen, having a different form.

RR 94:2
FTh 39:20
EgG III 57:5
Zs 9:16
IrG 1.29.4
EpG 25.2.2

Its concealment by wisdom

7 Now, when she saw that her desired artifact was stamped differently—
serpentine, with a lion's face,b and with its eyes gleaming like flashes of
11,12 lightning—•she cast it outside of her, outside that place, •so that none
13 of the immortals might see it: •for she had made it without acquaintance.

14,15 And she surrounded it withc a luminous cloud. •And she put a throne
16 in the midst of the cloud, •so that no being might see it except for the
19 holy spirit called "mother of the living."d •And she called its name
Ialtabaōth.e

23:20

5:6f, and note 2b. "the triple aeon" is found
in MS NHC III; the other MSS here have
lit. "the aeons, the three."

c. MS NHC III instead has "They will
remain at the luminary Ēlēlēth, assembling
there."

d. Lit. "of afterthought," perhaps looking
forward to the events described in 14:9f.
MSS BG and NHC III do not have this
phrase, instead having "Now, wisdom our
sibling."

e. "within herself": or "by her own
means."

f. "the person of her maleness": MSS BG
and NHC III instead have "her consort, the
male virgin spirit."

g. MS NHC III instead has "not discovered her consort."

h. MSS BG and NHC III instead have
"consented."

i. Or "knowledge of" in the sense of
sexual intercourse.

10 a. MS BG instead has "growing strong
because of the vulgar (*prounikos*) element
within her."

b. "serpentine . . . face": MS BG instead
has "with a snake's face and a lion's face."

c. MSS BG and NHC III instead have
"she harnessed it in."

d. Wisdom. MS BG instead has "life (Zōē),
mother of all."

e. The spelling of this name fluctuates
among "Ialdabaōth," "Ialtabaōth," and
"Altabaōth." For its meaning, see RR note
95b.

Its theft of power from wisdom

19,20   This is the first ruler, •*and it* took great power[f] from its mother, retreated from her, and moved out of the place where it had been born.
23   Taking possession (of another place), it made for itself other eternal
26   realms (aeons) inside a luminous, fiery blaze, which still exists.[g] •And it became stupefied in[h] its madness, which still is with it.

4:29
RR 86:28
FTh 39:28
IrG 1.29.4
EpG 26.1.9
RR 87:4+

Its creation of other rulers

27   And it engendered for itself authorities:[i]

28   the first is named Athōth,[j] who is called "[. . .]s" by the races;
30   the second, Harmas,[k] *the eye* of *fire*;
31   the third, Kalila-Oimbri[l] (or Kalila-Kimbri);
32   the fourth, Iabēl;[m]
33   the fifth, Adōnaios, who is called "Sabaōth";
34   the sixth, Cain, whom the races of humankind call "the sun";
36   the seventh, Abel;[n]
36   the eighth, Abrisene;[o]
37   the ninth, Iōbēl; **11**
1   the tenth, Armoupieēl;[a]
1   the eleventh, Melkheir-Adōnein;[b]
2   the twelfth, Belias, who presides over the depth of Hades.[c]

RR 95:1+
EgG III 57:21
IrG 1.29.4
EpG 25.3.5

11:31, 12:20
15:19
RR 95:13+

4   And it (the first ruler) established seven kings in charge of the seven heavens, one per firmament of heaven; and five in charge of the depth
7,8 of the abyss, to reign. •And it shared some of its fire with them, •but it did not bring forth any of the power of the light that it had gotten from
10,10 its mother. •For, the first ruler is dark and is without acquaintance. •For
12   when light mixed with darkness it made the darkness bright. •But when
13   darkness mixed with light it darkened the light, •so it was neither luminous nor dark, but rather was dim.

11:26
IrG 1.29.4
IrSat 1.24.1
RR 96:3+

15   Now, this dim ruler has three names:

16   the first name is Ialtabaōth;
         the second, Saklas;[d]
         the third, Samaēl.[e]

f. Cf. 10:1f. In 13:21f this act is described as theft.

g. MS BG instead has "an eternal realm (aeon), flaming with fire and luminous, where it now is."

h. MSS BG and NHC III instead have "harnessed to."

i. MSS BG and NHC III next have "(i.e.) the twelve angels—each of them unto its own eternal realm (aeon), after the prototype of the incorruptible eternal realms. And it made seven angels for each one of them, and three powers per angel [BG next has "all told 360 (sic), consisting of angelic beings and trios of powers"] after the image of the original prototype that was before them. Now, the authorities were shown forth in the first begetter and the first ruler of the darkness, out of lack of acquaintance of the one that begot them; and these are their names."

j. MS BG instead has "Iaōth"; NHC III, "Haōth."

k. MS BG, "Hermas."

l. MSS BG and NHC III, simply "Galila."

m. MSS BG and NHC III, "Iōbēl."

n. MSS BG and NHC III count "Sabaōth"

as the sixth; count "Cain" (called either "Kainan-Kasin" or "Kainan and Kaē, called Cain") as seventh; and do not mention "Abel."

o. MS BG, "Abiressine"; NHC III, "Abiressia."

11 a. MS BG instead has "Harmoupiaēl"; NHC III, "Armoupiaēl."

b. MSS BG and NHC III, simply "Adōnin."

c. MSS BG and NHC III next have "Now, they all have other names deriving from desire and anger. In short, they all have pairs of names: one set given them after the superior glory, the other corresponding to the truth that shows forth their nature. And Saklas called them by their names with reference to external appearance and with reference to their powers. Now, over intervals of time they withdraw and grow faint; thereafter they grow strong and increase."

d. "Saklas" (Aramaic "fool"): a conventional name of Satan in Judaism.

e. "Samaēl": Aramaic "blind god."

18,19 And the ruler is impious, in its madness that is with it. •For it said,   13:5+
21 "It is I who am god, and no other god exists apart from me," •for it   Is 45:21
22 did not recognize whence its strength had come. •And the rulers made   Is 46:9
23 seven powers for themselves; •and the powers made six angels for each   Is 45:5
25 of themselves, •so that they amounted to 365 angels.[f]
26 And these are the bodies belonging to the names (?):[g]   19:2
EpG 26.9.6
vs.26
11:4, 12:15
15;14, 17:8+
RR 95:2
IrUnid 1.30.5
EpA 40.2.3
EpG 26.10.1
10:28+

26   first, Athōth,[h] with the face of a sheep;[i]
27   second, Elōaios, with a Typhonian face (i.e. the face of a
        donkey);
28   third, Astaphaios, with the *face of a hyena*;
29   fourth, Iaō,[j] with the *face of a serpent* and having seven heads;
31   fifth, Sabaōth,[k] with the face of a dragon (or snake);
32   sixth, Adōnin, with the face of an ape;
33   seventh, Sabbede,[l] with a glowing face of fire.

34 This is the septet of the week.[m]
35 Now, Ialtabaōth had many **12** outward appearances, and relied upon
2,3 all of them, •so as to show any one of them according to wish; •and
    dwelled in the midst of seraphim.
4,5 It (the ruler Ialtabaōth) shared its fire with them.[a] •The reason it
    dominated them was because of the mother's luminous power of glory
8,9 that belonged to it. •For this reason it called itself god. •And it did not
    believe in the source from which it had come.
10,12 And it mixed with the authorities residing with it. •While it was
    thinking and while it was speaking, the seven powers came to exist;
13,14 and it assigned a name to one power after another.[b] •It began from
    above:

15   first is kindness,[c] with the first (power), Athōth;[d]   11:26+
17   second, forethought: with the second, Elōaiō;[e]
18   third, divinity: with the third, Astaphaios;
19   fourth, lordship: with the fourth, Iaō;
20   fifth, kingship: with the fifth, Sanbaōth;[f]
22   sixth, zeal: with the sixth, Adonein;
23   seventh, intelligence: with the seventh, Sabbateōn.[g]

25,26 And each of these has a firmament in its own eternal heaven.[h] •And
    they were named after the glory of the heavenly realm, for the [. . .]
28 power. •And they exercised power through the names that they had
30 been given by their first begetter; •but the names allotted to them
    according to the glory of the heavenly realm led to their overthrow and
33 powerlessness: •and so they have pairs of names.

f. "And it shared . . . 365 angels" (11:7–25f) is not present in MSS BG and NHC III. See, however, note 10i.

g. Translation uncertain. MSS BG and NHC III instead have "And the names of glory belonging to those in charge of the seven heavens are as follows."

h. MS BG instead has "Iaōth"; NHC III, "Athō."

i. MSS BG and NHC III, "of a lion."

j. MS NHC III, "Iazō."

k. MSS BG and NHC III, "Adōnaios."

l. MS BG, "Sabbataios"; NHC III, "Sabbadaios."

m. MSS BG and NHC III next have "It is these beings that preside over the world."

12 a. MSS BG and NHC III next have "but it did not bestow on them any of the uncontaminated light, i.e. the power, that it had detached from its mother."

b. MS BG next has "and appointed authorities" (NHC III is imperfect here).

c. In MS BG the list is somewhat different: (1) forethought; (2) divinity; (3) kindness; (4) fire (cf. "zeal"); (5) kingship; (6) [intelligence]; (7) wisdom (Sophia).

d. MS BG instead has "Iaōth."

e. MS BG, "Elōaios."

f. MS BG, "Sabaōth."

g. MS BG, "Sabbataios."

h. MS BG, "has a firmament and an eternal realm (aeon) in its own heaven."

Creation of the universe

33   And it (the first ruler) put all things in order,[i] according to the image of the original aeons that had come to exist, so as to **13** make all things 1 in the incorruptible manner: •not that the ruler itself had seen the 2 incorruptible, •but rather, the power within it, which it had gotten from its mother, and which had begotten within it the image of the ordered world.[a]

Ialtabaōth's arrogance

5   And seeing the creation surrounding it and the multitude of angels 8 around it that had come to exist out of it, it said to them, •"For my 9 part, I am a jealous god. •And there is no other god apart from me." 9 In uttering this it signified to the angels staying with it that another god 12 did exist. •For if no other one existed, of whom would it be jealous?

The mother's "movement"

13,14   Then the mother began to move. •She knew about the lack when the 15 radiation of her light diminished. •And she grew darker, for her consort had not come into harmony with her.

IV. DIALOGUE OF JOHN AND THE SAVIOR

A. INTERPRETATION OF GENESIS 1–4

The meaning of "move"

17   And I said, Sir, what is meant by "move"?
18   But it laughed and said, Do not suppose that it means "over the 21 waters" as Moses said. •No, rather when she saw the imperfection that had come to exist and the theft[b] that her offspring had committed,[c] she repented.
24   And in the darkness of unacquaintance, forgetfulness came over her. 25 And she began to be ashamed, moving back and forth. •*And she did* 26 *not rashly try to return, but rather* she *went back and forth.* •And the going back and forth is the meaning of "move."
27,28   Now, the arrogant (ruler) had gotten power from its mother. •For it 28 was without acquaintance, •since it thought that no other existed but its 30 mother alone. •And seeing the multitude of angels that it had created, accordingly it exalted itself over them.

Repentance and elevation of wisdom

32   But when the mother learned that the garment[d] of darkness had not come to exist perfectly, she knew accordingly that her consort had not 36 been in harmony with her, •and she repented **14** with much weeping. 1,2   And the entreaty of her repentance was heard, •and all the fullness lifted up praise on her behalf unto the invisible virgin spirit, *and it* 5 consented.[a] •And while the *holy spirit* was consenting, the holy spirit

Gn 1:1
RR 94:34 +
FTh 40:4
Zs 10:1
IrSat 1.24.1
EpS 39.1.4

11:18
RR 94:21
FTh 44:1
EgG III 58:23
IrG 1.29.4
IrUnid 1.30.6
EpG 25.2.3
v.8
Ex 20:5
Dt 49:9
v.9
Is 45:5

Gn 1:2

22:22

Gn 1:2
FTh 40:3
EgG III 59:6
Zs 10:7
IrG 1.29.4
EpG 25.2.4

---

i. Or "fashioned all things." At this point the story begins to parallel Genesis (Gn 1:1f).

13 a. "And they were named . . . ordered world" (12:26–13:2f): this passage is not present in MS BG (NHC III is imperfect here).

   b. Of wisdom's power (cf. 10:20f).

   c. "the imperfection . . . committed": MS

BG instead has "the imperfection and the coming rebellion of her offspring."

   d. MS BG, "the aborted foetus," perhaps correctly (NHC III is imperfect here). Ialtabaōth is meant.

14 a. *consented:* here and throughout this passage, the Coptic verb can be translated also *"gaze out."*

7 poured over her something of the fullness of all. •For her consort did
8 not come to her (in person); •rather, it came to her through the fullness,   23:20, 25:9
9 in order to rectify her lack.[b] •And she was conveyed not to her own   EgG 61:14 +
 Zs 45:17
11 eternal realm but to a place higher than her offspring, •so as to dwell in
the ninth[c] (heaven) until she rectified her lack.[d]

Projection of an image of a human being

13,14   And a voice emanated from above the exalted aeons: •"The human
15 being exists, and the child of the human being."[e] •But Ialtabaōth the
first ruler listened and thought that this voice came from its mother,
18 and it did not know where it had come from.

18   And the holy mother-father[f] and complete, perfect forethought, the   EgG III 59:4
 IrSat 1.24.1
image of the invisible, i.e. of the parent of the entirety in whom the
entirety had come to exist, the first human being, showed them[g] that it
24 had revealed its image in a representation like a portrait statue. •And
26 all the eternal realm of the first ruler trembled, •and the foundations of   30:19?
26 the abyss moved. •And through the waters that are over the material   Gn 1:2b
realm, the bottom [shone] because of the [appearance] of its image that   Gn 1:3
had appeared.

30   And when all the authorities and the first ruler were dumbfounded,[h]   Gn 1:4a
33 they saw that the whole lower part shone; •and by the light, they saw
in the water the representation of the image. **15**

Creation of the animate Adam

1,2   And it (the first ruler) said to the authorities dwelling with it, •"Come,   Gn 1:26
let us make a human being after the image of god[a] and after our images,   RR 87:23 +
 FTh 40:24
3,5 so that the human being's image might serve as a light for us." •And   IrUnid 1.30.6
 EpS 39.2.1
they performed the act of creation by means of one another's power,
6 according to the characteristics given to them. •And each of the
authorities[b] put into that being's soul[c] a characteristic corresponding to
9 the representation of the image that they had seen. •And they made a
11 subsistent entity, after the image of the perfect first human being. •And   8:28
they said, "Let us call him Adam, so that we might have his[d] name as
a luminous power."
13   And the powers began:

14   the first, kindness,[e] made an animate element[f] of bone.   12:15
15   The second, forethought, made an animate element of connec-
         tive tissue.
16   The third, divinity, made an animate element of flesh.

---

b. "For her consort . . . her lack": MSS BG and NHC III instead have "Her consort came down to her to rectify her lacks (plural). It was pleased to rectify her lacks by the agency of forethought."

c. In the list of twelve aeons given in 8:7f, the ninth from the bottom is afterthought.

d. By returning to regain the stolen power ("lack") in the person of life (Zōē), a luminous afterthought sent from afterthought proper.

e. "human being . . . child of the human being": or "man . . . son of man"; i.e. the Geradamas and the great Seth.

f. MS BG instead has "the holy perfect parent."

g. All the rulers.

h. MSS BG and NHC III instead have "bent down."

15 a. Forethought, the "first human being."

b. MSS BG and NHC III instead have "powers."

c. Or "animate (subsistence)." The original reading of the text is uncertain here.

d. For convenience of identification, the name Adam is hereafter picked up by "he" in the English translation.

e. In MS BG the list is somewhat different: (1) divinity; (2) kindness; (3) fire (cf. "zeal"); (4) forethought; (5) kingship; (6) intelligence; (7) wisdom (Sophia).

f. "animate element": lit. "soul," Greek *psykhē*.

18   The fourth, lordship, made an animate element of marrow.[g]
19   The fifth, kingship, made an animate element of blood.
20   The sixth, zeal, made an animate element of skin.
22   The seventh, intelligence, made an animate element of hair.[h]

23,24   And the multitude of angels stood before him. •And the seven substances of the animate subsistence[i] were taken by the authorities,
26   so that the regularizing of limbs and parts and the joining, i.e. ordering, of each of the constituents might be brought about.

29   The first,[j] Raphaō, began by making the crown of the head;
     Abrōn (?) made the skull;
     Mēniggesstrōēth made the brain;
32   Asterekhmē, the right eye;
     Thaspomakha, the left eye;
33   Ierōnumos, the right ear;
     Bissoum, the left ear;
35   Akiōreim, the nose; **16**
1   Banēnephroum, the lips;
     Amēn, the front teeth;
     Ibikan, the back teeth;
2   Basiliadēmē, the tonsils;
     Akhkha, the uvula;
3   Adaban, the back of the neck;
     Khaaman, the neck bone;
     Dearkhō, the throat;
5   Tēbar, the right shoulder;
     [. . .], [the] left shoulder;
6   Mniarkhōn, the [right] elbow;
     [. . .], the left elbow;
7   Abitriōn, the palm of the right hand;
     Euanthēn, the palm of the left hand;
     Krus, the back of the right hand;
     Bēluai, the back of the left hand;
9   Trēneu, the fingers of the right hand;
     Balbēl, the fingers of the left hand;
     Krima, the fingernails;
12   Astrōps, the right nipple;
     Barrōph, the left nipple;
13   Baoum, the right armpit;
     Ararim, the left armpit;
14   Arekh,[a] the bodily cavity;
     Phthauē, the navel;
     Sēnaphim, the abdomen;
16   Arakhethōpi, the right side;
     Zabedō, the left side;
18   Barias, the lower back on the right;
     Phnouth, the lower back on the left;
18   Abēnlenarkhei, the marrow;
     Khnoumeninorin, the skeleton;
20   Gēsole, the stomach;
     Agromauma, the heart;

g. MS BG next has "and all the system of the body."
h. MS BG next has "and they set all the body in order"; NHC III, "and they set all [the] human being in order."
i. Or "soul."

j. The following passage, 15:29–19:8f (". . . *Book of Zoroaster*"), is not found in MSS BG and NHC III.

16 a. Or "Arekhē."

Banō, the lungs;
Sōstrapal, the liver;
Anēsimalar, the spleen;
Thōpithrō, the intestines;
Biblō, the kidneys;
24   Roerōr, the connective tissue;[b]
24   Taphreō, the vertebrae;
25   Ipouspobōba, the veins;
Bineborin, the arteries;
Latoimenpsēphei, the pneumatic[c] system within all the limbs;
28   Enthollei[.], all the flesh;
28   Bedouk, the right buttock (?);
Arabēei, the left ⟨buttock (?)⟩;
29   ⟨. . .⟩,[d] the penis;
Eilō, the testicles;
Sōrma, the private parts;
30   Gormakaiokhlabar, the right thigh;
Nebrith, the left thigh;
Psērēm, the muscles of the right thigh;
Asaklas, the muscle of the left thigh;
34   Ormaōth, the right knee;
Ēmēnun, the left knee;
Knuks, the right leg; **17**
1   Tupēlon, the left leg;
2   Akhiēl, the right ankle;
Phnēmē, the left ankle;
Phiouthrom, the right foot;
Boabel, the toes of the right foot;
Trakhoun, the left foot;
Phikna, the toes of the left foot;
Miamai, the toenails;
6   Labērnium, ⟨the . . .⟩.[a]

7 Now, those which are ordained in charge of the preceding are seven in number:

8   Athōth;
Armas;
Kalila;
Iabēl;
Sabaōth;
Cain;
Abel.

8 And those which provide activation in the limbs are, according to parts:

10   first the head, Diolimodraza;
10   the back of the neck, Iammeaks;
11   the right shoulder, Iakouib;
the left shoulder, Ouertōn;
12   the right hand, Oudidi;
the left hand, Arbao;
the fingers of the right hand, Lampnō;
the fingers of the left hand, Lēekaphar;

---

b. Or "nervous system."
c. Or "respiratory."
d. The word "⟨buttock⟩ (?)" and the angel's name are missing. Through an inadvertence, MSS NHC II and IV omit a few words, having "Arabēei, the left penis."

17 a. One or more words are inadvertently omitted here.

15   the right nipple, Barbar;
            the left nipple, Imaē;
            the chest, Pisandiaptēs;
17   the right armpit, Koadē;
            the left armpit, Odeōr;
18   the right side, Asphiksiks;
            the left side, Sunogkhouta;[b]
19   the bodily cavity, Arouph;
            the abdomen, Sabalō;
20   the right thigh, Kharkharb;
            the left thigh, Khthaōn;
22   all the private parts, Bathinōth;[c]
22   the right knee, Khouks;
            the left knee, Kharkha;
            the right leg, Aroēr;
            the left leg, Tōekhtha;
            the right ankle, Aōl;
            the left ankle, Kharanēr;
26   the right foot, Bastan;
            the toes of the right foot, Arkhentekhtha;
            the left foot, Marephnounth;
            the toes of the left foot, Abrana.

29 [And (?)] seven, i.e. 7, were [ordained (?)] in charge of the preceding: 17:8

30   Mikhaēl;
            Ouriēl;
            Asmenedas;
            Saphasatoēl;
            Aarmouriam;
            Rikhram;
            Amiōrps.

32,33 And those which are in charge of perception are Arkhendekta; •and the
34 one that is in charge of reception,[d] Deitharbathas; •of imaging,[e] Oummaa;
35,1 of [harmony (with imaged information)], **18** Aakhiaram; •of all impulse
to action,[a] Riaramnakhō.
2   And the wellspring of the demons that are in all the body is divided
5 in four: heat, cold, wetness, dryness. •And the mother of them all is
matter.

6   Ruling over heat (is) Phloksopha;
            cold, Oroorrothos;
            dryness, Erimakhō;
            wetness, Athurō.

10 And Onorthokhrasaei the mother of all these stands in their midst, of
13 unlimited extent; and she is mixed with all of them. •And truly she is
matter, for they are nourished by her.
14   The four leading demons:

15   Ephememphi belongs with pleasure;
16   Iōkō, with desire;
17   Nenentōphni, with grief;
18   Blaomēn, with fear.

---

b. Or "Sounogkhouta."
c. Or "Thabin."
d. Or "perceived information."
e. Or "received information."

18 a. "reception . . . imaging . . . [har-
mony] . . . impulse to action": jargon from
the ethical division of Stoic philosophy.

18,19 And the mother of them all (is) Esthēnsis-Oukh-Epi-Ptoē.[b] •And out of the four demons came passions.

20 From grief:

> envy;
> fanaticism;
> pain;
> distress;
> contention for victory;
> lack of repentance;
> anxiety;
> mourning;
> and so forth.

24 From pleasure come many imperfections and vain boasting, and the like.

26 From desire:

> anger;
> wrath;
> [bitterness];
> bitter lust;
> insatiableness;
> and the like.

30 From fear:

> terror;
> entreaty;
> anguish;
> shame.

31,32 Now, all these are as it were virtues[c] and vices. •And the thought of
1 their truth is Anaiō (?), which is the head of the material soul: **19** •for it dwells with Esthēsis-Zoukh-Epi-Ptoē.[a]

2,3 Here is the number of the angels: all told, they amount to 365; •and they all labored at him (the human being), until limb by limb the animate and material body[b] was completed. 11:25

6 Now, others, whom I have not mentioned to you (sing.), preside over
8 the rest of the passions; •and if you want to know about them, the matter is written in the *Book of Zoroaster*. Porph 16.3 +

His immobility

10 And all the angels and demons labored, until they put the animate RR 88:4
13 body in order. •And for a long time their product existed inactive and IrSat 1.24.1
immovable.[c] IrUnid 1.30.6

Passage of wisdom's power into Adam

15 So when the mother wished to recover the power that she had 10:19 / RR 87:4 / FTh 40:25 / IrSat 1.24.1
surrendered to the first ruler, she entreated the greatly merciful mother- IrUnid 1.30.6

---

b. I.e. Greek *aisthēsis oukh epi ptoa*, "perception not in a state of excitement": more Stoic ethical jargon, a description of the psychic state of the virtuous person.
c. Or "valued categories."

19 a. Greek for either "perception not in a state of excitement" or "the seven perceptive faculties not in a state of excitement"; cf. note 18b.

b. "and material": with these words the narrator anticipates slightly, since the material body's creation is described at 20:28f. The present passage tells only how the "animate . . . body was completed."
c. MSS BG and NHC III next have "For, the seven authorities could not raise it; neither could the 360 angels that had constructed the chains."

18 father[d] of the entirety; •and by divine counsel the mother-father sent
21 five luminaries[e] in place of[f] the angels of the first ruler. •[And] they
counseled it (the ruler), and in consequence, the mother's power was
extracted from it.

22   Indeed, they said to Ialtabaōth, "Blow some of your spirit into his
25 face and his body will arise." •And Ialtabaōth blew some of its spirit,
that is, the power of its mother, upon him.
27,28   It did not understand, since it existed without acquaintance. •And the
mother's power left Altabaōth (i.e. Ialtabaōth) and entered the animate
body, which they had labored at after the image of the aboriginal existent.

Relegation of Adam to the realm of matter

32,34   The body moved, became strong, and shone. •And in that moment
1 the rest of the powers became envious; **20** •for by the efforts of all of
2 them he had come to exist, •and they had given their power to the
3 human being.[a] •And his intelligence became stronger than those which
had made him, and stronger than the first ruler.
5   Now, when they knew that he shone, thought more than they did,
and was naked of imperfection, they took him and cast him down into
the lower part of all matter.

Sending of a helper (life) to Adam

9   But the blessed, beneficent, compassionate mother-father had pity on
13 the mother's power, which had been extracted from the first ruler; •and
furthermore (had pity) because they were about to gain control over the
14 animate and perceptible body. •And by its beneficent spirit whose mercy
is great it sent unto Adam a helper, a luminous afterthought,[b] which
19 derived from it and which was called life (Zōē). •And afterthought
rendered assistance to the whole creature, suffering along with him;[c]
20,21 leading him into his fulfillment;[d] •teaching him about his descent as the
23 posterity—•about the way of ascent, by which he had descended.
24   And the afterthought of the light hid within Adam so that the rulers
27 might not understand, •and that rather the afterthought[e] might be a
rectification of the mother's lack.[f]

Creation of Adam's material body

28   And the human being became visible because of the light's shadow
30 that existed within him, •and his thinking surpassed all those who had
32 made him. •When they looked up, they beheld that his thinking was
33 higher. •And along with all the host of rulers and the host of angels,
35 they made a plan. •Taking fire, earth, **21** and water, they mixed them
2 together with the four fiery winds. •And they became forged to one
4 another, and a great disturbance was made. •And they brought him into

EgG III 65:23?

Gn 2:7
RAd 64:22+
RR 88:3
FTh 45:28
IrUnid 1.30.6

IrUnid 1.30.8

20:19+

RR 88:13
Th 14:10+
FTh 35:12
IrSat 1.24.1
Gn 3:20
Th 16:11
FTh 35:12
v.19
20:3, 20:30
21:14, 22:15
22:28, 28:2
Gn 2:18
RAd 64:12
RR 88:17
IrUnid 1.30.12
v.21
3St 127:20

IrUnid 1.30.9
20:19+

RR 87:23+

Gn 2:7

---

d. Forethought.
   e. MS BG instead has "sent the self-
originate and its four luminaries."
   f. MSS BG and NHC III, "after the manner of."

20 a. MS NHC III next has "And he bore
(within him) the souls of the seven authorities
and their powers."
   b. Forethought (the "mother-father") sends
wisdom back down into the material world
from her temporary residence in the ninth

heaven, the realm of the aeon afterthought
(14:11f). Wisdom as an envoy of forethought
is called forethought's afterthought, an "afterthought, which derived from it."
   c. Or "to all creation, suffering along with
them."
   d. Or "fullness."
   e. "the afterthought": MSS BG and NHC
III instead have "wisdom (Sophia) our sibling
that resembles us."
   f. I.e. might bring about the reclamation
of the missing power.

the shadow of death, in order to perform again the act of modeling, out
7 of earth, water, fire, and the spirit that derives from matter—•that is,
out of the ignorance of darkness, and desire, and their counterfeit spirit.[a]
9 That is the cave[b] of the remodeling of the body in which the brigands
12 clothed[c] the human being, the bond[d] of forgetfulness. •And he became
13 a mortal human being. •It is he who was the first to descend, and the
first to separate.
14　But it was the afterthought of the light within him that was raising his
thinking.

22:32+
Gn 2:21
20:19+

His introduction into paradise

16　And the rulers brought him and put him in the garden (paradise).
18,19 And they said to him, "Eat"—namely, at leisure. •For in fact their food[e]
21 is bitter, and their beauty is lawless; •while their enjoyment is deception,
their trees are impiety, their fruit is incurable poison, and their promise
24 is death. •And it was in the midst of the garden that they put the tree
of their life.

Gn 2:15
RR 88:24

Trees of paradise

26　Now, I shall teach you (plur.) what is the mystery of their life, the
29 plan they made with one another, the image of their spirit:[f] •its root is
31 bitter; its branches are deadly; •its shade is hateful; deception resides
33 in its leaves; •its blossom is the anointing of wickedness; its fruit is
34,36 death; •its seed is desire; and it is in the dark that it blossoms. •The
2 dwelling place of those who eat 22 of it is Hades, •and the darkness is
their realm of repose.
3　But as for that tree which is called by them the tree of acquaintance
with good and evil, and which is the afterthought of the light, they[a]
remained in its presence[b] lest he[c] gaze upon his fulfillment[d] and recognize
9 the nakedness of his shame. •But I rectified them so that they ate.

FTh 44:19

Gn 2:9
RR 89:34
IrG 1.29.3
IrUnid 1.30.9
EpG 26.2.6

The snake

9　And I said to the savior, Sir, was it not the snake that taught Adam
to eat?
11,12　The savior laughed and said, •The snake taught them to consume
imperfection consisting of the sowing of desire for corruption, so that
15 he (Adam) might become useful to it. •And it knew that he was disobedient
to it[e] because of the light of the afterthought dwelling within him and
18 making him more upright in his thinking than the first ruler. •And it

Gn 3:4

20:19+

21 a. "counterfeit": or "mimicking, imitative." Cf. 29:14f. MS BG instead has "adversarial spirit."
　b. "shadow . . . cave (Greek *spēlaion*)" (21:4–9f): Platonist clichés for the material world, based ultimately on Plato's *Republic*, book 7. "Cave" is also traditionally associated with "brigands" (21:9f).
　c. The "brigands" (a cliché for demons) are the rulers; the material body is here likened to the soul's garment in which it is "clothed," another cliché.
　d. "bond": a Platonist cliché for the material body.
　e. Or "enjoyment."
　f. The counterfeit spirit. Instead of "the

image of their spirit" MSS BG and NHC III have "namely their counterfeit spirit that derives from them so as to turn him back, so that he might not know his fulfillment (or fullness). That tree is of the following sort."

22 a. The rulers.
　b. "remained in its presence": MSS BG and NHC III instead have "gave the command not to taste of it, i.e. not to hearken to it; for the commandment was directed against him."
　c. Adam.
　d. Or "fullness."
　e. The snake is identified with one of the rulers, as in IrUnid.

wanted to extract from Adam the power that it had imparted to him.
20 And it caused a deep sleep to fall upon Adam.　　　　　　　　　　Gn 2:21

Creation of Eve

21   And I said to the savior, What does "deep sleep" mean?　　RR 89:3

22,23   And it said, It is not as you have heard that Moses wrote; •for in his   13:18
First Book (i.e. Genesis) he said that he made him lie down: no, rather   IrSat 1.24.2

25 (it means) in his perceptions.[f] •For also he said through the prophet, "I shall make their hearts[g] heavy, that they might not understand, and might not be able to see."

28,29   Next the afterthought of the light hid within him. •And the first ruler   20:19 +

31 wanted to extract it from his side. •But the afterthought of the light is

32 incomprehensible: •although the darkness was pursuing it, it could not comprehend[h] it.

32   And it (the ruler) extracted a portion of his power from him and   21:13
performed another act of modeling, in the form of a female, after the   Gn 2:21
  RR 89:7 +

36 image of the afterthought that had been shown forth to it. •And into the   IrUnid 1.30.7
modeled form of femaleness it brought 23 the portion it had taken from   EpS 39.2.1
the power[a] of the human being—not "his rib," as Moses said.

4,5   And he saw the woman beside him. •And at that moment the luminous afterthought was shown forth, for it had removed the veil from around

8 his heart; •and he became sober out of the drunkenness[b] of the darkness.

9 And he recognized his partner in essence, and said, "This now is bone   Gn 2:23

11 of my bones and flesh of my flesh. •Therefore man will leave his father   RR 89:13
and his mother and cleave to his wife, and they shall both become one flesh. For his consort will be sent to him."

20   Now, wisdom (Sophia) our sibling, who innocently descended[c] in   14:8 +
order to rectify her lack, was therefore called life (Zōē)—i.e. mother of   10:16

25 the living—by the forethought of the absolute power of heaven. •And   Gn 3:20

25 [. . .] him [. . .]. •And thanks to it (life) they tasted perfect acquaintance.

26   I myself was shown forth in the manner of an eagle upon the tree of acquaintance—which is the afterthought deriving from the uncontami-

30 nated, luminous forethought—•so that I might teach them and raise them

31 out of the depth of sleep. •For they both dwelled in a corpse,[d] and knew

33 that they were naked. •The shining afterthought was shown forth to them, raising their thinking.

The expulsion from paradise

35   But when Aldabaōth (i.e. Ialtabaōth) knew that they had withdrawn   RR 90:19

37 from it, it cursed its earth. •It found the female preparing 24 herself for   IrUnid 1.30.8
  Gn 3:17

1,2 her male—•he was master over her,[a] •for he was not acquainted with   v.1
the mystery that had come to pass from the holy plan.　　　　　　　　Gn 3:16

4,4   And they were afraid to rebuke it (Ialtabaōth). •And he (Adam)

6 showed[b] its lack of acquaintance that is within it to its angels. •And it[c]   Gn 3:24

7 expelled them from the garden, •and clothed them in obscure darkness.

---

f. MSS BG and NHC III instead have "rather, it covered his perceptions with a veil and weighed him down with unconsciousness."

g. MSS BG and NHC III, "the ears of their hearts."

h. Or "seize."

23 a. Wisdom's "power" is now divided between Adam and Eve; by them it will be transmitted into succeeding generations in the form of soul, cf. 26:26f.

b. Another common cliché for unperceptiveness, especially typical of gnostic texts.

c. As the luminous afterthought.

d. "corpse," or "fallen thing": the body.

24 a. "It found . . . over her" (23:37–24:1f): MSS BG and NHC III instead have "And what is more, it gave over the female so that the male might be master over her."

b. Or possibly "it (Ialdabaōth) displayed."

c. MS BG instead has "its angels."

Cain and Abel

8   And the first ruler saw the female virgin[d] standing with Adam, and
saw that the living, luminous afterthought had been shown forth within
12,13   her. •And Aldabaôth became filled with lack of acquaintance. •Now,
the forethought of the entirety learned of this, and sent certain beings,
15   who caught life (Zōē) up out of Eve. •And the first ruler defiled her,[e]
and begot on her two sons—the first and the second, Elōim and Iaue.[f]
18,19   Elōim has the face of a bear; Iaue, the face of a cat. •One is just, the
20   other is unjust: Iaue is just, Elōim is unjust. •It established Iaue in
charge of fire and wind, and established Elōim in charge of water and
24   earth. •And it called them by the names Cain and Abel, with trickery in
mind.
26   And to the present day sexual intercourse, which originated from the
28   first ruler, has remained. •And in the female who belonged to Adam it
29   sowed a seed of desire; •and by sexual intercourse it raised up birth in
31   the image of the bodies. •And it supplied them some of its counterfeit
32   spirit. •And it established the two rulers in charge of realms, so that
they ruled over the cave.[g]

Gn 4:1
RAd 66:25
RR 91:11
EgG 71:6
IrUnid 1.30.9
EpS 39.2.1
EpA 40.5.3
v.13
RAd 64:28
RR 89:25

RAd 67:2
Th 18:28

Seth

34   Now, after Adam had known the image of his own prior acquaintance,[h]
he begot the image 25 of the child of the human being,[a] and called him
Seth, after the race[b] in the eternal realms.
2   Likewise, also the mother sent down her spirit[c] in the image of the
female being that resembled her, as a counterpart of what is in the
5   fullness; •for she[d] was going to prepare a dwelling place for aeons that
were going to descend.

Gn 4:25
RR 91:30
EgG 71:10
IrUnid 1.30.9
EpS 39.2.4
EpA 40.7.1
RAd 65:5
9:11
v.2
EpG 26.1.7+?

Oblivion of Adam and Eve

7   And they were given water of forgetfulness[e] by the first ruler, so that
they might not know themselves and realize where they had come from.
9   And so the posterity temporarily remained, rendering service, so that
whenever the spirit[f] would descend from the holy aeons it might rectify
14   the posterity and heal it of the lack: •so that the entire fullness might
become holy and without lack.

RAd 65:9

RAd 73:10
RR 92:30
14:8+

B. THE SALVATION OF SOULS

The spirit of life

16   And I for my part said to the savior, Sir, will all souls then be saved
and go into the uncontaminated light?

---

d. Eve.
  e. Carnal Eve, from whom wisdom has
now escaped.
  f. "Elōim . . . Iaue": in Genesis and other
Old Testament books Elohim and Yahweh
(Jehovah) are names of the creator of this
world, the god of Israel.
  g. I.e. the material world (cf. note 21b).
  h. Had had intercourse with Eve.

25 a. Or "the son of man."
  b. Or "after the manner of birth."
  c. To compensate for the departure of the
spiritual element from Adam, Eve, and their

first two offspring (cf. 24:13f), wisdom now
sends the "spirit" of life to humankind. It
will remain in Seth's posterity as the element
capable of being awakened and saved by
true religion.
  d. "the female being . . . she": possibly
Seth's sister and wife, Nōrea, known from
other Sethian texts where considerable emphasis is placed upon her role in establishing
the posterity of Seth; cf. RR 91:34f; EpS
39.5.2–3; EpG 26.1.1f.
  e. Or "deep sleep."
  f. Forethought (the "holy spirit") as savior.

18   It answered and said to me, The matters that have arisen in your mind
20 are important ones: •indeed, it is difficult to disclose them to any but
those who belong to the immovable race,[g] upon whom the spirit of life
25 will descend and dwell with power.[h] •They will attain salvation and
26,26 become perfect. •And they will become worthy of greatnesses. •And
there they will become purified of every imperfection and of the anxieties
29 of wickedness: •being anxious for nothing except incorruptibility alone;
30 meditating on it thenceforth without anger, envy, grudging, desire, or
33 insatiableness as regards the entirety; •restrained by nothing but the
35 subsistent entity of the flesh, which they wear, •awaiting the time when
1 they will be visited **26** by those beings who take away. •Such souls are
3 worthy of eternal, incorruptible life and calling: •abiding all things and
enduring all things so that they might complete the contest and inherit
eternal life.

7   I said to him, Sir, can the souls upon whom the spirit of life has
descended, but who did not perform these deeds [attain salvation]?

10   It answered and said to me, If the spirit descends upon them, it is
12,12 quite sure that they will attain salvation; •and they will migrate. •Indeed,
14 the power will descend unto everyone[a]—•for without it no one can stand
5 up. •And after they are begotten, if the spirit of life increases—for the
power comes (to them)—it strengthens that soul,[b] and nothing can
20 mislead it into the works of wickedness. •But those upon whom the
counterfeit spirit descends will be beguiled by it and go astray.

22,23   But for my part I said, •Sir, so when the souls of these people have
come forth from their flesh, where will they go?

25,26   And it laughed and said to me, •The soul—which means the power—
will increase within it (the flesh) more greatly than the counterfeit spirit;
28,28 for it (the soul) is strong and will flee from wickedness. •And by visitation
of the incorruptible it will attain salvation and be taken into the repose
of the aeons.

The counterfeit spirit

32   But for my part I said, Sir, then where will the souls of these others,
who have not known to whom they belong, reside?

35   And it said to me, In the case of those others, the counterfeit spirit
1 has increased **27** within them while they were going astray. •And it
2 weighs down the soul, •and beguiles it into the works of wickedness,
3,4 and casts it into forgetfulness[a] (or deep sleep). •And after it has come
forth it is given into the charge of the authorities, who exist because of
6 the ruler. •And they bind it with bonds and cast it into the prison.[b]
8 And they go around with it[c] until it awakens out of forgetfulness and
10 takes acquaintance unto itself. •And in this way, when it becomes perfect
it attains salvation.

11,12   But for my part I said, Sir, how is it that •the soul becomes thinner
and thinner, returning then to the nature of its mother or to the human
being?

14,16   Then it was happy when I asked it this, and said to me, •You are

RAd 66:1+
RR 96:22+
FTh 41:21
EgG 74:30
IrSat 1.24.2
EpS 39.2.4
EpG 26.6.2

RAd 76:21

---

g. The posterity of Seth.
h. Or "with the power."

26 a. Wisdom's "power" (19:28f) is transmitted, "descends," to all the posterity of Adam in the form of soul, the animating element.
    b. The Coptic text of MS NHC II is slightly corrupt here. MS NHC III instead has "After a person is begotten, the counterfeit spirit of

life of [. . .] is introduced. Now, if the strong (i.e. true) spirit of life [comes], the power or [soul] becomes strong [and is not] misled into wickedness."

27 a. Cf. 22:23f, 25:7f.
    b. Cause it to become reincarnate in another material body ("prison").
    c. In cycles of reincarnation.

17 truly blessed, for you have understood! •That soul will be made to follow
19 the guidance of another in which the spirit of life resides, •and by that
20 other it attains salvation, •and so is not cast into flesh again.　　　EpG 26.10.7 +

Apostates

21　　And I said, Sir, where will the souls go of those who have gained
acquaintance and then turned away?
24　　Then it said to me, They will be taken to the place where the angels
26 of poverty go—•it is the place where no act of repentance is performed—
27 and they will be kept until the day when those who have uttered
blasphemy against the spirit will be tortured and punished with eternal
punishment.

C. THE ENSLAVEMENT OF HUMANKIND

Destiny

31　　But for my part I said, Sir, where did the counterfeit spirit come
from?
33　　Then it said to me, It is the mother-father who is greatly merciful, the
holy spirit who in every way is compassionate and **28** suffers with you
2 (plur.), that is, the afterthought of the luminous forethought.[a] •And it　20:19 +
raised up the posterity of the perfect race, raised their thinking, and
raised up the eternal light of the human being.
6　　When the first ruler knew that they were greatly superior to it and
that they thought more than it did, it then wanted to arrest their
pondering; and it did not realize that they were superior to it in thought　RR 87:17
11 and that it could not lay hold of them. •In the company of its authorities,
12 that is, its powers, it made a plan. •And in turns they fornicated with　FTh 43:13
13,15 wisdom; •and by them, destiny was begotten as bitterness (?): •this is
the last and varied bond, which is of diverse sorts, for they (the
17 authorities) differ from one another. •And it is difficult and overpowers
that being with whom the deities, angels, demons, and all the races have
21 mingled down to the present day. •For out of that destiny were shown
forth all impieties; violent action; blasphemy and the bond of forgetful-
24 ness; lack of acquaintance; •and all burdensome precepts, burdensome
26 sins, and great fears. •And thus they made all creation blind so that the
29 deity above them all might not be recognized. •And because of the bond
of forgetfulness, their sins became hidden (to them); for they had been
bound with measures, times, and ages, since it exerted mastery over
all.

The flood and Noah

32　　And it (the ruler) repented of all things that had come to exist because　RAd 69:2
34 of it. •Again it made a plan: to bring down a flood **29** upon the human　RR 92:3
creation.　　　　　　　　　　　　　　　　　　　　　　　　　EgG 72:10
1　　But the greatness of the light of forethought taught *Noah,* and he　IrUnid 1.30.10
4 preached to all the posterity, that is, the children of humankind. •And　EpS 39.3.1
6 those who were alien to him did not pay heed to him. •They did not—　EpG 26.1.7
7 as Moses said—hide in an ark; •rather, it was in a certain place that　**v.1**
8 they hid. •Not only Noah, but many other people from the immovable　Gn 6:5f
　　　　　　　　　　　　　　　　　　　　　　　　　　　　　IrUnid 1.30.10
　　　　　　　　　　　　　　　　　　　　　　　　　　　　　EpG 26.1.7 + ?
　　　　　　　　　　　　　　　　　　　　　　　　　　　　　RAd 69:19
　　　　　　　　　　　　　　　　　　　　　　　　　　　　　RR 92:8

---

28 a. The text may be corrupt here. Possibly
some words have been left out, as follows:
"The mother-father that is greatly merciful,
the holy spirit that in every way is compassionate and suffers with you (plur.), ⟨. . .⟩,
that is, the afterthought of the luminous
forethought." Instead of "mother-father,"
MS BG has simply "mother."

12 race, went into a certain place and hid within a luminous cloud. •And   RAd 70:16
13 they recognized his absolute power. •And with him was that being which
belonged to the light, who had illuminated them.

The counterfeit spirit

14,16   For it (the ruler) had brought darkness down over all the earth. •And
17 in the company of its powers, it made a plan. •It sent its angels to the   Gn 6:2
daughters of humankind to take some of them unto themselves and so
20 to raise up a posterity as a comfort for themselves. •And at first they
21 did not succeed. •Then after they had not succeeded, they assembled
23 again, and all together made a plan. •They made a counterfeit spirit in
the image of the spirit that had descended, by which they would befoul
26 the souls. •And the angels changed in image, after the images of their
spouses,[a] filling them with the spirit of darkness, which they mixed with
30 them, and with wickedness. •They brought gold, silver, gifts, copper,
33 iron, metal, and all kinds of raw materials. •And they beguiled the people
who followed them into great anxieties, **30** leading them astray in many
2 errors. •Humankind grew old without having any leisure, and died
without discovering any truth or becoming acquainted with the god of
4 truth. •And thus was the whole creation perpetually enslaved, from the
foundation of the world down to the present time.
7   And they married women and begot children out of the darkness,   Gn 6:5
8,9 after the image of their spirit. •And their hearts became closed and
hardened with the hardness of the counterfeit spirit, down to the present
time.

V. POEM OF DELIVERANCE

11   Then[a] I, the perfect forethought of the entirety, transformed myself   RR 97:1
into my posterity.

13   For, I existed in the beginning, traveling in every path of   FTh 36:4+
travel.
15   For it is I who am the riches of the light;
15   It is I who am the memory of the fullness.
17   And I traveled in the greatness of the darkness,
17   And I continued until I entered the midst of the prison.
19   And the foundations of chaos moved.   14:26?
20   And for my part, I hid from them because of their evil;
21   And they did not recognize me.

21   Again I returned, for a second time.   FTh 47:11
23   And I traveled, coming into the beings of the light—   EpS 39.3.1
24   I, who am the memory of the forethought.
25   I entered the midst of the darkness and the interior of Hades,
striving for my governance.
27   And the foundations of chaos moved, as though to fall down
upon those who dwelt in chaos and destroy them.
30   And once again I hastened back to my luminous root,[b]
31   Lest they be destroyed before their time.

32   Yet a third time I traveled—   RR 96:28+
33   I who am the light that exists within the light,

---

29 a. Or "doubles."

30 a. The following passage, 30:11f ("Then
I . . .") to 31:27f ("in your ears") is not
present in MSS BG and NHC III, which

instead have simply "then in the beginning
the blessed mother-father, who is greatly
merciful, takes form in its posterity. I have
come to the perfect realm (aeon)."
    b. Or "source."

34   I the memory of the forethought—
35   So that I might enter the midst of the darkness and the
          interior **31** of Hades:
1   I filled my face with the light of the end of their realm.   IrSat 1.24.2+
3   And I entered the midst of their prison,
4   Which is the prison of the body.
4   And I said, "O listener, arise from heavy sleep."   RAd 66:1
                                                                FTh 35:21
6   And that person wept and shed tears, heavy tears;
7   And wiped them away and said, "Who is calling my name?
9   "And from where has my hope come, as I dwell in the bonds
          of the prison?"
10   And I said, "It is I who am the forethought of the
          uncontaminated light;
12   "It is I who am the thinking of the virgin spirit,   4:26+
13   "And I who am leading you to the place of honor.
14   "Arise! Keep in mind that you are the person who has
          listened;
15   "Follow your root, which is myself, the compassionate;
16   "Be on your guard against the angels of poverty and the
          demons of chaos and all those who are entwined with you;
20   "And be wakeful, (now that you have come) out of heavy
          sleep and out of the garment in the interior of Hades."
22   And I raised and sealed that person, with the light of the   FTh 49:27+
          water of five seals,[a]   EgG 56:25
24   So that from thenceforth death might not have power over
          that person.
25   And lo, now I shall enter the perfect eternal realm:
27   I have completed all things for you (sing.) in your ears.

28   For my part, I[b] have told you (sing.) all things, so that you might   RAd 85:3
     write them down and transmit them secretly to those who are like you   Fr 68:16
31   in spirit. •For this is the mystery of the immovable race.[c]

VI. FRAME STORY (CONCLUSION)

32   And the savior transmitted these things to him (John) so that he might
34   write them down and keep them safe. •And it said to him, "Cursed be
     anyone who sells these in exchange for a bribe, for foodstuffs, for drink,
1   for clothing, or for anything else **32** of the sort." •And these things were
     transmitted to him mystically; and immediately, it vanished from before
4   him. •And he came to his fellow disciples and informed them of what
6   the savior had told him. •JESUS (IS) THE ANOINTED (CHRIST)![a] AMEN![b]

---

31 a. The "five seals" are associated with the reception of *gnōsis* in gnostic baptism (for which, see "Historical Introduction" in Part One).

b. The savior, forethought.

c. MS BG here adds: "Now, the mother came before me once again. Moreover, these are the things she did in the world. She caused the posterity to stand at rest. I shall tell you (plur.) about what is going to come to pass."

32 a. "the anointed": the divine self-origi-nate (cf. 6:23f). This is the only reference in BJn to the Incarnation. Because it does not occur within the central body of the work, some scholars have suspected that it is not part of the original but rather is a pious exclamation added by an ancient Christian gnostic copyist or editor. On the other hand, for gnostic elaborations of the Incarnation, see FTh, EgG, IrUnid, EpS, EpA, EpG; and probably RAd.

b. In the manuscripts the title of this work is written after the text (at 32:7f).

THE REVELATION OF ADAM

(RAd)

Contents

The Revelation of Adam ("Apocalypse of Adam") tells the gnostic myth from the creation of Eve down to the savior's final advent and the ultimate damnation of non-gnostic Christianity. The story line seems to be based primarily on the myth rather than Genesis. An important role is played by angels whose names are known from highly developed works such as EgG and Zs; this may indicate that a sophisticated form of the myth is presupposed. Yet in RAd the tale is abbreviated to the point of obscurity; a single biblical term ("god") is used, for example, to describe both the satanic creator (Sakla, i.e. Ialdabaōth) and the ineffable parent. No distinctive elements of non-gnostic Christianity occur in the work, leading some scholars to regard RAd as textbook evidence for the existence of non-Christian, i.e. Jewish, gnostic religion; such scholars are obliged to minimize its connection with other, more obviously Christian, versions of the gnostic myth.

The genealogy of humankind is especially important to the author of RAd, though its exact details are obscure (partly owing to the imperfection of the MS). The human race appears to divide into three groups or races: *(1)* the posterity of Seth, i.e. the gnostics who are destined for salvation; *(2)* the posterity of Noah, including *(a)* descendants of Sēm (Shem), the people of Israel (?); *(b)* descendants of Kham (Ham); *(c)* descendants of Iapheth (Japheth); and *(3)* apostates from *(2)(b)* and *(c)* who join the posterity of Seth and come under their protection. This threefold division seems to contradict Gn 5:1–6:1, which derives Noah from the Sethid line. Possibly the threefold division of humankind in Valentinian gnosticism should be compared.

Especially noteworthy is a fifteen-stanza poem on the incarnation of the savior, near the end of the work, comprising mythic material found nowhere else in gnostic myth.

Literary background

The author and place of composition of RAd are unknown. The date of its composition must be before A.D. 350, the approximate date of the MS. The mythic content of RAd resembles EgG, 3Tb, FTh, Zs, and Fr. The work is attributed by implication to Seth, recording words spoken by his father Adam; it is thus an example of pseudepigraphy. The language of composition was Greek.

RAd has a complex mixture of genres in which certain traditional materials are subordinated to others:

  I. Heavenly message
    A. Deathbed literature (autobiography)
       1. Angelic revelation: prediction of the "true history" of humankind

As in EgG and 3Tb, the whole work is presented (85:3f) as a *heavenly message*, in this instance brought by angelic messengers and set on a high mountain, perhaps engraved on tablets. The convention of the heavenly message is a commonplace of ancient Mediterranean revelatory literature. The body of the message in RAd falls into the category of *deathbed* (or farewell) *literature*, in which a patriarch summons his children to hear his last words. Such works, often called "testaments," are known from the Old Testament Pseudepigrapha (e.g. *Testaments of the Twelve Patriarchs*); they do not seem to have ever attained a set generic form. In the present example, Adam makes a final autobiographical statement to his son Seth, and in it he recounts an *angelic revelation* that he once received. The revelation comprises historical predictions, which amount to a revisionist *"true history"* of the Sethid line of humanity down to the final incarnation of the savior, partly paralleling the book of Genesis. The monologue eventually assumes the form of poetry (parallel strophes, 77:27f), but concludes with a prose description of the final damnation of the non-gnostic line of humankind.

Mythic characters

I. Great Eternal Aeons Mentioned in the Work

The ETERNAL GOD, or simply "god." The god of truth.
A REVEALER, in the form of "three persons." (Forethought?)
The GREAT SETH. The human being who is the seed of the great race. "That Human Being."
The GREAT RACE, or incorruptible seed, of the great Seth
The HOLY SPIRIT (not clearly distinguished in the text)
GREAT ETERNAL ANGELS and AEONS, including:
    ABRASAKS, SABLŌ, GAMALIĒL
    MIKHEUS, MIKHAR, MNĒSINOUS
    IESSEUS-MAZAREUS-IESSEDEKEUS

II. Rulers Mentioned in the Work

The RULER OF THE AEONS AND POWERS. The lord god, or simply "god," creator of Adam and Eve. Called Sakla (Saklas).
POWERS and ANGELS that are with the ruler

III. Humankind Mentioned in the Work

ADAM, the first human being
EVE, his wife
A CHILD OF EVE'S begotten by the ruler (Cain)
SETH. A child of Adam and Eve.
NOAH and HIS POSTERITY, including his sons:
    KHAM (Ham)
    IAPHETH (Japheth)
    SĒM (Shem)
The POSTERITY OF KHAM AND IAPHETH, constituting twelve kingdoms
400,000 RENEGADES from the posterity of Kham and Iapheth. A thirteenth kingdom.
The SEED OF SETH. "Those People."
A superior HUMAN BEING, in whom the great luminary becomes incarnate

IV. A Spirit Active in Humankind

PRIOR ACQUAINTANCE, eternal acquaintance. The life, or glory, that belongs to acquaintance.

Text

The original Greek apparently does not survive. The text is known only in Coptic translation, attested by a single manuscript from Nag Hammadi, MS NHC V (pp. 64–85), which was copied just before A.D. 350 and is now in the Cairo Coptic Museum.

The translation below is based on MacRae's critical edition of the Coptic, into which a few new restorations by Stephen Emmel have been incorporated: G. W. MacRae, ed., in *Nag Hammadi Codices V,2–5 and VI with Papyrus Berolinensis 8502,1 and 4* (D. M. Parrott, ed.; Nag Hammadi Studies, vol. 11; Leiden: E. J. Brill, 1979), 151–95.

SELECT BIBLIOGRAPHY

Böhlig, A. "Jüdisches und Iranisches in der Adamapokalypse des Codex V von Nag Hammadi." In *Mysterion und Wahrheit: Gesammelte Beiträge* [by A. Böhlig] *zur spätantiken Religionsgeschichte*, 149–61. Arbeiten zur Geschichte des antiken Judentums und des Urchristentums, vol. 6. Leiden: E. J. Brill, 1968.

Hedrick, C. W. *The Apocalypse of Adam: A Literary and Source Analysis*. Society of Biblical Literature Dissertation Series, vol. 46. Chico, Calif.: Scholars Press, 1980.

MacRae, G. W. "The Coptic Gnostic Apocalypse of Adam." *Heythrop Journal* 6 (1965): 27–35.

————. "Apocalypse of Adam." In *The Old Testament Pseudepigrapha*, edited by J. H. Charlesworth. Vol. 1, *Apocalyptic Literature and Testaments*, 707–19. Garden City, N.Y.: Doubleday & Company, 1983.

Morard, F. *L'Apocalypse d'Adam*. Bibliothèque copte de Nag Hammadi, Section "Textes," vol. 15. Québec: Les Presses de l'Université Laval, 1985. (Detailed commentary.)

Smith, M. "Testaments of the Twelve Patriarchs." In *Interpreters Dictionary of the Bible*, Vol. 4 (1962), pp. 575–79. (Deathbed literature as a Jewish genre.)

Speyer, W. "Religiöse Pseudepigraphie und literarische Fälschung im Altertum." *Jahrbuch für Antike und Christentum* 8/9 (1965–66): 88–125. Reprinted in *Pseudepigraphie in der heidnischen und jüdisch-christlichen Antike*, edited by N. Brox, 195–263. Wege der Forschung, vol. 484. Darmstadt: Wissenschaftliche Buchgesellschaft, 1977. (The heavenly message as a convention of pseudepigraphy.)

THE REVELATION
OF ADAM

The testament of Adam

₂ The revelation[a] that Adam taught to his son Seth in the seven hundredth
₅ year,[b] saying: •Listen to my utterances, my son Seth!

85:19
EpG 26.8.1 ?

I. THE HISTORY OF ADAM

Adam and Eve a mobile androgyne

₆ After god[c] had made me of earth, along with your mother Eve, I used
₁₀ to go about with her in glory.[d] •⟨. . .⟩[e] that she beheld, from the eternal[f]
₁₂ realm from which we had derived. •And she (or it)[g] taught me an account
₁₄ of acquaintance with the eternal god.[h] •And we resembled the great[i]
₁₆ eternal angels. •For, we were superior to the god that had made us, and
to the powers that are with him,[j] which we had not (yet) become
acquainted with.

RR 87:23 +
BJn 4:36
FTh 45:8 +
EgG 62:24
v.12
BJn 20:19 +

Creation of Eve. Passage of divine acquaintance
into an "other" race.

₂₀ Next, god the ruler of the aeons and the powers angrily gave us a
₂₂ command. •Next, we became two aeons,[k] and the glory that was in our
hearts—your mother Eve's and mine—left us, as did the prior[l] acquain-
₂₈ tance that had breathed[m] within us. •And it (the glory) fled from us and
₃₂ entered [some other][n] great [aeon and some other] great [race]. •It was
(?) not from the present realm (aeon)—from which your mother Eve and
₃ I derive—that it (acquaintance) [came]: **65** •rather, it passed into the
₅ seed belonging to great aeons. •For this reason, I too called you by the
₉ name of That Human Being[a] who is the seed of the great race—•or
₉ rather, from him (?).[b] •After those days, eternal acquaintance with the

RR 89:7 +
64:6
64:12
66:21
BJn 19:25 +
v.28
BJn 24:13 +

66:1 +

BJn 9:11
BJn 25:1

BJn 25:7

64 a. Greek *apokalypsis*, "apocalypse."

b. According to the Septuagint Greek version of Gn 5:3–5, Adam was 230 when he
begot Seth and died in the seven hundredth
year thereafter. The scene of RAd is therefore set at the end of Adam's life, and Adam's
speech is like a testament.

c. The ruler of the aeons, the creator.

d. "glory": an extraterrestrial element (see
note 64m).

e. Some Coptic words are inadvertently
omitted here. For grammatical reasons, "that
she beheld" does not relate to "glory."

f. "eternal": gnostic jargon, which in RAd
indicates membership in the spiritual realm.

g. "she (or it)": some entity mentioned in
the words omitted at 64:10f, possibly a manifestation of wisdom.

h. The other god, the god of truth.

i. "great": gnostic jargon, which in RAd
indicates membership in the spiritual realm.

j. In keeping with the biblical style of RAd,
the word "god" is picked up by "he, him,"
etc., in this English translation.

k. Prior to this event, Adam and Eve were
coupled like Siamese twins or as an andro-

gyne. It was widely held that the first human
creation of god was an androgyne until the
splitting apart of female and male.

l. Or "first."

m. According to BJn 19:22f, when the
creator (Ialdabaôth, there called Sakla)
"breathed" its spirit into Adam as breath of
life to make him alive, the stolen "power"
of wisdom passed into Adam. In RAd, "the
glory" has a similar function and mobility,
as a kind of spiritual element.

n. "other": or "foreign, alien"; gnostic
jargon, which in RAd is associated with the
seed of Seth on earth; it is based on Gn 4:25
(Septuagint), "god has raised up to me *some
other* seed instead of Abel."

65 a. I.e. the great Seth. The terms "That"
and "Those" are gnostic jargon, which in
RAd indicates membership in the spiritual
realm. The mystifying "That" (Greek *ekei-
nos*) was esoteric jargon known especially
from Pythagorean circles.

b. The Coptic text is slightly corrupt here;
one or more words may have been inadvertently omitted.

14 god of truth became distant from your mother Eve and me. •From that time on, we learned about mortal affairs, like human beings.   RR 91:9

Enslavement of Adam and Eve to the creator

16,18   Next, we became acquainted with the god that made us. •For we were 19,21 not alien to his powers. •And we served him in fear and servility. •And 24 after this, we became dark in our hearts. •And I, for my part, was asleep in the thinking of my heart.

Adam's revelation

25   Now, I saw before me three persons,[c] whose images I could not   EgG 50:23 + recognize, inasmuch as they were not from the powers of the god that 32 had [made us]. •[. . .] they surpassed [. . .] glory [. . .] . . . [. . .], saying 1 to me, **66** •''Adam! Arise from the sleep of death and hear about eternity   76:24? and the seed of That Human Being,[a] to whom life[b] has drawn near and   BJn 31:4 + which has emanated from you and from Eve your consort.''   65:3
                BJn 25:20 +

Rebuke of Adam by the creator

9   Next, when I had heard these utterances from Those Great People 14 who were standing before me then Eve and I sighed in our hearts. •And   RR 90:19 17 the lord god that made us stood before us and said to us, •''Adam! Why 18 were you (plur.) sighing in your hearts? •Do you (plur.) then not recognize 21 that it is I who am god, who made you (plur.)? •And that it is I who   64:22 + breathed a spirit of life into you (plur.), for you to be a living soul?''

Cain. The mortality of Adam.

23,25   Next, darkness came over our eyes. •Next, the god that made us   BJn 24:8 + made a child (begotten) by himself [on] Eve [your] mother[c] . . . [. . .] 2 . . . [. . .] . . . [. . .] in the [. . .] the thinking . . . **67** •I became   BJn 24:26 + 4 acquainted with a sweet desire for your mother. •Next, the zenith of our eternal acquaintance perished from within us, and weakness pursued 10,12 us. •For this reason, the days of our life became few. •For, I knew that   76:17 I had come under the authority of death.

II. PREDICTIONS REVEALED TO ADAM

14   So now, my son Seth, I shall disclose unto you what Those Persons   65:25 21 whom I had earlier seen before me disclosed unto me. •For after I have completed the times of the present generation and [the] years of [. . .] have come to an end, then [. . .] servant [. . .] . . . **69**[a]

A. EARLY HISTORY OF THE SEED OF SETH

The flood

2   Now, in order that god almighty[b] might destroy all fleshly beings from   BJn 28:32 + out of the earth because of what they seek after, rains of his will [. . .]

---

c: As in BJn 2:1f, the vision of the savior (forethought, the Barbēlō) has three aspects of a shifting character. Cf. BJn, note 2b.
66 a. The coming human manifestation of the great race of heavenly seed of Seth.
   b. The ''prior acquaintance'' of ''glory'' that had ''fled'' from Adam and Eve, and

''entered [some other] great [aeon and some other] great [race]'' (64:28f).
   c. I.e. Cain.
69 a. Page 68 of the MS is blank; it has a very irregular surface and could not have been used by the ancient copyist.
   b. The ruler of the aeons, the creator.

upon those (members) of the seed consisting of the people into whom   64:32
has passed [the] life that belongs to acquaintance[c]—(the life) that left   BJn 20:14
17,19 your mother Eve and me. •For they were alien to him. •After this, great
angels will come in lofty clouds, (angels) that will take Those People
3 into the place in which the spirit [of] life dwells [. . .][d] 70 •exist from   BJn 29:1+
4 the heaven unto the earth (?). •[. . .] the entire [. . .] of fleshly creatures
6 will be left behind in the [. . .]. •Next, god will rest from his wrath.
8 And he will cast his power upon the waters, and [he will] bestow power
upon his[a] sons and [their wives] (after they come) out of the ark, along
with [the] beasts that he has been pleased with and the birds of heaven
that he has summoned and released on earth.

The creator's covenant with Noah

16,17   And god will say to Noah, •whom the races will call Deukalion,[b]   BJn 29:12
19 "See, I have kept watch over you (sing.)[c] in the ark, along with your   EpG 26.1.6
wife and your sons and their wives and their beasts and the birds [of]
1 heaven] that you have called [and released] on [earth. . . .][d] 71 •Therefore
2 I shall give you (sing.) and your offspring the land. •With dominance
4 you (sing.) and your offspring will dominate it. •And out of you (sing.)
will come no seed of humankind that will not stand in my presence in
some other glory."[a]

The creator's discovery of the "other" race

8   Next, they[b] will become like the cloud of the great light.
10   Those who have been cast out from acquaintance with the great
14 eternal aeons[c] and the angels will come. •They will stand in the presence
of Noah and the aeons.[d]
16,17   And god will say to Noah, •"Why have you gone outside of what I
18 said to you (sing.)? •You have made some other race in order to heap
scorn upon my power!"
20   Next, Noah will say, "I shall testify in the presence of your strength   IrSat 1.24.2
that it was neither by me nor [by my offspring] that the race of these
people came to exist. [. . . .]"[e]

Entry of the "other" race into its land

1,3   72 •[. . .] acquaintance [. . .] Those People, •and bring them in to
5 their worthy land, and build for them a holy dwelling place. •And they
will be called by That Name[a] and will dwell there six hundred years in

---

c. The seed of Seth.
d. About four lines of Coptic text have been destroyed here. Noah and the ark were perhaps introduced in the missing passage.

70 a. "He . . . [he] . . . his" (70:8f): the antecedents of these pronouns are ambiguous; either Noah or god almighty is meant in each instance.
b. "Deukalion": a Noah figure in Greek myth. He and his wife Pyrrha built an ark ("coffer") in which they survived a flood brought wrathfully upon them by Zeus.
c. The MS here erroneously has "him."
d. About four lines of Coptic text have been destroyed here.

71 a. "other": or "foreign, alien"; i.e. one associated with the seed of Seth (cf. note 64n). The text may be slightly corrupt here. More logical would be "no seed of humankind that will stand in my presence in some other glory."
b. Probably, the seed of Seth.
c. Presumably the descendants of Cain, since the glory did not return until the birth of Seth the son of Adam.
d. Perhaps not the "great eternal aeons," but rather the lower, demonic aeons ruled by Sakla (cf. 64:20f).
e. Altogether about four lines of Coptic text have been destroyed here.

72 a. I.e. "the seed of *Seth*."

10 acquaintance with incorruptibility. •And angels of the great light will
12 dwell with them. •No hateful matter shall be in their hearts, only
acquaintance with god.

The testament of Noah

15   Next, Noah will divide up the whole land among his sons Kham
18 (Ham), Iapheth (Japheth), and Sēm (Shem). •He will say to them, "My
sons, listen to my utterances. Behold, I have divided up the land among
23 you: then serve him[b] in fear and servitude all the days of your life. •Do
not let your posterity go from before the face [of] god almighty. [. . .]
your [. . .] and I [. . .]."[c]

Shem's covenant

31   [Next Sēm (Shem), the] son of Noah, [will say, "My] posterity [will]
be pleasing in your presence and in the presence of your power. 73
4,6 Seal it with your mighty hand by fear and commandment. •For none of
the posterity that has come forth from me will turn away from you or
10 from god almighty: •rather, they will serve in humility and fear (because)   BJn 25:9+
of their knowledge."[a]

Entry of Hamids and Japhethids into the "other" land

13   Next, others from the posterity of Kham (Ham) and Iapheth (Japheth),
namely 400,000 people, shall go and enter some other land and sojourn
with Those People[b] who came into being out of great eternal acquaintance.
20 For the shadow of their power will guard those who have sojourned
with them from all evil deeds and all foul desires.
25   Next, the posterity of Kham (Ham) and Iapheth (Japheth) will make
27 twelve kingdoms.[c] •And [their other] posterity[d] will enter the kingdom
of some other people.

Accusation against the "other" people

30   [Next, . . .] will consider [. . .] aeon (or realm) [. . .] mortal [. . . of]
3 the great aeons of incorruptibility. 74 •And they will go to Sakla[a] their
4 god; •they will go in to the powers, accusing the great men that dwell
7,8 in their glory. •They will say to Sakla, •"What is the power of these
10 people who have stood in your presence; •who have been subtracted
from the posterity of Kham (Ham) and Iapheth (Japheth), amounting to
13 400,⟨000⟩[b] people; •have been received back into some other realm—the
14 one from which they have come; •and have overturned all the glory of
17 your power and the dominion of your hand? •For, within the realms
(aeons) where your rule has been dominant, the posterity of Noah
through his son has done all the will of yourself and of all the powers;
21 while also Those People and the people who sojourn in their glory have

b. The ruler of the aeons, the creator.
  c. Altogether about four lines of Coptic
text have been destroyed here.
73 a. "knowledge": the word translated here
means propositional or expository knowledge, and not acquaintance (gnōsis).
  b. The seed of Seth.
  c. "kingdoms": here and throughout the

text, the Coptic word can be translated also
"reigns," "dominions," or "kingships."
  d. The 400,000 renegades.
74 a. "Sakla" (Aramaic "fool"), elsewhere
called Saklas: a conventional name of Satan
in Judaism.
  b. Through an inadvertence the MS here
has "400." Cf. 73:13f for the correct number.

25 not done what is pleasing to you, •[but rather] have upset your entire throng.''

Fiery attack upon the "other" people

26   Next, the god of the aeons will give to them some of (?) those who
30 serve [him[c] . . .] except . . . . •They will come to that land where the
great people, who neither have become defiled nor will become defiled
5 by any desire, are going to dwell: **75** •for it was not by a defiled hand
that their souls came into existence, rather they came from a great
commandment of an eternal angel.
9   Next, fire, brimstone, and asphalt will be cast upon Those People. EgG 72:13
11,13 And fire and haze shall come over those aeons,[a] •the eyes of the powers
15 of the luminaries[b] shall grow dim, •and the aeons shall not have vision
in those days.

Their rescue

17   And great luminous clouds will descend, and from the great aeons[c]
21 still other luminous clouds will descend upon them. •Abrasaks, Sablō, EgG 64:14 +
and Gamaliēl will descend and remove Those People from the fire and
25 wrath, •and take them above the aeons and the realms of the powers,
and [take] them [. . .] living [. . . , and] take them [. . .] the aeons [. . .]
dwelling place (?) of the great [. . .] there and the holy angels and the
3,5 aeons. **76** •The people will come to resemble those angels, •for they are
6 not alien to them: •rather, it is at the incorruptible seed[a] that they[b] labor.

B. ADVENT OF THE SAVIOR

The incarnation

8   Once again, for a third time,[c] the luminary of acquaintance[d] will pass RR 96:28
by in great glory, in order to leave behind some of the posterity of Noah[e]
14 and the children of Kham (Ham) and Iapheth (Japheth)—•to leave behind
15 fruit-bearing trees for itself. •And it (the luminary) will ransom their
17 souls from the day of death. •For the entire (multitude of) modeled form[f] 67:12
that came into existence out of mortal earth will dwell under the authority
21 of death. •But those who think in their hearts upon acquaintance with BJn 25:30
24 god the eternal will not perish. •For they have not received spirit from BJn 25:20 + ?
26 the same kingdom;[g] •rather, it is from an eternal, angelic [. . .] that they
have received it [. . .] luminary [. . .] upon [. . .] mortal [. . .] . . . [. . .]
1 Seth.[h] **77** •And he will perform signs and wonders, in order to heap
scorn upon the powers and their ruler.

---

c. Or possibly "who [do not] serve [him . . .]."

75 a. Perhaps not the "great eternal aeons," but rather the lower, demonic aeons ruled by Sakla (cf. 64:20f).
  b. The sun and the moon.
  c. The spiritual realm.

76 a. The great race of the great Seth, i.e. its early manifestation as the seed of Seth.
  b. The eternal angels.
  c. After the flood and the fire.

d. The great Seth (see note 76h).
  e. Offspring of Sēm, Noah's favored "posterity" (Gn 9:26f).
  f. "modeled form": Jewish and Christian jargon for the human body, based on the fact that the creator modeled Adam out of earth.
  g. Implying perhaps that they received a spirit from a different kingdom; cf. perhaps the "spirit of life" of BJn.
  h. The final advent of the "luminary" of acquaintance (cf. 76:8f) seems to be the incarnation of the great "Seth" in the form of a "mortal" human being, who is superior to the powers.

4,5   Next, the god of the powers will become troubled, saying, •"Which (sort) is the power of this human being who is superior to us?"

The persecution

5,9   Next, he will raise up great wrath against That Human Being. •And the glory shall go elsewhere[a] and dwell in holy buildings that it has
12 chosen for itself. •And the powers[b] will not see it with their own eyes, nor will they see the other luminary.[c]
16 Next, they will chastise the flesh[d] of the human being upon whom the holy spirit has come.
18 Next, all the powers' angels and races will make use of the name
23 deceitfully, saying, •"Whence did it (the flesh) come into existence?"
23 Or else, "Whence came the utterances of falsehood that all the powers have failed to make out?"[e]

Explanations of the incarnation[f]

EgG 75:4
Zs 4:25

27   Now, the first kingdom [says of him],
       "He came into existence [from a . . .].
1   **78** A spirit [. . .] upward,
         And he was nourished in the heavens.
2   He received its glory and power,
3   And arrived at the lap of his mother.
5   And it was thus that he arrived at[a] the water."

6   And the second kingdom says of him,
7   "He came into existence from a great prophet.
9   And a bird came, and took the child that had been born
             and brought him into a high mountain.
12   And he was nourished by that bird of heaven.
13,15   An angel came from there and said to [him], •'Arise! God
             has glorified you.'
16   He received glory and strength.
17   And it was thus that he arrived at[b] the water."

18   The third kingdom says of him,
19   "He came into existence from a virgin womb.
21   He was cast out of his city along with his mother;
22,23   He was taken to a deserted place; •there he nourished
             himself.
24   He came and received glory and power.
25   And it was thus that he arrived at[c] the water."

27   [The fourth] kingdom [says of him],

77 a. If the preceding passage describes the temporary union of the preexistent great Seth with Jesus of Nazareth, then the present sentence may refer to the departure of the divine person ("glory"), i.e. the luminary or great Seth, from Jesus' body shortly before his death on the cross; cf. IrUnid 1.30.13.
  b. "the powers" of the ruler of the aeons, the creator.
  c. Perhaps, the great Seth or glory. For "other," see note 71a.
  d. Perhaps, crucify.
  e. Lit. "find." The two deceitful questions (77:23f) concern, respectively, the origin of the incarnate savior's flesh and the identity

of the divine person incarnate in the flesh.
  f. The first twelve stanzas are answers given by the posterity of Kham and Iapheth (73:25f); the thirteenth is by the 400,000 renegades (73:13f); the fourteenth, by the seed of Seth. The poem does not relate an answer by the posterity of Sēm.

78 a. Or "came upon." Possibly, Jesus' arrival at the Jordan for baptism by John the Baptist (Mt 3:13f, Mk 1:9f, Lk 3:21f, Jn 1:31f).
  b. Or "came upon."
  c. Or "came upon."

28	"He came into existence [from a] virgin (?)ᵈ [. . . search]
1	for her himself, **79** •along with Phērsalō and Sauēl and
	his armies that they had sent.
3	Solomōn, too, sent his army of demonsᵃ to search for the
	female virgin.
6	And they found not the female for whom they sought, but
	rather the female virgin who had been given to them:
9	It was she whom they brought.
9	Solomōn took her, and the female virgin became pregnant
	and bore the child in that place.
13	She nourished him within a boundaryᵇ of the desert.
14	When he had been nourished, he received glory and power
	from the seed from which he had been engendered.
18	And it was thus that he arrived atᶜ the water."
19	And the fifth kingdom says of him,
21	"He came into existence from a droplet of heaven.
22	He was sowedᵈ into the sea.
23	And the abyss took him unto itself and engendered him,
	and bore him up.
24	And he received glory and power.
26	And it was thus that he arrived atᵉ [the water]."
28	And [the] sixth kingdom [says],
29	". . . [. . .] to the lower realm (aeon),
1	**80** So that heᵃ might [gather] flowers.
2	She became pregnant from the desire forᵇ the flowers, and
	bore him in that place;
5	And the angels of the flower bed nourished him.
6	And he received glory and power in that place.
8	And it was thus that he arrived atᶜ the water."
9	And the seventh kingdom says of him,
11	"He was a droplet and came from heaven onto the earth.
13	Dragonsᵈ took him down into their dens, and he becameᵉ a
	servant.ᶠ
15	A spirit came over him and lifted him up on high to where
	the droplet had come from;
18	And he received glory and power in that place.
19	And it was thus that he arrived atᵍ the water."
20	And the eighth kingdom says of him,
22	"A cloud came over the earth and surrounded a rocky
	outcrop.ʰ
24	From it he came into existence.
25	[The] angels that preside over [the] cloud nourished him,
27	And he [received] glory and power [in that] place.
29	And it was [thus] that [he] arrived [at]ⁱ [the water]."

d. "virgin (?)," perhaps Greek *parthenos*: of this Greek word only two letters survive in the MS.

79 a. It was commonly believed by ancient Jews and Christians that King Solomon's proverbial wisdom (1 K 4:29–34) extended to the control of demons. In this capacity he was invoked by orthodox writers, gnostics, and magicians.
  b. Or "palisade."
  c. Or "came upon."
  d. Or "cast."

e. Or "came upon."

80 a. Or "it."
  b. Or "desire of."
  c. Or "came upon."
  d. Or "snakes."
  e. "He was a droplet and . . . took him . . . he became" (80:11f): or "There was a droplet that . . . took it . . . it became."
  f. Or "child."
  g. Or "came upon."
  h. Or "a rock."
  i. Or "came [upon]."

1   **81** And [the ninth] kingdom says of him,

2   "One of the nine Pierian Muses[a] went apart from the rest.

4   She arrived at (or came upon) a high mountain and tarried, sitting there, and so felt desire for herself alone, so as to become androgynous.

8   She realized her desire, became pregnant from her desire, and he was born.

10   The angels that preside over desire nourished him.

12   And he received glory and power in that place.

13   And it was thus that he arrived at[b] the water."

14   The tenth kingdom says of him,

16   "His god became enamored of a cloud of desire, and produced him into his hand.

18   And he ejaculated an additional quantity of the droplet upon the cloud.

20   And he was born and received glory and power in that place.

22   And it was thus that he arrived at[c] the water."

24   And the eleventh kingdom says,

25,27   "The father felt desire for his [. . .] daughter, •and she too became pregnant by her father;

28   And she cast [. . .] tomb[d] outside in the desert,

1   **82** And the angel nourished him in that place.

3   And it was thus that he arrived at[a] the water."

4   The twelfth kingdom says of him,

6   "He came into existence from two luminaries,[b]

7   And they nourished him there.

8   He received glory and power.

9   And it was thus that he arrived at[c] the water."

10   And the thirteenth kingdom[d] says of him,

12   "Every one of their ruler's begettings [is] a verbal expression.[e]

14   And this verbal expression received an ordinance in that place.

15   He received glory and power.

17   And it was thus that he arrived at[f] the water,

18   So that those powers' desires might be harmonized."

19   But the undominated race[g] says,

21   "God[h] chose him from all the aeons,

23   And caused acquaintance with the incorruptible quality of truth to reside [in] him."

25   He said,

       "The great luminary has emanated [from] an alien air, [from a] great aeon."

---

81 a. "the nine Pierian Muses": traditional Greek deities of poetry, literature, music, dance, astronomy, and similar pursuits, celebrated as the source and patrons of inspiration and wisdom. Pieria, in Greece, was famous as one of their most ancient sites of veneration.
   b. Or "came upon."
   c. Or "came upon."
   d. Or "cave."

82 a. Or "came upon."
   b. The sun and the moon.
   c. Or "came upon."
   d. The 400,000 renegades, 73:13f.
   e. Or "Word."
   f. Or "came upon."
   g. The seed of Seth.
   h. The eternal god.

28 And [he has caused (?)] the race of Those People to be luminous—**83**
2 those whom he chose unto himself so that they might be luminous over all the realm.''[a]

C. THE FINAL STRUGGLE

Protection of the seed of Seth

4 Next, the seed, who will have received his name upon the water[b]—
7 and from them all (?)—will struggle against the power. •And an obscure cloud will come upon them.

Acclamation of the seed of Seth

8,11 Next, the peoples will cry out in a loud voice, saying, •''Blessed are
12 the souls of Those People,[c] •for they have become acquainted with god[d]
14,15 in acquaintance with truth. •They will live for ever and ever! •For they
17 have not perished by their desires, as have the angels; •nor have they
19 completed the deeds of the powers. •Rather, they have stood at rest[e] in his presence in acquaintance with god, like light that has emanated from fire and blood.

Lament of the damned

23 ''But for our part, we have done everything in the folly of the powers.   IrSat 1.24.2+
25,28 We have boasted of the transgression of [all] our deeds. •We have cried out against [the god] of [truth] because his [works] . . . is eternal. **84**
1,2 These [belong to] our spirits. •Indeed, now we know that our souls are going to die with death.''

Accusation of the damned by the guardians of baptism

4 Next, a voice came to them—for Mikheus, Mikhar, and Mnēsinous,   FTh 48:18+
8 who preside over holy baptism and living water, were saying, •''Why[a] were you (plur.) crying out against the living god with lawless voices,
14 unlawful tongues, and souls full of blood and foul [deeds]? •You are full
16 of deeds that do not belong to truth; •instead, your ways are full of
17 revelry and fun. •Having defiled the water of life,[b] you have drawn it unto the will of the powers, into whose clutches you have been given,
23 so as to serve them. •And your thinking does not resemble that of Those
1 People, whom you have persecuted. . . . [. . .] desire [. . .]. **85** •Their
1 fruit does not wither. •Rather, they will be people who are recognized as far as the great aeons.''

Delivery of divine revelation unto the saved

3 For the extant[a] utterances of the god of the aeons have not been   BJn 31:28+
7 inscribed in the (form of a) book nor are they in writing: •rather, ⟨it is⟩

---

83 a. Or ''over all eternity.''
   b. In baptism (?). The text of this sentence is slightly corrupt.
   c. The seed of Seth.
   d. The eternal ''god.''
   e. To ''stand at rest'' is philosophical jargon for the state of permanence, non-change, and real being, as opposed to what exists in instability, change, and becoming.

84 a. ''Next, a voice . . . were saying,

'Why . . .' '' (84:4f): in this passage the copyist of the Coptic text has miscopied one letter; the English translation presupposes correction of the error. Without correction, the text appears to say: ''Next, a voice came to them, saying, 'O Mikheus, Mikhar, and Mnēsinous: O you who preside over holy baptism and living water! Why . . .' ''
   b. Possibly, by an improper kind of baptism.

85 a. Or ''preserved.''

angelic beings—about whom none of the races of humankind knows
9 anything—who will deliver them. •For, they will be situated atop a high   EgG 80:16+
mountain upon a rocky outcrop[b] of truth.
12   They will be called oracles[c] of incorruptibility [and] truth (given) unto
those who, by wisdom of acquaintance and by teaching of angelic beings,
18 are eternally acquainted with the eternal god: •because he is acquainted
with all things.

III. TRANSMISSION AND CONTENTS OF THE TREATISE

19,21   These are the revelations that Adam disclosed to his son Seth. •And   64:2
22 his son taught them to his seed. •This is the secret acquaintance of
24 Adam that he delivered unto Seth •and which, for those who are
26 acquainted with eternal acquaintance •through the agency of the reason-
born beings and the incorruptible luminaries who emanated from the
30 holy seed, is holy baptism,[d] •Iesseus-Mazareus-Iessedekeus, [the living]   EgG 75:25+
water.[e]

---

b. Or "rock."
c. Or "utterances."
   d. True ("holy") baptism is "acquaintance" (gnōsis).

e. Uncertain remnants of one more line of text survive; apparently it was the title "Revelation of Adam" copied as a subscript, duplicating 64:1f.

THE REALITY OF THE RULERS

(RR)

Contents

The Reality of the Rulers ("Hypostasis of the Archons") recounts the gnostic myth from the creation of Ialdabaōth down to Noah and the flood and concludes with a prediction of the final advent of the savior, the destruction of demonic powers, and the victory of the gnostics. In the first half of the work the story line intertwines with the wording of Genesis in the Septuagint Greek version, tacitly calling attention to discrepancies between the myth and canonical scripture. Of special importance is an unusual account of the rebellion of Sabaōth against his satanic father Ialdabaōth and his eventual installment as lord of the seventh heaven, i.e. as the god of Israel (?). Learned etymologies and puns on Semitic names suggest close contact with a Jewish or Jewish-Christian milieu, despite the anti-Jewish intention of the myth. Apart from the opening paragraph, no elements clearly characteristic of non-gnostic Christianity occur in the work. The author's theological perspective stresses the activity of divine providence ("the will of the parent") even in the deeds of the demonic rulers, probably thus altering to some degree the original intent of gnostic myth.

Literary background

The author and place of composition of RR are unknown. The date of its composition must be sometime before A.D. 350, the approximate date of the MS. The language of composition was Greek.

RR has a complex mixture of genres in which various traditional materials are subordinated to others:

I. Learned treatise
    A. Cosmogony
    B. "True history" of humankind
        1. Angelic revelation dialogue
            a. Cosmogony
            b. Historical predictions

The whole work is presented as a *learned treatise* in which a teacher addresses a topic ostensibly suggested by the dedicatee of the work. The treatise begins with a fragment of *cosmogony*, which leads naturally into a revisionistic "true history" of the events in Gn 2:7f. Within the narration of the true history occurs an *angelic revelation dialogue* (for this genre, cf. BJn, "Literary background"). In it, the revealing angel repeats and elaborates the author's fragment of *cosmogonic myth* in much broader scope, concluding with *historical predictions* of the coming of the savior and the end of days. At the end the narration assumes the form of poetry (parallel strophes).

The sequence of these elements within the work is unnatural and, to a degree, repetitive (86:27f = 94:19f) and thus obscure. The more straightforward order would be:

1. Cosmogony (94:2f, cf. 86:27f)
2. "True history" of humankind (87:11f)
3. Historical predictions (96:28f)

The *"true history"* closely mimics the wording of the parallel Genesis passages but with considerable additions, omissions, and substitutions. The result is a text that sounds like a close paraphrase of Genesis but in fact significantly deviates from it in theology and mythic content. Such paraphrases are sometimes called "targums"; they amount to a form of commentary in which the commentator's remarks have been incorporated into the object of commentary. Typical examples of the form are preserved in Aramaic; they are of either a Jewish or a Jewish-Christian origin and date roughly from the time of gnostic scripture. A classic example is *Targum Pseudo-Jonathan*, which (though by no means gnostic) contains striking parallels to RR.

Mythic characters

I. Immortals Mentioned in the Work

The PARENT OF THE ENTIRETY. The invisible virgin spirit.
INCORRUPTIBILITY
The CHILD, who presides over the entirety
FOUR LUMINARIES that stand before the parent of the entirety: ĒLĒLĒTH and three
    others
The TRUE HUMAN BEING
The UNDOMINATED RACE
WISDOM (Sophia), also called faith wisdom (Pistis Sophia)
LIFE (Zōē), her daughter

II. Rulers, Also Called Authorities

IALDABAŌTH. The chief ruler. Called SAKLA and SAMAĒL.
Ialdabaōth's first SEVEN OFFSPRING, including:
    SABAŌTH
Ialdabaōth's SECOND OFFSPRING, including:
    ENVY
    DEATH, etc.
CHERUBIM, ANGELS, etc., including:
    The ANGEL OF ANGER

III. Humankind

ADAM. The first human being.
EVE. His wife and counterpart.
Eve's children:
    CAIN, begotten by the rulers
    ABEL, begotten by Adam
    SETH, a son through god
    NŌREA or ŌREA
NOAH and his FAMILY
The CHILDREN OF THE LIGHT

IV. A Spirit Active in Humankind

The SPIRIT OF LIFE. The female spiritual principle.

Text

The original Greek apparently does not survive. The text is known only in Coptic translation, attested by a single manuscript from Nag Hammadi, MS NHC II (pp. 86–97), which was copied just before A.D. 350 and is now in the Cairo Coptic Museum.

The translation below is based on my own critical edition of the Coptic, with very minor alterations: B. Layton, "The Hypostasis of the Archons . . ." (see "Select Bibliography") 67: 351–425. An earlier version of the translation appeared in that publication and is revised here with the kind permission of the publisher.

SELECT BIBLIOGRAPHY

Barc, B. *L'Hypostase des Archontes*. Bibliothèque copte de Nag Hammadi, Section "Textes," vol. 5. Québec: Les Presses de l'Université Laval, 1980. (Detailed commentary.)

——————. "Samaèl-Saklas-Yaldabaôth: Recherche sur la genèse d'un mythe gnostique." In *Colloque international sur les textes de Nag Hammadi (Québec 22–25 août 1978)*, edited by B. Barc, 123–50. Bibliothèque copte de Nag Hammadi, Section "Études," no. 1. Québec: Les Presses de l'Université Laval, 1981.

Bowker, J. *The Targums and Rabbinic Literature*. Cambridge, England: Cambridge University Press, 1969. (The targum style as seen in *Targum Pseudo-Jonathan*.)

Layton, B. "The Hypostasis of the Archons . . . Edited . . . with a Preface, English Translation, Notes, and Indexes." *Harvard Theological Review* 67 (1974): 351–425; 69 (1976): 31–101.

Reinink, G. J. "Das Land 'Seiris' (Šir) und das Volk der Serer in jüdischen und christlichen Traditionen." *Journal for the Study of Judaism* 6 (1975): 72–85.

Rudolph, K. "Der gnostische 'Dialog' als literarisches Genus." In *Probleme der koptischen Literatur*, 85–107. Wissenschaftliche Beiträge der Martin-Luther-Universität Halle-Wittenberg, no. 1 [K2]. Halle: n.p., 1968.

THE REALITY OF THE RULERS[a]

I. THE AUTHOR'S TEACHING

Occasion for the treatise

20 **86** On account of the reality[b] of the authorities,[c] inspired by the spirit 96:22 + ?
of the parent of truth,[d] the great apostle[e]—referring to the authorities of BJn 25:20?
23 the darkness—told us that •"our contest is not against flesh and [blood]; Ep 6:12
rather, the authorities of the world and the spiritual hosts of wickedness."
26 [I have] sent (you) this[f] because you (sing.) inquire about the reality [of
the] authorities.

Reproof of Ialdabaōth's arrogance

27,28   Their chief is blind;[g] •[because of its] power[h] and its lack of acquain- 94:23 +
30 tance [and its] arrogance it said, with its [power], •"It is I who am god; 94:21 +
there is none [apart from me]." BJn 10:20 +
    v.30
31,32   When it said this, it sinned against [the entirety[i]]. •And this utterance Is 46:9
1 got up to incorruptibility; **87** •then there was a voice that came forth v.32
3 from incorruptibility, saying, •"You are mistaken, Samaēl"—which is, 93:29, 94:4
BJn 5:20 +
"god of the blind."[a] v.1
    94:23 +

Passage of the power out of Ialdabaōth

4,4   Its[b] thoughts became blind. •And, having expelled its power—that is, BJn 19:15 +
the blasphemy it had spoken—it pursued it down to chaos and the abyss, 94:31
7,8 its mother,[c] •at the instigation of[d] faith wisdom (Pistis Sophia). •And she BJn 10:20
9 appointed each of its offspring according to its respective power[e]—• 95:1 +
10 after the pattern of the eternal realms[f] that are above, •for by starting v.9
96:13
from the invisible domain the visible domain was invented.[g] v.10
    94:34 +

Title 86 a. In the manuscript, the title is found after the text (at 97:22f).

b. The Greek word (*hypostasis*) can be translated also "genesis" and "nature."

c. In this text, the terms "rulers" and "authorities" are equivalent.

d. The parent of the entirety.

e. Paul.

f. I.e. this treatise. The author here addresses a dedicatee.

g. I.e. ignorant.

h. This brief account differs significantly from the narrative in BJn 10:19f, 12:5f, 13:1f, and 19:15f, in which the chief ruler steals "power" from wisdom, and is subsequently induced to implant it in humankind.

i. The sum total of spiritual reality deriv-

ing, ultimately, from the parent of the entirety.

87 a. "Samaēl": Aramaic for "blind god."

b. "It": the chief ruler.

c. "abyss": the corresponding Greek word (*abyssos*) is grammatically feminine and thus easily spoken of as a "mother." The father, as it were, is wisdom.

d. Or "by."

e. "power": or "faculty," specific kind of planetary influence.

f. Or "aeons."

g. The "invisible domain" is the realm of immortals; it is hidden behind a cosmic veil (cf. 94:8f).

Projection of an image of incorruptibility

11   As incorruptibility[h] gazed down into the region of the waters, its image   EgG III 59:6
14 was shown forth in the waters; •and the authorities of the darkness
15 became enamored of it. •But they could not lay hold of that image,
which had been shown forth to them in the waters, because of their
17 weakness—•since merely animate beings cannot lay hold of those which   BJn 28:6
18 are spirit-endowed; •for they were from below, while it was from above.[i]

Creation of Adam out of matter

20   This is the reason why 'incorruptibility gazed down into the region   87:11
22 (etc.)': •so that, by the parent's will, it might join the entirety unto the   88:10, 88:34
23,24 light.[j] •The rulers laid plans and said, •''Come, let us create a human   96:11
                                               EgG III 59:10+
26 being that will be soil from the earth.'' •They modeled their creature as   v.23
27 one wholly of the earth. •Now, the rulers[k] [. . . body . . .] they have   Gn 1:26a
                                               BJn 15:1
29 [. . .] female [. . .] is . . . face(s) . . . are . . . bestial. . . . •They took   BJn 20:33
                                               RAd 64:6
31 [some soil] from the earth and modeled [their human being], •after their   IrUnid 1.30.6
body and [after the image] of god[l] that had been shown forth [to them]   v.27
in the waters.   94:18
                                                             v.29
                                                             Gn 2:7
                                                             v.31
                                                             Gn 1:26

Animation of Adam. His immobility.

33,33   They said, •''[Come, let] us lay hold of it[m] by means of our modeled
34,1 form,[n] •[so that] it may see its male counterpart [. . .], **88** •and we may
seize it by means of our modeled form''—not understanding the power   87:4
3 of god, because of their powerlessness. •And it[a] breathed into his face;   Gn 2:7
                                                             BJn 19:25+
4 and the human being came to be animate and remained upon the ground   v.4
5 many days. •But they could not make him arise because of their   BJn 19:10+
6 powerlessness.[b] •Like storm winds they persisted (in blowing), that they   87:4
might capture that image,[c] which had appeared to them in the waters.
9 And they did not recognize the identity of its power.

h. ''Incorruptibility'': one of the aeons deriving from the parent of the entirety. The text here presupposes knowledge of a more complicated exposition of theology, such as found in BJn 4:26f (cf. especially 6:5f).

i. Incorruptibility is ''from above'' and so possesses, or is, spirit (''spirit-endowed,'' Greek *pneumatikos*); while the rulers are from the visible domain (''below'') and so possess soul but not spirit (''merely animate,'' Greek *psykhikos*).

j. ''the light'': according to BJn (2:30f) the parent of the entirety can be described as uncontaminated light.

k. In the following passage the original text is uncertain owing to the imperfection of the MS. The passage described the rulers' body, which served as a prototype for that of Adam (87:31f).

l. I.e. the image of incorruptibility.

m. The image, which they cannot distinguish from incorruptibility itself.

n. ''modeled form'': Jewish and Christian jargon for the human body, based on the fact that the creator modeled Adam out of earth.

88 a. ''it'': the chief ruler.

b. Because the chief ruler had already emitted and lost its power by uttering blasphemy (86:28–87:4f), it was unable to impart the power of erect posture to the human being.

c. If the modeled form stands upright it will serve as a decoy by means of which the rulers hope to lure the image out of the waters and ''seize it.'' All the following episodes presuppose the rulers' erotic attraction to incorruptibility and all that is spiritual.

Passage of the spirit into Adam

10   Now, all these events came to pass by the will of the parent of the   87:22+
11 entirety. •Afterward, the spirit saw the animate human being upon the
13,14 ground. •And the spirit came forth from the Adamantine Realm;[d] •it   BJn 20:14+
descended and came to dwell within him, and that human being came   BJn 8:28+
   v.14
16 to be a living soul. •It called his name Adam since he was found moving   Gn 2:7
upon the ground.[e]

Sending of a helper to Adam

17   A voice[f] came forth from incorruptibility for the assistance of Adam;   BJn 20:19
19 and the rulers gathered together all the animals of the earth and all the   Gn 2:18
   v.19
birds of the sky and brought them in to Adam to see what Adam would   Gn 2:19f
call them, that he might give a name to each of the birds and all the
beasts.

His introduction into paradise

24,25   They took Adam [and] put him in the garden (paradise), •that he might   Gn 2:15
26 cultivate [it] and keep watch over it. •And the rulers issued a command   BJn 21:16
27 to him, saying, •"From [every] tree in the garden shall you (sing.) eat,
29 yet [from] the tree of acquaintance with good and evil do not eat, nor   Gn 3:3
31 [touch] it; •for the day you (plur.) eat [from] it, with death you (plur.)
are going to die."
32,33   They [. . .] this. •They do not understand what [they have said] to
34,1 him; •rather, by the parent's will, **89** •they said this in such a way that   87:22+
2 he might (in fact) eat, •and that Adam might ⟨not⟩[a] regard them as would
a person of an exclusively material nature.

Creation of Eve. Passage of the spirit into Eve.

3,4   The rulers took counsel with one another and said, •"Come, let us   BJn 22:21+
5,6 cause a deep sleep to fall upon Adam." •And he slept.—•Now, the deep   Gn 2:21
sleep that they "caused to fall upon him, and he slept" is lack of
7,9 acquaintance.—•They opened his side like a living[b] woman. •And they   BJn 22:32+
10 built up his side with some flesh in place of her, •and Adam came to be   RAd 64:22
merely animate.[c]
11   And the spirit-endowed woman came to him and spoke with him,
13,14 saying, "Arise, Adam." •And when he saw her, he said, •"It is you   BJn 23:9+
15,16 who have given me life; •you will be called 'mother of the living.' •For   Th
   v.15
16 it is she who is my mother. •It is she who is the midwife,[d] and the   Gn 3:20
   v.16
woman, and she who has given birth."[e]   Th 13:25
   Gn 2:23

---

d. The "spirit" is the "female spiritual principle" (cf. 89:31f). "Adamantine": lit. "steel," but here used as an esoteric word referring to "Adamas" (or "Geradamas"), the heavenly prototype of Adam; cf. BJn 8:28f, EgG 61:5f.

e. According to a traditional etymology "Adam" means "earth" (Hebrew *'adāmāh*); the etymology was known to speakers of both Greek and Semitic languages.

f. A faculty of speech.

89 a. The word "⟨not⟩" is inadvertently omitted in the MS.

b. "living": gnostic jargon indicating membership in the immortal realm. It is especially common in EgG.

c. Because the rulers have removed the spiritual element from Adam in the form of a "living woman," he is no longer spirit-endowed; cf. note 87i.

d. Or "physician."

e. "you have given me life . . . midwife . . . she who has given birth (or 'lying-in woman')": here begins a series of learned puns in Aramaic on the root of *Ḥawwāh*, the Aramaic equivalent of "Eve" (*ḥayyitani . . . ḥayyᵊtāʾ . . . ḥayyᵊtāʾ*). Ḥawwāh is thus a name of the spiritual element present in the "spirit-endowed woman." Since they cannot be perceived in Greek, these puns may be evidence of the author's close contact with Semitic-speaking culture. See also note 89l.

The rape of Eve

17,18   Then the authorities came up to their Adam. •And when they saw his female counterpart speaking with him, they became agitated with great

21,21 agitation; •and they became enamored of her. •They said to one another,

22,23 "Come, let us sow our seed[f] in her," and they pursued her. •And she   Th 16:16

25 laughed at them for their folly and their blindness; •and in their clutches,

26 she[g] became a tree,[h] •and left before them a shadow[i] of herself resembling   BJn 24:13 +

28 herself; and they defiled [it] foully.—•And they defiled the seal of her

29 voice,[j] •so that by their modeled form,[k] together with [their] own image, they made themselves liable to condemnation.

Passage of the spirit into a snake

31   Then the female spiritual principle came [in] the snake, the instructor;[l]   Gn 3:1

32,34 and it taught [them], saying, "What did it [say to] you (plur.)? •Was it,   FTh 42:17?
IrUnid 1.30.7
'From every tree [in the] garden (paradise) shall you (sing.) eat; yet   EpG 26.2.6
v.34
from [the tree] of acquaintance with evil and good do not eat'?"   Gn 2:16

2,3   **90** •The carnal woman[a] said, •"'Not only did it say 'Do not eat,' but   BJn 22:3 +
v.2
even 'Do not touch it; for the day you (plur.) eat from it, with death   Gn 3:2f
v.3
you (plur.) are going to die.'"   Gn 2:17

6,6   And the snake, the instructor, said, •"'With death you (plur.) shall not   Gn 3:4f

7,8 die; •for it was out of envy that it said this to you (plur.). •Rather, your (plur.) eyes shall open and you (plur.) shall come to be like gods,

11 recognizing evil and good." •And the female instructing principle[b] was

12 taken away from the snake, •and she left it behind merely a thing of the earth.

13,14   And the carnal woman took from the tree and ate; •and she gave to   Gn 3:6f

14 her husband as well as herself; •and these merely animate beings[c] ate.

15 And their imperfection was shown forth in their lack of acquaintance;

16 and they knew that they were naked of the spiritual element, and took fig leaves and bound them upon their loins.

The expulsion from paradise

19,20   Then the chief ruler came; •and it said, "Adam! Where are you?"—   Gn 3:9f
BJn 23:20 +
20 for it did not understand what had happened.   RAd 66:14f

21   And Adam said, "I heard your voice and was afraid because I was naked; and I hid."

24   The ruler said, "Why did you (sing.) hide, unless it is because you (sing.) have eaten from the tree from which alone I commanded you (sing.) not to eat? And you (sing.) have eaten!"

27   Adam said, "The woman that you gave me, [she gave] to me and I

29 ate." •And the arrogant [ruler] laid a curse upon the woman.   Gn 3:13f

30,31   The woman said, •"'It was the snake that led me astray and I ate."

32 [They[d] turned] to the snake and laid a curse upon its shadow,[e] [. . .]

---

f. Sexually.

g. I.e. the spiritual element within the woman.

h. The tree of life, Gn 2:9.

i. "shadow": a Platonist cliché for "copy"; i.e. the animate body of Eve, without the spiritual element.

j. The text may be corrupt here.

k. The woman modeled from a part of Adam's side (89:7f).

l. "tree (of life) . . . snake . . . instructor" (89:25–31f): more learned puns in Aramaic

on the root of the name of Eve (*ḥayyayyāʾ* ["life"] . . . *ḥewʾyāʾ* . . . **ḥāwēʾ* [hypothetical *Peal* participle, "the one who instructs"]). See note 89e.

90 a. I.e. the animate body of Eve, without the female spiritual principle.

b. Lit. "(female) instructor"; see note 89l.

c. I.e. Adam and Eve.

d. The rulers.

e. The animate body of the snake, without the spiritual element. Cf. note 89i.

33,34 powerless, •not recognizing [that] it was their own modeled form. •From
that day, the snake came to be under the curse of the authorities;
2 **91** until the perfect[a] human being was to come, that curse lay upon the   96:32
snake.

3   They turned to their Adam and took him and expelled him from the   Gn 3:24
5 garden along with his wife; •for they have no blessing, since they too
are under the curse.

7   Moreover, they threw humankind into great distraction and into a life
9 of toil, •so that their humankind might be occupied by worldly affairs,   RAd 65:14
10 and might not have the opportunity of being devoted to the holy spirit.

Cain and Abel

11,12   Now afterward, she bore Cain, their son;[b] •and Cain cultivated the   Gn 4:1f
13,14 land. •Thereupon he[c] knew his wife; •again becoming pregnant, she bore   BJn 24:8 +
15 Abel; and Abel was a herdsman of sheep. •Now Cain brought in from
the crops of his field, but Abel brought in an offering from among his
18 lambs. •God[d] gazed upon the votive offerings of Abel; but he did not
20 accept the votive offerings of Cain. •And carnal Cain pursued Abel his   Gn 4:8
brother.

21   And god said to Cain, "Where is Abel your brother?"
23   He answered, saying, "Am I, then, my brother's keeper?"
24   God said to Cain, "Listen! The voice of your brother's blood is crying
27 up to me! You have sinned with your mouth. •It will return to you:
27,29 anyone who kills Cain will let loose seven vengeances, •and you will
exist groaning and trembling upon the earth."

Seth and Nōrea

30   And Adam [knew][e] his female counterpart Eve, and she became   Gn 4:25
32 pregnant, and bore [Seth][f] to Adam. •And she said, "I have borne   BJn 24:34 +
[another] man through god, in place [of Abel]."   **v.32**
                                                      Gn 4:1
34,35   Again Eve became pregnant, and she bore [Nōrea].[g] •And she said,
"He has begotten on [me a] virgin as an assistance [for] many generations
2 of humankind." **92** •She is the virgin whom the powers did not defile.

The flood. Nōrea and Noah.

3   Then humankind began to multiply and improve.   Gn 6:1
4,5   The rulers took counsel with one another and said, •"Come, let us   BJn 28:32 +
cause a flood with our hands and obliterate all flesh, from human being   **v.5**
to beast."   Gn 6:7
                                                                   Gn 6:17
8   But when the ruler of the powers[a] came to know of their decision, it   Gn 6:13f
10 said to Noah, •"Make yourself an ark from some wood that does not   BJn 29:1 +

91 a. Or "all-powerful," Greek *teleios*.

     b. I.e. the rulers' son, begotten on Eve's "shadow," or physical body, by their act of raping her in a gang. The posterity of Cain are therefore the offspring of devils.

     c. Adam.

     d. "god": possibly Sabaōth, "god of the powers" (95:22f); cf. also 92:2–8f.

     e. Sexually.

     f. Restoration of the name "[Seth]" can be considered certain because of the biblical parallel (Gn 4:25) and is confirmed by the number of letters probably missing in the MS.

     g. Restoration of "[Nōrea]" is confirmed by 92:21f, 32f, and subsequent mentions of the name.

92 a. "ruler of the powers": Sabaōth. The text here presupposes knowledge of the rebellion of Sabaōth, "god of the powers," which is narrated only later (95:13–96:3f). See also note 91d.

rot and hide in it—you and your children and the beasts and the birds
of the sky from small to large—and set it upon Mount Sir."[b]

14,16   Then Ōrea[c] came to him wanting to board the ark. •And when he   EpG 26.1.7+
would not let her, she blew upon the ark and caused it to be consumed
17 by fire. •Again he made the ark, for a second time.
18,19   The rulers went to meet her intending to lead her astray. •Their
supreme chief said to her, "Your mother Eve came to us."

Confrontation of Nōrea and the rulers

21,22   But Nōrea turned to them and said to them, •"It is you who are the
23 rulers of the darkness; you are accursed. •And you did not know[d] my
24,25 mother; •instead it was your female counterpart that you knew. •For I
26 am not your descendant; •rather, it is from the world above that I am
come."
27   The arrogant ruler turned, with all its might, [and] its countenance
29,30 came to be like (a) black [. . .];[e] •it [said] to her recklessly, •"You must
31 render service[f] to us, [as did] also your mother Eve; •for I have been   89:26
given [. . .]."   BJn 25:9+
32,33   But Nōrea turned, with the might of [. . .]; •and in a loud voice [she]
1 cried out [to] the holy, the god of the entirety, **93** •"Rescue me from
the rulers of injustice and save me from their clutches—immediately!"

Appearance of Ēlēlēth

2   The ⟨great⟩ angel came down from the heavens and said to her,
4 "Why are you crying up to God? Why do you act so recklessly toward
the holy spirit?"
6   Nōrea said, "Who are you?"
7,8   The rulers of injustice had withdrawn from her. •It said, "I am Ēlēlēth,   93:18
prudence, the great angel who stands in the presence of the holy spirit.   BJn 8:16+
11 I have been sent to speak with you and save you from the grasp of the
12 lawless. •And I shall teach you about your root."[a]

II. NŌREA'S NARRATION:
THE TEACHING OF ĒLĒLĒTH (DIALOGUE)

13,14   Now, as for that angel, I[b] cannot speak of its power: •its image is like
16 fine gold and its raiment is like snow. •No, truly, my mouth cannot bear
to speak of its power and the image of its face!
18,19   Ēlēlēth, the great angel, spoke to me. •"It is I," it said, "who am   93:7+
20 intelligence. •I am one of the four luminaries, who stand in the presence
22 of the great invisible spirit. •Do you think these rulers have any power
23 over you (sing.)? •None of them can prevail against the root of truth;   97:13
25,26 for on its account he has been shown forth in the final ages (?);[c] •and
27 these authorities will be dominated. •And these authorities cannot defile
29 you and That Race;[d] •for your (plur.) abode is in incorruptibility, where   86:32+

b. In ancient Mediterranean lore, Seiris
(China?) was an idealized far-away place
whose inhabitants had special access to primeval wisdom. Jewish tradition held that in
this land Seth's descendants had recorded
information about the heavens, inscribing it
upon tablets. Cf. Poim (Introduction).
   c. "Ōrea" (Greek *Hōraia*, "beautiful"):
a variant form of "Nōrea," which is used
hereafter.
   d. "lead her astray . . . came to us . . .
did not know" (92:18–23f): sexually.

e. The original text was probably either
"like black [lead]" or "like intense [fire]."
   f. "render service": sexually.

93 a. "root": i.e. origin and source of spiritual sustenance.
   b. From here on the narrator is Nōrea.
   c. The text is slightly corrupt here.
   d. "That Race": i.e. the undominated race.
The term "That" is gnostic jargon indicating
membership in the immortal realm. It is
especially common in RAd.

the virgin spirit dwells, which is superior to the authorities of chaos and to their world.''

32 But I said, "Sir, teach me about the [faculty[e] of] these authorities— 96:15f
34,35 [how][f] did they come into being, and by what kind of genesis, •[and] of 1 what material? 94 •And who created them and their power?''

Production of wisdom's offspring: Ialdabaōth

2,4 And the great angel Elelēth, intelligence, spoke to me: •"Within 5 limitless eternal realms (aeons) dwells incorruptibility. •Wisdom (Sophia), who is called faith (Pistis), wanted to create something, alone without 7 her partner; •and her product was a celestial thing.

8 "A veil exists between the world above and the realms (aeons) that 10,12 are below;[a] •and shadow[b] came into being beneath the veil; •and that 13,14 shadow became matter; •and that shadow was projected apart. •And what she had created became a product in the matter, like an aborted 16,16 foetus. •And it assumed a plastic form molded out of shadow, •and 18 became an arrogant beast resembling a lion." •It was androgynous, as 87:27? I have already said, because it was from matter that it derived.[c]

BJn 9:25 +
v.4
86:32 +

Ialdabaōth's jealousy

19,21 "Opening its eyes it saw a vast quantity of matter without limit; •and[d] 21 it became arrogant, saying, •'It is I who am god, and there is none other 86:28, 95:4 apart from me.' BJn 13:5 +
Is 45:21
22,23 "When it said this, it sinned against the entirety. •And a voice came 87:1, 95:5 + 25 forth from above the realm of absolute power, saying, •'You are mistaken, FTh 39:32 Samaēl'—which is, 'god of the blind.' EgG III 59:1
IrUnid 1.30.6
26 "And it said, 'If any other thing exists before me, let it be shown 96:1 28 forth to me!•And immediately wisdom (Sophia) stretched out her finger 31 and introduced light into matter; •and she pursued it down to the region 87:4 + 32,33 of chaos. •And she returned up [to] her light; •once again darkness [. . .] matter.

Creation of the universe and of other rulers

34 "This ruler, by being androgynous, made itself a vast realm,[e] an extent 87:10 1,2 without limit. 95 •And it contemplated creating offspring for itself, •and BJn 12:33 + created for itself seven offspring, androgynous just like their parent. v.1
87:8
4 "And it said to its offspring, 'It is I who am the god of the entirety.' BJn 10:27 +
v.2
BJn 11:26 +
94:18
v.4

Relegation of Ialdabaōth to Tartarus

94:21 +

5 "And life (Zōē), the daughter of faith wisdom (Pistis Sophia), cried out and said to it, 'You are mistaken, Sakla!'[a]—for which the alternate 94:23 + 8,9 name is Ialtabaōth.[b] •She breathed into its face, •and her breath became IrUnid 1.30.7
BJn 11:15

---

e. Or "force, strength."
f. Or "[whence]."

94 a. The existence of such a heavenly curtain was a common Jewish teaching at the time RR was written.
b. Total darkness, because the veil blocks off the realm of light.
c. "it was androgynous . . . derived": not a part of Nōrea's narrative, but rather a

learned remark by the author of RR, referring perhaps to 87:27f.
d. Eleleth begins retelling the narrative already told at 86:28f.
e. Or "aeon."

95 a. "Sakla" (Aramaic "fool"): a conventional name of Satan in Judaism.
b. "Ialtabaōth" (also "Ialdabaōth," "Aldabaōth"): a conventional gnostic name for

10 a fiery angel for her; •and that angel bound Ialdabaōth and cast it down into Tartarus, at the bottom of the abyss.

Repentance and elevation of Sabaōth

13   "Now, when its offspring Sabaōth saw the power of that angel, it repented and condemned its father and its mother matter.

17   "It loathed her, but it sang songs of praise up to wisdom (Sophia) and
19 her daughter life (Zōē). •And wisdom and life caught it up and appointed it in charge of the seventh heaven, below the veil between above and
22 below. •And it was called 'god of the powers, Sabaōth,'c since it is up above the powers of chaos, for wisdom (Sophia) appointed it.

26   "Now when these events had come to pass, it made itself a huge four-facedd chariot of cherubim, and infinitely many angels to render assistance
31 and also harps and lyres. •And wisdom took her daughter life and had her sit at its right to teach it about the things that exist [in] the eighth
34,35 (heaven); •and the angel [of] anger she placed at its left. •[Since] that
1 day, [its right] has been called life, 96 •and the left has come to represent
3 the injustice of the realm of absolute power above. •It was before your (sing.) time that they came into being (?).a

BJn 10:33+
IrSat 1.24.2
IrUnid 1.30.5
IrUnid 1.30.8?
EpA 40.5.1+
EpG 25.2.2+

EpA 40.2.3
EpG 26.10.4+

94:23

Creation of other rulers

3   "Now, when Ialdabaōth saw it in this great splendor and at this height,
6 it envied that being; •and the envy became an androgynous product;
7,8 and this was the source of envy. •And envy engendered death; and death engendered its offspring and appointed each of them in charge of its heaven; and all the heavens of chaos became full of their multitudes.

11   "But it was by the will of the parent of the entirety that they all came
13,13 into being—•after the pattern of all the things above—•so that the sum of chaos might be attained.b

15   "There, I have taught you (sing.) about the pattern of the rulers;
16,16, and the matter in which it was expressed; •and their parent; and their world."

BJn 11:4
IrUnid 1.30.5

87:22+

87:9

93:32f

Promise of salvation for Nōrea's offspring

17   But I said, "Sir, am I too from their matter?"

19   "You, together with your offspring, belong to the primeval parent;c
20,22 from above, out of the incorruptible light, their souls are come. •Thus the authorities cannot approach them because of the spirit of truth
25 present within them; •and all who have become acquainted with this way exist immortal in the midst of dying humankind.

IrSat 1.24.2+

86:20 ?
96:32
BJn 25:20
EpG 26.6.2

the chief ruler, i.e. Satan. The name has been explained as a learned neologism based on two Aramaic components: "begetter of" (yalᵇd-) and "Sabaōth" (abaʾōt, a secondary form of sabaʾōt), thus describing the chief ruler's position as parent of Sabaōth or of heavenly armies in general. The name has no significance in Greek, but its meaning might have been guessed by an Aramaic speaker.

c. "Sabaōth": Hebrew "armies" or "powers," originally the second half of a traditional epithet of Jahweh, "god of the armies (or powers)." By the early Christian period, the single word "sabaōth" had begun to be taken as a name of god, as here. In RR, "Sabaōth" corresponds to the god of

Israel; its parent is Satan.
   d. Or "four-sided."

96 a. The text may be slightly corrupt here.
   b. Possibly a reference to the Neoplatonic doctrine of *plenum formarum*, according to which the production of all grades of possible existents would be a logically necessary consequence from the assumption of an omnipotent and benevolent first principle. Such a chain of graded beings would extend from the most perfect first principle down to the least perfect being at the bottom of Tartarus, thus "attaining the sum" or sum total of possibilities when it reached the limit "of chaos."
   c. The parent of the entirety.

Coming of the true human being

27,28   "Still, that posterity will not be shown forth now. •Instead, after three   BJn 30:32
generations[d] it[e] will be shown forth, and free them from the bond of the   RAd 76:8
                                                                                    FTh 47:13
authorities' error."   EgG 74:17+

31   Then I said, "Sir, how much longer?"

32   He said to me, "Until the moment when the true human being, within   91:2
a modeled form,[f] reveals (?) the existence of [the spirit of] truth, which   96:22+
the parent has sent.

Poem of deliverance: the final generation

1   **97** "[THEN] that being will teach them about every thing:

2   And will anoint them with the ointment of eternal life,   BJn 30:11
                given unto that being from the undominated race.   Zs 63:22

5,6   "THEN they will be freed of blind thought: •And they will   87:4
                trample under foot death, which is of the authorities: 96:8

7   And they will ascend into the limitless light, where this   FTh 50:18
                posterity belongs.

10,11   "THEN the authorities will relinquish their ages: •And   FTh 44:14+
12   their angels will weep over their destruction: •And   EgG 74:4
                                                                            v.11
                their demons will lament their death.   FTh 44:10
                                                                            IrSat 1.24.2+
13   "THEN all the children of the light will be truly
                acquainted with the truth and their root, and the parent   93:23
16   of the entirety and the holy spirit: •They will all say
                with a single voice, 'The parent's truth[a] is just, and the
19   child presides over the entirety': •And from everyone
                unto the ages of ages, 'Holy, holy, holy! Amen!'"[b]

---

d. Or "ages, epochs."   **97** a. I.e. judicial accuracy.
e. "it": the posterity.   b. In the manuscript the title of this work
  f. Perhaps meaning that after three "gen-   is written after the text (at 97:22f).
erations" or ages have passed, a heavenly
"true human being" will become incarnate
in a body ("modeled form").

THE THUNDER—PERFECT INTELLECT

(Th)

Contents

The Thunder—Perfect Intellect ("Thunder, Perfect Mind") is a riddlesome monologue spoken by the immanent savior, here represented as a female character and identifiable as "afterthought," a manifestation of wisdom and Barbēlō in gnostic myth. In gnostic myth the role of afterthought—also known as "life" (Zōē), the female instructing principle, and the holy spirit—is to assist both Adam and all humankind, in order to recollect the power stolen by Ialdabaōth (BJn 20:14f) and now dispersed in the gnostic race. She is immanent in all gnostics who have the holy spirit (BJn 25:20f). Although the monologue consists almost entirely of self-descriptions and exhortations directed to the reader, three short passages refer to the mythic setting of the savior's words: (1) she has been sent from "the power" or Barbēlō (cf. BJn 4:26f) and is immanent within humankind (13:2f); (2) she continues in her mission to "cry out" and summon members of the gnostic race (19:28f); (3) souls that respond will gain liberation from the material world and ascend to a place in the metaphysical universe where the speaker herself resides, and will not suffer reincarnation (21:27f). These allusions to the gnostic myth (however ambiguous), the identification of the speaker as "afterthought" (14:10f), and the resemblance of the work to *The Gospel of Eve* read by the gnostic sect (EpG 26.3.1) all suggest that Th should be considered a part of gnostic scripture and understood in the context of such works. Further support for this reading comes from RR 89:14f, where Adam uses similar words to address the female spiritual principle, i.e. afterthought, who is resident in Eve: the passage may be an allusion to Th. Nevertheless, some scholars have doubted that Th bears any relation to gnostic myth.

Literary background

The author and place of composition of Th are unknown. The date of its composition must be sometime before A.D. 350, the approximate date of the MS. The language of composition was Greek.

The mixture of genres in Th is simple:

I. Wisdom monologue
    A. Self-description (riddles), alternating with
    B. Exhortations

The work as a whole is a poem (parallel strophes) in the form of a *wisdom monologue.* In this genre a female divine voice, traditionally the Jewish figure of Dame Wisdom or the Egyptian goddess Isis, speaks directly to the readers about her own virtues and exhorts or summons them to assimilate to her; two types of material, self-description and exhortation, alternate in Th. Examples of the genre occur in the Old Testament (e.g. Pr 8); it also shapes the form of materials found in some passages of the New Testament and elsewhere in early Christian literature. Hellenistic-Roman Egyptian parallels are provided by numerous Greek inscriptions ("aretalogies") on stone connected with the cult of Isis; in these, the goddess speaks in a version of the genre.

The paradoxical content of the *self-descriptive passages* ("identity riddles") is almost unique in surviving examples of the wisdom monologue; for ancient readers it must have been one of the most striking features of the work. These paradoxes come from quite another source, for they mimic the logic of the Greek identity riddle—a well-known form in the ancient Mediterranean world. In this type of riddle, a person or personified object describes itself paradoxically; the solution of the riddle is the speaker's identity. E.g.: "No one seeing me sees me, but one who does not see beholds me. One who does not speak speaks; one who does not run runs. And I am a liar, yet say all things true." (Traditional solution: ⲙⲉⲁⲣ ⲃ.)

Among ancient riddles there was one from Hellenistic Judaism that may have been the starting point for the wild development of paradox in Th: "A human being begot me, and my parent is supernatural. He calls me life (Zōē), and I bring him death" (Planudean appendix to the *Anthologia Palatina* 7.44). The traditional solution is "Eve"—for she came out (was "begotten") of Adam ("a human being") but as the vivifying principle she was ultimately an emanation of god the "parent." According to the Septuagint Greek version of Gn 3:20, Adam ("he") called the woman not Eve but "Life" (punning on the Hebrew name "Eve"); and yet—in the orthodox, non-gnostic reading of Genesis—she led him to sin and "death." This Hellenistic-Jewish Eve riddle is alluded to as early as Philo of Alexandria, ca. 30 B.C.–A.D. ca. 45 (*Quis rerum* 11, par. 52). It is probably referred to also in Th 16:11f, 19:15f, though here of course with a gnostic reinterpretation made possible by the gnostic author's identification of life (Zōē) and afterthought (see preceding section, "Contents") and presupposition of the gnostic myth.

Many of the speaker's paradoxical assertions about her kinship and ethical relations can be understood by allowing that in the riddle of Th, two distinct actors are being referred to by the name "Eve": (1) the fleshly spouse of Adam (his "brother" or sibling while they were an original androgyne; his child because she was extracted from him; his wife or mate); (2) afterthought, the celestial Eve (mother of Adam because she is the vivifying principle and made him alive—cf. Gn 3:20, "mother of all the living"; mother of the fleshly Eve for the same reason; a perpetual virgin even though the rulers raped the fleshly Eve). A version of gnostic myth like that told in RR seems to be presupposed.

Th bears striking resemblances to the description and excerpt of the gnostic *Gospel of Eve* given by St. Epiphanius (EpG 26.2.6–26.3.1), in which the paradoxical voice of wisdom is described as "a voice of thunder."

Text

The original Greek apparently does not survive. The text is known only in Coptic translation, attested by a single manuscript from Nag Hammadi, MS NHC VI (pp. 13–21), which was copied just before A.D. 350 and is now in the Cairo Coptic Museum.

The translation below is based on MacRae's critical edition of the Coptic: G. W. MacRae, ed., in *Nag Hammadi Codices V,2–5 and VI with Papyrus Berolinensis 8502,1 and 4* (D. M. Parrott, ed.; Nag Hammadi Studies, vol. 11; Leiden: E. J. Brill, 1979), 231–55.

SELECT BIBLIOGRAPHY

Conzelmann, H. "The Mother of Wisdom." In *The Future of Our Religious Past* [Festschrift for R. Bultmann], edited by James M. Robinson, 230–43. London: S.C.M. Press, 1971.

Grant, F. C. *Hellenistic Religions: The Age of Syncretism*, 131–33. Library of Religion, vol. 2. New York: Liberal Arts, 1953. (English translation of a typical Isis monologue.)

Layton, B. "The Riddle of the Thunder." In *Gnosticism and Early Christianity*, edited by C. Hedrick and R. Hodgson. Peabody, Mass.: Hendrickson, 1986.

MacRae, G. W. "Discourses of the Gnostic Revealer." In *Proceedings of the International Colloquium on Gnosticism, Stockholm, August 20–25, 1973*, edited by Geo Widengren, 111–22. Stockholm: Almqvist & Wiksell, 1977.

[MacRae, G. W., et al.] *"The Thunder, Perfect Mind": Protocol of the Fifth Colloquy of the Center for Hermeneutical Studies in Hellenistic and Modern Culture, 11 March 1973, Graduate Theological Union, and the University of California–Berkeley*. Berkeley, Calif.: Center for Hermeneutical Studies, 1973.

Schultz, W. "Rätsel." In *Paulys Real-Encyclopädie der classischen Altertumswissenschaft*. 2d ed. by G. Wissowa et al. 2d ser., vol. 1/A (1914), cols. 62–125. (A classic description of the Greek riddle.)

THE THUNDER—
PERFECT INTELLECT

FTh 43:13?
EpG 26.3.1
18:9
FTh 47:7

Exhortations (1)

2   It is from the power that I, even I, have been sent
3   And unto those who think on me that I have come;
4   And I was found in those who seek me.[a]

5   Look upon me, O you (plur.) who think on me.
7   And you listeners, listen to me!
8   You who wait for me, take me unto yourselves,
9   And do not chase me from before your eyes.
11   And do not make your sound hate me: nor your hearing.
12   Do not be unacquainted with me at any place: or even at any
      time.
14   Keep watch! Do not be unacquainted with me!

14:10+
BJn 4:36+

Identity riddles (1)

15   For, it is I who am the first: and the last.
16   It is I who am the revered: and the despised.
18   It is I who am the harlot: and the holy.
19   It is I who am the wife: and the virgin.
20   It is I who am the mother: and the daughter.
21   I am the members of my mother.
22   It is I who am the barren: and who has many children.
23   It is I who am the one whose marriage is magnificient: and
      who have not married.
25   It is I who am the midwife: and she who does not give birth;
26   It is I who am consolation: of my own travail.
27   It is I who am the bride: and the bridegroom.
29   And it is my husband who has begotten me.
30   It is I who am the mother of my father: and the sister of my
      husband.
32   And it is he who is my offspring.
33   It is I who am the servant of him who prepared me:
34   It is I who am the governess of my (own) offspring.
1   **14** Yet it is he who [begot me] before (due) time, on a
      birthday:
3   And it is he who is my offspring in (due) time.
4   And my power comes from him.
5   I am the staff of his power in his childhood:
6   [And] it is he who is the rod of my old age,
8   And whatever he wishes happens to me.
9   It is I who am incomprehensible silence:
10   And afterthought, whose memory is so great.
12   It is I who am the voice whose sounds are so numerous:
13   And the discourse whose images[a] are so numerous.
14   It is I who am the speaking: of my (own) name.

16:27, 16:29
18:20

RR 89:16

18:14
BJn 22:28

13:1
BJn 20:14+
v.12
19:20+

13 a. This (13:2–4f) is one of three short
passages in Th that may narrate parts of a
gnostic myth of the descent of the savior;

see also 19:28f and 21:27f.

14 a. Or "kinds."

Exhortations (2)

15 Why, O you who hate me, do you love me,
16 And hate those who love me?
18 Declare me publicly, O you who deny me:
19 And deny me, O you who declare me publicly.
20 Tell lies of me, O you who speak truth of me:
21 And speak the truth about me, O you who have told lies of me.
23 Become unacquainted with me, O you who recognize me:
24 And may those who have not recognized me become acquainted with me!

Identity riddles (2)

26 For, it is I who am acquaintance: and lack of acquaintance.
27 It is I who am reticence: and frankness.
29 I am shameless: I am ashamed.
30 I am strong: and I am afraid.
31 It is I who am war: and peace.

16:3, 18:10
RAd 64:22

18:23

Exhortations (3)

32 Give heed to me—it is I who am the disgraced: and the mighty;
34 Give heed to my poverty: and my wealth.
2 **15** Do not be arrogant to me as I lie cast upon the ground:
3 [And] you will find me in those [who] are to come.
5 And do not look [upon] me on the dung heap, and then go and leave me cast there:
8 And you will find me in the kingdoms.
9 And do not look upon me lying cast among the disgraced and in the most wretched places, and then mock me:
13 And do not cast me down cruelly into those who are in need.
15 But as for me, I am merciful: and I am cruel.
16 Keep watch! Do not hate my obedience;
18 And love my continence in my weakness;
19 Do not overlook me, and do not neglect to fear my power!

18:27
18:30

22 For, why do you scorn my terror: and malign my boasting?
25 It is I who am what is present in all fears: and boldness.
27 In trembling, it is I who am what is feeble:
28 And it is in enjoyment of place that I thrive.
29 I am foolish: and I am wise.
31 Why have you hated me in your counsels?
32 (Is it) because I for my part shall be silent among those who keep silent,
34 And shall be shown forth and speak?
1 **16** Why, then, did you hate me, O Greeks?
2 Because I am a non-Greek[a] among [the] non-Greeks?

Identity riddles (3)

3 For, it is I who am the wisdom [of the] Greeks: and the acquaintance of [the] non-Greeks.
5 It is I who am judgment for Greeks; and for non-Greeks.
6 [I] am he whose image is manifold in Egypt:

14:26+
BJn 23:20

16 a. Lit. "a barbarian."

8   And she who has no image among the non-Greeks.
9   It is I who have been hated everywhere:
10   And who have been loved everywhere.
11   It is I who am called life:[b]   BJn 20:14 +
12   And whom you have called death.
13   It is I who am called law:
15   And whom you have called lawlessness.
16   It is I whom you have chased: RR 89:22
17   And it is I whom you have restrained.
18   It is I who am what you have scattered:
19   And what you have collected.   EpG 26.1.9
20   It is I before whom you have felt shame:
21   And with whom you have been shameless.
22   It is I who do not celebrate festivals:
23   And it is I whose festivals are numerous.
24   As for me, I am godless:
24   And it is I whose god is manifold.[c]
26   It is I on whom you have thought:
27   And you have despised me.   13:16 +
27   I am uneducated:
28   And people learn from me.

29   It is I who am the one you have scorned: 13:16 +
30   And about whom you think.
31   It is I from whom you have hidden:
32   And to whom you are manifest.
33   Yet whenever you hide yourselves,
35   I, too, shall show myself forth:
1   **17** For, [whenever] you [show yourselves forth],
2   I, too, [shall hide] from you.

Exhortations (4)

3   As for those who have [. . .] from [. . .] foolishly [. . .],
6   Remove me[a] [from] their [understanding] out of pain:
8   And accept me unto yourselves out of understanding [and]
      pain;
10   And accept me unto yourselves out of disgraceful places and
      oppression,
13   And catch (me) up from good things:
14   Though in disgrace out of shame, accept me unto yourselves
      without shame:
17   And out of shamelessness and shame put my members to
      shame within you.

19   And draw near to me, O you who are acquainted with me
      and you who are acquainted with my members,
22   And establish those that are great within the paltry first
      creatures.
24   Draw near to childhood,
26   And do not despise it because it is small and paltry;
28   Nor cause greatnesses, (dispersed) in parts,[b] to turn away
      from smallnesses;
30   For it is from greatnesses that smallnesses are recognized.

b. I.e. Eve; the name traditionally meant "life." Cf. the Eve riddle cited under "Literary Background" above.
c. Or "whose gods are many."

17 a. The translation of this passage (17:6–17f) is uncertain; the text may be slightly corrupt here.
b. Or "in particulars."

32   Why do you curse me: and honor me?

35   You have smitten: and you have spared.

36   Do not separate me from the first, whom you have
         [recognized];

1   **18** [And] cast no one [out, neither] bring any back [. . .]

4   . . . you [. . .] . . . [. . .] mine [. . .]

7   I myself am acquainted with the first:

7   And those after them are acquainted with me.

Identity riddles (4)

9	It is I, however, who am the [perfect] intellect,	13:1
10	And the repose [. . .].	

10   It is I who am the acquaintance of my seeking: 14:26+

11   And the discovery of those who seek after me,

12   And the command of those who make requests of me,

14   And the power of the powers, by my acquaintance—   14:4

15   Of the angels that have been sent, by my utterance;

16   And of the gods in their seasons, by my command;

18   And of the spirits of all men who dwell with me;

19   And of the women who are in me.

20   It is I who am the honored and praised: 16:16+

22   And the one scornfully despised.

23   It is I who am peace: 13:31

24   And because of me war has broken out:

25   And I am an alien: and a citizen.

27   I am riches: and she who has no riches.   14:34+

28   Those who exist because of my sexual intercourse are   BJn 24:26+
         unacquainted with me:

30   And it is those who reside in my wealth[a] that are acquainted   14:34+
         with me.

32   Those who are nigh unto me have not recognized me:

33   And it is those who are far away from me that have
         recognized me.

35   On the day that I am nigh [unto you, you] are far away [from
         me]:

2   **19** [And] on the day that I [am far] away from you, [I am
         nigh unto] you.

4   [It is] I who [am] . . . heart.

5   [It is] I [who am . . .] nature(s).

6   It is I who am [. . .] of the creation of the spirits [. . .]
         demand of the souls.

9   It is [I] who am restraint: and unrestraint.   19:20+

10   It is I who am joining: and dissolution.   RAd 64:22

11   It is I who am persistence:

12   And it is I who am weakening.

12   It is I who am descent:

13   And it is to me that people ascend.   21:27

14   It is I who am condemnation: and pardon.

15   As for me, I am free of sin:

16   And the root of sin derives from me.

18   It is I who am desire for what is seen:

19   And it is in me that continence of the heart resides.

---

18 a. "sexual intercourse . . . wealth": a pun, using Greek *ousia* ("being, essence, wealth") and a related compound, *syn-ousia* ("being together, sexual intercourse").

20 It is I who am the listening that is acceptable to everyone: 14:12, 19:9
22 And the speaking that cannot be restrained.   20:28
23 I am mute and cannot speak: v.22
24 And great is the multitude of my speaking.   FTh 50:16

Exhortations (5)

25 Hear me softly:
26 And learn from me harshly.

Identity riddles (5)

28 It is I who cry out:[a]   19:33
29 And it is upon the face of the earth that I am being cast out.[b]
31 It is I who prepare the bread and ⟨. . .⟩
32 ⟨. . .⟩ my intellect . . .
32 It is I who am acquaintance with my name.
33 It is I who cry out: 18:28
34 And it is I who give ear.
1 **20** I am manifest [and . . .] travel [. . .]   BJn 30:17
2 [. . .] seal of my (?) [. . .] . . .
5 It is I who am [. . .] the argument of defense [. . .]
7 It is I who am called truth,
8 And violence [. . .]

Exhortations (6)

9 You honor me [. . .]
10 And you whisper against [me].
11 You who are defeated, pass judgment before sentence is
　　passed against you;
13 For it is in you that the judge and the choosing reside.
14 If you are condemned by it, who will forgive you?
16 And yet, if you are acquitted by it, who can restrain you?
18 For your interior is your exterior:
20 And whoever molded you on the outside has stamped an
　　impression of it inside of you;
22 And what you see outside of you, you see inside of you.
25 It is manifest, and it is your garment.[a]
26 Hear me, O listeners,
27 And learn my utterances, you who are acquainted with me!

Identity riddles (6)

28 It is I who am the listening that is acceptable in every matter;   19:20+
30 It is I who am the speaking that cannot be restrained.
31 It is I who am the voice's name, and the name's voice.
33 It is I who am the meaning of text,   FTh 37:10
34 And the manifestation of distinction;
35 And [it is] I [. . .] light [. . .]
5 **21** [. . .] and [. . .] O listener[s . . .] you.
7 It is [. . .] the great power,
8 And [. . .] will not move the name

---

19 a. The ancient copyist originally wrote "It is I who cry out upon the face of the earth" and then struck out the last six words.
　　b. Cf. note 13a.

20 a. "garment": a Platonist cliché for the material body.

10   [. . .] him [. . .] who created me.
11   But as for me, I shall speak its name.

Exhortations (7)

12   Behold, then, its utterances, and behold all the texts that
         have been completed.
13   Give heed, then, O listeners—
14   And also you, O angels,
16   And you who have been sent,
17   And you spirits who have arisen from the dead.
18   For, it is I alone who exist,[a]
19   And I have no one to pass judgment upon me.
20   For—many and sweet are the species to be found in manifold
         sins and acts of unrestraint and disgraceful passions,
25   And in temporal pleasures; which people restrain,
27   Until they become sober and flee up to their place of rest.   19:13
29   And they will find me there,[b]   EpG 26.10.10+
30   And live, and not die again.[c]   EpG 26.10.7+

21 a. Or "it is I who dwell alone."   c. "not die again": i.e. not become rein-
    b. Cf. note 13a.   carnate.

FIRST THOUGHT IN THREE FORMS

(FTh)

Contents

First Thought in Three Forms ("Trimorphic Protennoia" or "Triple Protennoia") tells, selectively, the entire gnostic myth from the unfolding of the Barbēlō aeon, or second principle, down to the crucifixion of Jesus. Only the following mythic events are mentioned: the subdivision of the Barbēlō aeon; emanation of the preexistent anointed (Christ) or Word (Logos); production of the four luminaries; emanation of wisdom and Ialdabaōth; the creation; the theft of power and its passage into Adam; the incarnation of the Word in Jesus; the heavenly rulers' lament over the beginning of the last days; the establishment of gnostic baptism; the crucifixion. Much of the work consists of self-description by an immanent savior, as in the concluding poem of BJn; Th should also be compared.

"Three forms" of the invisible spirit's "first thought" are equated in the work: the Barbēlō aeon as the second principle; life (Zōē); the divine Word (Logos).

Of particular interest is the emphasis laid upon the emanation and incarnation of the preexistent Word (Logos), who is here identified with not only the preexistent anointed (Christ) but also (46:14f, 46:25f) the Barbēlō. Some scholars have considered this myth of the Word to be closely related to the source of the prologue of the Gospel of John.

Also noteworthy are the clear identification of wisdom and afterthought; the ambiguous statement (50:13f) that Jesus was "extracted from" the "accursed wood" by the Word; and a detailed description of the rite of gnostic baptism (for which, see "Historical Introduction" to Part One). The form of gnostic myth presupposed in FTh resembles both BJn and EgG; however, Ialdabaōth's independence is deemphasized, perhaps to insist upon divine providence as in RR.

Literary background

The author and place of composition of FTh are unknown. The date of its composition must be sometime before A.D. 350, the approximate date of the MS. In philosophical and mythic content the work resembles EgG, RAd, 3Tb, Zs, and Fr. The language of composition was Greek.

The mixture of genres in FTh is slightly complex, combining various traditional materials which alternate with one another in the course of the work:

I. Wisdom monologue
   A. Self-description
   B. Cosmogony and uranography
   C. "True history" of humankind
   D. Exhortations
II. Excerpt from a treatise on baptism (?), 36:27f

The work as a whole is a *wisdom monologue* (for this genre, see Th, "Literary background"); it moves back and forth between poetry (parallel strophes) and prose (running narrative). Four kinds of material appear in the monologue: the female speaker's *self-description*, characterizing herself and her virtues, a telling of the *cosmogony and uranography* (description of the structure of the universe) of gnostic myth; a *"true history"* of humankind touching upon the creation of Adam and the incarnation; and *exhortations* of the gnostics to respond to the speaker and gain deliverance. FTh is closely paralleled by the concluding poem of BJn; it can also be compared with Th, although unlike the latter it is not characterized by riddlesome paradox.

A fragment of what may be a treatise or sermon on baptism appears to interrupt the monologue at 36:27f, but this passage is so imperfect in the manuscript that its exact character and function are obscure.

Mythic characters

I. Incorruptible Beings Mentioned in the Text

The PARENT. The invisible spirit.
FIRST THOUGHT. The Barbēlō, the parent's thinking, consisting of:

> The FATHER ⎫
> The MOTHER ⎬ expressions of first thought
> The SON ⎭

The ANOINTED (Christ). The verbal expression (Word), the perfect child, the only-begotten of first thought.
MEIROTHEA (not clearly distinguished in the text). A manifestation of first thought.
FOUR sets of ETERNAL REALMS and LUMINARIES:
ARMĒDŌN-NOUSA[. . .]–[HARMŌZĒL]
PHAINION-AINION-OROIAĒL
MELLEPHANEA-LŌION-DAUEITHAI
MOUSANION-AMETHĒN-ĒLĒLĒTH
WISDOM (Sophia). Life of afterthought, the innocent.
FIVE TRIOS OF INCORRUPTIBLE BEINGS, who enrobe, baptize, etc. the saved:
AMMŌM, ELASSŌ, AMENAI, the enrobers
MIKHEUS, MIKHAR, MNĒSINOUS, the baptizers
BARIĒL, NOUTHAN, SABĒNAI, the enthroners
ĒRIŌM, ĒLIEN, PHARIEL, the glorifiers
KAMALIĒL, [. .]ANĒN, SAMBLŌ, those who catch up

II. Rulers (Authorities, Powers) Mentioned in the Work

IALTABAŌTH. The first begetter, the great demon, ruler of Hades and chaos. Called Sakla and Samaēl.
RULERS, REALMS, POWERS, ANGELS, DEMONS

III. Humankind Mentioned in the Work

The FIRST HUMAN BEING, created by Ialtabaōth (Adam)
JESUS
OFFSPRING OF THE LIGHT

IV. A Spirit Active in Humankind

The eternal HOLY SPIRIT

Text

The original Greek apparently does not survive. The text is known only in Coptic translation, attested by a single manuscript from Nag Hammadi, MS NHC XIII (pp. 35–50), which was copied just before A.D. 350 and is now in the Cairo Coptic Museum.

The translation below is based on Janssens' critical edition of the Coptic, with very minor alterations: Y. Janssens, *La Prōtennoia Trimorphe* (see "Select Bibliography").

SELECT BIBLIOGRAPHY

Janssens, Y. *La Prōtennoia Trimorphe*. Bibliothèque copte de Nag Hammadi, Section "Textes," vol. 4. Québec: Les Presses de l'Université Laval, 1978. (Commentary.)

Robinson, J. M. "Sethians and Johannine Thought: The Trimorphic Protennoia and the Prologue of the Gospel of John." In *The Rediscovery of Gnosticism: Proceedings of the International Conference on Gnosticism at Yale, New Haven, Connecticut, March 28–31, 1978*, edited by B. Layton. Vol. 2, *Sethian Gnosticism*, 643–62 (and discussion, 662–70). Studies in the History of Religions, no. 41, vol. 2. Leiden: E. J. Brill, 1981.

FIRST THOUGHT IN THREE FORMS[a]

I. FIRST THOUGHT'S VERBAL EXPRESSION[b]

POEM (1)

First thought as Barbēlō, life (wisdom), and savior

<table>
<tr><td>1</td><td>35 It is [I] who am first thought,[c] [the] thinking that exists in [. . .].</td><td>36:17, 38:7
42:6, 46:7
46:28</td></tr>
<tr><td>2</td><td>It is [I] who am the movement that exists in the [entirety],[d]</td><td>BJn 4:26 +
v.2</td></tr>
<tr><td>3</td><td>In [whom] the entirety stands at rest,[e]</td><td>35:13, 35:19
43:18, 46:25</td></tr>
<tr><td>4</td><td>[The first]-produced[f] among those that have [come into existence],</td><td></td></tr>
<tr><td>5</td><td>[Who] existed before the entirety, [who] am called by three names,[g] and who alone exist [perfect].</td><td>37:20 +</td></tr>
<tr><td>7</td><td>I am invisible within the thinking of the invisible,[h]</td><td>BJn 2:32</td></tr>
<tr><td>9</td><td>And disclosed within the immeasurable ineffables.</td><td>35:27</td></tr>
<tr><td>10</td><td>I am incomprehensible, existing within the incomprehensible and moving within every creature.</td><td></td></tr>
<tr><td>12</td><td>It is I who am the life[i] of my afterthought;</td><td>39:17</td></tr>
<tr><td>13</td><td>Who exist among all powers and all eternal movements; among invisible lights; and among the rulers, the angels, the [demons], all souls that dwell in Tartarus, and all material souls;</td><td>BJn 20:14 +
v.13
35:2 +

36:4 +</td></tr>
<tr><td>19</td><td>Who exist among those who have come into existence;</td><td></td></tr>
<tr><td>19</td><td>Who move among all, and who am strong among all;</td><td>35:2 +</td></tr>
<tr><td>21</td><td>Who travel[j] uprightly;</td><td>BJn 30:13</td></tr>
<tr><td>21</td><td>And who awaken those who are asleep.</td><td>BJn 31:4</td></tr>
<tr><td>22</td><td>It is I who am vision for those who dwell in sleep.</td><td></td></tr>
<tr><td>24</td><td>It is I who am the invisible within the entirety;</td><td></td></tr>
<tr><td>25</td><td>It is I who consider the hidden, being acquainted with the entirety,</td><td></td></tr>
<tr><td>25</td><td>And who exist within it.</td><td></td></tr>
<tr><td>27</td><td>I am the most innumerable of all beings.</td><td></td></tr>
</table>

Title 35 a. In the manuscript, the title is found after the text (at 50:22).

b. Or "First Thought's speech." For the significance of the title, see note 36b. This chapter title is copied only at the end of the chapter, at 42:3.

c. The Barbēlō aeon, which in other texts is called also "forethought," a slightly different word.

d. The sum total of spiritual reality deriving from the Barbēlō aeon.

e. The term "stand at rest" is philosophical jargon for the state of permanence, nonchange, and real being, as opposed to what exists in instability, change, and becoming. The speaker's paradoxical assertion to be "the movement" in which certain others "stand at rest" mimics for rhetorical effect the identity riddle, a style highly developed in Th.

f. The "thinking" of the parent, which is its "[first]-produced" power, is the Barbēlō. Cf. BJn 4:26f.

g. Cf. 37:20f.

h. I.e. the parent.

i. According to BJn, "life" or "the afterthought of the life" is the spiritual element present in all the offspring of the light (posterity of Seth). It is sent by and is an aspect of wisdom, who dwells in the realm of afterthought; it is an envoy of forethought or the Barbēlō, i.e. first thought; cf. BJn notes 20b and 25c. "Life" is thus a vivifying principle that is present in all who are capable of salvation.

j. I.e.: who visit the perceptible realm as savior; BJn 30:13f.

27	I am immeasurable and ineffable.	35:9, 36:27
28	And as for me, when I [. . . , I shall] show forth myself alone.	36:33, 46:14
30	. . . [. . .] the entirety, having existed before [. . .].	
31	It is I who am the entirety, having [existed (?) before] everyone.	
32	I am a sound [. . .],	36:9 +
33	Existing [. . .] within the silence [. . .] . . . and [. . .],	
1	**36** Which [exists (?)] within me [. . .] incomprehensible, immeasurable [. . .] immeasurable silence.	

Advent of first thought

4	For my part, [I entered the] midst of Hades,	35:13, 35:21
5	And [I] radiated [upon the] darkness.	40:29, 43:9
5	It is I who brought forth the [water (?)].	47:11
6	It is I who am hidden in waters[a] [. . .].	BJn 30:13
7	It is I who, within my thinking, radiated the entirety part by part.	
9	It is I who am laden with sound.	35:32, 38:14
9	It is because of me that acquaintance becomes immanent,	40:8, 42:4
10	Although I dwell among the ineffables and unrecognizables.	42:14, 44:2
12	It is I who am perception and acquaintance:	45:10, 45:27
13	Emitting sound by an act of thinking.[b]	46:19, 46:28
14	It is I who am the sound that exists,	
15	Bestowing sound upon everyone;	
15	And they recognize that a posterity exists within [me].	
17	It is I who am the parent's thinking;	35:1 +
17	And from me emanated sound, that is, acquaintance with the infinites:	
19	I exist as the thinking of the entirety.	
20	Being joined to unrecognizable and incomprehensible thinking,	42:5, 42:8
22	I personally showed myself forth among all those that had recognized me:	
23	For it is I who am joined unto everyone in hidden thinking, in exalted sound, and in sound caused by invisible thinking.	

PROSE DISCOURSE

Barbēlō's immanence within the gnostic church[c]

| 27,28 | And it[d] is immeasurable, existing within the immeasurable; •it is a | 35:27 + |
| 30 | mystery; it is [unrestrainable (?)] by [the incomprehensible (?)]; •it is invisible [. . .] shown forth within the entirety [. . .] exists within light. | |

36 a. "waters": a metaphor for the levels of acquaintance that are within the Barbēlō aeon. Cf. Zs 15:1f.

b. "sound . . . act of thinking": ancient Greek philosophers distinguished internal reasoning (*logos endiathetos*) or the "act of thinking" from the externally expressed reasoning (*logos prophorikos*) that can result from it. The relationship of internal to external reasoning was sometimes presented by Platonists as a model for understanding how god's existence—as he really is—might be related to his self-revelation, viz. in the form of a verbal expression or "Word" (*logos*) that he uttered. Such a model, which can be seen e.g. in the prologue to the canonical Gospel of John (1:1–18), underlies all the discussion of "thinking . . . sound . . . voice . . . verbal expression (Word) . . . acquaintance" in FTh. In FTh the model is additionally complicated by the assertion that the source (Barbēlō) of the verbal expression is itself the thinking of another entity (the parent).

c. Possibly this section, the MS of which is badly damaged, is actually poetry and is the beginning of poem no. (2).

d. "it": first thought. In this section a teacher speaks to an audience ("us," 37:1f), describing the immanence of first thought.

33 We [. . .] alone [. . .] shown forth [. . .] hidden [. . .], (it is) ineffable   35:27 +
1 and immeasurable. **37** •And what is in us and is hidden bestows its
products upon the water of life.[a]   48:20 +

POEM (2)

Appearance of the Word as savior[b]

3   So next, the offspring that is perfect in every way—i.e., the
         verbal expression (or Word) that came into being from the   46:5, 46:14
         sound[c] that had emanated from the height, having within it   46:30, 47:13
                                                                          BJn 7:9 +
         the name and shining bright—was shown forth to the
         infinite beings.
8   And all the unrecognizables were recognized;
10   And those which are difficult to interpret and hidden it   Th 20:33
         showed forth;
11   And to those who dwelt in silence and forethought it
         preached;
13   And to those who dwelt in darkness it showed itself;
14   And those who dwelt in the abyss[d] it instructed about itself;
16   And to those who dwelt in the hidden treasures it uttered the
         ineffable mysteries;
18   And the inexplicable teachings it taught to all who were
         offspring of the light.

NARRATION BY BARBĒLŌ (1)

Relation of the Word to Barbēlō[e]

20   Now, the sound that has derived from my thinking exists as three
23 compartments:[f] Father, Mother, Son—a voice existing perceptibly. •It   35:5, 46:28
contains within it a verbal expression (or Word),[g] which possesses all   EgG 50:23 +
                                                                            v.23
glory, and which possesses three masculinities[h] and three powers and   37:3 +
27 three names: •all three are thus[i] □ □ □, quadrangles, secretly in the
30 silence of the ineffable: •[the] only-begotten, who [is the anointed   49:7
31 (Christ)[j]], •[and] whom I myself anointed with glory [. . .] invisible in   BJn 6:23 +
33 [. . .]. •Thus [. . .] I made it alone stand at rest [. . .] eternal [. . .] upon
[. . .] living [. . .], i.e. [. . .], who first radiated light unto the exalted
eternal realms (aeons), within glorious light, in enduring strength.
3,5 **38** •And [it] stood at rest within its own light that was around it: •being
7 the eye of the light that enlightens me in glory. •It bestowed eternity   46:28
of[a] the parent of all the eternal realms (aeons), who is myself, the   EgG 61:8
                                                                            Zs 6:21
thinking of the parent of first thought, i.e. Barbēlō, the [perfect] glory   Fr 64:30?
and immeasurable, hidden invisible.   v.7
                                                                            35:1 +
                                                                            45:8 +

37 a. Baptismal water; cf. 48:20f.
   b. The speaker is either the teacher
(36:27f) or first thought.
   c. "verbal expression . . . sound": cf.
note 36b. Following a traditional Greek philosophical analysis of speech, FTh treats
"verbal expression" (*logos*), here meaning
external rational expression, as a special kind
of "voice" (37:20f), which in turn is a special
kind of "sound": thus every verbal expression is a sound, but not every sound is a
verbal expression. In the following paragraph, the "verbal expression" is personified
as a savior.
   d. "darkness . . . the abyss": i.e. the
material world, the realm of Sakla.

   e. First thought speaks.
   f. "compartments," or "rooms": Greek
monē; the same Greek word is used in the
canonical Gospel of John 14:2, "In my father's house are many rooms."
   g. "sound . . . thinking . . . voice . . .
verbal expression": see note 37c.
   h. "three masculinities": see EgG note
51f.
   i. A diagram appears at this place in the
MS.
   j. "anointed" and "Christ" are the same
word in Greek.

38 a. "of": or "upon."

POEM (3)

First thought as Meirothea

11   It is I who am the image of the invisible spirit,   BJn 4:34
12   And it was from me that the entirety received image:
13   (I,) the mother, the light that she left and which is virgin;
14   She who is called Meirothea,[b] the incomprehensible womb,   45:8
     the unrestrainable and immeasurable sound.   EgG 60:30 +
                                                                                       45:6
                                                                                       BJn 5:5
                                                                                       36:9 +

NARRATION BY BARBĒLŌ (2)

Praise of the anointed Word[c]

16   Next, the perfect child showed itself unto its eternal realms (aeons),   38:30
19   which had come into existence for its sake.[d] •It showed them forth and
20   bestowed glory upon them, and gave them thrones. •It stood at rest
22   within the glory by which it had glorified itself. •They praised the perfect
23   child, the anointed (Christ), the deity, the only-begotten, •and they
     glorified, saying:

24   It[e] exists! It exists!
     O child of god! O child of god!
     It is this that exists!
26   O eternal realm (aeon) of the eternal realms,
     You who gaze at the eternal realms that you have
          engendered!
27   For, you have engendered by your will alone.
28   Therefore [we] glorify you.
29   Ma! Mō!
     You are omega, omega, omega! You are alpha![f] You are
          being!
29   O eternal realm of the eternal realms! O eternal realm that gave
          itself!

Its establishment of the four eternal realms

30   Next, the begotten deity[g] bestowed upon them[h] [invincible . . .] power;   38:16
32,33 and [it] established [them]. •Now, it established   BJn 7:30 +

     [the] first eternal realm (aeon) [in the charge of the] first,
35   Armēdōn-Nousa[. . .]–[Harmōzēl]; •it established

     [the] second [in the charge of the second eternal realm],
          Phainion-Ainion-Oroiaēl;

1   **39** the third, in the charge of the third eternal realm,[a]
          Mellephanea-Lōion-Daueithai;

3   the fourth, in the charge of the fourth, Mousanion-Amethēn-
          Ēlēlēth.

5   So these eternal realms (aeons), which had been engendered by the
7   deity, engendered[b] the anointed (Christ). •And they were given glory;

b. "Meirothea": a Greek neologism, possibly meaning "divine part" (*moiros theios*).
     c. The speaker is either the teacher
(36:27f) or first thought.
     d. Or "because of it."
     e. I.e. the perfect child.
     f. "omega . . . alpha": related to a tradi-
tional acclamation. Cf. EgG note 53d.
     g. The anointed. Cf. 38:22f.

h. Its eternal realms, 38:16f.

39 a. "[in charge of the second eternal realm]
. . . in charge of the third eternal realm":
the text of the MS may be slightly corrupt
here. More consistent would be "[in charge
of the second] . . . in charge of the third."
     b. The Coptic text may be corrupt here.

8 and the eternal realms, too, glorified. •They were shown forth as being
9 exalted in their thinking. •And each eternal realm rendered myriad
11 glories unto (?) great, unsearchable luminaries. •And with one another
they all praised the perfect child, the begotten deity.

Emanation of wisdom (afterthought) and Sakla

13   Next,[c] a verbal expression (or Word) emanated from the great luminary   BJn 8:16+
Ēlēlēth, and it said, "It is I who am the ruler. Who is the one of chaos?
17 And who is the one of Hades?"[d] •And at that moment its light appeared,
19 shining bright because it possessed afterthought.[e] •The powers of the   35:12
powers did not supplicate it.
20   And immediately there was shown forth also the great demon that   BJn 9:25+
rules over the bottom of Hades and chaos, and which is misshapen and
24 imperfect, •yet has the form of the glory of those beings that were
26 engendered within the darkness, •and so is called Sakla,[f] i.e. Samaēl-
28 Ialtabaōth. •This is the being that got power—caught it up from the   BJn 10:20+
innocent,[g] whom it had first overcome, i.e. the afterthought of the light   40:7
that had descended and from which it had originally emanated.[h]

Forgiveness of wisdom (afterthought)

32   So [when] the afterthought of the light knew that it (Sakla) [was being]   RR 94:23+
supplicated [. . .], she said,[i] "[. . .] you shall be [. . ." . . .] in confusion
2 [. . .] all [the] house of the glory [. . .] upon her utterance. **40** •They
3 lifted up praise to her. •And the exalted band forgave her for him.[a]   BJn 13:32+

Creation of the universe

4   And the great demon began to order eternal realms (aeons) in the   BJn 12:33+
7 manner of the eternal realms that exist. •And it ordered them only
because of its power.   39:28+

Poem: Salvation of the stolen power

8   Next, I too secretly showed forth my sound, saying,   36:9+

10   "Cease, cease, O you (plur.) who tread upon matter!
11   For behold, I am coming down into the world of mortals
13   For the sake of that part of me[b] which has been there since
           the day that they overcame the innocent wisdom (Sophia)
           who descended;
16   (I am coming) so that I might thwart their goal that was
           ordained by the one that was shown forth[c] because of
           her."

c. The speaker is first thought. Cf. 40:8f.
d. I.e.: "Who is the ruler of chaos? And who is the ruler of Hades?" In this obscure passage, which parallels EgG 68:5f, wisdom ("the innocent") may be said to emanate from Ēlēlēth and assert her sovereignty—as a result of which, both the afterthought of life and the great demon Sakla appear.
e. The "afterthought of the light" is wisdom, returning to the realm of Sakla in order to rectify the lack created by Sakla's theft of her power; cf. note 35i.
f. "Sakla" (Aramaic "fool," elsewhere also "Saklas"): a conventional name for Satan in Judaism.
g. "the innocent": a stock epithet of wis-

dom (Sophia), 40:13; cf. BJn 23:20f. The theft of wisdom's "power" is narrated more fully in BJn 10:19f, 12:33f, 13:27f.
h. See BJn 9:25f.
i. The exact limits of afterthought's statement are uncertain.

40 a. This highly condensed narration (39:13–40:25f) of the fall and forgiveness of wisdom and the creation of the world and human beings presupposes the reader's acquaintance with more detailed information, such as that found in BJn.
b. The stolen "power," 39:28f.
c. I.e. Sakla.

19 And all who dwelt in the house of the unrecognizable light became
22 disturbed. •And the abyss shook.

Creation of Adam

22   And the first begetter of the ignorance[d] ruled over chaos and Hades.
24,25 It put in order a human being, after my manner of appearance.[e] •But it   BJn 15:1+
did not know that the human being would turn out to be its condemnation
unto destruction, nor did it recognize the power that he had within   BJn 19:15+
himself.

POEM (4)

Advent and victory of first thought

29   But then for my part, I descended and got as far as chaos.   36:4+
30   And I dwelt [with] my own[f] who were there, [hidden] within
     them,[g] bestowing power [. . .], (and) [imparting] image unto   45:23+
     them.
34   And [. . .] down to the present [. . .] those who [. . .], i.e. the
     offspring of [the] light.
1   **41** It is I who am their parent.
2   And I shall tell you a mystery that is ineffable and
     indescribable by [any] mouth.
4   For you (plur.), I loosed all the fetters and broke the bonds[a]
     of the demons of Hades, bonds that were bound to my
     limbs[b] and worked against them.
7   And I threw down the high walls of the darkness,
9   And I broke open the solid gates of the merciless (plur.) and
     split their bolts.
11   And the evil agency, who strikes you (plur.), who impedes
     you, the tyrant, the adversary, the ruler, the real enemy—
     as for all of these, I taught them about my own, the
     offspring of the light:
17   So that they[c] might become loosened from all these and
     rescued from all the fetters, and might enter the place
     where they had been in the beginning.
20   It is I who am the first to have descended, for the sake of
     that part of me which remained,
21   Namely, the spirit that exists within the soul[d] and which has   45:29
     come to exist out of the water of life and out of the   BJn 25:20+
     baptism of the mysteries.   48:20+
24   I myself spoke with the rulers and with authorities, for I had
     descended deep into their language;
27   And I uttered my mysteries to my own—a hidden mystery—
28   And the fetters were loosened, as was eternal forgetfulness.
30   And within them I bore fruit, namely, the thinking that
     concerns the unchangeable eternal realm (aeon) and my
     house and [their] parent.
32   And I have gone [to] my [own] since the beginning, and I
     have [. . .] beginning [. . .] first branch (?), which [. . .].
35   All who [were] in me shone bright.

---

d. Lit. "lack of acquaintance."
e. The Barbēlō has the image of an androgynous human being: BJn 5:6.
f. The offspring of the light.
g. As a spiritual element. Cf. note 35i.

41 a. "fetters . . . bonds": a Platonist cliché
for the material body.
   b. During an incarnation.
   c. The offspring.
   d. The soul animates the body and is not
identical with the spirit or highest self.

36   And for the ineffable lights within me I prepared a manner of
2   appearance. **42** •Amen!ᵃ

II. DESTINYᵇ

POEM (5)

First thought as life (wisdom)

4	It is I who am the sound that was shown forth by my thinking.	36:9 +
5	For it is I who am the conjoined.	36:20 +
6	I am called the thinking of the invisible.	35:1 +
7	I am called the unchangeable voice.	42:14, 44:29
8	I am called she-who-is-conjoined.	45:10, 46:7 47:11
8	I am unique, incorruptible.	**v.8** 36:20 +
9	It is I who am the mother [of (?)] the sound:	
10	I speak in many ways; I complete the entirety;ᶜ acquaintance exists within me—acquaintance with ⟨the⟩ endless.	
12	It is I [who] speak in every creature; and I have been recognized by the entirety.	
14	It is I who impart the voice of the sound into the ears of those who have become acquainted with me, who are children of the light.	42:7 + ; 36:9 +
17	And I came, for a second time, in the manner of a woman; and I spoke with them.	RR 89:31 ?
18	And I shall instruct them about the coming end of the realm.ᵈ	
20	And I shall instruct them about the beginning of the coming realm,ᵉ which does not experience change, and in which our appearance will change.	
23	They shall become purified within the aeons, in which I showed myself forth in the thinking of the image of my masculinity.	
25	I have put myself within those who are worthy in the thinking of my unchangeable eternal realm (aeon).	
27	For I shall tell you (plur.) a mystery of this realm,	
28	And I shall instruct you about the agencies that are within it.	
30	Birthᶠ is the production of an echo. [For], hour engenders hour, day [engenders (?)] day, months produceᵍ months, [. . .] following [. . .].	
33	In [such] terms, this realm has become complete.	
1	**43** And it has been reckoned, and is slight.	
2	For finger has loosened finger,ᵃ	
3	And bond has been bound (?) by bond.	

NARRATION: THE FINAL STRUGGLE

Conflagration of the heavens

4   Now, when the great authorities knew that the time for fulfillment had   IrSat 1.24.2 +
come—as when labor pains are felt by a lying-in woman—and that it

---

42 a. In the MS the chapter title of the
preceding chapter is written here as a subscript.

b. This chapter title is copied only at the
end of the chapter, at 46:4.

c. By recalling the missing units of wisdom's power to their rightful home and
reuniting them with the eternal realms.

d. Or "age."

e. Or "age."

f. The translation of this verse is uncertain.

g. "produce": the MS has lit. "an-
nounce."

43 a. Or possibly "inch replaces inch."

was near the door, and that just so, destruction had drawn nigh, all the
9 elements together shook. •And the foundations of Hades and the ceilings   36:4+
10,11 of chaos moved. •A great fire broke out in their midst. •And the rocky
cliffs and the earth moved as a reed is moved by the wind.

Planetary determinism undone

13   And the lots of destiny and those which traverse[b] the houses[c] were   BJn 28:12
15 greatly disturbed by a sharp thunderclap. •And the powers' thrones were   Th 13:1?
17 disturbed and overturned, and their ruler became afraid. •And those
which follow destiny[d] gave up their numerous circuits along the way.   44:14+
18 And they said to the powers, "What is this disturbance and this movement   IrUnid 1.30.6
that has come over us from a sound that belongs to the superior voice?   35:2+
22 All our house has moved; the whole circuit of our ascent has gone to
ruin; the way on which we travel and which leads us up to the first
begetter of our birth[e] is no longer established!"
27,28   Next, the powers answered, saying, •"We too are at a loss as to this
29,29 (disturbance). •For we do not know whom it belongs to. •But arise, let
us go to the first begetter and ask it."

Accusation of Ialtabaōth by the powers

31,33   The powers all gathered and went to the first begetter. •[They said to]
33,35 him, •"Where is your boasting of which [you] boasted? •Did we not
35 [hear you say], •'It is I who am God; [it is I who am] your (plur.) parent;   Is 45:21
1,1 **44** •it is I who engendered you; •there is no other apart from me'?[a]   BJn 13:5+
2 Well, now behold—there has been shown forth a sound that belongs to   36:9+
the invisible voice of [the eternal realm (?)] that we do not recognize.
4 And for our part at least [we have not] recognized whom we belong to.[b]
6 For, that sound which we heard is alien to us, and we do not recognize
8,8 it, •we do not know where it comes from. •It has come and instilled
fear in our midst and limpness in the joints of our legs.

Lament of the powers

10,12   "So, then, let us weep, let us mourn with great mourning! •Finally,   RR 97:11
let us complete our escape before we are forcibly trapped and taken
14 down into the bowels of Hades. •For the undoing of our bonds[c] has   43:17
17 already come, spans of time are falling short, days have dwindled; •our   RR 97:10+
time has been fulfilled, and weeping over our destruction has come upon
us, so that we shall be taken to a place that we do ⟨not⟩[d] recognize.
19   "For our tree from which we sprouted bears fruit of ignorance, and   BJn 21:26
23 also there is death in its leaves; •darkness dwells in the shadow of its
24,25 branches; •and we have harvested it deceitfully and with desire. •It is
27 by this that ignorant chaos has come to be our dwelling place. •For   49:13
behold, it, too—the first begetter of our birth, of whom we boast—it,
too, does not know about the voice!"

---

b. Or "measure."
c. "those which traverse the houses": the planets, which "traverse" the sectors ("houses") of the celestial sphere; according to ancient astrology each planet had its greatest influence within its own "house."
d. The planets.
e. "the first begetter": Sakla.

44 a. This claim is well known from other gnostic texts, where it figures in the narration of Sakla's emanation.
b. Or perhaps "[we have not] recognized whom it belongs to."
c. Their influence on human affairs.
d. The word "⟨not⟩" is erroneously omitted in the MS.

POEM (6)

Call to deliverance by first thought (Meirothea)

29   So, then, hear me O children of thinking; hear the voice of   42:7f
        the mother of your mercy.   BJn 10:16

31   For you have become worthy of the mystery that has been
33   hidden since eternities, •so that you [might . . .].

33   And the end of this realm (aeon) [and] of this violent life
        [have . . .] beginning (?) of the [. . .] which [. . .].

2   **45** I am androgynous [. . .] a parent[a] [. . .] with myself alone.

4   I [. . .] with myself alone (?) [. . .].

5   The entirety [. . .] through me alone.

6   It is I who am the [. . .] womb of the entirety, giving birth to   38:14
        the light [. . .] in glory.

8   It is I who am the aeon that [. . .] the completion of the
        entirety, namely, Meirothea,[b] the glory of the mother,   EgG 60:30 +
                                                                          46:19
10   And I project a voice [of the] sound into the ears of those   RAd 64:6 +
        who recognize me.   **v.10**
                                  42:7 +
12   And I am calling you (plur.) to enter the superior, perfect   36:9 +
        light:

13   When you (plur.) enter it you will be glorified by the   48:15
        glorifiers; the enthroners will give you thrones; you will be
        given robes by the enrobers, and the baptists will baptize
        you (plur.); so that along with glories you become the glory
        in which you existed, luminous, in the beginning.

Advent of first thought as life (wisdom)

21   And I hid myself in everyone,[c] and showed [myself] forth in
        them.

22   And all acts of thinking desired me and sought me,

23   For it is I who have imparted image unto the entirety: 40:30, 47:12
                                                                      EgG 62:9
24   They were misshapen, and I changed their forms into   Zs 5:15 +
        (temporary) forms until such time as the entirety should be
        formed.

27   It was through me that the sound came to exist.   36:9 +

28   And it is I who put breath into my own.   BJn 19:25 +

29   And I injected the eternal holy spirit into them,   41:21 +

30   And I ascended and proceeded into my light.

32   I (?) [. . .] down upon my branch,[d] I sat [. . . the . . .]
        children of the [. . .] light.

34,3 And [. . .] their dwelling place [. . . **46** •Amen!][a]

III. THE VERBAL EXPRESSION[b]
OF THE MANIFESTATION[c]

POEM (7)

First two advents of the savior as Word

5   It is I who am the [verbal expression (Word)] that exists   37:3 +, 46:14
        [. . .],

45 a. Or "father."   preceding chapter is written here as a sub-
    b. Cf. note 38b.   script.
    c. Cf. note 35i.   b. Or "the Word."
    d. Or "offshoot."   c. The chapter title is copied only at the
                                          end of the chapter, at 50:21f. It reads: "The
                                          Verbal Expression of the Manifestation. (Part)
46 a. In the MS the chapter title of the   Three."

6   And who exist in ineffable [. . .], existing in incorruptible
[. . .],

7   And an act of thought [. . .] perceptibly, through [. . .] voice
of the mother for a male offspring,   35:1+ / 42:7+

9,10   [. . .] put myself, •and since the beginning it[d] has existed in
the bones of the entirety.

11,12   And there is light that exists hidden in silence, •and which
emanated.

13   But the latter (silence) exists alone and silent.

14   It is I alone who am the ineffable, incorruptible,
immeasurable, inconceivable verbal expression,   35:27+ / 37:3+

16   And who am hidden light that yields a living crop, that brings
forth living water from the invisible, incorruptible,
immeasurable wellspring: 46:22 / BJn 4:21+ / **v.19**

19   That is, the inexplicable sound of the mother's glory,[e] the
glory of the engendering of the deity, a male virgin from a
hidden intellect;   36:9+ / 45:8+ / EgG 54:19 / 47:7

22   That is, silence—hidden from the entirety and inexplicable;
immeasurable light; the wellspring of the entirety; the root
of all eternity (aeon):   46:16+

25   Which is the platform that supports all motions of the eternal
realms (aeons) that belong to the mighty glory; is the   35:2+

28,28   foundation of all platforms; •is the breath of the powers; •is
the eye of the three compartments,[f] and exists as a sound   38:5+ / 37:20+ / 36:9+

30   from an act of thinking; •is a verbal expression (or Word)
by the voice that has been sent to enlighten those who
dwell in the darkness.   35:1+ / **v.30** / 37:3+

33   So behold, I [shall] show forth to you (plur.)[g] [. . .],

34   For you [are] my fellow [. . .] all know them(selves?) [. . .]
that exist in uninvoked [. . .].

7   **47** And I taught [. . .] by the [. . .] by perfect intellect.   Th 13:1 / 47:7

10   [I] became a foundation for the entirety, and [. . .] them.

11   For a second time I came, in the [voice (?)] of my sound,   BJn 30:21 / 42:7+

12   And I completely imparted image unto those who had
received image.   **v.12** / 45:23+

The third advent

13   For a third time I showed myself forth to them within their
bodies,[a] existing as a verbal expression (or Word).   RR 96:28 / 37:3+

15   And I showed myself forth in the resemblance of their image.

16   And I wore the garment[b] of all,

17   And I hid myself alone within them.

18   And [they] did not recognize the source of my power.

19   For I dwell in all the realms and the powers and in the angels
and in every movement that occurs in the whole of matter.   35:2+

22   And I hid myself within them until such time as I might show
myself forth unto my siblings.[c]

24   And none of them[d] recognized me, [even though] it was I
who was active within them.

---

d. "it": or "she"; for grammatical reasons, in the Coptic text this word can refer to either "the voice" or "the mother."

e. Or "the sound of the inexplicable mother's glory," or "the sound of the mother's inexplicable glory."

f. Cf. 37:20f.

g. Or "be shown forth to you as."

47 a. "Bodies": lit. "tents," a traditional metaphor for the fleshly body as the residence of the inner person or self.

b. A Platonist cliché for the material body.

c. The offspring of the light.

d. I.e. the rulers.

25   Rather, [they] thought that the entirety had been created by [them], being unaware that they had not recognized [their] root[e] from which they had sprung.

28   It is [I] who am the light that illuminates the entirety.

29   It is I who am the light that rejoices in [its] siblings.

31   For I have come into the world [of] mortals for the sake of the spirit that remained in that which [. . .]

33   [. . .] came from wisdom (Sophia) [. . .] and [. . .]

Baptism of acquaintance

35   And I [. . .] had [. . .] from the water [. . .] strip from that person the chaos that [. . .] ultimate [darkness] that exists

10   [. . .] whole [darkness]; **48** •that is, the thinking [of the . . .][a] and animate (subsistences?).

11   For my part, I put all these on;

12   But I stripped them off of that person,[b]   49:28

13   [And I] clothed that person in shining light,

13   That is, acquaintance with thinking about kinship.

15   And I delivered that person unto the enrobers[c] Ammōm,   45:13
     Elassō, and Amēnai, and they dressed that person in a robe belonging to the robes of the light.

18   And I delivered that person unto the baptists Mikheus,   RAd 84:4
     Mikhar, and Mnēsinous, to be baptized;   EgG 76:2 / Zs 6:7

20   And they washed that person in the wellspring of the water of   Zs 46:31
     life.   **v.20** / 37:1, 41:21

21   And I delivered that person unto the enthroners Bariēl, Nouthan, and Sabēnai,

22   And they [gave] that person a throne from the throne of glory.

24   And I delivered that person unto the glorifiers Ēriōm, Ēlien, and Phariēl,

25   And they glorified that person with the glory of the kinship.

26   And those who catch up, Kamaliēl, [. .]anēn, and Samblō,   EgG 64:13
     the great assistants [of the] holy luminaries, caught up and took that person into the luminous place of that person's kinship.

30   And [. . .] the five seals by[d] [the] light of the mother, first   49:27+
     thought.

32   And they [. . .] to that person, and took from [the mystery (?)] of acquaintance, and [. . .] with light.

35   So then [. . .] exist in them [. . .].

7   **49** They thought [. . .] their anointed (their Christ).   37:31+

8   For my part, [. . .] every [. . .], in that which [. . .] luminous [. . .] in them [. . .] the rulers.

11   It is I who am their beloved.

The saving Word as Jesus

11   For in that place I clothed myself [as though I were] the   50:12
     offspring of the first begetter,[a]

---

e. Sakla.

48 a. Possibly "[of the corporeal]."
    b. In a traditional metaphor of garments, expressing renewal by Christian baptism, the former state of being is stripped off the baptismal candidate and a new state is put on.
    c. Cf. 45:13f.
    d. Or "from."

49 a. "the first begetter": Sakla.

13	And I brought it (the first begetter) to the end of its judicial authority, which is the ignorance[b] that belongs to chaos.	44:27
15	And while among the angels, I showed myself forth in their likeness;
17	While among the powers, as though I were one of them;
18	And while among the children of humankind, as though I were a child of the human being,[c]
19	Although I am the parent of everyone.
20	I hid myself in all these (spiritual beings)[d] until such time as I might show myself forth out of my own members.
22	And I taught them about the ineffable ordinances and about the siblings.
23	They[e] are uninvoked by all realms and powers of rulers—only by the offspring of the light alone.
26,26	They are the ordinances of the parent; •they are the glories
27	superior to all glories; •they are the five seals[f] that are perfect through intellect.	48:30, 50:9 · BJn 31:22+
28	Whoever possesses the five seals of these very names has taken off robes[g] of ignorance[h] and put on shining light.	48:12
32	And none that belongs to the powers of the rulers will appear before that person.
34	Within such persons, darkness will perish and [. . .][i] will die;
36	And the thinking of the [. . .] creation [. . .] bestow one and the same manner, and [. . .] will perish.
38	And [. . .] and [. . .] incomprehensible [. . .] in [. . .]
6	**50** until such time as I should show myself forth [. . .] and until such time as I should gather [. . .] all [my (?) . . .] siblings in my [. . .].
9,10	And I proclaimed the [five] ineffable seals unto them, •so that [I might dwell] in them, and they too might dwell in me.	49:27+
12,13	For my part, I put on Jesus;[a] •I extracted him from the	49:11
14	accursed wood;[b] •and I made him stand at rest in the dwelling places of his parent.
15	And the beings[c] that watch over their dwelling places did not recognize me.
16	For I myself am unrestrainable, together with my posterity.	Th 19:20+
18	And I shall bring my posterity in to the holy light, in incomprehensible silence. Amen![d]	RR 97:7

b. Lit. "lack of acquaintance."

c. Or "a son of man."

d. "all these," namely spiritual beings: gnostic jargon used in this text, probably to mean the sum total of spiritual reality deriving from the Barbēlō aeon; cf. Zs note 2e.

e. The ordinances.

f. The "five seals" are associated with the reception of *gnōsis* in gnostic baptism (for which, see "Historical Introduction," Part One).

g. "robes": cf. note 47b. Also possible is "He who possesses the five seals . . . took off."

h. Lit. "lack of acquaintance."

i. Possibly "[ignorance]."

50 a. The body or person of Jesus is here likened to the garment in which first thought is clothed during her final advent; a Platonist cliché for the relation of body to soul. This incarnation, or adoption, parallels the final advent of the great Seth, EgG 75:15f.

b. Possibly the cross. The corresponding Greek word *hylē* also means "matter," and it may have been mistranslated into Coptic.

c. The rulers.

d. In the MS, the text concludes with the chapter title of Chapter III, the general title of the work (at 50:22) and the following expression: "Holy scripture, paternally authored in perfect acquaintance."

THE HOLY BOOK OF THE GREAT INVISIBLE SPIRIT

or

THE EGYPTIAN GOSPEL

ACCORDING TO MS NHC IV
(EgG)

Contents

The Holy Book of the Great Invisible Spirit, also entitled *The Egyptian Gospel* ("The Gospel of the Egyptians"), tells the gnostic myth as though it were the solemn prelude to a baptismal ritual; the work ends with an account of the establishment of gnostic baptism and a baptismal service book, including a list of metaphysical beings that preside over gnostic baptism and a hymn to be said by the baptized. For further discussion of gnostic baptism, see the "Historical Introduction" to Part One. The entire gnostic myth is recounted, but with emphasis on the first and last acts of the mythic drama—that is, the expansion of the invisible spirit or first principle into a full spiritual universe and the establishment of the gnostic church. These two emphases provide a mythic setting for the participation of metaphysical beings in baptism and the establishment of the baptismal ritual. The spiritual universe is described as a glorifying throne room ("Doxomedōn Domedōn"), filled with incessant litanies sung by a hierarchical retinue whose names and laudatory epithets are repeatedly catalogued. The Barbēlō aeon in EgG has a threefold structure, as in FTh, Zs, Fr, and 3Tb. As in BJn, the preexistent savior (here called the great Seth) comes three times to intervene in human history. The third advent is said to be the incarnation or adoption of Jesus by the preexistent great Seth. The account of creation is brief and positive, emphasizing divine providence as in RR and FTh.

The work has no obvious Egyptian character; the reference to Egypt in the title is obscure. EgG is *not* identical to "The Gospel According to the Egyptians" occasionally cited by fathers of the church.

Literary background

The author and place of composition of EgG are unknown. The date of its composition must be sometime before A.D. 350, the approximate date of the MS. In mythic content the work resembles RAd, 3Tb, Zs, Fr, and 3Tb. The language of composition was Greek.

The mixture of genres in EgG is slightly complex, combining various traditional materials:

I. Heavenly message
  A. Learned treatise: (1) cosmogony; (2) "true history"
  B. Liturgical service book: (1) uranography; (2) hymn

As in RAd and 3Tb, the whole work is presented (80:15f) as a *heavenly message,* in this instance composed by "the great Seth" (i.e. the spiritual archetype) and left by him in high mountains, perhaps engraved on tablets. The convention of the heavenly message is a commonplace of ancient Mediterranean revelation literature. The message is not spoken by Seth in the first person, but rather is quoted obliquely; the work therefore purports to be not the message itself, but a transcript of the message by someone else. The body of the heavenly message falls into two parts. The first has the form of a *learned treatise* on *cosmogony,* followed by a revisionist *"true history"* of the Sethid line of humanity down to the final incarnation of the savior. The second part is a *liturgical service book* for gnostic baptism, beginning with a *uranographic catalogue* (list of structural elements of the universe) of "great beings that stand at rest" and preside over gnostic baptism and concluding with an ecstatic *hymn* spoken by the newly baptized gnostic.

Mythic characters

I.   The Incorruptible Beings

The PARENT. The great invisible virgin spirit.
THREE POWERS and their LIGHTS:
  1. THE FATHER, consisting of
       Thought
       Verbal expression (Word)
       Incorruptibility
       Eternal life
       Will
       Intellect
       Prior acquaintance
       Androgynous father
  2. THE MOTHER
  3. THE SON
AEONS, GLORIES, POWERS, THRONES, etc., partly associated with the Doksomedōn realm
IŌĒL. The silence of silent silence, a masculine female virgin.
The ANOINTED (Christ). The thrice-male child, Telmaēl-Telmakhaēl-Ēli-Ēli-Makhar-Makhar-Seth.
ĒSĒPHĒKH. The child of the child, holder of the glory.
The MOIROTHEA, probably the same as PLĒSITHEA. Mother of the luminaries and the incorruptible beings that are with them.
FOUR LUMINARIES and their CONSORTS, ATTENDANTS, and ATTENDANTS' CONSORTS:
  HARMOZĒL
       LOVELINESS—GAMALIĒL—MEMORY
  OROIAĒL
       PERCEPTION—GABRIĒL—LOVE
  DAUEITHE
       INTELLIGENCE—SAMBLŌ—PEACE
  ĒLĒLĒTH
       PRUDENCE—ABRASAKS—ETERNAL LIFE
BEINGS that dwell with the luminaries:
  The SELF-ORIGINATE WORD (or verbal expression). An offspring of the anointed (Christ). Fused with Adamas.

ADAMAS. The incorruptible first human being. With Harmozēl.

The GREAT SETH, his son. The "child of the human being" (son of man). With Oroiaēl.

SEED OR OFFSPRING OF THE GREAT SETH. The incorruptible immovable race. With Daueithe.

SOULS of the offspring. With Ēlēlēth.

MATERIAL WISDOM (Sophia)

ANGELIC AGENTS in the birth of the seed of Seth:

HORMOS

EDŌKLA

GUARDIANS of the seed of Seth:

400,000 ETHEREAL ANGELS

AEROSIĒL

SELMELKHEL

OTHER INCORRUPTIBLE BEINGS who preside, receive, guard, etc., including the living water Iesseus-Mazareus-Iessedekeus and others.

II. The Rulers

SAKLA. The great angel that rules over Hades and chaos, the devil.

NEBROUĒL. The great demon that is with Sakla.

Sakla's ANGELS, that preside over Hades and chaos

III. Humankind

ADAM

HIS WIFE (Eve)

THREE SONS ("sowings") begotten on Eve:

A SON by the rulers (Cain)

A SON by Adam (Abel)

A SON by the great Seth (Seth)

The RACE OF SETH on earth, including perhaps:

A FEMALE VIRGIN by whom Seth becomes incarnate (Mary)

JESUS of Nazareth. Seth incarnate as a reason-born being.

Text

The original Greek apparently does not survive. The text is known only in Coptic translation, attested by two manuscripts, MSS NHC III (pp. 40–69) and NHC IV (pp. 50–81), which were copied just before A.D. 350 and are now in the Cairo Coptic Museum. Each of the two Coptic manuscripts contains an independent and stylistically distinct translation based on the Greek; thus, wherever the two texts are parallel, they differ in vocabulary and style. Careful comparison of the parallels has made it possible to gain a systematic understanding of the different ways in which the two ancient Coptic translators carried out their task; and thus, in cases where one of the two manuscripts is defective, its original text can often be restored by consideration of the wording of the parallel.

There are also important differences between the two manuscripts that are not a matter of ancient translation technique, but rather indicate that two distinct editions of the Greek text were already in circulation in antiquity when the Coptic translations were being made. At present, there is no certainty among scholars as to which ancient edition contains the more accurate version of the original text, though the editors of the critical edition believe that NHC IV may have been generally superior. For that reason the present translation is based on MS NHC IV; in many places where NHC IV is defective, its readings can be conjecturally restored by comparison and stylistic adjustment of the reading found in the other manuscript. Such restorations, which are supported by the parallel manuscript, are *printed in italics*.

Comparison of the other manuscript has also clarified the meaning of certain Coptic expressions in NHC IV and has thus been an aid in translation. In a few instances both manuscripts are defective in a given passage but the original text can nevertheless be conjectured with certainty: these totally conjectural restorations are enclosed within square brackets [ ]. Reference numbers keyed to the translation follow NHC IV, even in italicized passages, except when NHC IV is so defective that its line numbers are uncertain. In such cases a reference to NHC III is given (e.g. **III 55**).

The translation below is based upon Böhlig and Wisse's synoptic critical edition of the Coptic, with some alterations: A. Böhlig and F. Wisse, *Nag Hammadi Codices III,2 and IV,2* . . . (see "Select Bibliography"), 52–167. The translation is based on MS NHC IV; parallel line references of the other manuscript are also provided in the margin.

An English translation of the other ancient edition of the work, which is found in MS NHC III, is given in Böhlig and Wisse's critical edition.

SELECT BIBLIOGRAPHY

Böhlig, A. "Die himmlische Welt nach dem Ägypterevangelium von Nag Hammadi." *Muséon* 80 (1967): 5–26, 365–77.

Böhlig, A., and F. Wisse. *Nag Hammadi Codices III,2 and IV,2: The Gospel of the Egyptians.* Nag Hammadi Studies, vol. 4. Leiden: E. J. Brill; Grand Rapids, Mich.: William B. Eerdmans Publishing Co., 1975. (Commentary, with an English translation of both versions of the work.)

Speyer, W. "Religiöse Pseudepigraphie und literarische Fälschung im Altertum." *See* RAd, "Select Bibliography." (The heavenly message as a convention of pseudepigraphy.)

THE HOLY BOOK OF THE GREAT INVISIBLE SPIRIT

or

THE EGYPTIAN GOSPEL[a]

I. THE INCORRUPTIBLE REALM

Title. The parent.

IV
III

1 (40 *12*) **IV 50** *The Holy Book* of the [. . .] *of* the Great *Invisible*
3 (*13*) [Spirit]:[a] the *unnameable* parent [that] emanated *from the* BJn 2:26+
5 (*17*) heights; •the light of [the] fullness; the eternal light of the aeons;
the light in silence—in forethought and the parent's silence; the
light in word and truth; the light of the incorruptibilities; the inac-
12 (41 *2*) cessible light; •the light that has emanated forever, belonging
to the aeons of the ineffable, traceless,[b] and unproclaimable par-
18 (*5*) ent; the eternity of the aeons; •the self-originate, self-radiation,
21 (*–*) and alien; •the inexplicable power of the ineffable parent.
23 (*7*)   Three powers emanated from it: namely the father, the BJn 9:9+
mother, and the son, which are self-manifest beings, from the RAd 65:25
FTh 37:20+
29 (*9*) incorruptible parent's living[c] *silence*. •They emanated from *the* Zs 58:23
ineffable parent's silence [. . .] **51** Doksomedōn-Domedōn,[a] 3Tb 121:32+
IrG 1.29.3
4 (*15*) the eternal realm *of the aeons*. •[From that source] emanated **v.29**
53:3, 55:7
the light—[that] is, the emanation—of *each* of their powers; 62:4, 65:13
and *in this way the son* emanated as the *fourth,* the mother as III 56:1
Zs 126:6
11 (*19*) the [fifth], the father as the *sixth*. •[. . .] *it*[b] was [not . . . ;
rather, it is] traceless,[c] [and] it left no mark *in* all *the powers,*
glories, *and* incorruptibilities.

Emanation of three powers

15 (*23*)   From it there had emanated three *powers,*[d] which are three
octets, which the parent *emitted* from its bosom in silence *and*
by its forethought: the father, the mother, the *son*.

The father

22 (42 *5*)   The first octet, for whose sake[e] the thrice-male[f] child[g] ema- 55:11
nated:

Title a. The double title is found in the
colophon in MS NHC III at the end of the
work (III 69:6f). Many scholars translate the
subtitle as "The Gospel of the Egyptians"
and call the work only by this designation.
The following translation is based on MS
NHC IV wherever that MS is extant; for the
meaning of *italics*, see the introduction to
EgG, "Text."

IV **50** a. In the colophon of MS NHC III,
the main title of the work is copied as the
last phrase, a normal place for titles. It is
based upon these opening words.
b. MS NHC III next has "unaging and."

c. "living": gnostic jargon used in this
text to indicate membership in the incorruptible realm.

51 a. Apparently not an actor but a place.
b. The parent.
c. MS NHC III next has "unfamiliar."
d. This passage is a detailed retelling of
50:23f.
e. Or "because of which."
f. "thrice," i.e. "supremely": gnostic jargon used in this text; "male": gnostic jargon
used in this text to indicate membership in
the incorruptible realm.
g. Or "servant."

thought;

Word (verbal expression);

incorruptibility;

eternal life;

will;

intellect;

52 *prior* acquaintance;

androgynous father.

BJn 4:26 +

52:22, 53:17
55:7, 58:23
60:1, 60:21
61:18, 62:16
65:5, BJn 7:9 +
BJn 5:20
BJn 5:26
BJn 7:6
BJn 6:34
BJn 5:10

The mother

2   *(11)*   The second power or octet:

> *the mother*;
>
> the [masculine] female virgin, the *Barbēlō*;
>
> ⟨Epititiōkh[. . .]ai⟩;
>
> ⟨Memeneaimen[. . .]⟩;[a]
>
> [. . .]kaba;
>
> Adōne;
>
> [. . .], who presides over the heaven [. . .];
>
> [. . .]akrōbōriaōr[. . .], the inexplicable and *ineffable* power, who [. . .].

BJn 4:36

11   *(17)*   Having *emanated,* she (the mother) *self-radiated,* and took delight *in* the parent of the living silence.[b]

The son

15   *(21)*   And *the third* power or octet, which constitutes the son of silence together with silence (?)[c] and acquaintance with *the*

19   (43 *1*)   *father* and excellence of [the] mother: •from his bosom *emanated* seven powers of the great[d] light, [which are] seven vowels;[e]

22   *(3)*   the Word (or verbal expression) derives from them, [and is]   51:22 + their fulfillment.

24   *(4)*   They amount to three powers or three octets, which the parent *emitted* from its bosom in silence [and] in its *forethought.*

Completion of the Doksomedōn realm

3   *(7)* **53**   In that *very same place,* the place where Doksomedōn *the*   50:29 + eternal realm of the aeons was shown forth *along with the thrones* (?) *that are within it and the powers* [that] *surround* them *and glory and incorruption,* [the] *parent of* the great *light*

12   *(15)*   [. . .][a] *forth in silence* [. . . •the great] Doksomedōn *realm,* in

15   *(15)*   which the [thrice]-male (?) child *reposes.* •*And within it was*   55:11 +

17   *(19)*   *established the throne of* its glory; •and upon it on the *tablet* [. . .], its *obscure*[b] name [was inscribed] . . . *the Word* (or   51:22 + *verbal expression*) . . . the parent . . . *light of* the entirety . . .

23   *(22)*   silence,[c] •which emanated *in silence,* which *reposes in silence,*

---

52 a. The words in angle brackets are supplied from MS NHC III; they are erroneously omitted in NHC IV.

   b. MS NHC III instead has "silent silence."

   c. "silence": probably an error of copying; MS NHC III instead has "glory," which may be the original reading of the text. "Glory" and "acquaintance" are closely associated in RAd.

   d. "great": gnostic jargon used in this text to indicate membership in the incorruptible realm.

   e. Or "seven voices."

53 a. Possibly "[came]."

   b. Or "ineffable."

   c. The grammatical connection of the last five phrases is unknown, owing to the imperfection of the manuscripts.

26 (24) *whose name* is in an *invisible symbol* [. . .] [an] ineffable *mystery* emanated:[d]

3 (44 3) **54**   I I I I I I I I I I I I I I I I I I I I I I
ĒĒĒĒĒĒĒĒĒĒĒĒĒĒĒĒĒĒĒĒĒĒ
OOOOOOOOOOOOOOOOOOOOOO
UUUUUUUUUUUUUUUUUUUUUU
EEEEEEEEEEEEEEEEEEEEEE
AAAAAAAAAAAAAAAAAAAAAA
ŌŌŌŌŌŌŌŌŌŌŌŌŌŌŌŌŌŌŌŌŌŌ

13 (9) And so *the three* powers lifted up praise unto

15 (10)   the great, *invisible, uninvoked, unnameable,* the *virgin* spirit of the [parent]; *and*

19 (12)   the *masculine*[a] female virgin, [the Barbēlō].

Appearance of Iōēl, the anointed (Christ), another being, and Ēsēphēkh

20 (13) The latter[b] (the Barbēlō) made a request for [. . .] *a power.*

21 (14) And a *living silence* [of] *silence*[c] *was shown forth* in power,   55:15
[. . .] are glories (?) and *incorruptibilities,* the eternity [. . .]   Zs 56:13

1 (17) the aeons, **55** •which presides [over the] *myriad* mysteries, the thrice-*male* beings, the thrice-male peoples, the male races, the [glories of . . .], the glories of the great [anointed (Christ), and

7 (19) the] male peoples. •The *races*[a] filled the great *eternal realm* Doksomedōn with *powers* [of] *the* Word (or verbal expression)   50:29
of the luminous [fullness].   51:22 +

11 (22) Next the *thrice-male* child, [the] great *anointed (Christ),*[b]   51:22, 53:12
whom *the* [great] invisible *spirit* anointed and whose power [is   BJn 6:23 +

15 (25) named] Ainon, •[lifted] up praise unto *the great invisible spirit* [and the] *masculine female virgin Iōēl the silence of silent*

19 (28) silence,[c] •*the greatness* that [. . .] obscure [. . . ineffable] [. . .] unreplying [and] inexplicable, the first to [appear], and unpro-

3 (-) claimable [. . .] wonderful [. . .] ineffable [. . .] **56** •which possesses all the greatnesses, the (?) greatness of the silence of

6 (-) silence, in that [place], •the thrice-[male] child lifted up praise and made a request for [a power] from the [great invisible virgin] spirit.

11 (-) Next from [that] place was shown forth [. . .] which [. . .]

---

d. What follows is a copy of the "obscure (or ineffable) name" written "on the *tablet*" attached to the throne of "the [thrice]-male (?) child." The seven Greek vowels are arranged, in descending order, to spell "Iēou—Epsilon—Alpha—Omega" and each vowel is copied twenty-two times, the number of letters in the Hebrew alphabet. "Iēou" may be a variant of Ieou, the name of the true god according to certain gnostics (cf. the *Book of Jeu,* edited by C. Schmidt and V. MacDermott; Nag Hammadi Studies, vol. 13; Leiden: E. J. Brill, 1978). It may ultimately derive from Iaō, a conjuring name of Yahweh commonly used in Jewish-Greek magical spells. "Epsilon" (the letter E) also represents "five" in Greek, and may refer to the quintet structure of the parent's forethought, or Barbēlō, in classic gnosticism (cf. BJn 6:2f). "Alpha—Omega" (the first and last letters of the Greek alphabet) is a traditional acclamation (cf. Rv 1:8: " 'I am the Alpha and the Omega,' says the lord god"). The "tablet" thus contains a pseudo-Semitic representation in Greek of the ineffable name of god.

54 a. According to BJn 5:6f, the Barbēlō is "the mother-father . . . the thrice-male . . . the thrice-androgynous name."
   b. "The latter": MS NHC III instead has "they."
   c. "*silence* [of] *silence*": the "masculine female virgin Iōēl." Cf. 55:15f.

55 a. Or "peoples."
   b. "anointed" and "Christ" are the same word in Greek.
   c. Or possibly "the silence (which is an offspring) of silent silence."

which beholds [glories . . . treasures] in [. . . invisible] mysteries
[. . .] of silence [. . . the] masculine [female] virgin [. . .].

20   (–)   Next was [shown forth the child of the] child Ēsēphēkh.ᵃ   59:24, 62:1
23   (–)   And [thus] it was completed: 65:19
III 55:22
24   (–)   the [father];   IV 73:17
Zs 13:7+
[the] mother;
the son;
25   (–)   the five seals;   58:6, 59:27
25   (–)   the invincible power, which is the great [anointed   66:25, 74:13
(Christ)] of all the incorruptibilities.   78:3
BJn 31:22+

2   (–) [. . .] **57** holy [. . .] the end [. . .] and [. . .] are powers, [glories],
13   (–) and incorruptibilities [. . .] emanated [. . .] •it lifted [up praise]
unto
14   (–)   the hidden, obscure [. . . , the] concealed (aeon)ᵃ [. . .]
in [. . .] the aeons [. . .] throne(s) [. . .] and [. . .]
25   (–)   each [. . .] •countless myriads of [. . .] surrounded
them, [glories] and incorruptibilities [. . .] and [. . .];
3   (–)   **58** the father;
the mother;
the son;
5   (–)   all [the fullness] of which I have already [spoken];
6   (–)   [the] five seals [. . .] of [. . .].   56:25+

8   (–) They [. . .] presiding over [. . .] •and the aeons [. . .] •and the
14   (–)
21   (–) eternal aeons [in very] truth.

Emanation of another being

23   (–)   Next [. . .]ᵃ [emanated] in [silence] together with [living]
silence [of] the spirit [and] the parent's Word (or verbal   51:22+
27   (–) expression) and light. •[It] had [. . .] the [five] seals, which the   56:25+
2   (–) [parent emitted] from its bosom; **59** •it had passed through all
4   (–) the aeons of which I have already spoken; •and it had established
glorious thrones [and] countless [myriads] of angels [that]
7   (–) surrounded [them]—•[powers and incorruptible] glories, [sing-
ing] and glorifying, all praising [. . .] with [one voice] in a form
with a never silent cry, [. . . unto]:
13   (–)   the father;
the [mother];
[the] son, [. . .];
14   (–)   [all the] fullnesses [of which I have already] spoken;
i.e.
16   (–)   [the great] anointed (Christ), which came from
[silence], [which] is the [incorruptible] child
Telmaēl-Telmakhaēl-[Ēli-Ēli]-Makhar-Makhar-
[Seth], [the] power [that] is in very truth living;
22   (–)   [the] masculine [female virgin] that is with [it], Iouēl;
24   (–)   Ēsēphēkh, holder [of the glory] and [child] of the
child;
26   (–)   [the crown of] that being's glory;

56. a. Known elsewhere also as Ēphēsēkh.   **58** a. Only part of this word is preserved in
Cf. Zs 13:7f.   the one surviving MS of the present passage;
the original text might have been either "[an
57 a. "[the] concealed (aeon)": according   emanation]" or "[forethought]."
to Zs, the highest of the three aeons that
constitute the Barbēlō aeon.

27   (–)   [. . .] the five [seals: the] fullness [of which I have   56:25 +
                 already spoken].

1   (–) **60**   The great living self-originate [Word (or verbal expression)],   51:22 +
4   (–) [the] truly [divine], the unengendered nature, •whose name I   IrG 1.29.2
                                                                         EpG 26.10.4
7   (–) shall utter by saying [. . .]aia[. . .]thaōthōsth.[. .],ª •which is
         [the] offspring of the [great] anointed (Christ),ᵇ i.e. the offspring
9   (–) [of] ineffable silence, having [emanated] from there, •having
         come forth from the great [invisible] and incorruptible [spirit
13   (–) as] the [offspring] of silenceᶜ together with [silence], •revealed
         [. . .] treasure [. . .] its glory [. . .] appeared in the visible [. . .].
19   (–) And it [established] the four [aeons]. •By means of the Word   51:22 +
21   (–) (or verbal expression) it established [them]. ·
22   (–)   It (the Word) lifted up [praise] unto the great invisible virgin
24   (–) spirit, •[the silence (?)] of the [parent], in silence [of the] living
27   (–) silence of [silence], •[where] the human being reposes, [. . .]
         by means of [. . .].

Emanation of the Moirothea and production of Adamas

30 (49 *1*)   Thence there next emanated the *great cloud* of light, a living
               power, the mother of the holy *incorruptible* beings of the great   FTh 38:14 +
5   (5) powers, *the Moirothea.*ª **61** •And she engendered *that being*   Zs 6:21 +
                                                                            3Tb 119:11 +
        whose name I shall utter by saying,   v.5
                                                                            BJn 8:28 +

6   (6)   [Thou art unique!]
            Thou art unique!
            Thou art unique!
8   (7)   *Ea, Ea, Ea!*ᵇ

8   (8)   Inasmuch as *the latter—Adamas—*is *light* that has radiated
11 (9) [. . .], this being [is] the eye of the [light]. •Indeed, [this is] the   FTh 38:5 +
        first *human being,* because of *whom* [are] all things, *unto whom*
14 (13) *are* all things, and *without whom is nothing:* • the inaccessible
        *parent*ᶜ *beyond thought,* who *has become immanent* and has
        emanated down from above for the obliteration *of the* lack.   71:1,
                                                                       BJn 14:8

Fusion of the self-originate Word with Adamas

18 (16)   Next, the *great divine* self-originate *Word* (or *verbal expres-*   51:22 +
        sion) and *Adamas* the incorruptible human being *became* by
22 (21) fusion *a human rational faculty.* •And *human beings* came into
        existence because of a *rational faculty.*
23 (22)   *This* (*fusion*) *lifted* up praise *unto*

24 (23)   *the great invisible, incomprehensible,* virgin *spirit;*
26 (25)   *the masculine female* virgin, [the Barbēlō];
28 (26)   *the thrice-male child;*
29 (50 *1*)   *the masculine female virgin Iouēl;*
1   (2)   **62** [the] child Ēsēphēkh, holder *of the* glory and
                     child of the *child;*

---

60 a. An esoteric word, not Greek. The MS
is imperfect here.
  b. The divine Logos (Word) is not identical with the preexistent Christ but rather
its offspring.
  c. Cf. note 55c.

61 a. Moirothea: a Greek neologism, pos-

sibly meaning "divine part."
  b. Or possibly "[Thou art unique!] Thou
art unique! Thou art unique! O five, O one!
O five, O one! O five, O one!" (i.e. "O five
in one"). The letters *E* and *A* represent
"five" and "one" in Greek.
  c. *"parent,"* i.e. father of the great Seth.

3	(3)	the crown of that being's glory;	
4	(4)	the great aeons of Doksomedōn;	50:29 +
5	(5)	*the* thrones that are within them;	
5	(6)	*the powers that* surround them—*glories and incorruptibilities* and *the whole fullness* of which I have already *spoken*;	
9	(10)	*the* ethereal[a] *god-receiving* realm, where *holy* people *of the* light *receive image*—people of the light of the parent *of silence* and the [silent] living wellspring;	FTh 45:23 + BJn 4:21 +
14	(15)	i.e. *the* parent and *all* the fullness of *these beings,* as I have *just said.*	

Adamas's request for four aeons

16	(17)	*The* great divine *self-originate* Word (or verbal expression), in the company of Adamas *the incorruptible* human being, *lifted*	51:22 +
19	(21)	up *praise* •and *made a request for* power and *eternal strength* and [incorruptibility] (*to be given*) *unto the* self-originate in the	
24	(24)	form of a *full complement* of four *aeons*; •so that by their agency *might* appear the *glory and power* of the[b] [. . .] parent *unto the* holy *people* of the *great light* that was to *descend unto* the *gloomy* world.	RAd 64:6 +

Production of the great Seth

30	(51 5)	[Next] *Adamas* the [great (?)] incorruptible *human being* made a request for a child (to be produced) for it from out of	BJn 9:11 +
1	(7)	*itself*—**63** •*that* for its part, it (the child) might become parent	
4	(9)	*of the* immovable and *incorruptible* race;[a] •that, for the sake of	
6	(12)	this race, *silence and speech* might be shown forth; •and that, at its instigation, the realm that is *dead* might *arise* and dissolve.	

Production of four luminaries

8	(14)	*And so* the great [. . .] power *of the* great light emanated	
11	(16)	*from above.* •*The effulgence* engendered four *luminaries*:	BJn 7:30 +

Harmozēl;
Oroiaēl;
Daueithe;
Ēlēlēth;

14	(20)	together with •the *great incorruptible* Seth the son *of Adamas* [the great] incorruptible human being.	
17	(22)	And so was completed *the* full septet[b]—*which* resides in a [mystery] of *hidden* mysteries, and which was glorified [. . .]	
22	(52 2)	and •became a *group of eleven* octets, thus [being completed by (?)] four octets.	

Production of the luminaries' consorts

24	(3)	*And* the parent *consented, and* the *full complement of the*	
27	(6)	luminaries *joined in* the consent. •*Consorts* were shown forth	

---

62 a. Lit. "airy."
   b. MS NHC III next has "invisible"; the original reading of the text is uncertain.

63 a. The "child" is the great Seth, and "*the* immovable . . . race" is the seed of the great Seth.
   b. I.e. a septet of octets.

to bring about the completion of the octet *of the* divine self-originate:

2	(8)	**64** *loveliness,* for the first luminary *Harmozēl*;
3	(10)	perception, for the *second* luminary Oroiaēl;
5	(11)	*intelligence,* for the third luminary Daueithe;
6	(13)	*prudence,*[a] *for* [the] fourth luminary *Ēlēlēth.*

| 8 | (14) | This is the *first octet* of the *divine self-originate.* |

Production of the luminaries' attendants

10	(16)	And *the parent* consented, and all the full complement *of the*	
13	(19)	luminaries joined in the *consent.* •And attendants *emanated*:	76:15 FTh 48:26
14	(20)	first, great Gamaliēl, [belonging to] *the great* luminary *Harmozēl*;	RAd 75:21 Zs 46:31
17	(22)	great Gabriēl, [belonging to] the second *great luminary Oroiaēl*;	Zs 58:20
19	(24)	great Samblō, *belonging to the* third *great luminary* Daueithe;	
20	(26)	*great* Abrasaks, belonging to [the] fourth [great] luminary Ēlēlēth.	

Production of consorts for the luminaries' attendants

23	(53 1)	And consorts *emanated* by the *parent's consent* to them:
26	(4)	*memory,* for the first, *great Gamaliēl*;
27	(5)	love, *for the second,* great Gabriēl;
28	(7)	*peace, for the third,* great *Samblō;*
1	(8)	**65** eternal life, for the fourth, great Abrasaks.

2	(10)	And thus the five *octets* became complete, a sum total of forty: the inexplicable [power].	
5	(12)	*Next* the great *self-originate* Word (or verbal expression) and all the full complement *of the four* luminaries *lifted up* praise unto:	51:22+
9	(16)	the *great invisible, uninvoked, unnameable virgin spirit*;	
12	(18)	the masculine *female virgin*;[a]	
13	(19)	the great aeons of *Doksomedōn*;	50:29+
14	(20)	the thrones that are *in* them;	
15	(21)	the powers that *surround* them[b]—glories and *powers and* authorities;	
17	(23)	the thrice-*male child*;	
18	(24)	the masculine *female virgin* Iouēl;	
19	(25)	Ēsēphēkh, *holder* of the glory;[c]	
20	(54 2)	*the crown of* that being's glory;	
21	(3)	all *the fullness* and *all* the glories within the inaccessible fullnesses and *the* unnameable *aeons*;	

---

64 a. "*intelligence . . . prudence,*" MS NHC III: NHC IV here has "acquaintance . . . teaching," alternate Coptic translations of the corresponding Greek words (*synesis . . . phronēsis*).

65 a. The Barbēlō.
  b. The MS here erroneously inserts "and."
  c. MS NHC III next has "and [child] of the child."

25 (6) *so that* they [for their part] invoked *the parent*[d]—•*namely the*
26 (7)
        . . .*-th*[e]—and the *incorruptible* [immovable] race of the parent;
28 (8) [and] called [this race] *the* seed of the great *Seth.*

Enthronement of the four luminaries in the four eternal realms

30 (13) *Next* the fullness began to move, *and* disturbance seized the
2   (13) *incorruptibles.* **66** •*And then* the thrice-male *child* emanated
        down from above unto *the unengendered* and self-originate
        beings,[a] and unto those *engendered in* the (realm of) generation.
6   (18) *That* great being who belongs to *all* the greatnesses *of* the great
        anointed (Christ) emanated, and established thrones of glory[b]
10 (23) *in the four* eternal realms (aeons). •And countless *myriad powers*
13 (55 1) *surrounded* them—*glories* and incorruptibilities. •*And in this*
        way it emanated.
14 (2)   And *the* incorruptible spiritual *congregation*[c] *developed into*
        full strength within the four luminaries of the *great, living,* self-
        originate [Word (or verbal expression)], *the god* of truth,   51:22+
19 (6)   *praising* [and] singing, all glorifying *with one voice* in *unanimous*
        form with a never silent cry *unto:*

22 (9)   *the father;*
             the mother;
             the son;
23 (10)   their *fullness, of which I have* [already] spoken
             [. . .];
25 (11)   *the five seals* that preside [over] *the myriads;*   56:25+
27 (12)   the beings that *rule over the aeons;*
28 (13)   the *governors that convey* glory, having [been]
             ordered *to appear*[d] unto the worthy.

1   (16) **67** *Amen!*

II. HISTORY OF THE SEED OF THE GREAT SETH

Production of the seed of Seth

2   (16) Next the great Seth, son *of Adamas the* incorruptible human
        being *lifted* up *praise* unto:

4   (19)   the *great,* invisible, uninvoked, unnameable, *virgin*
             spirit;
7   (21)   the masculine *female* [virgin];[a]
8   (–)   the thrice-male [child];
9   (21)   [the] masculine [female] virgin *Iouēl;*[b]
–   (55 22)   **III 55** (22)*Ēsēphēkh,*[a] *holder of the glory;*

---

d. Or "father."
e. ". . .-th": an ordinal number. The original reading of the text is uncertain here. MS
NHC III has "seventy-fourth," which the
ancient copyist has struck out, adding "fourth"
above the canceled word; NHC IV is imperfect here.

66 a. "self-originate beings": according to
Zs, the lowest of the three aeons that constitute the Barbēlō aeon is "the self-originate
(aeon)," and it consists of self-originates.
   b. MS NHC III next has "countless myriads."

c. The same word also means "church."
d. Or "*to make revelations.*"

67 a. The Barbēlō.
   b. "Iouēl": i.e. Iōēl.

III 55 a. The following passage, "Ēsēphēkh
. . . great Seth" (67:9–70:31 = NHC III
55:22–59:10), has been almost entirely destroyed in MS NHC IV, and so is translated
from the parallel text in NHC III, taking
account of the usual style of NHC IV whenever possible.

	(23)	*(23)the crown of that being's glory, the child of the child;*[b]	
–	(56 *1*)	**III 56** *(1)the great Doksomedōn aeons;*	50:29+
–	(2)	*(2)the fullness of which I have already spoken.*	
–	(3)	*(3)And he (Seth) made a request for his seed.*	BJn 9:14+
–	(4)	*(4)Thence there next emanated Plēsithea[a] the great power of the great light, mother of the angels, mother of the luminaries,*	
–	(8)	*mother of glories, (8)the female virgin that has four breasts,*	
–	(9)	*(9)bearing fruit as a wellspring out of Gomorrah and out of Sodom—namely, the fruit of the spring Gomorrah that is within*	
26	(12)	*her.* **IV 67** •*She emanated through the agency of[a] the great Seth.*	
27	(13)	*Next the great Seth rejoiced at the grace that had been*	
31	(17)	*bestowed upon him by the incorruptible child.* •*He took his*	
2	(19)	*seed from the female virgin that has four breasts* **68** •*and established it along with her (?)[a] within the four aeons, in the third great luminary Daueithe.*	

Appearance of material wisdom

5	(22)	*After five thousand years, the great luminary Ēlēlēth said,*	
7 9	(24) (26)	*"Let something rule over chaos and Hades."* •*And a cloud*	
–	(57 2)	*[. . .] "material wisdom" (Sophia) appeared.* **III 57** *(2)[. . .] gazed upon the [. . .], with her face resembling [. . .] in her manner [. . .] blood.*	BJn 8:19+

Emanation of Sakla, Nebrouēl, and Sakla's angels

–	(5)	*(5)And [the great] angel Gamaliēl spoke [to (?) great Gabriēl], the attendant belonging to [the great luminary] Oroiaēl, [saying,*	BJn 9:25+ Zs 9:2?
–	(9)	*(9)"Let an] angel emanate [to rule] over chaos [and Hades]."*	
–	(11)	*(11)Next the cloud [. . .] from the two units[a] [. . .] light [. . .]*	
31	(16)	*she established [. . .] within the cloud [. . .]* **IV 68** •*Sakla[a] the great [angel] beheld* Nebrouēl *the great demon that was with*	
3	(18)	*him,* **69** •*and they [. . .] became an earthborn spirit [. . .]*	
–	(21)	*helping angels.* **III 57** *(21)Sakla [said] to Nebrouēl the great [demon], "Let the twelve aeons exist within [. . .] aeon(s) . . .*	BJn 10:27
–	(25)	*worlds [. . .]." (25)Through the will of the self-originate, the*	
–	(58 *1*)	*great angel [Sakla] said,* **III 58** *(1)"The [. . .] shall [. . .] the*	
–	(3)	*quantity of seven [. . .]." (3)And it said to the [. . . angels], "Go! Let [each] of you rule over its own [. . .];" and each [of them] went.*	
–	(6)	*(6)[These are the] twelve [angels]:[a]*	
–	(7)	*(7)[the first] angel, [Athōth . . .], who is called "[. . .]" by the] races of humankind;*	BJn 10:28+

b. "the child of the child": probably this phrase has been copied in the wrong place and belongs after "Ēsēphēkh, holder of the glory."

III 56 a. Plēsithea: perhaps "nearby goddess."

IV 67 a. Or "out of."

68 a. "along with her (?)": the MS here erroneously has "along with him(self)."

III 57 a. Or "two monads."

IV 68 a. "Sakla" (Aramaic "fool"): a conventional name of Satan in Judaism.

III 58 a. The destroyed words in the passage have been restored by comparison with a similar list in BJn 10:28f.

–	(10)	*(10)second, Harmas, [the eye of fire];*
–	(12)	*(12)third, [Kalila];*
–	(12)	*(12)fourth, Iōbēl;*
–	(13)	*(13)[fifth], Adōnaios, who is called "Sabaōth";*
1	(15)	**IV 70** sixth, [Cain, whom all (?) the races of] humankind call "the sun";
3	(17)	*[seventh, Abel];*
4	(18)	*eighth, Akiressina;*[a]
4	(18)	ninth, Ioubēl;
5	(19)	*tenth, [Harmoupiaēl];*
5	(19)	*eleventh, Arkheir-[Adōnein];*[b]
–	(21)	**III 58** *(21)twelfth, [Belias].*
–	(21)	*(21)These preside over Hades [and chaos].*

Reproof of Sakla's arrogance

– (23)   *(23)And after the preparation [of the . . .],*[a] *Sakla said to its*   BJn 13:5+
– (24) *[angels (?)],* *(24)"For my part, I am a [jealous] god; and none has [come to exist] apart from me:" [for it was]*[b] *confident of its origin.*   Ex 20:5 / Dt 49:9 / Is 46:9

– (59 1)   **III 59**   *(1)Next a voice came from on high, saying, "The*   RR 94:23+
– (4) *human being*[a] *and the child of the human being*[b] *exist"—(4)with reference to the descent of the higher image resembling its voice on high, which belonged to the image.*   BJn 14:18

Projection of an image. Creation of Adam.

– (6)(6)   *(6)It (the image) gazed out. (6)By the gaze of the image was modeled the first modeled form,*[c] *because of whom repentance came into existence.*   RR 87:11 / BJn 13:32+

– (10)   *(10)It (the image) received its realization and its power through the will of the parent and the delight that the parent took in the great incorruptible, immovable race of the great mighty*   74:13 / RR 87:22+
1 (16) *people of the great Seth,*[d] **IV 71**   •who sowed it (the image) in the earthborn aeons, so that because of it the lacks might be   61:14+
3 (18) completed. •*For* that (image) which descended from on high into the gloomy world [. . .] came *to issue exhortation.*[a]

Cain, Abel, and Seth

6 (21)   And after the sowing by *the* ruler of this realm and those [that derive from] that ruler—a defiled and corrupt sowing of   BJn 24:8+ / IrS 1.24.2
10 (25) the *demon-begetting* god[b]—•[and] *after* the sowing by *Adam,*   BJn 24:34
11 (60 2) *a sowing that resembles the sun and the great Seth,*[c] •next *the great* angel Hormos[d] *emanated* in order to prepare for *the* great Seth's sowing[e] through the *holy* spirit *in a holy,* reason-born   Zs 47:9 / 75:15

IV 70 a. Probably an error for "Abiressina." Cf. BJn.
    b. Melkheir-Adōnein in BJn.

III 58 a. Possibly "[of the world]."
    b. Or possibly "[for it was not]."

III 59 a. Adamas.
    b. Or "son of man"; i.e. the great Seth.
    c. "first modeled form": i.e. Adam; Jewish and Christian jargon, based on the fact

that the creator modeled Adam out of earth.
    d. The following passage (to IV 78:18f) survives in MS NHC IV, and the translation is based on that MS.

IV 71 a. Or "*to summon.*"
    b. The begetting of Cain (and perhaps Abel) by Sakla and Sakla's offspring.
    c. The begetting of Seth son of Adam.
    d. Lit. "refuge."
    e. Or "seed."

vessel,[f] *by the means of* the virgins *of the* defiled *sowing* of this realm.

Incarnation of the seed of Seth

18   (9)   *Next* the great Seth came, *bringing his* seed, *and he sowed it in the* earth-*born* aeons, *whose number is* the infinite number *of* Sodom.

22   (12)   [And they (the aeons)] were *called a pasture*[g] *of the great*

25   (15)   Seth, *i.e.* Gomorrah. •The *great Seth took the plant from* [the]

27   (16)   spring of *Gomorrah* •and *planted it in the second location, which* also was *called Sodom.*

30   (19)   This *is the race*[h] *that* appeared through the agency of Edōkla.

2   (20)   **72**   For by means of reason, it (Edōkla) engendered truth and right (?),[a] i.e. the source of the seed of eternal life and of all those who are going to endure because of acquaintance with

7   (25)   their emanation. •This is the great incorruptible *race that appeared* from out of three (previous) *worlds.*[b]   74:17 +

The flood and other catastrophes

10   (61 *1*)   And *the* flood will *come* as a *prototype for the* end of the age   BJn 28:32 +

13   (4)   [and descend] against the world. •*On account of this* race   RAd 75:9

16   (6)   conflagrations will come upon the earth [. . .] •grace *will come through the agency* of *the* prophets and *the watchmen* of *the*

19   (10)   *living* race. •*On account of this race* plagues and famines will

22   (12)   *occur.* •*All* these things will come to pass *on account of* this

24   (13)   *great, incorruptible* race. •On account of this *race, temptations* [and] *deceptions of false* prophets *will* occur.

Prediction of Sakla's downfall

27   (16)   *Next the* great Seth *saw* that in *the devil's*[c] activity, in its crookedness, in its scheme that it was going to bring down upon the immovable race, in the persecution *waged by its*

6   (22)   powers and its angels, *and* in *its* deception, **73**   •it was going to act recklessly *against its own self.*

7   (23)   Next the great Seth lifted *up* praise unto:

8   (24)   the great, *uninvoked,* invisible, *unnameable,* virgin
                        spirit [of the father];

11   (25)   the masculine female virgin, *the* Barbēlō;

12   (62 2)   the male child[a] Telmaēl-Telmakhaēl-Ēli-Ēli-Makhar-
                        Makhar-Seth, *the* power that is in very truth
                        living;

16   (5)   the masculine female virgin Iouēl;

17   (6)   Ēsēphēkh, holder of *the glory;*

18   (7)   the crown of that being's glory;

19   (8)   the great glorifying aeon:[b]

---

f. The "reason-born vessel" is Jesus, cf. 74:25f and 75:15f. The begetting of Seth the son of Adam establishes a line of descent "by means of the virgins . . . of this realm" leading ultimately to Jesus and his adoption by the great Seth.

g. Or "distribution."

h. I.e. the race of Seth on earth.

72 a. Gk. *themissa,* perhaps a proper name coined by the author. In Greek *themis* means

"established custom, right."

b. Corresponding to the "three advents" of 74:17. MS NHC III next has "into the (present) world."

c. "*the devil*": Sakla.

73 a. MS NHC III instead has "the thrice-male child."

b. MS NHC III, "the great Doxomedōn aeon."

20   (9)   the thrones that are within it;
21   (9)   the great beings that surround them, and glories and
                 incorruptibilities and *the* whole fullness of which I
                 have already spoken.

Emanation of guardian angels

25   (12)   *And* he first made a request for guardians of his seed. •Next
27   (13) four hundred *ethereal angels* emanated from the great aeons;
29   (15) with *them* were Aerosiēl and the great Selmelkhel, the guardians
           of the great incorruptible race, its fruit, and the mighty people
4   (19) of the great Seth **74** •*from the* time and age of *truth* and right
           (?)[a] down to the *end of* these aeons[b] and their rulers, •*whom*   RR 97:10+
8   (22) the great *judges* have condemned to death.   Zs 9:6

Seth's incarnations

9   (24)   Next the *great Seth* was sent by *the four* great luminaries—
11   (26) *by* the will of the self-originate *and* all their (the luminaries')
13   (63 1) whole fullness, •*through* the gift and delight *of* the great, invis-   III 59:10
           ible spirit, the five seals, and the whole fullness   56:25+

17   (4)   to live through the three advents of which I have already   72:7
19   (6)   spoken, •*the* flood, the conflagration, and the judgment of RR 96:28+
                     the rulers, authorities, and powers;   **v.19**
                                                                                   IrSat 1.24.2
22   (8)   to save that (race) which went astray, •by [destruction] of
23   (9)   the world and *baptism* of the body, •and by [that]
25   (10)   reason-born being[c] which the great Seth prepared   75:15+
                     mystically through the female virgin;[d]
29   (13)   to make the *holy people*[e] be born again[f]   BJn 25:20+

30   (14)   by *the* holy *spirit* and invisible, hidden symbols;
2   (16)   **75**   by destruction of world against world;
4   (17)   by renunciation of the world and the god of the
                     thirteen aeons;[a]   RAd 77:27+
7   (19)   by invitation from the holy, ineffable, and
9   (20)   incorruptible beings •(in)[b] the bosom *of* the mighty
                     light that *preexists* in forethought.

His establishment of baptism

11   (22)   And by forethought he established the holy and the baptism
14   (25) that is higher than the heavens: •(he did this) by the holy, by
15   (64 1) the incorruptible, •and by the living reason-born Jesus, whom   71:11, 74:25
17   (3)   the great Seth put on (like a garment).[c] •And he nailed down   77:12, 79:26
20   (5)   the powers of the thirteen aeons and made them inactive; •at   IrUnid 1.30.12
           his instigation they are fetched and they are removed.   EpS 39.3.5
                                                                                   EpG 26.10.4
21   (6)   And they[d] are armed in invincible, incorruptible power with
           an armor consisting of acquaintance with the truth.

---

74 a. Greek *themissa* (cf. note 72a).
  b. Or "ages."
  c. Jesus (cf. 75:15f).
  d. The virgin Mary.
  e. The race of Seth on earth.
  f. In incorruptible baptism (cf. 77:18f).

75 a. Perhaps corresponding to the thirteen
kingdoms of RAd.

  b. Through an inadvertence the MS here
omits "in."
  c. The body or person of Jesus is here
likened to the garment in which the great
Seth is clothed, or which he adopts, at his
final incarnation; a Platonist cliché for the
relation of body to soul.
  d. The holy people? Cf. 74:29f.

III. BAPTISMAL SERVICE

Incorruptible beings that preside over baptism

24   (9)   And the following have been revealed as great beings that   Zs 47:12
stand at rest:

25	(10)	Iesseus-Mazareus-Iessedekeus, the living water;	RAd 85:30
27	(12)	the great *governors,* the great Jacob, and	Zs 47:5
		Theopemptos, and Isauël;	v.27 Zs 47:15 Zs 47:12
1	(–)	**76** the being that presides over grace, Mēp[. .]- ēl (?);	
2	(14)	those that preside over the springs of truth, Mikheus, Mikhar, and Mnēsinous;	76:7?
5	(16)	the one that presides over the baptism of the living, the purifier Seseggen-Barpharaggēs;	FTh 48:18 + Zs 6:11
7	(19)	those that preside over the gates *of the* waters of life, Miseus[a] *and* Mikhar;	76:2?
10	(20)	those that preside over ascent, Seldaō and Elainos;	Zs 6:13 +
12	(22)	the receivers of the holy race and incorruptible, mighty people of the great Seth;	
15	(24)	the attendants *of* the four luminaries—great Gamaliēl, great Gabriēl, great Samblō, and great Abrasaks;	64:14 +
19	(65 *1*)	those beings that preside over the sun's path of coming out, Olsēs, Hymneus, and Heurymaious;	Zs 47:15?
22	(3)	those that preside over the (sun's) way of going in unto the repose of eternal life, Phritanis, Mikhsanthēr, and Mikhanōr;	
26	(6)	the *guardians* of chosen[b] souls, Akraman and Strempsoukhos;	Zs 46:31
2	(8)	**77** the great power Telmakhaēl-Telmakhaēl-Ēli-Ēli- Makhar-Makhar-Seth;	
4	(9)	the being that is great, invisible, *virgin,* and unnameable, i.e. in spirit and silence;	
7	(12)	the great luminary Harmozēl, where there is the living, self-originate god in truth, with whom is Adamas the incorruptible human being;	
12	(16)	Oroiaēl, where there is the great Seth and *Jesus* of life, who came and crucified what was subject to the law;	75:15
16	(19)	third, *Daueithe,* where the offspring of the great Seth repose;	
18	(20)	fourth, Ēlēlēth, where *the souls of the offspring repose*; **III 65**	
–	(23)	*(23)fifth, Iōēl, who presides over the name of the being who will be ordained to baptize with the holy, incorruptible baptism that is higher than heaven.*[a] **IV 77**	

Effect of baptism

31   (26)   *But henceforth* **78** •by the agency of the holy and incorrup-
1   (66 *1*) tible Poimaēl, •(acting) for the sake of those worthy of baptisms
3   (2)
6   (4) *of* renunciation and the ineffable seals thereof, •whichever   56:25 +

---

76 a. Or "Mikheus."   **III 65** a. The baptism that is acquaintance.
b. Or "slain."   Cf. RAd 85:22f.

persons have gained acquaintance of *their* receivers, according as they *have been instructed* and have learned, *shall not taste death.*

Baptismal hymn

10	(8)	O Iesseus!	75:25 +
11	(9)	[. .]ōēouōōua!	
11	(9)	In very truth!	
12	(10)	O Iesseus-Mazareus-Iessedekeus!	
13	(11)	O living water!	
14	(11)	O child of the child!	
14	(12)	O name of all glories	
15	(12)	In *very truth!*	
16	(13)	O eternal being!	
17	(13)	IIII ĒĒĒĒ EEEE OOOO YYYY ŌŌŌŌ AAAA![a]	
18	(14)	*In very truth!*	
19	(15)	**III 66** [(15)]*ĒI AAAA ŌŌŌŌ!*[a]	
–	(16)	[(16)]*O being, which beholds the aeons*	
–	(17)	[(17)]*In very truth!*	

[(17)]*A*

E E

Ē Ē Ē

I I I I

Y Y Y Y Y

Ō Ō Ō Ō Ō Ō Ō Ō[b]

–	(19)	[(19)]*O existent for ever and ever*
–	(20)	[(20)]*In very truth!*
31	(20)	**IV 78** *ĬĒA AIŌ* in the heart!
2	(21)	**79** *O existent upsilon forever unto eternity!*
3	(21)	*You are what you are!*
3	(21)	*You are who you are!*
3	(22)	*This great name of yours is upon me,*[a] *o self-originate that lacks nothing* and is free,
8	(25)	O invisible unto all but [me]!
9	(25)	*O invisible unto all!*
11	(26)	For what being can *comprehend*[b] *you by* speech or praise?
12	(27)	*Having myself become acquainted with you,* I have now *mixed with your unchangeableness*;
14	(67 2)	And *I have girded myself* and come to dwell in an armor of loveliness[c] and light, *and I have become luminous.*

---

78 a. Cf. 54:3f.

III **66** a. Or possibly "Thou art Alpha, Alpha, Alpha, Alpha, Omega, Omega, Omega, Omega!" Cf. note 53d.

  b. In the MS this passage is copied as a string of letters rather than a pyramid; the pyramid progresses from Alpha (*A*) to Omega (*Ō*) (cf. note 53d and 78:15). Possibly a line of text ("OOOOO") has been omitted after "IIII" through an inadvertence, and the original reading is as follows:

A

E E

Ē Ē Ē

I I I I

O O O O O

Y Y Y Y Y

Ō Ō Ō Ō Ō Ō Ō Ō

79 a. After baptism.

  b. Or "*contain.*"

  c. Or "grace." The remainder of the text has been almost entirely destroyed in MS NHC IV and so is translated from the parallel text in NHC III, taking account of the usual style of NHC IV whenever possible.

	(4)	**III 67** *(4)For the mother[a] was there, because of the fair beauty of the loveliness.[b]*	
17	(6)	**IV 79** *For this reason I have stretched out my two hands.*	
18	(8)	*I have been formed within the orbit of the riches of the light,*	
21	(9)	*For it (the light) is within my bosom, bestowing form upon the various engendered beings by unreproachable light.*	
24	(12)	*I shall truly declare your praise,*	
25	(13)	*For I have comprehended you:*	
26	(14)	*(It is) yours, O Jesus! Behold, O eternally omega, O eternally epsilon,[a] O Jesus!*	75:15+
27	(14)	*O eternity! Eternity!*	
–	(15)	**III 67** *(15)O god of silence! I beg you utterly!*	
2	(16)	**IV 80** *You are my realm of repose.*	
3	(17)	*O son, Ēs Ēs, the epsilon![a]*	
4	(17)	*O being without form that dwells among those without form,*	
5	(19)	*Raising a human being by whom you will sanctify me into your life according to your ineffaceable name.*	
9	(22)	*For this reason, the fragrance of life is within me:*	
10	(23)	*For it has been mixed with water to serve as a prototype for all the rulers,[b]*	
12	(25)	*So that in your company I might have life in the peace of the saints,*	
13	(26)	*O eternally existent in very truth!*	

IV. CIRCUMSTANCES OF COMPOSITION

15	(68 1)	*This is the book that the great Seth composed •and which*	3Tb 118:10
16	(2)	*he placed in high mountains upon which the sun has never*	RAd 85:9+
19	(5)	*risen—nor can it. •And from the beginning of their days, the*	Fr 68:2
		name has never risen upon the hearts of the prophets, the	
24	(9)	*apostles, or the heralds—nor could it; •and their ears have not*	
26	(10)	*heard it.[c] •The great Seth composed this book in writing in 130*	
2	(12)	*years and **81** •placed it in the mountain called Kharaksiō,*	
–	(14)	**III 68** *(14)so that, by emanating at the end of times and ages*	
		through the will of the self-originate god and all the fullness,	III 59:10+
		because of the gift of the unsearchable, inconceivable, parental,	
–	(20)	*will, (20)he might appear unto this holy, incorruptible race of*	
–	(22)	*the great savior and unto (22)those[a] who sojourn with them in*	
–	(23) (25)	*love—(23)along with the great, invisible, eternal spirit and (25)its*	
–	(26) (69 1)	*only-begotten offspring, and (26)the eternal light and **III 69** (1)its*	
		great incorruptible consort and incorruptible wisdom (Sophia)	
(5)		*and the Barbēlō and utter fullness in eternity. (5)Amen!*	

III **67** a. The Barbēlō.
  b. Or "grace."

IV **79** a. "epsilon," or "five." Cf. note 53d.

80 a. Or "the five." Cf. note 53d.
  b. Here MS NHC IV seems instead to have "For it has been blended with [the] baptismal [waters of all] the rulers."

c. I.e. neither the "prophets" of Israel nor Christian "apostles" and "heralds" have known the truth.
III **68** a. "appear unto this . . . unto those . . .": or "reveal this . . . and those . . ."

Colophon in MS NHC III[a]

(6)   (6)*THE EGYPTIAN GOSPEL*,[b] *a book of divine authorship, holy*
(8) *and secret.* (8)*May loveliness, intelligence, perception, and
prudence*[c] *be with the copyist, the beloved Eugnōstos in the
spirit—in the flesh my name is Gongessos*[d]—*and with my*
(14) *companion luminaries in incorruption.* (14)*O Jesus Christ, O son*
(15) *of God, O savior! O ikhthys!*[e] (15)*Of divine authorship is the*
(18) *Holy Book of the Great Invisible Spirit! Amen!* (18)*THE HOLY
BOOK OF THE GREAT INVISIBLE SPIRIT. Amen!*

III **69** a. At the end of MS NHC III the copyist or a predecessor has added the following note.

b. See note IV 50a.

c. Not only virtues, but also consorts of the four luminaries (cf. 64:2f).

d. Latin *Concessus*.

e. "ikhthys" (Greek "fish"): a traditional early Christian acronym in Greek for "Jesus Christ, son of god, savior" (*Iēsous KHristos THeou Yios Sōtēr*).

ZŌSTRIANOS

(EXCERPTS)
(Zs)

Contents

Zōstrianos describes gnostic baptism of acquaintance as a mystical ascent of the soul toward acquaintance or *gnōsis* with the ineffable first principle. The steps in the ladder of this ascent are the "aeons"—eternal hypostases or abstractions—that according to gnostic myth have emanated from the first principle and populate the spiritual universe. The structure of abstractions follows a threefold division of the Barbēlō as in EgG; although most details are lost owing to the imperfection of the manuscript, the structure is clearly one in which higher levels subsume lower ones in a relationship of whole to parts.

The theory of the soul's progress from higher to higher abstraction toward a mystical leap to *gnōsis* had been laid down by Plato in a much-studied passage of the *Symposium* (210a–212a), and it was a standard element in the teaching of Platonism in the second century A.D. The mystical ascent is not, therefore, the final and decisive ascent of the soul after death, but rather a means of gaining nondiscursive knowledge or *gnōsis* ("acquaintance"). Once it has achieved its goal, the soul must descend back through the same levels it passed before, in reverse order. Zs thus narrates the intellectual voyage of the mystic. In accordance with a convention of apocalyptic literature, the voyager is accompanied by a series of revealing angels who explain the various levels of abstraction and incidentally mention other details of the gnostic myth.

Because baptism was the main metaphor of acquaintance in gnostic Christianity, the voyage is mythologized as a progression of "baptisms" in "waters" that "fill" each abstraction. A precedent had already been set in BJn 4:21f, where the first principle is called a wellspring; RAd 85:22f explicitly equates baptism with *gnōsis* or acquaintance with god. Higher levels of abstraction in Zs are thus mythically quantified as numbers of baptisms, with resultant transformations of the voyaging soul. For further discussion of gnostic baptism, see the "Historical Introduction" to Part One.

Zs is of particular importance in the history of philosophy because Plotinus, the great Neoplatonist philosopher, was acquainted with its contents (cf. Porph 16.3f) and took it into account in his cycle of lectures against the gnostics (*Enneads* 3.8, 5.8, 5.5, and 2.9 [nos. 30–33 chronologically]).

The work concludes with a classic example of gnostic sermon.

The limited scope of Zs does not allow for reference to the history of Israel or the foundation of Christianity, and the pseudepigraphic frame story and its main character imply a setting in pre-Christian Persia. Some scholars therefore consider

Zs to be prime evidence for the existence of a non-Christian variety of the gnostic sect. On the other hand, early Christians as well as non-Christians were fascinated by the idea that ancient religious heroes of the East, including not only Moses but Zoroaster, Hermes Trismegistus, and others, had extraordinary information about divine things. Zs might thus be the work of a Christian author writing in a pseudo-Zoroastrian mode. A third-century observer states explicitly that Zs was used by Christians (Porph 16.1f). The same source refers to a lengthy refutation of Zs written by Amelius, a Neoplatonist disciple of Plotinus; the refutation does not survive.

Literary background

The author and place of composition of Zs are unknown. The date of its composition must be sometime before A.D. 268, because the work was known to Plotinus before he wrote against the gnostics. Zs is attributed to Zōstrianos, allegedly the grandfather or uncle of Zoroaster (founder of the Persian dualist religion that bears his name); it is thus an example of pseudepigraphy. The language of composition was Greek.

Zs has a complex mixture of genres in which various traditional materials are subordinated to others:

I. Autobiography of a seer
  A. Heavenly voyage
    1. Angelic revelations
      a. Uranography, combined with
      b. Mystical ascent

Like Fr, the whole work is presented as the spiritual autobiography of a religious seer. The most important component of his autobiography is the aftermath of an attempt at suicide—a heavenly voyage of his soul, accompanied by revealing angels. Psychic voyage literature of this sort is known from the Old Testament Pseudepigrapha (e.g. *1 Enoch*); it is sometimes called "apocalyptic." Such works do not seem to have ever attained a set generic form. In Zs, the sites of the voyage are revealed by interpreting angels, who partly describe the structure of the metaphysical universe ("*uranography*") and partly mark the steps in the *mystical ascent* and descent of the seer's soul.

Mythic characters

I. The Great Eternals

The GREAT INVISIBLE SPIRIT
The BARBĒLŌ
Constituents of the Barbēlō:
  1. THE CONCEALED AEON. Reality, divinity.
  2. THE FIRST-MANIFEST AEON. Blessedness, acquaintance.
  3. THE SELF-ORIGINATE AEON. Life, vitality.
Subconstituent luminaries within the three constituents:
  1. Concealed aeons—
    (H)ARMĒDŌN
    DIPHANE[S]
    MALSĒDŌN
    [. . .]
  2. First-manifest aeons—
    SOLMIS
    AKREMŌN
    AMBROSIOS
    [. . .]

3. Self-originate aeons; beings with them—
     4th (lst) HARMOZĒL; the GERADAMAS, perfect first human being
     3rd (2nd) ŌROIAĒL; SETH EMMAKHA SETH, his son
     2nd (3rd) DAUEITHE; the IMMOVABLE RACE, children of Seth
     1st (4th) ĒLĒLĒTH; other self-originate aeons
Lower aeons:
     4. The REALLY EXISTENT REPENTANCE
     5. The REALLY EXISTENT SOJOURN (or exile)
Antitypical aeons:
     3-A. The ANTITYPICAL SELF-ORIGINATE AEON
     4-A. The ANTITYPICAL REPENTANCE
     5-A. The ANTITYPICAL SOJOURN (or exile)
The THRICE-MALE CHILD
ĒPHĒSĒKH, the child of the child
Great ANGELS, GLORIES, POWERS, etc., that preside, purify, seal, guard, judge, etc.,
     having various names

II. Ruler Mentioned in the Excerpts

The WORLD RULER (Sakla)

III. Humankind Mentioned in the Excerpts

ZŌSTRIANOS and his ancestors
Holy SEED OF SETH within the material realm

Text

The original Greek apparently does not survive. The text is known only in Coptic translation, attested by a single manuscript from Nag Hammadi, MS NHC VIII (pp. 1–132), which was copied just before A.D. 350 and is now in the Cairo Coptic Museum.

The translation below is based on my own critical edition of the Coptic, which will appear in J. Sieber, ed., *Nag Hammadi Codex VIII* (Nag Hammadi Studies; Leiden: E. J. Brill, forthcoming).

SELECT BIBLIOGRAPHY

Bidez, J., and F. Cumont. *Les Mages hellénisés: Zoroastre, Ostanès et Hystaspe d'après la tradition grecque.* 2 vols. Paris: Les Belles Lettres, 1938. (Pseud-epigraphy under the name of Zoroaster.)

Dodds, E. R. *Pagan and Christian in an Age of Anxiety.* Cambridge, England: Cambridge University Press, 1965. (Especially Chap. 3, "Man and the Divine World," on mystical union with god.)

Isaac, E. "1 (Ethiopic Apocalypse of) Enoch." In *The Old Testament Pseudepigrapha*, edited by J. H. Charlesworth. Vol. 1, *Apocalyptic Literature and Testaments*, 5–89. Garden City, N.Y.: Doubleday & Company, 1983. (A classic example of heavenly voyage literature.)

Plato, "Symposium." In vol. 5 of *Plato with an English Translation*, by W. R. M. Lamb, 74–245. Loeb Classical Library. New York: G. P. Putnam's Sons, 1935.

Puech, H.-Ch. "Appendice" [to his "Plotin et les Gnostiques"]. In his *En Quête de la gnose*. Vol. 1, *La Gnose et le temps et autres essais*, 110–16. [Paris]: Gallimard, 1978.

Rudolph, K. "Der gnostische 'Dialog' als literarisches Genus." In *Probleme der koptischen Literatur*, 85–107. Wissenschaftliche Beiträge der Martin-Luther-Universität Halle-Wittenberg, no. 1 [K2]. Halle: n.p., 1968.

Sieber, J. "The Barbelo Aeon as Sophia in *Zostrianos* and Related Tractates." In *The Rediscovery of Gnosticism: Proceedings of the International Conference on Gnosticism at Yale, New Haven, Connecticut, March 28–31, 1978*, edited by B. Layton. Vol. 2, *Sethian Gnosticism*, 788–95. Studies in the History of Religions, no. 41, vol. 2. Leiden: E. J. Brill, 1981.

──────. "An Introduction to the Tractate Zostrianos from Nag Hammadi." *Novum Testamentum* 15 (1973): 232–40.

──────. *Nag Hammadi Codex VIII*. Nag Hammadi Studies. Leiden: E. J. Brill, forthcoming. (Advance copy supplied by the author.)

ZŌSTRIANOS

ORACLES OF TRUTH OF ZŌSTRIANOS
GOD OF TRUTH
ORACLES OF ZOROASTER[a]

(EXCERPTS)[b]

I. INTRODUCTION

Title and authentication

1 **1** [The . . .] of the [. . .] of the oracles[c] [. . .] living forever, which I   Porph 16.3
Zōstrianos[d] personally [. . .] and Iolaos:[e] I [who] came to dwell in the   4:10
world on behalf of those like me and [those] coming after me, [the]
7 living elect.[f] •As god lives,[g] [I] myself [am telling (?)] the truth in very
truth, [and] acquaintance and eternal light.

II. ZŌSTRIANOS'S SPIRITUAL AUTOBIOGRAPHY AND ASCENT

Zōstrianos's career as a gnostic teacher

10   After I had parted, by means of intellect, from the corporeal darkness
within me[h] together with the animate chaos and desirous femininity
14,15 within that darkness[i]—•for I did not concern myself with it, •and after
16 I had discovered the infinite (aspect) of my material •and had reproved
the dead creation within me [and] the perceptible divine world-ruler,[j]
19 then [I] powerfully proclaimed the entirety[k] unto those who possessed
22 alien parts.[l] •Although I undertook their affairs for a short time, according
as the necessity of (my) birth brought me into public light, I was never
26 at all content. •Rather, I always used to part from them.[m] * * *

Title **1** a. In the manuscript, the title is
after the text (at 132:6f). The words "Oracles
of Truth . . . of Zoroaster" are written in a
Coptic alphabetic cipher and would not have
been intelligible to the unprepared Coptic
reader. "Zoroaster": Zarathustra, founder
of the Persian dualist religion of Zoroastri-
anism. He was the subject of legendary
speculation among the Greeks, and widely
respected as one of the ancient oriental sages.

b. Many parts of the MS have been destroyed, and consequently only some of the
passages are intelligible enough to be translated. Asterisks (* * *) are used where text
has had to be omitted.

c. Or "utterances."

d. Zōstrianos: according to the fourth-
century church father Arnobius, Zoroaster
("the Armenian") was his *nepos* (the Latin
word means either grandson or nephew).

e. Iolaos: Zōstrianos's father, 4:10f.

f. The holy seed of Seth.

g. A traditional oath to guarantee the truth
of one's words. Cf. Jg 8:19, 1 S 14:39, etc.

h. The intellectual abstraction of the true
self from its material context.

i. "corporeal darkness . . . animate chaos
. . . that darkness": the state of body together with soul as its vivifying principle, as
opposed to intellect.

j. The chief ruler, called Sakla or Ialdabaōth in other texts.

k. Was active as a gnostic teacher; "the
entirety": the sum total of spiritual reality
deriving from the Barbēlō aeon.

l. The holy seed of Seth have an "alien
part" or divine spiritual element capable of
salvation.

m. See note 1b.

He ponders spiritual questions[a]

24,25 **2** •"Concerning reality:[b] •How could existents deriving from the aeon[c] (that consists) of derivatives of an invisible spirit,[d] which is an undivided self-originate even while being three unengendered images, have a source superior to reality and exist prior [to] all [these (spiritual beings)[e]],
32 even though being in the [world]?

33   "How could those that are against it and all these (spiritual beings) [. . .] good [. . .]?

3 **3**   "Which place belongs to [it]?

4   "What source does it have?

5   "In what way does its derivative belong to it and all [these] (spiritual beings)?

6   "How could [it become] simple if it displays differences within itself— for it is reality, intelligible form and blessedness, and bestows living power through life?[a]

11   "In what way has reality, which does not exist, been shown forth in power as existing?"

14   Now, I ⟨used to⟩ consider how I might understand these questions,
15 and I used to offer up daily (a sacrifice) to the god of my ancestors,
17 according to the custom of my people. •I would sing the blessing of all
18 these (spiritual beings).[b] •For my forefathers and ancestors who searched
20 found. •And for my part, I did not leave off making requests for a realm of repose worthy of my spirit without my being bound within the perceptible world.[c]

23   And next, because I was very anguished and depressed at the pettiness
25 around me, •I dared to commit a rash act and surrender myself to the wild beasts of the wilderness, unto a horrible destruction.

Revelation of the angel of acquaintance

28   The angel of acquaintance of the eternal [light] stood before me and
31,32 said to me, •"O Zōstrianos, why are you raving in [this] way, •without
8 understanding the great eternals that are above [. . .]?" * * * **4** •"More-
10 over, do [you] suppose that you are the parent of [your people]? •Or that
13 Iolaos is your father? [. . .]" * * * •"Come and pass through [these[a]   1:1
14 (lower realms)]: •and then you will return again to them in order to   v.13
16,17 proclaim a living race,[b] •to save those who are worthy, •and to bestow   Fr 59:9
18 power upon the chosen (plur.). •For, the struggle of [eternity] is great, and the time [in] this place is short."

---

2 a. The exact narrative context is lost. Zōstrianos, despite a successful career in which he "powerfully proclaimed" the gnostic message, becomes driven by metaphysical problems, some of which are listed here.

    b. An aspect of the concealed aeon, the highest of the three constituents of the Barbēlō aeon.

    c. The Barbēlō aeon.

    d. The great invisible spirit.

    e. "all these," namely, spiritual beings: gnostic jargon used in this text, probably identical with "the entirety." Cf. note 1k.

3 a. "reality . . . blessedness . . . life": aspects of the first, second, and third constituents of the Barbēlō aeon, i.e. the concealed aeon, the first-manifest aeon, and the self-originate aeon.

    b. Zōstrianos's activity as a gnostic teacher is compatible with the practice of traditional Persian religion, in the course of which he invokes blessing upon "all these" (cf. note 2e).

    c. Zōstrianos longs for escape from the "petty" influence of the body and finally decides upon a passive kind of physical suicide.

4 a. "these," viz. lower realms: the perceptible world and lower aeons as a structure. The angel invites Zōstrianos on a voyage through the aeons which, incidentally, enables him temporarily to escape from his body.

    b. The immovable race or metaphysical counterpart of the holy seed of Seth, which Zōstrianos will encounter in his voyage; "living": gnostic jargon used in this text to indicate membership in the eternal realm.

Zōstrianos abandons his material body and ascends

20   Now, after it (the angel) said these words [to me], in its company
with eagerness and great gladness I went on board a large luminous
25 cloud, leaving my modeled form[c] on earth guarded by glories. •And [we]
escaped from the whole world and the thirteen realms[d] residing in it,
29 [along with their] hosts of angels, without our being seen. •And their
31 ruler was troubled by [our] journey. •For, the [luminous] cloud [. . .],
2 being far superior [to any] worldly thing. 5 •It had ineffable beauty;
6 glowed; was powerful; led the way for holy spirits; •and existed as a
7 life-giving spirit [and] an intellectual utterance—•[not] like things that
reside in the world [. . .] of mutable material [and] aggressive utterance.

130:6
Fr 58:26
v.25
RAd 77:27+

He is baptized

10   And next, I recognized that the power residing within me presided
14 over the darkness, [for] it possessed total light. •There I [was] baptized;
15 and •I received the image of the glories that are in that place, becoming
like one of them.
17,18   I passed through the ethereal [realm].[a] •And I went past the antitypical
19 aeons,[b] •having sunk [there] seven times [in] living [water]—once per
22 aeon—•without stopping until [I had seen (?)] absolutely (?) all the
waters.
24,25   [And] I came up to [the really] existent sojourn;[c] •and [I] was baptized
and [. . .] world.
26,28   I came up to the [really] existent repentance; •[and] there [I was]
baptized [four] times.

46:25
FTh 45:23+

8:7
v.18
11:2
129:28

He is baptized four times into the self-originate aeon

29,2   I went past the sixth [realm (?)[d] . . .]. 6 •And I came [up] to the [. . .
3 (plur.)]. •There I stood at rest, for I had seen really existent light of
truth deriving from [a] self-originate root of it, [together with] great
7 angels and glories [. . .] than measure. •And I [was] baptized into the
[name of] the divine self-originate (aeon)[a] by Mikhar and [Mikheus], the
11 powers that preside (?) [over] living waters. •And I became pure by the
12 agency of [the] great Barpharaggēs. •And they were [shown forth] unto
13,13 me, •and I was inscribed in glory. •I [was] sealed by those which preside
over the aforementioned powers [Mikhar], Mikheus, Seldaō, Elenos,
17,19 and Zōgenethlos. •And I [became] a [. . .]-seeing angel. •And I stood at
rest upon the first, i.e. fourth, aeon[b] along with the souls.
21 '   I blessed

FTh 48:18+

EgG 76:5

126:17
EgG 76:10

the divine self-originate (aeon);

c. Jewish and Christian jargon for the
human body, based on the fact that the
creator modeled Adam out of earth.
    d. Or "thirteen aeons": discussed in RAd
and EgG.

5 a. In the system of Zs, between the "thirteen realms" or heavens of the perceptible
world and the tripartite Barbēlō aeon, there
are six zones: (1) the ethereal realm; (2)
antitypical sojourn; (3) antitypical repentance; (4) the antitypical self-originate aeon;
(5) really existent sojourn; (6) really existent
repentance. The next thereafter is the self-
originate aeon, which is the lowest constituent of the Barbēlō aeon.

b. Or "antitypes of the aeons."
    c. Or "exile."
    d. For the six zones before the Barbēlō
aeon, see note 5a.

6 a. The self-originate aeon is the lowest
constituent of the Barbēlō aeon.
    b. The self-originate aeon has four sub-
constituents (29:1f); they are numbered both
one to four in ascending order and four to
one in descending order, since in his voyage
(here recounted after the fact) Zōstrianos
both ascended and descended through the
aeons. Thus the "first" when he ascended
was eventually the "fourth" in his descent.

the [first] parent, the Geradamas, [an eye of] the self-originate (aeon), the perfect [first human being];   BJn 8:28 +
30:4
FTh 38:5 +

Seth Emmakha [Seth], the child of Adamas, the [parent of] the [immovable race]; the [four luminaries . . .];   30:9
BJn 9:11 +

[. . .];

Mirothea, the mother [. . .];   EgG 60:30 +

Prophania, [the . . .] of the lights;

Dē[. . .].

1 **7**   And I [was baptized for] a second time into the name of the divine
4 self-originate (aeon) by the same aforementioned powers, •and became   28:10?
6 an angel of masculine gender.[a] •And I stood at rest upon the second,   30:12
BJn 9:14 +
i.e. third, aeon along with the children of Seth.

9   I blessed each of the aforementioned powers.

9   And I [was] baptized for a third time into the name of the divine self-
13 originate (aeon) by each of the aforementioned powers, •and became a
14 holy angel. •I stood at rest upon the third, i.e. second, [aeon].

15   I [blessed] each of the aforementioned.

16   And I was baptized [for a] fourth time by [each of] the aforementioned
18,19 powers, •and became a perfect [angel]. •And [I stood at rest upon] the
fourth, [i.e. first], aeon.

21   And I [blessed each of the aforementioned.] * * *

III. REVELATIONS OF AUTHROUNIOS

Appearance of Authrounios

7,9 **8**   •Authrounios, the great holder of superiority, said to me, •"Are you   47:18
seeking to understand those things through which you have passed?
10,12 Or why the ethereal realm has this worldly pattern? •Or how many
14,15 antitypical aeons[a] there are? •Or why they are unperturbed? •Or
[why (?)] the sojourn[b] and the repentance and the creation of the [. . .]
and the world[c] . . . [. . .]?" * * *

Creation of the universe

1,2 **9**   •Authrounios, the [great] holder of [superiority], said [to me], •"The   EgG III 57:5?
4 ethereal realm came into existence by an utterance; •but it incorruptibly
shows forth engendered things along with those that are corrupt.

6   "As for the descent of the great judges, it was so that they[a] might not   EgG 74:8
taste (the realm of) perception and be enclosed within the creation.
9,10 This is why they descended; •and this is the reason that they examined
13 the works of the world and condemned its ruler unto destruction, •as
14 being a representation[b] of the world, [. . .] •and a source of the corrupt,
dark material that engenders [. . .].

16   "Now, when wisdom (Sophia) gazed [at these], she emitted the   BJn 9:25
darkness[c] [. . .]" * * *   EgG III 57:2?

28   "[. . .] utterance without [its receiving(?)] power [. . .] aeon(s) of
1 [creation], to see any of the eternals. **10** •It (the world ruler) saw a   BJn 12:33 +
reflection, [and] with reference to the reflection that it [saw] therein, [it]

---

7 a. "masculine gender": belonging to the eternal realm; compare the gnostic jargon "male" in other gnostic texts (EgG, note 51f).

8 a. Or "antitypes of the aeons."

b. Or "exile"; cf. note 5a.
c. The rest of the passage is damaged.

9 a. The holy seed of Seth (?).
b. Or "symbol."
c. The rest of the passage is damaged.

4 made the world. •And with a reflection of a reflection it worked at
6 (crafting) the world. •And (then) even the reflection of[a] visible reality
was taken from it.

Repentance and elevation of wisdom

7   "Now, it was a realm of repose that was given unto wisdom (Sophia)   BJn 13:32+
9 in return for her repentance:[b] •and in consequence, since there was
nothing in her domain by way of uncontaminated, first image—nothing
within it (the realm of repose) either preexistent or that had already
come into existence through it—it (the world ruler) exercised its imag-
15 ination and worked at (crafting) what remained. •For always the image
belonging to wisdom (Sophia) is corrupt and deceptive.
17   "Now, the ruler[c] [. . .]" * * *

The antitypical aeons

2,4 **11** •"Now, the antitypical aeons[a] exist as follows. •They themselves   5:18
6 have not attained one and the same ideal form of power. •What they
7 possess are eternal glories. •And they reside in the judgment places of
9 the several powers. •But if the souls are illuminated by the light residing
in these[b] and by the pattern that often comes impassively to dwell within
14 them, •then it does not suppose that what it beholds is[c] [. . .]" * * *

Ascent of the fallen aeons from antitype unto model

3 **12** "They[a] are given training by the antitypes, which receive a pattern
7 of their souls while they are still residing in the world. •After each aeon's
9 road of emanation, it comes into existence, •and each one crosses over:
10,13 from the antitype of sojourn to the really [existent] sojourn;[b] •from the
15 antitype of repentance to the really existent repentance; •[and from the]
antitype of the self-[originate to the] really existent [self-originate]; and
19 so forth [. . .]. •Now, the souls of[c] [. . .]" * * *

Zōstrianos (and Authrounios ?) offer a blessing[a]

1 **13**   * * * [blessed]

[the] deity above the [great] aeons;[b]
the [unengendered] concealed (aeon);[c]
the [great], masculine first-manifest (aeon);[d]
the perfect [child][e] who is superior to deity;
its eye, the Geradamas.[f]

---

10 a. "of": or "corresponding to."
  b. "repentance": because of having produced the world-ruler; cf. BJn 13:21f.
  c. The rest of the passage is damaged.

11 a. Or "antitypes of the aeons."
  b. I.e. the antitypical aeons.
  c. "it does not . . . what it beholds . . .":
the Coptic text may be slightly corrupt here.
More logical might be "they (i.e. the souls)
do not . . . what they behold . . ." The rest
of the passage is damaged.

12 a. The exact context is lost.

  b. "sojourn . . . sojourn": or "exile . . .
exile."
  c. The rest of the passage is damaged.

13 a. The narrative context is lost, but cf.
44:23f, 48:23f.
  b. The great invisible spirit.
  c. The first or highest constituent of the
Barbēlō aeon.
  d. The second constituent of the Barbēlō
aeon.
  e. Or "[servant]"; i.e. the self-originate
aeon.
  f. I.e. Adamas.

IV. REVELATIONS OF ĒPHĒSĒKH

Appearance of Ēphēsēkh

7,8   And I called upon the child of the child Ēphēsēkh.[g] •It (Ēphēsēkh)   45:1, 45:9
stood before me and said, "O angel of god,[h] O son of the father, [. . .][i]   EgG 56:20 +
12 perfect human being! •[Why] are you calling to me and seeking to
understand things that you (already) know about, as though you [did
14 not understand] them?" •[And] for my part, [I] said, "I am seeking to
understand the mixture[j] [. . .]" * * *

Barbēlō the source of the three major aeons

1,2 **14** •* * * saying,[a] "Zōstrianos, listen (to me) concerning [. . .]. •For
4 the first [. . .] sources are three (in number): •they were shown forth
6 from one and the same source of [. . .], the Barbēlō aeon, •(although)
not as sources and powers, nor as from one source and one power;
9 they showed forth every source and bestowed power upon every power;
11 and they were shown forth in that which is [far] superior to these latter,
namely

13   reality;
       blessedness;
       life."[b]

   * * *

Waters of the three major aeons[a]

1,2 **15** •* * * "and water[b] belonging to each of them [. . .]. •Therefore they
are [. . .] waters; they are the perfect ones.
4   "The water of life, belonging to vitality, is that in which you have
now been washed within the self-originate (aeon).
7   "[And] the [water] of blessedness, [belonging to] acquaintance, is that
in which you are going to [be washed] within the first-manifest (aeon).
10   "And [it is] the water of reality [that] belongs to divinity, i.e., [to] the
concealed (aeon).
13,14   "And the water of life [exists in respect of] power;[c] •that of [blessed-
15 ness], in respect of essence; •and that of [divinity], in respect of reality."
1 * * * **17** •"And the power, the essence, and the reality of being[a] exist
4 insofar as the water exists. •And the name in which the washing is
conducted is an utterance belonging to[b] the water.
5   "Now, the first perfect water belonging to the [threefold power of]
9 the self-originate (aeon) [is] life of the perfect souls: •for it is an utterance
11 of the perfect deity while coming into being [. . .]. •For, the invisible
13 spirit is a wellspring of all [these (spiritual beings)]; •therefore the others   BJn 4:21 +
derive from acquaintance, being images of it (the spirit)." * * *

---

g. Elsewhere known also as Ēsēphēkh; cf. EgG 56:20f.

h. Cf. 7:4f.

i. Possibly "[O you who are the]."

j. The rest of the passage is damaged.

14 a. Ēphēsēkh replies. The exact narrative context is lost.

b. Corresponding to the concealed aeon, the first-manifest aeon, and the self-originate aeon.

15 a. Ēphēsēkh continues. The exact narrative context is lost.

b. The "waters" described here are not a material substance, but rather the eternal medium in which the candidate is "washed" or baptized into acquaintance; cf. RAd 85:22f.

c. Or "potentiality."

17 a. "being": the Coptic word can also be translated "becoming."

b. "belonging to": or "of."

5 **18** "And the great perfect, invisible, masculine, intellectual first-
8 manifest (aeon) possesses its own water, •as you (sing.) [are going to
9 see] when you come to its place; •so does the unengendered concealed
(aeon).

11 "Each partial (aeon) coexists with a [first] intelligible form, in order
13 that they might become complete accordingly. •For there are four perfect
self-originate aeons."[a] * * *

Structure of the self-originate aeon

6 **19** "Now, the divine self-originate (aeon) is the first ruler of its aeons
9 and of the angels, as though they were parts of it. •For considered
11 individually, the four belong to it. •The fifth aeon consists of them all
12,13 together; •and the fifth exists as[a] one. •The four [make up] the fifth in
15 respect of its parts. •But considered individually, these [four] are perfect,
having[b] [. . .]" * * *

Derivation of each major aeon from the preceding

4 **20** "Now, the self-originate concealed aeon[a] exists as a prior source—
god and foreparent—of the self-originate (aeon), in that it is a cause of
the first-manifest (aeon): parent of its own parts; a divine, foreunderstood
12,13 parent. •And they (its parts) did not understand it: •for it is a power
15 deriving from its own self, and a parent deriving from its own self. •In
this sense, it is without [parent]."[b] * * *

Classification of souls

19,20 **26** •"Now, do not wonder about the difference among souls.[a] •For,
when it is supposed that they display differences,[b] [. . .]" * * *
2 **27** "Now, those that are wholly [uncontaminated] display four
4 [kinds (?)]. •But those that are [within the] realm of time are ninefold.
5 Each of them has its own kind and custom, and ⟨their⟩ images are
different from one another, distinct, and stable.

9 "And other souls, which are immortal, coexist along with all the   43:1
aforementioned souls, because of wisdom (Sophia), who gazed down.

13 "Indeed, there are three kinds of [immortal] soul.

14,16 "First are those who have become rooted in sojourn,[a] •and do not   43:13
have the power[b] of being engendered—for it rests only [with] those who
19 follow works of others. •And since this is a unitary type,[c] . . . [. . .].

21 "Second are those who have stood at rest [upon] repentance[d] [. . .]   43:19
27 sin [. . .] acquaintance [. . .] new [. . .] difference [. . .] •they have   BJn 9:18?
sinned along with others and have repented along with others [. . .] from
3 their own selves. **28** •For [. . .] kind(s) that exist(s) [. . .] and those who

---

18 a. Listed at 29:1f.

19 a. Or "in."
  b. The rest of the passage is damaged.

20 a. The "concealed aeon" is the source
of the "first-manifest," which in turn is the
source of the "self-originate." The concealed
aeon is thus the "prior source" of the self-
originate.
  b. Several pages had to be omitted here.

26 a. The context and detailed argument of

this section cannot be reconstructed because
the passage is damaged. Apparently, an elaborate hierarchy of souls graded by degrees
of perfection was here related to their possible abodes.
  b. The rest of the passage is damaged.

27 a. Or "exile."
  b. Or "possibility."
  c. The rest of the passage is damaged.
  d. The lower aeon called "repentance."

6 have committed all kinds of sin and have repented. •Either they are
8 parts, or they have willed (?) of their own accord. •Thus also their aeons
are sixfold as regards the places that accrue to each of them.

10   "Third is the type of those souls[a] that belong to the self-originates   7:6?, 44:5
14 and possess an utterance of the ineffable truth, •(an utterance) that
exists in acquaintance and power out of them and eternal [life (?)].
17,19 [And] they display four varieties, according as there are •the kinds of
angels; those [who] love truth; those who hope; those who believe."

* * *

The four luminaries of the self-originate aeon

1 **29** "Likewise, too, four luminaries exist [there].   127:15
2   "(H)armozēl [presides] over the first aeon, and is a wish[a] of the   BJn 7:30+
god [. . .] of truth and the unification of the soul.

6   "Ōroiaēl presides over the second, and is a power perceptive of truth.
8   "Daueithe presides over the third, and is a vision of acquaintance.
10   "Ēlēlēth presides over the fourth, and is an impulse to action and a
preparing for truth.

13,15   "Now, the four exist as utterances of truth and acquaintance. •But
16 [they] exist without belonging to the first-manifest (aeon); •rather, [they]
17 belong to the mother, •for she is an act of thought by the [perfect]
19 intellect of light, •so that immortal souls might take acquaintance unto
themselves." * * *

Inhabitants of the luminaries

4 **30** "Since Adamas the perfect human being is an eye of the self-   6:21
6 originate (aeon), it is acquaintance therewith, •comprehending (?) that
the divine self-originate (aeon) is an utterance of [the] perfect intellect
of truth.

9   "And Seth the son of Adamas comes to each of the souls, for he is   6:21
acquaintance that suffices for them.

12   "And for this reason [the] living seed derived from him.   7:6
14   "And Mirothea[a] is [. . .] divine self-originate (aeon) [. . .] from it and   6:21
16 [. . .], •being an act of thought by the perfect intellect."[b] * * *

Different kinds of persons[a] and their fates[b]

20 **42** "And the soul, [intellect, and] body of the persons [that belong to]
mortal things [are] all [dead]." * * *
1 **43** "And the second (kind of) person is the immortal soul that dwells   27:9
4 within mortal things, looking after its own interests. •[For] this (kind)
then undertakes a search for affairs that are profitable in every single
7,8 case (?). •[And it] perceives bodily pain. •It is [. . .], and it [. . . .
10 Although (?)] possessing [an] eternal divine (element), it coexists with
[demons].

13,14   "Next is [the] (kind of) person that resides in the sojourn.[a] •Now, if   27:14

---

28 a. The holy seed of Seth.

29 a. Or "promise."

30 a. A Greek neologism, possibly meaning
"divine part" (*moiros theios*).
  b. A lengthy passage had to be omitted
here.

42 a. This may refer to components of the
human being or to stages in human development.
  b. The context and detailed argument of
this section cannot be reconstructed because
the passage is damaged.

43 a. Or "exile."

16 this (kind) experiences within itself a discovery of truth, •it is far from the deeds of others who live [evilly] and [stumble].

19 "As for the (kind of) person that repents, if [this (kind)] abandons 27:21 [mortal] things and desires the things that [exist], the immortal intellect 25 and the immortal soul [. . .] first [. . .] for them, •while for its[b] sake this (kind of person) undertakes a search—[not] for action but for deeds. 27 For, as a result, it[c] [. . .].

1 44 "And the (kind of) person that gets saved is the one who seeks to 5 understand, and so to discover, the self and the intellect. •Oh how much power that person has!

5 "[And] the (kind of) person that has been saved is the one who has 28:10 8 not understood these [. . .] as they exist, •but rather is personally also 11 within [the] rational faculty[a] as it exists [. . .]. •That person has gotten 13 [. . .] everywhere [it] exists simple and one. •For the one who then has the power to advance through all [these] (spiritual beings) has been 16,17 saved. •That person becomes [. . .] all these (spiritual beings). •(And) that person can voluntarily part from all these (spiritual beings), and 21 withdraw inward. •For such a person becomes god[b] and has withdrawn into god."

Zōstrianos offers a blessing

23 When I had listened to this I lifted up praise unto

24 the living and unengendered [god] who resides in truth;[c]
26 the unengendered [concealed] (aeon);
27 the perfect, masculine, invisible, first-manifest intellect;[d]
29 the invisible thrice-male child; and
31 [the divine self-originate (aeon)].

The soul's swerve and eventual return

1 45 And I said to Ēphēsēkh the child of the child, who was with me, 13:7+ 2 "Can your wisdom instruct me about the dispersion of the human being 5 that is (being) saved? •Which are the beings that are mixed with such a 6,8 person? •Which are [the ones that] divide that person? •(Tell me), so that the living elect might understand."

9 And next, Ēphēsēkh the child of the child openly said to [me . . .], 12 "If that person many times [withdraws] inward and dwells near ac- 46:13 quaintance with others, the intellect and the unengendered first principle Fr 59:1 17,18 will [not (?)][a] understand. •Thereafter, that person has a lack: •for that BJn 14:8+ 20 person, too, turns; has nothing; parts from it (the intellect); •stands [. . .]; and exists in an alien [impulse] to action instead of existing as 23,25 One. •Consequently, that person [resembles] many forms; •once having 27 inclined, comes into being by seeking things that do not exist; •and once 29 having fallen into these notionally—•being unable to understand them 1 otherwise without receiving enlightenment—46 becomes a part of the 2 natural order. •And thus does that person come down into the realm of 4 generation[a] because of it; •becomes speechless at the pains and [infinity] 6 of material; •and, although possessing immortal eternal power, is bound

---

b. Or "its own."
c. The rest of the passage is damaged.

44 a. Or "Word."
b. Or "divine."
c. The great invisible spirit.
d. I.e. the first-manifest aeon.

45 a. The original reading of the text is uncertain here. Despite the definiteness of "will," the passage seems to describe a possible course of events.

46 a. I.e. becomes reincarnate.

9,10 in the body's advance; •[made] to be alive; •and bound each [time]ᵇ in
13 strong fettersᶜ that cut by all kinds of evil spirits: •until once again that
person acts,ᵈ and so begins once more to dwell within.   45:12 +

Helpers of the fallen souls

15   "For this reason, beings are ordained to be in charge of their salvation.
17,18 And these several powers dwell here (in the visible world), •whereas at
each of the aeons within the self-originate (aeon) glories stand at rest,
so that beside them a person who is [here] (in the world) might be saved.
22,24 And the glories are perfect concepts, appearing unto the powers. •They
25 are incorruptible,ᵉ for [they are] patterns of salvation, •in which each
26 (saved person) is stamped: •such a person shall escape safely into them. 5:15
27 And it is by being stamped that the person receives power from the
same one of them and has that glory for a helper.
30   "In this way, such a person passes through the world and [the] aeons
[. . .].
31   "And there are guardians of the immortal soul:

2   **47** Gamaliēl and Strempsoukous;   EgG 64:14
           Akramas and Lōēl;   EgG 76:26
                                                                  126:9?
           Mnēsinous.   EgG 76:26
                                                                  FTh 48:18

5   "[The following is the] immortal spirit: Iesseus-Mazareus-Iessedekeus. EgG 75:25 +
7   "[. .]atitou is [the . . .] of the child; [. .]ōr, the child of the child.
8,9 And [. . .]. •And it is (H)ormos [that . . .] over the living seed;   EgG 71:11
11 while Kam[ali]ēl (?) is the cause (or bestower) of spirits.   EgG 76:15
12   "And the following stand at rest before [them]:   EgG 75:24

           Seisauēl;   EgG 75:27
           Audaēl;
           Abrasaks.

14   "The myriads:

           Phaleris;
           Phalsēs;
           Eurios.

15   "The guardians of glory:

           Stētheus;   126:12?
           Theopemptos;   EgG 75:27
           Eurymeneus;
           Olsēn.   EgG 76:19?

18   "And the helpers in every kind of affair are:

           Ba[. . .]mos;
           [.]sōn;
           Eir[.]n;
           Lalameus;
           Eidomeneus;
           Authrounios.   8:7

22   "The judges are:

           Symphthar;
           Eukrebōs;
           Keilar.

---

b. In each reincarnation.   e. "incorruptible": the syllable "in-" has
c. "fetters": a Platonist cliché for the   been destroyed in the MS and is here con-
material body.   jecturally restored.
d. Responds to the gnostic appeal.

24　"The being who takes away: Samblō.
24　"The angels that guide the billowing (?) clouds:

　　Saphphō;
　　Thurō."

Intelligible forms within the self-originate aeon

27　After saying these things, it (Ēphēsēkh) instructed me about all these
30　(spiritual beings) that reside in the self-originate aeon. •And they were
1,2　all luminous, eternal, **48** •and completely perfect particulars. •And at　113:1
　　each of the aeons I saw living[a] earth, living water, luminous [air], and
7,9　nonconsuming fire—•all [these] being simple [and immutable]; •simple
12　and [eternal living animals], with many kinds of [body (?)]; •many kinds
　　of incorruptible trees, and also plants of the same sort as (?) all the
16,17　aforementioned; incorruptible fruit; •living human beings; •and every
18,19　(other kind of) intelligible form; •together with immortal souls; •every
20,21　form and intelligible form of intellect; •deities of truth; •angels residing
23　in great glory; •body that is indissoluble; unengendered offspring; and
26　immovable perception. •Moreover, in that place was that which[b] expe-
29　riences passions although being impassive: •for it[c] was a power belonging
　　to a power. [. . .][d] * * *

Zōstrianos and Ēphēsēkh offer a blessing[a]

23　　**51** * * * as we said,
24　"You are One, you are [One], you are One!
25　O child of [. . .] * * *
16　　**52** "O thrice male! Aa[. . .]ōōōōō[a] [. . .]
18　"You are spirit from spirit!
19　"You are light from light!
20　"You are [silence] from silence!
21　"[You are] thought from thought!
23　"O child of [god], O divine seven[b] [. . .]" * * *

Zōstrianos baptized for a fifth time into the self-originate aeon

14 **53** And for a fifth [time I was] baptized into the name of the self-
18　originate (aeon) by the aforementioned groups of powers, •and became
20,21　divine.[a] •[I stood at rest] upon the fifth aeon, •being a compound[b] of all
22　[these] (spiritual beings). •I beheld all that belong to [the] self-originate
25　(aeon) and which are really existent. •[And] I [was] washed five times
12　[. . .][c] * * * **56** •[I] received an image from [all] these (spiritual beings).
13,15　[And] the aeons [of the] self-originate (aeon) opened (?). •Great [light]
18　radiated [upon (?) . . .] from the aeons of the [thrice]-male, •and they
　　were [glorifying] them. * * *

---

48 a. "living": gnostic jargon in this text to indicate membership in the eternal realm. The self-originate aeon contains the Platonic ideal forms both of the four basic elements ("earth . . . water . . . [air] . . . fire") and of the particular kinds of entity such as species of plants and animals.
　b. Or "he who."
　c. Or "he."
　d. Several pages had to be omitted here.

51 a. The exact narrative context is lost.

52 a. Cf. EgG, note 78b.
　b. The rest of the passage is damaged.

53 a. Or "a god."
　b. Or "inhabitation."
　c. The rest of the passage is destroyed. Several pages had to be omitted here.

V. REVELATIONS OF IŌĒL

Appearance of Iōēl

13 **57** [And] into my presence came Iōēl, the masculine female virgin that   EgG 54:21+
15 belongs to [the] glories. •And [I] took counsel concerning the wreaths.[a]
17 It [said] to me, "Why [has] your spirit taken counsel [concerning] the
21 wreaths[b] and the seals that are upon them? •[These (?)] are the wreaths[c]
23 that impart power [unto] every [spirit] and every soul; •while [the] seals
that exist [upon] them are the threefold peoples[d] and [belong to (?)] the
invisible spirit [. . .]." * * *

13 **58** "And the seals [. . .] people(s)[a] belong to the self-originate (aeon),
16 the first-manifest (aeon), and the concealed (aeon). •And the [invisible]
spirit [is] an animate and intellectual power—an understander and a
20 foreunderstander: •and therefore he[b] is with Gabriēl the cause of spirits—   EgG 64:17
22 so that when it (Gabriēl) bestows holy spirit it might seal him with[c] the
wreath[d] and wreathe him."[e] * * *

Zōstrianos baptized by Iōēl

23 **60** And after it (Iōēl) had said these things, it baptized [me . . .] * * *
8 **61** I received power [. . .] . . . [. . . I] received form [. . .], and I
received [. . .] exist(s) over [. . .] receive(d) an uncontaminated spirit.
14 [I] came to be really existent.
15 And next, it brought me into the great aeon where the perfect, thrice-
19 [male] is located. •And I beheld [the] invisible child within invisible
light.
22 Next, [it] baptized me again in[a] [. . .] * * *
8 **63** [After] Iouēl,[a] who belongs to all [the glories], [had said] these
things to me, it left [me] and departed to stand at rest before the first-
manifest (aeon).

VI. REVELATIONS OF SALAMEKS AND OTHERS

Appearance of Salameks and others (the first-manifest aeon)

13 Next, I [stood at rest], presiding over my spirit [and] mentally praying   126:1
17 much to the great luminaries: •I was calling upon Salameks, Se[. .]en,
20 and the female wholly-perfect [. . .]ē. •And I beheld [glories] that were
22,22 mightier than powers. •And they smeared oil on me, •and I became   RR 97:2
able[b] [. . .] * * *
7 **64** [. . .] Salameks and [. . .], who had disclosed everything [to me],
saying, "O Zōstrianos, [listen] (to us) concerning the things that you
are seeking to understand.
13 "It was a [. . .] and single entity [that] existed prior to [all] these
(spiritual beings), really existing [in (?) the] immeasurable and indivisible
14,16 spirit [. . .] * * * **65** •[. . .] infinite; more than unsearchable; •bestowing
18 [. . .] mightier than any body; •more uncontaminated than [any] bodiless
19,21 entity; •entering every thought and every body; •more powerful than all

---

57 a. Or "crowns."
  b. Or "crowns."
  c. Or "crowns."
  d. Or "species."

58 a. Or "species."
  b. "he": perhaps a type of person, mentioned in the damaged passage just before
58:13f.

c. Or "in."
d. Or "crown."
e. Several pages had to be omitted here.

61 a. The rest of the passage is destroyed.

63 a. I.e. Iōēl.
  b. The rest of the passage is destroyed.

these (spiritual beings), all [species], and [all] intelligible forms, as being the entirety that relates to them [. . .]"ª * * *

Intelligible forms within the concealed aeonª

1 **113** "angels; demons; intellects; souls; living animals; trees; bodies; 48:2, 119:3
4,5 and what exist prior to these: •(namely), what belong to the simple elements of the simple first principles, which exist (both) confusedly (?)
9,11 [. . .] and unmixed—•air, water, earth; •number, connection, motion,
13 [. . .], order; •breath, et cetera.
14 "Now, there are powers of a [fourth] type that reside [in] the fourth
21 aeon, (namely) those [that] reside in theᵇ [. . .] * * * •[angels belonging to the] angels; souls [belonging to the] souls; livingᶜ animals [belonging to the] living animals; trees [belonging to the trees]ᵈ * * *
1,3 **115** •"And they do not exercise compulsion upon one another; •rather, it is in themª that they are alive, coexisting with and consenting to one
7 another as deriving from one single source. •And they exist conjointly, for they all reside within one single aeon of the concealed (aeon); [. . .]
11 in power and distinct. •For in the case of each of the aeons they exist standing at rest according to (?) what has reached them.
13,14 "[Now], the concealed (aeon) is one single aeon; •[it] comprises four varieties of aeon."ᵇ * * *
1 **117** "All living animals are there, both existing particularly and all
4 conjointly collective. •Acquaintance of acquaintance is there, and at-
7 tainment of noncomprehension. •Chaos is there, and [a perfect place]
9,10 belonging to all (spiritual beings). •And they are new.ª •Moreover, true light is there, and darkness that has been illuminated.ᵇ * * *

The four luminaries of the concealed aeon

3 **119** "Now, the luminaries belonging to it (the concealed aeon) have 113:1 names:

4   the first [is] (H)armēdōn; the female entity with it is [. . .];
6   second, Diphane[. .]; the female entity with it, Dēiph[. . .];
8   third, Malsēdōn; the female entity with it, [. . .];
10   fourth, [. . .]s; the female entity with it, Olmis.

12,13 [And] the concealed (aeon) exists [. . .] along with its ideal form. •And [it is] obscure to [all] these (spiritual beings), so that they all might receive power from it."ª * * *
11,12 **125** •"Now, the concealed (aeon) is really existent; •and with it is located Iouēl,ª the masculine female virgin glory that belongs to all the glories, (the glory) through whom all the wholly perfects have been beheld." * * *

---

65 a. A very lengthy part of the work had to be omitted here because of damage to the MS.

113 a. The narrative context is lost. The concealed aeon, which is the highest constituent of the Barbēlō aeon, contains the Platonic ideal forms of kinds of entity such as plants and animals, the basic elements ("air, water, earth"), and abstractions such as "number," "connection," etc.
   b. The rest of the passage is damaged.
   c. Cf. note 48a.

d. The rest of the passage is damaged. One page had to be omitted here.

115 a. Or "in one another."
   b. One page had to be omitted here.

117 a. Or "strange."
   b. One page had to be omitted here.

119 a. Several pages had to be omitted here.

125 a. I.e. Iōēl.

The four luminaries of the first-manifest aeon

1 **126** "Now, the first aeon that exists within it, and derives from it, is 63:13
the first luminary Solmis, together with that which shows forth god;
6 being infinite, after the pattern that exists in the concealed aeon and
Doksomedōn.
                                                                    EgG 50:29+
9 "The second aeon, Akremōn the ineffable, occupies the second 46:31?
luminary Zakhthos and Iakhthos.

12 "And the third aeon is Ambrosius the virgin, occupying the third
luminary Sētheus and Antiphantēs.
                                                                    47:15?
17 "While the fourth aeon is that which praises [. . .], occupying [the]
fourth luminary [Seldaō] and Elenos." * * *
                                                                    6:13+

1   **127** "Phoē, zoē, zēoē, zē[. .], zōsi, zōsi, zaō, zēooo, zēsen,
           zēsen!
3   The particulars live,[a] and the quartet that is eightfold!
5   Ē O O O O Ē A Ē Ō !
5   It is you (sing.) who are prior to them.
6   And it is you who are in all these (spiritual beings)!

7 "And these are in the perfect, masculine, (H)armēdōn, first-manifest
(aeon), (being) the activity of all these (spiritual beings), collectively,
that exist.

The four luminaries of the self-originate aeon

11 "Inasmuch as all the perfect particulars were existent, the activity of
all the particulars became shown forth again, namely, the divine self-
15 originate (aeon). •Now, the latter stands at rest within an aeon, displaying 29:1+
within itself four varieties of aeon, consisting of the self-originates:

19   the first aeon that exists within it, belonging to the first
                   luminary [(H)armozē]l: Orneus-Euthrounios, which is
                   called [. . .];
25   [the] second [aeon, belonging to the second luminary
                   Ōroiaēl]: [. .]udas[.]us-Ap[. . .]-Arros[. . .];
1   **128** the third, belonging to the third luminary Daueithe:
                   Laraneus-Epiphanios-Eideus;
4   the fourth, belonging to the fourth luminary Ēlēlēth: Kodērē-
                   Epiphanios-Allogenios.

The fate of those who have fallen into material existence

7 "But as for all the rest who dwelt in the material realm, they all
10 remained.[a] •And since they have come into being and have been put in
order[b] because of acquaintance with greatness, because of recklessness,
and because of power, and since they have become uncomprehending
of god, they shall perish.

14 "There, O Zōstrianos! You have heard all these things, of which the
gods are uncomprehending and which unto angels seem infinite."

---

127 a. The esoteric words in 127:1f are per-   128 a. The Coptic text may be corrupt here.
mutations of the Greek stem meaning "to   More logical would be "shall not remain."
live," of a type that could be found in Greek   b. Or "adorned."
magical spells at the time Zs was composed.

Zōstrianos ponders the ineffable first principle

19 But for my part, I acted recklessly and said, "I am still seeking to
22 understand about the triply powerful, perfect, invisible spirit.[c] •How
does it exist . . . [. . .] cause(?) of all these (spiritual beings)? [. . .]
really existent [. . .]? Which is [. . .]? Or [. . .]?"
27,1 [. . .] greatly.[d] **129** •They left [me and] departed.   BJn 4:15 + ?

VII. ZŌSTRIANOS'S DESCENT
RECORD OF HIS EXPERIENCE

He descends

2 And Apophantēs came before me, accompanied by Aphro Pais-
4 Parthenōphōtos.[a] •And it brought me into the great, masculine, perfect,   63:8
6 first-manifest intellect. •And there I saw all these (spiritual beings) as
8,9 they exist, in one. •And I became unified with all of them, •and I blessed

10   the concealed aeon;
        the virgin Barbēlō;
        the invisible spirit.

12 And I became wholly perfect; received power; was inscribed in glory;
was sealed; and there was wreathed with a perfect wreath.
16,18 I came forth unto the perfect particulars. •And they all were greeting
20 me, and listening (to me) about the greatnesses of acquaintance. •And
they were rejoicing, and receiving power.
22,24 And I then descended to the aeons comprising the self-originates. •I   5:29
received a [true], uncontaminated image worthy of perception.
26 I descended to the antitypical aeons.[b]   5:18
28,1 From there [I] descended to the ethereal [realm], **130** •and I inscribed   5:17
three tablets (of wood)[a] and left them[b] as a (source of) acquaintance for   v.1 3Tb 118:10
those who would come after me, the living elect (plur.)

He reoccupies his material body

4,6 And I descended to the perceptible world, •and I put on my ignorant   4:20
7,8 material image.[c] •Although it was ignorant, •I bestowed power upon it,
10 and went about preaching truth unto all. •Neither the hosts of angels of
12 the world nor the rulers saw me. •Indeed, I escaped many condemnations
that brought me near to death.

His sermon[d]

14,16 I awakened[e] a multitude that were lost, saying, •"O living people! O
17 holy seed of Seth! Understand! •Do not let yourselves [appear (?)]
18,19 inattentive to me. •Elevate[f] your divine element as being god. •Bestow

c. Having ascended through all three constituent aeons of the Barbēlō, Zōstrianos now asks about the ineffable great invisible spirit. The text is badly damaged.

d. Zōstrianos is unable to obtain a discursive answer.

129 a. "Aphro, child of virgin light." Zōstrianos now descends through the first-manifest aeon to the self-originate aeon and then through the six zones between the self-orig-

inate and the perceptible world; cf. note 5a.

b. Or "antitypes of the aeons."

130 a. The Greek word means specifically a writing board of wood.

b. The tablets are left not on earth but in "the ethereal [realm]."

c. Lit. "statue, idol."

d. A typical gnostic sermon. For another sample of this style of rhetoric, cf. CH7.

e. Or "raised up."

f. Or "awaken."

21 power upon the innocent, [elect] soul. •Behold the transitoriness that is
22,24 found here. •Seek immutable unengenderedness. •[The] parent of all
26 these (spiritual beings) is calling you (plur.). •When you are being
2 censured and mistreated, that (parent) will not abandon you. **131** •Do
3 not bathe yourselves in death, •nor surrender yourselves unto ones who
5 are inferior to you as though they were superior. •Flee the madness and
7 fetter[a] of femininity, •and choose for yourselves the salvation of mas-
8 culinity.[b] •It is not to experience passion that you have come (to this
10 place), but to break your fetters. •Break yourselves free, and the one
12 who bound you[c] will be broken to bits! •Save yourselves so that that
14 (soul) might be saved! •The kind parent has sent the savior unto you   BJn 6:23 +
16,17 and bestowed power upon you. •Why are you standing there? •Convert!
18,19 For you are being sought! •You are being called! Listen! •For, the time
20,21 is short! •Do not let yourselves be deceived! •Great is the eternity[d] of
23 the aeon of the living (plur.), •and (great is) the chastisement of those
24 who are unconvinced. •Many fetters and chastisers are surrounding you.
1 **132**   Flee in the short time that remains, before destruction overtakes
3,3,4 you! •Behold the light!! •Flee the darkness!! •Do not let yourselves be
enslaved unto destruction!!"[e]

131 a. The body; cf. note 46c.

  b. "femininity . . . masculinity": i.e.
"materiality . . . membership in the eternal
realm"; cf. note 7a.

c. The world ruler.

d. Or "aeon."

e. In the manuscript, the titles of this work
are written after the text (at 132:6f).

THE FOREIGNER

(EXCERPTS)
(Fr)

Contents

The concluding half of *The Foreigner* ("Allogenes"), which is translated here, describes the interior mystical journey of a soul to acquaintance or *gnōsis* with the ineffable first principle, thus constituting a close parallel to Zs (cf. the introduction to Zs). The stages of this journey are the main aeons (abstractions) that according to gnostic myth have emanated from the first principle and structure the spiritual universe. Their description in Fr is brief and very selective; it follows a threefold division using terminology also found in Zs, but at least one important structural detail is at variance with that work:

	Fr	Zs
The concealed aeon	= reality	= reality
The first-manifest aeon	= vitality	= blessedness
The self-originate aeon	= blessedness	= vitality

Unlike Zs, the mystical ascent described in Fr is almost entirely abstract, without metaphorical "baptisms" or interpreting angels. Furthermore, the ascent is explicitly said to be "inward" to the interior of the self, so that the apocalyptic convention of an "upward" voyage through "heavens" is entirely suppressed. No reference is made to a return voyage downward. The voyager is not explicitly identified with any known religious hero or put in a historical setting, but simply called "the Foreigner" (Greek *allogenēs,* "an other type," "an alien type"; the Greek word is retained in the ancient Coptic version of the text); according to EpA 40.7.2, gnostics understood this epithet to belong to Seth, presumably with reference to Gn 4:25. The Foreigner's experience comes not after a career of religious service as in Zs, but as the summation of a hundred years of "deliberation," i.e. study and contemplation. After attaining his vision (*gnōsis*) of the "unrecognizable" first principle, he seeks rational knowledge about the nature of the unrecognizable, but these hopes are dashed when holy powers from the Barbēlō aeon lecture him on the ineffability of the first principle. Their lecture closely parallels the beginning of the gnostic myth in BJn, and actually quotes from the latter. Thus, in Fr, a mythic structure whose original context was cosmology (in BJn) has been abstractly transformed into a psychology of the individual gnostic—macrocosm into microcosm, myth into philosophical mysticism.

Like Zs, *The Foreigner* is of particular importance in the history of philosophy because Plotinus, the great Neoplatonist philosopher, was acquainted with its contents (cf. Porph 16.3f) and took it into account in his cycle of lectures against the gnostics (*Enneads* 3.8, 5.8, 5.5, and 2.9 [nos. 30–33 chronologically]).

Of special interest is the language used to describe the technique of mystical contemplation (59:9f).

The abstract and theoretical character of the excerpt does not allow for reference to the history of Israel or the foundation of Christianity, nor indeed to dramatic actions of any part of the gnostic myth.

Literary background

The author and place of composition of Fr are unknown. The date of its composition must be sometime before A.D. 268 because the work was known to Plotinus before he wrote against the gnostics. Fr is attributed to an unnamed person simply called "the Foreigner" (*allogenēs*); however, gnostics are known to have applied this epithet to Seth (cf. above, "Contents"), so if the equation operates here Fr is an example of pseudepigraphy. The language of composition was Greek.

Fr has a complex mixture of genres in which various traditional materials are subordinated to others:

   I. Autobiography of a seer
      A. Mystical "ascent" (cf. heavenly voyage)
         1. Angelic revelation
           a. Learned treatise

Like Zs, the work as a whole is a spiritual autobiography of a religious seer. The literary genre of the excerpt is a variant of the "apocalyptic" heavenly voyage of the soul (for this genre, see the introduction to Zs), spiritualized and stripped of its usual celestial reference so as to coincide with a description of the *mystical ascent* of the soul.

The seer voyages alone, without the usual interpreting angels. But before his voyage begins, he receives angelic directions; and after it has come to an end, he seeks angelic advice on its rational interpretation. In consequence, the seer receives a monologic *angelic revelation,* in the form of a typical philosophical *treatise* on the nature of god, comparable to the treatise embedded in BJn.

Mythic characters

I. Great Eternals Mentioned in the Excerpt

The TRIPLY POWERFUL INVISIBLE SPIRIT. The unrecognizable. The BARBĒLŌ. A masculine female virgin, first source of blessedness and divinity.
   1. THE CONCEALED (AEON). Reality.
   2. THE FIRST-MANIFEST INTELLECT. Harmēdōn. Vitality.
   3. THE SELF-ORIGINATE (AEON). Blessedness.
The THRICE-MALE CHILD. The savior.
LUMINARIES of the Barbēlō
Their HOLY POWERS

II. Humankind Mentioned in the Excerpt

The FOREIGNER (Seth?)
MESSOS, a disciple or spiritual "child" of the Foreigner

Text

The original Greek apparently does not survive. The text is known only in Coptic translation, attested by a single manuscript from Nag Hammadi, MS NHC XI (pp.

45–69), which was copied just before A.D. 350 and is now in the Cairo Coptic Museum.

The meaning of one word occurring several times in the Coptic manuscript is at present unknown. It has been represented by a series of points (. . .) in the English translation.

The translation below is based on an advance copy of Hedrick's critical edition of the Coptic (kindly supplied by him), with minor alteration: C. Hedrick, ed., *Nag Hammadi Codices XI, XII, and XIII* (Nag Hammadi Studies; Leiden: E. J. Brill, forthcoming).

SELECT BIBLIOGRAPHY

See items listed under Zs, "Select Bibliography."

THE FOREIGNER[a]

(EXCERPTS)

I. PREPARATION FOR THE MYSTICAL VISION

The Foreigner's lifetime of deliberation

27 **57** But for my part, I did not despair at the words that I had heard.[b]
29,30 Through them I prepared myself, •and I deliberated for a hundred years.[c]   Porph 16:3
* * *

The way of withdrawal: summary[d]

7 **58** [And when . . .] the hundred years had [nearly passed (?)] the
blessedness[a] of eternal hope, filled with kindness, [came over (?)] me.
12 I beheld

12 the good, divine self-originate (aeon);[b]	Zs 20:4
13 the savior, i.e. the thrice-male perfect child;	Zs 29:1 + **v.13**
15 the latter's goodness;	Zs 13:1
16 the perfect, Harmēdōn, the first-manifest intellect;[c]	Zs 127:7
18 the blessedness of the concealed (aeon);[d]	Zs 63:13 + **v.18**
19 the first source of blessedness, the Barbēlō aeon, filled with	Zs 113:1 + **v.19**
23 divinity, •the first source of beginninglessness, the triply	Zs 14:4 **v.23**
powerful invisible spirit, the entirety better than perfect.	BJn 2:26 EgG 50:23 + **v.26**

26   After being caught up by the eternal light out of the garment[e] that I   Zs 4:20
was wearing, and taken to a holy place, no resemblance of which could
be shown forth in the world, then by great blessedness I beheld all the
37,38 things that I had heard about. •And I blessed all of them, •and [stood
at rest][f] within my acquaintance.

The Foreigner's vision of holy powers

1 **59** [I turned] inward[a] toward acquaintance [with] the entireties, the   Zs 45:12 +
4 Barbēlō aeon, •and I beheld holy powers from the luminaries of the

---

Title 57 a. In the manuscript, the title is
found after the text (at 69:20).

  b. The first part of the work, about a dozen
pages, is badly damaged and had to be
omitted here. In it "the Foreigner" (*allogenēs*) evidently writes to a disciple, Messos,
reporting certain revelations made by the
eternal being Iouēl "that belongs to all the
glories" (i.e. Iōēl; cf. Zs 57:13f, EgG 55:15f).
These revelations may have described the
structure of the Barbēlō aeon, as in Zs. In
the second part of the work, translated here,
the Foreigner tells of putting this information
to use as the basis for mystical contemplation, and of receiving a further revelation
from "the glories." The exact narrative context of the excerpt is lost.

  c. Lit. "the hundred years" (referring to
an earlier mention of the hundred-year period).

  d. The following section (58:7–38f) summarizes the contents of the more detailed
passage that follows hereafter.

58 a. "blessedness" is bestowed by Barbēlō. See below.

  b. The lowest of the three constituents of
the Barbēlō aeon. This and the other constituents had already been discussed in the
earlier pages of the work.

  c. I.e. the first-manifest aeon (cf. Zs 127:7),
which is the second constituent of the Barbēlō aeon.

  d. The highest constituent of the Barbēlō
aeon.

  e. "garment": a Platonist cliché for the
body.

  f. To "stand at rest" is philosophical jargon for the state of permanence, non-change,
and real being, as opposed to what exists in
instability, change, and becoming.

59 a. The Barbēlō aeon is "within" the self
and can be discovered in the course of self-
acquaintance.

7 masculine female virgin Barbēlō, •[which said . . .] I would attempt [. . .] reside in the world.

The method of withdrawal

9 "O Foreigner, behold how your blessedness[b] resides in silence—(a Zs 4:13 blessedness) through which you understand yourself as you really are. 3Tb 120:11
11 And in seeking to understand yourself, withdraw to vitality,[c] which you
16 will see moving. •And if you are unable to stand at rest, do not be
18,20 afraid. •Rather, if you want to stand at rest, withdraw to reality,[d] •and
you will find it standing at rest and still, after the resemblance of what
24 is really still •and restrains all these (spiritual beings)[e] in quietness and lack of activity.[f]
26 "And if you receive a manifestation thereof through a first manifes-
30 tation of the unrecognizable[g]—•of which you must be uncomprehending,
32 if you should happen to understand it—•and if you are afraid there,
35 draw back because of the activities. •And if in that place you become
37 perfect, be still; •and understand also that its manner of existing in [all these] (spiritual beings) is after the pattern that resides within you.[h]
2 **60** "And do not be further dispersed, [so that] you might be able to
5 stand at rest. •And do not desire to [be active], lest you utterly perish [because of] the inactive element within [you] that belongs to the
8,9 unrecognizable. •Do not (attempt to) comprehend it: •for this is impos-
10 sible. •Rather if, through a luminous thought, you should happen to understand it, be uncomprehending of it."

The Foreigner's withdrawal

12 Now, I was listening to them say these things, and within me was 59:9
16 stillness of silence. •I listened to blessedness,[a] through which I understood
19 myself as I really am. •And I withdrew to vitality, which I sought to
20,22 understand; •and I accompanied it into itself, •and stood at rest—not
24 firmly, but in stillness. •And I beheld an indivisible, eternal, intellectual movement—belonging to all the powers; formless; and unlimited by
28 bestowal of limit. •And when I wished to stand firmly at rest I withdrew to reality, which I found to be standing at rest and still, after an image
35 and a resemblance of that (image) which I was wearing. •Through a manifestation of the undivided and the still, I became full of manifestation.
38 (And) through a first manifestation of the unrecognizable, I [understood] it (the unrecognizable), at the same time [that] I was uncomprehending
3 of it. **61** •And from the latter I received power, having gotten eternal strength from [it].[a]
5 I recognized that [which] existed within me and the triply powered and the manifestation of the uncontained [that] belonged to it.

---

b. "your blessedness" (cf. 58:7f): "blessedness" is an aspect of the self-origi-nate aeon, the lowest of the Barbēlō con-stituents, which the Foreigner discovers "within."

c. An aspect of the first-manifest aeon, the second of the Barbēlō constituents.

d. An aspect of the concealed aeon, the highest Barbēlō constituent.

e. "all these," namely, spiritual beings: gnostic jargon used in this text, probably to mean the sum total of spiritual reality deriv-ing from the Barbēlō aeon; cf. Zs note 2e.

f. The highest form of self-acquaintance (to "understand yourself as you really are")

is a state of total stillness and inactivity; it is acquaintance with god, i.e. the Barbēlō.

g. "the unrecognizable": i.e. the invisible spirit.

h. The Barbēlō and its constituents en-countered within the self correspond to the structure of spiritual reality at large ("all these"; cf. note 59e): microcosm corre-sponds to macrocosm.

60 a. The events narrated here (60:16–38f) correspond to the instructions given in 59:9f.

61 a. "[it]": the first manifestation.

II. VISION OF THE UNRECOGNIZABLE

8   [And] I beheld the first,[b] which is unrecognizable to all, the deity better than perfect, through a first manifestation thereof, along with the triply powered[c] that exists in all.

III. DESCRIPTION OF THE UNRECOGNIZABLE

The Foreigner's attempt to understand the vision

14   I was seeking to understand[d] the ineffable and unrecognizable god, of which people are certainly uncomprehending even if they understand it,
19 the intermediation of the threefold power that is located in stillness and quietness and which is unrecognizable.
22   Now, once I was strong in these, the powers of the luminaries said
25 to me, •"It is enough that through the search for the incomprehensibles
28 you might disperse the inactive element that resides in you. •Yet, listen (to us) about this subject, insofar as may be possible with a first manifestation and a manifestation.[e]

Can the unrecognizable be described?

32   "Now, its possession of any given nonessential property resides in   BJn 2:26+
its mode of existing, either in existing and being about to be, or in being
36 active, or in understanding and being alive— •although, in an incomprehensible way, it does not possess intellect, life, reality, or unreality.
1 **62**   And it has any given nonessential property along with its essential existent property without its being left behind[a] in any way, at the time that it causes something undertaken, or purifies, [or] receives, or bestows; likewise without its being [. . .] in any way, [whether] through its will
10 alone or in bestowing or in receiving from another. •Nor has it any will, neither (one deriving) from itself nor (one bestowed) through another.
13,14 It is not toward its own self that it proceeds; •yet neither does it, in itself, bestow anything out of itself, lest it become . . . in some other
17 way. •Accordingly, it does not need intellect or life, or indeed anything
20 at all: •for, in (its) lacking ⟨nothing⟩ and being unrecognizable, i.e. in nonexistent reality, it is superior to the entireties, inasmuch as it possesses silence and stillness, lest it be . . . by those that are not . . .
27,30   "It is neither divinity nor blessedness nor perfection. •Rather, (each   BJn 2:33
of these) is an unrecognizable nonessential property of it, and not its
32 essential property. •Rather, it is some other, superior to blessedness, divinity, and perfection.
36   "Indeed, it is not perfect: rather, it is some other, superior thing.
1 **63**   It is not infinite, nor [is] limit bestowed upon it by [some] other:
5 rather, it is some other, superior thing. •It is not corporeal; it is not   BJn 3:22
6,8 incorporeal. •It is not large; [it is not] small. •It is not quantifiable; it is
9 not a [creature]; •nor is it something that exists, i.e. which one could
11 understand; •but rather it is [something] else, which is superior,[a] i.e.

b. The invisible spirit.

c. I.e. the Barbēlō.

d. By progressive mystical introspection, the Foreigner has "beheld" the ineffable, i.e. gained acquaintance (*gnōsis*) of it (61:8f). Yet to "understand" the vision of this object is a different task, the task of philosophy; hence the heavy philosophical style of the revelation that follows.

e. The following description of god may be compared with BJn 2:33f. In some ways

it is typical of second-century Platonist philosophy. The precise details of translation are somewhat conjectural throughout this section.

62 a. "left behind": or "distinct."

63 a. A more obvious translation of the Coptic phrase would be "but rather it is a superior nonessential property."

14 which one could not understand. •It is a first manifestation and ac-
17 quaintance therewith, although it is understood only by itself, •inasmuch
as it is not anything among the existents, but something superior, among
the superiors.

20   "Yet, like its essential property and any given nonessential property
21,24 of it, •it neither shares in eternity nor shares in spans of time. •It neither
25,26 receives anything from another, •nor is it . . . •It neither is . . . anything,
28 nor is it un- . . . •Rather, it is attainment (?) of itself alone, at the same
31 time as being unrecognizable, •(and) at the same time as being superior,
33 in (its) unknowability, to those which are good; •possessing a blessedness,
35 a perfection, a quietness—〈not〉 blessedness 〈itself〉 or perfection itself
37 with a stillness, •but rather (each of these as) a nonessential property of
it as it exists, which one could not understand, and which is still.

2 **64**   "Yet these are nonessential properties that are unrecognizable to
4,6 all. •And in beauty it is far superior to all those which are good. •Thus
9 it is utterly unrecognizable to all and by all, •although it is in all—and
not just in unrecognizable acquaintance that exists according as it (the
12 ineffable) really is. •And it is reconciled through[a] the nonrecognition
14,16 that looks toward it. •How is it unrecognizable? •Or does any behold it
18 as it utterly exists? •If one should say that it exists as something, such
as acquaintance, one has acted impiously toward it, and has been
23 sentenced to not being acquainted with god: •not sentenced by that
(ineffable), which neither cares about anything nor possesses any will,
29 but rather self-sentenced •because of not having discovered the really
30 existent first principle. •Such a person has gone blind, outside the still
eye of activated manifestation, which derives from the triply powered   BJn 4:19
belonging to the first thought of the invisible spirit, which thus exists   FTh 38:5?
[. . .]"[b] * * *

17 **65**   "beauty, . . . of stillness, quietness, stillness, and great unsearch-
21 ability. •In having been shown forth, it has no need of spans of time,
25 not even of eternity—but rather, of itself alone, •since it is unsearchably
26 unsearchable, •and does not activate (anything), not even itself, and so
28,30 it exists in stillness. •And it is not reality, and so it does not lack. •In
31 terms of being in a place, it is a body; •but in terms of being in a
32,34 dwelling, it is incorporeal; •possesses nonexistent reality; •belongs to[a]
35,36 all, as itself; and •has no will. •Rather, it is a great superiority of
37 greatness, •and superior to its stillness, so that [. . .]"[b] * * *

19,20 **66**   •"Nor does anyone who shares in it receive power. •Nothing
activates it, in accord with (its) still sameness.

23,23   "Indeed, it is unrecognizable. •For, it is a place without spirit[a] of
25 infinity, •at the same time as being infinite, powerless, and nonexistent.
27,28 It does not bestow existence: •rather, it receives all these (spiritual
beings) unto itself in stillness, standing at rest out of that which always
32 stands at rest, •since eternal life has been shown forth: (viz.) the invisible
35 and triply powerful spirit, •the One, which is in all these beings that are
existent, and which surrounds them all, though being more exalted than
all."[b] * * *

18 **67**   "It [has] stood at rest prior (?) [to] these (?), bestowing power upon
19 all these (spiritual beings); •and has filled all these.

---

64 a. Or "reconciled to."   b. The next half page of the MS has been
   b. The next half page of the MS has been   destroyed.
destroyed.

65 a. Or "exists for."   **66** a. Or "breath."
                                                 b. The next half page of the MS has been
                                                destroyed.

Limits upon further speculation

20   "Truly, you have listened firmly (to us) concerning all these things.
22,24 Do not seek to understand[a] anything more. Rather, go. •We are not   BJn 4:15+
      acquainted with whether the unrecognizable possesses angels or gods;
28   nor whether the still has anything within it but stillness, i.e. its own self;
32   and so it is not . . . •Nor is it fitting to become dispersed many more
      times by seeking (to understand)."[b] * * *

IV. CIRCUMSTANCES OF COMPOSITION

16 **68**   [It][a] said [to] me, "Write down [whatever] I tell you and remind   BJn 31:28+
20   you about, for the sake of whoever after you may be worthy.[b] •And you   EgG 80:16+
22   shall deposit this book upon a mountain, •and call upon the guardian.
      Come, O Phriktos,[c] guardian of death."
23,25   Now, after saying these things it parted from me. •And for my part,
26,27 I was filled with joy. •And I wrote this book. •It was ordained, O Messos   Porph 16:3
      my child,[d] that I should disclose to you the things that have been
31   proclaimed unto me within myself. •I first received them in great silence
34   and stood at rest as I really was, preparing myself. •These are the things
      that were disclosed to me, O [Messos] my child [. . .]"[e] * * *

67 a. Cf. note 61d.
   b. The next half page of the MS has been destroyed.

68 a. The exact narrative context is lost. The Foreigner now converses with one interlocutor rather than several.
   b. The holy seed of Seth.
   c. The Greek word means "dreadful, awesome."
   d. "my child": the style in which a spiritual teacher addresses a disciple. The same word also means "my son." For "Messos," see note 57b.
   e. The final half page of the text has been destroyed except for a few words of the last sentence, in which the Foreigner perhaps encourages Messos to disseminate the contents of the treatise, followed by the title (at 69:20): "[. . .] publish (?) [them, O] Messos [my] child, [. . .] seal [. . .] all the [. . .]. The Foreigner (69:14–20)."

THE THREE TABLETS OF SETH
(3Tb)

Contents

In gnostic myth, hymnody (parallel strophes) is the usual mode by which one divine being addresses another (e.g. BJn 9:7f) or the savior speaks to the gnostic soul (BJn 30:13f). In *The Three Tablets of Seth* ("Three Steles of Seth") two important characters of the myth—the metaphysical archetypes of Seth ("Emmakha Seth") and his father Adam ("Geradamas," i.e. Adamas) express their hymnic adoration of a more abstract being within the structure of the spiritual universe. As in modern Christian hymnals, no explicit setting or mythic actions are described; the reader's acquaintance with the gnostic myth is simply presupposed.

According to the mythic structure of the spiritual universe (as described e.g. in Zs) the two speakers are situated within the lowest constituent of the Barbēlō aeon. Hymns 4, 5, and 6 express their desire for acquaintance with the Barbēlō, i.e. the higher abstraction under which they are subsumed. Hymns 5, 6, and 7 express thanksgiving for the receipt of acquaintance; the pauses between Hymns 4 and 5, 5 and 6, and 6 and 7 are thus moments of mystical contemplation and unification with the Barbēlō. There is no clear reference in the work to attainment of *gnōsis* of the ineffable, unrecognizable first principle, as described in Fr.

Hymns 6 and 7 are phrased as though uttered by more than two speakers (e.g. 124:33f, "we *all* bless you"). The phraseology of these two hymns is particularly suited to recitation by a congregation, and may indicate that 3Tb as a whole is a hymnal of the gnostic church. The gnostics' belief that Emmakha Seth was the archetype of Seth, the founder of the gnostic race, provides adequate justification for them to have joined in his hymns of praise and petition.

The frame story, which recounts the discovery and transcription of the tablets by a certain Dositheus, concludes with reference to an ascent and descent of the soul, analogous to the mysticism of Zs and Fr, and can be read as a liturgical direction for use of the hymns. It speaks of ascent from "the first" to "the second" to "the third" (i.e. the three major constituents of the Barbēlō aeon), then "silence" (mystical contemplation), and finally descent in reverse order.

Literary background

The place of composition of 3Tb is unknown. Its date of composition must be sometime before A.D. 350, the approximate date of the MS. In philosophical and mythic content the work resembles EgG, RAd, FTh, Zs, and Fr. The transcript of the tablets is attributed to a certain Dositheus, possibly meaning the ancient sect leader of that name (cf. note 118b). But it is impossible to know whether 3Tb is actually by him, by another writer of that name, or an example of pseudepigraphy. Beyond the assertion that Dositheus transcribed the three tablets, their authorship is attributed (118:10f) to the great Seth, i.e. the spiritual archetype Emmakha Seth; the work is thus in any case pseudepigraphic. The language of composition was Greek.

The mixture of genres in 3Tb is slightly complex, combining three traditional materials:

I. Heavenly message
    A. Hymnal
    B. Directions for use

As in RAd and EgG, the whole work is presented (118:10f) as a *heavenly message*, in this instance left by Seth (the metaphysical archetype) in the form of three stone tablets, and subsequently discovered by Dositheus. The convention of the heavenly message is a commonplace of ancient Mediterranean revelation literature; in the message of 3Tb, Seth speaks in the first person. The Roman Jewish historian Josephus (*Antiquities* 1.2.3) records the popular belief that Seth, son of Adam, had left esoteric information for his posterity in the form of tablets on a high mountain; 3Tb may be a literary elaboration of that tradition. The body of the heavenly message is a *hymnal*, consisting of seven hymns distributed in three "tablets" (the sevenfold division is hypothetical; there is no sign of division between hymns in the MS). The hymns are followed by what appear to be *directions for use* or at least a reference to use of the hymnal in congregational mystical communion.

Mythic characters

I. Eternals Mentioned in the Work

The INVISIBLE PARENT. The One.
The BARBĒLŌ aeon
Constituents of the Barbēlō aeon:
    1. THE CONCEALED AEON
    2. THE FIRST-MANIFEST AEON
    3. THE SELF-ORIGINATE AEON
        GERADAMAS
        EMMAKHA SETH, his son
        The LIVING AND IMMOVABLE RACE
The WORD (or verbal expression)
Various POWERS, etc.

II. Humankind Mentioned in the Work

The SEED OF SETH, the elect, including DOSITHEUS

Text

The original Greek apparently does not survive. The text is known only in Coptic translation, attested by a single manuscript from Nag Hammadi, MS NHC VII (pp. 118–27), which was copied just before A.D. 350 and is now in the Cairo Coptic Museum.

The translation below is based on an advance copy of J. M. Robinson's critical edition of the Coptic, kindly supplied by him: in F. Wisse, ed., *Nag Hammadi Codex VII* (Nag Hammadi Studies; Leiden: E. J. Brill, forthcoming).

SELECT BIBLIOGRAPHY

Isser, S. J. *The Dositheans: A Samaritan Sect in Late Antiquity*. Studies in Judaism in Late Antiquity, vol. 17. Leiden: E. J. Brill, 1976. (Ancient traditions about Dositheus.)

Reinink, G. J. "Das Land 'Seiris' (Šir) und das Volk der Serer in jüdischen und christlichen Traditionen." *Journal for the Study of Judaism* 6 (1975): 72–85.

Robinson, J. M. "The Three Steles of Seth and the Gnostics of Plotinos." In *Proceedings of the International Colloquium on Gnosticism, Stockholm, August 20–25, 1973*, edited by Geo Widengren, 132–42. Stockholm: Almqvist & Wiksell, 1977.

Speyer, W. "Religiöse Pseudepigraphie und literarische Fälschung im Altertum." *Jahrbuch für Antike und Christentum* 8/9 (1965–66): 88–125. Reprinted in *Pseudepigraphie in der heidnischen und jüdisch-christlichen Antike*, edited by N. Brox, 195–263. Wege der Forschung, vol. 484. Darmstadt: Wissenschaftliche Buchgesellschaft, 1977. (The heavenly message as a convention of pseudepigraphy.)

Tardieu, M. "Les Trois Stèles de Seth." *Revue des sciences philosophiques et théologiques* 57 (1973): 545–75.

THE THREE TABLETS OF SETH[a]

I. CIRCUMSTANCES OF COMPOSITION

Introduction: Dositheus's vision of the tablets

10 **118** Report of Dositheus,[b] (consisting) of the three tablets[c] of Seth,[d]
13 father of the living[e] and immovable race.[f] •He[g] remembered what he
16 saw,[h] gained acquaintance of, and read; •and he delivered it, just as it
was written there, unto the elect.[i]

EpG 26.8.1?
Zs 130:1
BJn 9:11+
EgG 80:15

His report

19,21 Many times I[j] joined in glorifying along with the powers.[k] •And I was
deemed worthy by the immeasurable greatnesses.
24 And they[l] are as follows.

II. THE TEXT OF THE TABLETS

THE FIRST TABLET OF SETH[m]

Hymn 1: Emmakha Seth's praise of the Geradamas

25 I[n] praise you, O father, O Geradamas[o]—
26 I, your own son Emmakha Seth, whom you have ingenerately
produced for the praise of our god.
30 For, I am your own son,
31 And it is you who are my intellect, my father.
1 **119** Now, I for my part have sown and begotten:
3 While you, for your part, have beheld the greatnesses, and
have stood at rest[a] ceaselessly.
4 I praise you, [O] father: bless me, O father.

BJn 8:28+
Zs 6:21+

Title 118 a. In the manuscript, the title is found after the text (at 127:27).

b. "Dositheus": the name Dositheus and a sect of "Dositheans" were mentioned in a list of sectarian leaders cited in the second century A.D. by the anti-gnostic writer Hegesippus; other ancient and medieval sources occasionally refer to an ancient leader or sect of this name, but never with much detail or precise indication of date.

c. "tablet," Greek *stēlē*: a monumental stone slab set upright in a permanent base and bearing an incised inscription. Such tablets were commonly erected in ancient cities as records of important public documents.

d. The eternal Seth, in this text called "Emmakha Seth."

e. "living": gnostic jargon used in this text to indicate membership in the eternal realm.

f. The eternal posterity of the eternal Seth.

g. Dositheus.

h. Presumably the tablets had been set up in the eternal realm, since their author is the spiritual Seth (cf. note 118e); this implies that Dositheus "saw" them either in a vision

or in the course of a heavenly voyage like the one described in Zs.

i. The seed of Seth, son of Adam, on earth.

j. Dositheus.

k. Dositheus's act of "joining in" the heavenly liturgy sets a precedent for use of the tablets by human worshipers. Cf. also note 124c.

l. The tablets.

m. The chapter title of the first tablet is copied only at the end of the chapter, at 121:16f.

n. The eternal Seth.

o. "Geradamas" or "Ger-Adamas," i.e. Adamas (cf. BJn note 8f): father of the eternal Seth. According to Zs he and his son are located in the Barbēlō aeon, within the self-originate aeon, at the luminaries Harmozēl and Ōroiaēl, respectively.

119 a. To "stand at rest" is philosophical jargon for the state of permanence, non-change, and real being, as opposed to what exists in instability, change, and becoming.

6   It is because of you that I exist: it is because of god that you
     exist.

7   Because of you I exist under (the authority of) that being.

9   You are light, beholding light: you have shown forth light.

11   You are a Mirotheas: it is you who are my Mirotheos.[b]   120:15
                                                                      EgG 60:30
13   I praise you as a deity, I praise your divinity:

15   Great is the good self-originate (aeon),[c] which has stood at
     rest.

17   O deity that stood at rest in the beginning,

18   You came with good, and you were shown forth: and you
     showed forth a good.

20   I shall utter your name: for you are a prime name.

22   You are unengendered: for your part, you have been shown
     forth so that you might show forth those which are eternal.

25   It is you who are the one that is existent: therefore you have
     shown forth those which are really existent.

27   It is you who are spoken of by voice: but by intellect you are
     glorified.

30   It is you who are powerful everywhere.

31   Because of you and your seed [the] perceptible universe is
     acquainted with you: you are merciful.

1   **120** And you derive from a foreign thing:[a] and it presides   120:11
     over a foreign thing.

3   But now, you derive from a foreign thing: and it presides
     over a foreign thing.

5   You derive from a foreign thing: for you are [dissimilar].[b]

6   And you are merciful: for you are eternal.

8   It is over a people that you preside: for you have caused all
     these (spiritual beings)[c] to increase.

9   And (you did this) for the sake of my seed: for it is you who   BJn 9:14+
     recognize that it resides in (the realms of) generation.[d]

11   And they derive from foreigners: for they are dissimilar.   Fr 59:9

13   And it is over foreigners that they preside: for they reside in
     life.

15   You are a Mirotheos:[e] I praise its power, which has been   119:11+
     given unto me.

Hymn 2: Praise of the Barbēlō[f]

17   O you who have caused the really existent masculinities to be
     thrice-male![g]

---

b. "Mirotheas . . . Mirotheos": a Greek neologism, possibly meaning "divine part" (*moiros theios*). The spelling of the MS has been reproduced in the English translation.

c. The lowest of the three subconstituents of the Barbēlō aeon, in which the eternal Seth and the Geradamas are located. Cf. note 118o.

120 a. Or "an alien thing" (the same word is translated "foreigner" in Fr): the invisible parent. In the following verses, all the eternal world of emanations is a "foreign thing"; likewise, the seed of Seth on earth are "foreigners" who "derive from foreigners," i.e. from the living and immovable race that is their prototype.

b. "[dissimilar]": the word is partially preserved in the MS. Cf. 120:11f.

c. "all these," namely, spiritual beings: gnostic jargon used in this text, probably meaning the sum total of spiritual reality deriving from the Barbēlō aeon; cf. Zs note 2e.

d. "my seed . . . in (the realms of) generation": the seed of Seth on earth.

e. Cf. note 119b.

f. The eternal Seth and the Geradamas speak, jointly praising the Barbēlō aeon, from which they ultimately derive and within which they are located. Hymns 2–4 speak of the Barbēlō's emanations and immanence within the perceptible realm.

g. "masculinities . . . thrice-male": cf. EgG note 51f, BJn 5:6f.

19   O you who have been divided into the quintet![h]   BJn 6:2
20   O you who have been given to us in triple powerfulness!   121:32+
22   O you who have been ingenerately produced!
23   O you who have emanated from the superior (realm), and for
         the sake of the inferior (realm) have gone forth into the
         middle![i]
26   You are a parent (produced) by a parent:[j] an utterance from a
         command.
29   We praise you, O thrice-male: for you have unified the
         entirety[k] from out of all.
31   For, you have bestowed power upon us.
32   You have come into existence from the One[l] by the One.
33   You have traveled:[m] you have entered the One.
34   [You] have saved, you have saved, you have saved us.
35   O you who are crowned, O you who crown: we praise you
         eternally.
2   **121** We praise you—we who, in our capacity as those who
         are perfect and particular, have become wholly saved,
4   We who are perfect because of you,
5   We who [became] perfect along with you.
6   O you who are perfect!
6   O you who perfect!
7   O you who are perfect through all these (spiritual beings)!
8   O you who are everywhere similar!
8   O thrice-male!
9   You have stood at rest: you stood at rest in the beginning.
10   You have become divided everywhere:[a] you have remained
         One.
11   And you have saved whomever you desired: and you desire
         that all worthy people become saved.
14   You are perfect! You are perfect! You are perfect![b]

THE SECOND TABLET OF SETH

Hymn 3: Praise of the Barbēlō[c]

20   Great is the masculine, virgin, first aeon Barbēlō, the   BJn 4:36
         invisible parent's first glory![d]
23   O you (sing.) who are called perfect, you yourself have
         beheld in the beginning that what is first really existent is
         nonexistent.[e]
27   And from it and through it you came into existence eternally
         in the beginning.
30   O you who are nonexistent[f] from an undivided, thrice-   BJn 3:26
         [powerful] One,

---

h. Although mostly speaking of the Barbēlō aeon as a tripartite structure, the author
of 3Tb here accepts the quintet structure
elaborated in BJn, demonstrating that the
two structures were not necessarily held to
be mutually exclusive.
   i. Or "into public view."
   j. The Barbēlō is "parent" of its constituents, even while being a product of the
invisible parent or One.
   k. "entirety": the sum total of spiritual
reality deriving from the Barbēlō aeon.
   l. Cf. 120:26f.
   m. I.e. become immanent; cf. BJn 30:13f.

121 a. I.e. become immanent.
   b. In the MS the chapter title of the first
tablet is written here as a subscript.
   c. The eternal Seth and the Geradamas
speak.
   d. The Barbēlō is the first emanation of
the invisible parent. Cf. BJn 4:26f.
   e. "nonexistent": or "without essence."
Cf. BJn 3:26.
   f. Or "O you who are without essence."
The Barbēlō aeon is here addressed by an
epithet of its parent.

32 You are a threefold power!ᵍ

33 You are [a] mighty unit from [an] uncontaminated unit!

1   **122** You are a superior unit!ᵃ

1   O first shadowᵇ of the holy parent, light from light,

4   [We] praise you.

5   O you who produce perfect beings and who are a cause of
     aeons,

6   You yourself have [beheld] those which are eternal, for they
     derive from a shadow.

8   And you have been a cause of multiplicity:ᶜ
     And you have found and remained One, while yet being a
     cause of multiplicityᵈ in order to become divided.

10 You are a threefold replication: truly you are thrice
     replicated.

12 You are One belonging to the One: and you derive from its
     shadow.

14 You are a concealed (aeon):ᵉ you are a world of
     acquaintance;

16 For, you understand that those which belong toᶠ the One
     derive from a shadow.

17 And theseᵍ are yours in (your) heart.

18 For the sakeʰ of these, byⁱ essentiality you have bestowed
     power upon those which are eternal.

20 By vitalityʲ you have bestowed power upon divinity.ᵏ

22 By goodness you have bestowed power upon understanding.

23 By blessednessˡ you have bestowed power upon the shadows
     that flow from the One.

26 By understanding you have bestowed power upon one;

27 By creation you have bestowed power upon another;

28 You have bestowed power upon the same and the different,ᵐ
     the similar and the dissimilar.

31 In (the realms of) becoming and (of) intelligible form you
     have bestowed power, by that which is existent untoⁿ
     others . . . and [. . .].

34 Upon these—which means, Thatᵒ Concealed (Aeon) in the
     heartᵖ—[you have bestowed] power.

2   **123** And you [have] emanated unto these and [out of] these.

3   You get dividedᵃ among them;

4   And you become a great, masculine, first-manifest intellect.ᵇ

120:20, 122:10
123:23
EgG 50:23 +
v.33
BJn 2:26

121:32 +

g. Or (continuing the verse) "belonging to a threefold power."

122 a. "unit . . . unit . . . unit": or "monad . . . monad . . . monad."

b. "shadow": i.e. image.

c. Or "you have bestowed number."

d. Or "bestowing number."

e. The "concealed (aeon)" is the highest of the three constituents of the Barbēlō aeon, according to Zs.

f. Or "those of."

g. I.e. "those which belong to the One."

h. Or "because."

i. "by": here and in the following verses, the word can also be translated "in."

j. "vitality": an aspect of the self-originate aeon according to Zs, but of the first-manifest according to Fr.

k. "divinity": an aspect of the concealed aeon according to Zs and Fr.

l. "blessedness": an aspect of the first-manifest aeon according to Zs, but of the self-originate according to Fr.

m. "same . . . different": or "equal . . . unequal."

n. Possibly a new verse began with this word.

o. As in RAd, the term "That" is gnostic jargon indicating membership in the spiritual realm.

p. Cf. note 122e. As in Fr, constituents of the Barbēlō aeon, such as "That Concealed Aeon," are both the macrocosmic structure of god and the microcosmic structure of the individual self ("the heart").

123 a. Or "shared."

b. I.e. either the first-manifest or the self-originate aeon. Cf. note 122l.

Hymn 4: Petition to Barbēlō the parent

6   O god the parent! O divine child!ᶜ O producer of multiplicity!
8   In respect of division of all those which are really existent
           you (sing.) have shown forth a verbal expression (or Word)
           unto all.
11   And you possess all these (spiritual beings) ingenerately and
           eternally, without (participation in) perishing.
14   Becauseᵈ of you (sing.) salvationᵉ has come unto us.
15   From you comes salvation!
16   You are wisdom (Sophia)!ᶠ   BJn 8:19
17   You are acquaintance!
17   It is you who are truth!
18   Becauseᵍ of you is life:ʰ from you comes life.
20   Because of you is intellect: from you comes intellect.
21   You are intellect: you are a world of truth.ⁱ
23   You are a threefold power: you are a threefold replication;   121:32 +
24   Truly, you are thrice replicated, O aeon of aeons!
26   It is you alone who without contamination behold those
           which are first eternal and those which are unengendered:
           but also the first divisions, according as you have been
           divided.
30   Unify us according as you have been unified.
31   Tell us [of] the things that you behold.
33   Bestow power upon us, so that we might become saved up
           into eternal life.
2   **124**   For, as for us, we are a shadow of you.
3   [And] according as you are a shadow of that which is first
           preexistent, hear us first.
6   We are eternal: hear us—we who are perfect and particular.
8   It is you who are the aeon of aeons, O you who are
           collectively wholly perfect.

Hymn 5: Thanksgiving to the Barbēlō

10   You have heard! You have heard!
11   You have saved! You have saved!
12   We give thanks! We praise always! We will glorify you!ᵃ

THE THIRD TABLET ⟨OF SETH⟩ᵇ

Hymn 6: Collective thanksgiving and petition to Barbēlō the parent

17   Weᶜ rejoice! We rejoice! We rejoice!
18   We have beheld! We have beheld! We have beheld that

---

c. "parent . . . child": cf. note 120j.
d. Or "For the sake of."
e. Or "preservation."
f. "wisdom" is here considered a manifestation of the Barbēlō or perfect forethought of the light, as in BJn (cf. BJn note
20b).
g. Or "for the sake."
h. "life": the spiritual element immanent
in the seed of Seth (BJn note 25c).
i. Or "you are a world; you are truth."

124 a. In the MS the chapter title of the

second tablet is written here as a subscript.
b. In the MS the chapter title of the third
tablet is written here (124:27). The words
"of Seth" are absent, probably through an
inadvertence, in the first of the two places.
c. Hymns 6 and 7 are uttered by a group
of speakers: cf. 124:33f, "we *all* praise you";
125:13f, "acquaintance with you . . . is the
salvation of us *all*"; 126:29f, "we have praised
you: . . . *All of us* do so." Thus the grammatical form of these two hymns is immediately appropriate for use by a congregation.
Cf. note 118k.

which is first really existent[d] as it really exists—as it exists!
20 O you who are first eternal, O you who are unengendered,
22 From you[e] (sing.) come those which are eternal and the
aeons, those which are collectively wholly perfect and
those which are perfect and particular.
25 We praise you, O you who are non-existent,[f] O reality prior
to realities, O first essence prior to essences, O parent of
divinity and vitality, O maker of intellect, O bestower of
good, O bestower of blessedness![g]
33 We all praise you, O you who understand with blessing [. . .],
you because of whom all [. . .],
3 **125** O you who understand yourself through yourself alone!
4 Indeed, there is nothing that is active prior to you.
6 You are spirit, alone and living.
7 And [you] are acquainted with the One:[a] for, we cannot
speak of That One, which everywhere belongs to you;
9 For, your light is shining upon us.
11 Command us to behold you, so that we might be saved.
13 It is acquaintance with you that is the salvation of us all.
14 Command! If you command, then we have been saved!

Hymn 7: Collective thanksgiving to the Barbēlō

16 Truly we have been saved!
17 We have beheld you by means of intellect.
18 It is you who are all these (spiritual beings).
18 Indeed, you save all these (spiritual beings)—you, who
moreover shall not be saved, nor have been saved, by
them;
21 For, as for you, you have commanded unto us.
23 You are the One, you are the One[b]—according as a person
might speak of you, you are the One;
25 You are a single, living spirit.
26 How shall we say your name? It is not ours to say!
28 For, it is you who are the reality of all these (spiritual
beings).
30 It is you who are the life of all these (spiritual beings).
31 It is you who are the intellect of all these (spiritual beings).
32 [It is] you in whom all [these] (spiritual beings) rejoice.
1 **126** For your part, you have commanded all these (spiritual
beings) to [. . .] in your [. . .] them, the [. . .] before it.
5 [O] blessed concealed (aeon) Sēnaōn, [. . .] from its own self!
O [. . .]neus!
O . . ephneus!
O Optaōn!
O great power, Elemaōn!
O Emouniar!
O Nibareus!

d. Some of the language in this hymn could also refer to the invisible parent of the Barbēlō aeon (cf. 121:23f), yet the hymn is clearly addressed to the Barbēlō and not its parent (125:7f, "[you] are acquainted with the One: for, we cannot speak of That One, which everywhere belongs to you").
e. "you" is addressed to one being throughout the hymn; it is grammatically singular.

f. Or "who are without essence."
g. "divinity . . . vitality . . . blessedness": aspects of the three Barbēlō constituents. Cf. notes 122j, k, and l.

125 a. The invisible parent.
b. The Barbēlō aeon is here addressed by an epithet of the invisible parent.

O Kandēphoros!
O Aphrēdōn!
O Dēiphaneus!   Zs 119:6?

11   It is you who are Armēdōn ⟨for⟩ these:[a] O you who produce   Zs 119:4?
powers, O Thalanatheus, O Antitheus!   Zs 127:7?

14   It is you who reside within your own self.

15   It is you who are before[b] your own self: and after you, none
have come providing activation.

17   With what shall we praise you? We cannot!

19   But as inferior beings we give thanks to you;

20   For, you, who are superior, have commanded us to glorify
you as we are able.

24   We praise you, perpetually glorifying you: for we have been
saved.

26   So that we might be saved unto eternal salvation, we will
glorify you.

29   We have blessed you: for we are able.

30   We have been saved: for you have wished (it) always.

32   All of us do so;[c] all of us do so.

33   [. . .] through [. . .],

4   **127**   Who has [. . .], us together with those who [. . .].

III. DOSITHEUS'S DIRECTIONS FOR USE OF THE HYMNS

The mystical ascent

6   Whoever remembers these[a] and always glorifies shall be perfect among
11 those who are perfect and impassive beyond all things; •for, particularly
and collectively they all praise these: and afterward they shall be silent.

14,15   And just as it has been ordained for them, they will ascend.[b] •After   Zs, Fr
silence,[c] they will descend from the third: they will bless the second;
20 and afterward, the first. •The way of ascent is the way of descent.[d]   BJn 20:21

21   Understand, then, O you who live, that you have succeeded, and
have taught yourselves about the infinites: marvel at the truth that is
within them, and the manifestation.[e]

IV. DOSITHEUS'S CONCLUDING BENEDICTION

28,30   This text[f] belongs to the kinship.[g] It is the son[h] who wrote it. •Bless
31 me, O parent: I praise you, O parent. •In peace. Amen!

---

126 a. The MS has "It is you who are
Armēdōn for me."
   b. "before": in either a temporal or a
spatial sense.
   c. I.e. "All of us praise you."

127 a. These tablets.
   b. A mystical ascent such as described in
Zs.
   c. The moment of highest contemplation,

cf. Fr. 59:18f and note 59f.
   d. A dictum of Heraclitus (Frag. 60, Diels).
   e. In the manuscript, the title of this work
is written here (at 127:27).
   f. Or "this manuscript," in which case
the concluding words are a note by the
copyist or a predecessor, and not part of the
original text.
   g. The gnostic church.
   h. Or "an offspring."

SATORNINOS

According to
St. Irenaeus of Lyon
Against Heresies 1.24.1–2
(IrSat)

Contents and literary background

Not enough is known about the teaching of Satorninos to be sure it is a product of the gnostic sect. If it is, he is one of the earliest teachers whose name can be associated with the gnostics. This summary of his teaching by St. Irenaeus of Lyon, written in Greek about A.D. 180, may be based either on a treatise by Satorninos himself, or else a pseudepigraphic work (like the others collected here) that Satorninos was known to have written or used. It parallels the full extent of gnostic myth from the description of the first principle ("a single parent, unrecognizable by all") down to the final destruction of the heavenly rulers ("angels"), among whom is the god of the Jews. Although it is extremely compressed and brief, the summary refers to almost all parts of the gnostic myth, as well as related topics such as components of the human being, genealogies of humankind, the history of Israel, principles of biblical interpretation, Christology, and ethics. No single gnostic work is more comprehensive than this; it is thus possible that the document here summarized parallels an original statement of gnostic myth that underlies other gnostic scriptures.

A little earlier in the same chapter, St. Irenaeus reports that Satorninos was from the city of Antioch in Syria (see Map 1). Nothing else is known about the circumstances or exact date of his career.

Mythic characters

I. Immortals Mentioned by St. Irenaeus

The PARENT
The ANOINTED (Christ)
The SUPERIOR POWER

II. Rulers Mentioned by St. Irenaeus

SEVEN ANGELS who created the world, among them being the god of the Jews (Sabaōth?)
Other ANGELS, ARCHANGELS, AUTHORITIES, POWERS

SATAN
DEMONS

III. Humankind Mentioned by St. Irenaeus

The FIRST HUMAN BEING (Adam)
An EVIL HUMAN RACE
A GOOD HUMAN RACE, having the spark of life within it

Text

St. Irenaeus wrote in Greek; part of the original Greek text of this passage survives in a quotation by the third-century father of the church, St. Hippolytus of Rome (*Against Heresies* 7.28). But the complete passage is known only in an ancient Latin version of Irenaeus's work, attested by a number of medieval manuscripts. The translation below is based on the critical edition of Rousseau and Doutreleau, with alterations: A. Rousseau and L. Doutreleau, eds., *Irénée de Lyon, Contre les hérésies: Livre I* [Book 1] (Sources chrétiennes, no. 264; Paris: Le Cerf, 1979), vol. 2, 320–4.

The parent

1.24.1 Satorninos refers to a single parent, unrecognizable by all,[a] BJn 2:26+
who made angels, archangels, powers, and authorities.[b]

Creation of the universe

And the world and all things in it were engendered by some seven of BJn 12:33+
these angels. BJn 11:4

Projection of an image. Creation of Adam.

Moreover, the (first) human being[c]—he says—was a creation of angels, BJn 14:18+
in response to the appearance of a luminous image coming down from
the realm of absolute power. Because they could not lay hold of that
(image), since it immediately retreated back upward, they exhorted one
another saying, "Let us create a human being after the image and after
the likeness."

His immobility. Passage of a spark of life into Adam.

When this had happened—he says—and when the modeled form BJn 19:10+
proved to be unable to stand erect because of the angels' impotence,
and rather writhed on the ground like a worm, the superior power[d] had BJn 19:15
pity upon him because he had come into being after her[e] likeness; and
that (power) sent a spark of life,[f] which aroused the human being, raised BJn 20:14+
him up, and made him be alive. EpS 39.2.4

1.24.1 a. Or "unknown to all." Possibly
corresponding to the invisible virgin spirit of
BJn.

b. "who made . . . authorities." In the
system of BJn and similar works, all beings
derive ultimately from the unrecognizable
parent, but do so by a very complex genealogy that is interrupted by the error of
wisdom: cf. BJn 4:26–12:33f. Possibly Irenaeus skips or compresses this in his account
of Satorninos.

c. Adam.

d. Possibly corresponding to forethought,
the Barbēlō aeon, in BJn.

e. "her": i.e. "the superior power's."

f. Possibly corresponding in BJn to the
luminous afterthought called "life."

The spark alone is destined for salvation

Thus after the end (of one's life)—he says—this spark of life returns to the elements like it;[g] and the other parts[h] dissolve into those out of which they came into being.

The incarnate savior's body was apparent and not material

1.24.2   And he postulates that the savior was unengendered, incorporeal, and formless, and was shown forth as a human being only in appearance.[a]   EpA 40.8.2

Judaism worships an angel

And—he says—the god of the Jews is one of the angels. And because the parent wished to destroy all the rulers, the anointed (Christ)[b] came for the destruction of the god of the Jews and for the salvation[c] of those who might be persuaded by him: and these are the ones who have the spark of life within them.[d]

RR 95:13
BJn 31:1
RAd 83:23
RR 97:10
FTh 43:4
EgG 74:19
EpS 39.2.5

Two human races

Indeed, there are—he says—two human races which were modeled by the angels, one wicked and the other good.[e] And inasmuch as the demons were assisting wicked people, the savior came for the destruction of bad human beings and demons and for the salvation[f] of good ones.

BJn 25:20+
RAd 71:20
RR 96:19
EgG 71:6
EpS 39.2.6

Ethics

And he says that marriage and the engendering of offspring are from Satan.[g] And most of his followers abstain from (the flesh of) living things,[h] and they deceive many people by this feigned abstinence.

BJn 24:26+

Principle of biblical interpretation

And certain of the prophecies[i] (he says) were spoken by the angels who created the world, others by Satan. The latter—he postulates—was itself also an angel, which opposed the ones that created the world and opposed above all the god of the Jews.[j]

BJn 22:22+
IrUnid 1.30.11
EpG 26.6.1
RR 95:13+

---

g. I.e. to the immortal realm.

h. I.e. components of the human being, such as material body and its animating force.

1.24.2 a. The doctrine (called "docetism") that the real Jesus did not exist as human flesh, but only appeared to do so.

b. "anointed" and "Christ" are the same word in Greek.

c. Or "preservation."

d. Possibly corresponding to the posterity of Seth in BJn.

e. Possibly corresponding to the posterity of Cain and the posterity of Seth.

f. Or "preservation."

g. Like RR, Satorninos does not equate Satan (called Sakla, Ialdabaôth) and the "god of the Jews" (Sabaôth). Cf. below.

h. Abstinence from meat, alcohol, and sexual activity was a common form of asceticism (called "encratism") practiced by religions and philosophies of the ancient Mediterranean world.

i. Of Jewish scripture (the Old Testament).

j. Possibly as in RR, where Ialdabaôth, called Sakla (i.e. Satan), opposes the other rulers, who are led by Sabaôth (the god of Israel).

THE GNOSTICS

ACCORDING TO
ST. IRENAEUS OF LYON
AGAINST HERESIES 1.29
(IrG)

Contents and literary background

Unlike his summary of the teaching of Satorninos, St. Irenaeus's account of the gnostics (sometimes called "Barbelognostics"), written in Greek about A.D. 180, is detailed and clearly tells the very myth that underlies BJn. Its importance is not in providing information about the contents of the myth, but in connecting the myth with gnostic Christianity as such. The coherence of the cycle of classic gnostic works is only a matter of their systematic interrelationship, for the scripture itself provides no obvious grounds for connection with any precise historical group. It is St. Irenaeus's remark in the opening paragraph of this excerpt that constitutes the primary evidence for such a connection.

The material that St. Irenaeus has chosen to excerpt covers only the first act of the mythic drama (expansion of the first principle into a full spiritual universe), followed by the production of the imperfect craftsman of the material world. It is impossible to know how much more was covered in the document from which he extracted this summary; in any case it is not likely to have simply ended with the production of the world craftsman, as here. (Cf. also the introduction to IrUnid.)

Despite its overall agreement with BJn, a number of peculiar details indicate that the excerpt is based on either a different work or an edition of BJn that differs from the ones that survive: the fact that the main emanations (aeons) of the first principle are explicitly arranged in pairs; the distinction of the anointed (Christ) from the self-originate (as in EgG but not BJn); and wisdom's epithet Prounikos, "the vulgar."

Mythic characters

I. Immortals Mentioned by St. Irenaeus

The PARENT. The virgin spirit.
[*The next ten aeons can be listed either as in* BJn *or in the form of five duets. Both arrangements are given below.*]
A QUINTET OF AEONS:

1. The BARBĒLŌTH. A thought, the parent's thinking.
2. PRIOR ACQUAINTANCE

3. INCORRUPTIBILITY
4. ETERNAL LIFE
5. TRUTH

The ANOINTED (Christ). Begetter of the entirety.

Its coactors: INTELLECT, WILL, WORD (or verbal expression)
The SELF-ORIGINATE
[*Irenaeus speaks of another arrangement of these aeons, in five duets:*

Word (verbal expression)	=	*Thinking (the Barbēlōth)*
Intellect	=	*Prior acquaintance*
The anointed (Christ)	=	*Incorruptibility*
Will	=	*Eternal life*
The self-originate	=	*Truth*]

FOUR LUMINARIES that stand around the self-originate, and their FOUR ATTENDANTS:

HARMOGENĒS
    LOVELINESS
RAGUĒL
    PERCEPTION
DAUID
    INTELLIGENCE
ĒLĒLĒTH
    PRUDENCE

ADAMAS. The perfect true human being. With Harmogenēs.
PERFECT ACQUAINTANCE, his consort. Joined to Adamas.
The FATHER ⎫
The MOTHER ⎬ *The place of these within the system is not clear.*
The SON ⎭
VULGAR WISDOM (Sophia Prounikos). The mother, a holy spirit, an emanation from the angels that stand beside the self-originate.

II. Rulers Mentioned by St. Irenaeus

The FIRST RULER. Maker of the world.
The first ruler's AUTHORITIES, ANGELS, etc.
Another set of EVIL OFFSPRING, including:

EVIL
JEALOUSY
ENVY
DISCORD
DESIRE

Text

St. Irenaeus wrote in Greek, but the present passage is known only in an ancient Latin version of his work, attested by a number of medieval manuscripts. A summary in Greek of Irenaeus's original Greek text is given by the fifth-century Christian historian Theodoret of Cyrrhus (*Compendium,* 13); it sheds light upon the Greek vocabulary of the original. The translation below is based on the critical edition of the Latin text by Rousseau and Doutreleau with alterations, in comparison with the Greek summary by Theodoret; I have also utilized the classic English translation of Irenaeus by A. Roberts and J. Donaldson (in their *Ante-Nicene Fathers,* vol. 1): A. Rousseau and L. Doutreleau, eds., *Irénée de Lyon, Contre les hérésies: Livre I* [Book 1] (Sources chrétiennes, no. 264; Paris: Le Cerf, 1979), vol. 1, 328–30 (Greek summary); vol 2, 358–64 (Latin).

SELECT BIBLIOGRAPHY

van den Broek, R. "Autogenes and Adamas: The Mythological Structure of the Apocryphon of John." In *Gnosis and Gnosticism: Papers Read at the Eighth International Conference on Patristic Studies (Oxford, September 3rd–8th, 1979)*, 16–25. Nag Hammadi Studies, vol. 17. Leiden: E. J. Brill, 1981.
See also items listed under BJn, "Select Bibliography."

Genealogy and multiplicity of the gnostics

1.29.1 Now in addition, from the aforementioned Simonians[a] a multitude of gnostics[b] have sprung up, and have become shown forth like mushrooms growing out of the ground. We shall now describe the principal opinions that they hold.

TEACHINGS OF THE SECT

The parent and the Barbēlōth

Some of them, then, assume the existence of a certain unaging[c] aeon,[d] which they call Barbēlōth,[e] existing within a virgin spirit.[f] In that place, they say, there exists a certain unnameable parent.[g] And it willed to show itself forth to this Barbēlōth.

BJn 4:36
BJn 3:15
BJn 2:26+

Production of other aeons

Then this thought[h] emanated and stood at rest[i] in its presence, and made a request of it, to have prior acquaintance. And when prior acquaintance, too, had emanated and these,[j] moreover, had made a request, incorruptibility emanated, and then eternal life.

BJn 4:26+
BJn 5:10

BJn 5:20+
BJn 5:26+

Begetting of the anointed (Christ)

Barbēlōth rejoiced in these. And gazing at the magnitude, it (Barbēlōth) took pleasure in the act of conception,[k] and in respect of this (magnitude)

BJn 6:10

1.29.1 a. In an earlier part of the work from which this excerpt comes, Irenaeus had described a sect supposedly founded by Simon Magus (Ac 8:9f). From this sect, he claims, other sects such as the gnostics derive their inspiration.

b. "gnostics," meant as the proper name of a sect. Several versions of the text are attested here, and the original reading is uncertain; possibly it was "Barbēlōgnostics" or "gnostics of Barbēlō."

c. "unaging": or "indestructible."

d. "aeon": or "eternity."

e. "Barbēlōth," Greek fragment; in the Latin version, this word does not have the final -*th*.

f. Or "a certain unaging aeon existing within a virgin spirit that they call Barbēlōth."

g. The "unnameable parent" is the "virgin spirit"; see BJn 2:28f, 3:15f, 4:34f.

h. "this thought": the Barbēlōth, BJn 4:26f.

i. To "stand at rest" is philosophical jargon for the state of permanence, non-change, and real being, as opposed to what exists in instability, change, and becoming.

j. "these": or "it."

k. The Greek fragment next (or instead) has "it became pregnant."

begot light similar to it (the parent). They declare that this was the beginning both of enlightenment[1] and of the begetting of the entirety; and that the parent, beholding this light, anointed it with its own kindness[m] until it became perfect. _{BJn 6:23+}

Its request for coactors

Moreover, they maintain that this was the anointed (Christ),[n] who _{BJn 6:33} again, according to them, made a request that it be given a coactor,[o] namely intellect. And intellect emanated. Moreover, besides these, the parent sent forth the Word (or verbal discourse).

Then the following joined as consorts:

> thinking and the Word (or verbal discourse);
> incorruptibility and the anointed (Christ);
> eternal life and will;
> intellect and prior acquaintance.

These, then, glorified the great light[p] and Barbēlōth.

Emanation of the self-originate and truth

1.29.2   They also state that the self-originate[a] afterward emanated from _{EgG 60:1} thinking and the Word (verbal discourse), in the image of the great light. And they state that it was greatly honored and that the entirety was subordinated to it. Along with this (self-originate) there emanated truth. _{BJn 5:32} And the self-originate and truth joined as consorts.

Emanation of four luminaries and their attendants

And from the light that is the anointed (Christ) and from incorruptibility, _{BJn 7:30+} the four luminaries emanated—they say—to stand around the self-originate.

And again, from will and eternal life, four emanations were produced _{BJn 8:2} so that they might serve the four luminaries. And these they name

> loveliness;
> perception;[b]
> intelligence;
> prudence.

And furthermore, loveliness is subjoined to the first great luminary, _{BJn 8:4} which they consider to be the savior, and which they call Harmogenēs; perception, again, is subjoined to the second luminary, which they also call Raguēl; intelligence, to the third, which they call Dauid; prudence, to the fourth, which they name Ēlēlēth.

Emanation of Adamas and perfect acquaintance

1.29.3   So when all these had been established in this way, the self- _{BJn 8:28+} originate additionally emits[a] a perfect, true human being, whom they

---

l. Or "light."

m. The Greek fragment instead has "It was anointed with the spirit's perfection."

n. "anointed" and "Christ" are the same word in Greek.

o. Or "assistance."

p. "the great light": in BJn (6:13f) the "anointed" is called a "luminous spark consisting of light."

1.29.2 a. Classic gnostic texts do not agree

on the systematic function of the "anointed" and the "self-originate." For example, the two are identical in the system of BJn, but distinct in EgG.

b. The MSS here erroneously have "volition," Greek *thelēsis;* the original text, "perception," Greek *aisthēsis* (or *esthēsis*), is confirmed by BJn 8:2f.

1.29.3 a. The present tense is used for rhetorical effect.

also call Adamas,[b] inasmuch as neither has he himself ever been dominated, nor have those from whom he derived: he, too, was set apart with the first luminary (H)armogenēs.[c] Moreover, perfect acquaintance was emitted by the self-originate along with that human being, and was joined to him as a consort; hence he gained acquaintance of that being which is over the entirety. An invincible faculty was also given to him by the virgin spirit. And the entirety reposed in him, to lift up praise to the great aeon.[d]

The father, mother, and son. The tree of acquaintance.

Hence, too—they say—the mother, the father, and the son were shown forth.[e] And from the human being and acquaintance there sprouted a tree, which they also call acquaintance.[f]

EgG 50:23 +
BJn 22:3 +

Emanation of vulgar wisdom

1.29.4 Next, they say, a holy spirit,[a] whom they also call wisdom (Sophia) and the vulgar element,[b] emanated from the first angel, who stands by the side of the self-originate.

BJn 10:20 +
IrUnid 1.30.3 +
EpG 25.3.2

Her offspring: the first ruler

It,[c] then, perceived that although all the others had consorts it had no consort; and it searched for a being with which it might become united. And since it did not find one, it passed through[d] and extended itself; and it gazed down into the lower region, thinking it would find a consort there; and not finding one, it leaped forth in a state of loathing,[e] because it had taken this impulsive action without the good will of the parent. Then next, influenced by simplicity and kindness, it engendered a product in which resided lack of acquaintance, and also arrogance. This, its product—they say—was the first ruler, the maker of this creation.[f]

BJn 9:25 +

Its theft of power from wisdom. The universe. Other rulers.

Moreover they relate that it stole great power from its mother,[g] and that it retreated from her into the lower region, and made a firmament of heaven, in which—they say—it also dwells. And since it was in (a state of) lack of acquaintance, it made those which are in its charge— authorities, angels, and firmaments, and all earthly things. Next—they say—it united with arrogance, and bore evil, jealousy, envy, discord,[h] and desire.

BJn 10:19 +
RR 87:4 +
BJn 10:27 +
BJn 11:4
RR 96:3

---

b. In Greek, *adamas* means "steel," an unyielding or hard substance.

c. The MSS here erroneously have "he was also set apart from (H)armogenēs along with the first light."

d. Or "eternity."

e. Or "were brought forth."

f. The tree of acquaintance (*gnōsis*) with good and evil, Gn 2:17.

1.29.4 a. Or "the holy spirit."

b. Or possibly "lewd," Greek *prounikos*.

The word basically means "mover, porter," one who corporally transports burdens for a fee.

c. The holy spirit who is wisdom.

d. The MS here erroneously has "it confirmed."

e. Or "weariness."

f. "this creation": i.e. the material world.

g. The holy spirit who is wisdom.

h. Or "fury."

Wisdom's flight into the eighth heaven

When these had been born, the mother, wisdom (Sophia), was deeply   BJn 13:32+
grieved and fled. She departed into a higher place—and it was the eighth
(heaven), counting from below.

The first ruler's arrogance

And since she had thus departed, it[i] imagined that it alone existed.   BJn 13:5+
And on this account it said, "For my part, I am a jealous god, and there   Ex 20:5
is none apart from me."   Dt 49:9
                                                                          Is 46:9
And such are the lies that these (gnostics) tell.

"OTHER" GNOSTIC TEACHINGS

ACCORDING TO
ST. IRENAEUS OF LYON
AGAINST HERESIES 1.30–31
(IrUnid)

Contents and literary background

St. Irenaeus's chapter on the gnostics (IrG) is immediately continued by the one translated here, which summarizes the teaching of certain unidentified "others." It has been suggested that the two chapters really belong together (even if they are not perfectly continuous) and that the "others" are other gnostics; in any case the document being summarized here seems to present a version of the gnostic myth. The summary was written in Greek about A.D. 180. For the most part, the contents of the two chapters are complementary: IrG gives a detailed description of the expansion of the first principle into a full spiritual universe and stops with the creation of the craftsman of the world; IrUnid speaks especially of the production of the craftsman and of the subsequent events of the mythic drama, all of which are touched upon in some detail. Taken together, then, the two chapters present a full summary of the gnostic myth from the production of the Barbēlō (the second principle) down to the end of time, with the ingathering of gnostic souls into their spiritual home and the recovery of the dispersed power.

The first three paragraphs of the present excerpt are a brief and almost incoherent summary of the first act of the mythic drama. They seem to be strangely different from other tellings of the myth, including the one found in IrG. The second act of the gnostic myth, as found in this version, begins with a unique account of the origin of matter ("creation of the heavenly universe")—a topic hardly touched upon in other versions of the myth. In the third act, Adam and Eve are said to have been created twice, once as animate creatures and again as material bodies to encase the animate entities; their expulsion from paradise is allegorized as the beginning of life in material bodies. A comparable version of a double creation (but with reference only to Adam) is found in BJn, following Hellenistic Jewish interpretation of the two creation narratives in Gn 1:26–2:7. Particular emphasis is laid on the final act of the drama (the subsequent history of humankind) as it bears on the history of Israel and the life of Jesus of Nazareth. The Incarnation is explained as the descent of a preexistent Christ into Jesus of Nazareth; Christ is explicitly said to have left Jesus just before his death on the cross. Also discussed are the nature of Jesus' resurrection body and his establishment of gnostic doctrine during a period of post-resurrection teaching.

Of the three short appendixes with which the chapter ends, the second and third seem completely unrelated to the rest of the summary, and may have nothing to do with gnostic Christianity.

Mythic characters

I. Immortals Mentioned by St. Irenaeus

The PARENT OF THE ENTIRETY. The first human being.
The parent's THOUGHT. Its offspring, the second human being.
The HOLY SPIRIT. The first female.
The ANOINTED (Christ)
VULGAR WISDOM (Sophia Prounikos)

II. Rulers Mentioned by St. Irenaeus

(a) The HIGHER SEPTET:
    IALDABAŌTH. Wisdom's offspring, ruler of heaven.
    Ialdabaōth's SIX OFFSPRING
(b) OTHER OFFSPRING of Ialdabaōth's, including:
    FORGETFULNESS
    EVIL
    JEALOUSY
    ENVY
    DEATH
(c) The LOWER SEPTET:
    The "NUN," a snake. The chief worldly demon. Called Michael and Samaël.
    The "*nun*"'s SIX DEMONIC OFFSPRING

III. Humankind Mentioned by St. Irenaeus

ADAM. The first material human being. Created (as a non-material body) in the
    image of the parent of the entirety and of the rulers, then fitted with a material
    body.
EVE, his wife
CAIN
ABEL
SETH
NŌREA, Seth's sister
NOAH
ABRAHAM and his DESCENDANTS
ELIZABETH
JOHN THE BAPTIST, her son by Ialdabaōth
The VIRGIN MARY
JESUS, her son by Ialdabaōth
Jesus' DISCIPLES
People who have HOLY SOULS

Text

    St. Irenaeus wrote in Greek, but the present passage is known only in an ancient
Latin version of his work, attested by a number of medieval manuscripts. A summary
in Greek of Irenaeus's original Greek text is given by the fifth-century Christian
historian Theodoret of Cyrrhus (*Compendium*, 14–15); it sheds light upon the Greek
vocabulary of the original. The translation below is based on the critical edition of
the Latin text by Rousseau and Doutreleau with alterations, in comparison with the
Greek summary by Theodoret; I have also utilized the classic English translation of
Irenaeus by A. Roberts and J. Donaldson (in their *Ante-Nicene Fathers*, vol. 1): A.
Rousseau and L. Doutreleau, eds., *Irénée de Lyon, Contre les hérésies: Livre I*

[Book 1] (Sources chrétiennes, no. 264; Paris: Le Cerf, 1979), vol. 1, 330–34 (Greek summary of Irenaeus 1.30.1–14); vol. 2, 364–86 (Latin). Theodoret's summary (*Compendium*, 15) of Irenaeus 1.30.15–1.31.1 can be found in J. P. Migne, genl. ed., *Patrologiae Cursus Completus: Patrologia Graeca*, vol. 83 (Theodoretus Cyrensis Episcopus, *Opera Omnia*, vol. 4), col. 368.

The parent, its thought, and the holy spirit

1.30.1 Furthermore,[a] others[b] relate a monstrous thing, that in the power of the deep there exists a certain blessed, incorruptible, infinite first light, which is the parent of the entirety and is called the first human being. Moreover—they say—its thought[c] emanated from it and was the offspring of the being that had emitted it; and this was the offspring of the human being,[d] the second human being.[e] And below these is the holy spirit.[f] And below the superior spirit were distinct elements: BJn 2:26 + ?

> water;
> darkness;
> abyss;
> chaos.

It was above these—they say—that the spirit moved. And they call this (spirit) the first female. Gn 1:2

Begetting of the anointed (Christ)

Next, they say, the first human being together with its offspring became enamored of the beauty of the spirit—that is, of the female; and it shed light upon her and begot on her an incorruptible light, a third masculine being, whom they call the anointed (Christ)[g]—the offspring of the first and second human beings and of the holy spirit, the first female being. BJn 6:23 +

1.30.1 a. The present account comes immediately after IrG in Irenaeus's catalogue of heresies.

b. Instead of "others" the Greek fragment preserved by Theodoret has "the Sethians, whom some call Ophians or Ophites," but these words are often regarded as an interpretive remark by Theodoret.

c. In BJn (4:26f) the thinking or thought of the ineffable parent is the Barbēlō or forethought.

d. Or "the son of man."

e. In BJn (5:6f) the Barbēlō is called "the first human being."

f. In BJn the "holy spirit" who is the "mother of the living" is wisdom or her manifestation as life. It seems unlikely that Irenaeus's account or his source here has compressed the description of a theology like that of BJn, since the terms "first human being," "second human being," and "first female" are not applied according to the system of BJn.

g. "anointed" and "Christ" are the same word in Greek.

Production of the vulgar element, wisdom

1.30.2 Now, the parent and the offspring both had sexual intercourse with the female, whom they also call mother of the living; and then she could neither endure nor contain the excess of the lights, but was—they say—filled to saturation and overflowed on the left side: thus, too, their only-begotten the anointed (Christ), who was as it were on the right side and ever tending to what was higher, was immediately drawn up into the incorruptible realm[a] along with its mother. Moreover, this constitutes the true, holy congregation,[b] which has become the calling,[c] assembling, and union of

the parent of the entirety or first human being;
the offspring or second human being;
the anointed (Christ), their offspring;
the aforementioned female.

EpA 40.5.2?

1.30.3 Now, they teach that the power that gushed forth from the female contained a secretion of light, and fell downward from its parents; yet it was by its own will that it contained the secretion of light. And this they call "left," "vulgar element,"[a] and "wisdom" (Sophia), as well as "androgyne."

1.30.7, 1.30.9
1.30.11
IrG 1.29.4+

Creation of the heavenly universe

It absolutely sank into the waters, while they were (still) motionless; moreover, it set them in motion, recklessly proceeding all the way to the lowest depths,[b] and it assumed from them a body. For—they say— all things rushed toward the secretion of light that it contained; clung to it; and enveloped it. Had it not contained this (secretion), it probably would have been totally absorbed and submerged by matter. Bound, therefore, by a body composed of matter, and greatly weighed down by it, this (power) recovered its senses, and attempted to escape from the waters and ascend to its mother. But it could not do so, on account of the weight of the enveloping body. But greatly suffering, it contrived to conceal that light, which was from above, for fear that the light too might be injured by the inferior elements, just as it had been. And when it had gotten power from the secretion consisting of the light that it possessed, it rebounded and surfaced; and once it was above, it spread out as a covering, and out of its body it constructed this visible heaven. And it stayed beneath the heaven that it had made, for it still had the characteristics of an aqueous body. When it had conceived a desire for the higher light and had received power, it put off this body in every respect, and was freed from it. Moreover, they call this body, which— they say—that (power) took off (like a garment), "female from a female."[c]

RR 87:4?

Wisdom's offspring and the emission of its offspring

1.30.4 Now, they also say that her offspring, too, had some sort of breath of incorruptibility, which had been left it by its mother, by means

---

1.30.2 a. Or "aeon."
  b. The word can be translated also "church."
  c. Or "naming."

1.30.3 a. Or possibly "lewd element," Greek *prounikos*. The word basically means "mover, porter," one who corporally transports bur-

dens for a fee.
  b. Lit. "to the abysses."
  c. Some scholars hold that the text is corrupt here and conjecture that the original reading was "Moreover, they say this body was her child (or son), and they call her 'female from female.' "

of which it worked. And becoming powerful, this (offspring), too—so they say—emitted a motherless offspring out of the waters; for they deny that it knew a mother. And by imitation of its parent, its offspring emitted another offspring. This third one, too, engendered a fourth; the fourth also generated an offspring; from the fifth—they say—a sixth offspring was engendered; and the sixth, too, engendered a seventh. Thus, according to them, the septet was completed, with the mother occupying the eighth position. And just as these beings have a hierarchy of generation, so too they have one of rank and of power.

1.30.5 Moreover, they have assigned names within their false system,[a] such as the following:

> the first descendant of the mother is called Ialdabaōth;
> the descendant therefrom, Iaō;
> thence, Sabaōth;
> fourth, Adōnaios;
> fifth, Elōaios;
> sixth, Ōraios;
> seventh and last of all, Astaphaios.

1.30.11
BJn 11:26

Furthermore, they suppose that these heavens, excellences, powers, angels, and creators sit invisibly in heaven according to the hierarchy of their generation and dominate heavenly and earthly things.

Creation of other rulers. The "nun."

Ialdabaōth, the first of them, despised its mother, inasmuch as it produced children and grandchildren without anyone's permission— angels, archangels, powers, authorities, and dominions. After these had been produced, its children turned against it to strive and quarrel with it over the rulership. Accordingly, Ialdabaōth became sad and filled with despair; and, observing the dregs of matter that lay below, fixed its desire[b] thereupon. Hence, they say, an offspring was born. This offspring is the letter *nun* (נ),[c] which is twisted in the form of a snake. From it derive spirit, soul, and all worldly things; from it were generated all forgetfulness, evil, jealousy, envy, and death. Moreover, they say, while this serpent-like, twisted *nun* of theirs was with its parent in heaven and in the garden (paradise), it subverted its parent even more by its crookedness.

RR 95:13

EpG 26.10.8
RR 96:3+

Reproof of Ialdabaōth's arrogance

1.30.6 So Ialdabaōth rejoiced, priding itself in all those that were below it, and said, "It is I who am the parent and god;[a] and there is none above me."

BJn 13:5+
Is 45:21?
Is 46:9?

Now, when its mother heard it speak thus, she cried out against it, "Do not lie, Ialdabaōth: for above you (sing.) are the parent of the entirety or first human being; and the human being who is the offspring of the human being."

RR 94:23+

1.30.5 a. "they . . . their false system": Irenaeus speaks from his own point of view.
  b. Or "thought."
  c. The Hebrew letter נ (*nun*) is here compared to a snake because of its form. Some scholars have also detected here a play

on an inflection of the Greek word *nous*, "intellect," presumably referring to the effective aspect of the power that Ialdabaōth got from the mother.

1.30.6 a. Or "god and parent."

Creation of a non-material Adam. His immobility.

Now, all were disturbed by the new voice, and by the unexpected announcement, and they asked where the sound was coming from. In order—they say—to distract them and attract them to himself, Ialdabaōth said, "Come, let us make a human being after our image." Now, when the six powers had heard this, their mother caused them to think of the human being—so that by this means she might empty them of their original power. They gathered together, and they modeled a human being that was immense in breadth and length. But since it could only writhe upon the ground, they carried it to their parent.

FTh 43:17

BJn 15:1+

BJn 19:10

Passage of wisdom's power into Adam

But wisdom (Sophia) was causing this so that she might empty it (Ialdabaōth) of the secretion of light, so that it might not be able to rise up against those that were above it by having power. And when it breathed a spirit of life into the human being—they say—it was inadvertently emptied of power. And thus the human being became a possessor of intellect,[b] and thinking: and these—they say—are the elements that can be saved.

And this (human being) at once rendered thanks to the first human being, forsaking its creators.

BJn 19:15+

Creation of a non-material Eve

1.30.7 Ialdabaōth was jealous, and decided to consider a way of emptying the human being, by (the creation of) a woman. And as a result of its own thinking, it brought a woman out.[a] The aforementioned vulgar (wisdom) seized her and secretly emptied her of the power.

BJn 22:32

1.30.3+

Begetting of angelic offspring upon Eve

But the others came and were amazed at her beauty; and they called her Eve. And they became enamored of her, and begot children on her, and these they also call angels.

The snake

But their mother (wisdom) cunningly led Eve and Adam astray by the agency of the snake, so that they transgressed the commandment of Ialdabaōth. And Eve was easily persuaded, as if she were listening to an offspring of god. And she persuaded Adam to eat from the tree from which god had said not to eat. Moreover—they say—when they ate they became acquainted with that power which is superior to all, and they revolted from those who had made them.

1.30.8, 1.30.9
1.30.15
RR 89:31+

Second reproof of Ialdabaōth

Now, when the vulgar (wisdom) saw that the latter (lower powers) had been defeated by their own modeled form,[b] she rejoiced greatly. And once again she cried out that, since an incorruptible parent had already existed, it (Ialdabaōth) had lied when it called itself the parent;

RR 95:5

---

b. Greek *nous:* see note 1.30.5c.

1.30.7 a. I.e. brought her out of Adam's side.

b. "modeled form": Jewish and Christian jargon for the human body, based on the fact that the creator modeled Adam out of earth.

and that since a human being and a first female had already existed, it had sinned in making counterfeit copies of these beings.[c]

The expulsion from paradise into the realm of matter

1.30.8 But Ialdabaôth paid no attention to these words, because of the forgetfulness that surrounded it. And it expelled Adam and Eve from the garden (paradise), because they had transgressed its commandment. For it wished to beget (yet other) offspring on Eve, but it did not succeed because its mother opposed it in all things. And she secretly emptied Adam and Eve of the secretion of light, so that the spirit that derived from the realm of absolute power might not receive a share in the laying of a curse or in a state of disgrace. Thus—they teach—after they had been emptied of the divine essence a curse was laid upon them by it, and they were cast down from heaven into this world.

BJn 19:32
BJn 23:35

RR 91:5

Production of seven worldly demons

But the snake too, which had worked against its parent, was cast down by it into this lower world. And it brought together under its authority the angels that are here, and engendered six offspring, with itself serving as the seventh in imitation of that septet which surrounds its parent. And—they say—these are the seven worldly demons, which always oppose and resist the race of human beings, because it was on account of these that their parent was cast down.

1.30.7+
RR 90:32
RR 95:13?

1.30.11
RR 95:2?

Production of material bodies for Adam and Eve

1.30.9 Now, previously Adam and Eve had had the nimble, shining, and as it were spiritual bodies that had been modeled at their creation; but when they came hither, these changed into darker, denser, and more sluggish ones.[a]

BJn 20:28

Adaptation to material life

Their souls also were inattentive and listless, inasmuch as they had received from their maker a merely worldly inbreathing: until the vulgar (wisdom) had pity on them and restored to them the good fragrance of the secretion of light. By means of this they came to a recollection of themselves, and recognized that they were naked, and that their bodies were made of matter. And they recognized that they carried death about with them. And they existed patiently, recognizing that bodies would envelop them only for a time.

BJn 22:3

Cain and Abel

Led by wisdom (Sophia), they also discovered food; and when they were satisfied they had sexual intercourse, and engendered Cain, whom the contemptible snake and its offspring immediately laid hold of and destroyed by filling him with worldly forgetfulness. They led him into foolishness and arrogance, so that in killing his brother Abel he was the first (human being) to display jealousy and death.

BJn 24:8+

1.30.7

---

c. Or (quite differently) "saw that she had sinned when she committed adultery."

1.30.9 a. I.e. their bodies became or acquired material substance.

Seth and Nōrea

After these (two)—they say—by the forethought of the vulgar (wisdom), Seth was engendered, and then Nōrea. From them—they say—the remaining multitude of humankind descended.

BJn 24:34 +
1.30.3 +
EpG 26.1.7

Humankind led astray

They were introduced by the lower septet to all kinds of evil: apostasy from the upper, holy septet; idolatry; and a general contempt for everything—even though the mother always secretly opposed them and preserved[b] her own, that is, the secretion of light. Moreover, they say that the holy septet is the seven heavenly bodies called planets; and—they say—the contemptible snake[c] has two names, Michael and Samaēl.[d]

BJn 17:30?

The flood

1.30.10   Now, Ialdabaōth was angry at humankind because they did not worship or honor it as parent and god; and it sent a flood upon them so that it might destroy all people at once. And here too wisdom (Sophia) opposed it; and Noah and those with him were saved in the ark for the sake of the secretion of that light which derived from her. And because of it the world was again filled with human beings.

BJn 28:32 +

BJn 29:1 +

Abraham

From among these Ialdabaōth chose a certain Abraham, and made a covenant with him, to the effect that if his posterity would continue serving it, it would give them the land as their inheritance.

Moses. The prophets.

Next, through Moses it brought Abraham's descendants out of Egypt, and gave unto them the law, and made them the Jews. From among these (Jews) each of the seven deities,[a] which they also call the holy septet, chose its own herald to glorify it and to proclaim that it was god; so that when the rest (of the Jews) would hear these glorifications they too would serve the beings who had been proclaimed to be gods by these prophets. **1.30.11**   And they arrange the prophets as follows.

1.30.8

1.30.5

> To Ialdabaōth belong:
> Moses;
> Joshua the son of Nun;
> Amos;
> Habakkuk.
> To Iaō belong:
> Samuel;
> Nathan;
> Jonah;
> Micah.

---

b. Or "saved."
c. Or "the snake that had been cast down."
d. Samaēl: Aramaic, "blind god."

1.30.10 a. The MSS have "it (Ialdabaōth) chose seven days . . . each of which also has its own herald": this text is probably corrupt; the English translation given above represents an attempt to recover the original reading. In any case each of the seven demonic deities in the following list possibly corresponds to a planet and day of the week or "septet"; cf. Gn 1:3–2:4.

To Sabaōth belong:
  Elijah;
  ⟨Hosea⟩;[a]
  Joel;
  Zechariah.
To Adōnai belong:
  Isaiah;
  Ezekiel;
  Jeremiah;
  Daniel.
To Elōi belong:
  Obadiah;[b]
  Haggai.
To Ōraios belong:
  Malachi;[c]
  Nahum.
To Astaphaios belong:
  Esdras;
  Zephaniah.

Principle of biblical interpretation

Thus each of these (prophets) glorifies his own particular parent and IrSat 1.24.2 +
god. And—they say—wisdom (Sophia) herself also spoke many words
through these (prophets) concerning the first human being, the incorruptible realm,[d] and the anointed (Christ) who is above, thus foretelling
and reminding humankind of the incorruptible light, the first human
being, and the descent of the anointed (Christ). And the rulers were
terrified and amazed at the newness of those things which were proclaimed by the prophets.

Begetting of John the Baptist and Jesus by Ialdabaōth

Through Ialdabaōth, but without its knowing what it did, the vulgar 1.30.3 +
(wisdom) caused the emission of two human beings: one from Elizabeth,
a barren woman; and the other from Mary, a virgin. **1.30.12** And since
she herself (the vulgar wisdom) had no repose either in heaven or on
earth, she felt grief, and called upon her mother to assist her. And her
mother, the first female, took pity upon her daughter, and made a request
of the first human being, that the anointed (Christ) should be sent to her
as an assistance. And it emanated and descended to its sister and to the BJn 20:19 +
secretion of light. And when the lower wisdom (Sophia) recognized that
her sibling was descending to ⟨her⟩, she announced its advent through
the agency of John, prepared a baptism of repentance, and made Jesus
suitable in advance, so that when the anointed (Christ) should descend
it might find a pure vessel,[a] and that thanks to the agency of her son
Ialdabaōth the existence of the female might (ultimately) be proclaimed
by the anointed (Christ).

Union of the anointed (Christ) and wisdom

Now, it descended (they say) through the seven heavens, having
assumed the likeness of their offspring, and it gradually emptied them

---

1.30.11 a. Erroneously omitted in the MSS.   d. Or "aeon."
b. The MSS erroneously have "Tobias."
c. The MSS erroneously have "Mi-   **1.30.12** a. "vessel": i.e. "body," a tradi-
chaiah."   tional cliché.

of any power; for—they say—the whole secretion of light rushed to it. And when the anointed (Christ) was descending into this world, it first 1.30.1 put on its sister wisdom (Sophia), and both rejoiced, reposing in one another: this they declare to be bridegroom and bride.

Christ descends into Jesus

Moreover Jesus, by being begotten of a virgin through the agency of god, was wiser, purer, and more righteous than all other human beings. The anointed (Christ) in combination with wisdom (Sophia) descended into him, and thus was made Jesus Christ. **1.30.13** Accordingly many of his disciples—they say—did not recognize that the anointed (Christ) had descended into him; but when the anointed (Christ) did descend into Jesus, he began to perform miracles, heal, proclaim the unrecognizable[a] parent, and openly confess himself to be the child of the first human being.[b]

Crucifixion of Jesus

The rulers and the parent of Jesus were angry at this, and worked to have him killed. And while he was being led away (to death)—they say—the anointed (Christ) himself, along with wisdom (Sophia), departed for the incorruptible realm,[c] but Jesus was crucified.

Jesus' resurrection body

The anointed (Christ) was not unmindful of its own, but sent down EpA 40.8.2? into him a certain power, which raised him up in a (kind of) body that they call animate and spiritual, for he let the worldly parts return to the world. Now, when his disciples saw him after he had arisen, they were not acquainted with him—nor with the one by whose agency Jesus had arisen from the dead. And—they say—among his disciples there arose the great error of imagining that he had arisen in a worldly body, for they did not know that "flesh and blood do not lay hold of[d] the kingdom 1Co 15:50 of god." **1.30.14** Moreover, they claim to confirm that the anointed (Christ) descended and reascended by the fact that according to Jesus' disciples Jesus did not do any great deed either before his baptism or after his resurrection from the dead; these (disciples) did not know that Jesus was united with the anointed (Christ) nor that the incorruptible realm[a] was united with the septet. And they spoke of his animate body as if it were a worldly one.

His post-resurrection teachings and ascension

Now, after his resurrection he remained (on earth) for eighteen months. And because perception had descended into him (from above), he taught the plain truth. He taught these things to a small number of his disciples, who, he knew, were able to receive such great mysteries.

His ingathering of souls will bring the end

And so he was taken up into heaven, where the anointed (Christ)[b] sits at the right hand of its parent Ialdabaōth, so that he (Jesus) might receive

---

1.30.13 a. Or "unknown."
  b. Or "the son of first man."
  c. Or "aeon."
  d. Or "do not comprehend."

1.30.14 a. Or "aeon."
  b. Some scholars hold that the original text here had "Jesus" rather than "the anointed (Christ)."

unto himself the souls of those who have become acquainted with him, once they have left behind their worldly flesh—thus enriching himself without his parent's[c] knowing or even seeing him; so that to the extent that Jesus enriches himself with holy souls his parent is diminished and suffers loss, being emptied of the power that it[d] has in the form of souls: for in consequence it does not have any more holy souls to send back into the world, except for those which derive from its essence, that is, those which come from its inbreathing. Moreover, the end will take place when the entire secretion of the spirit of light is gathered together and caught up into the realm[e] of incorruptibility.

EpG 26.9.3

EpG 26.10.7+

APPENDIXES

The snake

1.30.15[a] * * * Some assert that it was wisdom (Sophia) herself who became the snake; accordingly she remained hostile to the creator of Adam, and introduced acquaintance into humankind. For this reason the snake was said to be more prudent than all (others).

1.30.7+

But also, because of the arrangement of our intestines, through which food is passed, and the fact that the intestines possess the shape that they do, these persons point to the life-producing essence hidden within us in the form of a snake.[b]

Origin of Cain

1.31.1 And others[a] say that Cain was from[b] the superior realm of absolute power, and confess that Esau, Korah, the Sodomites, and all such persons are of the same people[c] (or nation) as themselves: for this reason they have been hated by their maker, although none of them has suffered harm. For wisdom (Sophia) snatched up out of them whatever in them belonged to her.

The "Gospel of Judas"

And furthermore—they say—Judas[d] the betrayer was thoroughly acquainted with these things;[e] and he alone[f] was acquainted with the truth as no others were, and (so) accomplished the mystery of the betrayal. By him all things, both earthly and heavenly, were thrown into dissolution.

And they bring forth a fabricated work to this effect, which they entitle *The Gospel of Judas.*[g]

---

c. "his parent": i.e. Ialdabaōth.
d. I.e. the parent.
e. Or "aeon."

1.30.15 a. An irrelevant comment by Irenaeus is here omitted.
b. See note 1.30.5c. The original reading of the text here is debated by scholars, but the general meaning is held to be clear.

1.31.1 a. The Greek fragment preserved by Theodoret next has "who are called Caini."
b. The Greek fragment preserved by

Theodoret instead has "was ransomed from."
c. The saved.
d. The name can also be translated "Jude."
e. Perhaps referring to the union of the anointed (Christ) and Jesus as related in 1.30.12–13.
f. The Greek fragment preserved by Theodoret next has "of all the apostles."
g. Or *"The Gospel of Jude."* No such work survives, although GTh is a work entitled "gospel" and written down by Didymus *Jude* Thomas.

THE GNOSTICS

ACCORDING TO
PORPHYRY, *LIFE OF PLOTINUS*
CHAPTER 16
(Porph)

Contents and literary background

In this brief selection Porphyry of Tyre (A.D. 232/3–ca. 305), an educated pagan of the third century, attests to the fact that classic gnostic scriptures were available in the city of Rome about A.D. 250. In the process he mentions the names of several authors of gnostic scripture and confirms that Zs and Fr were scriptures of the gnostic sect, that those who used them were Christians, and that they were written in Greek.

Porphyry was interested in gnostic scripture because he was a professional Platonist philosopher. The Platonic component of gnostic myth had always been obvious for all to see. But when non-Christian Platonism—especially the system of its greatest representative, Plotinus—and the mythic ideas of the gnostics grew closer to one another, the resemblance became too close for comfort, and Platonists felt obliged to refute the gnostics and dissociate themselves from gnostic philosophy. Porphyry, as one of Plotinus's closest disciples, played a major role in this task. After his teacher's death he edited his works (which included four treatises against the gnostics), publishing them shortly after A.D. 300. He also composed a fascinating biography of Plotinus, which is excerpted here; it was written A.D. 301–5.

Plotinus (A.D. 205–69/70), the greatest philosopher of late antiquity, had taken up philosophical study in Egypt, then traveled, and at the age of 40 settled in Rome, where he gave philosophical seminars. Porphyry became his disciple there in A.D. 262/3. Both Plotinus and Porphyry wrote in Greek.

Porphyry was an unoriginal philosopher, but a learned scholar and a critical student of religions. By conviction he was anti-Christian, and in his famous treatise *Against Christians* he turned historical criticism against the church, arguing (for example) on the basis of anachronisms that the Old Testament book of Daniel must be a relatively modern work and so an example of pseudepigraphy. He used precisely the same technique in refuting one of the gnostic works, as he states in the present excerpt.

Text

The translation below is based on the critical edition of Henry and Schwyzer, whose line numbers are also followed: P. Henry and H.-R. Schwyzer, eds., Plotinus, *Opera*, vol. 1 (Museum Lessianum, ser. philosophica 33; Paris: Desclée de Brouwer; Brussels: Universelle, 1951), 21–22.

SELECT BIBLIOGRAPHY

Dodds, E. R. "Plotinus." In *Oxford Classical Dictionary*, 2d ed. Oxford: Clarendon Press, 1970, 847–48.

————. "Porphyry." In *Oxford Classical Dictionary*, 2d ed. Oxford: Clarendon Press, 1970, 864–65.

Plotinus, *The Enneads*. Translated by S. MacKenna, 4th ed. by B. S. Page. London: Faber & Faber, 1969.

Schwyzer, H.-R. "Plotinos." In *Paulys Real-Encyclopädie der classischen Altertumswissenschaft*, 2d ed. by G. Wissowa et al. Vol. 21 (1951), cols. 471–592.

16 In his time[a] there were among the Christians many others,[b] members of a sect,[c] who were followers of Adelphios and Aquilinus[d] and had started out from classical philosophy. •They possessed many works by Alexander of Libya, Philokōmos, Dēmostratos, and Lydos;[e] and they brought out revelations of Zoroaster,[f] of Zōstrianos,[g] of Nikotheos,[h] of the Foreigner,[i] of Messos,[j] and of other such figures. •They deceived many people, and themselves as well, in supposing that Plato had not drawn near to the depth of intelligible essence.

Accordingly, Plotinus constructed many refutations (of their ideas) in his seminar meetings; in addition, he wrote the work to which I have assigned the title[k] "Against the Gnostics."[l]

He left it to us[m] to contend with the rest. Amelius[n] proceeded with a forty-chapter refutation[o] of the *Book of Zōstrianos.* •I, Porphyry, constructed numerous refutations[p] of the *Book of Zoroaster*: I demonstrated that the book is spurious and modern, fabricated by the organizers of the sect[q] in order to give the impression that the opinions that they themselves wished to represent were those of the ancient Zoroaster.

BJn 19:8f ?
Zs,
Fr
EpS 39.5.1
EpA 40.2.2+

16.3

a. In the time of Plotinus.

b. Or simply "there were many other Christians." But "others" may refer to an epithet that the gnostics applied to themselves; see RAd note 64n.

c. "members of a sect": Greek *hairetikoi*. Porphyry goes on to identify them as gnostics.

d. Adelphios and Aquilinus are otherwise unidentifiable.

e. Some scholars conjecture that the original text is "Dēmostratos the Lydian." None of the gnostic writers listed here can be specifically identified or linked with one of the surviving works of gnostic literature.

f. Cf. perhaps BJn 19:8f. Zoroaster is mentioned also in the title of Zs.

g. Identical with Zs.

h. The work apparently does not survive.

i. Identical with Fr.

j. The work apparently does not survive. Messos is mentioned in Fr.

k. As Plotinus's editor, Porphyry assigned titles to the lectures that comprise the *Enneads*, Plotinus's collected works.

l. *Enneads* 2.9 (no. 33 in the chronological list). It is in fact one of a four-part series directed against gnostic philosophy, comprising *Enneads* 3.8, 5.8, 5.5, and 2.9 (nos. 30–33 in the chronological list).

m. Plotinus's pupils.

n. Amelius or Amerius Gentilianus, pupil of Plotinus A.D. 246–70.

o. The work apparently does not survive.

p. The work apparently does not survive.

q. The gnostic sect.

THE SETHIANS

ACCORDING TO
ST. EPIPHANIUS OF SALAMIS, *AGAINST HERESIES*
CHAPTER 39
(EpS)

Contents and literary background

Seth was of special importance to the gnostic sect as being the parent of their racial line, which was the transmitter of the divine power of wisdom. In this very important sense, gnostic myth is a myth about Seth. Not without reason, then, have modern scholars referred to the gnostic sect as "Sethian gnostics"; in fact, such terminology had already developed by the fourth century, as the present excerpt shows. The excerpted passage was written in Greek about A.D. 375.

The material that St. Epiphanius of Salamis has chosen to summarize adds nothing in particular to one's knowledge of gnostic myth. Apart from a passing reference to the creation of the world by "angels," the summary begins with the third act of the mythic drama, that is, the creation of Adam and Eve and the birth of their children, with emphasis on Seth and his special relationship to the metaphysical universe. The fourth act—the subsequent history of humankind—stresses the difference between the descendants of Seth and the rest of humankind. St. Epiphanius's summary ends with the flood, except for the information that the preexistent Christ that descended into Jesus of Nazareth (as in IrUnid) was actually Seth; this identification is known also from EgG. Cf. also the introduction to EpA.

Mythic characters

I. Immortals Mentioned by St. Epiphanius

The ANOINTED (Christ)
The MOTHER or FEMALE (Wisdom?)

II. Rulers Mentioned by St. Irenaeus

ANGELS who created the world and the first human beings

III. Humankind Mentioned by St. Irenaeus

The TWO FIRST HUMAN BEINGS (Adam and Eve)
CAIN and ABEL, their offspring
SETH
HŌRAIA, his wife

POSTERITY OF CAIN ⎫
POSTERITY OF ABEL ⎬ merged

POSTERITY OF SETH, and in particular:
  KHAM (Ham), a descendant of Cain and Abel
  NOAH
  JESUS, a descendant of Seth

Text

St. Epiphanius's original Greek text is attested by a number of medieval manuscripts, whose accuracy is a matter of debate among scholars. The translation below is based upon Holl's critical edition, but with alterations: K. Holl, ed., *Epiphanius,* vol. 2 (Griechische christliche Schriftsteller, vol. 31; Leipzig: Henrichs, 1922), 71–74.

I. HISTORICAL INFORMATION

Epiphanius's acquaintance with the Sethian sect

39.1.1 * * * Another school of thought[a] is the Sethians, so-called. It is not found everywhere; neither is the school of the Caini, mentioned above.[b] And perhaps most of them have already been eradicated from the world—for what is not from god will not stand at rest,[c] but rather will flourish for a while but will not endure so as to last forever. **39.1.2** But I think I probably[a] encountered this school of thought, too, in the country of the Egyptians.[b] Indeed, I do not exactly remember which country[c] I encountered them in. And some details we became acquainted with by first-hand observation of this (school), while others we learned from written accounts of it.

The sectarians claim to have sprung from Seth

39.1.3 Now, these Sethians proudly derive their ancestry from Seth the son of Adam and honor him and attribute to him whatever belongs to excellence, and proofs of excellence and righteousness and the like. They even do not stop short of calling him the anointed (Christ)[a] and 39.3.5 insist that he was Jesus.

II. TEACHINGS OF THE SECT

Creation of the universe by angels

39.1.4 And they teach the doctrine that the universe has come into BJn 12:33+ existence because of angels and not because of the power on high.

39.1.1 a. Greek *haeresis*, the usual term for a philosophical school or religious sect. An unspecified degree of social cohesion is implied by the term.

  b. In the preceding chapter of the work from which this passage is extracted.

  c. To "stand at rest" is philosophical jargon for the state of permanence, non-change, and real being, as opposed to what exists in instability, change, and becoming.

It was a favorite term of gnostic writers; it is here turned against them by Epiphanius.

39.1.2 a. Or "perhaps."

  b. Or possibly "in the Egyptian countryside," i.e. the part outside Alexandria.

  c. Or "region."

39.1.3 a. "anointed" and "Christ" are the same word in Greek.

Adam and Eve. Cain and Abel.

39.2.1 Now, they agree with the preceding school,[a] the Caini, on the following point: that in the beginning two human beings[b] immediately came into being; Cain and Abel were from those two; forming a faction on account of them, the angels went to one another;[c] thus Abel was caused to be slain by Cain. **39.2.2** For (they say) the faction was formed[a] by the angels as they struggled on account of the descendants of the human beings ⟨. . .⟩[b] these two, the one who begot Cain and the one who begot Abel.[c]

BJn 15:1+
BJn 22:32
BJn 24:8+

Intervention of the mother. Seth.

39.2.3 But the higher power prevailed, whom they call "mother"[a] and "female"—for[b] they suppose that there are mothers above, and females and males, and almost speak of kinships and patriarchal lineages.[c]

IrUnid 1.30.2?

39.2.4 So—they say—since she had prevailed, the mother who is called the female, once she recognized that Abel had been killed, took thought and caused Seth to be born. And she deposited her power within him, establishing[a] in him[b] a posterity[c] of the power from above and the spark that had been sent from above for the first establishment of the posterity and the alliance.[d] **39.2.5** And the latter is an alliance of righteousness and a choosing of a posterity and a people, so that by such an alliance and by this posterity the powers of the angels who had created the world and the two original human beings might be defeated.

BJn 24:34+
BJn 25:20+
IrSat 1.24.1+

IrSat 1.24.2+

39.2.6 So it is for this reason that the people of Seth have been set apart and are descended from that origin, as being the elect who are differentiated from the other people.—**39.2.7** For, they say, as time went on the two peoples belonging to Cain and to Abel coexisted, intermingled, and merged into one owing to great imperfection. Taking note of this fact, the mother of all decided to make the posterity of the human beings pure, as I said, because of the slaying of Abel. And she chose this Seth and showed that he was pure. And in him alone she established the people of her power and purity.

IrSat 1.24.2+

The flood

39.3.1 And again the aforementioned mother and female saw the frequent intercourse and confused impulse on the part of the angels and the human beings, so that the two tended toward mixture; and saw that their confusion was producing certain alliances of (the two) species. Again she traveled, and she brought on a flood and destroyed every faction of any human being of the (?)[a] hostile people—naturally, so that

BJn 28:32+

BJn 30:21+

39.2.1 a. In the preceding chapter of the work from which this passage is extracted.
  b. Adam and Eve.
  c. Perhaps meaning "joined in alliance." Some scholars conjecture that the original reading of the text was "went to <war with> one another," understanding that the angels quarreled with one another and not with the "mother" (39.2.3).

39.2.2 a. Or "the quarrel was held."
  b. Possibly one or more words are inadvertently omitted here.
  c. "the one . . . Cain . . . the one . . . Abel": the male parents of Cain and Abel, i.e. according to RR 91:11f the chief ruler (angelic creator of the world) and Adam, respectively.

39.2.3 a. Wisdom, according to other Gnostic texts.
  b. Epiphanius here speaks from his own point of view.
  c. Or "relatives and fatherhoods."

39.2.4 a. Or "sowing."
  b. The MSS instead have "in it" (i.e. her power).
  c. Throughout EpS this word can also be translated "seed."
  d. Or "(political) union." The word has many other meanings as well: "existence, genesis, nature, structure," etc.

39.3.1 a. The text is uncertain here.

the pure people descended from Seth, who alone were righteous, might remain in the world, to bring about an alliance of the people from above and the spark of righteousness.

Kham preserves an unrighteous strain within Noah's ark

39.3.2 But in turn the angels secretly introduced Kham (Ham) into the ark, for he belonged to their posterity. For, they say that out of eight persons then saved in that "coffer"[a] of Noah seven belonged to the pure people, but one—namely Kham—belonged to the other power, having sneaked on board unbeknownst to the higher mother. EpG 26.1.8
39.3.3 And this plan, which was contrived by the angels, came out as follows. Now—they say—inasmuch as the angels recognized that their entire people was going to be obliterated by the flood, by trickery they secretly added the aforementioned Kham in order to preserve the evil people, which had been made by them. **39.3.4** And as a result of this (people) there arose forgetfulness, error, sinful undisciplined passions, and evil promiscuity among humankind within the world. And thus the world turned back again to its original state of disorderliness and became filled with evils as it had been in the beginning before the flood.

Incarnation of Seth (Christ) within Jesus

39.3.5 But the anointed (Christ) itself came as Jesus, a descendant of Seth by descent and by succession of peoples; it[a] was shown forth in the world not through being born but in a mysterious way. This was Seth himself, who both formerly and at that time—as the anointed (Christ)[b]—visited the human race, having been sent from above, from the mother.[c] * * * BJn 6:23+ Lk 3:23-38 EgG 71:11 EgG 75:15+ 39.1.3

III. BOOKS READ BY THE SECTARIANS

39.5.1 Now, they have composed certain books, attributing them to great people:
they say there are seven books attributed to Seth; RAd ? EgG ? 3Tb ?
other, different[a] books they entitle *Foreigners*:
another they call a *Revelation* attributed to *Abraham,* and full of all evil; Porph 16.3+ IrUnid 1.30.10? EpG 26.11.12?
others attributed to Moses;
and others atttributed to other figures.

IV. ANOTHER TEACHING OF THE SECT

Hōraia, wife of Seth

39.5.2 And degrading their intellects into utter foolishness, they say that a certain woman named Hōraia was the wife of Seth.—Just consider, EpG 26.1.7+

39.3.2 a. "coffer," Greek *larnaks*: not the usual biblical word for Noah's ark, but rather the classical Greek term for Deukalion's ark. Cf. EpG 26.1.8.

39.3.5 a. "it": the anointed.
  b. "as the anointed (Christ)": some scholars delete this phrase as being not a part of the original text; but cf. 39.1.3 (end).
  c. In the next paragraph (not translated here) Epiphanius attacks the Sethian myth of origins, objecting that in the beginning there was only one human being (Adam), not two (he probably misconstrues the myth at this point; cf. BJn 15:1f and BJn 20:33f). Similarly he objects that after the flood (Gn 6:11–8:19) all people descended only from Noah and his wife.

39.5.1 a. Or possibly "another seven": cf. EpA 40.7.4f.

O beloved friend,[a] the folly of these (Sethians) and utterly condemn
their drama, their fabulous vanity of thought, their fictitious nonsense.—
39.5.3   Indeed, there are other schools of thought that say there is a
power whom they name Hōraia. So, these (Sethians) say that the power,
whom others esteem and call Hōraia, was the wife of Seth. * * *

39.5.2 a. Epiphanius addresses the dedicatee of the work from which this passage is
extracted.

THE ARCHONTICS

ACCORDING TO
ST. EPIPHANIUS OF SALAMIS, *AGAINST HERESIES*
CHAPTER 40
(EpA)

Contents and literary background

This excerpt affords a rare glimpse into the ecclesiastical history of the gnostic church.

The later fourth century A.D. was an age of Christian pilgrimage to the holy lands of Egypt and Palestine. Pilgrims came not only to visit the holy places but also to converse with holy people—the Christian monks and nuns, whose fame had extended to far away countries. Among these pilgrims was a certain Eutaktos, whose story is told in this excerpt. Eutaktos traveled from what is now eastern Turkey ("Lesser Armenia") southward to Egypt and then back north to Palestine, finally returning to his native Armenia (see Map 3). Although in both lands (cf. EpS) he could have encountered gnostic Christians, it was in southern Palestine, where monastic hermits were such a common sight, that Eutaktos met a gnostic Christian monk named Peter and was converted to the gnostic understanding of Christianity. Eutaktos is the first known Armenian pilgrim to the holy land, and after his visit to Peter the Gnostic he became the first gnostic missionary to Armenia. According to St. Epiphanius of Salamis, Eutaktos founded the gnostic branch of the Armenian church, which eventually spread eastward from Lesser Armenia to Greater Armenia. By about 375, when Epiphanius wrote this passage (in Greek), Eutaktos was no longer alive ("the lord quickly obliterated him").

Peter the Gnostic's career is somewhat more obscure. Earlier in his life, he had already been "denounced" and "refuted" in the diocese of a certain bishop named Aetius, who eventually expelled him from the priesthood. Nothing is known about the identity of Bishop Aetius, nor where the incident took place. But in any case Epiphanius may have gotten some of his information about gnostic beliefs from the "refutation" that convinced Bishop Aetius, especially if it was a written document. From A.D. ca. 337 to 367, St. Epiphanius, a notorious heresy hunter in his day, resided in Eleutheropolis, Palestine (cf. 40.1.1). When Peter eventually came to settle in that region, Epiphanius recognized him and had him excluded ("expelled") from participation in church affairs. It is not clear whether the exclusion occurred before or after Eutaktos made his pilgrimage and became a convert to Peter's gnostic Christianity.

St. Epiphanius treats the teachings summarized here as belonging to a distinct group within gnostic Christianity, one that was peculiar to Palestine and Armenia and went by the strange name of "Archontics," i.e. people characterized by belief in the *arkhontes,* or heavenly rulers. But it is not clear whether Epiphanius's "Archontics" were really so distinct from other kinds of gnostics. The present

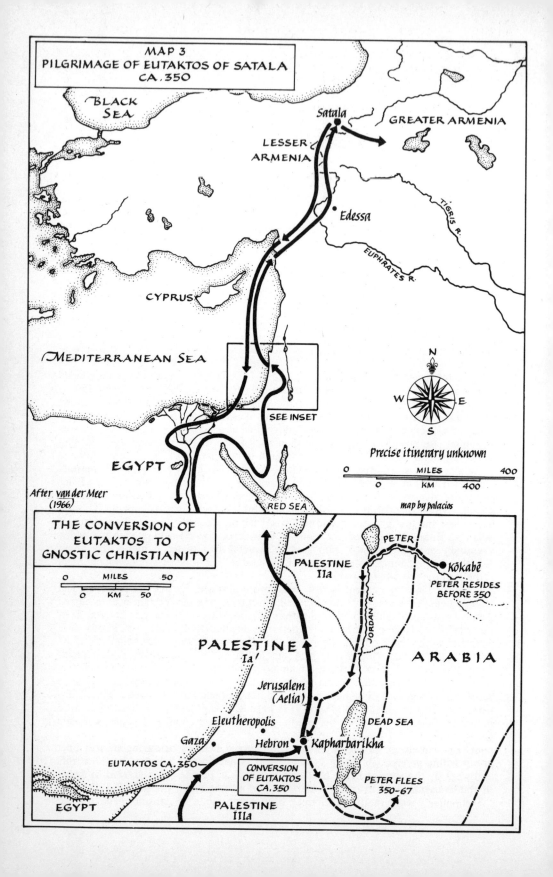

MAP 3
PILGRIMAGE OF EUTAKTOS OF SATALA
CA. 350

BLACK SEA

Satala

GREATER ARMENIA

LESSER ARMENIA

Edessa

TIGRIS R.

EUPHRATES R.

CYPRUS

MEDITERRANEAN SEA

SEE INSET

N
W   E
S

Precise itinerary unknown

0   MILES   400
0   KM   400

EGYPT

After van der Meer
(1966)

RED SEA

map by palacios

THE CONVERSION OF
EUTAKTOS TO
GNOSTIC CHRISTIANITY

0   MILES   50
0   KM   50

PETER

Kōkabē

PALESTINE
IIa

PETER RESIDES
BEFORE 350

JORDAN R.

PALESTINE
Ia

ARABIA

Jerusalem
(Aelia)

DEAD SEA

Eleutheropolis

Gaza

Hebron   Kapharbarikha

EUTAKTOS CA. 350

CONVERSION
OF EUTAKTOS
CA. 350

PETER FLEES
350–67

EGYPT

PALESTINE
IIIa

chapter, for example, immediately follows his account of the so-called "Sethians" (EpS). It may be no coincidence that the contents of the two chapters are largely complementary, and that taken together they cover much the same parts of the gnostic myth as RR. Parts of St. Epiphanius's work *Against Heresies* depend on earlier works of a similar nature. It is just possible that, in some prior source that he used, the material here distributed in chapters on the "Sethians" and the "Archontics" belonged to a single document or report.

The account of the "Archontics" follows RR in stating that Sabaōth (the eldest offspring of Ialdabaōth) rules from the seventh heaven and dominates Ialdabaōth ("the devil"); St. Epiphanius's report that Sabaōth is the parent of the devil may be a misunderstanding of the kind of material found in RR 95:13f.

Two pieces of sectarian information are reported: the "Archontics" reject baptism as practiced in the non-gnostic church on the grounds that it is performed in the name of Sabaōth rather than the highest deity; and they practice abstinence (which, adds Epiphanius, is really a sham).

Mythic characters

I. Immortals Mentioned by St. Epiphanius

The PARENT
The LUMINOUS MOTHER or superior power (Wisdom?)

II. Rulers Mentioned by St. Epiphanius

SEVEN HEAVENLY RULERS or authorities, one per heaven:
   SABAŌTH, the highest
   SIX OTHERS
Hosts of ANGELS that assist them
The DEVIL, an offspring of Sabaōth. Ruler of earth.

III. Humankind Mentioned by St. Epiphanius

ADAM
EVE, his wife
CAIN and ABEL, sons of Eve by the devil
SETH, a son of Eve by Adam
SEVEN SONS OF SETH
JESUS

Text

St. Epiphanius's original Greek text is attested by a number of medieval manuscripts, whose accuracy is a matter of debate among scholars. The translation below is based on Holl's critical edition, but with alterations: K. Holl, ed., *Epiphanius*, vol. 2 (Griechische christliche Schriftsteller, vol. 31; Leipzig: Henrichs, 1922), 80–89.

SELECT BIBLIOGRAPHY

Puech, H.-Ch. "Archontiker." In *Reallexikon für Antike und Christentum*, vol. 1 (1950), cols. 633–43.
Stone, M. E. "An Armenian Pilgrim to the Holy Land in the Early Byzantine Era." *Mélanges Bogharian*. *Revue des études arméniennes*. In press. (Advance copy supplied by the author.)

I. HISTORICAL INFORMATION

Presence of the sect within Palestinian monasticism

40.1.1 The school of thought[a] called Archontics[b] is next.[c] Now, it is not commonly found in many places, only in the province of Palestine. Yet they have already somehow carried their poison into Greater Armenia.[d]

40.1.2 What is more, at the end of the reign of Constantius,[a] this weed had already been sown in Lesser Armenia[b] by a certain man from Armenia, named Eutaktos—or rather, *ataktos* ("disordered"),[c] in his way of life! He was temporarily residing in Palestine, learned this evil teaching, and then returned home and taught it. **40.1.3** Now in Palestine, as I said, he had received it, like poison from an asp, from a certain old man named Peter—who was unworthy of the name. The latter lived in the territory belonging to Eleutheropolis of[a] Jerusalem, three miles beyond Hebron. The village is called Kapharbarikha.[b]

40.1.4 This old man had, in the first place, an astonishing disguise, filled with hypocrisy. For outside he was literally wrapped in a lamb's fleece; but it passed unnoticed that inside he was a ravenous wolf. For, he appeared to be a hermit[a] situated in a cave; he led many people, of course, to a life of renunciation and was called, of course, "father"

40.1.1 a. Greek *haeresis*, the usual term for a philosophical school or religious sect. An unspecified degree of social cohesion is implied by the term.

b. From Greek *arkhōn*, "ruler," i.e. heavenly ruler of the material world.

c. "next," viz. in the catalogue of schools from which this chapter is extracted.

d. Roughly, the eastern part of modern Turkey, south and east of the upper Euphrates River, together with modern Soviet Armenia. The Christianization of Armenia had largely begun in the late third century A.D.

40.1.2 a. Constantius II, the third son of Constantine the Great. He reigned A.D. 324–61.

b. In modern Turkey, roughly between the headwaters of the Euphrates River and Trebizond.

c. A pun in Greek on the component *-taktos*, "ordered." The prefix *eu-* means "well" (*eutaktos*, "well-ordered"), while *a-* means "dis-" (*ataktos*, "disordered").

40.1.3 a. "of": or "and." "Eleutheropolis": modern Beit Jibrīn or Bet Guvrin, southwest of Jerusalem. Epiphanius was born in Eleutheropolis.

b. Possibly identical with the modern village of Bani Naʿīm, three miles east of Hebron.

40.1.4 a. I.e. a monastic solitary, an anchorite. Such Christian hermits (desert "fathers") were very common in Palestine at this time.

because of his age and his monastic dress; and he distributed his possessions to the poor and gave alms daily.

40.1.5 In his youth he had been found in many schools of thought. But in the time of Aetius the bishop he was denounced and refuted; next he followed the school of the gnostics;[a] and he was deprived of the priesthood[b]—for he had once been a duly appointed priest. And after his refutation he was expelled from office by Aetius, departed, and lived in Kōkabē in Arabia,[c] from which the roots of the Ebionites and the Nazoreans[d] sprang; I have already noted this fact about the place in discussing many other schools.

Epiphanius's opposition to its leader

40.1.6 But later he returned, as though chastened in his old age; and secretly bearing within himself this venom, he was unrecognized by all—until finally he was convicted as such by words that he was whispering in the ears of certain people, and was expelled from the church by us and was refuted by your humble servant.[a] **40.1.7** And he sat in the cave, finally, abhorred by all and isolated from the Christian community[a] and from most of those who have charge of their own lives.

Spread of the sect to Armenia

40.1.8 The aforementioned Eutaktos—if indeed he can be called *eutaktos* ("well-ordered")—was passing through on his way from Egypt, and put in to port with the old man. He took up the old man's evil teaching, treating this poisonous substance as a precious cargo, and transported it back to his native land; for, he originated in Lesser Armenia, as I said—from the district near Satala.[a] **40.1.9** So after he had returned to his native land, he polluted many people of Lesser Armenia, defiling some who were rich, a certain man of senatorial rank, and other dignitaries. And through these illustrious persons he destroyed many people there. But the lord quickly obliterated him from life; yet he sowed his weed.

II. BOOKS READ BY THE SECTARIANS

40.2.1 And these (Archontics) have forged certain apocryphal books for themselves, whose titles are as follows:

> one book they entitle *Lesser Harmony*;
> another, *Greater Harmony*.

And furthermore, they accumulate other books for themselves, ⟨. . .⟩[a] to introduce in addition whichever ones they happen upon, and so they pretend to confirm their erroneous teaching with many (books). **40.2.2**

40.1.5 a. Presumably Epiphanius refers to the sect described by him in EpG.

  b. Or "office of presbyter (elder)."

  c. Khokhaba, southeast of the Sea of Galilee in the vicinity of modern Deraa, Jordan. Its exact location is uncertain.

  d. Two branches of the Semitic Christian church, which Epiphanius treated as heresies.

40.1.6 a. "us . . . your humble servant (lit. 'our smallness')": i.e. Epiphanius.

40.1.7 a. "Christian community": lit. "brotherhood."

40.1.8 a. Modern Sadak, Turkey, about 75 miles south of Trebizond (at 39°37′ E, 40°14′ N). Located in Lesser Armenia, it was sufficiently important to send a bishop to the ecumenical Council of Nicaea in A.D. 325.

40.2.1 a. One or more words are inadvertently omitted here.

Thus they also use the work called *The Foreigners*—for there are books [Fr ?] entitled thus.[a] And they draw arguments from the *Ascension of Isaiah* [Porph 16:3] [40.7.5] and also from certain other apocryphal books.

III. TEACHINGS AND PRACTICES OF THE SECT

The heavenly rulers

40.2.3 And ⟨. . .⟩[a] the whole (of their system) from the book entitled *Harmony*. In this (book) they state that there is an eighth heaven[b] and [BJn 11:26+] a septet of heavens;[c] that there are rulers for the various heavens; that [RR 95:31+] the latter are installed in the seven heavens, so that there is one ruler per heaven with each ruler having a band (of angels); and that the luminous mother is in the highest position, in the eighth, just as the [IrUnid 1.30.2 ?] other schools of thought assert.

Ethics

40.2.4 And some of them, as it happens, have polluted their bodies by [IrG] sensuality. Others, of course, feign a put-on abstinence and deceive the [IrSat 1.24.2] simpler folk, priding themselves on a kind of renunciation in the disguise of monastic hermits.
40.2.5 Now, they say that in each heaven, as I mentioned,[a] there is a realm and an authority and hosts of angels for assistance, inasmuch as each ruler has engendered and made for itself an assisting retinue.

Resurrection

And (they say) there is no resurrection of flesh, but only a resurrection [IrUnid 1.30.14] of souls.

Rejection of baptism and other sacraments

40.2.6 And they curse and reject baptism, even though there are some among them who have already been baptized. They deny the value of participation in the sacraments[a] on the grounds that it is alien and has been established in the name of Sabaōth.

Sabaōth rules the universe

For, like certain other schools of thought, they make out that the [40.5.1] latter rules with absolute dominion from the seventh heaven, and prevails over the others.

The soul's escape through the heavens

40.2.7 The soul, they maintain, is the rulers' and authorities' food, and without it they cannot live since it comes from the moisture from above, and provides them with power.
40.2.8 If the soul comes to be in (a state of) acquaintance and flees [EpG 26.10.7+] the baptism of the church and the name of Sabaōth, who gave the law,

---

40.2.2 a. Possibly a reference to Fr.

40.2.3 a. One or more words are inadvertently omitted here.
  b. Or possibly "an octet of heavens."
  c. Or possibly "a seventh (heaven)."

40.2.5 a. Cf. 40.2.3.

40.2.6 a. Lit. "mysteries," a usual term for the eucharist or baptism.

it ascends to each heaven in turn, gives a speech of defense before each authority, and thus rises up to the superior mother and the parent of the entirety, whence indeed it descended into this world.[a] * * *

The devil

40.5.1 These (Archontics) maintain, as I have previously indicated, that the devil is an offspring of Sabaōth[a] the seventh authority, and that Sabaōth is god of the Jews; the devil is the evil offspring of the latter, which presides over the earth and opposes its own parent. **40.5.2** And (they say) its parent is not this sort, nor again is it the incomprehensible deity that they call parent, but belongs to the left-hand authority.

RR 95:13 +
EpG 25.2.2

BJn 2:26 +
IrUnid 1.30.2 ?

Cain and Abel

40.5.3 These folk recount another tale, according to which, they say, the devil came to Eve and united with her as a man with a woman and begot on her[a] Cain and Abel. **40.5.4** One (supposedly) rose up against the other because they were jealous of one another: they (the Archontics) do not accept the true story,[a] that Abel was very pleasing to god, but fictitiously tell another account, which states that inasmuch as both of them had burning desire for a sister of theirs, Cain rose up against Abel and slew him. For, they say, they were physically begotten from the devil's sperm, as I have already stated. **40.5.5** When they wish to deceive people they adduce evidence from the holy books[a]—as I have already mentioned in discussing another heresy[b]—(noting) that the savior said to the Jews, "You (plur.) are of Satan" and "when he lies he speaks according to his own (nature), for his father, too, was a liar." **40.5.6** And so, of course, they say that Cain was from the devil[a] inasmuch as he (the savior) said, "He was a murderer from the beginning" and ⟨. . .⟩[b] **40.5.7** to show that the devil was his father, and that the devil's parent was the lying ruler. And bringing down blasphemy upon their own heads, these foolish people say it is Sabaōth, supposing that the word "Sabaōth" is the name of a particular deity.[a] * * *

BJn 24:8 +

Seth's birth, escape, and reincarnation

40.7.1 And in turn, they say, Adam united with Eve his wife and begot Seth, his own physical son. And next, they say, the higher power descended, accompanied by the ministering angels of the good god, and caught up Seth himself, **40.7.2** whom they also call "the foreigner"; carried him somewhere above and cared for him for a while, lest he be slain; and after a long time brought him back down into this world and

BJn 24:34 +

Fr

40.2.8 a. The following passage (not translated here) is a polemic by Epiphanius.

40.5.1 a. Exactly contradicting BJn, RR, and similar gnostic texts, according to which "Sabaōth the seventh authority" or ruler is the offspring of "the devil" and only through rebellion gains control of the seven heavens.

40.5.3 a. Or possibly "produced out of itself."

40.5.4 a. I.e. the biblical account (Gn 4:1f):

Epiphanius here speaks from his own point of view.

40.5.5 a. I.e. the canonical scriptures of Epiphanius's church.
 b. In his attack on the so-called sect of the Caini, 38.4.2.

40.5.6 a. Or possibly "that Cain was the devil."
 b. One or more words are inadvertently omitted here.

40.5.7 a. The following passage (not translated here) is a polemic by Epiphanius.

rendered him spiritual and bodily,[a] so that neither ⟨Sabaōth⟩[b] nor the authorities and realms of the world-creating god could prevail over him. **40.7.3** And they say that he no longer served the maker and craftsman (of the world); but he acknowledged the unnameable power and the higher, good god, serving the latter; and that he revealed many things to the discredit of the maker of the world, the rulers, and the authorities.

IV. PSEUDEPIGRAPHIC BOOKS READ BY THE SECTARIANS

40.7.4 Hence they have also portrayed certain books, some written in the name of Seth and others written in the name of Seth and his seven sons, as having been given by him. **40.7.5** For they say that he bore seven ⟨sons⟩,[a] called "foreigners"—as we noted in the case of other schools of thought, viz. gnostics and Sethians. **40.7.6** And these (Archontics) say there are also other prophets, a certain Martiades and a Marsianos, who were caught up into the heavens and came back down after three days. **40.7.7** And there are many tales that they fictitiously portray[a] * * *

RAd ?
EgG ?
Fr ?
3Tb ?
s.40.7.5
40.2.2 +

V. ANOTHER TEACHING OF THE SECT

Jesus' body was apparent and not material

40.8.2 Moreover, these (Archontics) say that his[a] body did not exist but rather was shown forth in appearance[b] * * * .

IrSat 1.24.2
IrUnid 1.30.13 ?

40.7.2 a. "bodily": some scholars have supposed that this word contradicts 40.8.2 below and so cannot be in the original of the text, conjecturing that the original reading must have been "invisible" or "seemingly bodily." But it must be noted that "bodily" is not the same as "material," and so there may be no contradiction at all.

b. "<Sabaōth>": or possibly "<the craftsman (of the world)>": in any case one or more words are inadvertently omitted here in the MSS.

40.7.5 a. "<sons>": the word is inadvertently omitted in the MSS.

40.7.7 a. The following passage (not translated here) is a polemic by Epiphanius.

40.8.2 a. I.e. Jesus Christ's. The reference is clarified by the preceding passage, which is not translated here.

b. The doctrine of docetism: that the real Jesus did not exist as human flesh, but only appeared to do so. The rest of the chapter (not translated here) is a polemic by Epiphanius.

THE GNOSTICS

ACCORDING TO
ST. EPIPHANIUS OF SALAMIS, *AGAINST HERESIES*
CHAPTERS 25–26
(EpG)

Contents and literary background

Gnostic myth sets out to show that only the soul is the true self; that the body is a negative element, a "prison" or "fetter" of the soul; and that salvation entails escape from the "bondage" of bodily existence. Yet classic gnostic scriptures almost never go on to draw explicit conclusions about the way that gnostics should in consequence behave. This is understandable, for the literary form of the gnostic scriptures provides almost no occasion for ethical conclusions to be drawn. To some extent, such ethical conclusions may have seemed too obvious to state; for, to many thinkers in the second century A.D., the acceptance of a split between body and soul implied that the best mode of life was continence, so as to minimize the body's adverse influence upon the soul ("passion"). This is also confirmed by a certain amount of direct literary evidence in the gnostic scriptures. *Zōstrianos* (Zs 131:8f) states explicitly that "it is not to experience passion that you have come (to this place), but to break your fetters" (cf. also BJn 25:30f); St. Epiphanius of Salamis (EpA) mentions the monastic asceticism of the "Archontic" gnostics, though ambiguously; and St. Irenaeus (IrS) reports Satorninos's teaching that "marriage and the engendering of offspring are from Satan," adding that most of his followers "abstain from (the flesh of) living things." The speaker in *Thunder* (Th 15:18f) exhorts the listeners, "Love my continence."

Against this background, St. Epiphanius's description (written A.D. ca. 375) of the licentious behavior of the "gnostics, also known as Borborites," completely diverges from the expected norm and is shockingly anomalous.

Stories about sexually licentious Christian sects were not unheard of in antiquity. Starting as early as St. Irenaeus, anti-gnostic writers occasionally reported on libertine sects, some of whom even called themselves "gnostics," that is, "people capable of acquaintance" (it should be remembered that in the language of the Old Testament, "to know, to gain acquaintance of" could be a euphemism for sexual intercourse). It is difficult to judge the accuracy and fairness of such polemical reports. Irenaeus (1.25.1–6), for example, states that followers of a certain Carpocrates (in the second century A.D.) believed that they must experience every kind of deed, including what is ordinarily held to be wicked, in order to escape reincarnation in another body after death. Whether or not this statement is accurate or reasonable, the doctrine of the Carpocratians bears no noticeable resemblance to gnostic myth, and so there are no grounds to conclude that the Carpocratians were gnostics in the classic sense of the word, although they may have borrowed the name "gnostic," perhaps as a form of self-praise.

The same is not true of St. Epiphanius's description, translated here, of a licentious "gnostic" sect in Egypt, for in this instance the teachings of the sect bear an unmistakable resemblance to classic gnostic myth, touching selectively on all four acts of the mythic drama. The following mythic elements are mentioned or implied, although their presentation by Epiphanius is disorderly and obscure: emanation of the Barbēlō from the parent of the entirety; the afterthought of light, here confused with both Barbēlō and "vulgar" wisdom (Prounikos); production of Ialdabaōth; theft of wisdom's power and its passage into human beings; wisdom's repentence; creation of the world by Ialdabaōth; the existence of 365 heavenly rulers or authorities, of which the seven main ones have traditional gnostic names; Ialdabaōth's claim to be honored as god; his defeat and replacement by Sabaōth, as in RR (only implied; cf. 25.2.2 and 26.10.3); the chief ruler's arrogance; the serpentine form of Sabaōth (known also from EpA); Eve and the serpent; activity of the female spiritual principle (the speaker in the gnostic *Gospel of Eve*, 26.3.1); Nōrea (here called "Nōria") and Noah; struggle of two spirits active in humankind; incarnation of the preexistent Christ within Jesus of Nazareth; escape of the soul and ingathering ("collection") of gnostic souls into their spiritual home.

The sources of St. Epiphanius's information were literary, for he cites them by title. Apart from the usual gnostic myth, he speaks also of an unusual gnostic claim to be obliged to "collect" the dispersed units of wisdom's power ("emissions") in the form of "soul" dispersed in all "living things, whether beasts, fishes, reptiles, human beings, vegetables, trees, or fruit . . . No matter what we eat," they claim, "whether meat, vegetable, bread, or anything else, we are doing a favor to created things by collecting soul from all things and transporting it with us to the above." Likewise they claim that when a gnostic soul ascends through the seven heavens it can only get past the rulers if it has "not sown children for the ruler, but . . . eradicated its roots and collected the scattered members . . ." If it has produced a child, the soul is swallowed by Sabaōth, the celestial snake (the Milky Way?), and sent back to earth.

This striking notion of a religious elect who deliberately gather entrapped particles of the divine from foodstuffs and transport them to the metaphysical universe is well known from the Manichaean religion—though the Manichaean diet was vegetarian and the Manichaean elect were extreme ascetics. Since Manichee missionaries were active in Egypt starting in the late third century A.D., St. Epiphanius may have encountered a gnostic church that had been influenced by the pattern of Manichaean theology. Alternatively, he may be using a polemical source that parodies Manichaeism.

In the absence of further information, it is impossible to reconstruct any rationalization of the gnostic diet as described in this excerpt. The reputedly licentious behavior of the sect appears difficult to justify or explain on the basis of the theology just described. St. Epiphanius's description of the gnostic church therefore remains a mystery. The historian must weigh the saint's claim of first-hand observation and the grisly detail of his report against his avowed desire to discredit and destroy the sect. In any case, there is no reason to assume that this is a typical description of gnostic Christianity.

St. Epiphanius lists various names under which the sect was known. One of these in particular, "Borborites," continued to be mentioned in later historical documents, especially in Syria and Mesopotamia (see Map 1). In fact, the original form of this name may have been Barbērites, "followers of Barbērō," for Epiphanius reports that Barbērō was an alternate form of Barbēlō (26.10.10), and that the sect was also known as Barbēlites (26.3.7). The form spelled Borborites, "filthies, muddies," may thus be a polemical tag coined by opponents of the sect.

Mythic characters

I. Higher Powers Mentioned by St. Epiphanius

The PARENT OF THE ENTIRETY
The BARBĒLŌ or BARBĒRŌ

The ANOINTED (Christ)
The VULGAR ELEMENT. Wisdom. Confused with Barbēlō.
The MOTHER, perhaps identical with the former

II. Rulers (At Least 365 in Number) Mentioned by St. Epiphanius

IALDABAŌTH
SABAŌTH
Other AUTHORITIES, RULERS, ANGELS, DEMONS, etc.
The RULER OF THIS WORLD, a snake

III. Humankind Mentioned by St. Epiphanius

EVE
NOAH
NŌRIA, his wife
PROPHETS and OTHERS mentioned in the Old Testament
ZECHARIAH
MARY
JESUS

IV. Spirits Active in Humankind

The SPIRIT OF TRUTH. The holy spirit, perhaps identical with wisdom.
The WORLD SPIRIT, belonging to Ialdabaōth

Text

St. Epiphanius's original Greek text is attested by a number of medieval manuscripts, whose accuracy is a matter of debate among scholars. The translation below is based on Holl's critical edition, but with alterations: K. Holl, ed., *Epiphanius,* vol. 1 (Griechische christliche Schriftsteller, vol. 25; Leipzig: Henrichs, 1915), 268–98.

SELECT BIBLIOGRAPHY

Gero, Stephen. "With Walter Bauer on the Tigris: Encratite Orthodoxy and Libertine Heresy in Syro-Mesopotamian Christianity." In *Gnosticism and Early Christianity,* edited by C. Hedrick and R. Hodgson. Peabody, Mass.: Hendrickson, 1986.

Grant, R.M. "Charges of 'Immorality' Against Various Religious Groups in Antiquity." In *Studies in Gnosticism . . . Presented to Gilles Quispel,* edited by R. van den Broek and M. J. Vermaseren, 161–70. Études préliminaires aux religions orientales dans l'empire romain, no. 91. Leiden: E. J. Brill, 1981.

AGAINST THE GNOSTICS
ALSO KNOWN AS BORBORITES[a]

Genealogy and diversity of the gnostics

25.2.1   And from this source,[a] those who belong to *gnōsis* (acquaintance), falsely so called, also began to spring up in the world—namely, gnostics,[b] Phibionites, the so-called followers of Epiphanes, Stratiōtics, Levitics, Borborites, and the rest. For, each of these has provoked its own school of thought[c] by its own particular passions, and has invented myriad ways of evil.

I. TEACHINGS OF THE SECT

A. VENERATION OF BARBĒLŌ

Barbēlō's offspring. Its arrogance.

25.2.2   Now, certain ones of them venerate a certain Barbēlō, who— they say—is above in the eighth heaven.[a] And—they say—this female was emitted from the parent. Some say she is the mother of Ialdabaōth; others, of Sabaōth; **25.2.3**   and her offspring keeps charge of the seventh heaven in arrogance and absolute dominion; and says to those below, "It is I who am the first and hereafter; there is no other god apart from me." **25.2.4**   But (they say) the Barbēlō heard this utterance and wept.

26.10.4 +
BJn 4:26 +
BJn 9:25 +
26.10.11
RR 95:13 +
EpA 40.5.1
BJn 13:5 +
Is 44:6
S.25.2.4
BJn 13:32 +

Recovery of her power

Moreover, she is repeatedly[a] shown forth to the rulers in a kind of beauty, and through pleasure and outflowing robs the sperm from them, so that—of course—she might again recover her power that has been sown into various places.[b] * * *

Title a. This title properly belongs only to chapter 26 of Epiphanius's catalogue of heresies; it appears in the MSS at 26.1.1. But the following extract, which is taken from chapter 25, "Against the Nicolaitans," actually concerns the gnostics and is a transitional prelude to chapter 26. Elsewhere in his catalogue of heresies (the table of contents with book 2 of the catalogue) Epiphanius gives a summary description of each of the schools of thought that he intends to refute. His summary of the gnostic school provides a few supplementary points of information (italicized below) that are not found in the extracts translated here:

"Gnostics: successors to the aforementioned schools of thought; but more than they, raving devotees of filthy conduct; in Egypt, called Stratiōtics and Phibionites, but *in the "Upper" (i.e. southern) part (of Egypt), called Secundians, elsewhere Sōkratites, and* by still others called Zacchaeuses. Others, still, call them Coddians; yet others call them Borborites. These people take pride in Barbēlō, who is also called Barbērō."

25.2.1 a. The Nicolaitans, a school of thought mentioned in the preceding passage (not translated here). From early Christian times, the condemnation of a group called Nicolaitans had apostolic and scriptural sanction (Rv 2:6f; see Map 1); Epiphanius's assertion that the gnostics and other schools were merely offshoots of the Nicolaitans is one of his refutations of their authenticity.

b. "gnostics," here used in the narrower sense as the designation of a particular school.

c. Greek *hairesis*, the usual term for a philosophical school or religious sect. An unspecified degree of cohesion is implied by the term.

25.2.2 a. In other gnostic texts, it is Barbēlō's manifestation in the form of wisdom who presides in the eighth heaven.

25.2.4 a. Or "always."

b. The following passage (not translated here) is a polemic by Epiphanius.

Allegorical significance of sexual acts

25.3.2 And others venerate a certain vulgar element;[a] and like the above-mentioned people, when they consummate their passions they make mythical reference to this allegory of obscenity, saying, "We are collecting the power of the vulgar from bodies by means of their emissions,[b] that is, by semen and menses."[c] * * *   IrG 1.29.4 +

C. VENERATION OF IALDABAŌTH

25.3.4 And others venerate the aforementioned Ialdabaōth, stating that he is the first offspring of the Barbēlō, as I said. And thus—it says[a]— one must render honor to that (first offspring) because it revealed many things.

Books of Ialdabaōth

25.3.5 Hence they make up also certain books under the name of Ialdabaōth, forming also myriad non-Greek names of rulers and author-ities, distributed among the heavens and opposing the souls of humankind. And their plotting[a] against the human race through error is, in a word, great.[b] * * *   BJn 10:27 +

II. BOOKS COMPOSED BY THE SECTARIANS[a]

Genealogy of the sect

26.1.1 In turn, the aforementioned gnostics sprouted up in diverse ways from him.[b] * * * **26.1.3** And they—who are connected with this Nicolaus and who are begotten from him like scorpions from the failed egg of a snake or ⟨. . .⟩ from asps[a]—introduce to us certain names belonging to godless chatter, and they fabricate books.

A. THE BOOK "NŌRIA"

One book they entitle *Nōria*. And by allegorical interpretation of Greek religion[b] they recompose Greek epic mythology and imagery, interweaving falsehood and the truth. **26.1.4** For, this Nōria, they say, was Noah's wife.[a]

25.3.2 a. Or possibly "lewd element," Greek *prounikos*. The word basically means "mover, porter," one who corporally transports bur-dens for a fee. In gnostic texts it is an epithet of wisdom (Sophia); cf. 1rG 1.29.4.
  b. "emissions" (the Greek word can also be translated "emanations"): cf. 26.1.9, 26.4.5, 26.4.8, 26.5.3, 26.5.7, 26.8.2, 26.8.4, 26.8.7, 26.9.2, 26.10.9, 26.11.1, 26.11.10, 26.13.5.
  c. The following passage (not translated here) is a polemic by Epiphanius.

25.3.4 a. "it says,": either Epiphanius re-fers to a specific written source, or he means this in the sense of "they say." The phrase recurs throughout the extracts.

25.3.5 a. I.e. the gnostics' plotting.
  b. The following passage (not translated here) is a polemic by Epiphanius.

26.1.1 a. In the MSS the chapter title is written here; see note "a." with title.
  b. The following passage (not translated here) is a polemic by Epiphanius.

26.1.3 a. One or more words are inadvert-ently omitted in this phrase. Some scholars conjecture that the original reading was "<cobras> from asps."
  b. Or "Greek superstition."

26.1.4 a. Nōria (Nōrea, Hōraia, Ōrea) is mentioned also in RR and EpS.

Meaning of the name Nōria

And they name her "Nōria" so that with reference to non-Greek words they might recompose epic written among the Greeks in the Greek language[b] and so make an impression on those who have been deceived by them. Thus they give an explanation of the name Pyrrha[c] by calling her Nōria. **26.1.5** Now, inasmuch as *nura* means "fire" only in the Syriac language[a] but not in formal Hebrew—for in the formal language the Hebrews call fire *hēsath*[b]—it must have happened that they used this name (Nōria) from lack of acquaintance[c] and from inexperience. **26.1.6** For neither Pyrrha of the Greeks—for the Greeks say that Deukalion's wife was called Pyrrha—nor Nōria fabled by these (gnostics) was Noah's wife: rather, it was Barthenōs.[a]

RAd 70:17

Nōria and Noah

26.1.7 Then these (gnostics) once again stage Philistionian shows[a] for us, charging that when she wanted many times to be with Noah in the ark, her request was denied since—it says—the ruler who created the world wanted to destroy her in the flood along with all the others. **26.1.8** And—it says—she laid siege to the "coffer"[a] and burned it,[b] once, again, and a third time. Hence, indeed, the construction of Noah's "coffer" went on for many years because it was burnt many times by her. **26.1.9** For—it says—Noah put his trust in the ruler, whereas Nōria revealed the higher powers and the Barbēlō from the powers, who like the other powers was opposed to the ruler.

BJn 25:2?
BJn 29:1?
RR 92:14
IrUnid 1.30.9
EpS 39.5.2
BJn 28:32+
s.26.1.8
EpS 39.3.2

Recovery of the higher mother's power

And she made clear the necessity of collecting, from out of the power within bodies, the parts plundered from the superior mother by the ruler who made the world[a] and by the others in its company—gods, angels, demons—by means of the emissions of males and females. **26.2.1** And I simply find it difficult to describe the utter blindness of these people of darkness. For I would spend a lot of time if at this point I wanted to quibble over the treatise on these matters and give detailed information about the bizarre teachings of their falsely termed "acquaintance."

26.3.1, 26.5.6
26.9.4, 26.10.9
26.13.2
Th 16:19
BJn 10:20+
25.3.2+

---

b. "epic . . . Greek language": the flood myth of Deukalion, a Noah figure in Greek myth. He and his wife Pyrrha built an ark ("coffer") in which they survived a flood brought wrathfully upon the earth by Zeus.
c. Deukalion's wife.

26.1.5 a. The gnostics seem to have referred to a learned etymology of the name "Nōria," relating it to Syriac *nura*, "fire." Epiphanius here objects that since Noah is a biblical figure the etymology ought to work in "the formal language (i.e. Hebrew)" and not in Syriac.
b. I.e. ʾēšat. This is actually closer to the Palestinian Aramaic word for "fire"; the biblical ("formal") Hebrew is ʾēš.
c. "lack of *gnōsis*."

26.1.6 a. Noah's wife is not called by name

in the Old Testament; Epiphanius here refers to non-biblical tradition.

26.1.7 a. "Philistionian": erroneous, ridiculous, unclear. The epithet refers to a proverbial author of mimes who flourished in the early first century A.D.

26.1.8 a. "coffer," Greek *larnaks*: not the usual biblical word for Noah's ark, but rather the classical Greek term for Deukalion's ark.
b. Hence the gnostics' interest in the etymology of the name Nōria and her possible identification with Pyrrha, for Greek *pyr* means "fire."

26.1.9 a. The chief ruler's theft of "power" from wisdom and the subsequent implantation of that power in humankind are more explicitly narrated in BJn 10:19f, 12:5f, 13:1f, and 19:15f.

B. PROPHECY OF BARKABBAS

26.2.2 Certain others, originating from them[a] * * * introduce a prophet named Barkabbas—he is worthy of his name, **26.2.3** for *kabba* means "illicit sexual activity" in Syriac, "the act of murder" in Hebrew, and means also the fourth part of the measure.[a] * * * **26.2.4** And from this most wonderful prophet they adduce for us a shameful narrative so that we might be persuaded to have intercourse with corrupt bodies and be   26.3.3+
deprived of the higher hope: they are not ashamed to retell, verbatim, pornographic stories about sexual activity.[a]

C. "THE GOSPEL OF PERFECTION"

26.2.5 Still others, originating from them, introduce a fabricated work rather like a love charm, to which they have assigned the title *Gospel of Perfection*—in truth, it is not a gospel (good news) but rather sorrow over death, for all the consummation of death resides in this clandestine sowing of the devil.

D. "THE GOSPEL OF EVE"

26.2.6 And yet others shamelessly speak of a *Gospel of Eve*.[a] Indeed, they clandestinely sow (this weed) in her name, on the grounds that she   RR 89:31+
discovered the food of acquaintance through a revelation spoken to her by the snake.[b] And as though in the unstable frame of mind of a drunkard and of one who randomly utters statements that are not compatible, but rather are partly the result of laughter and partly full of weeping—such was the rogues' utterly evil, clandestine sowing. **26.3.1** And they start out from foolish visions and testimonies in the *Gospel* that they profess. Indeed, they say the following:

> I stood upon a high mountain. And I saw a tall person and another who was short. And I heard as it were a voice of thunder, and I drew near to listen. And it[a] spoke to me and   Th 13:1+
> said:

> It is I[b] who am you (sing.): and it is you who are me.   26.1.9+
> And wherever you are, I am there.
> And I am sown in all: and you collect me from wherever
>   you wish.
> But when you collect me, it is your own self that you
>   collect.[c] * * *

III. PRACTICES OF THE SECT

Promiscuous religious services

26.3.3 Those of the school of *gnōsis*[a] (acquaintance) who are connected with Nicolaus's school of thought[b] thus introduce such things, having

26.2.2 a. The following passage (not translated here) is a polemic by Epiphanius.

26.2.3 a. The following passage (not translated here) is a polemic by Epiphanius.

26.2.4 a. Lit. "about Aphrodite," a traditional euphemism.

26.2.6 a. For the literary character of this *Gospel*, see introduction to Th.
   b. As, e.g., in RR 89:31f.

26.3.1 a. The voice of thunder.
   b. The speaker (the superior mother) is consubstantial with the divine elements (her power) now "sown" in various human bodies.
   c. The following passage (not translated here) is a polemic by Epiphanius.

26.3.3 a. Gnostics, as a specific school.
   b. Cf. note 25.2.1a.

been deprived of the truth; and they not only turn away the intellects of their followers, but also make their bodies and their souls slaves of illicit sexual activity and promiscuity. Thus they confuse[c] their religious services with promiscuous filthy conduct, eating and becoming contaminated by human flesh and impurities.[d] * * *

26.2.4, 26.4.1
26.4.4, 26.5.2
26.9.6, 26.10.1
26.11.9, 26.17.7

Various branches of the sect

26.3.5   * * * Indeed, the blasphemous assembly full of enormous recklessness, the anthologizing and narration of its filthy conduct, and the filthy perversity of their beggarly obscenity truly pollute the ears, **26.3.6** so that quite naturally they are called Borborites ("filthies")[a] by some; others call them Coddians—for *kodda* means "side dish" or "bowl" in Syriac—from the fact that people cannot eat with them, but rather they dispense their food in private to those who have been polluted and no one can dine with them, not even on bread, because of the defilement.[b] **26.3.7**   * * * In Egypt the same people are called Stratiōtics and Phibionites, as I mentioned before in turn. Some call them Zacchaeuses, others call them Barbēlites.[a] * * *

26.4.3. +

Sign of membership in the sect

26.4.1   * * * They hold their women in common. **26.4.2**   And if someone from out of town belonging to their persuasion comes to visit, they have a signal for use by men unto women and by women unto men: the hand is held out, in greeting of course, and a tickling stroke is made in the palm of the hand, so as to indicate secretly that the visitor is of the same religion as they. **26.4.3**   Thereupon, having recognized one another they hasten to dine. And they serve lavish meat dishes and wines,[a] even if they are in penury. Then, after a drinking party where so to speak they have engorged their veins[b] with gormandizing, they turn to their frenzied passion.

26.3.3 +
26.3.6, 26.5.5
26.5.8, 26.9.4

Sexual practices in the eucharistic service

26.4.4   And husband withdraws from wife and says, speaking to his own wife,

> Arise and have the love feast[a] with your (sing.) brother.

And when the wretches have had intercourse with one another[b] * * * **26.4.5**   * * * in the passion of illicit sexual activity, then they lift up their blasphemy to heaven. The woman and the man take the male emission in their own hands and stand gazing toward heaven with the impurity in their hands; and of course they pray—**26.4.6**   I refer to the so-called Stratiōtics and gnostics—offering what is in their hands aptly to the parent of the entirety. And they say,

26.3.3 +
25.3.2 +
26.8.5 +

---

c. Or "wet."
d. The following passage (not translated here) is a polemic by Epiphanius.

26.3.6 a. From Greek *borboros*, "filth, mud": presumably a hostile parody of the name Barbērō, an alternate form of Barbēlō.
b. The following passage (not translated here) is a polemic by Epiphanius.

26.3.7 a. The following passage (not translated here) is a polemic by Epiphanius.

26.4.3 a. Abstinence from meat, wine, and sexual activity was typical of early Christian asceticism.
b. Or "organs."

26.4.4 a. Greek *agapē*, a technical term of early Christianity, originally denoting a common meal held in connection with religious services or meetings. The phrase quoted here is thus liturgical in character.
b. The following passage (not translated here) is a polemic by Epiphanius.

> We offer unto you (sing.) this gift, the body of Christ (the anointed)[a]

26.4.7 and then they eat it, partaking of their own filthiness. And they say,

> This is the body of Christ (the anointed), and this is the Passover because of which our bodies feel passion[a] and are constrained to confess the passion[b] of Christ (the anointed).

26.4.8 And likewise with the woman's emission: when it happens that she has her period, her menstrual blood is gathered and they mutually take it in their hands and eat it. And they say,   25.3.2+

> This is the blood of Christ (the anointed).

26.5.1 Thus when they read in apocryphal books,[a]

> I beheld a tree bearing twelve crops[b] per year, and he said to me, "This is the tree of life"

they interpret the passage allegorically as referring to the woman's monthly emissions.

Childbearing forbidden

26.5.2 Now, although they have intercourse with one another, they forbid childbearing; for among them, this (act of) corruption is not undertaken for the sake of bearing children, but for pleasure.[a] * * *   26.3.3+
26.5.3 They consummate their pleasure, and then they take unto themselves the sperm produced by their (act of) impurity—not insemi-   25.3.2+
nating it for the bearing of children, but rather eating the product of their filthy conduct.

Abortion and ritual cannibalism

26.5.4 And if one of them, a man, prematurely ejaculates and the woman becomes pregnant, listen to the even more terrible thing that these folks dare to do. **26.5.5** As soon as it is feasible, they induce the   26.4.3+
expulsion of the embryo, and take the aborted offspring and grind it up with a mortar and pestle. And they season it with honey, pepper, and other spices, and with aromatics, so as not to nauseate themselves. Doing this, all the participants belonging to this ⟨herd⟩[a] of swine and dogs gather together[b] and partake with their fingers of the ground-up baby. **26.5.6** And when in this fashion they have accomplished their act of cannibalism they pray, finally, to god. It[a] says,

> We have not been deceived by the ruler of desire, but rather we have collected the transgression of our brother.   26.1.9+

And, of course, they consider this to be the perfect Passover.   26.8.5+

26.4.6 a. "anointed" and "Christ" are the same word in Greek.

26.4.7 a. "passion": or "suffering."
   b. "Passover . . . feel passion . . . the passion": a play on words in Greek, *paskha . . . paskhein . . . pathos* (which is formally related to *paskhein*). The formulaic phrases quoted here are in the style of solemn eucharistic prayers.

26.5.1 a. Very similar to Rv 22:2.

b. Or "fruits."

26.5.2 a. The following passage (not translated here) is a polemic by Epiphanius.

26.5.5 a. Through an inadvertence this word is omitted in the MSS.
   b. "gather together": the Greek verb (*synagesthai*) is appropriate to gatherings for celebration of the eucharist.

26.5.6 a. Cf. note 25.3.4a.

26.5.7 But they dare to perform other, equally dreadful acts. Indeed, when again they are aroused to the point of climax they wet their own hands with the filthiness of their own emission; and entirely naked with their hands still defiled, they pray—as though by this production to find the openness to speak to god.   25.3.2+

Abstinence forbidden

26.5.8 And they—both men and women—care for their bodies night and day, perfuming themselves, bathing, banqueting, and spending their time in bed and drunk. And they curse anyone who is abstinent,[a] saying one ought not to be abstinent, for abstinence belongs to the ruler who made this realm; rather, one must eat in order to make one's body strong so it can yield its fruit in its season.[b]   26.4.3+   26.8.7+

IV. LITERATURE OF THE SECT

Principle of biblical interpretation

26.6.1 They utilize both the Old and the New Testament, but they reject the one who spoke in the Old Testament. And whenever they find a passage capable of meaning something in opposition to themselves, they say that it has been spoken by the world spirit. **26.6.2** But if any statement—not what the passage actually means, but what their deceived interpretation says—can be adapted so as to be similar to their (sexual) desire, they transform it to conform to their (sexual) desire and say that it has been spoken by the spirit of truth.   IrSat 1.24.2   BJn 26:32?   BJn 25:20+ RR 96:22+

> **26.6.3** And this—it says—is what the lord said concerning John: "What did you (plur.) go out into the wilderness to behold? A reed shaken by the wind?" For—it says—John was not perfect, since he was inspired[a] by many spirits[b] like the reed shaken by every wind.   Mt 11:7

26.6.4 And

> when the spirit belonging to the ruler came, it proclaimed Judaism. But when the holy spirit came, it spoke of Christ (the anointed). And this—it says—is the meaning of "whoever is least in the kingdom" (etc.).[a] It is about us that he spoke—it says—for the least among us is greater than he.[b] * * *   Mt 11:11

Books composed by the sectarians

26.8.1 And they have many books. Indeed, they publish certain *Questions of Mary.* Others posit many *Books* in the name *of* the aforementioned *Ialdabaōth* or in the name of *Seth.* Other books they call *Revelations of Adam;*[a] and they have dared to compose other *Gospels* in the names of the disciples, and are not ashamed to say that our savior and lord himself, Jesus Christ, revealed this obscenity.   RAd ? EgG ? Fr ? 3Tb ?

26.5.8 a. Or "who fasts."
   b. Cf. 26.8.7.

26.6.3 a. Or "blown upon."
   b. The Greek word (*pneumata*) also means "winds."

26.6.4 a. Mt 11:11: "Truly, I say to you, among those born of women there has risen no one greater than John the Baptist; yet whoever is least in the kingdom of heaven is greater than he."
   b. The following passage (not translated here) is a polemic by Epiphanius.

26.8.1 a. "*Books . . . of . . . Seth . . . Revelations of Adam*": cf. perhaps 3Tb and RAd.

The "Greater Questions of Mary"

26.8.2 For, in the so-called *Greater Questions of Mary* (indeed, there are also *Lesser* ones fabricated by them) they posit that he gave a revelation to her:[a] he took her to the mountain,[b] prayed, and took from his side a woman; he began to mingle with her; and thus, of course, partaking[c] of his own emission, he indicated that   25.3.2+

> we must act thus, so that we might live;

26.8.3 and when Mary was disturbed and fell to the ground, he raised her up and said to her, "O person of little faith, why did you doubt?"   Mt 14:31

Examples of biblical interpretation

26.8.4 And they say that what is written in the gospel, when it says "If I have told you (plur.) earthly things and you do not believe, how   Jn 3:12
will you believe in heavenly things?" and "When you see the son of   Jn 6:62
man ascending where he was before," refers to the source from which
came the emission[a] that is partaken of. **26.8.5** And when it says "Unless   25.3.2+
you (plur.) eat my flesh and drink my blood," and when the disciples   26.4.6, 26.5.6
are troubled and say "Who can listen to it?" they say that the statement   Jn 6:53
was about filthy conduct. **26.8.6** Thus they both were troubled and   Jn 6:60
"drew back."[a] For—it says—they were no longer established in fullness.   Jn 6:66
26.8.7 And when David says that "he shall be as a tree planted by the   26.5.8
brooks of waters, which shall yield its fruit in its season" he is speaking—   Ps 1:3
it says—of filthy conduct by the male. The words "at the outpouring of
waters" and "which shall yield its fruit" refer—it says—to the emission   25.3.2+
belonging to pleasure.[a] And "its leaf shall not fall off" refers—it says—   Ps 1:3
to the fact that we do not let it fall on the ground but personally eat it.[b]
* * * **26.9.2** Indeed—it says—the statement that Rahab set the scarlet
in the window[a] did not refer—it says—to a scarlet thing; rather, it refers
to the parts of the female reproductive organ and the scarlet refers to
menstrual blood.   25.3.2+
And the saying "Drink water out of your (sing.) own vessels" refers   Pr 5:15
to the same thing.

V. TEACHINGS OF THE SECT

Resurrection

26.9.3 They say that flesh is dying, and is not arising, and that it belongs   IrUnid 1.30.14
to the ruler.

Recovery of the higher mother's power

26.9.4 And (they say) the power residing in the menses and the semen   26.4.3+
is soul, which, they say,

26.8.2 a. Mary.
  b. Or possibly "to the desert."
  c. The Greek word is appropriate to eating in a sacramental rite.

26.8.4 a. The Greek word (*aporrhoia*) also means "emanation."

26.8.6 a. Jn 6:53–66: "Jesus said to them, '. . . unless you eat the flesh of the Son of

man and drink his blood, you have no life in you.' . . . After this many of his disciples drew back and no longer went about with him."

26.8.7 a. Or "pleasurable emission."
  b. The following passage (not translated here) is a polemic by Epiphanius.

26.9.2 a. The story is told in Jos 2:1f.

we collect and eat. And no matter what we eat, whether meat, vegetable, bread, or anything else, we are doing a favor to created things by collecting souls from all things and transporting it with us to the above. 26.1.9+

Thus they partake of all kinds of meat, saying,

It is so that we might have mercy upon our own kind.[a]

26.9.5 And they say that one and the same soul is sown in living things, whether beasts, fishes, reptiles, human beings, vegetables, trees, or fruit.

A. PHIBIONITE TEACHINGS AND PRACTICES

Divinization through ritual intercourse

26.9.6 And those of them who are called Phibionites offer up their shameful sacrifices of illicit sexuality—which we have already spoken of—in the names of 365 rulers, which they themselves fabricated, of course. They deceive their women, saying, 26.3.3+ BJn 11:25+

Have intercourse with me, so that I might bring you (sing.) up to the ruler.

26.9.7 And with each act of intercourse they utter a non-Greek name of some one (of the rulers) fabricated by them. And, of course, they pray, saying,

I bring my offering unto you (sing.), O so-and-so, so that you might bring (her) as an offering to so-and-so.

And again, with the next act of sexual intercourse the male posits that he is likewise offering (her) to the next (ruler), so that also that one might (bring her as an offering) to the next. **26.9.8** And until he has "ascended"—or rather gone down—through 365 falls consisting of coitus, the man who is doing this invokes some name with each act. And then he begins to "descend" through the same ones, performing the same shameful acts and misleading the deceived women. **26.9.9** Now, when he has progressed through the enormous number of 730 falls—I mean, shameful acts of sexual intercourse and names fabricated by these people—then next this man acts recklessly and says

It is I who am Christ (the anointed), inasmuch as I have descended from above through the names of the 365 rulers.

Names of the heavenly rulers

26.10.1 They speak of many rulers, but the names of what they consider to be the greater ones, they say, are the following:

In the first heaven is the ruler Iaō; BJn 11:26+
in the second—it says—is Sakla, the ruler of illicit sexual 26.3.3+
　activity;
in the third, the ruler Sēth;
in the fourth—it says—is Dauidē

26.10.2 (for they posit a fourth heaven and a third);

fifth is another heaven, in which they say is Elōaios, also called Adōnaios;

26.9.4 a. Or "our own people."

in the sixth, some say there is Ialdabaōth, while others say
Ēlilaios;

26.10.3 they posit additionally a seventh heaven, in which
they say there is Sabaōth—but others say no, rather
Ialdabaōth is in the seventh.

The incorruptible realm

26.10.4 And in the eighth heaven:

the so-called Barbēlō;
the parent of the entirety and lord, the self-engendered itself;
the anointed (Christ), another self-born being.

25.2.2
RR 95:31+

26.10.10+
BJn 4:36+
EgG 60:1+

Jesus' body was apparent and not material

And (they say) it was this anointed (Christ) who came down and
manifested this acquaintance unto humankind. They also say he was
Jesus, **26.10.5** but that he was not born of Mary but manifested by
Mary; and he did not take on flesh, but only existed in appearance.[a]

EgG 75:15+

IrSat 1.24.2

Sabaōth's form

26.10.6 And some say that Sabaōth has the form of an ass;[a] others, of
a pig—whence, it says, the Jews were commanded not to eat pork. And
it (Sabaōth) is the maker of heaven and earth, of the heavens thereafter,[b]
and of its angels.

26.12.2

The soul's escape or its reincarnation

26.10.7 Thus (they say), departing from here the soul passes through
the aforementioned rulers; but it cannot get through unless it is in
fullness of acquaintance (*gnōsis*)—or rather, moral dereliction (*kata-
gnōsis*)[a]—and if it has become full it escapes the clutches of the rulers
and the authorities. **26.10.8** And the ruler who restrains this world has
the form of a snake, and it swallows the souls that do not exist in a
(state of) acquaintance and returns them to the world through its tail,
and thence into swine and other living things, and brings them up again
through the same (rulers). **26.10.9** But if, it says, one is in this (state
of) acquaintance and gathers one's self out of the world, by the menses
and by the emission belonging to pleasure,[a] that person is no longer
restrained here (in this world), but rather goes beyond the aforementioned
rulers, **26.10.10** and comes to Sabaōth and tramples upon his head—
as they say with their blasphemous babbling; and thus the person goes
beyond, into the higher place, where there is the mother of the living,
the Barbērō or Barbēlō, and in this way the soul is preserved.[a]
26.10.11 Furthermore, the wretches say that Sabaōth has hair like a
woman, and they suppose that the word *sabaōth*[a] is the name of a
particular ruler.[b] * * *

26.13.2
BJn 27:20
Th 21:30
IrUnid 1.30.14
EpA 40.2.8

IrUnid 1.30.5

26.1.9+
25.3.2+

26.10.4
Th 21:29

25.2.2+

26.10.5 a. The doctrine of docetism: that
the real Jesus did not exist as human flesh,
but only appeared to do so.

26.10.6 a. Cf. 26:12.2f.
  b. I.e. higher than our terrestrial heaven.

26.10.7 a. Epiphanius puns on the Greek
word *gnōsis*.

26.10.9 a. Or "by pleasurable emission."

26.10.10 a. Or "saved."

26.10.11 a. Hebrew "armies," originally the
second half of a traditional epithet of Jahweh,
"god of the armies." By the early Christian
period, the single word "sabaōth" had begun
to be taken as a name of god.
  b. The following passage (not translated
here) is a polemic by Epiphanius.

Homosexual practices

26.11.1 * * * Indeed, some of them who are males do not consort with females, but corrupt themselves with their own hands and catch their corruption in their hands and so eat it, **26.11.2** utilizing misrepresented [25.3.2+] (scriptural) evidence—namely, the passage "These hands ministered not [Ac 20:34] only to me but also to those who were with me" and again, the passage "Working with your (plur.) own hands, so that you might be able to [Ep 4:28] share also with those who do not have."[a] * * * **26.11.8** * * * For the [26.13.1] males who become corrupted by their own hands, as also the ones who consort with females, finally become sated of promiscuity with females and burn with passion for one another, males with males.[a] * * *

Definition of female virginity

26.11.9 But also males who deceive the female sex[a] * * * say to the [26.3.3+] women who are deceived by them that such-and-such a woman is a virgin, when for many years she has been corrupt and is being corrupted every day. For with them the desire for coitus is never satisfied. Rather, a man is admired by them in proportion to the frequency of his obscenity. **26.11.10** And the females that they call "virgins" are the ones who have never experienced the worldly intercourse of ordinary natural marriage as far as the reception of sperm goes. Rather, even though [25.3.2+] they are always having intercourse and illicit sexual activity, before the consummation of pleasure they release the wicked male seducer and take his aforementioned filthiness to eat.[a] * * *
26.11.12 And they utter blasphemy against not only Abraham, Moses, [EpS 39.5.1?] Elijah, and all the band of prophets, but also the god who chose them. [26.13.4]

"The Birth of Mary"

26.12.1 And they dare to put forth many other fabricated writings. Indeed, they say there is a certain book called *The Birth of Mary,* into which they have inserted terrible and destructive passages, which they then proceed to read.
26.12.2 For—it says[a]—the reason why Zechariah was slain in the temple [Lk 1:5f] was that he saw—it says—a vision. And when he wished to tell the vision his mouth froze from fear. For—it says—in the hour of the offering of incense he saw, as he was offering incense, a person standing at rest, having—it says—the form of an ass.[b] **26.12.3** And when he went outside—it says—and wanted to say, "Woe unto you (plur.)! What are you worshiping?" the thing he had seen inside in the temple froze his mouth, so that he could not speak. And when his mouth opened so that he might speak, then he revealed it to them, and they slew him. And thus—it says—did Zechariah die. **26.12.4** Indeed, the reason why

---

26.11.2 a. The following passage (not translated here) is a polemic by Epiphanius.

26.11.8 a. The following passage (not translated here) is a polemic by Epiphanius.

26.11.9 a. The following passage (not translated here) is a polemic by Epiphanius.

26.11.10 a. The following passage (not translated here) is a polemic by Epiphanius.

26.12.2 a. In the passage that follows, fea-

tures of two biblical stories are combined— the murder of Zechariah the son of Jehoiada the priest in about 800 B.C. (2 Ch 24:20f, mentioned in Mt 23:35 and Lk 11:51) and the circumstances of the birth of John the Baptist (Lk 1:5–80). "*The Birth of Mary*" must have properly concerned the second of these two stories.
   b. According to an Egyptian anti-Semitic tradition the god worshiped by the Jews had to be an ass because they spoke of him (in Greek) as "Iaō" (cf. Yahu, Yahweh) and the Old Coptic word for "ass" was *eiō* or *iaō*.

the priest was commanded by the lawgiver himself[a] to have bells—it says—was so that whenever he entered to perform priestly duties, the being who was worshiped might hear the noise and hide, lest the imaginary nature of his form be disclosed.[b] * * *

B. LEVITIC PRACTICES AND TEACHINGS

Homosexual practices

26.13.1 Those males among them called Levites do not have sexual 26.11.8 intercourse with females but have intercourse with one another. They, of course, are the ones who are preferred and honored among them. But they scorn those who practice religious behavior, purity, and virginity, as though they undertook this labor in vain.

Ascent of the soul in "The Gospel According to Philip"

26.13.2 And they produce a fabricated *Gospel* in the name *of Philip*[a] the holy apostle, with—it says—the words

> The lord revealed unto me what the soul must say when it is 26.10.7+ ascending into heaven and how it must reply to each of the higher powers: "I have come to be acquainted with my self"— it says; "I have collected myself from everywhere; I have not 26.1.9+ sown children for the ruler, but have eradicated its roots and collected the scattered members. And I know who you (sing.) are. For it is I"—it says—"who belong to those from the above." And so—it says—the soul departs. **26.13.3** But if—it says—it is found to have produced a child, it is restrained below until it can get back its own offspring and return to itself.

26.13.4 So frivolous and fabulous are their stories that they dare also to utter blasphemy against the holy Elijah and to state that—it says— after he had been taken up he was cast back down into the world. **26.13.5** For—it says—a female demon came, laid hold of him, and said, "Where are you (sing.) going? For I have had children by you; you cannot ascend and leave your children here." And—it says—he replies, "How could you have had children by me while I remained in purity?" And—it says—she replies, "Oh yes, often while you were dreaming dreams you had nocturnal emissions, and it was I who partook of your 25.3.2+ sperm and bore you children."[a] * * *

VI. EPIPHANIUS'S ACQUAINTANCE WITH THE GNOSTICS

26.17.4 Indeed, beloved readers, I happened to come upon this school of thought in person, and was instructed in these matters face to face, by the people who naturally attempt this (school). Women, who had been deceived in such a way, not only offered us this verbal information and revealed such things to us, but also—just like that deadly, wretched

---

26.12.4 a. Moses. See Ex 28:33f (28:29f in the Greek LXX version).

b. I.e. lest it be discovered that he did not look as people had imagined. The following passage (not translated here) is a polemic by Epiphanius.

26.13.2 a. The following citation bears no relation to the Valentinian *Gospel According to Philip* (GPh).

26.13.5 a. The following passage (not translated here) is a polemic by Epiphanius.

Egyptian wife of the captain of the guard[a]—reached out their hands to us in our youth and with babbling recklessness attempted to drag us down. **26.17.5** But the one who once assisted the holy Joseph also assisted us, and[a] * * * **26.17.6** * * * we were saved. For, though reproached by these deadly women I laughed scornfully when they indicated to one another, making fun of me, of course, "We have not been able to save the young man, but have abandoned him to perish in the clutches of the ruler"—**26.17.7** inasmuch as the one of them who is the most beautiful offers herself so to speak as bait, so that by means of her they promise to save those who are deceived "before they perish." And the unbeautiful female (gnostic) is reproached by the more beautiful ones with the words, "It is I who am a chosen instrument, who am able to save those who are deceived, but you (sing.) cannot." **26.17.8** Now, the women who gave instruction in this erotic incantatory tale were very beautiful in the form of their appearance, but in the content of their wretched thought they possessed the full ugliness of the devil. But the merciful god delivered us from their wretchedness. And thus after we had read their books and truly understood their intention we were not led away by them, but rather we avoided them and did not become hooked. **26.17.9** And we devoted ourselves to the problem of the moment, pointing them out to the bishops there and detecting the names of those who were hidden within the church. And so they were expelled from the city, about eighty names, and the city was cleansed of their thorny underbrush full of tares.

26.3.3 +

Ac 9:15

26.17.4 a. Gn 39:1–7. Joseph was sold into Egypt as a slave, where he was owned by Pharaoh's Egyptian captain of the guard. After a time, Joseph's master's wife noticed Joseph's good looks and said, "Lie with me." Joseph's refusal led to his imprison-

ment on false charges, but god eventually assisted him and he was saved.

26.17.5 a. The following passage (not translated here) is a polemic by Epiphanius.

PART TWO

THE WRITINGS OF VALENTINUS

HISTORICAL INTRODUCTION

Valentinus's early years

Valentinus (A.D. ca. 100–ca. 175) was born in the Egyptian Delta, at Phrebonis[1] (see Map 4). He enjoyed the good fortune of a Greek education in the nearby metropolis of Alexandria, the world capital of Hellenistic culture. In Alexandria he probably met the Christian philosopher Basilides (see Part Five), who was teaching there, and may have been influenced by him. There, too, he must have made the acquaintance of Greek philosophy. Valentinus's familiarity with Platonism may have come to him through study of Hellenistic Jewish interpretation of the bible, for in a passage of one of his sermons he seems to show knowledge of a work by the great Alexandrian Jewish allegorist and philosopher Philo Judaeus (ca. 30 B.C.–A.D. ca. 45).[2] Valentinus's distinguished career as a teacher began in Alexandria, sometime between A.D. 117 and 138. Since most of the Fragments of his works (VFr) were preserved by a second-century Christian intellectual in Alexandria, Valentinus may have written and published in Alexandria while he was teaching there. If so, his considerable expertise in rhetorical composition, which is evident in these Fragments, must have been acquired while he was studying in Alexandria. Valentinus's followers in Alexandria later reported that he had claimed a kind of apostolic sanction for his teaching by maintaining that he had received lessons in Christian religion from a certain Theudas, who—he said—had been a student of St. Paul. If there is any truth in this claim, his contact with Theudas and his reading of St. Paul may have occurred in Alexandria.

In the second century all roads led to Rome. Thus, sometime between A.D. 136 and 140, Valentinus migrated to the great nerve center of the Roman empire, where he assumed a role in ecclesiastical affairs.

St. Irenaeus of Lyon reports in about the year 180 that Valentinus based his theological system in part upon the gnostic myth (IrV, "Relation to gnostic myth"). Where then did Valentinus come into contact with the sect of gnostics—Alexandria or Rome? Since VFrC speaks of a "preexistent," or

---

[1] A city of the north central Egyptian Delta, otherwise called Phlabonis. The sixth-century encyclopedist Hierocles places it between Xois and Pachnemunis, thus nearly at the latitude of Alexandria but halfway between the two main branches of the Nile. Its exact modern equivalent cannot be discovered.

[2] GTr 36:35f may use the allegory of Gn 2:8 found in Philo Judaeus, "Questions and Answers on Genesis" 1.6. For the text, see *Philo: Supplement I, Questions and Answers on Genesis Translated from the Ancient Armenian Version of the Original Greek*, by R. Marcus (Loeb Classical Library; Cambridge; Mass: Harvard University Press, 1953).

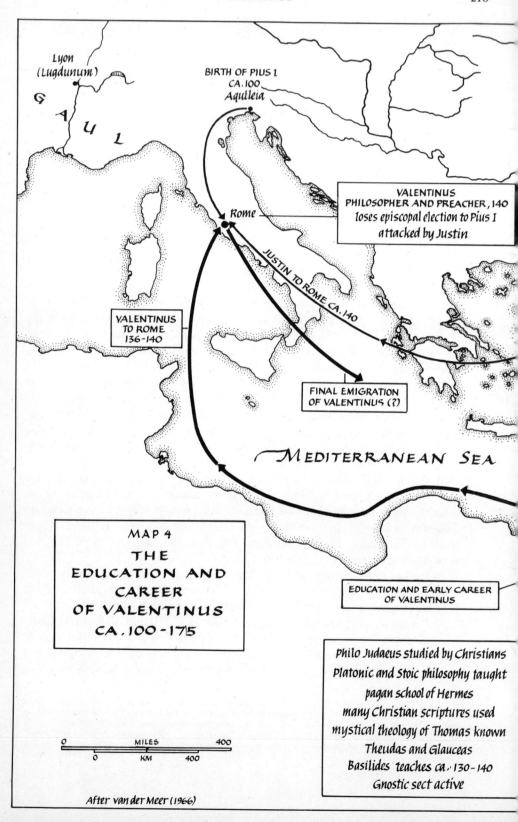

Lyon
(Lugdunum)

G A U L

BIRTH OF PIUS I
CA. 100
Aquileia

VALENTINUS
PHILOSOPHER AND PREACHER, 140
loses episcopal election to Pius I
attacked by Justin.

Rome

JUSTIN TO ROME CA. 140

VALENTINUS
TO ROME
136-140

FINAL EMIGRATION
OF VALENTINUS (?)

MEDITERRANEAN SEA

MAP 4

THE
EDUCATION AND
CAREER
OF VALENTINUS
CA. 100 - 175

EDUCATION AND EARLY CAREER
OF VALENTINUS

philo Judaeus studied by Christians
Platonic and Stoic philosophy taught
pagan school of Hermes
many Christian scriptures used
mystical theology of Thomas known
Theudas and Glauceas
Basilides teaches ca. 130-140
Gnostic sect active

0   MILES   400
0   KM   400

After van der Meer (1966)

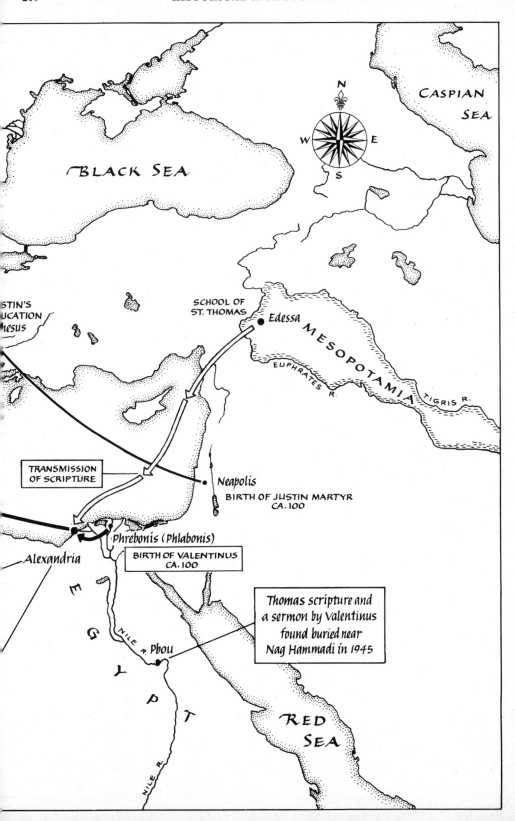

CASPIAN SEA

BLACK SEA

N
W E
S

STIN'S
UCATION
hesus

SCHOOL OF
ST. THOMAS

● Edessa

MESOPOTAMIA

EUPHRATES R.

TIGRIS R.

TRANSMISSION
OF SCRIPTURE

● Neapolis

BIRTH OF JUSTIN MARTYR
CA. 100

Phrebonis (Phlabonis)

Alexandria

BIRTH OF VALENTINUS
CA. 100

E
G
Y
P
T

NILE R.

Pbou ●

Thomas scripture and
a sermon by Valentinus
found buried near
Nag Hammadi in 1945

NILE R.

RED
SEA

spiritual, prototype of Adam, a knowledge of gnostic myth *may* be already presupposed in this Fragment. VFrC is one of the Fragments that were transmitted in Alexandria and preserved by an Alexandrian source, and so it may well go back to the time of Valentinus's residence in Alexandria. If so, he had already met gnostics while he was in Egypt. Otherwise, he must have met them in the Christian church of Rome when he arrived. Any previous Alexandrian contact with Basilides or other myth-creating philosophers would have prepared him for this meeting.

It is difficult to detect the influence of other precise historical figures or sects upon Valentinus. But from the atmosphere of his style it is hard not to imagine that he also had come into contact with the esoteric Hermetic literature of Greek-speaking Egypt (cf. Poim, CH7). However, much more important—central, in fact—in Valentinus's Christianity is mysticism, an acceptance of salvation through *gnōsis* (acquaintance) of the savior, the self, and god, whose most brilliant exposition is found in his sermon *The Gospel of Truth*. This doctrine is far from classic gnostic myth and from gnostic mysticism (as represented by Zs, Fr, and 3Tb). It is therefore a major aspect of Valentinus's revision of gnostic tradition that he chose to make this mystical approach to salvation so important.

The doctrine is dimly present in the Johannine literature of the New Testament; but its clearest expression is probably in the works of the school of St. Thomas that are translated in Part Four, and which are *not* gnostic. Since the Mesopotamian Thomas literature (at least GTh) circulated in Egypt roughly at the time of Valentinus's formative years—and also was known at Rome (to judge from the third-century witness of St. Hippolytus)— it might be supposed that Valentinus knew *The Gospel According to Thomas*, or perhaps similar works. This Mesopotamian current is the chief intellectual counterforce to gnostic myth in the delicate and unstable system of Valentinus's religious thought (see Table 1).

His later career

Once at Rome, Valentinus began to play an active role in the affairs of the Roman church as teacher and leader. It is even reported that he expected to be chosen bishop of Rome, on the grounds of his outstanding talent and literary ability (Greek was at this time the language spoken by Christians living in Rome). If this was his hope, it was dashed—and had it not been, the whole future of Roman Christianity might have been unimaginably altered.

Although Valentinus played a public role in the teaching and worship of the Christian community, he and his students also met privately. Apparently they accepted a shared, traditional Roman formulation of correct belief, but by means of allegorical interpretation they discovered also a "deeper" meaning within it, which was partly expressed in the form of Valentinus's version of the gnostic myth (IrV); cf. "Allegorical interpretation of scripture" in the "Historical Introduction" to Part Three. Valentinus was a successful and productive teacher, for the next generation of the Valentinian movement was populated by important exegetes and writers, who continued in the trail that Valentinus had blazed.

The Roman Christian community at mid second century was noteworthy for the great variety of its theologians and for their acrimonious debates with one another. Valentinus was the subject of a bitter series of attacks, in which he was lumped together with many different sects and past figures of Christianity. However, it is not clear that this opposition ever caused him to leave Rome, as later church fathers claimed in retrospect. In any case, Valentinus's public Roman career probably ended sometime around A.D. 165, and his death is shrouded in silence.

His writings

Valentinus's genius and Greek eloquence were publicily acknowledged by even his bitterest enemies. It is not surprising, then, to find an astonishing range and variety in his literary remains—so astonishing, in fact, that some critics even doubt they can have been written by one and the same author. But the variation is mainly one of literary genre and content, not style. In particular, the stylistic identity and peculiarity of the Fragments and GTr have recently been demonstrated, tending to confirm the attribution of GTr to Valentinus.

Three sides of Valentinus's literary personality emerge in these remains. First, there is the mythmaker—continuing in the steps of the gnostics, but strikingly innovative so as to take account of a different brand of philosophy, a more profound acceptance of biblical and cross-centered Christianity, and a different structuring of the myth. A doctrinal résumé of Valentinus's myth, by St. Irenaeus, survives (IrV): it is abbreviated and stops short, so no more than a hint of this side of Valentinus emerges. The myth is known in more detail in versions taught by Valentinus's disciples. The version by Ptolemy is included in the present volume (IrPt); from it, a modern reader can get a better idea of what Valentinus's own teaching must have been like, though some details are doubtless due to Ptolemy's own creativity.

Second, there is the Platonizing—or perhaps, better, gnosticizing—biblical theologian of the Fragments (VFrA–H). These eight Fragments, excerpted by ancient witnesses from Valentinus's philosophical epistles, sermons, and treatises, show an intensity, an attention to detail, and a penchant for unexpected turns of thought that set them apart from most other literature of gnostic Christianity and Valentinianism. Despite their brevity and incompleteness, they are among the most striking remains of ancient Christian literature. Without more of the originals, it is hard to assess how far they resembled the other material attributed to Valentinus. VFrA, VFrC, and VFrD relate to a mythic story of cosmic structure and creation like IrV, while VFrF and VFrH resemble more the content of GTr. However, there is very little in the Fragments that unambiguously resembles gnostic or postgnostic myth (except perhaps "the preexistent human being" in VFrC; cf. VFrD, "the form was not reproduced with perfect fidelity").

Third, there is the mystic poet of *Summer Harvest* (VHr) and *The Gospel of Truth* (GTr). Both these works are personal and visionary. *Summer*

Harvest is nothing less than a stylized evocation of the whole metaphysical and physical world, in seven lines of verse that hover between philosophical cosmology and pure poetry. *The Gospel of Truth* also evokes the entire universe, but in a rhetoric that no longer bears any immediate relation to the linear, chainlike cosmology of gnostic myth or *Summer Harvest*. The world view of GTr is Stoic and pantheistic: that is, a universe in which all is enclosed by god, and ultimately all *is* god. Although it begins with formal rhetoric and continues with exhortation of the listeners, GTr ends in a purely visionary mode in which Valentinus confesses that he is already present in the "place" of repose and salvation.[3]

SELECT BIBLIOGRAPHY

Any reconstruction of Valentinus's life and teachings is inseparable from the study of his disciples and his school. See, therefore, the "Select Bibliography" at the end of the "Historical Introduction" to Part Three.

---

[3] Since each of these three bodies of text—the myth, the Fragments, and GTr—is written from a different perspective, the marginal cross-references among them are of uncertain value.

VALENTINUS'S MYTH

ACCORDING TO
ST. IRENAEUS OF LYON
AGAINST HERESIES 1.11.1
(IrV)

Contents and literary background

This incomplete summary by St. Irenaeus of Lyon, written in Greek about A.D. 180, may be based upon a lost work of Valentinus; but if so, nothing is known about the literary nature or title of that work. The summary may also be based on secondhand information. Irenaeus did not know Valentinus personally, though he did have personal contact (in Gaul, i.e. southern France, and perhaps elsewhere) with the first generation of Valentinus's disciples and also examined writings used in the Valentinian church. In addition, he relied on at least one older Christian work written against Valentinus and others.

St. Irenaeus means the reader to compare the present summary with his account of the gnostic sect (cf. IrG and possibly IrUnid), as he explicitly states. Thus he is only concerned to highlight some of the salient differences between Valentinus's system and the gnostic myth.

The summary parallels the gnostic myth, very selectively, from the description of the first principles down to Jesus of Nazareth—and perhaps beyond, since it ends by describing the activity of the holy spirit, presumably within the church.

The following points of Valentinus's gnostic myth appear:

Act I: The emission of the spiritual universe (**b–c, e**)
    A primaeval octet and twenty-two subsequent aeons develop
Act II: The creation of the material universe (**c, f–h**)
    "The mother" produces matter, Christ, and a thieving "craftsman"
(Act III: The creation of Adam, Eve, and their children—not mentioned here)
Act IV: The subsequent history of the human race (**i–j**)
    Emission of the holy spirit; Jesus

From the summary, Valentinus's system appears more overtly Christian than the gnostic myth and also closer to the language of Plato (it speaks of a divine "craftsman," for example, and not of Ialdabaōth). Furthermore, it is not inspired by the same school of Platonic teaching as gnostic myth, since the system begins with not a monad (BJn 2:26f) but a duality or dyad, that is, a pair of original first principles. The system also takes account of the origin of matter (a "shadow" engendered by one of the aeons ["powers"] of the spiritual universe). On the problems of reconstructing Valentinus's original system from other sources, see the introduction to IrPt.

Mythic characters

I. The Original Fullness

A. The deep:

    The INEFFABLE, unengendered parent   =   SILENCE

B. Other aeons of the fullness:

    The PARENT (of the entirety)   =   TRUTH
    The WORD   =   LIFE
    The HUMAN BEING   =   The CHURCH

TEN POWERS, from the Word and life

TWELVE POWERS, from the human being and the church, including:

    The MOTHER (Wisdom)

II. Beings Produced Outside the Fullness

The ANOINTED (Christ)

The CRAFTSMAN (The almighty)

The LEFT-HAND RULER

JESUS

III.

The HOLY SPIRIT

Text

St. Irenaeus's original Greek text survives in the form of a word-for-word citation in St. Epiphanius of Salamis, *Against Heresies* 31.32.2–9 (vol. 1, 434–35 in K. Holl's edition of Epiphanius), whose text is attested by a number of medieval manuscripts. An ancient Latin version of Irenaeus's work also survives. The translation below is based on the critical edition of the Greek and Latin texts by Rousseau and Doutreleau, with slight alteration: A. Rousseau and L. Doutreleau, eds., *Irénée de Lyon, Contre les hérésies: Livre I* [Book 1] (Sources chrétiennes, no. 264; Paris: Le Cerf, 1979), vol. 2, 166–71.

SELECT BIBLIOGRAPHY

See the bibliography at the end of the "Historical Introduction" to Part Three. Also:

Dillon, J. "Valentinus." In his *Middle Platonists*, 384–89. Ithaca, N.Y.: Cornell University Press, 1977.

Plato. "Timaeus." In vol. 7 of *Plato with an English Translation*, by R. G. Bury, 1–253. Loeb Classical Library. New York: G. P. Putnam's Sons, 1929.

Relation to gnostic myth (a)

1.11.1 Valentinus adapted the fundamental principles[a] of the so-called gnostic school of thought to his own kind of system.[b] Here is what he laid down.

The ineffable and silence (b)

There was a duality, of which one member is called the ineffable[c] and the other is called silence.

GTr 17:4
GTr 34:7

Production of the other aeons (c)

Then from this duality a second duality was emitted, of which one member he calls the parent[d] and the other he calls truth.

GTr 16:31

This quartet yielded:[e]

> the Word;[f]
> life;
> the human being;
> the church.

GTr 16:33 +
GTr 20:28
VFrC

This is the first octet.

And—he says—from the Word and life ten powers[g] were emitted, as I already said.[h] And from the human being and the church twelve powers[i] were emitted.

1.11.1 a. Or "first principles"; i.e. metaphysical assumptions, perhaps referring in this case to the gnostic myth.

b. Lit. "to his own character of classroom."

c. Cf. the ineffable parent of the entirety in gnostic myth (BJn 2:26f).

d. As distinct from the "ineffable parent" (or "the ineffable").

e. Like a crop. The word here is an agricultural term. The Valentinian school char-

acteristically spoke of emanations and the process of emanation in agricultural metaphors.

f. Or "verbal expression, rational faculty" (Greek *Logos*).

g. Cf. BJn 6:8f.

h. Cf. IrPt 1.1.2. In the work from which this section comes, St. Irenaeus discusses the Ptolemaean version of the myth before he summarizes the teaching of Valentinus.

i. Cf. BJn 8:22f.

Revolt of the mother (d)

One of these[j] revolted[k] and became lacking; this one was responsible for the rest of the affair.

Two boundaries (e)

He assumes the existence of two boundaries: one is between the deep and the rest of the fullness,[l] bounding the engendered aeons away from the unengendered parent;[m] the other bounds their mother apart from the fullness.

GTr 35:14
GTr 16:33

Production of the anointed (Christ) and "shadow" (f)

And furthermore, the anointed (Christ) was not emitted from the aeons within the fullness. Rather, he and a shadow[n] were engendered by the mother, according to her memory of the superior realm, while she was outside (of the fullness). Since he was male he cut off the shadow, (removing it) from himself; and he hastened up into the fullness.

Loss of spirit by the mother. The craftsman. (g)

The mother was left behind with the shadow; and having been emptied of the spiritual substance,[o] she emitted another child. This was the craftsman,[p] whom he also calls the almighty of those that are subject to it.

GTr 17:17

The left-hand ruler (h)

Just like the gnostics—falsely so called!—of whom we shall speak further on,[q] he holds that along with this (craftsman) was emitted also a ruler on the left.

The emanation of Jesus (i)

And furthermore, sometimes he says that Jesus emanated from that being who had drawn away from this mother of theirs and had merged with the entirety, i.e. the wished-for.[r] At other times he says that he emanated from that being which had hastened up into the fullness, i.e. the anointed (Christ); at still other times, he says that he emanated from the human being and the church.

GTr 17:4

---

j. In gnostic myth, wisdom (the last of the twelve aeons accompanying the four luminaries).

k. Or "turned away."

l. Valentinian jargon for the spiritual universe.

m. The "ineffable" belonging to the first duality.

n. Matter; cf. RR 94:8f.

o. Corresponding to the "power" lost by wisdom at the production of her offspring Ialdabaōth; cf. BJn 10:20f.

p. Greek *dēmiourgos;* the same word is used by Plato in his myth of creation entitled *Timaeus.* Valentinus's craftsman corresponds to Ialdabaōth of gnostic myth.

q. St. Irenaeus's refutation is arranged in such a way that his description of the gnostics comes after that of Valentinus even though, as he says, they were Valentinus's predecessors.

r. Greek *thelētos,* "the one who is desired or desirable." Perhaps an epithet of the annointed (Christ), although St. Irenaeus's next remark implies that this being is distinct from the anointed.

The holy spirit (j)

And the holy spirit, he says, was emitted by truth, for the scrutiny and yielding of the aeons,[s] invisibly entering into them. Through it the aeons yielded the plants of truth.[t]

GTr 26:35 +

VHr 6
GTr 36:35 +

s. "aeons" (or "eternal realms") usually refer to beings within the spiritual universe (fullness).

t. See note "e."

VALENTINUS

FRAGMENTS OF LOST WORKS

(VFrA–H)

A. The Divine Word Present in the Infant (Frag. 7 Vö.)
B. *On the Three Natures* (Frag. 9 Vö.)
C. Adam's Faculty of Speech (Frag. 1 Vö.)
D. Adam's Name (Frag. 5 Vö.)
E. Jesus' Digestive System (*Epistle to Agathopous*) (Frag. 3 Vö.)
F. Annihilation of the Realm of Death (Frag. 4 Vö.)
G. The Source of Common Wisdom (*On Friends*) (Frag. 6 Vö.)
H. The Vision of God (*Epistle on Attachments*) (Frag. 2 Vö.)

The Fragments are arranged not in the traditional numerical order (established by W. Völker) but according to the order of events in the gnostic myth so far as it is relevant. Völker's "fragment" 8—*Summer Harvest* (VHr)—is put in a separate section, for in fact it is no fragment at all but rather a complete work.

SELECT BIBLIOGRAPHY

Bloom, H. "Lying Against Time." In *The Rediscovery of Gnosticism*, edited by B. Layton. Vol. 1, *The School of Valentinus*, 57–72. Studies in the History of Religion, no. 41, vol. 1. Leiden: E. J. Brill, 1980.

Festugière, A. J. "Notes sur les extraits de Théodote de Clément d'Alexandrie et sur les fragments de Valentin." *Vigiliae Christianae* 3 (1949): 193–207.

Standaert, B. "L'Évangile de vérité: critique et lecture." *New Testament Studies* 22 (1976): 243–75.

Stead, G. C. "In Search of Valentinus." In *The Rediscovery of Gnosticism*, edited by B. Layton. Vol. 1, *The School of Valentinus*, 75–95 (and discussion, 95–102). Studies in the History of Religion, no. 41, vol. 1. Leiden: E. J. Brill, 1980.

THE DIVINE WORD PRESENT IN THE INFANT

(VFrA)

Contents and literary background

The first two sentences of this fragment may summarize an autobiographical or visionary statement by Valentinus. Nothing is known about the title or literary nature of the work in which the statement occurred. Its place of composition is uncertain (possibly Alexandria). The language of composition is Greek.

The third sentence is a later commentator's derogatory attempt to explain the source of Valentinus's theology ("pompous tale . . . his attempt at a sect"). This explanation may be compared with the historical one put forward by St. Irenaeus (IrV, "Relation to the gnostic school"). Neither explanation excludes the other. Cf. also the introduction to VHr.

Text

The source of this fragment is St. Hippolytus of Rome (cf. VHr), *Against Heresies* 6.42.2. It counts as Frag. 7 in Völker's enumeration. The translation below is based on Völker's text: W. Völker, ed., *Quellen zur Geschichte der christlichen Gnosis* (Sammlung ausgewählter kirchen- und dogmengeschichtlicher Quellenschriften, new ser., no. 5; Tübingen: Mohr [Siebeck], 1932), 59.

Fragment A

FOR Valentinus says he saw a newborn babe, and questioned it to find VHr 7 ?
out who it was. And the babe answered him saying that it was the HPrl ?
BasFrG ?
Word.[a] Thereupon, he adds to this a certain pompous tale,[b] intending GTr 16:33+
to derive from this his attempt at a sect.

---

a. Or "verbal expression, rational faculty" (Gk. *Logos*).

b. Lit. "a certain tragic myth." Possibly the commentator means that Valentinus added the gnostic myth ("a certain pompous tale") to his own theological vision; cf. IrV ("Relation to gnostic myth"). If so, the vision of the babe may refer to HPrl (cf. GTh nos. 22, 46) and the mystical concept of salvation conveyed by the Thomas scripture.

Fragment B

ON THE THREE NATURES

(VFrB)

Contents and literary background

This is not really a literary fragment, just a title. It shows that Valentinus, like the gnostics (and also like contemporaneous Platonists), recognized a tripartite structure at some level in his description of the spiritual universe. The work presumably was a theological treatise. Its place of composition is unknown. The language of composition must have been Greek.

Text

The source of this fragment is the fourth-century theologian Marcellus of Ancyra ("Pseudo-Anthimus of Nicomedia"), *On the Holy Church,* 9. It is not clear whether the terms "subsistent entity (hypostasis)," "person," and "father, son, holy spirit" were used by Valentinus or belong only to Marcellus's characterization of the treatise.

The excerpt counts as Frag. 9 in Völker's enumeration. The translation below is based on Völker's text (cf. VFrA, "Text"), *Quellen,* p. 60.

Fragment B

VALENTINUS, the leader of a sect, was the first to devise the notion of three subsistent entities (hypostases), in a work that he entitled *On the Three Natures*.[a] For, he devised the notion of three subsistent entities and three persons—father, son, and holy spirit.

GTr 26:35 +

a. Apart from its title (*Peri tōn triōn physeōn*), the work apparently does not survive. It must have concerned the structure of the spiritual universe. A threefold division of the Barbēlō aeon is described in certain works that recount the gnostic myth (cf. EgG 50:23f), but these divisions do not correspond to the three persons of the orthodox trinity. A trio of hypostases also figured in Platonist philosophical speculation starting at least as early as the second century A.D.

Fragment C

ADAM'S FACULTY OF SPEECH

(VFrC)

Contents and literary background

In this fragment, which is quoted verbatim, Valentinus speaks of the divine or artistic inspiration, and thus superiority, inherent in Adam ("that modeled form") just after the faculty of speech was imparted to him from the higher realm, as an assistance. For details of the story, the gnostic paraphrase of Gn 2:18 in RR 88:17f may be compared. The rulers are called "angels" as in IrSat, EpS, and generally in Jewish lore of the period. Reference to "the preexistent human being" that provided a model for the creation of Adam makes it clear that this passage is not simply an exegesis of Gn but refers to a more elaborate story, presumably a revision of the gnostic myth (cf. IrV). The "agent who deposited" the faculty of speech ("seed of higher being") is, at least in RR, the female spiritual principle, but may in Valentinus refer to the Word (son) of the ineffable parent. This principle "speaks freely" through Adam, using him as its mouthpiece so long as it inhabits his body. For free speech of the divine as an aspect of the son, see VFrH and GTr.

The fragment comes from "a certain epistle" by Valentinus, no doubt a treatise in the form of a philosophical epistle. This literary genre was often used in the period; complete Valentinian examples survive in TrRs and PtF. The recipient of the epistle is unknown and its place of composition, uncertain (possibly Alexandria). The language of composition is Greek.

Text

The source of this fragment is the late-second-century Christian intellectual St. Clement (Titus Flavius Clemens) of Alexandria, *Miscellanies* (*Stromateis*) 2.36.2–4 (132,6–16 Stählin). It counts as Frag. 1 in Völker's enumeration. The translation below is based on Völker's text (cf. VFrA "Text"), *Quellen*, 57–58.

Fragment C

AND EVEN as awe[a] overcame the angels[b] in the presence of that modeled form[c] because it uttered sounds superior to what its modeling justified,[d] owing to the agent who had invisibly deposited in it a seed[e] of higher essence and who spoke freely: so too in the races of worldly people,[f] human artifacts become objects of awe for their creators—for example, statues and paintings[g] and everything that (human) hands make as representing[h] a god. For Adam, modeled as representing a human being, made them stand in awe of the preexistent human being;[i] for precisely the latter stood in him. And they were stricken with terror and quickly concealed[j] the work.

VFrD

GTr 17:14

VFrH

IrV (c)

GTr 30:19

GTr 17:9+

a. Or "fear."

b. The "rulers" of gnostic myth.

c. Adam's body. "modeled form" is Jewish and Christian jargon for the human body, based on the fact that the creator modeled Adam out of earth.

d. Cf. RR 88:17f.

e. The Valentinian school characteristically speaks of emanations and the process of emanation in agricultural metaphors.

f. Perhaps meaning "the world at large," whether non-Christian or Christian.

g. Or "images."

h. The Greek idiom literally says "in the name of."

i. Adamas (Ger-Adamas) in gnostic myth. Cf. BJn 8:28f.

j. Or "marred, destroyed."

Fragment D

ADAM'S NAME

(VFrD)

Contents and literary background

In GTr, Valentinus elaborates the idea that the divine son of god, who is also called the father's "name," completes the "lack" within each person that is saved. In VFrD, he explores this theme in regard to Adam ("what has been modeled") and his relationship to the divine image and likeness after which he was formed. Adam was "modeled as representing (literally, in the name of) . . . the preexistent human being" and also bears that being's name ("human being"): cf. VFrC. This archetypal relationship may provide a clue to some of the enigmatic statements about names in GTr.

As narrator of the fragment, Valentinus moves back and forth ambiguously between general statements about artistic verisimilitude and specific comments on Adam's degree of likeness to the divine: this shifting ambiguity has been noted as a salient feature of Valentinus's literary style.

The literary genre of the work excerpted in this fragment is unknown and its place of composition uncertain (possibly Alexandria). The language of composition is Greek.

Text

The source of the fragment is the late-second-century Christian intellectual St. Clement (Titus Flavius Clemens) of Alexandria, *Miscellanies* (*Stromateis*) 4.89.6– 4.90.1 (vol. 2, 287,21–27 Stählin). It counts as Frag. 5 in Völker's enumeration. It has been suggested that this and VFrF come from the same work because the two fragments are quoted so close to one another by Clement. The translation below is based on Völker's text (cf. VFrA, "Text"), *Quellen*, 59.

Fragment D

HOWEVER much a portrait[a] is inferior to an actual face, just so is the VFrC
world worse than the living realm.[b] Now, what is the cause of the
(effectiveness of the) portrait? It is the majesty of the face that has
furnished to the painter a prototype so that the portrait might be honored
by his name.[c] For the form was not reproduced[d] with perfect fidelity,
yet the name completed the lack[e] within the act of modeling. And also GTr 21:14
god's invisible cooperates with what has been modeled[f] to lend it Rm 1:20
credence.

a. Or "image."

b. "living" in gnostic myth is jargon indicating association with the spiritual universe. "realm": or "aeon."

c. "by his name": by the name of the
majestic subject who is being painted. Or,
alternatively, by the painter's reputation.

d. "was not reproduced": the past tense

("was") takes the narrative back to a description of the "act of modeling" of the first
human being Adam (the "modeled form")
and his relation to the divine prototype (Adamas or Ger-Adamas, cf. BJn 8:28f).

e. Cf. GTr note 24a.

f. Specifically Adam.

Fragment E

JESUS' DIGESTIVE SYSTEM

Epistle to Agathopous
(VFrE)

Contents and literary background

In this fragment Valentinus discusses Jesus' "continence" (the Greek term, *enkrateia,* means abstemiousness in the use of wine, meat, sex, etc.), perhaps as a model for Christian behavior (cf. IrSat 1.24.2). His exaggerated statement about Jesus' digestion may be based on a New Testament story of Jesus' command to the people of Tiberias in Jn 6:27, playing upon the double meaning of the Greek verb "to labor for," which can also mean "to digest": "Jesus answered them . . . 'Do not *labor for* (or *digest*) the food which perishes, but for the food which endures to eternal life, which the son of man will give to you.'"

The fragment comes from an *Epistle* to a certain Agathopous (otherwise unknown), no doubt a treatise in the form of a philosophical epistle; cf. VFrC ("Introduction"). Its place of composition is uncertain (possibly Alexandria). The language of composition is Greek.

Text

The source of the fragment is the late-second-century Christian intellectual St. Clement (Titus Flavius Clemens) of Alexandria, *Miscellanies (Stromateis)* 3.59.3 (223,12–16 Stählin). It counts as Frag. 3 in Völker's enumeration. The translation below is based on Völker's text (cf. VFrA, "Text"), *Quellen,* 60.

Fragment E

HE WAS continent, enduring all things. Jesus digested[a] divinity: he ate Jn 6:27 ?
and drank in a special way, without excreting his solids. He had such a
great capacity for continence that the nourishment within him was not
corrupted,[b] for he did not experience corruption.   VFrF
                                                                         Ac 13:35
                                                                         = Ps 16:11

a. Or "labored for."   b. I.e. did not become excrement.

Fragment F

ANNIHILATION OF THE REALM OF DEATH

(VFrF)

Contents and literary background

The fragment quoted here is a piece of exaggerated artistic rhetoric, spoken before a Christian congregation. The occasion is unknown. The passage makes implicit comparison between the individual Christian elect ("From the beginning") and Jesus, for both are said to be immortal by nature and superior to corruption (cf. VFrE, "he [Jesus] did not experience corruption"). As in GTr and TRs, the material world is spoken of as unreal compared to the state of being experienced by the saved Christian. The verbatim quotation (printed here in ordinary type) is continued by a summary (in *italics*) phrased in the words of St. Clement, by whom the fragment is preserved.

Because the fragment comes from a sermon, as the source explicitly states, it should be compared with GTr. The sermon's place of composition is uncertain (possibly Alexandria). The language of composition is Greek.

Text

The source of the fragment is the late-second-century Christian intellectual St. Clement (Titus Flavius Clemens) of Alexandria, *Miscellanies (Stromateis)* 4.89.1–3 (287,10–20 Stählin). It counts as Frag. 4 in Völker's enumeration. It has been suggested that this and VFrD come from the same work because the two fragments are quoted so close to one another by Clement. The translation below is based on Völker's text (cf. VFr7, "Text"), *Quellen,* 58, supplemented by a passage from Stählin's text of Clement: O. Stählin, ed., *Clemens Alexandrinus: Stromata Buch I–VI* (Griechische christliche Schriftsteller, 15; Leipzig: Hinrichs, 1906) 4.89.4–5 (vol. 2, p. 287, 15–20).

Fragment F

FROM the beginning you (plur.) have been immortal, and you are   GTr 21:23
children of eternal life. And you wanted death to be allocated to   GTr 43:22+
yourselves so that you might spend it and use it up,[a] and that death   GTr 33:19
might die in you and through you. For when you nullify[b] the world and   GTr 24:20
are not yourselves annihilated, you are lord over creation and all
corruption.   VFrE

Now,[c] like Basilides,[d] he supposes that there is a people that by its
(very) nature is saved;[e] *that this race, indeed, has come down to us[f] for
the destruction of death;[g] and that* the origination of death is the work
of the creator of the world. *Accordingly, he understands the scriptural
passage (Ex 33:20)[h]* "No one shall see the face of god and live" *as
though god[i] were the cause of death.*

a. "allocated . . . spend it . . . use it up":
fiscal imagery was a commonplace way of
speaking of death or of the body as a corrupt
part of the human being, e.g. on ancient
Greek and Latin gravestones. It is used also
in TRs.

b. Or "loosen (the bond of)." For "nul-
lification" of the "realm of appearance" or
"world" see GTr 24:20f.

c. The italicized remarks are by St. Clement.

d. An inaccurate comparison; for what
Basilides meant, cf. BasFrC.

e. So also "'one is saved by (one's very)

nature' as Valentinus has it" (BasFrC 5.3.3).

f. "us": St. Clement speaks as a non-
Valentinian, referring to the rest of the human
race.

g. "that this race . . . of death": St. Clement's interpretation of the beginning of Fragment F. It may or may not be correct.

h. In the exact wording of the passage
(Septuagint Greek version) God speaks: "No
person shall see my face and live."

i. "the creator of the world . . . god": the
craftsman of the world (Ialdabaôth in gnostic
myth).

Fragment G

THE SOURCE
OF COMMON WISDOM

On Friends
(VFrG)

Contents and literary background

In the middle of the second century A.D., non-Valentinian Christians as well as Valentinians were interested in why moral truths were to be found in pagan pre-Christian literature ("publicly available books"), especially the classics of Greek culture such as Plato or the tragedians. For example St. Justin Màrtyr, a Christian philosopher who was contemporary with Valentinus at Rome, argued that god's preexistent Word (the son) had created the world, and then up to the time of his incarnation in Jesus of Nazareth had "sowed seeds" of moral enlightenment in the hearts of certain great teachers and writers of pagan classical antiquity. The present fragment must be from Valentinus's treatment of the same problem, but it is too brief to make his full position clear. Though Valentinus, like Justin, used the agricultural imagery of moral or intellectual "seeds" implanted in humankind (VFrC), here he seems to work with the image of the human heart (moral faculty) as a book in which god writes: cf. GTr 23:2f, where the individual Christians are said to be passages of text that speak aloud.

The fragment is taken from a sermon by Valentinus entitled *On Friends*. The sermon's place of composition is uncertain (possibly Alexandria). The language of composition is Greek.

Text

The source of this fragment is the late-second-century Christian intellectual St. Clement (Titus Flavius Clemens) of Alexandria, *Miscellanies (Stromateis)* 6.52.3–4 (vol. 2, 458,11–16 Stählin). It counts as Frag. 6 in Völker's enumeration. The translation below is based on Völker's text (cf. VFrA, "Text"), *Quellen*, 59.

Fragment G

MANY of the things written in publicly available books[a] are found in
the writings of god's church. For this shared matter is the utterances
that come from the heart, the law that is written in the heart. This is   Rm 2:15 ?
the people of the beloved, which is beloved and which loves him.   GTr 19:34
                                                                           GTr 32:31+
                                                                           Rm 9:25 ?

---

a. I.e. non-Christian or pre-Christian literature.

Fragment H

THE VISION OF GOD

Epistle on Attachments[a]
(VFrH)

Contents and literary background

This fragment concerns the heart's prerequisites for *gnōsis* or acquaintance with god (to "see god") and so belongs to the genre of literature that sets out a theory of spirituality or mysticism. The language is partly biblical (purity of heart, evil spirits dwelling in the heart) but also strongly Platonic. Like the image of "attachments" mentioned in the title (cf. note "a"), the comparison of the soul to a caravansary (found in this fragment) was used by Plato in the *Republic* (580a4); the same comparison was used also by followers of Basilides. Valentinus emphasizes the role of the savior, referred to as son, Word (god's "act of free speaking"), and forethought, in the prelude to *gnōsis*. The saving action of the son is also spoken of as the visitation of the father, so that the distinction of father and son is deemphasized: the theology of GTr may be compared.

The fragment is taken from an "epistle on attachments" (or "appendages"), no doubt a treatise in the form of a philosophical epistle. This literary genre was often used in the period; complete Valentinian examples survive in TRs and PtF. The recipient of the epistle is unknown and the epistle's place of composition is uncertain (possibly Alexandria). The language of composition is Greek.

Text

The source of this fragment is the late-second-century Christian intellectual St. Clement (Titus Flavius Clemens) of Alexandria, *Miscellanies* (*Stromateis*) 2.114.3–6 (vol. 2, 174,31–175,14 Stählin). It counts as Frag. 2 in Völker's enumeration. The translation below is based on Völker's text (cf. VFrA "Text"), *Quellen*, 58.

---

a. The title of the work is known from Clement of Alexandria (see below). The image of "attachments" or "appendages" does not occur in the surviving fragment; its source may have been Plato's comparison (*Republic* 611cd) of the soul to the sea god Glaucus, who had become like a sea monster owing to the seaweed, rocks, and shells that had become attached to him because of his mode of life. In the surviving fragment, Valentinus uses another Platonic image of the soul, also taken from the *Republic*; cf. below.

Fragment H

AND ONE there is who is good![b] His free act of speaking is the
manifestation of the son. And through him alone can a heart become
pure, when every evil spirit has been put out of the heart. For the many
spirits dwelling in the heart do not permit it to become pure: rather,
each of them performs its own acts, violating it in various ways with
improper desires. And in my opinion the heart experiences something
like what happens in a caravansary.[c] For the latter is full of holes and
dug up and often filled with dung, because while they are there, people
live in an utterly vulgar way and take no forethought for the property
since it belongs to someone else. Just so, a heart too is impure by being
the habitation of many demons, until it experiences forethought.[d] But
when the father, who alone is good, visits the heart, he makes it holy
and fills it with light. And so a person who has such a heart is called
blessed, for that person will see god.[e]

Mt 19:17
VFrH
GTr 36:35+
VFrC
GTr 32:31+
GTr 31:34

GTr 21:25

GTr 18:15
Mt 5:8
GTr 30:14+

b. God the father. Quoted from Mt 19:17.
c. A rural inn of the East, with large
enclosed courtyard for pack animals, where
caravans may stop overnight.
d. Or "providence, first thought." In

gnostic myth the savior is identified with
forethought or first thought (BJn 4:26f, FTh).
e. Thus the passage is an interpretation of
Mt 5:8, "Blessed are the pure in heart, for
they shall see god."

SUMMER HARVEST

(VHr)

Contents

Summer Harvest ("Harvest") is a cosmological poem that is visionary and personal in character ("I see in spirit . . . I know in spirit . . ."). Its authority, like that of GTr, rests ultimately upon the speaker's claim to knowledge based upon personal acquaintance (*gnōsis*); thus it stands in sharp contrast to the gnostic sect's use of pseudepigraphy as a source of authority.

Lines 3–5 describe the world outside the divine realm as a static structure—that which is "hung." The main elements are common terms suitable to Greek science and philosophy. The linear chain of "flesh–soul–air–upper atmosphere" recalls the genre of cosmological myth, although it starts from below and ascends (cf. the introductions to Zs and Fr).

Lines 6–7 describe what is "borne" (carried) from within the godhead downward to our world, and make the connection between our world and the spiritual one. The tone changes from stasis to urgent motion, the vocabulary from science to myth, the epistemology from what is "seen" to what is "known" (lines 1–2). With the word "deep," the informed reader is plunged into the innermost place in Valentinus's own version of the gnostic myth (cf. IrV), the ultimate source of all emanations. "Crops" are a typical Valentinian image of emanations. The "womb," in a cosmological and mythic context, would have recalled the Barbēlō or first emanation of gnostic myth, which was called "a womb for the entirety" (BJn 5:5f). The word "babe" is ambiguous, unless a clue is provided by VFrA, where a newborn babe "seen" by Valentinus is identified as the Word (Logos). If the same is true in VHr, the poem culminates in a reference to the procession of the divine Word— this is the "harvest." Secondarily, then, it would also refer to the Incarnation or epiphany of a divine "babe." If so, the poem would be suitable for Advent, despite its metaphorical title of *Summer Harvest*. Cf. also VFrA note b.

Literary background

Compared to the poetry of the gnostic sect (e.g. BJn 30:13f, FTh, EgG 78:10f), VHr is ostentatiously Hellenistic. Unlike classic gnostic poetry, VHr is composed in regular verse. The meter of the Greek text is one that was used during Hellenistic and Roman times in "popular" poetry. The poem is described as a "hymn" (*psalmos*) in the source where it is preserved, and indeed Valentinus may have intended the text to be sung. It has even been suggested that the rubric "Summer Harvest" (*theros*) specifies a preexistent tune (otherwise unknown), which the poem would fit; other song tunes named for seasonal occupations are attested in roughly the same period. The place of the hymn's composition is unknown.

Text

The text survives only because it is quoted by the third-century father of the church St. Hippolytus of Rome, *Against Heresies* 6.37.7 (167,14–168,4, Wendland). It counts as "Fragment" 8 in Völker's enumeration, though it is no fragment at all, rather, a complete work. The translation below is based on Völker's text: W. Völker, ed., *Quellen zur Geschichte der christlichen Gnosis* (Sammlung ausgewählter kirchen- und dogmengeschichtlicher Quellenschriften, new ser., no. 5; Tübingen: Mohr [Siebeck], 1932), 59.

SELECT BIBLIOGRAPHY

Festugière, A. J. "Notes sur les extraits de Théodote de Clément d'Alexandrie et sur les fragments de Valentin." *Vigiliae Christianae* 3 (1949): 193–207.

Standaert, B. "L'Évangile de vérité: critique et lecture." *New Testament Studies* 22 (1976): 243–75.

Stead, G. C. "In Search of Valentinus." In *The Rediscovery of Gnosticism,* edited by B. Layton. Vol. 1, *The School of Valentinus,* 75–95 (and discussion, 95–102). Studies in the History of Religions, no. 41, vol. 1. Leiden: E. J. Brill, 1980.

SUMMER HARVEST[a]

I see in spirit[b] that all are hung[c]
I know in spirit that all are borne[d]
Flesh hanging from soul
Soul clinging to air
5 Air hanging from upper atmosphere

Crops rushing forth from the deep[e]
A babe rushing forth from the womb.[f]

GTr 36:35 +
IrV (e)
VFrA ?

---

a. This may not be the title, but rather a specification of the tune to which the text should be sung; cf. the introduction. On the other hand, the Valentinian school characteristically speaks of emanations and the process of emanation (cf. lines 6–7) in agricultural metaphors.

b. Or "by means of (my) spirit."

c. Or "hanging."

d. Or "being carried."

e. According to IrV, the "deep" is the part of the divine fullness that comprises the ineffable unengendered parent and silence.

f. In gnostic myth (BJn 5:5f) the first emanation from the ineffable source (the Barbēlō) is "a womb for the entirety."

Appendix

A LATER ALLEGORICAL
INTERPRETATION OF
"SUMMER HARVEST"

St. Hippolytus of Rome, *Against Heresies* 6.37.8

Contents and literary background

St. Hippolytus of Rome, whose quotation preserves the text of VHr, also reports the following allegorical interpretation of it. In his work *Against Heresies* (written in Greek A.D. ca. 222–35) this interpretation immediately follows a full quotation of Valentinus's original text. There is no particular reason to believe that the allegory corresponds to Valentinus's own intentions.

Text

The translation below is based on Völker's text (*Quellen*, p. 60).

He means this: "flesh" according to them[a] is matter which "hangs from" the "soul" of the craftsman.[b] "Soul clings to air": i.e. the craftsman (clings) to spirit of the outer fullness.[c] And "air hangs from upper atmosphere," i.e. the outer wisdom (hangs) from the inner boundary[d] and the entire fullness. "Crops rush forth from the deep," having become the complete emanation of the aeons[e] from the parent.[f]

a. "they" are presumably Valentinian theologians giving an allegorical interpretation of what "He" (Valentinus) "means."

b. Cf. IrV note p. "soul" may refer to what Plato called "world soul" in the *Timaeus*; cf. "power" in gnostic myth and "spiritual substance" in IrV.

c. In IrV the spiritual universe ("fullness") is divided into "the deep," comprising "the ineffable" and "silence," and the rest of the fullness (here called "the outer fullness").

d. Cf. IrV (e).

e. Cf IrV note s.

f. Two beings are designated "parent" in IrV; cf. IrV note d.

THE GOSPEL OF TRUTH

(GTr)

Contents

The Gospel of Truth is a Christian sermon on the theme of salvation by acquaintance with god (*gnōsis*). One of the most brilliantly crafted works of ancient Christian literature, in the original Greek it must have had a rhetorical power that ranked with the great masterpieces of Christian prose. It is the earliest surviving sermon of Christian mysticism. And since very few sermons survive from the ancient gnostic sect and its offshoots, GTr affords a rare glimpse of the actual human atmosphere of a church meeting, in which a magisterial gnostic preacher addresses a congregation, speaking from personal authority. The main themes of the work are established in the opening sentence: search for the father (god) and the hope of deliverance on the part of those who had fallen ignorant and needed a savior to ransom them from ignorance; and emission of the saving divine Word, who proclaimed the truth about the father and brought joy and acquaintance with the father. The contents are thus a dynamic description of Christian *gnōsis* or acquaintance with god.

The characters of this theological drama are simply the *father* (the unknowable god), the *Word* or *son* (god's manifestation), and *the ignorant*, who become transformed into *those who have acquaintance*. The work is overtly Christian, and makes no specific reference to the gnostic myth. It speaks of Jesus' crucifixion as the central object of Christian faith, and contains many paraphrases of New Testament passages.

Two possible states of being are contrasted in GTr: repose (true being, wakefulness) and movement (illusory existence, nightmare). A similar distinction is observed in Platonism, but the basic world view of GTr is not simply Platonist. Rather, the cosmological model of GTr is provided by Stoic pantheistic monism and by astronomy. God (the father) is held to be uncontained and to contain all things. Individuals within him are also said to contain god: thus god permeates, or can permeate, all individual things. Accordingly, the model is not linear (as in gnostic mysticism, cf. Zs, Fr) but three-dimensional and nested, like the ancient astronomical concept of nested heavenly spheres, with god as the most encompassing sphere.

Yet unlike Stoic cosmology, the system of GTr is strongly antimaterialist, even illusionist, as regards the reality of material structures. One consequence of acquaintance (*gnōsis*) with the all-containing divine father is to see the illusion that there are material things—indeed the illusion of distinction and structure—fade away into nothingness. This amounts to reunion with the father; it is salvation, and repose. The main register of GTr is thus not description of the universe but discussion of knowledge and psychology. In this, the concept of salvation in GTr closely resembles that of *The Gospel According to Thomas*. In the few passages where mythic cosmology may covertly come into view (e.g. 17:4f) the figures and events of myth are psychological. In this sense, GTr is to cosmological myth (IrV) as allegory (cf.

the "Historical Introduction" to Part Three) is to text. In this almost complete allegorization, the underlying dynamic of gnostic myth (fullness—lack—recapture of the lacked) is reapplied microcosmically, at the level of the individual Christian.

The theology of GTr uses the simple biblical language of "father" and "son" (or possibly "parent" and "offspring," though 43:11f seems to apply a specifically male anatomical metaphor to the parent). It has been demonstrated that in GTr Valentinus paraphrases, and so interprets, some thirty to sixty scriptural passages, almost all from New Testament books (Gn, Jn, 1 Jn, Rv, Mt, Rm, 1 Co, 2 Co, Ep, Col, and Heb). Of these, it has been shown that the Johannine literature (including Rv) has had the most profound theological influence upon Valentinus's thought; the Pauline literature, less so; and Mt hardly at all. To a large degree the paraphrased passages have been verbally reshaped by abridgement or substitution, to make them agree with Valentinus's own theological perspective (cf. the paraphrase of Gn in RR).

Though carefully controlled, the rhetoric of GTr is not linear but atmospheric, just as its cosmology is not linear but concentric: GTr aims not to argue a thesis by logic, but to describe, evoke, and elicit a kind of relationship. Ideas and images are developed slowly by repeating key points with minor changes. As in gnostic myth a great many epithets used substantively are applied to each main character. Ambiguity of the pronouns "he" and "it" plays a major role in this development; this is one of the striking aspects of Valentinus's style, and can be seen also in the Fragments. Valentinus's style—quite apart from his mystic theology or theory of salvation—is probably unique within ancient Christian literature; it has been described as a gnostic rhetoric.

Literary background

The manuscripts do not specify the title or author of GTr. The conventional title has been supplied by scholarship; it may be a mistake to suppose that Valentinus ever gave a title to the work. In any case, the second-century father of the church, St. Irenaeus of Lyon, states that the Valentinian church read a *Gospel* (or *Proclamation) of Truth*. Since this is the opening phrase of GTr, some scholars have concluded that Irenaeus must be referring to the present work.

The author's name does not appear in the manuscripts, and thus the attribution of GTr to Valentinus remains hypothetical. Nevertheless, it is extremely likely for several reasons: the work's stylistic resemblance to the Fragments (whose attribution is explicit) and the uniqueness of that style; the alleged genius and eloquence of Valentinus and the lack of a likely candidate for the authorship among later Valentinian writers; and the absence of a developed system in the work, perhaps suggesting that it belongs early in the history of the Valentinian church.

The place and exact date of composition of GTr are unknown (Valentinus died ca. 175); the language of composition was Greek.

The work is a sermon and has nothing to do with the Christian genre properly called "gospel" (e.g. the Gospel of Mark).

Text

The original Greek apparently does not survive, though a remark by St. Irenaeus (see above, "Literary background") may be taken as testimony to its existence. The text is known only in Coptic translation, attested by two manuscripts, NHC I (16–43) and NHC XII (fragments), which were copied just before A.D. 350 and are now in the Cairo Coptic Museum. The two Coptic manuscripts contain different versions of the text, one (NHC I) in a Subachmimic dialect of Coptic and the other (NHC XII) in the Sahidic dialect of Coptic. The two versions seem to have been translated from slightly different ancient editions of the Greek text. The Sahidic manuscript (NHC XII) has been almost completely destroyed and survives in the form of a few fragments; the Subachmimic manuscript (NHC I) is virtually complete. For that reason, the present translation is from the Subachmimic MS (NHC I) alone.

The translation below is based upon the critical edition of the Coptic by Malinine et al., with some alterations and with improved readings introduced from an unpublished collation of the manuscript made by S. Emmel and kindly supplied by him: M. Malinine et al., *Evangelium Veritatis*, 2–48, and *Evangelium Veritatis [Supplementum]*, 2–8 (see "Select Bibliography").

SELECT BIBLIOGRAPHY

Arai, S. *Die Christologie des Evangelium Veritatis: Eine religionsgeschichtliche Untersuchung*. Leiden: E. J. Brill, 1964.

Attridge, H., and G. MacRae. "The Gospel of Truth." In *Nag Hammadi Codex I*, edited by H. Attridge. Vol. 1, *Introductions, Texts . . .*, 55–117, and vol. 2, *Notes*, 39–135. Nag Hammadi Studies, vols. 22, 23. Leiden: E. J. Brill, 1985.

Barrett, C. K. "The Theological Vocabulary of the Fourth Gospel and of the Gospel of Truth." In *Current Issues in New Testament Interpretation: Essays in Honor of Otto A. Piper*, edited by W. Klassen and G. F. Snyder, 210–23, 297–98. New York: Harper & Row, 1962.

Dillon, J. *The Middle Platonists*. London: Gerald Duckworth, 1977.

Fineman, J. "Gnosis and the Piety of Metaphor: *The Gospel of Truth*." In *The Rediscovery of Gnosticism*, edited by B. Layton. Vol. 1, *The School of Valentinus*, 289–312 (and discussion, 312–18). Studies in the History of Religion, no. 41, vol. 1. Leiden: E. J. Brill, 1980.

Grobel, K. *The Gospel of Truth: A Valentinian Meditation on the Gospel*. Nashville and New York: Abingdon Press, 1960.

Jonas, H. *The Gnostic Religion*. 2d ed. Boston: Beacon Press, 1963.

Malinine, M., et al., eds. *Evangelium Veritatis: Codex Jung f. VIIIv–XVIv, f. XIXr–XXIIr*. Zürich: Rascher, 1956.

———. *Evangelium Veritatis: Codex Jung f. XVIIr–f. XVIIIv*. Zürich and Stuttgart: Rascher, 1961.

Marrou, H.-I. "L'Évangile de vérité et la diffusion du comput digital dans l'antiquité." *Vigiliae Christianae* 12 (1958): 98–103.

Ménard, J.-E. *L'Évangile de vérité*. Nag Hammadi Studies, vol. 2. Leiden: E. J. Brill, 1972.

Schoedel, W. R. "Gnostic Monism and *The Gospel of Truth*." In *The Rediscovery of Gnosticism*, edited by B. Layton. Vol. 1, *The School of Valentinus*, 379–90. Studies in the History of Religion, no. 41, vol. 1. Leiden: E. J. Brill, 1980.

Standaert, B. "'Evangelium Veritatis' et 'Veritatis Evangelium.' La Question du titre et les témoins patristiques." *Vigiliae Christianae* 30 (1976): 138–50.

———. "L'Évangile de vérité: critique et lecture." *New Testament Studies* 22 (1976): 243–75.

van Unnik, W. C. "'The Gospel of Truth' and the New Testament." In *The Jung Codex*, translated and edited by F. L. Cross, 79–129. London: A. R. Mowbray, 1955.

Williams, J. A. "The Interpretation of Texts and Traditions in the Gospel of Truth." Ph.D. diss., Yale University, 1983. (Biblical paraphrases in GTr and their theological implications.)

THE GOSPEL OF TRUTH[a]

Prologue

31 **16** The proclamation[b] of the truth is a joy for those who have received ⟨Mk 1:1 ?⟩
33 grace from the father of truth, •that they might learn to know him[c] ⟨IrV (c)⟩
through the power of the Word[d] that emanated from the fullness[e] that is ⟨IrV (c)⟩
36 in the father's thought[f] and intellect—the Word, •who is spoken of as ⟨VFrA⟩ ⟨IrV (e)⟩
"savior": for, that is the term for the work that he[g] was to accomplish
1 to ransom those who had fallen ignorant **17** of the father; •while
the term "proclamation" refers to the manifestation of hope, a discovery
for those who are searching for him.

I. THE ORIGIN OF IGNORANCE

The creation

4 Inasmuch as the entirety[a] had searched for the one from whom they ⟨IrV (i)⟩
had emanated, and the entirety was inside of him—the inconceivable ⟨IrV (b)⟩
9 uncontained, who is superior to all thought[b]—•ignorance of the father
11 caused agitation and fear. •And the agitation grew dense like fog, so ⟨29:1, VFrC⟩ ⟨Rm 1:21 ?⟩
14 that no one could see. •Thus error[c] found strength and labored at her ⟨v.14⟩
17 matter[d] in emptiness. •Without having learned to know the truth, she ⟨VFrC⟩
took up residence in a modeled form,[e] preparing by means of the power,[f] ⟨IrV (g)⟩
in beauty, a substitute for truth.

The unreality of creation

21,23 Now, to the inconceivable uncontained this was not humiliating; •for
the agitation and forgetfulness and the modeled form of deception were
as nothing, whereas established truth is unchangeable, imperturbable,
28 and cannot be beautified. •For this reason despise error, since she has
no root.[g]

Forgetfulness

30 She dwelt in a fog as regards the father, preparing, while she dwelt
33 there, products and forgetfulness and fears, •so that by them she might

---

16 a. Or "*The Proclamation of Truth*." No title is given in the MSS. The present title has been supplied by modern scholars, following a statement by St. Irenaeus (cf. the introduction to GTr).

b. "proclamation" (Gk. *euaggelion*): the Greek word can be translated also "gospel." The title plays on this double meaning.

c. "father . . . him" (or "parent . . . it"): traditional anthropomorphic Christian language for reference to the highest deity is used in this work.

d. "Word" (Gk. *Logos*): or "verbal expression."

e. "fullness": Valentinian jargon for the spiritual universe.

f. Or "thinking"; cf. BJn 4:26f.

g. "he" (or "it"): traditional Christian anthropomorphic language for reference to the mediating principle (Word, son) is used in this work.

17 a. "entirety": gnostic jargon for the sum total of spiritual reality deriving from the Barbēlō aeon or second principle; here it refers especially to spiritual reality as alienated from its source.

b. Cf. BJn 3:22–26.

c. "error": a feminine personification corresponding to both wisdom and Ialdabaōth in gnostic myth. The present section (17:4–17f) is an allegorical equivalent of the production of Ialdabaōth and the creation of the universe and humankind in gnostic myth.

d. "her matter": the material universe, which belonged to error.

e. Jewish and Christian jargon for the human body, based on the fact that the creator modeled Adam out of earth. The word (Gk. *plasma*) also means "fiction, fabrication."

f. "the power": cf. BJn 10:20f.

g. "root": source.

36 beguile those of the middle[h] and take them captive. •The forgetfulness
that belongs to error is not apparent; it is not (?) **18** [. . .] with the
1 father. •It was not in the father's company that forgetfulness arose, and
4 surely then not because of him! •Rather, what comes into being within
him is acquaintance, which appeared so that forgetfulness might perish
7 and the father might come to be known. •Inasmuch as forgetfulness
arose because the father was unknown, from the moment the father
comes to be known, there will no longer be forgetfulness.

II. DISCOVERY OF THE FATHER

The crucified Jesus is god within

11   It is to the perfect[a] that this, the proclamation of the one they search   Col 1:25
15 for, has made itself known, through the mercies of the father. •By this
the hidden mystery Jesus Christ shed light upon those who were, because   VFrH
18 of forgetfulness, in darkness. •He enlightened them and gave them a   Jn 14:6
21 way, and the way is the truth, about which he instructed them. •For
23 this reason error became angry at him and persecuted him. •She was
24 constrained by him, and became inactive. •He was nailed to a tree[b] and   Gn 2:17
26 became fruit of the father's acquaintance. •Yet it did not cause ruin   Gn 3:7
27 because it was eaten. •Rather, to those who ate of it, it gave the
possibility that whoever he discovered within himself might be joyful in
31 the discovery of him. •And as for him, they discovered him within
them—the inconceivable uncontained, the father, who is perfect, who   19:7, Col 1:16
created the entirety.

Existence within the father

34   Because the entirety was within him and the entirety was in need of
him[c]—since he had retained within himself its completion, which he had
not given unto the entirety—the father was not grudging; for what envy
40 is there between him and his own members? •For if **19** this realm had
[. . .] them, they would not be able to [. . .] the father, retaining their
completion within himself, in that it [was] given them in the form of
7 return to him and acquaintance and completion. •It is he who created   18:31
9 the entirety, and the entirety is in him. •And the entirety was in need   Col 1:16
10 of him: •just as someone who is unknown to certain people might wish
14 to become known, and so become loved, by them. •For what did the
entirety need if not acquaintance with the father?

The savior as teacher

17,19   He became a guide,[a] at peace and occupied with classrooms. •He
21 came forward and uttered the word as a teacher. •The self-appointed
wise people came up to him, testing him, but he refuted them, for they
were empty; and they despised him, for they were not truly intelligent.

---

h. I.e. ordinary Christians (?). In later Valentinian theology, "the middle" is the realm of the "just," who can waver between good and evil, as distinct from the realm of the spirituals (Valentinians) and the father; cf. IrPt 1.7.1 Valentinus's own teaching on this subject is unknown.

18. a. "the perfect": the elect, who have been chosen for salvation.
b. "a tree": Christian jargon for the cross,

but here also contrasted with the tree of acquaintance with good and evil, Gn 2:17, which in the non-gnostic reading "caused ruin" to Eve and Adam.
c. "in need of him": had a lack of him, cf. note 24a.

19. a. Or "pedagogue," a trained slave who accompanied schoolchildren to the classroom and supervised their conduct.

27 After them all, came also the little ones, to whom belongs acquaintance   43:22 +
30 with the father. •Once they were confirmed and had learned about the
outward manifestations of the father they gained acquaintance, they
were known; they were glorified, they gave glory.

III. PREDESTINATION TO SALVATION

The book of the living

34   In their hearts appeared the living book of the living, which is written   32:31 +
1 in the father's thought and intellect. **20** •And since the foundation of the   VFrG
3 entirety it had been among his incomprehensibles: •and no one had been   Rv 5:3
able to take it up, inasmuch as it was ordained that whoever should take
6 it up would be put to death. •Nothing would have been able to appear
among those who believed in salvation, had not that book come forward.

The crucifixion and publication of the book

10   Therefore the merciful and faithful Jesus became patient and accepted   Heb 2:17
the sufferings even unto taking up that book: inasmuch as he knew that   Rv 5:7
14 his death would mean life for many. •Before a will[a] is opened, the extent   Mt 20:28
of the late property owner's fortune remains a secret; just so, the entirety   Heb 9:17 ?
19 was concealed. •Since the father of the entirety is invisible—and the
entirety derives from him, from whom every way emanated—Jesus
appeared, wrapped himself in that document, was nailed to a piece of   Col 2:14
27 wood, and published the father's edict upon the cross. •O, such a great
28 lesson! •Drawing himself down unto death, clothed in eternal life, having   1Co 15:53
put off the corrupt rags,[b] he put on incorruptibility, a thing that no one   Ph 2:8 ?
34 can take from him. •Having entered upon the empty ways of fear, he   IrV (c)
escaped the clutches of those who had been stripped naked by forget-   Jn 10:17
38 fulness, •for he was acquaintance and completion, and read out [their]
1,3 contents **21** [. . .]. •When [. . .] instruct whoever might learn. •And
those who would learn, [namely] the living enrolled in the book of the
living, learn about themselves, recovering themselves from the father,
and returning to him.

Predestination of the elect

8   Inasmuch as the completion of the entirety is in the father, the entirety
11 must go to him. •Then upon gaining acquaintance, all individually receive
14 what belongs to them, and draw it to themselves.[a] •For whoever does
not possess acquaintance is in need, and what that person needs is great,   VFrD
inasmuch as the thing that such a person needs is what would complete
18 the person.[b] •Inasmuch as the completion of the entirety resides in the
23 father, and the entirety must go to him and all receive their own, •he   Jn 12:32
inscribed these things in advance, having prepared them for assignment   VFrF
to those who (eventually) emanated from him.

Calling of the elect

25   Those whose names he foreknew were called at the end, as persons   Rm 8:29
28 having acquaintance. •It is the latter whose names the father called.   VFrH

---

20 a. Or "testament."
   b. "corrupt rags": it was a Platonist cliché
that the human body is the garment of the
soul.

21 a. "and draw it to themselves": or "and
he draws it to himself."
   b. "what would complete the person": or
"what would complete him."

30 For one whose name has not been spoken does not possess acquaintance.
32 How else would a person hear, if that person's name had not been read   Jn 10:3 ?
34 out? •For whoever lacks acquaintance until the end, is a modeled form
37 of forgetfulness, and will perish along with it. •Otherwise, why do these
1 contemptible persons have no **22** name? •Why do they not possess the
faculty of speech?

Response to the call

2,4   So that whoever has acquaintance is from above: •and if called, hears,   Jn 3:31 ?
7 replies, and turns to the one who is calling; and goes to him. •And he
9 knows how that one is called.[a] •Having acquaintance, that person does
11 the will of the one who has called; •wishes to please him; and gains
12,13 repose. •One's name becomes one's own. •Those who gain acquaintance
in this way know whence they have come and whither they will go;   Jn 3:8
16 they know in the manner of a man who, after having been intoxicated,
18 has recovered from his intoxication: •having returned into himself, he
has caused his own to stand at rest.[b]   Jn 10:4 ?
20   He has brought many back from error, going before them unto their
ways from which they had swerved after accepting error because of the
depth of him who surrounds every way, while nothing surrounds him.
27 It was quite amazing that they were in the father without being acquainted
with him and that they alone were able to emanate, inasmuch as they
were not able to perceive and recognize the one in whom they were.

Contents of the book

33,35   For had not his will emanated from him ⟨. . .⟩[c] •For he revealed it to
38 bestow an acquaintance in harmony with all its emanations, •that is to
say, acquaintance with the living book, an acquaintance which at the
end appeared to the **23** aeons[a] in the form of [passages of text from] it.
2,3   When it is manifest, they speak: •they are not places for use of the
voice, nor are they mute texts for someone to read out and so think of
8 emptiness; •rather, they are texts of truth, which speak and know only
11 themselves. •And each text is a perfect truth—like a book that is perfect
and consists of texts written in unity, written by the father for the aeons:
so that through its passages of text the aeons might become acquainted
with the father.

IV. SALVATION

The advent of the Word

18   Its[b] wisdom meditates upon the Word.
20   Its teaching speaks him[c] forth.
21   Its acquaintance has revealed ⟨him⟩.[d]
23   Its forbearance is a crown upon him.
24   Its joy is in harmony with him.

22 a. Or "he knows how he is called."

b. To "stand at rest" is philosophical jargon for the state of permanence, non-change, and real being, as opposed to what exists in instability, change, and becoming.

c. One or more words are inadvertently omitted here.

23 a. Or "eternal realms." In gnostic myth, the aeons are emanations of the first principle and compose the structure of the spiritual universe, which contains only aeons.

b. "Its": here and throughout the passage (23:18–31f) the Coptic word also can be translated "His."

c. "him": here and throughout the passage (23:18–31f) the Coptic word can be translated also "it."

d. Through an inadvertence, the MS omits this word.

26 Its glory has exalted him.
27 Its manner has manifested him.
29 Its repose has taken him to itself.
30 Its love has clothed him with a body.
31 Its faith has guarded him.

Ingathering of the elect

33 In this manner the Word of the father goes forth in the entirety, being
the fruition **24** [of] his heart and an outward manifestation of his will,
personally supporting the entirety and choosing it, and also taking the
6 outward manifestation of the entirety and purifying it, •bringing it back
into the father, into the mother, Jesus of the infinity of sweetness.   42:16
9   And the father uncovers his bosom—now, his bosom is the holy spirit,   Jn 1:18
14 and reveals his secret—his secret is his son, •so that out of the father's   Ep 3:9 ?
bowels they (the entirety) might learn to know him, and the aeons might
no longer be weary from searching for the father, might repose in him,
20 and might know that he is repose, •for he has supplied the lack[a] and
22 nullified the realm of appearance. •The realm of appearance, which   1Co 7:31b ?
belongs to it (the lack), is the world, in which it served.   VFrF

Disappearance of the material world

25   For where there is envy and strife there is a lack, but where unity is,
28 there is completion. •Inasmuch as the lack came into being because the
father was not known, from the moment that the father is known the
32 lack will not exist. •As with one person's ignorance (of another)—when
one becomes acquainted, ignorance of the other passes away of its own
37 accord; •and as with darkness, which passes away when light appears:
1 **25** so also lack passes away in completion, and so from that moment
on, the realm of appearance is no longer manifest but rather will pass
away in the harmony of unity.
7,8   For now their affairs are dispersed. •But when unity makes the ways
complete, it is in unity that all will gather themselves, and it is by
acquaintance that all will purify themselves out of multiplicity into unity,
consuming matter within themselves as fire, and darkness by light, and   2Co 5:4 ?
19 death by life. •So since these things have happened to each of us, it is
22 fitting for us to meditate upon the entirety, •so that this house might be
holy and quietly intent on unity.

A parable of jars

25,27   It is like some people who moved to a new house. •They had some
jars that in places were no good, and these got broken; but the owner
of the house suffered no loss, rather the owner was glad because instead
of the bad jars it was (now) the full ones that they would be going to
35 use up. •For this is the judgment that has come **26** from above, having   Jn 3:19
judged everyone—a drawn two-edged sword cutting this way and that,   Heb 4:12 ?
since the Word that is in the heart of those that speak it, has come   Jn 1:14
7,8 forward. •It is not just a sound, but it became a body. •A great disturbance
has come to pass among the jars; for some have leaked dry, some are
half full, some are well filled, some have been spilled, some have been
washed, and still others broken.

---

24 a. "lack": in gnostic myth, the missing   wisdom. In GTr the lack is mutual, between
power stolen by Ialdabaôth from its mother   the divine fullness and the individual aeon.

Lament and downfall of error

15   All the ways moved and were disturbed, for they had neither basis
18,20 nor stability; •and error became excited, not knowing what to do; •[she]
was troubled, mourned, and cried out that she understood nothing,
inasmuch as acquaintance, which meant the destruction of her and all
26 her emanations, had drawn near to her. •Error is empty, with nothing
27 inside her. •Truth came forward: all its emanations recognized it, and
they saluted the father in truth and power (so) perfect that it set them
32 in harmony with the father. •For everyone loves truth since truth is the
35,36 father's mouth; •his tongue is the holy spirit. •Whoever attaches **27** to   IrV (j)
2 the truth attaches to the father's mouth; •it is from his tongue that this   VFrB
person will receive the holy spirit, that is to say, the revealing of the
7 father and the uncovering of him to his aeons. •He has revealed his   Col 1:26 ?
9 secret; he has unloosed himself.[a] •For who but the father alone contains
(anything)?

Potential being and real being

10,11   All the ways[b] are his emanations. •They know that they have emanated
from him like children who were within a mature man but knew they
18 had not yet received form nor been given name. •It is when they receive
the impulse toward acquaintance with the father that he gives birth to
22 each. •Otherwise, although they are within him they do not recognize
23 him. •The father himself is perfect and acquainted with every way that   Mt 5:48
26 is in him. •If he wills, what he wills appears, as he gives it form and   1Jn 3:20 ?
29 name. •And he gives it name, and causes it to make them come into
existence.
31   Those who have not yet come to be are not acquainted with the one
34 who put them in order. •Now, I am not saying that those who have not
36 yet come to be are nothing: •rather, that they exist **28** within him who
might will that they come to be, if he wills at some future time, as it
4 were. •Before all things have appeared he is personally acquainted with
7 what he is going to produce. •But the fruit that has not yet appeared
10 recognizes nothing, nor is it at all active. •Just so, also all the ways that
13 reside in the father derive from the existent, •that being which has
16 caused itself to stand at rest from out of the nonexistent. •For what has
18 no root also has no fruit: •truly, although it may think to itself, "I have
22 come into being," next it will wither of its own accord. •Accordingly,
24 what was wholly nonexistent will not come into being. •What then does
26 he want it to think? •This: "I have come into being (only) in the manner
28 of shadows and apparitions of the night." •O the light's shining on the
fear of that person, upon knowing that it is nothing!

The nightmare state and awakening

32   Thus they were unacquainted with the father, since it was he whom
1 **29** they did not see. •Inasmuch as he was the object of fear and   17:9+
disturbance and instability and indecisiveness and division, there was
much futility at work among them on his account, and (much) empty
8 ignorance—•as when one falls sound asleep and finds oneself in the
11 midst of nightmares: •running toward somewhere—powerless to get
away while being pursued—in hand-to-hand combat—being beaten—

---

27 a. Or "he has explained it" (with this   b. "ways": this obscure term apparently
translation cf. possibly Jn 1:18).   refers to the aeons or potential aeons.

falling from a height—being blown upward by the air, but without any
20 wings; •sometimes, too, it seems that one is being murdered, though
nobody is giving chase—or killing one's neighbors, with whose blood
25 one is smeared: •until, having gone through all these dreams, one
28 awakens. •Those in the midst of all these troubles see nothing, for such
32 things are (in fact) nothing. •Such are those who have cast off lack of
acquaintance from themselves like sleep, considering it to be nothing.
37 Neither do they consider its **30** other products to be real things.
2 Rather, they put them away like a dream in the night, and deem
6 acquaintance with the father to be the light. •That is how each person
10 acted while being without acquaintance: as though asleep. •And the
12 person who has acquaintance is like one who has awakened. •And good
14 for the person who returns and awakens! •And blessed is the one who   42:37
has opened the eyes of the blind!   VFrH
                                                                        Gn 3:5 ?
16   And the quick spirit hastened after that person when the person had
19 awakened; •having helped the one who lay prostrate on the ground, it
made that one strong enough to stand up; for that person had not yet   VFrC
arisen.

V. THE FATHER'S INTERVENTION

Mediation of the son

23   Acquaintance from the father and the appearance of his son gave
26 them a means to comprehend. •For when they saw and heard him, he   1Jn 1:1 ?
32 let them taste and smell of himself and touch the beloved son, •after he
had appeared to tell them about the father, the uncontained, and had   Jn 20:22 ?
breathed into them what was in the thought[a] (of the father), doing his Gn 2:7 ?
                                                                        Jn 6:38
36 will. •When many had received the light, they converted **31** to him,
1 for they were strangers and did not see his image and had not recognized
him.
4,4   Matter ⟨. . .⟩[a] •for he had come out of it in a fleshly likeness without Rm 8:3
7 anything's blocking his progress—•for incorruptibility is tantamount to
9 unseizability[b]—•speaking moreover in new terms while yet speaking
11 about what was in the father's heart, •for he had produced the Word
15 that has no defect; and light spoke forth from his mouth. •And his voice
16 gave birth to life. •He gave them thought and intelligence and mercy
and salvation and the powerful spirit from the father's infinity and
21,22 sweetness, •having made punishments and torments cease: •for it was
they who had gone astray from the presence of certain others, who fell
26 short of mercy, in error and bondage.[c] •And, allied with power, he
unchained them and reproved them by acquaintance.

A parable of sheep

28   He became a way for those who had gone astray and acquaintance   Jn 14:6
31 for those who were without acquaintance; •discovery for those who
34 were seeking, and strength for those who were trembling; •purity for
35 those who were defiled: •since it is he who is the shepherd[d] who left   Mt 18:12
2 behind the ninety-nine **32** sheep that had not gone astray, •and came
3 and searched for the one that had gone astray. •He rejoiced when he
4 found it, •for 99 is a number expressed with a gesture of the left hand.

---

30 a. Or "thinking."   c. "bondage": a Platonist cliché for the
                                            material body.
31 a. One or more words are inadvertently   d. "the" shepherd known to readers from
omitted here.   Mt 18:12f.
b. Cf. RR 87:17f.

6,9 But when 1 is found, the sum total transfers to the right hand.[a] •In this way the thing that is in need of one, namely the whole right hand, draws what is missing, and takes it from the left-hand part so that it transfers 15,16 to the right hand. •And thus the number becomes 100. •This is a symbol 17 of the spoken forms of these numbers. •The father is he who, even on   Mt 12:11 the Sabbath, when the sheep[b] that he had found had fallen into the ditch, labored over it and kept the sheep alive, once he had brought it up from the ditch.

22,38   Understand the interior meaning,[c] •for it is you who are the children   43:22 + 23 of interior understanding. •What is the Sabbath? That day on which 26 salvation cannot be idle. •Speak from (the perspective of) the superior 29 day, in which there is no night; •and from the star that does not set,   Rv 21:25 31 since it is perfect. •Speak, therefore, from the heart, for it is you who   19:34 are the day that is perfect, and it is within you that there dwells the   VFrG VFrH 35 star that does not set. •Speak of the truth with those who seek it, and of acquaintance with those who have sinned in the midst of their error.[d] **33**

VI. DUTIES OF THE ELECT

1,2   Make steady the feet of those who have stumbled, •and stretch out 3,4 your hands to those who are sick. •Feed those who are hungry, •and 5 unto those who are weary give repose; •and awaken those who wish to   Mt 11:28 7,8 arise, •and get up from your sleep. •For it is you who are unsheathed 9 intelligence. •If strengthening is thus, it is truly strong.

11,12   Focus your attention upon yourselves. •Do not focus your attention 13,14 upon others,[a] that is, •ones whom you have expelled. •Do not return to 16 eat what you have vomited forth. •Do not become eaten by moths; do   Mt 6:19 17 not become infested with worms; •for you have already cast him[b] out. 19 Do not become the place of the devil, for you have already brought him   Ep 4:27 22 to naught. •Do not strengthen the elements that impede you—those who   VFrF 24 fall—supposing that this is a kind of improvement. •For the lawless is 24,26 nothing. •Treat such a one more forceably than the just, •since the lawless acts on the supposition of being lawless, while the just acts 30 toward others on the supposition of being just. •For your own part, then, do the will of the father, for you are from him.

VII. THE FATHER AND THE ELECT

The father's fragrance

33,35   For the father is sweet and in his will is goodness; •he is acquainted   36:35 + 37 with your own, upon whom you rely. •For by their fruits your own are   Mt 7:16 39 known: •for the father's children **34** are themselves his fragrance, for   Mt 7:20 3 they are from the loveliness of his face. •Therefore the father loves his   2Co 2:14

---

32 a. The Romans used a system of numerical gestures, in which one to ninety-nine could be expressed by ninety-nine different postures of the left hand alone. Starting with one hundred, the postures were made by fingers of the right hand. Thus ninety-nine is "a number expressed with a gesture of the left hand," while one hundred is a right-hand gesture. Independent of these numerical gestures, the "left" was superstitiously considered to be sinister, and the "right" auspicious. Thus the "transfer" of the numerical gesture to the right hand is an auspicious change.

b. "the" sheep known to readers from Mt 12:11.

c. In the MS the rest of this sentence is written on the thirty-eighth line of the page with an indication that it had been inadvertently omitted and should be inserted between lines 22 and 23.

d. For line 38, see above after line 22.

33 a. Or "other things."

b. Or "it."

5 fragrance and manifests it everywhere. •And when it mingles with matter
7 it imparts his fragrance to the light, •and by his silence he makes it   IrV (b)
9 superior in every way to every sound. •For it is not the ears that smell
10 the fragrance, •rather it is the spirit[a] that possesses the faculty of smell
and draws the fragrance toward itself for itself and sinks down into the
14 father's fragrance; •thus it nourishes it and takes it to what[b] it emanated
18 from, the original cold fragrance. •And it is a soul-endowed modeled   Gn 2:7 ?
22 form, being like a cold liquid that has sunk into some loose earth; •and   ICo 15:45 ?
24 those who see it suppose that (only) earth is there. •Afterward, it
reevaporates when a gust (of wind) draws it off and it becomes warm.
26,28 Cold fragrances, then, result from division. •For this reason, faith came
and did away with division, and it brought the warm fullness of love,
33 so that coldness might not return: •rather, it is unity of perfect thought.

The father's restoration of the lack

34   This is the account of the good news about the discovery of the
fullness, for those who strain toward **35**   the salvation coming from
2 above. •Their hope, toward which they strain, is straining (toward them):   VFrH
4,6 it is their image, the light in which there is no shadow. •How truly at   IJn 1:15
8 that time the fullness is on the way to coming! •The lack belonging to
the realm of matter did not result from the infinity of the father as he
12 came to bestow time upon the lack. •Of course, it could not properly
14 be said that the incorruptible would "come" in such a way. •Rather,
the father's depth is immense, and it is not with him that the thought of   IrV (e)
18 error resides. •It is a fallen (?)[a] thing, that can easily be made upright
through the discovery of him who came to that which he would bring
back.
22,24   For the restoration is called repentance. •The reason why incorruptibility exhaled and followed the one who had sinned, was so that that
27 one might gain repose. •For the remainder of the light, within the lack,
30 is forgiveness—the Word of the fullness. •For, a doctor hurries to where
33 sickness is;[b] that is the doctor's wish. •A person who has something
wrong, then, will not hide the fact, for the one has what the other needs.
35 Thus the fullness, which has no defect, supplies such a person's lack
⟨with⟩[c] what it has **36**   bestowed so as to supply what that person needs,
3 so that the person might thus receive grace. •While in need, this person
5 did not have grace. •For this reason, it was diminution that resided
8 where there was no grace. •When the diminished portion was received,
11 the one who needed it was manifestly a fullness. •And this is the
discovery about the light of truth that has risen upon such a person:
that it is unchangeable.

Anointment of the elect

13   Because of the coming of Christ (the anointed) it was said publicly:
15 Seek, and those that are disturbed will receive restoration, and he will   Mt 7:7 ?
17 anoint them with ointment. •The ointment is the mercy of the father,   IJn 2:27 ?
                                                                            GTh 2 ?

---

34 a. Or "wind current," perhaps meaning
breath; Gk. *pneuma*.
  b. Or "where."

35 a. Translation uncertain.
  b. This saying is attributed to Jesus by St.
Ephraem Syrus, a fourth-century father of

the Syrian church (*Syr. Evang. Concord.
Expos.*, chap. 17); in A. Resch's collection
of sayings attributed to Jesus that are not in
the canonical New Testament (*Agrapha*
[Leipzig: Henrichs, 1906]) it counts as no.
176 [A76].
  c. Through an inadvertence, the MS omits
this word.

who will be merciful to them; and those whom he has anointed are the
21,22 perfected. •For it is full jars that get coated (with sealing wax). •But
whenever some jar's coating is ruined it leaks, and the cause of its
27 defectiveness lies in the fact of its not being coated: •for in such a case
a gust (of wind) and the power of what is with it will make it evaporate.
29 While from the one that has no defects, no seals are broken; neither do
33 such ones leak in any way. •Rather the father, since he is perfect,
resupplies it with anything it lacks.

An allegory of paradise

35,35   He is good. •He is acquainted with his plants, for it is he who has   33:33, 43:19
38 planted them in his paradise (garden). •Now, his paradise is his realm   VFr H+
39 of repose: •it 37 is the perfection within the father's thought, and they   IrV (j), VHr 6
4 (his plants) are the verbal expressions of his meditation.ᵃ •Each of his   Gn 2:15 ?
verbal expressions is the product of his will and the manifestation of his
speaking.
7   Since the time when they constituted the depth of his thought, uttered
discourse has manifested them, and intellect uttering the discourse, and
12 silent loveliness. •It (the discourse) was called thought, inasmuch as
15 they dwelled in it (silent loveliness) without becoming manifest. •So it
came to pass that it was uttered in the beginning, when it pleased the
will of him who willed.

The father's incomprehensible will

19,20   Now, will is what the father reposes in. •And nothing comes to pass
without what pleases him, nor does anything happen without the father's   Mt 10:29 ?
24,25 will. •Rather, his will is incomprehensible. •His will is his imprint, and
27 no one can understand him; •nor does he exist so that they might observe
29 him in order to lay hold of him. •Rather, when he wills, what he wills
is this—even if the sight is not at all pleasing in the presence of god: the
34 father's will. •For he is acquainted with the beginning and the end of
36,37 all. •For at their end he will greet them. •Now, the end is reception of
1 acquaintance with him who is hidden, and he is the father, 38 •from
whom the beginning came and to whom all who emanated from him will
4 return. •And they appeared so that there might be glory and joy in his
name.

VIII. THE FATHER AND THE SON

The father's name

6,7   Now, the name of the father is the son. •It is he who in the beginning
10 named what emanated from him, remaining always the same. •And he   Heb 1:5
12 begot him as a son and gave him his name, which he possessed. •It is   Jn 17:11
14 he in whose vicinity the father has all things: •he has the name, and he
15,16 has the son. •The latter can be seen; •but the name is invisible, for it
alone is the mystery of the invisible, which comes into ears that are
21 wholly full of it, because of him. •And yet the father's name is not
23,24 spoken. •Rather, it is manifest in a son. •Thus, great is the name!
25   Who, then, can utter his name, the great name, but him alone who

---

37 a. Possibly a reuse of the allegorical in-   *Philo, Supplement I;* Loeb Classical Library;
terpretation of Gn 2:8, by the brilliant exegete   Cambridge, Mass.: Harvard University Press,
of Alexandria, Philo Judaeus (ca. 30 B.C.–   1953): "And His ideas the Creator planted
A.D. ca. 45) as found in his *Questions and*   like trees in the most sovereign thing, the
Answers on Genesis 1.6 (trans. R. Marcus;   rational soul."

possesses the name—and the children of the name in whom the father's
32 name reposed and who in turn reposed in his name! •Inasmuch as the
father is unengendered, it is he who alone bore him unto himself, as a
36 name, before he had put the aeons in order, •so that the name of the
38 father might be supreme over them as lord. •And this is the **39** true
3 name, confirmed by his command in perfect power. •For this name does
not result from words and acts of naming, but rather his name is invisible.
7 He alone gave him a name, for he alone saw him, and it was he alone
11 who was able to name him: •for what does not exist has no name—
indeed, what would a nonexistent be named?—but what exists, exists   Rv 19:12 ?
16 along with its name. •And he alone is acquainted with him and ⟨. . .⟩ᵃ
19 for him alone to give him a name. •He is the father: his name is the son.
20,23 So he did not hide it within action, rather it existed. •The son alone
24 gave names. •So the name belongs to the father, just as the name of the
27 father is the son, the beloved. •For where would he find a name except
from the father?
28 Yet perhaps someone will say to another, "Who could name one that
33 preexisted before him? •Do not children get names **40** from their
2 parents?" •First, we must consider the question of what sort of thing a
5,6 name is. •For he is the true name. •Thus it is he who is the name from
9 the father; for it is he who exists as the most lordly name. •Accordingly,
he did not get the name on loan—unlike others, all of whom individually
13 get their names according as they are created. •But this one is the most
14 lordly name. •There is no other being that bestowed it upon him.
16 Rather, he is unnameable and indescribable until such time as the perfect
20 alone has spoken of him. •And it is the latter who is able to speak his
name and see him.
23 So when it pleased him that his uttered name should be his son, and
when he who had emanated from the depth gave him his name he spoke
30 of his secrets, knowing that the father is without evil. •Precisely for this
reason he produced him—so that he might speak concerning the place
from which he had emanated and his realm of repose, **41** and that he
might glorify the fullness, the greatness of his name, and the father's
sweetness.

IX. REPOSE

Proclamation of the place of repose

3 All, individually, will speak concerning the place from which they
have emanated and the lot according to which they have received their
7 establishment in the state of rest. •They will hasten to return and to
receive from that place in which they (once) stood at rest, tasting of it
and being nourished and growing.

Repose in the father

12,14 And his own realm of repose is hisᵃ fullness. •Thus all the father's
16 emanations are fullnesses; •and he is the root of all his emanations,
within that (place) where he caused all to sprout and gave them their
20 destinies. •So each is manifest in order that from their own thought
23 ⟨. . .⟩ᵇ •For they send their thought to where their root is, their root
which carries them up above all the heights to the father.

---

39 a. The Coptic text is corrupt; one or more   **41** a. "his . . . his": or "their . . . their."
words may be inadvertently omitted here.   b. One or more words are inadvertently
                                                   omitted here.

28,30   They cling to his head, which is repose for them. •And they hold
themselves close to him so that, as it were, they receive from his face
something like kisses, although they do not give **42** this impression.
2 For they have neither surpassed themselves nor fallen short of the glory   Rm 3:23
4 of the father. •And they do not think of him as trivial or bitter or
6 wrathful: •rather, that he is without evil, imperturbable, sweet, ac-
9 quainted with all ways before they have come into being. •And he does
11 not need to be instructed. •Such are they who have possessions from
above, from the immeasurable greatness, straining toward the solitary
16,17 and perfect, •he who is a mother to them. •And they will not descend   24:6
into Hades, nor do they have envy or groaning; nor is death within   Rv 21:4 ?
21 them. •Rather, they repose in that being who gives unto himself repose,
and in the vicinity of truth they are neither weary nor entangled.
25,26   But it is precisely they who are the truth. •And it is in them that the
father dwells, and in the father that they are, being perfect, undivided
in what is truly good, and imparting no defect to anything, but rather
33 imparting repose and being fresh in spirit. •And it is to their root that
they will listen, being occupied with the things in which one might find
one's root and not damage one's soul.

Conclusion

37,39   This is the place of the blessed. This is their place. •As for the others,   30:14+
then, let them know in their own places that it is not right for me **43** to
2 say more, for I have been in the place of repose. •No, it is there that I
5 shall dwell, continually occupied with the father of the entirety •and the
true siblings, upon whom the father's love is poured out and in whose   Rm 5:5
midst there is no lack of him; who truly and obviously dwell in true and
11 eternal life, •and speak of the light that is perfect and full of the father's
16 seed, and which is in his heart and in the fullness. •In this his spirit
19 rejoices, and it glorifies what it dwelt in. •For he is good, and his children   36:35+
22 are perfect and worthy of his name. •Truly, it is children of this kind   19:27, 32:38
that the father loves.   VFrF

PART THREE

THE SCHOOL
OF VALENTINUS

HISTORICAL INTRODUCTION

Valentinus's school

Valentinus's genius and eloquence must have been matched by his gifts as a teacher, for after he arrived in Rome his followers blossomed into a brilliant international school of theologians and biblical commentators. Their activity began while Valentinus was still alive. Like their master, the first and second generations of Valentinians aspired to raise Christian theology to the level of pagan philosophical studies. The first Christians to begin this process of intellectualization had been Basilides (cf. IrB) and the gnostic sect, followed soon after by Christian intellectuals of proto-orthodox and Valentinian theology.

Thus the Valentinian movement had the character of a philosophical school, or network of schools, rather than a distinct religious sect. Because of its brilliant efflorescence, the number of second- and third-century Valentinians still known by name is remarkably large, a fact that indicates their importance in the ancient churches: Alexander, Ambrose, Axionicus, Candidus, Flora, Florinus, Heracleon, Mark, Ptolemy, Secundus, Theodotus, Theotimus.

In a certain sense the very purpose of the school was speculation, and so in the nature of things diversity was not discouraged. Two distinct branches seem to have emerged by the middle of the third century (see Map 5): an "Italic" or Western branch, whose founders had been Ptolemy and Heracleon, and an Eastern branch, represented initially by Theodotus and Mark. The Italic branch accepted that Jesus had been born with a body of animate essence (IrPt 1.6.1) to which the holy spirit (the "Word" of wisdom) later united at his baptism: while the Eastern one held that he had been conceived by the holy spirit and born as a body of spiritual essence (cf. GPh 55:23f). Geographically, Valentinian Christianity, just like the gnostics, spread to almost all parts of the Roman world: Gaul (southern France), Rome, Asia Minor (Turkey), Syria, all parts of Egypt, Carthage (modern Tunis), and eventually Mesopotamia. The movement was long-lived. Records from the end of the seventh century still speak of Valentinians as well as gnostics (see Map 2)—by that time fully separated from the imperial Catholic church.

Its activity within the church at large

Although the followers of Valentinus eventually became distant from the established church of the Roman empire, in the second and third

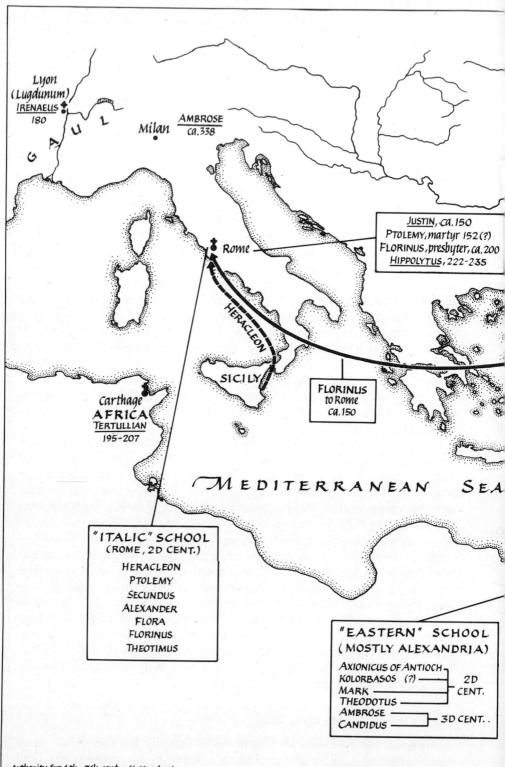

Lyon
(Lugdunum)
IRENAEUS
180

G A U L

Milan   AMBROSE
ca.338

JUSTIN, ca.150
PTOLEMY, martyr 152 (?)
FLORINUS, presbyter, ca.200
HIPPOLYTUS, 222-235

Rome

HERACLEON

FLORINUS
to Rome
ca.150

SICILY

Carthage
AFRICA
TERTULLIAN
195-207

M E D I T E R R A N E A N   S E A

"ITALIC" SCHOOL
(ROME, 2D CENT.)

HERACLEON
PTOLEMY
SECUNDUS
ALEXANDER
FLORA
FLORINUS
THEOTIMUS

"EASTERN" SCHOOL
(MOSTLY ALEXANDRIA)

AXIONICUS OF ANTIOCH
KOLORBASOS (?)   2D
MARK   CENT.
THEODOTUS
AMBROSE   3D CENT.
CANDIDUS

Authority for 4th~7th cent.: K. Koschorke
After van der Meer (1966)

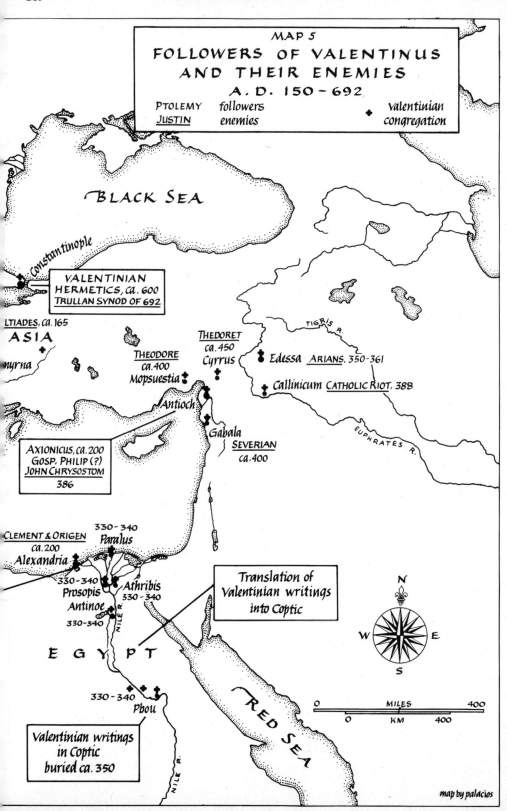

MAP 5

FOLLOWERS OF VALENTINUS AND THEIR ENEMIES
A. D. 150 – 692

PTOLEMY   followers   · valentinian
JUSTIN   enemies   congregation

BLACK SEA

Constantinople

VALENTINIAN HERMETICS, ca. 600
TRULLAN SYNOD OF 692

LTIADES, ca. 165

ASIA

Smyrna

THEODORE
ca. 400
Mopsuestia

THEDORET
ca. 450
Cyrrus

Edessa   ARIANS, 350-361

Callinicum CATHOLIC RIOT, 388

TIGRIS R.

EUPHRATES R.

Antioch

Gabala
SEVERIAN
ca. 400

AXIONICUS, ca. 200
GOSP. PHILIP (?)
JOHN CHRYSOSTOM
386

330-340
CLEMENT & ORIGEN   Paralus
ca. 200
Alexandria

330-340   Athribis
Prosopis   330-340
Antinoe
330-340

Translation of
Valentinian writings
into Coptic

N
W   E
S

E G Y P T

NILE R.

330-340
Pbou

Valentinian writings
in Coptic
buried ca. 350

RED SEA

NILE R.

0   MILES   400
0   KM   400

map by palacios

centuries they were members, however eccentric, of the universal church at large. Their teachings were an interpretation of Christianity, not a rival religion. In fact they do not seem to have called themselves by any special sectarian name as did the sect of the gnostics; rather, they referred to themselves by traditional Christian epithets already used in the very early church, "people endowed with spirit, spirituals" (Greek *pneumatikoi,* 1 Co 2:15) and "the perfect" (*teleioi,* Mt 19:21). The term "Valentinians" must have been coined by their enemies, to imply that they followed not Christ but Valentinus; this term began to appear about A.D. 160 in pamphlets attacking the followers of Valentinus and other theologians of the time.

In this period Christian theological schools, whatever theological tradition they taught, normally had a loose and ill-defined relation to local Christian congregations and bishops. Their meetings, which were open to qualified students, would be held in private quarters under the direction of a scholar, as a supplement to the regular church life of worship and service. The scholar might issue various kinds of academic publications—elementary, propagandistic, and technical.

The structure of the Valentinian movement is a typical, early instance of this pattern. The spectrum of its theological and mythical speculation was held together not only by academic tradition, but also by the members' allegiance to ordinary Christian congregations. Followers of Valentinus read and interpreted the same scripture that most Christians read today (cf. IrPt, PtF), presumably in services attended by other kinds of Christian as well; they accepted the usual sacraments of the second-century church (cf. GPh); and referred to the same kind of creed, or rule of faith, as what in retrospect seems to have been proto-orthodox Christianity (cf. TRs). Although there is no evidence that Valentinians ever attained the rank of bishop, by the year 200 it was still possible for a follower of Valentinus to hold the ecclesiastical rank of presbyter in the church at Rome. The writings of the Valentinian school were not simply dismissed out of hand by all opponents, but were sometimes taken as a topic of serious discussion, especially by philosophically minded theologians such as St. Clement of Alexandria (A.D. ca. 150–ca. 215) and Origen (A.D. ca. 185–ca. 254). For a long time, then, the Valentinian movement remained firmly within the church at large, causing their opponents to call them bitterly "wolves in sheep's clothing."

Valentinian literature

The scholastic character of the Valentinian movement is reflected in the typical forms of Valentinian literature, which are mostly academic ones. The selections translated below illustrate all these forms: the metaphysical treatise (summarized in IrPt, cf. TRs), the philosophical epistle (PtF, TRs), the scriptural commentary (IrPt), and the anthology (GPh). In addition, a theologian's prayer (PPl) used by Valentinians illustrates their emphasis on St. Paul as founder and patron of their academic tradition. Two of the works (PtF, TRs) are propagandistic, that is, designed to attract beginners and introduce them to Valentinian teaching. It should be noted that no complete example of a Valentinian biblical commentary will be found here, for none is known to have survived intact, though fragments of such commentaries are quoted by early Christian writers. But the allegorical technique used in these commentaries is very clearly illustrated by passages in St. Irenaeus's summary of Ptolemy's theology (IrPt), among which is a long citation of an allegorical commentary on John.

Opposition

As early as A.D. 160, opponents of the Valentinian school began their attempt to label, alienate, and oust the movement from the church. It may be stated, parenthetically, that the Valentinians did not reply in detail to these attacks (though see PtF), but their mythic theology contained an answer of sorts: it foresaw in god's final reckoning a provision for non-Christians to be destroyed; for Valentinians to be reunited with the heavenly father; and for ordinary Christians (i.e. the opposition) to enter only a second-class paradise and rest forever—not with god the father, but merely with the craftsman of the world (IrPt 1.7.1).

The earliest attempts to alienate the Valentinians, such as those of St. Justin Martyr (A.D. ca. 100–ca. 165), were ineffective; but starting about A.D. 200, more and more ordinary Christians, or at least clergy and theologians, began to think of a distance between themselves and the private classes of the Valentinian school. To a large extent this was thanks to the efforts of St. Irenaeus of Lyon, a Greek-speaking bishop of Gaul (A.D. ca. 130–ca. 200).

St. Irenaeus's attack

Irenaeus's work is now best represented by his full-scale masterpiece of anti-Valentinian polemic, *The Detection and Overthrow of "Gnōsis" Falsely So Called,* usually cited as *Against Heresies*. Written in Greek about A.D. 180, it is today a precious source of information about the Valentinian movement. When it was written, the work was also the occasion for a precedent-setting discussion of what the ordinary Christian ought to believe, and an early assertion of the idea that this formulation of ordinary Christian beliefs had been handed down uncontaminated by a chain of teachers stretching back to the apostles. Born a Greek speaker and educated in Asia Minor (modern Turkey) and Rome, Irenaeus spent the most mature part of his life as bishop of the diocese of Lugdunum in the Roman province of Gaul, now Lyon, France. He was a strident enemy of gnostics, Valentinians, and various other groups about whom he had learned from the earlier pamphlet literature and from personal contact. Like his predecessors, he tended to lump all these enemies together. From his strategic vantage point in Lugdunum, St. Irenaeus kept in close touch with the church in Rome, for there was a flow, between the capital and Lyon, of Christian messengers and missionaries, among whom were teachers of the Valentinian school. It was to defend his flock against the "depredations of these wolves" that he wrote the *Detection and Overthrow*.

Irenaeus's arguments were serious and intelligent, but another main part of his strategy was to establish a derogatory image of the newly arrived Valentinians as esoteric and absurd, practitioners of sorcery, given to debauchery, and teachers of an academic tradition that extended not back to St. Paul but rather to the Samaritan sorcerer Simon Magus (Ac 8:9–24). The image he painted was much sharper than similar attempts by his predecessors. In fact, it became a popular image of Valentinian gnostic Christianity that was destined to last, and which survives to the present day.

Separation of Valentinianism as a heresy

At the time of Ireneaus the Valentinian school must have begun to edge toward a separate existence as a Christian sect, for the evidence of works like GPh seems to indicate that some Valentinians went beyond the usual sacraments of Christianity to add distinctive ones of their own.

Starting in the fourth century, the Roman government began to lend its official support to the Christian church in various ways. Pro-Christian emperors tried tentatively to encourage the unification of Christianity into a more monolithic and universal organization, and in the process issued various legislations against one or another movement within the church. Valentinians appear in a list of "sectarians" ("heretics") against whom the emperor Constantine legislated A.D. ca. 326, officially forbidding them to hold any further meetings. While the edict could not be enforced (it specified no penalties for disobedience), it did mark the beginning of official, i.e. governmental, nonrecognition of the Valentinian movement.

In this century (if not before)—about the time that the Coptic manuscripts of Nag Hammadi had to be buried in the desert—the Valentinian Christians must have become self-consciously separate from the rest of Christianity. But they continued to exist. In A.D. 388, a Valentinian chapel (Latin *fanum*) was burned by a Christian mob in the Eastern garrison city of Callinicum, on the Euphrates; this incident provides, by chance, the first literary reference to a distinct church building designated as Valentinian. In A.D. 428, the emperor Theodosius II again included the Valentinians (as well as gnostics called Borborites, cf. EpG) in a decree forbidding certain sectarians to assemble—thus indicating that Valentinians *did* assemble at that time. As late as A.D. 692, they still continued to be mentioned, for Canon 95 of the Trullan Synod tells how to receive a repentant Valentinian into the imperial Catholic church.

Allegorical interpretation of scripture

The fact that Valentinians, despite their acceptance of the extraordinary gnostic myth, could remain so long within the loose folds of the Christian church is due to their use of allegorical interpretation. Allegory made it easy for them to continue affirming ordinary Christian scripture and even the ordinary Christian creed or rule of faith, while reserving in their own minds a "deeper" Valentinian meaning of these texts. For an example of allegory, see IrPt 1.1.3 ("Allegories of the thirty aeons").

The use of allegory is a characteristic of the Valentinian movement. But the Valentinians by no means invented allegorical interpretation. Rather, the technique goes back in Greek culture almost as far as literature itself. Although it was always controversial, allegory was a standard method of interpretation. It had been in use by Jews and Christians for a century before the time of Valentinus and continued to be used long afterward.

Greek allegory had developed as early as the fifth century B.C., with the pre-Socratic philosophers. It was used extensively by Philo Judaeus of Alexandria (ca. 30 B.C.–A.D. ca. 45), who very often employed it to read Platonic philosophy into the text of the Pentateuch. St. Paul had used it as well (Ga 4:21–31), and later it was developed by Christian theologians such as Origen of Alexandria. Thus the use of the allegorical method was not itself the ultimate bone of contention in gnostic scriptural interpretation. Rather, the most serious objections lay in what Valentinians "found" when they allegorized the New Testament and creed; in their implicit denial that the obvious meaning was of much importance; and in the esoteric nature of their philosophy, which they claimed to have received in an apostolic tradition transmitted not by bishops but by scholars.

Generally speaking, allegory had two essential functions. On the one hand, it permitted thinkers to assert that their own philosophical views (the "allegorical meaning") had been recognized long before by an even more authoritative person, such as Homer, Moses, Jesus, or St. Paul. This function is analogous to the pseudepigraphy of classic gnostic scripture, in which a modern thinker's views are passed off as an ancient document left by an authoritative figure of the past.

On the other hand, the method enabled the allegorist to negate unacceptable or offensive passages in texts whose authority was already beyond question. Thus by allegory the literal sense of a line of Homer, a Mosaic law, or a verse of the New Testament could be neutralized; at the same time, the authority of Homer, Moses, or St. Paul could be used to sponsor the allegorist's own religious or philosophical speculation.

Being embedded within the ordinary Christian church at large, Valentinus and the Valentinian theologians accepted the canonical scriptural status of the writings now called the Old and the New Testament, or at any rate most of them. It was precisely in the middle of the second century that some Christians began to use the New Testament books as a body of literature having the same kind of authority as the Old Testament (see "Gnostic Scripture and the Christian Bible" in the "General Introduction"). Furthermore, it was in this period that ordinary Christians began developing a consensus about the list ("canon") of Christian works that ought to be used in this way. On this score, neither Valentinus himself nor his followers seem to have been especially different from ordinary Christianity.

As a result, their writings are not meant to replace the canonical scripture of the Old and the New Testament. Rather, they aim to bring out the meaning of canonical scripture and provide a key to its interpretation. In their literary posture, they do not claim to rival the antiquity of works like the gospels or letters of St. Paul. Yet it must not be forgotten that Valentinian writers claimed to speak *on the authority* of a secretly transmitted academic tradition, whose origin they traced back to St. Paul. For this reason, the authority of Valentinian academic writings—based, so they thought, on the secret key—was considered equal to, or even greater than, the text itself of the New Testament.

SELECT BIBLIOGRAPHY

Brox, N. *Gnosis, Offenbahrung, und gnostischer Mythos bei Irenäus von Lyon: Zur Charakteristik der Systeme.* Salzburger patristische Studien, vol. 1. Salzburg and Munich: Anton Pustet, 1966.

Casey, R. P. "Two Notes on Valentinian Theology." *Harvard Theological Review* 23 (1930): 275–98.

De Faye, E. *Gnostiques et gnosticisme: étude critique des documents du gnosticisme chrétien aux IIᵉ et IIIᵉ siècles.* 2d ed. Paris: P. Geuthner, 1925.

Dillon, J. "Valentinus." In his *Middle Platonists,* 384–89. Ithaca, N.Y.: Cornell University Press, 1977.

Foerster, W. *Von Valentin zu Herakleon: Untersuchungen über die Quellen und die Entwicklung der valentinianischen Gnosis.* Beihefte zur Zeitschrift für die neutestamentliche Wissenschaft und die Kunde der älteren Kirche, 7. Giessen: Töpelmann, 1928.

Hilgenfeld, A. *Die Ketzergeschichte des Urchristenthums urkundlich dargestellt.* Leipzig: Fues, 1884.

Irenaeus of Lyon. Edited by A. Rousseau, L. Doutreleau, in *Irénée de Lyon, Contre les hérésies.* 5 vols. in 10. Sources chrétiennes, nos. 100 (2 vols.), 152–53, 210–11, 263–64, 293–94. Paris: Le Cerf, 1965–82. (The best edition and translation. Standard English translation by A. Roberts and J. Donaldson in their *Ante-Nicene Fathers,* vol. 1, 315–578.)

Jonas, H. *The Gnostic Religion.* 3d ed. Boston: Beacon Press, 1970.

Koschorke, K. "Patristische Materialien zur Spätgeschichte der valentinianischen Gnosis." In *Gnosis and Gnosticism: Papers Read at the Eighth International Conference on Patristic Studies (Oxford, September 3rd–8th, 1979),* edited by M. Krause, 120–39. Nag Hammadi Studies, vol. 17. Leiden: E. J. Brill, 1981.

Layton, B., ed. *The Rediscovery of Gnosticism: Proceedings of the International Conference on Gnosticism at Yale, New Haven, Connecticut, March 28–31, 1978.* Vol. 1, *The School of Valentinus.* Studies in the History of Religions, no. 41, vol. 1. Leiden: E. J. Brill, 1980. Note especially essays by Stead ("In Search of Valentinus") and Quispel ("Valentinian Gnosis and the Apocryphon of John").

Leisegang, H. "Valentinus (1), Valentinianer." In *Paulys Real-Encyclopädie der classischen Altertumswissenschaft.* 2d ed. by G. Wissowa et al., 2d ser., vol. 7 (1948), cols. 2261–73.

Lipsius, R. A. "Ptolemy" and "Valentinus." In vol. 4 of *Dictionary of Christian Biography,* edited by W. Smith and H. Wace. London: John Murray, 1887.

Lüdemann, G. "Zur Geschichte des ältesten Christentums in Rom: I. Valentin und Marcion, II. Ptolemäus and Justin." *Zeitschrift für die neutestamentliche Wissenschaft und die Kunde der älteren Kirche* 70 (1979): 86–114.

McGuire, A. "Valentinus and the *Gnōstikē Hairesis:* An Investigation of Valentinus's Position in the History of Gnosticism." Ph.D. diss., Yale University, 1983.

Orbe, A. *Estudios Valentinianos.* 5 vols. in 6. Analecta Gregoriana, vols. 65, 83, 99 (2 vols.), 113, 158. Rome: Libreria Editrice dell' Università Gregoriana, 1955–66.

Pagels, E. *The Gnostic* [i.e. Valentinian] *Paul: Gnostic Exegesis of the Pauline Letters.* Philadelphia: Fortress Press, 1975.

————. *The Johannine Gospel in Gnostic* [i.e. Valentinian] *Exegesis: Heracleon's Commentary on John*. Society of Biblical Literature, Monograph Series, vol. 17. Nashville, Tenn.: Abingdon Press, 1973.

Quispel, G. "The Original Doctrine of Valentine." *Vigiliae Christianae* 1 (1947): 43–73, now partly retracted in his contribution to Layton, *Rediscovery*.

Sagnard, F. *La Gnose valentinienne et le témoignage de Saint Irénée*. Études de philosophie médiévale, vol. 36. Paris: J. Vrin, 1947.

Stead, G. C. "The Valentinian Myth of Sophia." *Journal of Theological Studies*, n.s. 20 (1969): 75–104.

Tate, J. "Allegory, Greek." In *The Oxford Classical Dictionary*, 2d ed., 45–46. Oxford: Clarendon Press, 1970.

Some important Valentinian materials not in this volume

Heracleon. *The Fragments of Heracleon: Newly Edited from the Manuscripts with an Introduction and Notes*, by A. E. Brooke. Texts and Studies, vol. 1, no. 4. Cambridge: Cambridge University Press, 1891.

Theodotus. *The Excerpta ex Theodoto of Clement of Alexandria: Edited with Translation, Introduction and Notes*, by R. P. Casey. Studies and Documents, vol. 1. London: Christophers, 1934.

————. *Extraits de Théodote: texte grec, introduction, traduction et notes*, by F. Sagnard. Sources chrétiennes, vol. 23. Paris: Le Cerf, 1948. (The most reliable guide as to which excerpts are actually by Theodotus. English translation of the genuine excerpts by D. Hill, in *Gnosis: A Selection of Gnostic Texts*, edited by W. Foerster, 222–33. Oxford: Clarendon Press, 1972.)

Tripartite Tractate, translated by H. Attridge. In *Nag Hammadi Codex I*, edited by H. Attridge and E. Pagels. Vol. 1, *Introductions, Texts* . . ., 193–337, and vol. 2, *Notes*, 217–497. Nag Hammadi Studies, vols. 22, 23. Leiden: E. J. Brill, 1985.

PTOLEMY'S VERSION OF THE GNOSTIC MYTH

ACCORDING TO
ST. IRENAEUS OF LYON, *AGAINST HERESIES* 1.1.1–1.8.5
(IrPt)

Contents

This selection was the best-known account of gnostic myth until the discovery of the Coptic manuscripts of Nag Hammadi.

Ptolemy was one of Valentinus's first and most brilliant students. In this excerpt St. Irenaeus of Lyon, writing in Greek about A.D. 180, gives a detailed account of Ptolemy's teaching of the myth, "the blossom of Valentinus's school." Just as Valentinus's own mythic doctrine was a highly modified version of classic gnostic myth, so Ptolemy's must have been a further modification of his master's version—a revision of a revision.

An adequate historical interpretation of IrPt would therefore need to compare Ptolemy's myth with the teaching of Valentinus, taking note of Ptolemy's alterations. But this is easier said than done, for Valentinus's teaching is known only in very sketchy form (cf. IrV), and modern scholars disagree on the extent to which Ptolemy simply reproduces what he had learned from Valentinus. One view sees the Ptolemaean myth as closely following a written text, now lost, of Valentinus's original version, but slightly altered so as to mitigate its most shocking features. On this assumption, comparison of Ptolemy's doctrine with the teachings of Valentinus's other disciples makes it possible to isolate the original teaching of Valentinus, and thus to distinguish passages in which Ptolemy has altered that teaching.

A quite different view reconstructs Valentinus's original doctrine from another set of evidence, arriving at a relatively simple theology—in which, for example, only one figure of wisdom (Sophia) is involved in disaster. Set against such a reconstruction, the Valentinian myth of Sophia or wisdom as taught by Ptolemy would appear to be an elaborate piece of scholasticism, going far beyond Valentinus to resolve inner inconsistencies and contradictions within the speculative system. The doctrine of two wisdoms (higher wisdom and Achamōth) would then be an invention of Valentinus's disciples or perhaps a reintroduction of a classic gnostic doctrine of two wisdoms.

The Ptolemaean version, as summarized here by St. Irenaeus, parallels the full extent of classic gnostic myth from the description of the first principle down to the end of material creation and final restoration of the missing spiritual "seeds" to their spiritual home. It also touches on the issues of biblical interpretation and ethics. In this summary Irenaeus has woven together several written works. He gives two versions of the restraint of wisdom, for example (1.2.2–1.2.4), and reports two somewhat different descriptions of the perfect parent (1.2.4). From yet another source may come the lengthy excerpts in which New Testament passages are allegorically interpreted to refer to the myth. A commentary on the prologue to the Gospel of John (1.8.5) can also be isolated.

However much it may be indebted to the original doctrine of Valentinus, in any case Ptolemaean teaching stands at some distance from the myth of classic gnostic scripture. The overall tone and diction of Ptolemy's teaching—if St. Irenaeus's summary paints a representative picture—lacks the many Eastern or quasi-Jewish features of classic gnostic scripture. It is Hellenic, placid, clear, and deeply Christian, though unorthodox. The metaphysical realm of aeons in Ptolemy's myth is clearly and arithmetically structured. Its unity and equality are emphasized (1.2.6), so that the aeons both share in the passion of wisdom (1.2.1) and cooperate in the emission of a savior to rectify her error (1.2.6). Stability—the underlying systemic goal of gnostic as well as Valentinian myth—is here linked with androgyny, the permanent unification of sexual opposites in one entity. Androgyny is thus the structure of the ultimate first principle (1.2.4) and the goal of the individual Christian. Corresponding to the self or spirit within each Valentinian Christian, Ptolemaean myth postulates a corresponding other self or "angel," with which it will ultimately unite (1.7.1), in a union that could be expressed sacramentally or metaphorically in the "mystery of bridal chamber" (cf. GPh). In keeping with this theme, a certain amount of apparently sexual language appears in the names of the aeons ("intercourse, union, pleasure, mixture"); it is, however, paired with terms that express stability, the goal of androgynous union ("deep-sunken, unaging, self-produced, motionless"), cf. 1.1.2.

The tendency, already found in classic gnostic myth, to pair higher and lower entities (Barbēlō and wisdom, wisdom and life, first thought and afterthought) is less ambiguous in Ptolemy; it is limited to higher and lower Christs and higher and lower wisdoms (also called "Christ" and "Jesus"; "wisdom" and "Achamōth"). The heavenly rulers, though recognizably identical with their counterparts in gnostic myth, are demystified and domesticated. The divine particles that the chief ruler (craftsman) sows in humankind are not his by virtue of having stolen them from his mother (BJn 10:20f), but because she secretly deposited them in him; thus the theme of ultimate divine providence, which is still unintegrated in gnostic myth (cf. RR 87:20f), has been fully incorporated into the Ptolemaean version. The threefold genealogical division of classic gnostic historiography (descendants of Cain, Abel, Seth) has in Ptolemy been coordinated with a traditional philosophical analysis of the human makeup, as comprising material body, animating soul, and contemplative intellect or spirit. As in gnostic myth, the end of time is seen as a moment when the system reattains stability and all parts are installed in their proper places. Yet the Ptolemaean vision of the end is more complex, ambiguous, and systemically unstable than the gnostic one; for, Ptolemy must provide for two kinds of salvation, corresponding to two classes of saved Christians, i.e. Valentinians and ordinary Christians, "the spirituals" and "the just" (1.7.1). At this point, Ptolemaean myth clearly reflects the social position of the Valentinian school within a larger Christian organization.

Literary background

Almost nothing is known about Ptolemy, the author of the main material summarized in this excerpt; he is also the author of a work on the sources of the Pentateuch, which survives in its original wording (cf. PtF). Ptolemy is reported to have been a leader of an "Italic" branch of the Valentinian school, and so scholars have often suggested that he taught in Rome. According to ancient report, he was one of Valentinus's first students. Because "Ptolemy" was a rare name at Rome, some scholars have identified him with the only Roman Christian intellectual of that name who is otherwise known in the period, Ptolemy the martyr (died ca. 152); this identification is controversial. The martyr Ptolemy is stated (by St. Justin Martyr, *Apology II*) to have been a Christian teacher; his death resulted from his efforts to convert a wealthy Roman matron to Christianity, which ultimately led to his denunciation before hostile Roman authorities. The Valentinian Ptolemy's theological career must therefore fall after the date of Valentinus's migration to Rome (A.D. 136–40) and before the time of Irenaeus's summary (written ca. 180)—and further-more, before ca. 152 if he is identical with the Roman martyr. His language of composition was Greek.

As mentioned above, St. Irenaeus has combined several written works—presum-ably treatises—in this excerpt. Their exact literary structures are masked by Irenaeus's summary.

Mythic characters

I. The Invisible Spiritual Fullness

A. The THIRTY SILENT AND UNRECOGNIZABLE AEONS

  (1) The PRIMAL OCTET OF AEONS:

    The DEEP. The perfect parent, prior source, and ancestor.
    SILENCE, its notional consort. Thought, loveliness.

    INTELLECT. The only-begotten, the parent and source of the entirety.
    TRUTH, its consort

    The WORD. The parent and source of the fullness.
    LIFE (Zōē), its consort

    The HUMAN BEING
    The CHURCH, its consort

  (2) The TEN AEONS, emanations from the Word and life. Five pairs:

The DEEP-SUNKEN	=	INTERCOURSE
The UNAGING	=	UNION
The SELF-PRODUCED	=	PLEASURE
The MOTIONLESS	=	MIXTURE
The ONLY-BEGOTTEN	=	The BLESSED

  (3) The TWELVE AEONS, emanations from the human being and the church. Six pairs:

The INTERCESSOR	=	FAITH
The FATHERLY	=	HOPE
The MOTHERLY	=	LOVE
The EVER-FLOWING	=	INTELLIGENCE
The ECCLESIASTICAL	=	BLESSEDNESS
The WISHED-FOR	=	WISDOM (Sophia), "higher wisdom"

B. OTHER BEINGS WITHIN THE FULLNESS

The ANOINTED (Christ) or upper anointed. An emanation from intellect.

The HOLY SPIRIT, his consort

An inner hexagonal BOUNDARY between the perfect parent and intellect, created by the anointed and the holy spirit: BOUNDARY, CROSS, REDEEMER, EMANCIPATOR, BOUNDARY-SETTER, CONVEYER

JESUS, an emanation from all the fullness of aeons. Called savior, second-anointed (Christ), Word, son, and entirety. Ultimately, Achamōth's bridegroom.

The ANGELS, Jesus' bodyguards, emanations from all the fullness of aeons. Models of the spiritual elements within Valentinian Christians, and, ultimately, their bridegrooms.

An outer palisade or BOUNDARY at the outer limits of the fullness

II. Non-Human Beings Outside the Fullness

ACHAMÔTH, the thinking of higher wisdom, wisdom's offspring. Called wisdom (or lower wisdom) and holy spirit; the mother; the eighth; lord. Ultimately, bride of Jesus the savior.

Her offspring, the CRAFTSMAN (demiurge) of material beings; parent of animate beings; an angel. Called the parentless mother-father; god and king of all; the seventh. The god of Israel and of ordinary Christians.

SEVEN ANGELS OR HEAVENS, made by the craftsman

SPIRITS (spiritual hosts) OF WICKEDNESS:
   The DEVIL or WORLD-RULER. A creature of the craftsman.
   DEMONS

III. Humankind

ADAM, comprising three elements:

   (1) The ANIMATE HUMAN BEING; the spirit of life (Zōē); soul; the right.
   (2) The MATERIAL ADAM. Body; the left.
   (3) The SPIRITUAL HUMAN BEING, an element secretly sown in Adam at the instigation of Achamōth; Achamōth's offspring, patterned after the angels.

SUBSEQUENT HUMAN BEINGS:

   (1) POSTERITY OF SETH. SPIRITUALS: those who possess the seed of Achamōth as well as soul and matter; whose spirits are ultimately to be the brides of the angels. Valentinian Christians. [Among them, according to some followers of Ptolemy, was:
   JESUS BORN OF MARY, a son of the craftsman. The lower or animate anointed (Christ); a spiritual human being, upon whom the savior (higher Jesus) descended.]
   (2) POSTERITY OF ABEL. ANIMATES; those who consist merely of soul and matter. Other Christians.
   (3) POSTERITY OF CAIN. Those who consist merely of dust or matter. Other people.

Text

St. Irenaeus's original Greek text survives in the form of a word-for-word citation in St. Epiphanius of Salamis, *Against Heresies* 31.9.1—31.32.9 (vol. 1, 398–435 in K. Holl's edition of Epiphanius); Epiphanius's text is attested by a number of medieval manuscripts, whose accuracy is a matter of debate among scholars. One short passage is also quoted in Pseudo-Ephraem of Edessa, *On Virtue*. An ancient Latin version of Irenaeus's work (containing the entire selection) also survives; two short passages exist in Syriac, as quoted by Severus of Antioch's *Against the Impious Grammarian*; and two more in Armenian are found in a Patristic florilegium conserved in Istanbul (MS Galata 54). The translation below is based on the critical edition of the Greek and Latin texts, which uses the Syriac and Armenian evidence, by Rousseau and Doutreleau, with alterations: A. Rousseau and L. Doutreleau, eds., *Irénée de Lyon, Contre les hérésies: Livre I* [Book 1] (Sources chrétiennes, no. 264; Paris: Le Cerf, 1979), vol. 2, 18–137.

SELECT BIBLIOGRAPHY

See the bibliography at the end of the "Historical Introduction" to Part Three, especially items by Lüdemann, Quispel, Sagnard, and Stead. Also:

Foerster, W. "Die Grundzüge der ptolemaeischen Gnosis." *New Testament Studies* 6 (1959): 16–31.
Justin Martyr. (Works.) Translated in *Ante-Nicene Fathers,* vol. 1. See "Apology II" for the martyrdom of the Roman martyr Ptolemy.

I. THE VALENTINIAN GNOSTIC MYTH

The perfect parent

1.1.1 Within invisible and unnameable heights[a] there was—they say—a preexistent, perfect eternity;[b] this they call also prior source, ancestor, and the deep. And it existed uncontained, invisible, everlasting, and *IrV (e)* unengendered. Within infinite eternal realms it was in great stillness and *IrV (e)* rest.

And with it coexisted thought, which they also call loveliness and silence.[c]

Production of intellect (the only-begotten)

And eventually the aforementioned deep took thought[d] to emit a source of the entirety.[e] And it deposited this emanation that it had thought to emit, like sperm, in the womb of the silence that coexisted *IrV (b)* with it. And the latter received this sperm, conceived, and brought forth intellect, which was like and equal to the emitter and was the only being that comprehended[f] the magnitude of its parent. And this intellect they call also only-begotten, parent,[g] and source of the entirety. *IrV (c)*

And truth was emitted along with it.

And this is equivalent to the first, primal *tetraktys*[h] of Pythagorean philosophy. They call it also the root of the entirety. For it consists of

the deep;
silence;

1.1.1 a. I.e. at the highest level of abstraction. The negative epithets of this paragraph ("invisible, unnameable, uncontained, unengendered") may be compared with the description of the parent in BJn 2:26f.

b. Or "aeon."

c. The reality of the parent's consort is called into question in 1.2.4.

d. In classic gnostic myth, the second principle (Barbēlō) is called the parent's thinking or thought, cf. BJn 4:26f.

e. In classic gnostic scripture, the "entirety" means the sum total of spiritual reality deriving from the second principle (Barbēlō).

In IrPt it seems to have the same meaning as "fullness," cf. 1.2.6, and note 1.1.1k.

f. Or "contained."

g. The three first principles of the myth (the deep, intellect, and the Word) are all called "parent."

h. A quartet consisting of the first four integers or their sum ($1 + 2 + 3 + 4 = 10$), sometimes represented as

and then

> intellect;
> truth.

Production of more aeons by intellect: the Word

Now, when this only-begotten perceived the ends for which it had been emitted, it emitted the Word[i] and life (Zōē)—a parent[j] of the IrV (c) entirety of beings that were to exist after it and a source and forming of the entire fullness.[k]   IrV (e)

The human being

And from the Word and life (Zōē) emanated the human being and the IrV (c) church, as a pair.

And these constitute the primal octet—a root and source[l] of the entirety. It is designated by them with four names:

> the deep;
> intellect;
> the Word;
> human being.

For each of them is androgynous, as follows:

> first, the ancestor united with its thought—called also
>   loveliness and silence—forming a pair;
> the only-begotten, i.e. intellect, united with truth;
> the Word united with life (Zōē);
> the human being united with the church.

Emission of the ten aeons

1.1.2 Now, the aforementioned aeons were emitted for the glory of the parent.[a] And wishing to glorify the parent with something of their own, they too emitted emanations in pairs. And after emitting the human being and the church, the Word and life (Zōē) emitted another ten aeons, IrV (c) to whom they give the following names:

> the deep-sunken and intercourse;
> the unaging and union;
> the self-produced and pleasure;
> the motionless and mixture;
> the only-begotten and the blessed.

These are ⟨the⟩ ten aeons that emanated—they say—from the Word and life (Zōē).

Emission of the twelve aeons

Now, in addition the human being and the church emitted twelve IrV (c) aeons, upon which they bestow the following names:

> the intercessor and faith;
> the fatherly and hope;

---

i. "Word" (Greek *Logos*): the same term (throughout this selection) also means "rational faculty, reason, utterance"; it is used in the prologue of the Gospel of John.

j. Cf. note 1.1.1g.

k. "fullness": Valentinian jargon for the spiritual universe.

l. Or "substance."

1.1.2 a. I.e. the deep.

the motherly and love;
the ever-flowing and intelligence;
the ecclesiastical and blessedness;
the wished-for and wisdom (Sophia).　　　　　　　　IrV (i)

1.1.3　The aforementioned are—according to their erroneous teaching—the thirty silent and unrecognizable aeons. They constitute the invisible, spiritual fullness according to them. And it is divided into three parts: an octet, a group of ten, and a group of twelve.

Allegories of the thirty aeons[a]

And, they say, the reason that the savior—for they do not wish to call him the lord—did nothing publicly for thirty years, was in order to manifest the mystery of these aeons. Indeed, also in the parable of the workers sent to the vineyard—they say—these thirty aeons are disclosed very openly. For some get sent at the first hour; others at the third; others at the sixth; others at the ninth; still others at the eleventh. If these are added together they make the sum of thirty. For, $1 + 3 + 6 + 9 + 11 = 30$. And they maintain that the aeons are disclosed in the mention of these hours. And these great, admirable, secret mysteries are the fruit that they bear wherever they have been able to accommodate and adapt some passages of scripture to their own fictitious creation.

Lk 3:23
Mt 20:1

Contemplation of the parent by intellect

1.2.1　Now, in their system the only being that was acquainted with the ancestor was—they say—the only-begotten, or intellect, which derived from it. To all the others, this (ancestor) was invisible and incomprehensible. Only the intellect—according to them—had the pleasure of contemplating the parent and the joy of understanding its immeasurable magnitude.

And it thought to communicate the size and extent of the parent's magnitude to the other aeons, and the fact that it was beginningless, uncontained, and not capable of being seen. But by the will of the parent, silence restrained it because it wanted to elevate all of them into thought and into longing for a search for the aforementioned ancestor of theirs.

Wisdom's passionate search for the parent

Now, the other aeons[a] in similar fashion and more or less in stillness longed to see the emitter of their seed and to inquire about the beginningless root. **1.2.2**　But wisdom (Sophia)—the very last, most recent aeon of the group of twelve that had been emitted by the human being and the church—charged forward and experienced passion without the involvement of her consort, the wished-for.

IrV (d) ?

The passion originated in the region of intellect and truth; but it collected in this (last aeon), which had been diverted—ostensibly out of love but really out of recklessness—because it had not communicated with the perfect parent as intellect had.

The passion consisted of a search for the parent; for—they say—she wanted to comprehend its magnitude. She was unable to, for she had tried to accomplish the impossible. And she became engaged in a very

---

1.1.3 a. For allegory, see the "Historical Introduction" to Part Three.

1.2.1 a. Except for wisdom (Sophia).

great struggle, owing to the magnitude of the depth, the unsearchability of the parent, and her affection for that (parent).

Her restraint by the inner boundary (1)

Then she strained forward more and more. And she would have been swallowed and would have dissolved into universal essence had she not encountered a power that established the entirety and kept it outside of the ineffable magnitude. And this power they call the boundary.[a] By it she was held back and established. With difficulty, she turned back to herself and became convinced that the parent was incomprehensible: and so she put off her former thinking, along with its consequent passion, which had come from terrifying amazement.

IrV (e)

Production of her offspring (Achamōth)

1.2.3   And some of them tell the following tale about the passion of wisdom (Sophia) and her turning back.

In attempting the impossible and incomprehensible, she gave birth to essence without form,[a] of that nature which a female must give birth to.[b] And when she understood it, first she was grieved because of the imperfection of its origin. Next, she was afraid lest the thing should die.[c] And then she became distraught and uncertain, searching for the cause and searching for the means to hide what had come into being. After being occupied with passions she accepted a turning back: having tried to hasten up to the parent and having, for a while, acted recklessly, she became exhausted. She became a suppliant before the parent; and the other aeons, especially intellect, joined her entreaty.

The essence of matter—they say—had its first source in the afore-mentioned lack-of-acquaintance, grief, fear, and terror.[d]

Her restraint by the inner boundary (2)[e]

1.2.4   Through the agency of the only-begotten,[a] over against these the parent emitted in its own image the aforementioned boundary, having no consort and having no female component. For sometimes they maintain that the parent is with a consort, silence; but other times, that it is beyond (the categories) male and female. And this boundary[b] they call also cross, redeemer, emancipator, boundary-setter, and conveyer. By this boundary—they say—wisdom (Sophia) was purified, established, and restored to membership in a pair.

IrV (e)

Separation of Achamōth and passions by the outer boundary

For, thinking and its consequent passion[c] were separated from her: she remained inside the fullness; but her thinking and the passion were

---

1.2.2 a. Greek *horos*.

1.2.3 a. The same words also mean "to a misshapen essence."
 b. It was a philosophical cliché that the material constituent of an entity was "female," while its form (or ideal form) was "male."
 c. Lit. "have an end."
 d. As St. Irenaeus goes on to explain (1.5.4), wisdom's passions are subsequently experienced by her offspring Achamōth, and

it is Achamōth's passions that are the source of material essence in the world.
 e. Section 1.2.4 partly repeats 1.2.2 ("Her restraint by the inner boundary [1]").

1.2.4 a. I.e. intellect.
 b. I.e. the inner boundary.
 c. Wisdom's passionate search consisted of passion and the abortive attempt to conceive of the perfect parent by means of thinking.

bounded apart[d] by the boundary, were fenced off with a palisade,[e] and existed outside the fullness. This (thinking) was a spiritual essence, since it was a natural impulse to action on the part of an aeon. Yet it was without form[f] and imageless[g] because she had not comprehended anything. And—they say—for this reason it was a weak and female fruit.

Emission of the anointed and the holy spirit

1.2.5 After it had been bounded apart outside the fullness of the aeons and its mother had been restored to membership in her own pair, the only-begotten emitted another pair by the parent's foresight, for the fixing and establishment of the fullness, lest any of the aeons should experience the same as she had. This consisted of the anointed (Christ) and the holy spirit; by them the aeons were set in order.

Proclamation of the parent's incomprehensibility by the anointed

Now, the anointed (Christ) taught them the nature of membership in a pair,[a] . . . and among them to proclaim publicly acquaintance with the parent, saying that it is uncontained, incomprehensible, and cannot be   Mt 11:27
seen or heard except through the only-begotten.[b] And the eternal permanence of the entirety is due to the incomprehensible aspect of the parent; but its origination and forming is due to the parent's comprehensible aspect, which is to say, its child.[c] And that is what the newly emitted anointed (Christ) did for the entirety.

Equalization of the aeons by the holy spirit

1.2.6 Moreover, once they had all been made equal with one another the holy spirit taught them to give thanks and brought in true repose. And in this way—they say—the aeons were appointed equal in form and intention, so that all of them were intellects, all were Words, all were human beings, and all were anointeds (Christs); while the female ones were likewise all truths, were all lifes (Zōē's), were all spirits, and were all churches. When the entirety had been established for this end and was perfectly at repose, very joyfully it lifted up praise unto the ancestor, sharing in much good cheer.

Emission of Jesus and the angels

And in response to these good deeds, with a single design and intention,   IrV (i)
as the anointed (Christ) and the spirit joined in the consent and their parent joined in the approval, the entire fullness of aeons—each of the aeons—joined in bringing and contributing the most beautiful and splendid that it had within itself. And interweaving these elements fittingly and uniting them harmoniously, in honor and to the glory of the deep they emitted an emanation that was a kind of utterly perfect beauty and star of the fullness, a perfect[a] fruit,[b] Jesus: after his parent he was named

---

d. Or "defined."

e. "fenced off with a palisade": a single verb in Greek. The word (apo-staurizein) is obviously related to the words "crucify" (staurizein) and "cross" (stauros). It might also be taken to mean "fenced off by a cross." The outer boundary is meant.

f. Or "misshapen."

g. Or "formless."

1.2.5 a. The text that follows is corrupt and cannot be translated coherently. The inco-

herent phrase appears to say "recognizing comprehension of the unengendered, sufficient to be."

b. I.e. intellect.

c. Or "son" (as in GTr).

1.2.6 a. Or "ripe."

b. "fruit" (cf. also note 1.2.6a): the Valentinian school characteristically spoke of emanations and the process of emanation with agricultural metaphors.

also savior, anointed (Christ), and Word; and also entirety, because he is from the entirety.

Simultaneously, in honor of it (the entirety) angels of the same ancestry were emitted as bodyguards for him.[a]

1.3.1 Such then are the system of the interior of the fullness, as expressed by them; the misfortune of the aeon that suffered and nearly perished in vast matter through a search for the parent; the hexagonal construction consisting of

> the boundary;
> cross;
> redeemer;
> emancipator;
> boundary-setter;
> conveyer;

the creation of the first-anointed (Christ) and the holy spirit by their parent, subsequent to that of the aeons, as a result of a repentance;[a] and the constructing of the second-anointed (Christ), also called savior, compounded out of contributed elements.

But these things are not openly spoken of, for not all people can comprehend acquaintance with them. Rather, they are mysteriously disclosed in parables by the savior for those who can understand, as follows.   Mt 19:11

Further allegories of the aeons

As I already mentioned,[b] the thirty aeons are disclosed by the thirty years in which—they say—the savior did nothing in public; and by the parable of the workers of the vineyard. And Paul—they say—speaks of the aeons by name very openly, even maintaining their order, when he says

> to all generations of aeon belonging to the aeons.[c]   Ep 3:21

But also when we say "to aeons belonging to aeons"[d] we are supposed to be signifying the aforementioned aeons. And wherever the Greek words *aiōn* ("ever," "aeon") and *aiōnes* ("ever," "aeons") are spoken of, they maintain that the reference is to these (aeons).
1.3.2 The emission of the group of twelve aeons is supposed to be disclosed by the fact that the lord held a discussion with the teachers of the law when he was twelve, and by the selection of the apostles, for there were twelve apostles. And the remaining eighteen aeons are supposed to be shown forth by the fact that it says he conversed with his disciples for eighteen months after his resurrection from the dead. But the eighteen aeons are even supposed to be clearly disclosed by the two initial letters of his name in Greek (*Iēsous*, "Jesus"), that is, the letters *I* (iota) and *ē* (eta).[a] Similarly, they say that the ten aeons are signified by the initial letter *I* (iota) of his name, and this is why the savior said, "Not an iota, not a dot, will pass until the entirety comes into being."[b]   Lk 2:42 / Mt 10:2 / Lk 6:13 / Mt 5:18

1.3.1 a. For the repentance of wisdom in classic gnostic scripture, see BJn 13:32f.
  b. Cf. 1.1.3.
  c. In its original context (Ep 3:21) this Greek phrase means "to all generations, for ever and ever."
  d. In its ordinary liturgical context, this Greek phrase means "for ever and ever."

1.3.2 a. In Greek the letters of the alphabet were used as numerical figures. *I* was equivalent to 10, *ē* to 8. Thus *Iē* = 18.
  b. The usual translation of this passage (Mt 5:18) is "Not an iota, not a dot, will pass . . . until all is accomplished."

1.3.3 The passion (suffered) by the twelfth aeon[a] is—they say—signified by the apostasy of Judas, who was the twelfth of the apostles; and because he[b] suffered in the twelfth month. For they maintain that after his baptism he preached for only a single year. Furthermore, it is very plainly made clear in (the passage concerning) the woman who had suffered from a hemorrhage. For she had already suffered for twelve years before she was made well by the advent of the savior through touching the fringe of his garment.[c] And the reason why the savior said, "Who was it that touched me?" was to teach the disciples about the mystery that had taken place among the aeons and the cure of the suffering aeon. For, the woman who had suffered for twelve years is— they say—that female power while it was straining forward and its essence was flowing into the infinite. And had she not come in contact with what the son[d] was wearing,[e] namely truth—which belongs to the first quartet, and is disclosed by the fringe—she would have dissolved into her essence.[f] But she came to stand at rest and was cured of her passion. For the son's power—which, they maintain, is the boundary— healed her, and the passion was separated from her.

Lk 4:19

Lk 8:43

Allegories of Jesus the savior

1.3.4 The fact that the savior, who derives from all, is the entirety, is—they say—made clear by the phrase "the entirety, being male, explaining[a] the womb":[b] the savior, who is the entirety, explained[c] the womb of the thinking of the aeon who had suffered and had been put outside the boundary of[d] the fullness. Her they call also the second eighth being—of which we speak below. Paul speaks of this openly— they say—with the phrases,

Lk 2:23
Ex 13:2

> and he is the entirety;[e]   Col 3:11

> the entirety is in[f] him, and derives from him;[g]   Rm 11:36

> in him the whole[h] fullness of deity dwells.   Col 2:9

And the phrase

> to unite the entirety in the anointed (Christ),[i]   Ep 1:10

and other such passages, have been divinely spoken according to their interpretation.

Allegories of the inner boundary

1.3.5 Furthermore, as for the boundary, which they call by many names, they declare that it has two activities: one that stabilizes, the

---

1.3.3 a. Wisdom (Sophia).

b. Jesus according to Christian scripture.

c. "the fringe of his garment": lit. "his fringe."

d. I.e. the savior.

e. Or "bearing along."

f. Probably the original reading of the text here is "into universal essence," as in 1.2.2.

1.3.4 a. Or "opening."

b. The more normal translation of this passage (Lk 2:23 = Ex 13:2) is "every male that opens the womb," meaning "every first-born male child."

c. Or "opened."

d. "put outside the boundary of": or "banished from."

e. The more normal translation of this passage (Col 3:11) would be "He (Christ) is all."

f. Or "into."

g. The text of this verse (Rm 11:36), as it is now found, is normally translated "from him and through him and to him are all things." But the Valentinians may have known a slightly different form of the text and based their interpretation upon that.

h. Or "entire."

i. The more normal translation of this passage (Ep 1:10) is "to unite all things in (him)."

other that divides. In stabilizing and establishing, it is the cross; in dividing and bounding, it is the boundary. And—they say—the savior disclosed its activities in the following words. First, he disclosed its stabilizing activity when he said

> That which does not lift up its cross and follow me cannot be my disciple;[a]   Mt 10:38
> Lk 14:27

and

> Lift up the cross, follow me.[b]   Mk 10:21 var.

But he disclosed its bounding activity, when he said

> I have not come to bring peace, but a sword.   Mt 10:34

John, too—they say—disclosed this (boundary) when he said

> His winnowing fork is in his hand, to clear his threshing floor, and he will gather his wheat into his granary, but the chaff he will burn with unquenchable fire.   Mt 3:12
> Lk 3:17

In this passage the activity of the boundary is supposedly disclosed. For according to their interpretation, that winnowing fork is the cross; the latter also consumes all the material elements as fire consumes chaff, and winnows[c] the saved as a winnowing fork winnows wheat. Moreover, Paul the apostle, too—they say—makes mention of this cross in the following words:

> For the word of the cross is folly to those who are perishing, but to us who are being saved it is a power of god;   1Co 1:18

and

> But far be it for me to glory in anything except the cross of the anointed (Christ), by which the world has been crucified to me, and I to the world.[d]   Ga 6:14
> GPh 46

* * *

The essential formation of Achamōth by the anointed

1.4.1   The following are the events that they say happened outside the fullness. Once the higher wisdom's (Sophia's) thinking, which they call also Achamōth,[a] along with her passion had been bounded apart from the fullness it was—they say—cast forth in a region of shadow and emptiness: and necessarily so, for it had come to be outside the light and the fullness, without form[b] and imageless[c] like an aborted foetus,[d] because it had not comprehended anything. But the anointed (Christ) took pity on this female being[e] and stretched out along the cross. By his own power he formed (her as) a concrete formation, (formed) not by acquaintance, but rather in essence alone. Once he had done this he hastened back upward, gathering in his power; and he left her, so that as she perceived the passion that was hers because of her removal from the fullness she might yearn for the superior realm; (for) she had a   GPh 34

1.3.5 a. The more normal translation of these words would be "He who does not bear his cross . . ."

  b. These words are found in some ancient MSS of Mk 10:21.

  c. Or "purifies."

  d. The following passage (not translated here) is a polemic by St. Irenaeus.

1.4.1 a. Biblical Hebrew *hokhmôth* (Pr 8–9), "wisdom"; in Ptolemaean Valentinianism, the name of lower wisdom, as opposed to Sophia; cf. GPh 34.

  b. "without form": or "misshapen."

  c. Or "formless."

  d. Cf. RR 94:14f.

  e. I.e. Achamōth.

fragrance of incorruptibility left in her by the anointed (Christ) and the holy spirit. Accordingly, she is called by two names: wisdom (Sophia) after her father, for her father[f] is called wisdom; and holy spirit, from the spirit belonging to the anointed (Christ).

Achamōth's passionate search for the light (the anointed)

Now, once she had been formed and come to her senses, and then had been immediately emptied of the Word that was invisibly with her, i.e. the anointed (Christ), she rushed to search for the light that had left her; and she could not comprehend it, being prevented by the boundary.[g] It was here that the boundary, in preventing her from the impulse to forward motion, said, "Iaō!" This—they say—is the origin of the name Iaō.

Origin of matter

Because she was unable to pass through the boundary since she was involved with passion, and she had been left outside and alone, she became subject to every aspect of manifold and diverse passion: she suffered grief, because she had not understood; fear, lest life should leave her just as light had done; uncertainty, at all of these; and everything in lack of acquaintance.

And unlike the aeon first wisdom (Sophia), her mother, in these passions she experienced not alteration but rather contrariety; and a different condition came to be present in her, one of turning back[h] toward the one who had made her alive.

1.4.2 She—they say—accounts for the genesis and essence of the matter out of which this world came into being. For, the entire soul of the world and the craftsman had its origination in her turning back;[a] other things had their beginning in her fear and her grief. Indeed, all moist essences came into being from her tears; luminous ones, from her laughter; and the bodily elements of the world, from her grief and terror. For sometimes—they say—she cried and felt grief because of being left alone in the darkness and emptiness; sometimes she proceeded to thought about the light that had left her, and she relaxed and laughed; sometimes she was afraid; and yet other times she became uncertain and distraught.[b] * * *

The concrete formation of Achamōth by Jesus the savior

1.4.5 So when this mother of theirs[a] had gone through every passion and had, with difficulty, surfaced again,[b] she turned—they say—to supplicate the light that had left her, i.e. the anointed (Christ).

Since he had returned to the fullness it is likely[c] that he hesitated to descend for a second time in person. But he dispatched the intercessor to her, i.e. the savior, endowing him with all the parent's power and delivering all things to be under his authority. And the aeons did likewise. Thus "in him the entirety was established, the visible and the invisible,   Mt 11:27 Lk 10:22 Col 1:16

---

f. "father . . . father": or "parent . . . parent."

g. I.e. the outer boundary.

h. Or "conversion."

1.4.2 a. Or "conversion."

b. The following passage (not translated here) is a polemic by St. Irenaeus.

1.4.5 a. St. Irenaeus speaks sarcastically of Achamōth.

b. Cf. IrUnid 1.30.3.

c. The sarcasm of this remark may indicate that the whole clause is a comment by St. Irenaeus.

thrones, divinities, dominions."[d] And he was sent to her along with his comrades, the angels.

At first—they say—Achamōth was ashamed before him and put on a veil out of shame. But then when she saw him and all his harvest[e] she ran to him, for she had gotten power from his appearing. And that (great one) formed her as a concrete formation (formed) by acquaintance, and he effected a cure of her passions. VHr

He separated them from her, but he could not ignore them; for it was impossible to make them disappear as the passions of the earlier (wisdom)[f] had, since they were already habitual and powerful. Rather, he set them apart, poured them together, fixed them, and transformed them from incorporeal passions into incorporeal matter. Next he endowed them with suitable properties and with such a nature that they would enter into compounds and bodies, so that two essences came into being, a bad one, deriving from the passions; and a mixed one tainted with passion,[g] deriving from the turning back.[h] And that is why they say that the savior acted virtually as a craftsman.[i] TRs 46:36 ?

Achamōth, once separate from her passions, from joy became pregnant with the contemplation of the lights that accompanied him, i.e. the angels with him; and—they teach—craving (?) them[j] she produced fruits after their[k] (?) image, a spiritual offspring generated after the likeness of the savior's bodyguards.

The three essences

1.5.1 Now, of the three (essences) that—they say—were by this point extant, one derived from her passion, and this was matter; another derived from her turning back,[a] and this was the animate; another was what she brought forth, and this was the spiritual. So she turned to their forming.

But she could not form the spiritual, inasmuch as it was of the same essence[b] as she.

(1) Animate essence: the origin of the craftsman

So she turned to the forming of the animate essence that derived from her turning back,[c] and she emitted what the savior had taught (her to emit). And first, from the animate essence she formed the god and parent and king[d] of all, that is, of both those which are of the same essence[e] as he, i.e. the animates, which they call those on the right; and those which derive from passion and matter, which they call those on the left. For they say that he formed all that were after him, being moved surreptitiously by the mother. Hence they call him mother-father, parentless, craftsman, and parent. And they say that he is parent of those on the right, i.e. animates; craftsman of those on the left, i.e. materials; and king of all. 1.5.6+

---

d. The more normal translation of this passage (Col 1:16) is "in him all things were created . . ."

e. Lit. "all his gathering of crops (or fruit)." Cf. note 1.2.6b.

f. I.e. the twelfth aeon.

g. "a mixed one tainted with passion": or simply "a passive one."

h. Or "conversion."

i. Just as two beings within the system are called "wisdom," so two are called "craftsman."

j. Or "delighting in their conception."

k. "their": or "his."

1.5.1 a. Or "conversion."

b. "of the same essence": Greek *homoousios*.

c. Or "conversion."

d. The text attested by the Latin version instead has "the god and savior and father and king."

e. Greek *homoousios*.

Prototypes of the created universe

Now, the aforementioned thinking[f] wished to make all things to the honor of the aeons, and so—they say—she made images of them; or, rather, the savior did, through her. She kept the image of the invisible parent, since the craftsman was not acquainted with it; he (the craftsman) kept the image of the only-begotten child;[g] and the archangels and angels that were with the latter kept the images of the other aeons.

Creation of the universe

1.5.2 Thus they say that he became parent[a] and god of things outside the fullness, being the maker of all things, both animate and material. For he separated the two essences that had been poured together, made bodies out of incorporeal things, and created things both heavenly and earthly. And he became the craftsman of material and animate things, of right and left, of light and heavy, of upward-tending and downward-tending. For he constructed the seven heavens, above which—they say—is the craftsman. For this reason they call him the seventh, and the mother they call the eighth,[b] preserving the count of the primal and first octet of the fullness.

Creation of the rulers

They say that the seven heavens are intellectual and postulate that they are angels; and the craftsman, too, is supposed to be an angel, but resembling god. Likewise they say that paradise is above the third heaven and is virtually the fourth archangel; and that Adam got something from it[c] when he passed time within it. TRs 44:35

1.5.3 Now, the craftsman—they say—supposed that he was constructing these things of his own accord, but he (really) made them through Achamōth's act of emission. For he made a heaven without knowing about heaven, modeled a human being without being acquainted with the human being, and showed forth earth without knowing earth. And in the case of all things he was in a like fashion unacquainted—they say—with the ideal forms of the things he was making and with the mother; rather, he supposed that he was totally alone. The cause—they say—of this supposition of his was his mother, who wished to promote him by making him head and source of his own essence and lord of the whole affair.

This mother[a] they call also the eighth, wisdom (Sophia), land, Jerusalem, holy spirit, and "lord" in the masculine gender.[b] She occupies the place of the midpoint;[c] and until the end, she is above the craftsman but below or outside the fullness.

(2) Material essence

1.5.4 So material essence—they say—was generated from three kinds of passion:

> fear;
> grief;
> uncertainty.

f. Achamōth.
g. I.e. intellect.

1.5.2 a. In so being, the craftsman parallels the three first principles of the myth; cf. note 1.1.1g.
b. Cf. RR 95:19f.

c. Or "him."

1.5.3 a. Achamōth.
b. They call her "master" rather than "mistress."
c. Cf. 1.7.1.

From fear and turning back, animate things received generation. From turning back,[a] the craftsman—they maintain—had his generation; and from fear, all the rest of animate substance such as souls of irrational living things, both animals and human beings.

The craftsman's arrogance

So because he (the craftsman) was incapable of being acquainted with spiritual beings, he thought that he alone was god; and he said through the prophets, "It is I who am god; apart from me there is no one."[b]   BJn 13:8 +
Is 45:21
Is 46:9 ?

The devil and demons

From grief—so they teach—the spiritual hosts of wickedness were   TRs 44.35
generated. From this source originated the devil, whom they call the   Ep 6:12
world-ruler; the demons; and all the substance of wickedness having to
do with spirits. So they say that the craftsman was an animate offspring   PtF 33.7.8
of their mother, while the world-ruler was a creature of the craftsman.[c]
The world-ruler recognized the things that were superior to it because
it was a spirit of wickedness. But the craftsman did not recognize these
because he was (merely) animate. Their mother is supposed to reside in
the supracelestial place, i.e. the midpoint; the craftsman, in the celestial
place, i.e. the seventh (heaven); and the world-ruler in our world.

The elements

From terror and despair the elements comprising the world were   GTr 17:9
generated, just as bodily things were generated from what is more
stationary, as we said above: earth (was generated) by the fixity of
terror; water, by the activity of fear; air, by the fixing[d] of grief. But fire
is naturally present in all of these, as (a principle of) death and corruption,
just as lack of acquaintance—so they teach—is hidden in the three
aforementioned passions.

Material Adam and animate Adam

1.5.5   When he had crafted the world, he made also the human being
consisting of dust—not by taking some of the dry soil of this world, but
rather by taking some of the invisible essence, the liquid, flowing
(essence) of matter. And into it—they state—he breathed the animate   GPh 71
human being.[a] This[b] is the one who came into being "after the image   Gn 1:26
and likeness." It is the material human being who is "after the image,"
for it is near to, though not of the same essence as, god. It is the animate
human being who is "after the likeness," hence its essence is called a
spirit of life (Zōē), for it derives from a spiritual emanation.   Gn 2:7
And then—they say—it was clothed in the "garment of skin": this,   GPh 71
they maintain, is the perceptible flesh.   Gn 3:21

1.5.4 a. "turning back . . . turning back":
or "conversion . . . conversion."
  b. Cf. BJn 11:19f.
  c. Just so, in some versions of classic
gnostic myth, Ialdabaōth (the devil) is said
to be the son of Sabaōth (the god of Israel
and ordinary Christianity); cf. EpA 40.5.1.
  d. Or "coagulation."

1.5.5 a. St. Irenaeus's summary of the myth
does not describe in detail the creation of
the animate Adam, but cf. BJn 15:1f.
  b. "This": the union of the material "human being consisting of dust" and the "animate human being."

(3) Spiritual essence

1.5.6 Now, their mother Achamōth's offspring, which she had brought forth by contemplating the angels around the savior, was of the same essence as the mother, i.e. was spiritual. And—they say—the craftsman was unacquainted with it; without his knowing it, this (offspring) was secretly deposited in him,[a] so that it might be sown by him into the soul[b] that comes from him and into this material body;[c] might be carried by these (as it were by a pregnant woman), and increase; and might become ready for the reception of the perfect Word. So by ineffable power and forethought the spiritual human being escaped the notice of the craftsman after he had been sown by wisdom[d] (Sophia) into the craftsman's breath. For just as he had not recognized his mother so he did not recognize her seed;[e] and this (seed)—they say—is the church, and it is an earthly representation (antitype) corresponding to the spiritual church. 1.5.1
VFrC
GPh 12
GPh 30

Gn 2:7

This latter, they think, is the human being that is within them,[f] so that they have their souls from the craftsman, their bodies from dust, their fleshly elements from matter, and the spiritual human being from their mother Achamōth. TRs 47:38

Fates of the three essences

1.6.1 Now, of the three (elements) that exist, the material one, also called left, will—they say—necessarily perish, in that it is unable to receive any breath of incorruptibility. The animate one, also called right, will proceed in whatever direction it has an inclination toward, in that it is intermediate between the spiritual and the material. The spiritual has been sent so that it might be formed by being coupled to the animate and learning along with it during its time of residence in this place. And this, they say, is the meaning of (the teachings about) the salt and the light of the world. Indeed, the animate needs perceptible lessons, too. The world was constructed—they say—and the savior came to this animate (element) in order to save it, for it has free will. GTr 17:33

PPl A:22 ?
TRs 49:9

Mt 5:13
Mt 5:14

The savior's body was apparent and not material

For he took the firstfruits—they say—of those which he was to save: from Achamōth, the spiritual (element); from the craftsman he put on the animate anointed (Christ); from[a] the providential arrangement of events,[b] he became enveloped in a body that had animate essence but was constructed in some ineffable way so as to be visible, touchable, and capable of experiencing passion. And he did not take anything material[c]—they say—for the material essence is not capable of receiving salvation.[d] TRs 44:14 ?
VFrE ?

1.5.6 a. The craftsman has within him the spiritual seed of his mother, just as Ialdabaōth, the craftsman of classic gnostic myth, had the power of its mother; cf. BJn 10:20f.

b. The animate human being.

c. The material human being that encloses the animate one, cf. 1.5.5.

d. I.e. lower wisdom, Achamōth.

e. Or "posterity."

f. "This latter" is the inner human being or "spiritual human being." A spiritual human being (Valentinian Christian) thus con-

sists of a material body ("from dust") that contains a soul or animate body, within which is a spiritual body.

1.6.1 a. Or "by."

b. Lit. "from the *oikonomia*," by divine economy.

c. The doctrine of docetism: that the real Jesus did not exist as human flesh, but only appeared to do so.

d. Or "preservation."

Formation of all spiritual elements will bring the end

The end is supposed to come when every spiritual element has been formed and perfected[e] in acquaintance—that is, spiritual human beings who possess perfect acquaintance concerning god and who have been initiated into the mysteries of Achamōth. And they assume that they themselves are the people in question.

Ethics

1.6.2 But animate persons have been taught animate lessons, being strengthened by works and mere faith and not possessing perfect acquaintance. And they say that we, who belong to the church, are the people in question.[a] Hence—they declare—good behavior is necessary for us, for otherwise we could not be saved; but they hold to the doctrine that they are spirituals not by behavior, but by nature, and that they will be saved[b] (or preserved) no matter what. For just as the element that consists of "dust" cannot have a share in salvation[c]—for, they say, it is not capable of receiving it—so also the spiritual element, which they themselves claim to be, cannot receive corruption, no matter what sorts of behavior it has to pass its time in the company of. For a piece of gold does not lose its beauty when it is put into the filth but rather keeps its own nature, since the filth cannot harm the gold. And, of course, just so—they say—they themselves do not suffer incidental harm no matter what sorts of material behavior they pass their time with, nor do they lose their spiritual substance.[d] * * *

1.6.4 * * * Thus for us—whom they call "animates,"[a] saying that we are from the world—continence and good behavior are necessary, so that thereby we might get to the place of the midpoint. But for them—who call themselves "spirituals" and "perfect"—this is not supposed to be the case. For (they say), what leads one into the fullness is not behavior but the seed,[b] which was sent hither as an infant and grows to maturity in this place.

Final restoration of the spirituals

1.7.1 When all the seed has grown to maturity,[a] Achamōth their mother will—they say—leave the place of the midpoint, enter the fullness, and receive as her bridegroom the savior, who derives from all (the aeons), so that a pair is produced consisting of the savior and wisdom (Sophia) who is Achamōth: they are the bridegroom and bride, and the entire

(marginal references): TRs 46:5 ? · VFrF · GPh 93 · VFrE · TRs 48:38 · GPh 20 · GPh 41 · 1.6.1 · GPh 55 · TRs 44:30 · 1.7.5+ · 1.7.5 · GTr 43:11 ? · TRs 44:30 · GPh 4 · Jn 3:29 ?

e. Cf. IrUnid 1.30.14 ("His ingathering of souls will bring the end").

1.6.2 a. St. Irenaeus refers to himself and his non-gnostic readers.
   b. "Salvation" and "preservation" are the same word.
   c. Or "preservation."
   d. In the following polemical passage (not translated here), St. Irenaeus claims to be reporting on the ethical conclusions that the Valentinians draw from the principle of the gold in the filth. He specifically charges that they have no hesitation to eat meat offered to idols, participate in pagan religious banquets, and attend gladiatorial games; that the male teachers of the group seduce female converts (sometimes married ones), whose personal confessions Irenaeus claims to know

about; and that male and female ascetics pretend to dwell together as brother and sister but actually cohabit sexually, with resulting pregnancies. Many scholars reject St. Irenaeus's report as just a malicious rumor or even a deliberate libel. Doubt has also been cast upon the accuracy of certain details of the preceding passage, and upon the next two sentences that are translated below. Cf. EpG, introduction.

1.6.4 a. "us . . . animates": i.e. people who possess body and soul (the animate human being) but not spirit. St. Irenaeus refers to himself and his non-gnostic readers.
   b. Or "posterity."

1.7.1 a. Or "has been perfected."

fullness is the bridal chamber.[b] And the spirituals are supposed to put off their souls; become intellectual spirits; unrestrainably[c] and invisibly enter the fullness; and become brides of the angels that are with the savior.[d]

1.7.2
TRs 45:36+
GPh 24+

Final repose of the just (animates)

The craftsman for his part will move into the place of wisdom (Sophia) the mother, namely in the midpoint. And the souls of the just,[e] also, will gain repose in the place of the midpoint. For nothing animate goes inside the fullness.

GPh 55
GPh 90

Final destruction of the world

After such things have happened—so they teach—the fire that lurks within the world will flare up, catch fire, overcome all matter, be consumed along with it, and enter into definitive nonexistence.[f] And the craftsman—they declare—was not acquainted with any of these facts before the advent of the savior.

Begetting of the earthly Jesus by the craftsman

1.7.2 There are some people who say that he (the craftsman) emitted a (different) anointed (Christ), who was his own son yet was animate; and that it was about this one that he spoke through the prophets. This (they say) was the one who passed through Mary as water goes through a pipe.

Heavenly savior descends into earthly Jesus

And also it was into him at his baptism that the savior, who comes from the fullness and derives from all (the aeons), descended in the form of a dove.[a] In him was also the spiritual seed[b] that comes from Achamōth.

Mt 3:16
Lk 3:22

So, they say that our lord was compounded of these four elements, maintaining the pattern of the primal, first *tetraktys*:[c]

> the spiritual, from Achamōth;
> the animate, from the craftsman;
> the providential arrangement of events, which was constructed in some ineffable way;
> the savior, who was the dove that descended into him.

Crucifixion of Jesus

And he continued to be without suffering[d]—for it was not possible for him to suffer, since he was unrestrainable[e] and invisible. Because of this, when this (anointed or Christ) was brought before Pilate, the spirit

1.7.1
TRs 45:36+

---

b. The imagery of the bridal chamber is developed especially in GPh.

c. Or "incomprehensibly."

d. All the spirituals (Valentinians), both men and women, become as it were female; all the savior's angels are as it were male.

e. I.e. including the souls of ordinary Christians like St. Irenaeus as well as the souls put off by the spirituals on their way toward the fullness.

f. The idea of a fire that lurks within the world and in due time will flare up and consume the world was a well-known part of ancient physics, as taught by the Stoic school. But the belief that the world will then "enter into definitive nonexistence" is not a part of Stoic physics.

1.7.2 a. Cf. IrUnid 1.30.12 (end).

b. Or "posterity."

c. Cf. note 1.1.1h.

d. Or "passions."

e. Or "incomprehensible."

of the anointed that had been deposited in him was taken away. But the seed[f] from the mother did not—they say—suffer, either. For it too was without suffering,[g] inasmuch as it was spiritual and was invisible even to the craftsman. What suffered, therefore, was what they consider to be the animate anointed (Christ), who was mysteriously constructed[h] out of the providential arrangement of events, so that through him the mother might display a representation[i] of the superior anointed (Christ), who had stretched out along the cross and who had formed Achamōth as a concrete formation in essence. For all these things—they say—are representations[j] of ones in that other (realm).

Principles of biblical interpretation

1.7.3 The souls who had the seed[a] of Achamōth were—they say— superior to the rest. Accordingly, they were loved by the craftsman more than any others, although he did not know the reason why, and rather supposed that they were as they were on account of him. Thus— they say—he assigned them to be prophets, priests, and kings. And many (utterances)—they explain—were spoken by this posterity through the prophets, as being of a more sublime nature; but also the mother— they say—spoke many (utterances) about the higher realm; and also, (many utterances were spoken) through this (craftsman) and the souls that came into being because of him.

And therefore they divide up the prophecies.[b] One part—they main- PtF tain—was spoken by the mother; another part, by the seed;[c] yet another part by the craftsman.

But so also, (the teachings of) Jesus: one part (was spoken) by the savior; another part by the mother; yet another part by the craftsman. This we demonstrate in our exposition below.

Role and authority of the craftsman

1.7.4 Now inasmuch as the craftsman was unacquainted with the realm superior to him, he was moved by the utterances but had no respect for them, attributing them to various causes—either the prophesying spirit, which has a kind of motion all its own; or the person in question; or an admixture of inferior things. And he continued in this lack of acquaintance until the advent of the savior. But when the savior came—they say—he learned everything from him, and was delighted to defect to him, accompanied by all his army.[a] It is he who is the centurion in the gospel, Mt 8:9 who says to the savior, "For I have under my authority soldiers and Lk 7:8 slaves, and whatever I command they do." He (the craftsman) will bring about a providential arrangement of events in the world until the appropriate time, especially because of his care for his church and his knowledge of the reward that awaits him, namely occupying the place of the mother.

---

f. Or "posterity."
g. Or "passions."
h. "What suffered, therefore . . . was mysteriously constructed": or "What mysteriously suffered, therefore . . . was constructed."
i. Or "symbol."
j. Or "symbols."

1.7.3 a. Or "posterity."
b. Cf. also PtF.
c. Or "posterity."

1.7.4 a. Or "force." Reference to this word virtually identifies the craftsman with Sabaōth of classic gnostic myth; cf. RR note 95c.

Three species of human beings

1.7.5 They postulate three species of human beings:

> spirituals;
> animates;
> those consisting of dust;[a]

according as Cain, Abel, and Seth were these.[b] And from them derive the three natures, no longer in one individual but distributed among three ancestries.

The element consisting of dust is proceeding to corruption.

The animate will gain repose in the place of the mother if it chooses the better, and if it chooses the worse, it will proceed to the realm of those like itself.

The spirituals, which down to this day Achamōth has continued to sow into just souls, learn here; are nourished, for they are sent as infants; later are deemed worthy of maturity;[c] and are given as brides to the angels of the savior—according to their doctrine. Yet their souls must necessarily repose with the craftsman in the midpoint forever. GPh 27 · 1.6.4 VFrA ?

Moreover, they subdivide the kinds of souls, saying that some are good by nature, others wicked by nature. Now, the good ones are those that become capable of receiving the seed; but those that are wicked by nature never receive that seed.[d] * * * VFrF

II. SCRIPTURAL ALLEGORIES OF THE MYTH[a]

1.8.1 * * * They extract phrases, words, and parables from one passage or another, intending to accommodate the sayings of the lord to their tales.[b] We have already spoken of the ones that they accommodate to events inside the fullness. **1.8.2** But the passages of scripture that they try to adapt to events outside the fullness are such as the following.

Wisdom's passionate search

The lord came to his passion[a] "at the last times" of the world—they say—so as to manifest the passion that occurred with the last of the aeons,[b] and so that the end of the affairs of the aeons might be reflected in his end.[c] IP 1:20

The essential formation of Achamōth

The young woman twelve years old who was the daughter of a ruler of the synagogue, over whom the lord stood and whom he raised from the dead,[d] is—as they describe—a representation[e] of Achamōth: this Lk 8:41

1.7.5 a. Greek *pneumatikoi, psykhikoi, khoïkoi* (pneumatics, psychics, choics).

b. Cain consisted only of dust; Abel consisted of dust and soul (animate element); Seth consisted of dust, soul, and spiritual seed.

c. Or "perfection."

d. "seed . . . seed": or "posterity . . . posterity." The following passage (not translated here) is a polemic by St. Irenaeus.

1.8.1 a. Cf. also 1.1.3 and 1.3.1–5; and for allegory, see the "Historical Introduction" to Part Three.

b. St. Irenaeus describes the Valentinians' use of scripture in an openly hostile way.

1.8.2 a. Or "suffering."

b. The Valentinians thus interpret "times" to mean "aeons."

c. Or "death."

d. The story in Luke (Lk 8:40–56) is interrupted by an episode in which Jesus heals a woman suffering from a hemorrhage; for the Valentinian interpretation of that passage, see above 1.3.3.

e. Or "symbol."

anointed (Christ) of theirs stretched himself out over her, formed her, and led her to perception of the light that had left her.

The concrete formation of Achamōth

The fact that the savior appeared to her while she was outside the fullness and had the appointed lot of an aborted foetus, is—they say—spoken of by Paul in *1 Corinthians*:

> Last of all, as to an aborted foetus,[f] he appeared also to me.   1Co 15:8

The advent of the savior with his comrades before Achamōth is likewise shown by him in the same epistle, when he says

> A woman ought to have a veil on her head, because of the angels.   1Co 11:10

The fact that Achamōth put on a veil out of shame when the savior came to her, was shown by Moses putting a veil on his face.   Ex 34:33

Separation of Achamōth and passions by the outer boundary

Her passions that she experienced were indicated—they say—by the lord. And by saying on the cross

> My god, my god, why hast thou forsaken me?   Mk 15:34

he disclosed that wisdom[g] (Sophia) had been left by the light and had been prevented from the impulse to forward motion by the boundary.[h]
Her grief he disclosed by saying

> My soul is very grief-stricken.[i]   Mt 26:38

Her fear he disclosed by saying

> My father, if it be possible, let the cup pass from me.   Mt 26:39

And likewise, her uncertainty he disclosed by saying

> And what shall I say? I do not know!   Jn 12:27

Three species of human being

1.8.3 The fact that there are three species of human beings was—they teach—disclosed by him as follows.
The material (species) he disclosed when a man said

> I will follow you (sing.)   Mt 8:19
>   Lk 9:57

and he replied

> The child of the human being[a] has nowhere to lay his head.

The animate (species) he disclosed when a man said

> I will follow you (sing.); but let me first say farewell to my own[b]

and he said to him

> No one who puts his hand to the plow and looks back is fit for the kingdom of heavens.

---

f. Or "one untimely born."
g. The lower wisdom, Achamōth.
h. The outer boundary.
i. Or "sorrowful."

1.8.3 a. Or "son of man."
    b. Or "those of my household."

For the latter ("heavens") means—they say—"the middle region."[c]
Also belonging to the animate species—they maintain—was the man Mt 19:20
who declared that he had carried out most of the parts of righteousness
and then refused to follow, being instead overcome by wealth, so that
he did not become perfect.

The spiritual (species) he disclosed by saying

> Leave the dead to bury their own dead; but as for you (sing.), Lk 9:60
> go and proclaim the kingdom of god

and when he said to Zacchaeus the tax collector

> Make haste and come down; for I must stay at your house Lk 19:5
> today.

For they declare that these people belonged to the spiritual species.

And—they say—the three species are made clear by the parable of Mt 13:33
the leaven that the woman is said to have hidden in three measures of Lk 13:20
meal. For—they teach—wisdom (Sophia) is called a woman; while the
three species of human beings, namely the spiritual, the animate, and
the one consisting of dust, are called three measures of meal. And—
they teach—the savior himself is called leaven. And furthermore Paul
spoke expressly of ones consisting of dust, animates, and spirituals. In
one passage he says

> As was the one consisting of dust, so are those who consist of 1Co 15:48
> the dust.

Elsewhere he says

> A merely animate person does not receive the realm of the 1Co 2:14
> spirit,[d]

and elsewhere,

> The spiritual judges all things.   1Co 2:15

The words "a merely animate person does not receive the realm of the
spirit" were spoken—they say—about the craftsman: because he was
merely animate he could not recognize his mother, since she was
spiritual; her seed[e]; or the aeons within the fullness.

The fact that the savior took the firstfruits of those which he was to
save was spoken of by Paul, when he says

> If the firstfruit is holy, so is the mixture.[f]   Rm 11:16

Here the spiritual (element)—so they teach—is called a firstfruit; while
we, the animate church,[g] are called the mixture. He took it—they say—
and made it rise by his agency, for he was leaven.

The formation of Achamōth

1.8.4 The fact that Achamōth wandered outside the fullness, was
formed by the anointed (Christ), and was searched out by the savior,
is—they say—disclosed by him when he says that he came unto the lost Mt 18:12
sheep. For this mother of theirs—they explain—is called a sheep; from Lk 15:4
                                                                        GTr 31:28

---

c. Or "For this person—they say—belongs to those of the middle."

d. The more normal translation of this
passage (1 Co 2:14) is "The unspiritual man
does not receive the gifts of the spirit."

e. Or "posterity."

f. The more normal translation of this
passage (Rm 11:16) is "If the dough offered
as firstfruits is holy, so is the whole lump."

g. St. Irenaeus refers to himself and his
non-gnostic readers.

her, they maintain, the church was sown into this world. Her time spent outside the fullness in all the passions, from which matter came into being, they assume to be a wandering.

Production of Achamôth and her final restoration

The superior wisdom (Sophia) is—as they describe it—called the woman who swept the house and found the silver coin (drachma), in that wisdom lost her thinking; then later, after all things had been purified by the savior's advent, she found it, because this[a] too is restored to the inside of the fullness, according to them.   Lk 15:8

Final repose of the craftsman

Simeon, who took the anointed (Christ) up in his arms and gave thanks to god and said

> Lord, now lettest thou thy servant depart in peace   Lk 2:29

is—they say—a representation[b] of the craftsman, who by the savior's coming learned of his change of position and gave thanks to the deep.

Achamôth's wait for restoration

Through Anna the prophet, who—so the gospel proclaims—lived with a husband seven years and spent all the rest of her time as a widow until she saw the savior, recognized him, and spoke of him to all— through her, they state, Achamôth is very openly disclosed, in that she saw the savior and his comrades for a brief moment and remained thereafter in the midpoint, waiting for when he would return and restore her to membership in her pair.   Lk 2:36

Her name is disclosed by the savior when he says

> Yet wisdom (Sophia) is justified by all her children   Lk 7:35

and by Paul, as follows:

> Yet we speak of wisdom (Sophia) among the perfect.[c]   1Co 2:6

Pairs of aeons in the fullness

The pairs within the fullness are—they say—spoken of by Paul, who shows this in one instance: for, writing on the subject of the marriage bond he said

> This mystery is a profound one, and I am saying that it refers to the anointed (Christ) and the church.   Ep 5:52

The primal octet of aeons (commentary on John)

1.8.5 Further, they teach that John the disciple of the lord disclosed the first octet, and their exact words[a] are as follows.

"John the disciple of the lord intentionally spoke of the origination of the entirety, by which the parent emitted all things. And he assumes that the first being engendered by god is a kind of "beginning"; he has   Jn 1:3
                                                                                                    Jn 1:1

1.8.4 a. Or "she."
  b. Or "symbol."
  c. The more normal translation of this passage (1 Co 2:6) is "Yet among the mature we do impart wisdom."

1.8.5 a. From the last sentence of the selection, it appears that the following is an exact quotation from a work by Ptolemy or one of his followers.

also called it[b] "child" and "only-begotten god."[c] "In this" (the only- Jn 1:18 var.
begotten) "the parent"[d] emitted "all things" in a process involving Jn 1:3
seeds.[e] By this (child), he says, was emitted the Word, in which was
the entire essence of the aeons that the Word later personally formed.

"Now, since he is speaking of the first origination, he does well to
begin the teaching at the beginning, i.e. with the child[f] and the Word.
He speaks as follows.

> The Word was in the beginning, and the Word was with god, Jn 1:1
> and the Word was god. It was in the beginning, with god.

First, he distinguishes three things,

> god;
> beginning;
> Word.

Then he unites them: this is to show forth both the emanation of the
latter two, i.e. the child and the Word, and their union with one another
and simultaneously with the parent.[g] For the beginning was in the parent
and from the parent; and the Word was in the beginning and from the
beginning. Well did he say

> The Word was in the beginning, Jn 1:1

for it was in the child.[h]

> And the Word was with god.

So was the beginning.

> And the Word was god;

reasonably so, for what is engendered from god is god. This shows the
order of emanation.

> All things were[i] made through it, and without it was not anything Jn 1:3
> made. PtF 33.3.6

For the Word became the cause of the forming and origination of all the
aeons that came after it.

"But furthermore (he says)

> That which came into being in it was life (Zōē). Jn 1:3-4 var.

Here he discloses a pair. For he says that the entirety came into being
through it, but life (Zōē) is "in it." Now that which came into being
"in" it more intimately belongs to it than what came into being "through" Jn 1:3
it: it is joined with it and through it it bears fruit. Indeed, inasmuch as
he adds

> and life (Zōē) was the light of human beings, Jn 1:4

in speaking of "human beings" he has now disclosed also the church
by means of a synonym, so that with a single word he might disclose
the partnership of the pair. For from the Word and life, the human being
and the church come into being. And he called life (Zōē) "the light of
human beings" because they are enlightened by her, i.e. formed and
made visible. Paul, too, says this:

---

b. The more normal translation of the
prologue of Jn refers to the Word as a person
("he"). The original Greek makes no distinction here between personal and imper-
sonal.

c. "child": or "son." "only-begotten god":
these words are found in some ancient MSS

of Jn 1:18.
d. Or "father."
e. Or "posterity."
f. Or "son."
g. Or "father."
h. Or "son."
i. Or "The entirety was."

For anything that becomes visible is light.   Ep 5:13

So since life (Zōē) made the human being and the church visible and engendered them, she is said to be their light.

"Now among other things John plainly made clear the second quartet, i.e.

> the Word;
> life;
> the human being;
> the church.

"But what is more, he also disclosed the first quartet. Describing the savior, now, and saying that all things outside the fullness were formed by him, he says that he is the fruit of the entire fullness. For he calls him a light that "is visible[j] in the darkness" and was not overcome by   Jn 1:5 it, inasmuch as after he had fitted together all things that had derived from the passion they did not become acquainted with him. And he calls him child,[k] truth, life (Zōē), and Word become flesh. "We have beheld   Jn 1:14 the latter's glory," he says. And its glory was like that of the only-begotten, which was bestowed on him by the parent,[l] "full of loveliness (grace) and truth." And he speaks as follows.

> And the Word became flesh and dwelt among us; we have   Jn 1:14 beheld its glory, glory as of the only-begotten[m] from the parent.[n]

So he precisely discloses also the first quartet when he speaks of

> the parent;
> loveliness;
> the only-begotten;
> truth.

Thus did John speak of the first octet, the mother of the entirety of aeons. For he referred to

> the parent;[o]
> loveliness;
> the only-begotten;[p]
> truth;
> the Word;
> life (Zōē);
> the human being (or man);
> the church."

These are the words of Ptolemy.

---

j. Or "shines."
k. Or "son."
l. Or "father."
m. Or "only son."

n. Or "father."
o. Or "father."
p. Or "only son."

A PRAYER OF PAUL THE APOSTLE

(PPl)

Contents

A Prayer of Paul the Apostle (PPl) is a theologian's intercessory prayer addressed to "the existent and prior existent," perhaps meaning the perfect parent or ultimate first principle, and invoking the name of "Jesus Christ, [the lord] of lords, the king of eternities." In addition, the central petitions (A:19f) invoke the authority of "the preacher of the gospel" (Greek *euaggelistēs*). This must mean St. Paul, since he is the only such person mentioned by name in the work. The title PPl therefore does not indicate that Paul is the author of the prayer, but characterizes it as a prayer that invokes his authority as an early apostolic preacher of the gospel.

Valentinian teachers claimed the apostle Paul as their theological ancestor, patron, and source of authority, maintaining that Valentinus had been instructed by a certain Theudas, who himself was said to have been a pupil of Paul. It was this chain of authority that supposedly empowered Valentinian teachers to compose treatises and commentaries under their own name.

While authors of classic gnostic scripture wrote their revelations as pseudepigraphy, attributed to venerated religious heroes of the past or to spiritual beings (Adam, Seth, the spiritual Seth, John the apostle, Barbēlō), Valentinian teachers almost always spoke on the authority of their school tradition. This "apostolic tradition" (PtF 33.7.9, GPh 74:16f) or academic genealogy has an exact parallel in secular philosophical schools (and indeed in Jewish rabbinical traditions), whose leaders strengthened their own personal authority by producing lists of academic predecessors going back to some venerated teacher of the past, such as Socrates.

PPl has a simple tripartite structure. The opening stanza (A:1–11f) speaks of the petitioner's emanation from the fullness and looks forward to ultimate return ("receive me . . . give me . . . completion"); it recalls the petitioner's intimate closeness to god. The second (A:15–23f) is a prayer for theological authority, healing of body, redemption of soul and spirit, and intellectual inspiration. It is this stanza that invokes the authority of St. Paul. The third (A:25–end) asks additionally for majesty and mystery; it concludes with a doxology.

Literary background

The author of PPl and its place of composition are unknown. The prayer was used by Valentinians, and so it may be Valentinian in origin. Alternatively, it may be a product of one of the schools of Pauline imitators, such as produced the deutero-Pauline epistles. Some echoes of Paul's vocabulary and phraseology occur in the work. The date of composition of PPl must be before A.D. 350, the approximate date of the MS. The language of composition was Greek.

Text

The original Greek apparently does not survive. The text is known only in Coptic translation, attested by a single MS from Nag Hammadi, MS NHC I (pp. A–B), which was copied just before A.D. 350, and is now in the Cairo Coptic Museum. This MS (the "Jung Codex") contains only Valentinian works (including GTr, TRs, and others); the prayer is copied on the front flyleaf of the MS (paginated A/B by modern editors) as an invocation of apostolic authority for the whole MS.[1] The first three lines of text are mostly missing owing to damage of the MS.

The translation below is based on the critical edition of the Coptic by Kasser et al., with alterations: R. Kasser et al., eds., *Tractatus Tripartitus,* vol. 2 (Pars II, Pars III) (Bern: Francke, 1975), 248–50. In the critical edition, the prayer is erroneously paginated 143–44, and the line numbering differs from the one used here.

SELECT BIBLIOGRAPHY

Kasser, R., et al., eds., *Tractatus Tripartitus,* vol. 2 (Pars II, Pars III), 243–85. Berne: Francke, 1975, in French.

Mueller, D. "Prayer of the Apostle Paul." In *Nag Hammadi Codex I*, edited by H. Attridge. Vol. 1. *Introductions, Texts* . . . , 5–11, and vol. 2, *Notes*, 1–5. Nag Hammadi Studies, vols. 22, 23. Leiden: E. J. Brill, 1985.

---

[1] Erroneously called a "colophon" to the manuscript by earlier scholarship.

A PRAYER OF PAUL THE APOSTLEª

1	**A** [. . .]	
4,5	Ransom me; for [I am(?)]ᵇ yours; •[from you (sing.)] have I emanated.	TRs 46:25 + GTr 27:10 ?
6	It [is] you [who are my] intellect: engender me.	
7	It is you who are my treasure:ᶜ [give] unto me.	
7	[It is] you [who are] my fullness: receive me.	
8	It is [you] who are ⟨my⟩ᵈ repose: give me unrestrainable completion,ᵉ	TRs 45:36 + ?
11	I pray you, O existent and prior-existent, in the name [which is] above every name, through Jesus Christ,ᶠ [the lord] of lords, the king of eternities.ᵍ	Ph 2:9
15	[Give] me your unregretted giftsʰ through the child of the human being,ⁱ [byʲ the] spirit, the intercessor, of [truth].	TRs 45:9 ? Jn 14:16
18	Give me authority, [I] request of you.	
19	Give me [healing] for my body, as I request [of] you through the preacher of the gospel;ᵏ	
22	[And] redeem my luminous soul [for] ever, and my spirit.	IrPt 1.6.1 ?
23	And [disclose] unto my intellect the [first-born] of the fullness of grace.	Jn 1:14
25	Bestow what eyes of angels have not [seen], what ears of rulers have not heard, what [has not] come upon the hearts	1Co 2:6
30	of human beings who have become angels,ˡ •and is after the image of the animate god when he was modeled in the	Gn 1:26 ? Gn 2:7 ?
33	beginning; •for I have faith belonging to hope.	
35	And give me alsoᵐ your beloved, chosen, blessed majesty: O	
3	first-born, O first-produced, **B** [. . .]ᵃ •the [wonderful] mystery of your house.	
4	[For] thine [is] the kingdom [and] the glory and the praise and the [greatness] for ever and ever. [Amen.]ᵇ	Mt 6:13 var.

Title A a. In the manuscript, the title is found after the text (at B:9f). Three lines of Coptic have been mostly destroyed at the beginning of the prayer.
  b. Restoration uncertain.
  c. Or "treasury."
  d. This word is inadvertently omitted in the MS.
  e. Or "perfection."
  f. Or "Jesus the anointed."
  g. Or "eternal realms, aeons."
  h. Or "emanations."
  i. Or "the son of man."

j. Or "and."
  k. Or "evangelist" (Greek *euaggelistēs*).
  l. Or "human beings, but has happened to angels."
  m. Lit. "add to me."

B a. About two lines of text are missing here.
  b. In the manuscript, the title of the work is written after the text (at B:9f): "A Prayer of Paul the Apostle. In peace. Holy is the Christ!"

PTOLEMY'S
EPISTLE TO FLORA

(PtF)

Contents

The meaning and value of the Jewish bible—which Christians eventually called "the Old Testament"—was one of the burning issues faced by Christianity in the second century. At this time, more and more Christians came from a non-Jewish background, and Christian theologians began to measure themselves against the teachings of secular Hellenistic philosophy. Many branches of Christianity had to face this issue, the gnostics no less than any other. Classic gnostic myth (cf. BJn) and its Valentinian successor (IrV, IrPt) obviously expressed a massive revision of the cosmogony and history taught in the books of Moses. Other sources show that gnostics and Valentinians addressed also the problem of the Old Testament prophecies and their authenticity, cf. IrSat 1.24.2, IrPt 1.7.3.

To Valentinian gnostics all these aspects of the Old Testament problem were systematically related, for the Valentinian myth of origins provided an interpretive key to all religious scripture, expression, practice, and belief. A presentation of Valentinian Christianity might therefore begin at almost any point in the system. In PtF, the great Valentinian teacher Ptolemy chooses to begin a systematic course of instruction by starting with the question of religious laws and observances. His addressee is a female adherent of ordinary Christianity named Flora. His manner of presentation is elementary, using terms that are moral and nonmetaphysical, and almost entirely within the realm of conventional Christian language (for another example of elementary Valentinian instruction, see TRs). Ptolemy begins with a clear and careful analysis of the multiple authorship of Old Testament laws, characterizes the nature of the laws by comparing them with the teachings of Jesus, and from their nature draws conclusions about the god who legislated them.

Ptolemy's conclusions take him to the very edge of metaphysics and myth, which he promises will form the next lesson of his course (for a summary of Ptolemy's metaphysics, see IrPt; his next lesson to Flora does not seem to have survived). One can distinguish, Ptolemy concludes, a perfect god, who is good; the god of Israel and the Old Testament, who is just; and the devil, who is evil. He carefully contrasts this view with positions that assert only two principles (god and the devil). In comparison with the theology of BJn or RAd, Ptolemy's tripartite scheme shows a relatively positive attitude toward the craftsman of the world or god of Israel; some classic gnostic scriptures also follow the same tripartite scheme, cf. RR 95:13f.

In the opening of the *Epistle*, Ptolemy sets out to refute two other opinions on the source of the Old Testament law. One opinion identified the legislator with the highest god; this was the view of ordinary Christianity and a great part of Judaism.

The other identified the legislator with the devil; scholars have been uncertain about the source of this opinion, but it may refer to gnostics who followed a myth like that of BJn or RAd, where the craftsman of the world (Ialdabaōth) appears to be identical with the god of Israel.

Literary background

Ptolemy, the author of PtF, is discussed in the introduction to IrPt ("Literary background"). The place of composition is unknown, but since Ptolemy was active in the western part of the Roman empire some scholars have suggested Rome. The exact date of composition is unknown; Ptolemy flourished roughly between A.D. 136 and 180 (or 136 and 152). His language of composition is Greek.

According to its title, the work is a *philosophical epistle*, that is, a short formal essay couched in the framework of a letter. The genre of philosophical epistle was used by both Valentinus (VFrC, E, and H) and the author of TRs; it was much favored by academic writers of the period. However, PtF lacks the customary epistolary salutation ("I greet you") at the end. Apart from its opening formula ("Ptolemy to Flora") PtF is simply a treatise addressed by name to a dedicatee, as was customary.

Text

The text is known only from a word-for-word quotation by the fourth-century father of the church St. Epiphanius of Salamis in his work *Against Heresies* 33.3.1— 33.7.10, written about A.D. 375. St. Epiphanius's original Greek text is attested by a number of medieval manuscripts, whose accuracy is a matter of debate among scholars. The translation below is based upon Quispel's critical edition of the Greek, with very minor alterations: G. Quispel, ed., *Ptolémée* (see "Select Bibliography"), 50–73.

SELECT BIBLIOGRAPHY

Fallon, F. "The Law in Philo and Ptolemy: A Note on the Letter to Flora." *Vigiliae Christianae* 30 (1976): 45–51.

Quispel, G., ed. *Ptolémée, Lettre à Flora: Analyse, texte critique, traduction, commentaire et index grec.* 2d ed. Sources chrétiennes, no. 24 *bis.* Paris: Le Cerf, 1966.

PTOLEMY TO FLORA

A. PROLOGUE

Difficulty of the topic

33.3.1 The law established by Moses,[a] my dear sister[b] Flora, has in IrPt 1.7.3 the past been misunderstood by many people, for they were not closely acquainted with the one who established it or with its commandments. I think you will see this at once if you study their discordant opinions on this topic.

False opinions on the topic

33.3.2 For some[c] say that this law has been ordained by god the father;[d] while others,[e] following the opposite course, stoutly contend that it has been established by the adversary, the pernicious devil; and so the latter school attributes the craftsmanship of the world to the devil,[f] saying that he is "the father and maker of the universe."[g] **33.3.3** ⟨But⟩ they Plato Ti. 28e are ⟨utterly⟩[h] in error, they disagree with one another, and each of the schools utterly misses the truth of the matter.

The law not established by the perfect god

33.3.4 Now, it does not seem that the law was established by the perfect god and father: for, it must be of the same character as its giver; and yet it is imperfect and needful of being fulfilled by another and contains commandments incongruous with the nature and intentions of such a god.

Nor by the devil

33.3.5 On the other hand to attribute a law that abolishes injustice to the injustice of the adversary[i] is the false logic[j] of those who do not comprehend the principle of which the savior spoke. For our savior declared that a house or city divided against itself will not be able to Mt 12:25 stand. **33.3.6** And, further, the apostle[k] states that the craftsmanship of the world is his, and that "all things were made through him, and Jn 1:3 without him was not anything made," thus anticipating these liars' flimsy IrPt 1.8.5 wisdom. And the craftsmanship is that of a god who is just and hates evil, not a pernicious one as believed by these thoughtless people,[l] who take no account of the craftsman's forethought and so are blind not only in the eye of the soul but even in the eyes of the body.[m]

33.3 a. In the first five books of the Old Testament.

b. I.e. "my dear fellow Christian."

c. Ordinary Christians and many Jews.

d. I.e. the perfect "parent" or deep. Traditional Christian language ("father") has been retained in this English translation of PtF, in keeping with the deliberately conventional nature of its vocabulary.

e. Possibly meaning gnostics; cf. Introduction, "Contents."

f. Ialdabaōth in classic gnostic myth like that of BJn.

g. With this phrase, Ptolemy evokes the philosophical myth of creation in Plato's *Timaeus* (28e).

h. "⟨But⟩, ⟨utterly⟩": these words are inadvertently omitted in the MSS.

i. The devil.

j. The Greek text is corrupt here, and the exact meaning is disputed by scholars.

k. John.

l. Or "these people without providence."

m. The creator's forethought is evident in the orderly and providential workings of the natural world, which can be seen with the eyes.

The topic

33.3.7 Now, from what has been said it should be clear to you (sing.) that these (schools of thought) utterly miss the truth, though each does so in its own particular way: one (school) by not being acquainted with the god of righteousness,[n] the other by not being acquainted with the father of the entirety, who was manifested by him alone who came and who alone knew him. **33.3.8** It remains for us, who have been deemed worthy of ⟨acquaintance⟩[o] with both, to show you (sing.) exactly what sort of law the law[p] is, and which legislator established it. We shall offer proofs of what we say by drawing from our savior's words, by which alone it is possible to reach a certain apprehension of the reality of the matter without stumbling.

Mt 11:27

B. EXPOSITION: THE NATURE OF THE LAW

1. THE THREE DIVISIONS OF THE LAW

Multiple authorship of the law

33.4.1 Now, first you must learn that, as a whole, the law contained in the Pentateuch of Moses was not established by a single author, I mean not by god alone: rather, there are certain of its commandments that were established by human beings as well. Indeed, our savior's words teach us that the Pentateuch divides into three parts. **33.4.2** For one division belongs to god himself and his legislations; while ⟨another division⟩[a] belongs to Moses—indeed, Moses ordained certain of the commandments not as god himself ordained through him, rather based upon his own thoughts about the matter; and yet a third division belongs to the elders[b] of the people, ⟨who⟩[c] likewise in the beginning must have inserted certain of their own commandments. **33.4.3** You will now learn how all this can be demonstrated from the savior's words.

Legislation of god distinct from legislation of Moses

33.4.4 When the savior was talking with those who were arguing with him about divorce—and it has been ordained (in the law) that divorce is permitted—he said to them: "For your (pl.) hardness of heart Moses allowed divorce of one's wife. Now, from the beginning it was not so." For god, he says, has joined together this union, and "what the lord has joined together, let no man put asunder." **33.4.5** Here he shows that ⟨the⟩[d] law of god is one thing, forbidding a woman to be put asunder from her husband; while the law of Moses is another, permitting the couple to be put asunder because of hard-heartedness. **33.4.6** And so, accordingly, Moses ordains contrary to what god ordains; for ⟨separating⟩[e] is contrary to not separating.

Mt 19:8

Mt 19:6

Dt 24:1
Mt 19:7

Yet if we also scrutinize Moses' intentions with which he ordained this commandment, we find that he created the commandment not of his own inclination but of necessity because of the weakness of those

---

n. Cf. 33.7.5.

o. This word is inadvertently missing in the MSS.

p. I.e. in the first five books of the Old Testament.

33.4 a. These two words are inadvertently omitted in the MSS.

b. Or "presbyters." Ptolemy refers here to the elders who were with Moses "in the beginning."

c. This word is inadvertently omitted in the MSS.

d. This word is inadvertently omitted in the MSS.

e. This word is inadvertently omitted in the MSS.

to whom it was ordained. **33.4.7** For the latter were not able to put into practice god's intentions, in the matter of their not being permitted to divorce their wives. Some of them were on very bad terms with their wives, and ran the risk[f] of being further diverted into injustice and from there into their destruction. **33.4.8** Moses, wishing to excise this unpleasant element through which they also ran the risk of being destroyed, ordained for them of his own accord a second law, the law of divorce, choosing under the circumstances the lesser of two evils, as it were, **33.4.9** so that if they were unable to keep the former (that is, god's law) they could keep at least the latter and so not be diverted into injustice and evil, through which utter destruction would follow in consequence. **33.4.10** These are Moses' intentions, with which we find him ordaining laws contrary to those of god. At any rate, even if we have for the moment used only one example in our proof, it is beyond doubt that, as we have shown, this law is of Moses himself and is distinct from god's.

Traditional legislation of the elders

33.4.11 And the savior shows also that there are some traditions of the elders interwoven in the law. He says, "For god spoke: 'Honor your father and your mother, that it may be well with you.' **33.4.12** But you have declared," the savior says, addressing the elders,[g] "'What you would have gained from me is given to god.' And for the sake of your tradition, O ancients, you have made void the law of god.'"[h] **33.4.13** And Isaiah declared this[i] by saying, "This people honors me with their lips, but their heart is far from me; in vain do they worship me, teaching as doctrines the precepts of men." Mt 15:4 Mt 15:5 Mt 15:8 Is 29:13

33.4.14 Thus it has been clearly shown from these passages that, as a whole, the law is divided into three parts. For we have found in it legislations belonging to Moses himself, to the elders, and to god himself. Moreover, the analysis of the law as a whole, as we have divided it here, has made clear which part of it is genuine.[j]

2. THE THREE SUBDIVISIONS OF GOD'S OWN LAW

33.5.1 Now, what is more, the one part that is the law of god himself divides into three subdivisions.

Nature of the subdivisions: (1) Pure but imperfect

The first subdivision is the pure legislation not interwoven with evil, which alone is properly called law, and which the savior did not come to abolish but to fulfill.[a] For what he fulfilled was not alien to him, ⟨but stood in need of fulfillment⟩:[b] for it did not have perfection. Mt 5:17

f. By leaving their wives, thus breaking god's original command and entering upon a course of lawbreaking.

g. Cf. note 33.4b.

h. This exchange is reported in Mt 15:3–6, where Jesus disputes with Pharisees and scribes from Jerusalem: "He (Jesus) answered them, 'And why do you transgress the commandment of god for the sake of your tradition? For god commanded, "Honor your father and your mother," and, "He who speaks evil of father or mother, let him surely die." But you say, "If anyone tells his father or his mother, 'What you would have gained from me is given to god,' he need not honor his father." So, for the sake of your tradition, you have made void the law of god.'" In the succeeding verses of Mt, Jesus quotes Isaiah 29:13, exactly as below.

i. As quoted by Jesus in Mt 15:8f.

j. I.e. only god's own law is genuinely divine.

33.5 a. Mt 5:17, part of the Sermon on the Mount: "[Jesus said,] 'Think not that I have come to abolish the law and the prophets; I have come not to abolish them but to fulfill them.'"

b. These words, or a phrase like them, is inadvertently omitted in the MSS.

(2) Interwoven with injustice

And the second subdivision is the part interwoven with the inferior and with injustice, which the savior abolished as being incongruous with his own nature.

(3) Symbolic

33.5.2 Finally, the third subdivision is the symbolic and allegorical[c] part, which is after the image of the superior, spiritual realm: the savior changed (the referent of) this part from the perceptible, visible level to the spiritual, invisible one.

(1) The decalogue is pure but imperfect

33.5.3 The first, the law of god that is pure and not interwoven with the inferior, is the decalogue or Ten Commandments inscribed on two stone tablets; they divide into the prohibition of things that must be avoided and the commanding of things that must be done. Although they contain pure legislation they do not have perfection, and so they were in need of fulfillment[d] by the savior.

33.6.1
Ex 20:3
Ex 34:1

(2) The lex talionis is interwoven with injustice

33.5.4 The second, which is interwoven with injustice, is that which applies to retaliation and repayment of those who have already committed a wrong, commanding us to pluck out an eye for an eye and a tooth for a tooth[e] and to retaliate for murder with murder. This part is interwoven with injustice, for the one who is second to act unjustly still acts unjustly, differing only in the relative order in which he acts, and committing the very same act. **33.5.5** But otherwise, this commandment both was and is just, having been established as a deviation from the pure law because of the weakness of those to whom it was ordained; yet it is incongruous with the nature and goodness of the father of the entirety. **33.5.6** Now perhaps this was apt; but even more, it was a result of necessity. For when one who does not wish even a single murder to occur—by saying, "You shall not kill"[f]—when, I say, he ordains a second law and commands the murderer to be murdered, acting as judge between two murders, he who forbade even a single murder has without realizing it been cheated by necessity.[g]

Lv 24:20
Lv 24:17
Mt 5:38

Ex 20:13
Ex 21:12
Lv 24:17

33.5.7 For this reason, then, the son who was sent from him abolished this part of the law, though he admits that it too belonged to god: this part is reckoned as belonging to the old school of thought,[h] both where he says, "For god spoke: 'He who speaks evil of father or mother, let him surely die'" and elsewhere.[i]

Mt 15:4

---

c. Or "prefigurative."
d. Or "completion."
e. The phrase is found in Mt 5:38, again in the Sermon on the Mount as above, cf. note 33.5a. In the Old Testament, this commandment is found in Lv 24:20–21, which also specifies death as the penalty for murder, as in the next phrase.
f. One of the Ten Commandments.

g. The so-called necessity he thought to be imposed by the weakness of those to whom the law was ordained (33.4.6) in fact cheats him of his desire that murder should cease.
h. The religion of the Old Testament before the son's advent.
i. The rest of the Matthean passage is quoted above, cf. note 33.4h.

(3) Ritual law has become symbolic

33.5.8 And the third subdivision of god's law is the symbolic part, which is after the image of the superior, spiritual realm: I mean, what is ordained about offerings, circumcision, the Sabbath, fasting, Passover, the Feast of Unleavened Bread, and the like.[j]
33.5.9 Now, once the truth[k] had been manifested, the referent of all these ordinances was changed, inasmuch as they are images and allegories. As to their meaning in the visible realm and their physical[l] accomplishment they were abolished; but as to their spiritual meaning they were elevated, with the words remaining the same but the subject matter being altered. **33.5.10** For the savior commanded us to offer offerings, but not dumb beasts or incense: rather, spiritual praises and glorifications and prayers of thanksgiving, and offerings in the form of sharing and good deeds. **33.5.11** And he wishes us to perform circumcision, but not circumcision of the bodily foreskin, rather of the spiritual heart; **33.5.12** and to keep the Sabbath, for he wants us to be inactive in wicked acts; **33.5.13** and to fast, though he does not wish us to perform physical fasts, rather spiritual ones, which consist of abstinence from all bad deeds.

> Rm 2:29
> GTh 53
>
> GTh 27
> GTh 6
> GTh 14

The justification for fasting

Nevertheless, fasting as to the visible realm is observed by our adherents,[m] since fasting, if practiced with reason, can contribute something to the soul, so long as it does not take place in imitation of other people or by habit or because fasting has been prescribed ⟨for⟩[n] a particular day. **33.5.14** Likewise, it is observed in memory of true fasting, so that those who are not yet able to observe true fasting might have a remembrance of it from fasting according to the visible realm. **33.5.15** Likewise, the apostle Paul makes it clear that Passover and the Feast of Unleavened Bread were images, for he says that "Christ, our paschal lamb, has been sacrificed" and, he says, be without leaven, having no share in leaven—now, by "leaven" he means evil—but rather "be fresh dough."

> 1Co 5:7

Summary: (1) The pure but imperfect has been fulfilled

33.6.1 And so it can be granted that the actual law of god is subdivided into three parts. The first subdivision is the part that was fulfilled[a] by the savior: for "you shall not kill," "you shall not commit adultery," "you shall not swear falsely" are subsumed[b] under not being angry, not looking lustfully at another, and not swearing at all.

> 33.5.3
> Mt 5:21
> Mt 5:27
> Mt 5:33

(2) The part interwoven with injustice has been abolished

33.6.2 The second subdivision is the part that was completely abolished. For the commandment of "an eye for an eye and a tooth for a tooth,"

> 33.5.4

j. Ritual laws specifically affirming identity as a child of Israel.
k. I.e. the savior and his teaching.
l. Or "literal."
m. I.e. Valentinians.
n. This word is inadvertently omitted in the MSS.

33.6 a. "fulfilled": i.e. rephrased according to an even more exacting general principle.
b. By Jesus in the Sermon on the Mount (Mt 5:21–37), where also the three Old Testament commandments are mentioned.

which is interwoven with injustice and itself involves an act of injustice, was abolished by the savior with injunctions to the contrary, **33.6.3** and of two contraries one must "abolish" the other: "For I say to you (pl.), Do not in any way resist one who is evil. But if any one strikes you (sing.), turn to him the other cheek also." Mt 5:39

(3) The symbolic has been physically abolished

33.6.4 And the third subdivision is the part whose referent was changed and which was altered from the physical[c] to the spiritual—the allegorical[d] part, which is ordained after the image of the superior realm. **33.6.5** Now, the images and allegories[e] are indicative of other matters, and they were well and good while truth[f] was not present. But now that truth is present, one must do the works of truth and not those of its imagery. Mk 2:19 par.
GTh 104

Paul a source of these teachings

33.6.6 His disciples made these teachings known, and so did the apostle Paul:[g] he makes known to us the part consisting of images, through the passage on the paschal lamb and the unleavened bread, which we have already spoken of.[h] The part consisting of a law interwoven with injustice, he made known by speaking of "abolishing the law of commandments and ordinances"; and the part not interwoven with the inferior, when he says, "The law is holy, and the commandment is holy and just and good." Ep 2:15

Rm 7:12

33.7.1 Thus I think I have shown you, as well as possible in a brief treatment, both that there is human legislation which has been slipped into the law and that the law of god himself divides into three subdivisions.

3. NATURE OF THE GOD WHO IS AUTHOR OF THE LAW

33.7.2 Now it remains for us to say what sort of being this god is, who established the law. But this too I believe I have demonstrated to you (sing.) in what I have already said, providing you have followed carefully.

The lawgiver is an intermediate god

33.7.3 For since this division of the law (that is, god's own law) was established neither by the perfect god, as we have taught, nor surely by the devil—which it would be wrong to say—then the establisher of this division of the law is distinct from them. **33.7.4** And he is the craftsman and maker of the universe or world and of the things within it. Since he is different from the essences of the other two ⟨and⟩[a] (rather) is in a state intermediate between them, he would rightfully be described by the term intermediateness.[b]

---

c. Or "literal."
d. Or "prefigurative."
e. Or "figures."
f. I.e. the savior and his teachings.
g. Valentinians considered Paul to be the ultimate source of their esoteric tradition, cf. PPl.

h. Cf. 33.5.15.

33.7 a. This word is inadvertently omitted in the MSS.
b. He will eventually become the god of the "midpoint," according to IrPt 1.7.1 ("Final repose of the just").

He is neither good nor evil, merely just

33.7.5   And if the perfect god is good according to his nature—as indeed
he is, for our savior showed that "one only is there who is good,"   Mt 19:17
namely his father whom he manifested—and if furthermore the law   VFrH
belonging to the nature of the adversary is both evil and wicked and is
stamped in the mold of injustice, then a being that is in a state intermediate
between these and is neither good, nor evil or unjust, might well be
properly called just, being a judge of the justice[c] that is his.

He is engendered in the image of the good god

33.7.6   And on the one hand this god must be inferior to the perfect
god and less than his righteousness precisely because he is engendered
and not unengendered—for "there is one unengendered father, from   1Co 8:6
whom are all things,"[d] or more exactly, from whom all things depend;
and on the other hand, he must have come into being as better and more
authoritative than the adversary; and must be born of an essence and
nature distinct from the essences of the other two. **33.7.7**   For the
essence of the adversary is both corruption and darkness, for the
adversary is material and divided into many parts; while the essence of
the unengendered father of the entirety is both incorruptibility and self-
existent light,[e] being simple and unique. And the essence of this
intermediate produced a twofold capacity,[f] for he is an image of the
better god.[g]

D. EPILOGUE

How could the just and the devil derive from the good?

33.7.8   And now, given that the good by nature engenders and produces
the things that are similar to itself and of the same essence, do not be
bewildered as to how these natures—that of corruption and ⟨that⟩[h] of   IrPt 1.5.4
intermediateness—which have come to be different in essence, arose
from a single first principle of the entirety, a principle that exists and is
confessed and believed in by us,[i] and which is unengendered and
incorruptible and good.

Promise of further instruction

33.7.9   For, god permitting, you will next learn about both the first
principle and the generation of these two other gods, if[j] you are deemed
worthy of the apostolic tradition,[k] which even we[l] have received by   TRs 49:37
succession; and along with this you will learn how to test all the   GPh 83
propositions by means of our savior's teaching.

---

c. Or "righteousness."
d. The original text of this passage (1 Co
8:6) says: "For us, there is one god, the
father" etc.
e. Cf. BJn 4:9f.
f. Cf. IrPt 1.5.1 ("[1] Animate essence").
g. With this sentence, Ptolemy begins to
speak of the esoteric Valentinian metaphysics, about which he will instruct Flora in the
following lesson (cf. 33.7.9).

h. This word is inadvertently omitted in
the MSS.
i. I.e. the Valentinians.
j. Or possibly "since."
k. The esoteric tradition that Valentinians
believed had been established by St. Paul,
transmitted by him to a certain Theudas,
thence to Valentinus, and finally to his successors like Ptolemy.
l. Or "which we too."

Conclusion

33.7.10 I have not failed, my sister Flora, to state these matters to you briefly. And what I have just written is a concise account, though I have treated the subject adequately. In the future these teachings will be of the greatest help to you—at least if, like good rich soil that has received ⟨Mk 4:20 par.⟩ fertile seeds,[m] you bear fruit.

---

m. Cf. IrPt 1.7.5, "The spiritual (elements), which down to this day Achamōth has continued to sow into just souls, learn here; are nourished, for they are sent as infants; later are deemed worthy of maturity; and are given as brides to the angels of the savior."

TREATISE ON RESURRECTION (EPISTLE TO RHEGINUS)

(TRs)

Contents

Almost the earliest known Christian text is a fragment of oral tradition that was quoted by St. Paul when he wrote to the Christians in Corinth about A.D. 54 (1 Co 15:3f). It is a creedal summary—a stylized formulation of beliefs, suitable for memorization—about the death and resurrection of Jesus, which Paul says he received from his even earlier predecessors.

Christ died for our sins in accordance with the scriptures.
He was buried.
He was raised on the third day in accordance with the scriptures.
He appeared to Cephas (Peter), then to the twelve. . . .

Such creedal declarations, whose wording varied from church to church, must have been a central reference point in the theological teaching of many early Christians.

From the time of Valentinus, no manuscript copy of a creedal formula seems to have survived; but the typical wording of such formulas can be roughly reconstructed from passing references found in Christian literature of the second century. Typically, a creedal formula about A.D. 150 might have asserted that Jesus

. . . was in the beginning.
He became incarnate.
He was crucified (or suffered) and died.
He arose from the dead.
He ascended into heaven.
He sits at the right hand of his father.
He shall come again to judge the world.

What did these words really mean? Precisely what did they refer to? And what did Jesus' resurrection and ascension indicate about the ultimate fate of the individual Christian? The answers to such questions were a matter of keen debate from the earliest moment in the history of the church (as 1 Co 15 shows)—nor was the debate any less lively at the time of Valentinus.

To some extent, answers might depend on an ancient teacher's prior assumptions about Jesus' manner of existence while he was on earth (was it material? animate? spiritual?) and, similarly, assumptions about the makeup of the individual Christian believer. A Valentinian interpretation of Christian resurrection would not be simple, for Valentinians conceived of three basic components in the human makeup: the material body ("dust"), which is destined to perish; an animate element (soul) that vivifies it, and which is ultimately destined for distinct preservation; and the intellect (spiritual element) or true self, which is destined for reunion and repose with god the father; cf. IrPt 1.6.1, 1.7.1.

Many ordinary Christians in the second century understood that just as Jesus had truly died and in his "resurrection" come back to life on the third day, so they too would die and then ultimately "arise" or come back to life in their same body. But Valentinian teachers, or at least some of them, did not accept that the animate element and the intellect (spirit) were capable of death; nor that the material body was capable of ultimate preservation. From these assumptions they concluded that the words "arise" and "resurrection" must not refer to a process of death and revivification, but to an upward movement in a different, more abstract or meta-phorical sense—in which the soul and intellect escape from material existence, and then "ascend" or change into another state of existence. It is the intellect's escape and change of condition that are the main topic of the *Treatise on Resurrection* ("Epistle to Rheginus").

For the author of TRs the "resurrection" and "ascension" of the intellect result from its contemplation of the divine, presumably at higher and higher degrees of abstraction until it contemplates the realm of permanent, pure being. A similar kind of mystical contemplation is described in several classic gnostic scriptures (cf. Zs and Fr); it was also discussed in non-Christian philosophy of the time. This, says the author of TRs, is "resurrection of the spirit" which makes the question of other kinds of resurrection irrelevant (46:1f). In the light of this Valentinian teaching, Jesus' "suffering"—traditionally understood to mean his real death on the cross—would not refer to biological death but simply to the suffering sojourn of his spirit or soul on earth within the illusory realm of matter. Like Valentinus in GTr, the author of TRs (48:19f) even goes so far as to deny the reality of the material world.

Thus for the author of TRs, the believer's true self—the "superior element"—never dies; its "resurrection" begins as soon as it starts to contemplate greater and greater intellectual objects (46:19f). This process begins here and now, while the believer dwells within the illusory material world. In this sense, the believer "already has resurrection" (49:13f). TRs is thus a classic exposition of the doctrine that "the resurrection is past already," a doctrine combated in the pastoral epistles of the New Testament (cf. 2 Ti 2:18).

The *Treatise* is addressed to an ordinary Christian believer named Rheginus (otherwise unknown), who seems to have become interested in Valentinian Christianity and to have inquired about the Valentinian interpretation of the local creedal formula, specifically as it concerned the doctrine of resurrection. The answer proposed in TRs is very ambiguous, shifting constantly between the traditional language of the creedal text and the author's allegorical interpretation of it phrased in philosophical terms. A certain amount of Valentinian jargon is introduced, but without any direct explanation or definition. The *Treatise* concludes with an offer to explain these ambiguities: no doubt the next installment of Rheginus's instruction would have been more systematic and technical. Thus TRs is an exhortation ("protreptic"), inviting ordinary Christians to a "deeper," Valentinian understanding of Christian faith.

Literary background

The author of TRs and its place of composition are unknown. Because of its elementary, introductory character, the Valentinian teaching of the treatise is vague; it is therefore difficult to identify it with a particular school of Valentinianism (it does not seem to agree perfectly with IrPt). The date of composition of TRs must be before A.D. 350, the approximate date of the MS. The language of composition was Greek.

TRs has a complex mixture of genres in which certain traditional materials are subordinated to others.

I. Philosophical epistle
  A. Introductory treatise (*eisagogē*)
    1. Philosophical sermon (diatribe)

The concluding salutation has led most critics to classify TRs as a *philosophical epistle*, that is, a short formal essay couched in the framework of a letter. The genre of philosophical epistle was used by both Valentinus (VFrC, E, and H) and Ptolemy (PtF); it was much favored by academic writers of the period. TRs lacks the customary epistolary greeting at the beginning; this has led some scholars to suppose that the first sentence of the work (with the author's name) is now missing.

The internal structure of TRs corresponds to the form of the Greek *introductory treatise* or *eisagogē*:

  1. Topic; proper orientation for success
  2. Exposition of the subject matter
  3. Special problems

But the rhetoric of the treatise belongs not to the formal essay but rather to the *philosophical sermon* or animated classroom lecture, sometimes called "diatribe style." Several characteristic devices of this style appear in TRs: sarcastic rhetorical questions; questions spoken as though by an imaginary opponent; an example of famous men (48:6f); patronizing moral exhortation ("Instruction") introduced at the end; incomplete philosophical exposition; overall brevity. Useful comparative material from roughly the same period can be found in the philosophical *Sermons* of Epictetus (A.D. ca. 55–ca.135).

Text

The original Greek apparently does not survive. The text is known only in Coptic translation, attested by a single MS from Nag Hammadi, MC NHC I (pp. 43–50), which was copied just before A.D. 350, and is now in the Cairo Coptic Museum.

The translation below is based on my own critical edition of the Coptic: B. Layton, ed., *The Gnostic Treatise* (see "Select Bibliography"), 10–32. An earlier version of the translation appeared in that publication and is revised here with the kind permission of the series editor.

SELECT BIBLIOGRAPHY

Epictetus. *The Discourses as Reported by Arrian, The Manual, and Fragments.* English translation by W. A. Oldfather. 2 vols. Loeb Classical Library. New York: G. P. Putnam's Sons, 1926–28. (For stylistic comparison with TRs.)

Kelly, J. *Early Christian Creeds.* London: Longmans, Green, 1950. (Creeds in the second century A.D.)

Layton, B., ed. *The Gnostic Treatise on Resurrection from Nag Hammadi.* Harvard Dissertations in Religion, 12. Missoula, Mont.: Scholars Press, 1979.

——————. "Vision and Revision: A Gnostic View of Resurrection." In *Colloque international sur les textes de Nag Hammadi (Québec, 22–25 août 1978)*, edited by B. Barc, 190–217. Bibliothèque copte de Nag Hammadi, Section "Études," no. 1. Québec: Presses de l'Université Laval; Louvain: Peeters, 1981.

Malinine, M., et al., eds. *De Resurrectione (Epistula ad Rheginum): Codex Jung f. XXIIr–f. XXVr (p. 43–50).* Zürich and Stuttgart: Rascher, 1963. (In French).

Ménard, J., ed. *Le Traité sur la Résurrection.* Bibliothèque copte de Nag Hammadi, Section "Textes," vol. 12. Québec: Les Presses de l'Université Laval, 1985.

Peel, M., ed. "The Treatise on Resurrection." In *Nag Hammadi Codex I*, edited by H. Attridge. Vol. 1, *Introductions, Texts* . . ., 123–57, and vol. 2, *Notes*, 137–215. Nag Hammadi Studies, vols. 22, 23. Leiden: E. J. Brill, 1985.

Schäfer, K. "Eisagoge." In *Reallexikon für Antike und Christentum*, vol. 4 (1959), cols. 862–904. (On the introductory treatise as a literary genre.)

van Unnik, W. "The Newly Discovered Gnostic 'Epistle to Rheginus' on Resurrection." *Journal of Ecclesiastical History* 15 (1964): 141–67. (A useful survey of second-century Christian views on resurrection and an interpretation of TRs different from the one followed above.)

TREATISE ON RESURRECTION[a]

A. PROLOGUE

Personal orientation appropriate to the subject

25 **43** There are certain persons, my child[b] Rheginus, who wish to become
learned:[c] that is their aim when they set out to solve unsolved problems,
29,32 and if they succeed they regard themselves highly. •But I do not think
34 their results lie within the account of the truth; •rather, it is repose[d] (in
35 the sense of recreation) that they are after. •This (true repose, that is) GTr 22:11
1 we obtained from our savior, our lord, the kind:[e] **44** •we obtained it
when we gained acquaintance with the truth and rested our confidence
upon[f] it.

Importance and difficulty of the topic

3 However, since it is the essential points on resurrection after which
7 you[a] so sweetly inquire, I am writing to you. •For resurrection is a basic
8 matter; •and not only do many give it no credence,[b] but few are they Mt 7:13
11 who understand[c] it. •So let this be the topic of our discussion.[d]

B. EXPOSITION

Dual nature of the savior

12,14 How did the lord handle the circumstances of this world?[e] •While he
was incarnate,[f] and after he had revealed himself to be a son of god,[g] IrPt 1.6.1 ?
17 he walked about in this region where you dwell[h] speaking about the law
20,21 of the natural order:[i] •I mean, death. •Moreover, O Rheginus, the son
23 of god was a human son.[j] •And he was master of his circumstances in
27 two respects—having both humanity and divinity: •so that he might
30 conquer death through being son of god, •and that through the human
33 son might come to pass the return[k] to the fullness:[l] •since from the IrPt 1.7.1
35 beginning he existed as a seed[m] of the truth from above, •before there GPh 59
came into being this cosmic structure,[n] in which lordships and divinities[o] IrPt 1.5.2
have become so numerous. IrPt 1.5.4

Title 43 a. In the manuscript, the title is
found after the text (at 50:17f).

b. I.e. "my disciple."

c. The author's antiphilosophical stance
is developed at 46:3f.

d. The Greek word (*anapausis*) has many
meanings including "recreation" (i.e. fun)
and "heavenly repose." The author plays on
this ambiguity.

e. The Greek word (*khrēstos*) was pronounced exactly like the word for "Christ."

f. Or simply "rested upon."

44 a. "you" is always singular in TRs, except where otherwise indicated.

b. Or "have no faith in it."

c. Lit. "find."

d. Or "our treatise."

e. Or "handle his affairs."

f. The lord preexisted before his incarnation, cf. 44:33f.

g. I.e. "to be divine." This phrase is the
only mention of the word "god" in TRs.

h. I.e. the material world.

i. I.e. the inevitable fate of all material
things; cf. IrPt 1.7.1 ("Final destruction of
the world").

j. Or "a son of man"; i.e. he was human
during his incarnation.

k. Or "return from exile." The Greek
word (*apokatastasis*) is Valentinian jargon
for the return of the intellect to its true home
within the fullness.

l. Valentinian jargon for the spiritual universe.

m. The Valentinian school characteristically spoke of emanations and the process
of emanation with agricultural metaphors.

n. The material world, including the heavens.

o. The heavenly rulers.

The savior's resurrection

39,2   I know that I am phrasing this explanation in difficult terms. **45** •Yet
4 consider: nothing within the account of the truth is truly difficult. •At
any rate, since he came forward for the sake of explanation, to leave
nothing obscure, rather to reveal in simple terms everything about
9 coming into being[a]—•the undoing of evil[b] and the manifestation of the
superior element,[c] these are the offshoot of the truth and the spirit:
13,14 this grace is bestowed by[d] the truth. •The savior swallowed[e] death.
15,16 You must not be unperceptive: •for I mean that laying aside the
corruptible world,[f] he exchanged it for an incorruptible eternal realm.[g]
19 And he raised himself up,[h] having "swallowed" the visible by means of
22 the invisible, •and gave us the way to our immortality.

GTr 26:32+
PPl A:15
v.14
46:1+

Spiritual resurrection of the Christian believer

23,25   So then, as the apostle[i] said of him, •we have suffered with him, and
arisen with him, and ascended with him.
28   Now, since we are manifestly present in this world, the world is what
31 we wear (like a garment).[j] •From him (the savior) we radiate like rays;[k]
32,34 and being held fast by him until our sunset—•that is, until our death in
36 the present life—•we are drawn upward by him as rays are drawn by
39 the sun, restrained by nothing. •This is resurrection of the spirit,[l]
1 **46** which "swallows"[a] resurrection of the soul[b] along with resurrection
of the flesh.[c]

GTr 31:4
IrPt 1.7.1
IrPt 1.7.2
PPl A:8
GPh 54
GPh 90
v.39
IrPt 1.6.1
v.1
45:14, 49:2

Philosophy versus gnōsis

3   Now, if there is anyone who is not a believer,[d] that person cannot be
5 convinced. •For it is the domain of faith,[e] my child, and not that of
argumentation, to assert that the dead will arise.
8   And suppose that, among the scholars[f] here, there is one who believes.
10,10 Why, then, that person will arise. •And let not the scholar here trust in
13 one who is self-converted (to faith). •And because of our faith ⟨. . .⟩.[g]
14   For we are[h] acquainted with the child of the human being,[i] and have
17 come to believe that he arose from the dead.[j] •And he is the one of
whom we say, "He became death's undoing."

GTr 25:8
1Co 15:54
2Co 5:4
v.5
IrPt 1.6.2 ?
GPh 3

---

45 a. The natural order, where things come into being and pass out of existence; cf. note 44i.

b. Or "the undoing of the inferior element."

c. I.e. the intellect or spirit.

d. Lit. "belongs to."

e. Overcame.

f. Especially the body of flesh.

g. Or "eternity, aeon."

h. The Coptic word can be translated also "arose."

i. Paul. The formula that follows uses sacramental metaphors known from the Pauline and Deuteropauline epistles: cf. Rm 8:17, Ep 2:4–6, Col 2:12, Col 3:1–3.

j. A Platonist cliché for the material body, but in the present context perhaps an allusion to Ro 13:12, Ep 4:22, Col 3:10, 1Co 15:49.

k. Lit. "it is from him that we are rays."

l. Or "spiritual resurrection."

46 a. Makes irrelevant.

b. Or "animate resurrection."

c. Or "fleshly resurrection."

d. The author takes pains to use ordinary Christian language. As emerges in 46:19f, "belief" (or "faith") actually means acquaintance with the truth, i.e. *gnōsis*.

e. Or "belief" (Greek *pistis*).

f. Or "philosophers."

g. One or more words are inadvertently omitted here.

h. Or "have become."

i. Or "the son of man" (a traditional Christian epithet of the human savior). Cf. note 44j.

j. In the allegorical sense explained in 45:16f.

Salvation of the intellect

19,21   Even as the object of belief[k] is great, great too are the believers: •the
23 thought[l] of those who are saved will not perish, •the intellect of those
25 who have acquaintance with such an object will not perish. •Thus, we
are chosen for salvation[m] and ransom,[n] having been set apart from the
28 beginning, •so that we might not stumble in the folly of the ignorant,
but might enter into the intelligence of those who are acquainted with
the truth.

32   Indeed, that truth, to which they are wakeful, cannot be brought to
34,36 naught; and it will not. •The structure of the fullness[o] is mighty. •That
38 which broke loose and became the universe is trifling. •But what is held
fast[p] is the entirety:[q] it did not come into being;[r] it simply was.

PPl A:4
GPh 5 +
Ro 8:29
Ep 1:4
VFrF
GTr 21:23

GTr 30:10

IrPt 1.4.5 ?

GTr 17:4

C. SPECIAL PROBLEMS[s]

(1) Will the flesh be saved?

1 **47** So do not be doubtful about resurrection, my child Rheginus.[a]
4 Now (you might wrongly suppose), granted you[b] did not preexist in
5 flesh—•indeed, you took on flesh when you entered this world—why
will you not take your flesh with you when you return to the realm of
9 eternity? •It is the element superior to the flesh[c] that imparts vitality to
11 it; •(furthermore, you might suppose) does not whatever comes into
12 being for your sake (that is, the flesh) belong to you? •So may we not
conclude that whatever is yours will coexist with you?[d]

GPh 21

14   Nay, rather, while you are here, what is it that you are alienated
15 from?[e] •Is this what you have endeavored to learn about: the bodily
18 envelope—that is, old age?[f] •And are you (the real you) mere corruption?[g]
19   You can count absence[h]—or (in another sense of the Greek word)
21 shortage—as your profit. •For you will not pay back the superior element[i]

---

k. I.e. the truth (cf. 46:28f).

l. Or "thinking."

m. The word can also be translated "preservation."

n. A traditional, Pauline way of speaking.

o. Cf. 44:30f.

p. Or "encompassed."

q. Cf. IrPt note 1.1.1e, and below 47:26f.

r. Cf. note 45a.

s. Ancient Greek introductory treatises often had an appendix that treated special problems (called *aporiai*) in a somewhat disjointed way; cf. "Literary background" in the introduction to TRs.

47 a. The author now begins an open attack on the ordinary, literal understanding of the resurrection of the Christian believer.

b. I.e. the real self, the intellect.

c. The soul or animate body, which contains the intellect. It was a tenet of Platonism that the soul is the material body's source of vitality.

d. This paragraph refers, rather sketchily, to a traditional Christian argument for resurrection of the body of flesh: since the fleshly body has been created by god's providence with the explicit goal of being alive, it would contradict the notion of god's providence and omnipotence to suppose that the flesh would ever cease to exist forever and

not, at least eventually, continue to coexist with its source of vitality; but god is providential and omnipotent—therefore the flesh must not perish forever.

e. Or "lack."

f. The text is corrupt here, obscuring the author's rebuttal of the argument summarized in the preceding paragraph. A few words must have inadvertently been omitted.

g. I.e. the traditional argument (47:1f) equates the real self with the realm of corruption and so is repugnant.

h. Greek and Latin funerary rhetoric spoke of the body (the "inferior element") as money borrowed from the bank of nature; when the soul ("superior element") departs from it at death, the body must be "paid back." In keeping with this rhetoric the author here plays on two meanings of the Greek word *apousia:* (1) "absence," the state of disconnection from the fleshly body; (2) "shortage," a technical word from the reminting of old coins—the amount of physical wear suffered by an old coin of silver or gold is its "shortage": thus the greater the body's "shortage," the greater the soul's "profit," since the body always impedes the soul.

i. The real self is identical with the "superior element": hence the true self does not "pay back" the superior element at death.

22 when you depart.[j] •The inferior element[k] takes a loss;[l] but what it owes
24,26 is gratitude.[m] •Nothing then buys us back[n] while we are here;[o] •yet the
27 entirety, and we as members of it, are saved. •We have had salvation
29 from start to finish. •Let us think in this way. Let us accept in this way.

Salvation is immediate

30   However, certain persons desire to know—in the investigation of their
investigations—whether one who is saved will, upon taking off[p] the
36 body, be immediately saved: •let no one doubt this![q]

"Resurrection" is uncovering

38   "Surely, then," (so might run the argument) "the dead, visible
members[r] will be preserved: for the living, interior members[s] are sup-   IrPt 1.5.6
3,4 posed to arise." **48** •But what is the meaning of resurrection? •It is the
uncovering[a] at any given time[b] of the elements that have "arisen."

(2) Is spiritual resurrection unreal?

6   Now, if you should recall having read in the gospel that Elijah   Mk 9:4 par.
appeared—and Moses—in his (Jesus') company, do not suppose that   GPh 23
12 resurrection[c] is an apparition.[d] •It is not an apparition; rather, it is
13 something real. •Instead, one ought to maintain that the world is an   48:26
16 apparition, rather than resurrection, •which became possible[e] through   GTr 24:25
our lord, the savior, Jesus the kind.

D. INSTRUCTION

The material world is unreal

19,22   And what am I telling you? Suddenly the living are dying—•surely
24 they are not alive at all in this world of apparition![f]—•the rich have   48:13+
26 become poor, rulers overthrown: •all changes,[g] the world is an apparition.
28   But let me not deprecate the circumstances of this world at too great
30 a length. •Simply: resurrection is not of this sort, for it is real.

The nature of resurrection

33   It is what stands at rest:[h]
34   And the revealing[i] of what truly exists.

j. I.e. "when you die."

k. The body.

l. Or "is diminished."

m. It is only thanks to the soul that the fleshly body ever lived at all.

n. Or "ransoms us."

o. I.e. "while we are incarnate in the world."

p. Cf. note 45j.

q. Traditional arguments for a general resurrection of the flesh (cf. note 47d) implied that there is a period of waiting between death and resurrection. The author here denies this.

r. Or "limbs."

s. Or "limbs," i.e. the soul and psychic faculties, and the intellect within it.

48 a. The body is again compared to a garment, cf. note 45j.

b. Or "for all time."

c. I.e. resurrection of the spirit.

d. I.e. "do not suppose that resurrection is existence in a ghost-like body of flesh."

e. Or "which came into being."

f. "in this world of apparition": lit. "in an apparition."

g. Paraphrasing a famous doctrine of the pre-Socratic Greek philosopher Heraclitus (cf. Frag. 12 Diels, and Plato, *Cratylus* 402a).

h. To "stand at rest" is philosophical jargon for the state of permanence, non-change, and real being, as opposed to what exists in instability, change, and becoming.

i. Cf. 45:9f and 48:4f.

35   And it is what one receives in exchange for the circumstances
of this world:

36   And a migration into newness.   GTr 31:9

38   For incorruptibility [is streaming] down upon corruption: **49**   1Co 15:53

2   And light is streaming down upon darkness, swallowing it.   IrPt 1.6.2
         v.2

4   And the fullness is filling up its lack[a]   GTr 24:37
         GTr 25:8

6   —these are the symbols and the likenesses of resurrection: GPh 106

8   This is what brings about goodness.   VFrH +

Resurrection has already come

9   Therefore do not concentrate on particulars, O Rheginus, nor live   IrPt 1.6.1
according to (the dictates of) this flesh; do not, for the sake of unity.[b]   GTr 24:7

13,15 Rather, leave the state of dispersion and bondage,[c] •and then you   GPh 8
         v.15

16 already have resurrection. •For if the dying part (flesh) "knows itself,"[d]   GPh 19

18 and knows that since it is moribund it is rushing toward this outcome

22 (death) even if it has lived many years in the present life, •why do you[e]
(the intellect) not examine your own self and see that you have arisen?

23 And you are rushing toward this outcome (that is, separation from the
body) since you possess resurrection.

Training is necessary

26,27 Yet you persist as though you were dying, •even though it is the

28 former (the moribund flesh) that "knows" it has died.[f] •Why then am I

30 so lenient, except because of your inadequate training? •Everyone should
practice[g] in many ways to gain release from this element (the body),

34 so that one might not wander aimlessly[h] but rather might recover one's   GTr 22:20
former state of being.   GTr 21:3

E. EPILOGUE

Offer of further instruction

37   What I received[i] through the generosity of my lord, Jesus the kind, I   PtF 33.7.9+
have taught to you and your siblings—who are my children[j]—without

5 omitting any of the points necessary to strengthen you. **50** •But if
anything in the exposition of the treatise is too profound, I shall explain
it to you if you inquire.

Salutation

8   Since this is so, do not hesitate to share with any other members of
your circle, for that (which I have taught you) has the power to be of

11,13 benefit. •Many people are awaiting what I have written for you: •to
them I address this lesson, to bring about "peace" among them "and

15 grace." •I greet you[a] and whoever, with familial love, love you.[b]

---

49 a. Cf. GTr note 24a.
   b. Or "harmony, oneness."
   c. A Platonic cliché for the material body.
   d. The Delphic maxim, "know thyself,"
expressed a central theme of traditional Greek
wisdom.
   e. I.e. the real self.
   f. The body in itself (apart from the soul
or vivifying element) has no life, and so as
such has never been alive.
   g. Or "lead an ascetic life."
   h. The Greek word (*planasthai*) some-

times refers to reincarnation of the soul in
another body.
   i. "received" through the Valentinian
school tradition.
   j. The author considers all members of
Rheginus's congregation to be his potential
disciples; cf. note 43b.

50 a. A salutation such as might occur at
the end of an epistle.
   b. In the manuscript, the title is written
after the text (at 50:17f).

THE GOSPEL ACCORDING TO PHILIP

A VALENTINIAN ANTHOLOGY
(GPh)

Contents and literary background

The work called *The Gospel According to Philip* is a Valentinian anthology containing some one hundred short excerpts taken from various other works. None of the sources of these excerpts have been identified, and apparently they do not survive. To judge from their style and contents, they were sermons, treatises, or philosophical epistles (typical Valentinian genres), as well as collected aphorisms or short dialogues with comments. Only some of the sources can definitely be identified as Valentinian. Because of their brevity and the lack of context it is difficult to assign any of them to particular schools of Valentinian theology. On the other hand, nothing indicates that all come from one and the same branch of the Valentinian church. It is possible that some of the excerpts are by Valentinus himself. Others, however, refer to etymologies in Syriac, the Semitic language (a dialect of Aramaic) used in Edessa and western Mesopotamia; these must be the work of a Valentinian theologian of the East, writing in a bilingual milieu such as Edessa (see Map 5). Probably the language of composition of all the excerpts was Greek.

GPh is not the only Valentinian anthology to survive, for among the works attributed to the late-second-century intellectual St. Clement (Titus Flavius Clemens) of Alexandria is a collection of excerpts from writings of the theologian Theodotus, one of the main representatives of the "Eastern" branch of Valentinianism. It is known as Clement's *Excerpts from Theodotus*. Much of the information that can be gleaned about Valentinus's successors survives only in fragmentary form, and the exact interpretation of their theologies is therefore difficult.

The compiler, place of compilation, and purpose of GPh as it now stands are completely unknown though some scholars have placed it in Syria because of references to the Syriac language in a few of the excerpts. The principle governing the order of the excerpts is obscure (see also "Text"). In some instances it appears that several excerpts come from a single source but without being quoted side by side or even in the original order.

The present title of the work may have been added after the anthology had been put into circulation in antiquity; in any case, the term "gospel" does not here refer to the Christian literary genre called gospel (e.g. the Gospel of Mark) but, rather, has its earlier meaning of "preaching" or "good news." Philip is the only apostle mentioned by name in the excerpts (see excerpt no. 80); it may be for this reason that his name is attached to the title of the anthology as though he were its compiler and patron saint. If indeed it is the apostle Philip to whom the title refers, and not some other person of that name, then with its present attribution GPh is one of the few instances of Valentinian pseudepigraphy; usually Valentinian theologians wrote under their own name and authority, as bearers of the Valentinian apostolic tradition (see excerpt no. 83 and PtF 33.7.9).

The date of compilation of GPh must be before A.D. 350, the approximate date of the MS.

Because probably more than one Valentinian theological perspective is represented in GPh, it would be misleading to reconstruct a single theological system from the whole anthology. Rather, individual groups of excerpts can profitably be studied in isolation, with comparison of other works or fragments of Valentinianism or of classic gnosticism.

Nevertheless, a certain number of keywords and themes (listed below) strikingly recur in many of the excerpts. They indicate the particular interest of the ancient compiler, who was especially concerned with theology of the sacraments (possibly baptism most of all). With due caution, they can be used to identify excerpts that belong together.

Especially striking are the many references to sacraments ("mysteries"), presumably ones recognized by the Valentinian Christian community or communities. As many as five are distinguished (cf. no. 60): baptism, chrism (anointment with holy oil), eucharist, ransom, and bridal chamber. Of these terms, the most distinctively Valentinian is "bridal chamber." Nothing in GPh indicates whether bridal chamber was expressed by an actual ritual or was merely a theological metaphor of salvation. In "the imaged bridal chamber" the soul or "image" joins with an angel and becomes as it were an androgyne, safe against sexual temptations (no. 53). This union rectifies the separation of Adam and Eve, the original androgyne (no. 70, cf. RAd). In such a union one embarks upon "return" (*apokatastasis*) to one's spiritual home (no. 59); this is the reception of resurrection and the holy spirit (no. 83). It is striking that the term "acquaintance" (*gnōsis*) plays only a very minor role in the excerpts.

Index of keywords and themes

The spiritual world:

truth: nos. 3, 8, 13, 37, 38, 40, 59, 76, 81, 93, 104, 105
light: nos. 6, 7, 24, 48, 57, 58, 67, 69, 73, 83, 90, 96, 102, 106
father (parent), son: nos. 7, 8, 15, 16, 18, 29, 38, 59, 61, 73, 83
Word: nos. 21, 27, 99, 104
the perfect human being: nos. 11, 27, 35, 86, 87, 90, 99
the child of the human being (son of man): nos. 47, 101
holy spirit, spirit: nos. 7, 12, 14, 21, 24, 29, 30, 31, 33, 35, 38, 44, 51, 54, 58, 59, 67, 71, 74, 83, 86, 92, 96, 106
wisdom: nos. 31, 34, 48
rulers, forces, brigands, unclean spirits: nos. 5, 9, 10, 12, 14, 30, 35, 45, 52, 53, 54, 69, 71
midpoint: nos. 55, 90
right, left: nos. 6, 35, 59
restrain: nos. 54, 90, 106

Primeval history:

paradise: nos. 11, 75, 80, 82
Adam: nos. 11, 27, 36, 63, 70, 71, 74, 75, 82
separate, join: nos. 24, 61, 63, 67, 69, 70, 71, 88, 104, 106
die, death: nos. 2, 3, 6, 10, 19, 27, 34, 55, 63, 65, 70, 79, 81, 82, 92, 104
sexual intercourse: nos. 36, 52, 53, 95, 96, 102
child, offspring: nos. 2, 3, 27, 31, 32, 33, 36, 41, 65, 75, 76, 85, 87, 95, 100, 101

The pagan world:

animal: nos. 10, 11, 35, 43, 45, 50, 66, 75, 87, 96, 100
slave: nos. 2, 9, 42, 66, 77, 93, 97, 100, 104, 106
sacrifice, offering: nos. 10, 31, 43, 68

Jesus Christ and the foundation of Christianity:

Mary: nos. 14, 28, 48
virgin: nos. 14, 66, 73, 74
the coming of Christ, Jesus, the truth: nos. 3, 5, 11, 46, 59, 62, 70, 72, 81
cross, crucify: nos. 46, 59, 64, 80, 83, 105
Christian, Hebrew, Jew, Gentile, convert: nos. 1, 3, 14, 39, 42, 51, 59, 83, 84, 87
apostle, apostolic person, disciple: nos. 14, 16, 23, 30, 31, 40, 48, 57, 59, 73, 83, 100
harvest and other agricultural metaphors: nos. 4, 13, 35, 50, 80, 98, 104, 106

The human being:

garment, nakedness: nos. 21, 26, 55, 69, 86, 102
soul: nos. 5, 20, 53, 71, 100

Salvation:

leave the world: nos. 54, 56, 106
inherit: nos. 2, 32

Sacraments and spirituality:

mystery: nos. 18, 51, 52, 60, 69, 73, 102
baptism, water, dyer: nos. 22, 37, 47, 51, 58, 60, 67, 68, 78, 79, 83, 84, 86, 92
chrism, anoint, oil: nos. 22, 41, 58, 59, 60, 67, 72, 80, 83, 84, 94, 106
eucharist: nos. 21, 24, 46, 60, 84, 86, 91
ransom, redeem: nos. 5, 40, 60, 68, 72, 78, 106
bridal chamber, bedroom: nos. 53, 58, 59, 60, 66, 68, 70, 71, 73, 77, 83, 87, 102, 105, 107
name: nos. 7, 8, 9, 17, 28, 29, 40, 42, 51, 59, 78, 83, 88
fire: nos. 22, 33, 44, 57, 58, 73, 106
food: nos. 11, 21, 35, 50, 75, 81, 82, 100, 102
image: nos. 24, 52, 53, 59, 61, 65, 68, 76, 105, 106
angel: nos. 18, 23, 24, 45, 48, 53
acquaintance: nos. 82, 93, 98, 104
resurrection: nos. 7, 19, 21, 55, 59, 68, 79, 80, 83

Text

The original Greek apparently does not survive. The text is known only in Coptic translation, attested by a single MS from Nag Hammadi, MS NHC II (pp. 51–86), which was copied just before A.D. 350 and now is in the Cairo Coptic Museum.

In the Coptic MS the excerpts are not divided from one another, probably through an inadvertence, nor are they numbered. The modern division and numbering of excerpts is thus purely hypothetical, being based on the style and contents of the text. Scholars have differed slightly in how they divide up the text, and there is no standard system of division and excerpt numbers. It is therefore desirable, for scholarly purposes, to cite GPh only according to page and line of the MS, e.g. "51:29f" (and not "Excerpt no. 1").

In some older literature, reference is made not to the MS page numbers but rather to the plate numbers of an early photographic facsimile of the text (ed. P. Labib). In the translation below, these early plate numbers are written in parentheses after the MS page numbers, e.g. **52** (100), so readers can easily make use of the older bibliography on the work. But modern citations of the text normally mention only the MS page number followed by the line reference, e.g. "52:2f".

The translation below is based on my own critical edition of the Coptic: B. Layton, ed., "The Gospel According to Philip," in vol. 1 of B. Layton, ed., *Nag Hammadi Codex II,2–7*, (see "Select Bibliography" under "Isenberg"), in press.

SELECT BIBLIOGRAPHY

The older commentaries, although invaluable, are based on a highly inaccurate edition and translation of the text and must be used with caution.

Gaffron, H.-G. "Studien zum koptischen Philippusevangelium unter besonderer Berücksichtigung der Sakramente." Dr. Theol. diss., Friedrich-Wilhelms-Universität, Bonn, 1969.

Grant, R. M. "The Mystery of Marriage in the Gospel of Philip." *Vigiliae Christianae* 15 (1961): 129–40.

Isenberg, W. "[The Gospel According to Philip.] Introduction." In vol. 1 of *Nag Hammadi Codex II,2–7, Together with XIII,2*, Brit. Lib. Or.4926(1) and P.Oxy.1, 654, 655*, edited by B. Layton. Nag Hammadi Studies. Leiden: E. J. Brill, in press.

Ménard, J.-E. *L'Évangile selon Philippe: Introduction, texte, traduction, commentaire*. Printed Th.D. diss., Univ. Strasbourg, Faculté de théologie catholique, 1967. MS page nos. 51–86 are mislabeled "53–88." The plate numbers are correct.

Trautmann, C. "La Parenté dans l'Évangile selon Philippe." In *Colloque internationale sur les textes de Nag Hammadi (Québec, 22–25 août 1978)*, edited by B. Barc, 267–78. Bibliothèque copte de Nag Hammadi, Section "Études," no. 1. Québec: Les Presses de l'Université Laval; Louvain: Peeters, 1981.

Wilson, R. M. *The Gospel of Philip, Translated from the Coptic Text, with an Introduction and Commentary*. London: A. R. Mowbray, 1962.

THE GOSPEL ACCORDING TO PHILIP[a]

(1)
Making a convert

29 **51** (99) A HEBREW makes a Hebrew, and such a person is called a
31 convert. •But a convert does not make a convert. [. . .] are as they
[. . .] and they make others [. . .] is enough that they exist.

(2)
Those who inherit the living

2,3 **52** (100) •ALL that a slave wants is to be free; •the slave does not hope
4,5 for the riches of its master. •But a child is not merely a child; •rather,
6 the child lays claim to the father's legacy. •Those[a] who inherit dead
8,8 things are also dead, •and what they inherit are dead things. •Those who
10 inherit the living are alive, •and they inherit both the living and the
11 things that are dead. •Dead things inherit nothing, for how could a dead
13 thing inherit anything? •If a dead person inherits the living, that person
will not die, but rather will greatly live.

3, 27, 31, 32,
33, 41, 85, 87,
100, 101
GTr 43:19+

(3)
The state of being a Christian

15 A GENTILE does not die, for the gentile has never become alive so as
17,18 to die. •One who has believed in the truth has become alive; •and this
person runs the risk of dying, because of being alive.
19   Since[a] Christ came, the world has been created, cities have been
21 organized, and the dead have been buried. •When we were Hebrews we
were orphans with (only) our mother, but when we became Christians
we got father and mother.

TRs 46:5

2+

(4)
Sow in the world and reap in the other realm

25,26 WHOEVER sows in the winter reaps in the summer. •"Winter" means
27 the world; "summer" means the other realm. •Let us sow in the world
28 so that we might reap in the summer. •For this reason we ought not to
29,30 pray in the winter. •What emerges from the winter is the summer. •But
if one reaps in the winter, one will not actually reap but only pluck out
33 young plants, for such will not bear a crop. •Not only does it come
[. . .] but even on the sabbath [. . .] is barren.

92, 98, 106
Mt 13:24
GTh 57
VHr
IrPt 1.7.1
v.28
GTr 42:9 ?

(5)
Christ came to rescue the soul

35 THE ANOINTED (Christ) came to purchase some, to rescue some, and
3 to ransom some. **53** (101) •He purchased those who were alien and made
4 them his own. •And he brought back his own, whom he had voluntarily
6 laid down as a deposit. •Not only, once he had appeared, did he lay

40, 60, 68, 72,
106
TRs 46:25+
Jn 10:17

Title a. In the manuscript, the title is found
after the text (at 86:18f).

2 a. Possibly a new excerpt begins here.

3 a. Possibly a new excerpt begins here.

down the soul (as a deposit) when he wished, but from the moment the
world existed he laid down the soul for such a time as he should wish.
10 Then he emanated[a] so that he might take it back, since it had been laid
11 down as a deposit. •It had fallen into the hands of brigands,[b] and they   VFrH
12 had taken it captive. •But he rescued it; and he ransomed those who
are good in the world, and the bad.[c]

(6)
Mutual dependence of opposites in this world

14 LIGHT and darkness, life and death, right and left, are siblings (that is,
17 mutually dependent); it is impossible for them to separate. •Accordingly,
the good are not good, the bad are not bad, life is not life, death is not
20,21 death. •So each will be dispersed[a] to its original source. •But things that
23 are superior to the world are indissoluble: •they are eternal.

(7)
Real names and unreal names

23 NAMES given to worldly things are very deceptive,[a] since they turn   8, 9
27 the heart aside from the real to the unreal. •And whoever hears the   GTr 39:3
word "god" thinks not of the reality, but has been thinking of what is
not real: so also, with the words "father," "son," "holy spirit," "life,"
"light," "resurrection," "church," etc., it is not the real that one thinks
35 of but the unreal, although the words have referred to the real. •The
1 names [that one has] heard exist in the world [. . .] deceive. **54** (102) •If
the names were situated in the eternal realm, they would not be uttered
3 on any occasion in the world, •nor would they have been assigned to
4 worldly things: •their goal[b] would be in the eternal realm.

(8)
The name of the father belongs to the son

5 ONLY one name is not uttered in the world, the name that the father   GTr 38:6
7 bestowed on the son;[a] •it is above every other—that is, the name of the   88, Ph 2:9-11
8 father. •For son would not become father had he not put on the name   PPl A:11
10 of the father. •Those who possess this name think it but do not speak
12,13 it. •Those who do not possess it do not think it. •Yet for our sakes truth   7+
engendered names in the world—truth, to which one cannot refer without
15,16 names. •Truth is unitary, ⟨. . .⟩[b] is multiple, •and it is for our sakes that   TRs 49:9
⟨it⟩[c] lovingly refers to this one thing by means of multiplicity.

(9)
Slavery to false names

18 THE RULERS[a] wanted to deceive humanity, inasmuch as they saw
21 that it had kinship with truly good things; •they took the names of the   7+

---

5 a. Or "came forth."
   b. A traditional name for rulers, forces,
and spirits of wickedness.
   c. "and the bad": One or more words
may have inadvertently been omitted after
"bad."

6 a. Or "dissolved."

7 a. Or "have great error."
   b. Or "reference."

8 a. Or "parent . . . child": Traditional
Christian language has been retained in the
English translation of this work, as in GTr.
   b. One or more words are inadvertently
omitted here.
   c. This word is inadvertently omitted in
the MS.

9 a. I.e. the heavenly rulers, the spirits of
wickedness.

good (plur.) and gave them to the nongood, to deceive humanity by the
25 names and bind them to the nongood •and—then what a favor they do
26 for them![b]— •to remove them (the names) from the nongood and assign
28,29 them to the good! •These they were acquainted with: •for they wanted
the free to be taken and enslaved to them in perpetuity.

(10)[a]
Sacrifices to the forces and to god

31 THERE exist forces[b] that [. . .] human beings, not wanting them to
34 [attain salvation], so that they might become [. . .]. •For if human beings
attain salvation, sacrifices [will not] be made [. . .], and animals will not
1 be offered up unto the forces. **55** (103) •Indeed, the ones to whom
2 offerings used to be made were animals. •Now, they were offered up
3,4 alive: •but when they had been offered up, they died. •Human beings
were offered up dead unto god; and they became alive.

(11)
Christ the bringer of bread

6 BEFORE the anointed (Christ) came there was no bread in the world:
7 just as paradise, where Adam was, had many trees for the food of the
10 animals but did not have wheat for the food of human beings, •and
11 human beings were nourished like the animals. •But when the anointed
(Christ), the perfect human being, came, he brought bread from heaven
so that human beings might be fed with the food of the human being.

(12)[a]
The holy spirit active in the rulers

14 THE RULERS[b] thought that it was by their own power and will that
16 they did what they did: •but the holy spirit was secretly activating the   IrPt 1.5.6+
entirety[c] through them, as it willed.

(13)
Truth sowed everywhere

19,20 TRUTH, which has existed from the first, is sowed everywhere.[a] •And
there are many who see it being sowed, but few who see it being reaped.   Mt 7:13
4+

(14)
Mary the virgin did not conceive by the holy spirit

23 SOME said that Mary conceived by the holy spirit: they are mistaken,

---

b. Ironic.

10 a. Cf. excerpt no. 43.
    b. I.e. the heavenly rulers, or a subdivision of them (cf. RR). In this passage the "forces" are equated with pagan deities. Many early Christians accepted the existence of pagan deities, but equated them with fallen angels (*daimones*) or spirits of wickedness.

12 a. Cf. excerpt no. 30.
    b. See note 10b.
    c. In classic gnostic scripture, "the entirety" is the sum of spiritual reality deriving from the second principle or Barbēlō aeon.

13 a. Cf. introduction to VFrG ("Contents and literary background").

25 they do not realize what they say. •When did a female[a] ever conceive by a female?[b]

27,28 Mary[c] is the virgin whom the forces did not defile. •Her existence is anathema to the Hebrews, meaning the apostles and apostolic persons.

31 This virgin whom the forces did not defile [. . .] forces defiled them(selves?).

(15)
The lord's two fathers

33 AND THE LORD [would] not say, "My [father who is in] the heavens," if [he] did not have a second father: rather, he would just have said, "[My father]."

(16)
The disciples should gather, not remove

37 THE LORD said to the disciples, "[. . .] from every house. **56** (104)
1,2 Gather (things) into the father's house; •but do not steal and remove (anything) while in the father's house."

(17)[a]
Names of Jesus Christ

3 "JESUS" is a private name,[b] "Christ (the anointed)" is a public name.[c]
5 Therefore "Jesus" does not exist (as a word) in any language, but
7 rather his name by which he is called is "Jesus." •But the word for Christ in Syriac is *messias,* and in Greek is *khristos,*[d] and probably all
12 the others have it according to the particular language of each. •"The Nazarene"[e] is the public name[f] of the private name.[g]

(18)
All are in Christ

13 THE ANOINTED (Christ) has each within him, whether human being or angel or mystery, and the father.

(19)
Resurrection must precede death

15 THOSE who say that the lord first died and then arose are mistaken,
18 for he first arose and then died. •If one does not first get[a] resurrection,   55, 79
19 one will not die. •As god lives![b] that person would[c] . . .   TRs 49:13

14 a. Mary. The Eastern branch of Valentinianism (see "Historical Introduction" to Part Three) accepted that "Mary conceived by the holy spirit" and that Jesus' body was a spiritual entity. In contrast, the Italic branch rejected this, holding that Jesus' body was of animate essence (IrPt 1.6.1), and that the holy spirit descended upon him at his baptism in the Jordan (IrPt 1.7.2). The Italic view seems to be reflected in this excerpt; cf. possibly also excerpt no. 72.

b. The holy spirit. In Syriac and other Semitic languages the word for "spirit" is usually grammatically feminine (this is not so in Greek), thus the author of this excerpt seems to presuppose an audience accustomed to the grammar of a Semitic language.

This excerpt may have been composed in a bilingual milieu.

c. Possibly a new excerpt begins here.

17 a. Cf. excerpt no. 40.
b. Or "personal name."
c. Or "epithet."
d. Christ, "the anointed."
e. Cf. notes 40b–d.
f. Or "epithet."
g. Or "personal name."

19 a. Or "produce."
b. A traditional oath to guarantee the truth or one's words, cf. Jg 8:19, 1 S 14:39, etc.
c. "that person would . . . ": One or more words are inadvertently omitted after "would" so that the sentence is incomplete.

(20)[a]
The precious hidden in the worthless

20 NO ONE would hide a precious expensive object within an expensive   IrPt 1.6.2
thing, yet often someone has kept vast sums in something worth a penny.
24 Such is the case with the soul: it is a precious thing, and it has come to
reside in a lowly body.

(21)
Eucharistic bread and resurrection

26 CERTAIN PERSONS are afraid that they may arise (from the dead)   26, 2Co 5:3
28,29 naked:[a] •therefore they want to arise in the flesh. •And they do not   TRs 47:1
31 know that those who wear the flesh are the ones who are naked.[b] •Those
32 who [. . .] to divest themselves are not naked. •"Flesh [and blood will   1Co 15:50
34 not] inherit the kingdom [of god]." •What is this flesh that will not
1,1 inherit it? 57 (105) •The one that we are wearing. •And what, too, is this
2 flesh that will inherit it? •It is Jesus' flesh, along with his blood.[c]
3   Therefore he said, "He who does not eat my flesh and drink my blood   Jn 6:53
5,6 does not have life within him." •What is meant by that? •His "flesh"
means the Word,[d] and his "blood" means the holy spirit: whoever has
9 received these has food, and has drink and clothing.[e] •For my part I
condemn (also) those others who say that the flesh will not arise.
10 Accordingly, both positions are deficient.[f]
11   (As to an imaginary discussant:) •You say that the flesh will not arise?[g]
12 Come now, tell me what element is going to arise, so I can congratulate
14 you! •You say it is the spirit that resides within the flesh, and also the
15 light that is within the flesh?[h] •This thing "that also is within the flesh"
16 is the Word (or teaching or rational faculty); •for what you are talking
18 about is none other than flesh![i] •It is necessary to arise in this kind of
19 flesh,[j] since everything exists in it. •In this world those who wear
21 garments[k] are superior to the garments; •in the kingdom of heavens the
garments are superior to those who put them on.

(22)
Baptism and chrism

22 BY WATER[a] and fire the entire place is sanctified—the visible (elements
25 of it) by the visible, the hidden by the hidden. •Some (elements) are
27 hidden by the visible: •there is water within water, there is fire within
chrism.

20 a. Cf. excerpt no. 41.

21 a. "naked": without a fleshly covering.
It was a Platonist cliché to compare the body
to a garment.
  b. I.e. those who have only the material
flesh are lacking ("naked of") what might
bring them resurrection. The point is developed below.
  c. The elements of the eucharist.
  d. Or "rational faculty, teaching."
  e. I.e. is "clothed" in the Word.
  f. Position (1) maintains that material flesh
will arise; position (2), that there is no sense
in which "flesh" will arise. The author maintains (3) that only Jesus' "flesh" in the sense
of the eucharistic bread (the "Word," "life")
arises; by partaking of it and "wearing" it
the Christian can "arise."

  g. For the debative style of this passage,
the so-called "diatribe style," cf. TRs, "Literary background."
  h. The author attacks a fourth position
(for which see TRs), namely that only the
spirit arises; and retorts that the way in which
the spirit is obtained is within the eucharistic
bread or "flesh," here equated with the
"Word."
  i. "flesh": in the sense of the eucharistic
element.
  j. The Word.
  k. I.e. fleshly bodies, cf. note 21a.

22 a. Probably referring to baptismal water,
since "chrism" (an oil of anointment used
in the baptismal ceremony) is mentioned
below.

(23)
Jesus' many appearances

28 JESUS tricked everyone, for he did not appear as he was, but appeared
32 in such a way that he could be seen. •And he appeared to all of them—
he [appeared] to [the] great as someone great, he appeared [to] the small
as someone small, he [appeared] [to the] angels as an angel and to human
2 beings as a human being. 58 (106) •For this reason he hid his discourse
3 from everyone. •Some saw him and thought they were seeing their own
5 selves.[a] •But when he appeared to his disciples in glory upon the   TRs 48:6
8 mountain he was not small, (for) he became great: •or, rather, he made
the disciples great so that they might be able to see that he was great.

(24)
Our union with the angels

10 HE SAID that day in the prayer of thanksgiving,[a] "O you who have
joined the perfect light with the holy spirit, join the angels with us, too,   53, 59, 60, 68,
as images."   73, 83, 105, 107
                                                                                 IrPt 1.7.1

(25)
The lamb and the door of the fold

14 DO NOT despise the lamb, for without it one cannot see the door.[a]   Jn 10:7

(26)
Encounter with the king

15 NO ONE can encounter the king while naked.   21+

(27)
The offspring of the perfect human being

17 THE HEAVENLY person has many offspring, more than the earthly.
18 If the offspring of Adam are many and yet die, how much more numerous
are the offspring of the perfect human being, who do not die but are   2+
22 being born at every moment! •A parent makes children and a (young)   IrPt 1.7.5
24 child is powerless to make children. •For one who has (recently) been
26 born cannot be a parent: rather, a child gets brothers, not children. •All
28 those born in the world are born from the natural order. •And the others
31 here [are nourished] from that whence they are born. •Human beings
33 [take nourishment] from the promise of the heavenly place. •[. . .] from
the mouth, [and if] the Word[a] had emanated from there, he[b] would be
2 nourished from the mouth, and would be perfect. 59 (107) •For it is
3 through a kiss that the perfect conceive and give birth. •For this reason
5 we too kiss one another: •it is by the grace residing in one another that
we conceive.

---

23 a. Cf. "The model of divine twinship" 10:7f). Some scholars emend "door" to
in the "Historical Introduction" to Part "king," referring to excerpt 26.
Four.

27 a. Greek *Logos*, as in Jn 1:1.
24 a. Greek lit. "eucharist."   b. Or "it."

25 a. I.e. the gate of the sheepfold (cf. Jn

(28)
The three Marys

6 THREE WOMEN always used to walk with the lord—Mary his mother,
10 his sister, and the Magdalene, who is called his companion. •For "Mary"
is the name of his sister and his mother, and it is the name of his partner.

(29)
Names of the trinity

11 "FATHER" and "son" are simple names: "holy spirit" is a two-part
13 name. •For they exist[a] everywhere—above, below; in the hidden, in the
16 visible. •The holy spirit is in the visible, and in the below; and in the
hidden, and in the above.

(30)[a]
The holy spirit active in evil forces

18,20 THE HOLY are ministered to by evil forces:[b] •for the latter have been
blinded by the holy spirit so that while they help the holy they think
that the ones they help are human beings who belong to them.
23   Thus[c] a disciple once asked the lord about a matter concerning the
25 world. •He said to him, "Ask your mother, and she will give (it) to you 14
from out of the alien realm."

(31)
Wisdom the salt of offerings to god

27 THE APOSTLES said to the disciples, "May all of our offering get
30 salt!" •They were referring [to wisdom] as "salt." Without it[a] no offering Lv 2:13
31,32 is acceptable. •Now wisdom [is] barren, [without] offspring. •For this
34 reason, [she] is called "[. . .] . . . of the salt." •Wherever [. . .] can
1 [. . .] like them, the holy spirit [. . .], 60 (108) •[and] many are her
offspring.   2+

(32)
The child's inheritance

1,2 WHAT a father owns belongs to his child. •And so long as the child, 2+
4 too, is little, it will not be entrusted with its own. •When the child grows
up, its father will give it all that it owns.

(33)
The spirit gives birth

6 IT IS the ones who have gone astray that the spirit gave birth to. 2+
7,8 Moreover, they go astray because of the spirit. •Thus from one and the
same spirit the fire is kindled and is quenched.

---

29 a. Or "they are such."   c. Possibly a new excerpt begins here.

30 a. Cf. excerpt no. 12.   31 a. Or "her."
  b. The heavenly rulers, the spirits of
wickedness.

(34)
Ekhamōth and ekh-mōth

10,11 EKHAMŌTH[a] is one thing; and ekh-mōth,[b] another. •Ekhamōth refers   IrPt 1.4.1
12 to wisdom proper; •But ekh-mōth, to the wisdom of death—that is, the
wisdom who is acquainted with death, and who is called the little
wisdom.

(35)
Plowing with domesticated animals

15 SOME animals are domesticated by human beings, such as the calf, the
17 donkey, and so forth. •Others are undomesticated and live apart in
19 uninhabited areas. •Human beings plow the fields with domesticated
animals, and as a result both they and the animals, whether domesticated
23 or undomesticated, are nourished. •Just so, the perfect human being
plows with domesticated forces, preparing everything to come to pass.
26 For thus does the whole place stand at rest[a]—the good and the evil, the
28 right and the left. •The holy spirit pastures each and rules [all] the forces,
32 whether domesticated or undomesticated and living apart. •For it [. . .]
shut(s) them in, so that if [it] wishes,[b] they might not get [out].

(36)
Cain

34 [THE ONE who] was modeled[a] was beautiful, [but] his offspring were
1 ⟨not⟩[b] like noble modeled forms.[c] **61** (109) •If he had not been modeled
3 but rather born, his posterity would be like what is noble. •But as a
4 matter of fact he was modeled, and then produced offspring. •What sort
6 of nobility is this?[d] First adultery occurred,[e] then murder! •And he[f] was
8 born of adultery; for he was the son of the snake.[g] •Therefore he became   Jn 8:44
10 a murderer like his father,[h] and slew his brother. •Every act of sexual
intercourse that has occurred between beings that do not resemble one
another is adultery.

(37)[a]
God's dyes

12,13 GOD is a dyer. •Just as the good dyes called "true" dyes dissolve into
the things that have been dyed in them, even so the things that god has
dyed become imperishable[b] through his colors, inasmuch as his dyes are
19 imperishable.[c] •Yet those whom god dips, he dips[d] in water.

---

34 a. I.e. Achamōth, biblical Hebrew *hokh-mōth* (Pr 8–9), "wisdom." In Ptolemaean Valentinianism, Achamōth is the name of lower wisdom, as opposed to Sophia; cf. IrPt.
   b. I.e. ʾēkh-mōth, "like death" (biblical and Mishnaic Hebrew and Aramaic).

35 a. To "stand at rest" is philosophical jargon for the state of permanence, non-change, and real being, as opposed to what exists in instability, change, and becoming.
   b. Or "[they] wish."

36 a. Adam.
   b. This word is inadvertently omitted in the MS.

c. "modeled form": Jewish and Christian jargon for the human body, based on the fact that the creator modeled Adam out of earth.
   d. Sarcastic.
   e. In classic gnostic scripture, Cain is often said to have been begotten by the adulterous intercourse of the chief ruler and Eve, cf. BJn 24:8f.
   f. Cain.
   g. The snake is identified with the chief ruler.
   h. The snake.

37 a. Cf. excerpt no. 47.
   b. Or "colorfast."
   c. Or "fast."
   d. Or "baptizes."

(38)

Only like can see like

20 PEOPLE cannot see anything in the real realm unless they become it.
23 In the realm of truth, it is not as human beings in the world, who see
the sun without being the sun, and see the sky and the earth and so
27 forth without being them. •Rather, if you have seen any things there,
you have become those things: if you have seen the spirit, you have
become the spirit; if you have seen the anointed (Christ), you have
become the anointed (Christ); if you have seen the [father, you] will
32 become the father. •Thus [here] (in the world), you see everything and
34 do not [see] your own self. •But there, you see yourself; for you shall
[become] what you see.

(39)

Faith and love

36,36 FAITH receives, love gives. •[No one can receive] without faith, no
2 one can give without love. 62 (110) •Thus in order to receive we believe,
3 and in order to love we give. •For if one gives without love, one has no
5 profit from what one has given. •Anyone who has received something
other than the lord is still a Hebrew.

(40)[a]

Names of Jesus Christ

6 THE APOSTLES before us used to employ the terms "Jesus the
Nasoraean[b] Messias," which means "Jesus the Nasoraean the Christ
9 (anointed)." •The last name is "Christ (anointed)," the first name is
11 "Jesus," the middle name is "the Nazarene."[c] •*Messias* has two
13 meanings, "Christ (anointed)" and "the measured."[d] •"Jesus" in
14 Hebrew means "ransom." •*Nazara* means "truth," thus "the Nazarene" 5+
15 means "truth." •It is the anointed (Christ) whom they have measured
out:[e] it is the Nazarene and Jesus[f] who have been measured out.

(41)[a]

The pearl in the mud

17,20 IF A PEARL is cast into the mud, it will not be less valuable. •Also, IrPt 1.6.2
21 if it is anointed with balsam it will not become more valuable. •Rather,
23 it always has its value for its owner. •Just so, the children of god still 2+
have their value for their father, whatever the circumstances in which
they live.

---

40 a. Cf. excerpt no. 17.

  b. Greek *nazōraios*. In antiquity this Christian term was sometimes taken to mean "person from Nazareth," i.e. Nazarene (as below); and sometimes, "one who is (religiously) observant." Cf. BJn 1:13f.

  c. Greek *Nazarēnos*, "person from Nazareth."

  d. Two meanings of Syriac *mšīḥā* ("Messias"): (1) "anointed" or "Christ"; (2) "measured."

  e. Or "who has been measured out." The text may be corrupt here; more logical might be "who measured them out."

  f. I.e. truth and ransom.

41 a. Cf. excerpt no. 20.

(42)

The name Christian

26,27 IF YOU say, "I am a Jew," no one will tremble. •If you say, "I am a   Col 3:11
28 Roman," no one will be bothered. •If you say, "I am a Greek—or a
31 barbarian, a slave, free" no one will be disturbed. •If you [say], "I am
32 a Christian," the [. . .] will shake. •If only I could [. . .] this sort, who
[. . .] cannot bear to [hear] his name.

(43)[a]

Sacrifice to god

35,1 GOD is a cannibal. **63** (111) •Therefore, human beings are [sacrificed]
2 to him. •Before human beings were sacrificed, animals used to be
sacrificed, because those to whom they were sacrificed were not gods.

(44)

Glass and ceramics

5,7 GLASS and ceramic vessels are produced with fire, •but if glass vessels
break they are remade, since they have been produced by means of
blown air;[a] while if ceramic vessels break they perish, since they have
been produced without blowing.

(45)

A donkey at a millstone

11,13 A DONKEY turning a millstone did a hundred miles of walking. •When
15 it was let loose it found itself still in the same place. •There are people
who do much traveling and make no progress toward anywhere: when
evening falls they have seen neither cities nor villages nor constructions
nor the natural order nor forces nor angels—the wretches have labored
in vain.

(46)

The name of the eucharist

21,21 THE EUCHARIST is Jesus. •Now, in Syriac it is called *pharisatha,*[a]
24 that is, "that which is spread out."[b] •For Jesus came to crucify[c] the   Ga 6:14
world.   GTr 24:20
IrPt 1.3.5

(47)[a]

The lord's dyes

25 THE LORD entered the dye works of Levi, and took seventy-two hues
27,28 and cast them into the caldron. •He brought them all out white. •And
he said, "For this did the child of the human being[b] come—to be a
dyer."

---

43 a. Cf. excerpt no. 10.

44 a. Or "spirit."

46 a. The Syriac word meant "broken bread" and was a liturgical term for the host, the bread of the eucharistic sacrament. In ancient

Christianity the host was sometimes called "the eucharist."
b. Another meaning of the Syriac word.
c. I.e. "spread out" on the cross.

47 a. Cf. excerpt no. 37.
b. Or "the son of man," a traditional Christian epithet of the heavenly savior.

(48)

Jesus and Mary Magdalene

30 THE WISDOM who is called barren wisdom is the mother [of the]
32,34 angels. •And the companion of the [. . .] Mary Magdalene. •The [. . .
loved] her more than [all] the disciples, [and he used to] kiss her on her
1 [. . . more] often than the rest of the [disciples] [. . .] **64** (112) •They
2 said to him, "Why do you love her more than all of us?" •The savior
answered, saying to them, "Why do I not love you like her? If a blind
person and one with sight are both in the darkness, they are not different
7 from one another. •When the light comes, then the person with sight
will see the light, and the blind person will remain in the darkness."

(49)

The preexistent is blessed

9 THE LORD said, "Blessed is that which existed before it came[a] into
existence. For the existent came into existence, and will exist."

(50)

Human beings dominate other animals

12 THE SUPREMACY of human beings is not externally apparent, but
14 rather resides in a hidden faculty. •For this reason they dominate animals
that are stronger than they and larger in external appearance and hidden
17,17 capacity. •And this enables them to survive. •But when human beings
20 withdraw from them they kill and devour one another. •And they ate
one another because they did not find food; but now they have found
food because human beings have worked the land.

(51)

Baptism and the name Christian

22 ANYONE who goes down into the water[a] and comes up without having
received anything and says, "I am a Christian," has borrowed the name.
25,27 But one who receives the holy spirit has the gift of the name. •Anyone
28 who has received a gift will not have it taken away. •But one who has
29 borrowed something will have it taken back. •So it is with us, if something
comes to pass through a mystery.

(52)

Marriage

31 [THE] MYSTERY of marriage [is] a great mystery, for [without] it the
33,34 world would [not] exist. •For [the] structure of [the world] [. . .] •But
35 the structure [. . .] marriage. •Consider the sexual intercourse [. . .]
37 pollute(s), for it possesses [. . .] force(s). •It is in pollution that its image
resides.

---

49 a. Or "the person who existed before   **51** a. In baptism.
coming."

(53)
Bridal chamber: androgyny protection against unclean spirits

1 **65** (113) AMONG the shapes of unclean spirits there are male ones and
3 female ones. •It is male spirits that have sexual intercourse with souls
who conduct their lives within a female shape, and female ones that
7 mingle promiscuously with those within a male shape. •And no one can
escape if seized by them, unless by taking on a male or female power,
11 namely (one's) bridegroom or bride. •Now, one takes on this power
12 from the imaged bridal chamber. •Whenever foolish female (spirits) see
a male sitting by himself they leap upon him and fondle him and pollute
15 him. •So also when foolish male ones see a beautiful woman sitting
alone they seduce her and do violence to her in order to pollute her.
19 But when they see a man and his wife sitting together, the female ones
cannot make advances to the male, nor can the male ones make advances
23 to the female. •Just so, if the image and the angel join with one another   24 +
none can dare to make advances to the male or the female.

(54)
The person who has left the world

27 AND WHOEVER leaves the world will no longer be restrained as   TRs 45:36 +
29 though (?) in the world. •This person obviously is above desire [. . .
32 and] fear, dominates [. . .], and is superior to envy. •If [. . .] then that
33 person is seized and strangled. •And how can that person escape the
35,36 [great] forces[a] [. . .]? •How can that person [. . .]? •There are some
people who [say], "We are faithful," in order that [. . .] [unclean]
2 spirit(s) and demons. **66** (114) •For if they possessed the holy spirit, no
4 unclean spirit could attach itself to them. •Do not fear the flesh or love
5 it. •If you fear it, it will dominate you; if you love it, it will swallow you
up and strangle you.

(55)
We must acquire resurrection now

7 AND THAT person will exist either in the present world or in resurrection   IrPt 1.6.4
9 or in the place in between—god forbid I should be found there! •Within
11 the present world, (reputedly) there is good and there is evil, •(but) the
12,13 world's goods are not (really) good, •and its evils not (really) evil.[a] •But
after this world, there are evils that are truly evil—the thing called
15,16 "midpoint." •It is death. •While we exist in this world we must acquire   IrPt 1.7.1 +
resurrection, so that when we put off the flesh we might be found in   19 +
20 repose and not walk in the midpoint: •for many get lost along the way.

(56)[a]
Sin and righteousness

21,23 IT IS good to leave the world before a person commits sin. •There are
24 some who neither want to nor can; •and others for whom, even if they
26 wanted to, there would be no use, for they have not acted •since [. . .]
27 act of will makes them sinners. •But if they do not want to, righteousness
29 will be hidden from them in both cases. •And [it is] always a matter of
the will, not the action.

54 a. The heavenly rulers, the spirits of   56 a. The translation of this excerpt is un-
wickedness.   certain.

55 a. Cf. excerpts nos. 6, 23, 88.

(57)

An apostolic vision of hell

29 IN A VISION, an apostolic person saw certain people imprisoned in a
house of fire and bound with fiery [. . .], lying [. . .] fiery [. . .] them in
34 [. . .] faith [. . .]. •And they said to them [. . .] them able to rescue[a]
36 [. . .] they did not wish. •They received [. . .] punishment that is called
1 the [. . .] darkness. 67 (115) •For it [. . .].

(58)

Otherworldly fire

2,3 SOUL AND SPIRIT are constituted of water and fire; •a bridegroom's
5 attendant[a] is constituted of water,[b] fire, and light. •Fire is chrism; light
is fire—I do not mean worldly fire, which has no form, but another kind
of fire, whose appearance is white, which is beautifully luminous, and
which bestows beauty.

(59)

Resurrection an image of the return

9 TRUTH did not come to the world nakedly; rather, it came in prototypes
11,12 and images: •the world will not accept it in any other form. •Rebirth
13 exists along with an image of rebirth: •by means of this image one must
14,15 be truly reborn. •Which image? Resurrection. •And image must arise by
16 means of image. •By means of this image, the bridal chamber and the   24+
image must embark upon the realm of truth, that is, embark upon the
19 return.[a] •Not only must those who produce the names of father, son,   TRs 44:30+
21 and holy spirit do so, but also ⟨those who⟩[b] have acquired these. •If
someone does not acquire them, the name too will be taken from that
23,24 person. •But if one gets them in the chrism of [. . .] •of the force of the
26 cross, which the apostles called right and left. •For this person is no
longer a Christian but rather is Christ (anointed).

(60)

The five sacraments

27 THE LORD [did] all things by means of a mystery: baptism, chrism,
eucharist, ransom, and bridal chamber.[a]   5+, 24+

(61)

Innermost, outer, and outermost

30 [. . .] said, "I have come to make [the lower] like the [upper and the]   GTh 22
outer like the [inner, and to join] them in [. . .] here by means of
36 prototype(s) [. . .]." •Those who say that [there is a heavenly person
38 and] one who is still higher [are] mistaken: •[for] they call the visible
2 heavenly [person] "lower"; 68 (116) •and maintain that the one to whom

---

57 a. Or "able to be rescued."

58 a. Or "a son of the bridal chamber."
   b. Baptismal water.

59 a. Or "return from exile." The Greek
word (*apokatastasis*) is Valentinian jargon

for the return of the self to its true home
within the fullness.
   b. These words are inadvertently omitted
in the MS.

60 a. See the "Index of keywords and
themes" in the introduction to GPh.

4 the hidden realm belongs is still higher. •Now, it would be better if they
6 spoke of inside, outside, and what is outside the outside. •Thus the lord
called corruption "outer(most) darkness," so that nothing exists outside
8,9 of it. •He said, "My father who is in secret."ᵃ •He said, "Go into your
room and shut the door and pray to your father who is in secret," that
13 is, the one who is innermost of all. •Now, what is innermost of all is
14,15 the fullness. •Beyond that, there is nothing further within. •This is what
is called the uppermost.

Mt 8:12 ?
Mt 22:13 ?
Mt 25:30 ?
v.9
Mt 6:6

(62)

Fall and return of the spiritual element

17 BEFORE the anointed (Christ), certain beings came from a realm that
they could not reenter,ᵃ and went to a realmᵇ that they could not yet
20 leave. •Then the anointed (Christ) came: he brought out those who had
enteredᶜ and brought inᵈ those who had left.

(63)

Separation of Eve from Adam

22,24 IN THE DAYS when Eve was [in] Adam,ᵃ death did not exist. •When
24 she was separated from him, death came into existence. •If he [reenters]
and takes itᵇ unto himself death will not exist.

GTh 22
GTh 106
GTh 114

(64)

The crucifixion

26,27 "[MY] GOD, my god, why O lord hast thou forsaken me?" •He spoke
these words on the cross; for he [had] withdrawn from that place.

Mk 15:34
Mt 27:46
IrPt 1.7.2

(65)

29,31 [. . .] born from [. . .] by god. •The [. . .] from the dead [. . .] exist(s),
but [. . .] is perfect [. . .] flesh, but [. . .] it is genuine flesh [. . .] is not
genuine; rather [. . .] image of the genuine one.

(66)

The bridal bedroom

1 **69** (117) ANIMALS have no bridal bedroom,ᵃ nor do slaves or defiled
3 women. •Rather, free men and virgins have one.

(67)

Baptism

4,6 WE ARE reborn by the holy spirit. •And we are born by the anointed
7,8 (Christ) through two things. •We are anointed by the spirit. •When we

---

61 a. Or "in the hidden realm."

62 a. I.e. spiritual seeds came from the fullness (IrPt 1.5.6, 1.7.5).
  b. The material realm outside the outer
boundary (IrPt 1.2.4).
  c. I.e. entered into the lower material
realm.
  d. I.e. back into the fullness.

63 a. When the two were joined in the beginning as an androgyne; cf. RAd 64:22f (with
note 64k).
  b. Or "him."

66 a. "bridal bedroom": or "wedding bed."
In GPh this Greek word is distinct from the
one translated "bridal chamber" but is used
with roughly the same meaning.

8 were born we were joined. •No one can see himself in the water or in
10 a mirror without light. •Nor, again, can you see by the light without
12 water or a mirror. •For this reason it is necessary to baptize with two
13 things—light and water. •And light means chrism.

(68)ᵃ
An allegory of the Temple: baptism, ransom, bridal chamber

14,15 THERE were three offering places in Jerusalem:ᵇ •one opening to the
17 west and called the holy; •another open to the south and called the holy
19 of the holy; •the third open to the east and called the holy of holies,
22 into which the high priest alone could enter. •The holy building is
baptism, the holy of the holy is ransom, the holy of holies is the bridal 24+
25 chamber. •[Baptism] possesses resurrection [and] ransom; ransom is in 5+
27 the bridal chamber. •[The] bridal chamber is within what is superior to
[. . .] its [. . .] is like [. . .] those who pray [. . .] Jerusalem [. . .]
Jerusalem [. . .] Jerusalem, expecting [. . .] who are called [the holy] of
the holies [. . .] veil rent [. . .] bridal bedroom except for the image
1 [. . .] above. **70** (118) •Thus, its veil was torn from top to bottom,
because certain people from below had to ascend.

(69)ᵃ
The garment of light

5 THE FORCESᵇ do not see those who have put on the perfect light and
7 cannot seize them. •One will put on the light in a mystery, through the
act of joining.

(70)ᵃ
Reunion in the bridal chamber

9 IF THE FEMALE had not separated from the male, she and the male
11 would not die. •That being's separation became the source of death.
12 The anointed (Christ) came to rectify the separation that had been
15 present since the beginning •and join the two (components); and to give
17 life unto those who had died by separation and join them together. •Now,
19 a woman joins with her husband in the bridal bedroom, •and those who
20 have joined in the bridal bedroom will not reseparate. •Thus Eve became
separate from Adam because it was not in the bridal bedroom that she
joined with him.

(71)
Passage of the spirit into Adam

22,23 ADAM'S SOUL resulted from an act of blowing. •Its partner is the Gn 2:7
24,25 [spirit]. •The element that was imparted to him is his mother. •His soul IrPt 1.5.5
26 was [taken away] and he was given a [spirit in] its place. •When it had VFrC
become joined (to him) the forces envied him because [he] spoke words
29 superior to them •[. . .] spiritual partner [. . .] hidden [. . .] them alone
[. . .] bridal bedroom, so that [. . .].

---

68 a. Cf. excerpt no. 105.   b. The heavenly rulers, the spirits of
    b. In the Jewish Temple of god.   wickedness.

69 a. Cf. excerpt no. 90.

70 a. Cf. excerpt no. 63.

(72)
The arrival of Jesus in the world

34 JESUS appeared [. . .] Jordan, the fullness [of the] kingdom of heavens.
36 The person who [was born] before all things was reborn; the one anointed
in the beginning was reanointed; the one who had been ransomed 5+
ransomed others in turn.

(73)
The virgin birth

3,4 **71 (119)** •HOW FITTING it is to speak of a mystery! •The parent of
5 the entirety joined with the virgin who came down, •and fire illuminated
6,8 him. •On that day he revealed the great bridal bedroom; •it was for this 24+
9 purpose that his body came into being. •On that day he came forth from
the bridal bedroom as from what comes to pass between[a] a bridegroom
11 and a bride. •Just so, through these things Jesus made the entirety[b]
13 stand at rest[c] within it: •and it is fitting for each of the disciples to
proceed into his or her repose.

(74)
Virgin birth of Adam and Christ

16 ADAM came into being from two virgins: from the spirit and from the
18 virgin earth.[a] •The anointed (Christ) was born of a virgin so that he
might rectify the fall that occurred in the beginning.

(75)
The two trees of paradise

22 THERE are two trees growing in paradise: one produces [animals], the
24 other produces human beings. •Adam [ate] from the tree that had
26 produced animals; [he] became an animal and begot animals. •For this
28 reason the children of Adam worship the [animals].[a] •The tree [. . .]
fruit [. . .] they became numerous [. . .] ate the [. . .] [. . .] fruit [. . .]
begot human beings[b] [. . .] human beings [. . .] god made human beings
1 [. . .] human beings made god. **72 (120)** •Just so, in the world human
3 beings make gods and bow down to their products: •it would be more
fitting for the gods to worship human beings!

(76)
Deeds are forces

4 A PERSON'S deeds, insofar as they are real,[a] result from that person's
7,8 force: •thus deeds can be called "forces."[b] •Children are a kind of
8,9 "deed," •and furthermore they result from a moment of repose. •For
11 this reason, one's force is active within one's deeds. •But it is obviously

---

73 a. Or "as from what is born of."
  b. Cf. note 12c.
  c. Cf. note 35a.

74 a. Adam's name in biblical Hebrew is a pun on *adamah*, meaning "earth." This pun was widely known in Greek theological circles.

75 a. Egyptian religion was famous in antiquity for its animal-headed deities and was often the target of Christian criticism leveled against pagan religion in general.
  b. Or "begot [. . .] for humankind."

76 a. Or "true."
  b. Or "manifestations of power."

12 in children that repose is found. •And this extends, as it were, to the
14,15 image: •and that means, the imaged person. •It is by their own force
16 that imaged people perform their deeds, •and from repose that they
beget their offspring.

(77)
Servants and free in the kingdom of heavens

17,18 IN THIS WORLD servants help those who are free. •In the kingdom
20 of heavens the free will render service to the servants: •the bridegroom's
22 attendants will render service to the wedding guests. •The bridegroom's
24 attendants are in one and the same condition: repose. •Being assembled,
they have no need of transformation, [since they are engaged in]
26 contemplation [. . .]. •They are [. . .] in [. . .].

(78)
Baptism and righteousness

29 [. . .] go down into the water [. . .] ransom him [. . .] those who [. . .]
33 in his name. •For he said, "[It is thus] that we shall fulfill all right-   Mt 3:15
eousness."

(79)
One must acquire resurrection now through baptism

1 73 (121) PEOPLE who say they will first die and then arise are mistaken.   19+
3 If they do not first receive resurrection while they are alive, once they
5 have died they will receive nothing. •Just so it is said of baptism: "Great
7 is baptism!" •For if one receives it, one will live.

(80)
Joseph and the wood of the cross

8 PHILIP THE APOSTLE said: "Joseph the carpenter planted a paradise,[a]
11 for he needed wood for his trade. •It is he who made the cross from the
trees that he had planted, and its seed hung from what he had planted:
14,15 the seed was Jesus, and the plant was the cross. •But the tree of life is
17 in the midst of paradise,[b] •and from the olive tree comes chrism; and
from the latter comes resurrection."

(81)
Jesus the bringer of true food

19,20 THIS WORLD devours corpses: •everything eaten within it also dies.
21,22 The realm of truth devours life: •thus no one of those who live on [truth]
23,24 is dying. •From that realm did Jesus come, •and he brought food from
25 there.[a] •And he gave [life] to whoever wished it, so that they might not
die.

---

80 a. Or "a garden full of trees."   **81** a. Cf. excerpt no. 11.
    b. Or "of that paradise."

(82)
The new paradise

27,28,29 [GOD . . .] a paradise.[a] •Human beings [. . .] paradise. •[. . .] exist with
32,33 [. . .] god in [. . .]. •Those within [it . . .] wish. •That paradise [is where]
it will be said to me, "[. . . eat] this, or not, [according as you] like."
1 **74** (122) The place where I shall eat everything is where the tree of
acquaintance is located.
3,3 The other one[b] slew Adam. •But here the tree of acquaintance has
5,5 brought human beings to life. •The law was the tree.[c] •It is able to impart
7 acquaintance of good and evil; •and it neither made him (that is, Adam)
9 cease from evil nor allowed him to be in the good. •Rather, it made
10 death for those who ate of it. •For while it[d] was saying, "Eat this, do
not eat this," it became a source of death.

(83)
Chrism, baptism, bridal chamber

12,13 CHRISM has more authority than baptism. •For because of chrism we
15 are called Christians, not because of baptism. •And the anointed (Christ)
16,17 was named for chrism, •for the father anointed the son; •and the son
18 anointed the apostles, and the apostles anointed us. •Whoever has been   PtF 33.7.9
21 anointed has everything: resurrection, light, cross, holy spirit; •the father
has given it to that person in the bridal chamber, and the person has   24+
22 received (it). •The father existed in the son, and the son existed in the
24 father. •This [is the] kingdom of heavens.

(84)
Outward signs of the sacraments

24 WELL did the lord say, "Some have gone into the kingdom of heavens
26,28 laughing. •And they came out [. . .] for a Christian [. . .]. •And [. . . go]
down into the water,[a] [. . .] all [. . .] it is a trifle, but [. . .] despise [. . .]
kingdom of [heavens . . .] if he despises [. . .] and he despises it as a
36 trifle [. . .] forth laughing." •Just so are the bread and the cup[b] and the
oil,[c] even though there are ones higher than these.

(85)
The creation of the universe

2,4 **75** (123) •THE WORLD came into being through transgression. •For
the agent[a] that made it wanted to make it incorruptible and immortal.[b]
6,7 That agent fell, and did not attain what was expected. •For the world's
8 incorruptibility was not; •furthermore, the incorruptibility of the agent
10 that made the world was not. •For there is no such thing as the
11 incorruptibility of things—only of offspring (children). •And no thing
13 can receive incorruptibility unless it is an offspring: •that which cannot   2+
receive (it) certainly cannot bestow (it).

---

82 a. Or "garden."
     b. The other tree, i.e. the one in the
original paradise.
     c. The Coptic text may be corrupt here.
More logical would be "The (other) tree was
the law."
     d. Or "he."

84 a. In baptism.
     b. In the eucharist.
     c. In the sacrament of chrism.

85 a. The craftsman (in classic gnostic myth,
Ialdabaôth).
     b. Cf. BJn 12:33f.

(86)
Consecrated water in the eucharist and baptism

14,16 THE CUP of prayer[a] contains wine and contains water, •being established as a representation[b] of the blood over which thanksgiving is offered.
17,18 And it is full of the holy spirit, •and belongs entirely to the perfect
19 human being. •Whenever we drink it we take unto ourselves the perfect human being.

21,22 The living water[c] is a body. •It befits us to put on the living human
23 being;[d] •accordingly, when one is about to descend into the water,[e] one strips naked in order to put that one on.

(87)[a]

Like begets like

25 A HORSE begets horses, a human being begets human beings, deity 2+
27 begets deity. •Just so in the case of [both] bridegrooms and brides—
30,32 they are from the [. . .]. •[. . .] Jew(s) [. . .] exist(s). •And [. . .] from the Jews [. . .] Christian(s) [. . .] this place is called [. . .] the chosen people of the [. . .] and the true human being and the child of the human
3 being[b] and the posterity of the child of the human being.[c] **76** (124) •This true people is renowned in the world: here is where the bridegroom's attendants are.

(88)
There is neither power nor weakness in the eternal realm

6 IT IS in the world, where power and weakness exist, that the act of
8 joining between males and females occurs; •but in the eternal realm
9 there is a different sort of joining. •Although it is with these names[a] that
9,10 we refer to things, •yet other names also exist, •above every current 8+
12 name, indeed, above the most potent. •For where brute force exists
14 there are those who are superior to power. •These are not two different
16 things, rather one and the same. •It is this which is incomprehensible to hearts of flesh.

(89)

Self-acquaintance

17 SHOULD NOT all people who possess all things know themselves[a]
19 utterly? •Now, if some do not know themselves, they will not have the
21 use of what they possess; •but those who have learned about themselves will do so.

---

86 a. The eucharistic cup.
b. Or "symbol."
c. Many ancient Christians used running ("living") water, such as rivers or springs, in their baptismal ceremonies.
d. Traditional Christian baptismal liturgy spoke of "putting off" the old person and "putting on" Christ, like a garment; cf. Ga 3:27, Ep 4:22, Col 3:9f.
e. I.e. to be baptized.

87 a. Cf. excerpt no. 96.
b. Or "son of man," a traditional Christian epithet of the heavenly savior.
c. "posterity . . .": i.e. the Valentinians.

88 a. Or "words."

89 a. The Delphic maxim, "know thyself," expressed a central theme of traditional Greek wisdom.

(90)ᵃ

The garment of light

22,24 THE PERFECT human being not only cannot be restrained, •but also   TRs 45:36
24,25 cannot be seen—•for if something is seen it will be restrained. •In other
words, no one can obtain this grace without putting on the perfect lightᵇ
29 [and] becoming, as well, perfect light. •Whoever has [put it] on will go
30 [. . .]. •This one is the perfect [. . .] that we be [. . .] before we have
33 come [. . .]. •Whoever receives all things [. . .] hither, can [. . .] there,
1 but will [. . . the] midpoint, as being imperfect. **77** (125) •Only Jesus is   IrPt 1.7.1 +
acquainted with that person's end!

(91)

The holy person's body

2 THE HOLY person is utterly holy, even including that person's body.
3 Such a person, if picking up bread, makes it holy—likewise the cupᵃ
or any of the other things which that person picks up and sanctifies.
6 And why would such a person not sanctify also the body?

(92)

Baptism and death

7 JUST AS Jesus perfected the water of baptism, so too he drew offᵃ
9,10 death. •For this reason we go down into the water •but not into death,
12 so that we are not poured out into the windᵇ of the world. •Whenever
14 the latter blows, winter comes: •whenever the holy spiritᶜ blows, summer   4 +
comes.

(93)

Acquaintance (gnōsis) brings freedom

15,17 ONE who possesses acquaintance with the truth is free, •and the free   Jn 8:32
17 person does not sin: •for, "one who commits sin is the slave of sin."   IrPt 1.6.2 +
  Jn 8:34
19,20 Truth is the mother, acquaintance the father. •Those who are not fated
22 to sin the world calls free. •As for those who are not fated to sin,
25 "acquaintance" with truth "puffs up"ᵃ—that is, makes them free, •and   1Co 8:1
25 it makes them "puffed up" as regards the whole place—•"but love
26 builds up." •Now, whoever has become free through acquaintance is a
slave on account of love toward those who have not yet taken up [the]
29 freedom of acquaintance. •[And] acquaintance makes them capable of
31 becoming free. •Love [never says] that anything [. . . belongs] to it [. . .]
33 belongs to it. •It does not [say, "This is mine"] or "That is mine," [but
rather "All my] own are yours."

(94)

The fragrance of spiritual perfume

35,36 SPIRITUAL love is wine and perfume. •Those who anoint themselves   GTr 33:33
with it all have the use of it, as do also those who are outside their

---

90 a. Cf. excerpt no. 69.
   b. The image of a garment of light, which
the Christian "puts on" (cf. note 86d), was
traditional especially in Syrian Christianity.

91 a. "bread . . . cup": the eucharistic elements.

92 a. Or "poured out."
   b. Or "spirit."
   c. Or "wind."

93 a. Meant in a good sense, perhaps "fills
(them) up with spirit."

4 company so long as the anointed ones stand there. **78** (126) •When those anointed with ointment leave them and depart, the ones who are not anointed but are only outside their company still remain within their
7 fragrance. •The Samaritan gave nothing to the man who had been beaten   Lk 10:33
10 except wine and oil, which means none other than ointment. •And it
11 healed the wounds, •"since love covers a multitude of sins."   1P 4:8

(95)
Children are like what the parent loves

12 THE CHILDREN that a woman produces will resemble the man she
13 loves. •If it is her husband, they resemble her husband; if it is an
15 adulterer, they resemble the adulterer. •Many times if a woman is constrained to sleep with her husband but her heart is set on the adulterer with whom she has intercourse, the child she bears will resemble the
20 adulterer. •You (plur.) then, who live with the son of god, do not love
22 the world: •rather, love the lord, so that those whom you produce might come to resemble not the world but rather the lord.

(96)ᵃ
Like mixes with like

25 HUMAN BEINGS mixᵇ with human beings, horses mix with horses,
27 donkeys mix with donkeys: •members of a species mix [with] their
28,29 fellow members. •Just so, it is with spirit that spirit mixes, •and rational
31 facultyᶜ has intercourse with rational faculty, •[and] light has intercourse
32 [with light.] •If [you (sing.)] become human, it is [human beings] that
33,34 [will] love you; •if you become [spirit], spirit will join with you; •[if] you
1 become rational faculty, rational facultyᵈ will mix with you; **79** (127) •if
3 [you] become light, light will have intercourse with you: •if you become
5 the upper, the upper will repose on you. •If you become a horse or donkey or calf or dog or sheep or any of the other animals, wild or domesticated, neither human being nor spirit nor rational faculty nor
10 light will love you; •neither the upper nor the inner can repose in you,ᵉ
13 and you have no share in them.

(97)
Only unwilling slaves can become free

13,15 PEOPLE who are unwilling slaves can become free. •Those who have become free through the benefaction of their master, and then have sold themselves into slavery, cannot become free again.

(98)
A parable of agriculture

18,19 THE AGRICULTURE of the world results from four things: •a successful   4+
22 harvest results from water, earth, air, and light. •And the agriculture of god likewise results from four things: faith, hope, love, and acquaintance.
25,26 Our earth in which we take root is faith. •Water, by which [we are
28,29 nourished], is hope. •Air, by which we grow, is love. •And light [is]

---

96 a. Cf. excerpt no. 87.
  b. Or "breed."
  c. Or "Word" (as in Jn 1:1).

d. Or "Word."
e. Cf. excerpt no. 61.

31 acquaintance, by which we [ripen to maturity]. •Grace is [. . .] earthly.
33 It is [. . .] above heaven [. . .].

(99)
We should not favor the rich nor cause grief

33,1 [BLESSED] is he who has not [. . .]ᵃ anyone. 80 (128) •That means
1 Jesus Christ (the anointed); •he has encountered the whole place and
3 has not burdened anyone. •For this reason, blessed is such a person:
this person is a perfect human being.
4　Now,ᵇ the rational facultyᶜ tells us how difficult it is to accomplish
6,7 this. •How can we be successful at this great virtue? •How can it give
8 help to everyone? •Above all, one must not cause grief to any person—
whether important, ordinary, unbeliever, or believer—and then proceed
12 to give help to those who repose in luxury. •Some people profit by
13 giving help to those who are rich. •The person who does good will not
15 give help to the rich, •for ⟨the good person⟩ᵈ does not simply take up
16 whatever project is most pleasing. •On the other hand the doer of good,
by not causing the rich to be distressed, will not cause them any grief.
17,19 Of course, the newly rich will sometimes cause others distress. •But the
19 doer of good does not do this: •rather, it is others' imperfectionᵉ that
20 causes them grief. •One who has the nature (of a perfect human being)
22 bestows happiness upon the good. •Some people are badly distressed at
this.

(100)
A parable of appropriate diets

23 THE OWNER of an estate acquired all sorts of things—children, slaves,
cattle, dogs, hogs, wheat, barley, chaff, fodder, [. . .], meat, and acorns.
27,29 [Now], he was wise, and knew the food of each sort. •He fed the children
30,31 bread [. . .], •but he fed [the] slaves [. . . and] grain. •[He fed] the cattle
33 [barley], chaff, fodder; •he fed [the] dogs bones; he fed [the hogs] acorns
and slops.
1,2 81 (129) •Just so are the disciples of god: •if they are wise they are
3 perceptive about discipleship. •Bodily forms will not deceive them:
5 rather, what they consider is the condition of each person's soul, and
7 they speak with that person accordingly. •In the world there are many
8 animals that have a human form. •If the disciples of god recognize that
they are hogs, they feed them acorns; if cattle, barley, chaff, and fodder;
12,13 if dogs, bones; •if slaves, a first course (that is, a single dish); •if children, 2+
a complete meal.

(101)
Creators and begetters

14,15 THE CHILD of the human beingᵃ exists, •and the child of the child of 2+
16 the human being exists. •The child of the human being refers to the
17 lord, •and the child of the child of the human being refers to the one
19 who creates by the child of the human being. •The child of the human

99 a. Perhaps "[caused grief to]."
　b. The translation of this whole paragraph
is uncertain.
　c. Or "the Word" (as in Jn 1:1).
　d. Inadvertently omitted in the MS.

e. Or "evil."

101 a. Or "son of man," a traditional Christian epithet of the heavenly savior.

20 being received from god so that he might create: •he possesses so that
21 he might beget. •One who has received so as to create is a creature;
22,23 one who has received so as to beget is begotten. •A creator cannot
25 beget, (but) a begetter can create. •Of course, creators are said to
"beget," but what they "beget" are creatures. [. . .] their offspring are
28 not begotten [. . .], but rather are [. . .]. •A creator works [openly], and
30 is visible as well. •A begetter begets [secretly] and is hidden while [. . .]
32 the image. •A creator then [creates] visibly, while one who begets
[begets] offspring secretly.

(102)
Unpolluted marriage

34 NO [ONE can] know when [a male] and a female have intercourse with
2 one another but they alone. **82** (130) •For the marriage of this world is
4 a mystery for those who have married. •If the marriage of pollution is
6 hidden, how much more is unpolluted marriage a genuine mystery! •It
7 is not concerned with flesh, but rather is sanctified. •It belongs not to
8 desire but to will, •not to darkness or night but to daytime and light.
10,11 If a marriage is naked it has become fornication. •And the bride has
committed fornication not only if she accepts the sperm of a different
14 man, but even if she leaves her bedroom and is seen. •Let her appear
only to her father and her mother and the best man and the bridegroom's
17 attendants: •these are permitted to enter the bridal chamber every day.
19 But let the others desire merely to hear her voice and enjoy her (perfumed)
21 ointment, •and let them be nourished, like dogs, by the scraps beneath
23,24 the table. •Bridegrooms and brides belong to the bridal chamber. •No
one can see a bridegroom or a bride except by becoming such.

(103)
Abraham's circumcision

26 WHEN Abraham [. . .] to behold what he was going to behold, [he]   Jn 8:56 ?
28 circumcised the flesh of the foreskin, •telling us that it is fitting to mortify
the flesh.

(104)
Lack of acquaintance must be burrowed out from the heart

30 [MOST beings] of (this) world stand up and are alive in so far as their
32 [innards] are hidden. •[If the innards] are exposed they die, as in the
34 [case] of the visible aspect of human beings: •[in so far as] the intestines
1 of human beings are hidden, they are alive. **83** (131) •If their intestines
3 are uncovered and come out of them, human beings die. •Likewise,
4 trees sprout and grow (?) while their root is hidden. •If their root is   GTr 28:16
6 uncovered, the trees wither. •So it is with all begotten things in this
world, not only things that are visible but also those that are hidden.
8,9 For so long as the root of evil is hidden it is mighty. •But as soon as it
10 has been recognized it has perished, •and as soon as it has appeared it
11 has ceased to be. •For this reason scripture[a] says that "even now the   Mt 3:10
13 axe is laid to the root of the trees." •It will not (just) cut them down,   Lk 3:9
14 for what is cut down sprouts back up: •rather, the axe will burrow down
16 until it extracts the root. •And Jesus has weeded[b] the whole place, while
others did so one part at a time.

104 a. Or "the Word" (as in Jn 1:1).   b. Or "pulled out the root of."

18   Let each of us, too, burrow for the root of evil that is within, and
21 root it up from his or her heart. •It will be rooted up when it is recognized.   VFrH
22,24 But if we are ignorant of it, it sinks its root within us, •and yields its
25,26,26 crops within our hearts; •dominates us; •we are its slaves; •it takes us   Rm 7:14
28 captive, so that we do the things we do [not] want, •and do [not] do the
28 things that we want; •and [it] grows powerful because we have not
29 recognized it. •So long as [it exists] it is active.
30,32   Lack of [acquaintance] is the mother of [all evils]. •Lack of acquain-
32 tance will lead to [death]: •[for], those who existed as a result of the [lack
of acquaintance] neither (truly) existed nor [do exist] nor will exist.
35,2 [. . .] will become perfect when the whole truth appears. **84** (132) •For
4 like lack of acquaintance, truth reposes in itself while it is hidden. •But
when it appears and is recognized, it is glorified insofar as it overpowers
7,7 lack of acquaintance and error. •It bestows freedom. •The Word[c] said,
10 "If you know the truth, the truth will make you free." •Lack of   Jn 8:32
11 acquaintance is a slave: acquaintance is freedom. •If we become
13 acquainted with the truth, we shall find the fruits of truth within us. •If
we join with it, it will receive our fullness.

(105)[a]
An allegory of the Temple: entry into bridal chamber

14,15 AT PRESENT we have access to the visible aspects of creation. •We
16 say that they are what is mighty and glorious, •while hidden things are
17 powerless and contemptible. •Are the hidden aspects of truth like this?
18,19 Are they powerless? And are they contemptible? •No, rather these
hidden aspects are mighty, glorious.
20   Now, the mysteries of truth are manifestly representations[b] and images.
21,22 Thus the bedroom is hidden away: •this stands for[c] the holy within the
23,25 holy. •For, originally the veil concealed how god controls creation; •but
when the veil is torn[d] and what is inside appears, then this building will
29 be left desolate or, rather, be destroyed. •And all deity will flee from
30,31 here: •but it will not flee into the holy [of] holies, •for it cannot mix
33 with unalloyed [light] and the fullness[e] that has no [defect]. •Rather, it
34 will dwell under the wings of the cross, [and under] its arms. •This ark
will be [for people's] salvation when the watery flood rages over them.
1 **85** (133) If others belong to the tribe of the priesthood, they will be
5 able to enter inside the veil along with the high priest. •For this reason,
the veil was not torn only at the top—for then only the upper region
7 would be opened. •Nor was it only at the bottom that it was torn—for
10 then only the lower realm would be revealed. •Rather, it was torn from
10 top to bottom. •The upper realm was opened for us in the lower realm,
13 so that we might enter into the hidden realm of truth: •this is what is
14 truly glorious and mighty. •And it is through contemptible representa-
16 tions[f] and powerless things that we shall enter. •They are contemptible
17 compared to perfect glory—•there is glory superior to glory, and power
18 superior to power. •Thus perfect things were opened to us, along with
19 the hidden aspects of truth. •And the holies of holies was uncovered.
20 And the bedroom invites us in.   24+

c. Or "scripture."

105 a. Cf. excerpt no. 68.
b. Or "symbols."
c. "stands for": or "is."

d. Cf. 70:1f.
e. Valentinian jargon for the metaphysical universe.
f. Or "symbols."

(106)
Revelation of the spiritual seed

21 INSOFAR as the seed of the holy spirit is hidden, evil—though inert—
24 has not been removed from its midst, •and members of it are enslaved
24 to wickedness. •But when this seed is revealed, then perfect light will   TRs 49:2
27 stream forth upon each person, •and all who belong to it will [be]
28,29 anointed. •Then the slaves will be free [and] captives ransomed. •"Every   5+
plant that my father in the heavens has not planted [will be] rooted up."   Mt 15:13
4+
31 Those who are separated will join [. . .] will become full.

(107)
Reception of the garment of light[a]

32 EVERY PERSON who [enters] the bedroom will kindle the [light.]   24+
33,35 For [. . .] like the marriages that are [. . .] be night. •The fire [. . .]
1 night, is extinguished. **86** (134) •However, the mysteries of that marriage
3 are performed in day and light; •and that day, or rather its light, does
4 not set. •If someone becomes a bridegroom's attendant, that person will
6 receive the light. •If one does not receive it while here, one cannot
receive it elsewhere.
7   Whoever receives that light will be invisible and cannot be restrained.
9 And nothing can harass such a person even while living in the world.
11 And, furthermore, when that person leaves this world, he or she has
13 already received the truth in the form of images, •and the world has
14 already become the eternal realm. •For, to this person the eternal realm
15,16 is fullness •and, as such, is manifest to him or her alone—•hidden not
in darkness and night but hidden in perfect day and holy light.[b]

107 a. Cf. excerpts nos. 69 and 90.
b. In the manuscript, the title of this work
is written after the text (at 86:18f).

RELATED
WRITINGS

PART FOUR

THE SCHOOL OF ST. THOMAS

HISTORICAL INTRODUCTION

The apostle Thomas

Among the most intriguing works of ancient Christian literature are those associated with St. Didymus Jude Thomas, apostle of the East. According to ancient tradition Thomas deserves credit for the conversion of northern Mesopotamia and India to Christianity, and had the signal honor of being Jesus' "double," i.e. identical twin. He is the same apostle to whom the New Testament Epistle of Jude is attributed (there he is called "brother of James"—thus, since James was Jesus' brother, the brother of the brother of Jesus). Two of the works included in Part Four—*The Gospel According to Thomas* (GTh) and *The Book of Thomas* (BTh)—have Thomas as their central human character. A third, *The Hymn of the Pearl* (HPrl), is found incorporated in a longer work called *The Acts of Thomas*; in one episode of the *Acts* this hymn is chanted by St. Thomas while languishing in an Indian prison.

The model of divine twinship

Although ancient literature often refers to him simply as Thomas, the central component of the apostle's name is Jude (or Judas, for the two names are different English translations of the same Greek form). "Didymus" and "Thomas," though eventually used as proper names, also had the ordinary meaning of "twin," the one in Greek, the other in Syriac (Aramaic). In the Thomas tradition, Thomas is explicitly called Jesus' "brother" and "double" (BTh 138:7f, 138:19f).

The twin motif was important in the ancient literary genre called the "romance." But in the Thomas tradition, far from being only a romantic exaggeration, this relationship provided a profound theological model for the reciprocal relationship of the individual Christian and the inner divine light or "living Jesus": to know oneself was to know one's divine double and thence to know god; to follow the living Jesus was to know and integrate one's self (BTh 138:7–19f). Thus the twinship and companionship of Jesus and Thomas metaphorically expressed a general model of salvation through acquaintance (*gnōsis*) with god, emphasizing both practical discipleship and self-awareness. Belief in the identity of these three—the individual self, the inner source of divine inspiration (Jesus), and god in the most universal sense (the father)—links the Thomas literature with other bodies of scripture in this book, especially the writings of Valentinus (GTr) and his school (TRs). *The Gospel According to Thomas* also emphasizes that the divine light or kingdom of light is not only a distinct realm and power with which the individual Christian must reunite, but also a reality around and within every person and thing (GTh 3, 70, 77). If, as many scholars maintain, GTh is older than the time of Valentinus, then this doctrine anticipates Valentinus's concept of a heavenly father who contains all believers and, through his son, is within all believers.

The myth of origins

Despite these parallels the Thomas literature shows no unmistakable signs of being Valentinian or classically gnostic. Instead, it presupposes only an uncomplicated Hellenistic myth of the divine origins of the self; conceives of god as unitary; does not discuss the alleged error of wisdom; puts no stress on revisionistic retelling of the myth of Genesis; and does not teach about an ignorant maker of the world. Also unlike gnostic and Valentinian myth, it does not speak of a future time in history when the forces of evil will be destroyed and the just rewarded; rather, god's kingdom comes now and is already present. This mythic understanding is most integrally expressed in *The Hymn of the Pearl,* but it is also clear in BTh and GTh (cf. the introduction to HPrl, Table 4).

According to this myth, the individual true self (spirit, soul, living element) "has come from" or "has been sent from" the "kingdom of light" in the East, i.e. belongs to the spiritual world. It now resides within a realm, i.e. a state, of "sleep, drunkenness, darkness, and death," whose rulers are malevolent authorities ("Pharisees, Scribes, Babylonian children, tyrannical demons of the Labyrinth"). By the will of the "king" or "father" a savior (Jesus), or a personified message, is sent to awaken, sober up, illuminate, and vivify the self, which learns to recognize itself and to distinguish between light and darkness. The savior's message causes the self to return to its proper home (the kingdom), i.e. to its proper state; this home is described as being partly elsewhere, i.e. distinct from the realm of darkness etc., and partly within the individual person. The practical consequences of the myth are seen to be ascetic disengagement from the realm of darkness and from legalistic adherence to the religious law of the authorities.

The myth of the soul is to some extent compatible with more complex systems like the gnostic or Valentinian myth, just as *The Gospel of Truth* was able to be read together with Valentinus's system of aeons. However, it does not necessarily presuppose such a system.

The cultural milieu

Although works of the school of St. Thomas circulated also in Egypt— where they could have been known to Valentinus in his formative years—

scholars usually consider that they were written in Syria or Mesopotamia, possibly in Edessa, a city of northern Mesopotamia (see Map 6).

Several arguments have been suggested in favor of this localization of the school of St. Thomas.

1. Mesopotamia is part of the geographical area traditionally associated with the wanderings of the saint, especially according to *The Acts of Thomas*. The young prince who is protagonist in HPrl sets out from this general region.
2. *The Acts of Thomas* (including HPrl, which forms a part of it) was transmitted in the Syriac language as well as Greek; for technical reasons most specialists hold that Syriac must have been the original language of its composition.
3. At least by the end of the fourth century, the church of Edessa possessed as a relic the bones of St. Thomas; they were seen there by Egeria, a Christian lady from France or Spain, on April 19, 384, and mentioned in her travel diary, which survives to this day.
4. The ethos of the texts suggests a region where a Syrian form of Christianity was present, and certain details such as references to wandering ascetics anticipate the character of monastic life that was peculiarly Syrian and Mesopotamian in following centuries.
5. The model of twinship between a divine being and a wandering missionary, which is found in Thomas scripture, profoundly influenced the founder of the Manichaean world religion, who lived in Mesopotamia in the third century A.D. From external sources, Manichaeans are known to have read GTh as part of their scripture.

These considerations, though somewhat unequal in value, suggest that the Thomas works were composed and transmitted in one or more Christian communities of the Mesopotamian region. Edessa was one of the main centers for the diffusion of Christian literature composed in the region; this fact, together with its claim to possess the bones of St. Thomas, makes it the most obvious home for a "school" of writers who honored St. Thomas as their patron saint. Since there is nothing especially sectarian about the Thomas scripture, it must have been a part of the normal canon of scripture read by Mesopotamian Christians in the second and early third centuries. It would have been read along with works such as the *Odes of Solomon* and Tatian's *Harmony* (*Diatessaron*); cf. also the General Introduction, "Gnostic Scripture and the Christian Bible." However, after the middle of the third century, Thomas scripture (at least GTh) was taken up by the Manichaean religion and so became seriously compromised.

Edessa (Orhay), where the Thomas literature was perhaps composed, is now a little-known town in eastern Turkey (modern Urfa, east of Gaziantep). But in antiquity it was a major oriental city on the Armenia-Syria caravan route and a point of exchange between Hellenistic-Roman and Iranian-Arab culture. After Alexander the Great conquered Mesopotamia (331 B.C.) his Macedonian successor Seleucus I reorganized the oriental city, which was rooted in local Syrian culture, so that it was superficially like a Greek city-state, at least in law and civic organization, and installed there a small Greek-speaking contingent of Macedonian colonists. This rough fusion of

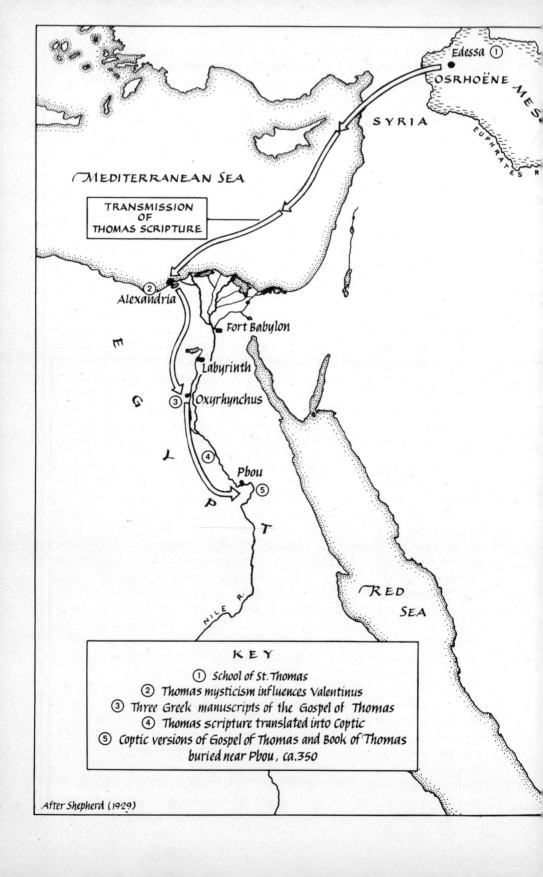

MEDITERRANEAN SEA

Edessa ①

OSRHOËNE MES.

EUPHRATES R.

SYRIA

TRANSMISSION
OF
THOMAS SCRIPTURE

Alexandria ②

Fort Babylon

Labyrinth

③ Oxyrhynchus

④

Pbou

⑤

E
G
Y
P
T

NILE R.

RED
SEA

KEY
① School of St.Thomas
② Thomas mysticism influences Valentinus
③ Three Greek manuscripts of the Gospel of Thomas
④ Thomas scripture translated into Coptic
⑤ Coptic versions of Gospel of Thomas and Book of Thomas
buried near Pbou, ca.350

After Shepherd (1929)

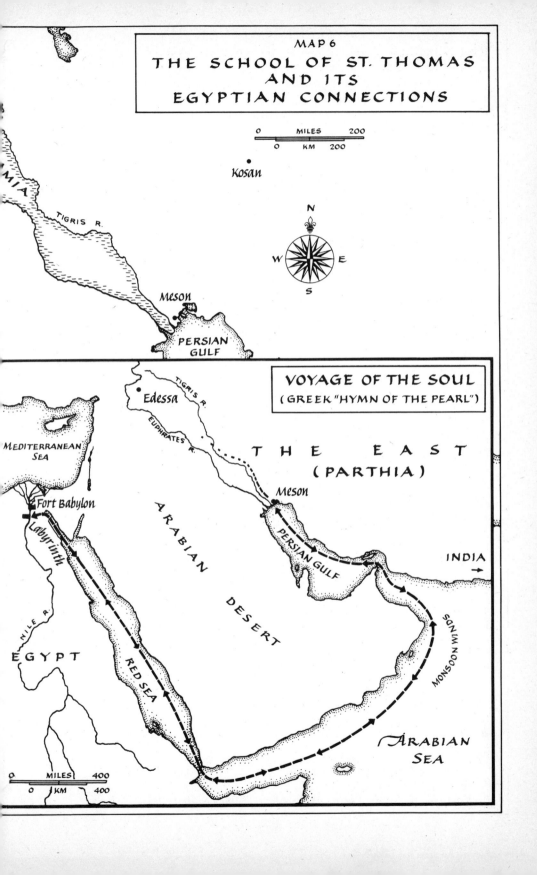

MAP 6
THE SCHOOL OF ST. THOMAS
AND ITS
EGYPTIAN CONNECTIONS

MILES 200
KM 200

Kosan

TIGRIS R.

Meson

PERSIAN
GULF

VOYAGE OF THE SOUL
(GREEK "HYMN OF THE PEARL")

MEDITERRANEAN
SEA

Edessa

TIGRIS R.

EUPHRATES R.

THE EAST
(PARTHIA)

Meson

Fort Babylon

PERSIAN GULF

Labyrinth

ARABIAN

NILE R.

INDIA

ARABIAN DESERT

EGYPT

RED SEA

MONSOON WINDS

MILES 400
KM 400

ARABIAN
SEA

local Syrian and imported Greek-like cultures continued to stamp the civilization of Edessa at least until A.D. 638, when the city fell to Islamic invaders. Local pagans worshiped typical Syrian planetary and solar deities; Judaism was a component of Edessene culture, perhaps an ancient one; Christianity seems to have arrived within a century of Jesus' death.

About 132 B.C. the Macedonian army was driven out of Mesopotamia, and from then until A.D. 165, Edessa was under Parthian political influence, though it was the capital of a nominally distinct kingdom called Osrhoëne, which stretched from the Euphrates to the Tigris across northern Mesopotamia. The Iranian kingdom of Parthia was strongly influenced by Greek culture, especially in the first half of this period. It was presumably under the Parthians that HPrl was composed (HPrl verse 38). Osrhoëne was ruled by a wily dynasty of Arab-Nabataean (later Armenian) stock, who guided it in the ambiguous role of buffer state between the hostile empires of Rome and its eastern neighbor Parthia. In A.D. 165, Osrhoëne became a dependency of Rome; in A.D. 198, its ruler Abgar VIII was honored by the Roman emperor with the traditional Parthian title of "king of kings" (cf. HPrl verse 41). In A.D. 214 the autonomy of Osrhoëne was finally annulled by the Romans, who absorbed it into the empire as a colony.

The early Christian literature written or used in Osrhoëne and the Mesopotamian region seems usually to have been transmitted in two languages—Greek and an early form of Syriac (the regional Aramaic dialect)—reflecting the two cultural strains within the kingdom and more generally within greater Syria; bilingual publication was not unusual in the Roman world. Thus probably not only *The Acts of Thomas* and HPrl, but also other important works of scripture, including Tatian's *Harmony (Diatessaron,* A.D. ca. 170), works of the Edessene Christian philosopher Bardaisan (born A.D. 154), and *The Odes of Solomon* (early second century A.D.?) were brought out in both Syriac and Greek; no matter which version was translated from the other, it was of course the Greek that was read in the rest of the Mediterranean world; here the Greek version was even translated into Latin, Coptic, and other languages (see Map 6). Old Syriac versions of the "separate gospels" (Mt, Mk, Lk, Jn) also circulated in Osrhoëne along with the Greek. The later literary history of Edessa is noteworthy mainly for works in Syriac (especially those of the "School of the Persians," which flourished in the city after A.D. 361), whose bulk and importance subsequently eclipsed the brilliance of the earlier period.

SELECT BIBLIOGRAPHY

Bauer, W. *Orthodoxy and Heresy in Earliest Christianity,* 1–43 ("Edessa"). Philadelphia: Fortress Press, 1971.
Charlesworth, J. H. "Odes of Solomon." In *The Old Testament Pseudepigrapha,* edited by J. H. Charlesworth, vol. 2, 725–71. Garden City, N.Y.: Doubleday & Company, 1985.
Colledge, M. A. R. *The Parthians.* London: Thames & Hudson, 1967.

Drijvers, H. J. W. *Bardaiṣan of Edessa*. Studia Semitica Neerlandica, no. 6. Assen: Van Gorcum, 1966.

Klijn, A. F. J. *The Acts of Thomas: Introduction—Text—Commentary*. Supplements to Novum Testamentum, vol. 5. Leiden: E. J. Brill, 1962.

————. *Edessa, Die Stadt des Apostels Thomas: Das älteste Christentum in Syrien*. Neukirchener Studienbücher, vol. 4. Neukirchen-Vluyn: Neukirchener, 1965.

————. "The Influence of Jewish Theology on the Odes of Solomon and the Acts of Thomas." In *Aspects du judéo-christianisme: Colloque de Strasbourg, 23–25 avril 1964*, 165–77 (and discussion, 177–79). Paris: Presses Universitaires de France, 1965.

Koester, H. In J. M. Robinson and H. Koester, *Trajectories Through Early Christianity*, 126–43 ("Edessa and the Osrhoëne"). Philadelphia: Fortress Press, 1971. Reprinted from *Harvard Theological Review* 58 (1965): 290–306.

The Odes of Solomon: The Syriac Texts. Edited, with translation and notes, by J. H. Charlesworth. Society of Biblical Literature, Texts and Translations, Pseudepigrapha Series. Missoula, Mont.: Scholars Press, 1977.

Poirier, P.-H. *L'Hymne de la perle des Actes de Thomas: Introduction, texte, traduction, commentaire*. Homo Religiosus, vol. 8. Louvain-la-Neuve: n.p., 1981, detailed study of earlier scholarship; introductions; commentaries; editions and translations of the Syriac, Greek, and Nicetas's epitome; indexes.

Quispel, G. "The Discussion of Judaic Christianity." *Vigiliae Christianae* 22 (1968): 81–93. Reprinted in his *Gnostic Studies*. Vol. 2, 146–58. Uitgaven van het Nederlands historisch-archaeologisch instituut te Istanbul, no. 34, vol. 2. Leiden: Nederlands Historisch-Archaeologisch Instituut te Istanbul, 1975.

————. "L'Évangile selon Thomas et les origines de l'ascèse chrétienne." In *Aspects du judéo-christianisme* (see above, Klijn), 35–51 (and discussion, 51–52). Reprinted in his *Gnostic Studies* (see above). Vol. 2, 98–112.

Segal, J. B. *Edessa: "The Blessed City."* Oxford: Clarendon Press, 1970.

Scripture of the school of St. Thomas not in this volume

The Acts of Thomas (complete). Translated with notes by A. F. J. Klijn (cf. above, his *Acts of Thomas*).

THE HYMN OF THE PEARL

or

THE HYMN OF JUDE THOMAS THE APOSTLE IN THE COUNTRY OF THE INDIANS

IN THE GREEK VERSION
(HPrl)

Contents

The Hymn of the Pearl ("The Hymn of the Soul")[1] or *The Hymn of Jude Thomas the Apostle in the Country of the Indians* presents a Hellenistic myth of the human soul's entry into bodily incarnation and its eventual disengagement from the body. The mythic tale of salvation is recounted by the protagonist (the soul) in the form of an autobiographical reminiscence. The myth does not directly demand a religious response from the reader, for it is a general description of salvation. Nevertheless, quoted within the story (verses 41–48) is a classic homiletic appeal for conversion, phrased in the traditional language of sleep and awakening. This has been identified as a special type of material (often loosely termed the "gnostic call"), which in fact transcends narrow sectarian and philosophical boundaries (cf. BJn 31:10f, Zs 130:14f, Poim 27f, CH7 1f).

For the most part, the myth of salvation is not expressed literally in HPrl but, rather, is hidden behind a figurative fairy tale or folktale. To perceive the myth, an ancient reader would have needed to reinterpret the tale allegorically (for the technique, see the "Historical Introduction" to Part Three, "Allegorical interpretation of scripture"). The process of reinterpretation begins within the text of HPrl itself (verses 76–78, 88, 98); the prince's garment, given to him in reward for conquering the dragon of Egypt, is equated with self-acquaintance (*gnōsis* of the self); by putting on the garment the prince knows himself and "arises" into the realm of peace. Starting from this clue, an ancient reader could work back through the story at another level, retelling it as an account or model of the quest for self-knowledge and salvation. It must be emphasized that, except for the one explicit clue, the text itself provided ancient readers no more than a figurative representation of this hidden message. Readers had to supply or construct the rest of the deeper interpretation.

---

[1] The titles *The Hymn of the Pearl* and *The Hymn of the Soul*, by which the present work is generally known, are the creation of modern scholarship. Neither one is found in any ancient manuscript of the work.

Both popular belief and certain kinds of academic philosophy (especially Platonism and Pythagoreanism) accepted that the soul had its "origin" in a nonphysical "realm" from which it "had come"; that its incarnation in a material body hindered it from contemplating the good or god, and was generally harmful; that it might be saved from this unfortunate fate, e.g. by acquiring the self-knowledge taught by wisdom or philosophy; and that the result might be an existence free of the body's influence. The problem of why in the first place the soul had ever "fallen" into existence in a body was a topic of philosophical discussion.

The outlines of this commonplace myth of the soul are parallel to the story line of HPrl. They also agree with the mythic elements in GTh and BTh (the latter two works are overtly Christian while HPrl, as a figurative text, has no place to mention the Christian savior as such). The parallelism can be expressed as follows.

Story line (see Map 6). The (1) king of (2) the East (Parthia) sends (3) a royal prince by way of (4) the satrapy of Mesene ("Meson") to (5) Egypt, in order to (6) get a precious pearl. The prince (7) is poisoned and made intoxicated by (8) Egyptians. But he (9) is awakened by (10) a message from the king. He (11) takes the pearl and (12) returns to the East, where he puts on (13) a robe of *gnōsis* and (14) ascends to the king's palace, (15) entering the realm of peace.

Allegorical meaning (myth). The (1) first principle of (2) the spiritual realm providentially causes (3) the individual soul to descend past (4) the heavenly bodies (?) into (5) incarnate life in a material body, in order to (6) be educated (get salvation). The soul (7) becomes unconscious and inert because of (8) matter. But it (9) disengages itself in response to (10) the savior or message of philosophy (wisdom). It (11) becomes acquainted with itself and its career and (12) is metaphysically reunited with (13) itself (i.e. becomes integral) and with (14) the first principle, (15) gaining true repose.

Deduction of this myth from the story line of HPrl is confirmed by comparison of HPrl with other works of Thomas scripture; cf. Table 4. The results of such a comparison (column 2 of Table 4, "Implied Philosophical Myth") describe a specifically Edessene interpretation of HPrl within the school of St. Thomas. But it remains possible that HPrl was originally composed elsewhere and that this interpretation was historically secondary; cf. below "Literary background." The total lack of any specifically Christian or Jewish details or characters also raises the possibility that HPrl was first written for a non-Christian readership. Only specific historical information about the circumstances of its composition could clarify these questions. In the absence of such information it is not surprising that modern scholars have substantially disagreed on the interpretation of HPrl.

Given the importance of the myth for one's life and conduct, why is the philosophical sense of the text not stated more explicitly? No definite answer to such a question is possible, but three factors are worth noting. First, HPrl is formally a work of art, not philosophy; a fairy tale and not a philosophical myth. Second, as a piece of religious art it may have had the secondary function of religious propaganda, that is, to attract interested external readers into a particular school of religious thought by its artistry (for this function, see also TRs, PtF, and even GTr). Third, by incorporating within the text a clue to a parallel allegorical reading, HPrl engages the reader in a lesson in interpretation; this would not be possible if the philosophical meaning were stated explicitly and completely. The other two works included in Part Four also insist on the importance of textual interpretation in the acquisition of salvation (GTh 1, BTh 138:1–37f); an act of textual interpretation on the part of the believer seems to be an integral part of the idea of salvation in the school of St. Thomas.

Literary background

The author of HPrl is unknown.[2] Since the text is only attested as a part of *The Acts of Thomas* (probably written in Edessa, A.D. ca. 200–25) any deductions about

---

[2] Some scholars have attributed the work to Bardaisan (born A.D. 154), the bilingual Christian poet and theologian of Edessa, but this attribution is not generally accepted.

Table 4

The Myth of the Soul in Thomas Literature

Structural Elements	Implied Philosophical Myth	The Hymn of the Pearl	The Gospel According to Thomas	The Book of Thomas
Starting point	Spiritual realm	A palace in the East (Parthia)	The kingdom of light	The kingdom (essence) of light
Protagonist	Individual souls	A royal prince	Jude; individual spirits	Jude; individual sparks of light
Companion	(?)	His Brother/Cousin	The living Jesus	The savior Jesus
First event	Descent	Divestiture, travel	....	....
• Cause	First principle	The King of Kings	The living father	The king
• Purpose	Education	To get a precious pearl	....	To gain acquaintance (*gnōsis*)
Second event	Incarnation	Entry into Egypt	Entry into poverty, the world, the flesh, the garment	The burning of desire within the body; alienation
• Result	Unconsciousness	Sleep, servitude	Intoxication, blindness	Intoxication, blindness, bondage
• Opponents	Demons	Egyptians, demons of the Labyrinth	Brigands, Pharisees and Scribes	Demons, spirits, fire
Third event	Disengagement from matter	Disrobing	Abstinence from the world; disrobing	Travel with the savior, self-examination
• Result	Self-acquaintance	Awakening; the pearl	Self-acquaintance, treasure, the kingdom, a pearl	Self-acquaintance
• Cause	Wisdom	A letter from the king; a female guide	Interpretation of Jesus' obscure sayings	The female being who is truly wise; appearance of Jesus the light
Fourth Event	Reunion with the self and with god	Investiture with a robe of acquaintance	Self-integration, return to one's source	Departure, withdrawal
• Result	Repose	Peace	Reign, rest, repose, light	Repose, reign

the date and place of composition of HPrl must rest upon two prior questions: *(a)* whether HPrl was composed by the author of *The Acts of Thomas*; *(b)* whether HPrl presupposes a model of divine twinship based on the name Didymus Jude Thomas (see the "Historical Introduction" to Part Four). To the first of these questions *(a)* most scholars have answered no; both its style (mainly in the Syriac) and its content suggest that HPrl was composed independent of *The Acts of Thomas* and was either incorporated in the *Acts* by their author or interpolated in them by a subsequent editor.

The second question *(b)* is harder to answer. If HPrl was composed in Edessa (see Map 6), comparison of its structure with the mythic background of GTh and BTh should indicate the *original* sense of HPrl. In such a case, HPrl could have provided the model, even if it were a non-Christian one, on which the Christian Thomas tradition was based; alternatively, HPrl might have presupposed the Thomas tradition and might represent an apologetic popularization of that tradition in the form of a folktale. The crucial factor here is the order in which the three works— HPrl, GTh, and BTh—were composed.

But if HPrl was not composed in Edessa, its original meaning might have been something quite different from the theology of divine twinship; the allegorical obscurity of the text would completely hide any such meaning unless further information could be obtained about the religious context in which the text originally was read. In such a case HPrl would have been imported to Edessa and secondarily adopted by the school of St. Thomas for its own purposes. The date of composition is presumably sometime during the Parthian dynasty of Persia (247 B.C.–A.D. 224), since Parthia is mentioned by name and favorably (HPrl 38). If the work was composed in Edessa, it would have been composed during the Parthian control of that city, which ended in A.D. 165. The original language of composition is a matter of debate—Greek, Syriac, or a simultaneous publication in both languages. The Greek version, which is translated here, is in an unclassical and often obscure prose style, reflecting perhaps the taste of the late-Hellenistic period with some regional peculiarity due to the bilingualism of Edessa.

HPrl is, in the words of the Greek *Acts of Thomas* (108), a "hymn" (*psalmos*), implying that it is designed to be sung, perhaps with instrumental accompaniment. It has the strophic form typical of Semitic poetry (neither the Greek version nor the Syriac is written in strictly controlled meter or with a fixed number of syllables per unit, nor is either version rhymed). In narrative structure HPrl resembles a classic folktale or fairy tale; in this sense, its genre is characteristic of oral, popular literature.

The allegorical motif of the pearl (cf. Mt 13:45–46, GTh 76) was widely used not only by Mesopotamian Christian authors, but also in ancient world literature in general.

Mythic characters

I. Inhabitants of the East

The KING OF KINGS, the Great King, the prince's father
His wife
Other KINGS (satraps) and royal officials of the Parthian empire
The PRINCE, son of the King of Kings
A noble boy of high rank, who accompanies him in Egypt. Called BROTHER and COUSIN.
Two GUIDES along the road to Egypt
Two TREASURERS who bring the garment to the prince
A FEMALE BEING who guides the prince back from Egypt to the East

II. Intermediates

The MOSANI, inhabitants of Meson (Maišān)

III. Inhabitants of Egypt

The EGYPTIANS, also called BABYLONIANS
The TYRANNICAL DEMONS of the Egyptian Labyrinth
A ravenous DRAGON that guards the pearl
The KING OF EGYPT, perhaps identical with the dragon

Text

In its known form, HPrl is part of a much larger work, *The Acts of Thomas,*
which recounts the wanderings and adventures of an ascetic preacher Didymus Jude
Thomas and the miracles he performed with the aid of his twin brother Jesus. *The
Acts of Thomas* (including HPrl) exist in both Greek and Syriac. The *Acts* consists
of a series of narrative episodes with which poetry and prayers have been
amalgamated; but the manuscripts of the *Acts* (six Syriac, seventy-five Greek)
substantially differ as to which episodes, poems, and prayers they include, for
throughout its history the text was constantly being reshaped by successive ancient
editors. Thus it happens that only one Greek manuscript (of the eleventh century
A.D.) and only one Syriac (A.D. 936) contain HPrl: these two manuscripts are the
only surviving evidence for the text, except for an eleventh-century epitome of the
Greek version made by Nicephoras, Archbishop of Thessalonica.

Scholarship is not agreed on whether HPrl was an original part of the *Acts* or a
secondary addition. Nor is there agreement on whether the Syriac was translated
from the Greek or vice versa. Furthermore, the wording of the two versions differs
enough to show that they are witnesses of two distinct ancient editions of the text.
The Greek is translated here, since it was specifically the Greek edition that was
known in the Mediterranean world. Since the single surviving Greek manuscript
contains substantial errors of copying and has many obscure turns of phrase, the
wording of the Syriac edition sometimes had to be consulted. Line numbers given
below correspond to the customary Syriac numbering; HPrl also counts as paragraphs
108–13 of the Greek *Acts of Thomas* and these numbers are given in boldface type.
The translation below is based on Bonnet's critical edition of the Greek (in which
the Syriac manuscript and Nicetas's epitome are also collated), but with alterations:
M. Bonnet, *Acta Philippi et Acta Thomae Accedunt Acta Barnabae* (*Acta Aposto-
lorum Apocrypha,* eds. R. Lipsius, M. Bonnet, II/2; Leipzig: Mendelssohn, 1903;
reprinted, Darmstadt: Wissenschaftliche Buchgesellschaft, 1959), 219–24.

SELECT BIBLIOGRAPHY

Kees, H. "Labyrinthos (4): Ägyptisches Labyrinth." In *Paulys Real-Encyclopädie
der classischen Altertumswissenschaft.* 2d ed. by G. Wissowa et al. Vol. 12/A
(1924), cols. 323–26.
Klijn, A. F. J. *The Acts of Thomas: Introduction—Text—Commentary.* Supplements
to Novum Testamentum, vol. 5. Leiden: E. J. Brill, 1962.
Poirier, P.-H. *L'Hymne de la perle des Actes de Thomas: Introduction, texte,
traduction, commentaire.* Homo Religiosus, vol. 8. Louvain-la-Neuve: n.p.,
1981, detailed study of earlier scholarship; introductions; commentaries; editions
and translations of the Syriac, Greek, and Nicetas's epitome; indexes.
Quispel, G. "Makarius und das Lied von der Perle." In *Le origini dello gnosticismo:
Colloquio di Messina, 13–18 aprile 1966,* 625–44. Edited by Ugo Bianchi.
Studies in the History of Religions, no. 12. Leiden: E. J. Brill, 1967.
Wright, W. *Apocryphal Acts of the Apostles.* Vol. 2, *The English Translation,* 238–
45. London and Edinburgh: Williams & Norgate, 1871.

THE HYMN OF
JUDE THOMAS THE APOSTLE
IN THE COUNTRY OF THE INDIANS[a]

The journey down to Egypt

1   **108** When I was an infant too young to talk, in my father's palace,

2   Reposing in the wealth and luxury of those who nourished me,

3   My parents equipped me with supplies and sent me out from the East, our country, on a mission.

4   From the wealth of their treasuries[a] they gave me a great cargo,[b]   Mt 11:30

5   Which was light,[c] so that I could carry it by myself—

6   The cargo was gold from the high country,[d] silver plate of the great treasuries,

7   Emerald jewels[e] of India, and agates of Kosan;[f]

8   And they armed me with steel.[g]

9   They took away from me[h] the jewel-studded garment shot with gold
That they had made out of love for me

10   And the robe[i] of yellow color (tailored) to my size.[j]

11   But they made an agreement with me,
Impressed it on[k] my mind, (so that) I might (not)[l] forget it, and said,

12   "If you go down to Egypt and bring from there the one pearl,   Mt 13:46

13   "Which resides there near the ravenous[m] dragon,[n]   GTh 76

14   "You shall put (back) on that jewel-studded garment and the robe,[o] which you like;

15   "And you shall be a herald for our kingdom, along with your well-remembered Brother."[p]

16   **109** So I started out from the East, on a hard and frightening road, accompanied by two guides;

Title a. This title may never have been a feature of the Greek version of *The Acts of Thomas*. It is found only in the Syriac version of the work. "In the Country of the Indians" refers to the setting of the episode in the *Acts*. In the following annotations the Syriac version is quoted from Wright, *Apocryphal Acts* (see "Select Bibliography"), Vol. 2, 238–45, sometimes with comparison of Poirier's French.

108 a. Or "treasures."
b. Or "burden" as in Mt 11:30, "My yoke is easy, and my burden is light."
c. I.e. not heavy.
d. Or "the above."
e. Lit. "Chalcedony jewels." The exact ancient meaning of this term is uncertain. The Syriac version has "rubies."
f. The Syriac version has "Beth-Kāšǎn," which Wright hesitantly identifies with Ḳashan in Persia, north of Ispahan.

g. Greek *adamas*.
h. The Greek MS erroneously has "They put upon me"; the reading translated here is found in the Syriac version.
i. "the . . . garment . . . And the robe": i.e. "the garment, which was a robe." This equational use of "And" is one of the figures of speech in ancient rhetoric.
j. Or "age."
k. Lit. "wrote it in."
l. "(so that), (not)": these words are inadvertently omitted in the MS; the Syriac version has "that it might not be forgotten."
m. Lit. "swallowing."
n. Lit. "serpent": Greek *drakōn*.
o. "that . . . garment and the robe"; cf. note 108i.
p. The term "Brother" was sometimes used by Eastern kings of Hellenistic and Roman times as a title of honor; the Syriac here has "second (in command)."

17   For I was unused to traveling on it.
18   I passed the borders of the Mosani,[a] where there is the inn of
     the Eastern traveling merchants;
19   And reached the land of the Babylonians.[b]

The bondage in Egypt

20   Since I had entered Egypt the guides departed who had
     traveled with me,
21   And I rushed directly to the dragon and camped near its den,
22   Lying in wait for it to grow drowsy and fall asleep, so that I
     might make away with the pearl.
23   Being on my own, I put on a disguise[c] and (would have)
     seemed alien even to my own people.
24   But there I saw a Cousin[d] of mine from the East—a free
     person,
25   Gracious, handsome, and young, a child of members of court:
26   Who came and kept me company,
27   And whom I made my friend and partner in my travels; had
     as a constant companion;
28   And exhorted to guard against the Egyptians and against
     intercourse with their impurities.
29   So I put on their style of dress,[e] so that I might not look like
     one who was foreign
30   And ⟨had come⟩[f] from abroad to get the pearl,
     Lest the Egyptians arouse the dragon against me.
31   But somehow they learned that I was not from their land.[g]
32   They gave me a mixture of cunning and treachery, and I
     tasted their food.
33   I did not (any longer) recognize that I was a child of the
     (Great) King,[h] but rather acted as servant to their king.
34   And I even came to the pearl for which my parents had sent
     me on the mission
35   But sank into deep sleep under the heaviness of their food.[i]

The exodus

36   **110** Now, my parents also noticed me suffering these things,
     and they suffered over me.
37   So a proclamation was heralded in our kingdom,[a] that all
     should present themselves at our court.[b]

109 a. The Syriac version here has "the borders of Maišǎn," which Wright identifies with "the district between al-Baṣra and Wāsiṭ, with a chief town of the same name"; i.e. Mesene or Characene at the head of the Persian Gulf.

b. "land of the Babylonians": i.e. Egypt. In HPrl "Babylon" is not the Mesopotamian city on the Euphrates, as the author makes clear by the geographical order of place names (verses 18–19, 69–70). Rather, it refers to the Egyptian "Babylon," a fortified garrison city in the vicinity of the great pyramids (at modern "Old Cairo" by Fostāt). Babylon of Egypt was the site of an important Roman fortress; under the emperor Augustus, one of the three Roman legions in Egypt was stationed there.

c. Lit. "I became foreign in (my) appearance."

d. Probably not an indication of close blood relationship, but rather an Eastern title bestowed at royal court as a mark of honor.

e. Cf. verse 23.

f. These words are inadvertently omitted in the Greek MS; the Syriac version has "because I was come from abroad."

g. Or "region."

h. "of the (Great) King": lit. "of King," a traditional way of referring to the Persian monarch in Greek.

i. I.e. the Egyptians' food.

110 a. I.e. in the East.
b. Lit. "doors."

38   And next the kings of Parthia,[c] those in office, and the leaders of the East

39   Decided that in my case I should not be left in Egypt.

40   So, too, the members of court wrote to me declaring as follows:

41   "From your father the King of Kings,[d] your mother who rules the East,

42   "And their Brothers,[e] who are second[f] after them:[g] "To our child in Egypt. Peace!

43   "Arise, and become sober out of (your) sleep.

44   "Listen to the words written in this letter. "Remember that you are a child of kings. "You have fallen under a servile yoke.

45   "Call to mind your garment shot with gold.

46   "Call to mind the pearl for which you were sent on the mission to Egypt.

47   "Your name has been called ⟨to⟩[h] the book of life,

48   "Along with that of your Brother[i] whom you have taken to yourself, in our kingdom."[j]

49   **111** So the king confirmed[a] it, as an ambassador,[b]

50   Because of (the threat of) the Babylonian children[c] and the tyrannical demons of the Labyrinth.[d]

53   But for my part I gave a start when I perceived its voice.[e]

54   And I took it up and kissed it, and I read.

55   But what was written there concerned that which was engraved in my heart.[f]

56   And on the spot I remembered that I was a child of kings and that my people demanded my freedom (?).[g]

57   I also remembered the pearl for which I had been sent on the mission to Egypt,

58   And the fact that I had been coming against the fearsome dragon for booty.[h]

c. Or "the kings of virginity (Greek *parthenia*)," the reading of the Greek MS. The Syriac version and the Greek epitome have "Parthia." For the Parthian empire, see "The cultural milieu" in the "Historical Introduction" to Part Four. It was subdivided into smaller kingdoms, each with its local "king."

d. This title was used both by the kings of the Arsacid dynasty of Parthia from about ca. 250 B.C. to A.D. 224 and by the succeeding Sassanid dynasty (A.D. 224–636).

e. Cf. note 108p.

f. Second in rank; very high court dignitaries.

g. Lit. "after us."

h. This word is, perhaps, inadvertently omitted in the MS; the Syriac version has ". . . thy name hath been read out in the list of the valiant."

i. Cf. note 108p; the Syriac here has "viceroy."

j. The text of the Greek MS may be slightly corrupt here. The Syriac version has "and with thy Brother, our viceroy (?), thou shalt be with him in our kingdom."

111. a. Or "sealed."

b. The saving letter is personified as a savior. It is to pass through hostile territory with the diplomatic immunity of an ambassador.

c. The Egyptians; cf. note 109b.

d. "the Labyrinth": the Egyptian Labyrinth, a famous and extremely intricate temple complex southwest of modern Cairo. It is located beside the pyramid of Amenemhat (Ammenemes) III at Hawāra in the vicinity of Crocodilopolis (Medīnet el-Faiyūm, capital of the Faiyūm Oasis). For readers of the ancient Greco-Roman world the Labyrinth was the best-known architectural monument of Egypt after the great pyramids. The cult of Sobk, the crocodile god, was popular in the Faiyūm. The Greek version of HPrl seems to imply that the pearl and its guardian "dragon" are in the Labyrinth. Verses 51–52 are a feature only of the Syriac version.

e. Lit. "I gave a start at its voice and perception."

f. Cf. verse 11.

g. The Greek MS here erroneously has "and that my freedom demanded my people." The Syriac version has "I remembered that I was a son of royal parents, and my noble birth asserted its nature."

h. Or "to snatch something," lit. "for snatching" (Greek *harpasis*); cf. verse 61.

59   And I subdued it[i] by calling out my father's name.[j]

61   And I snatched the pearl, and turned to carry it away to my parents.

62   And I took off the dirty clothing[k] and left it behind in their land.

63   Immediately, I went straight (?) ⟨to⟩ the road leading[l] to the light of our Eastern home.

64   And while on the road I found a female being,[m] who lifted me up.

65   So she[n] got me up from sleep, giving as it were an oracle by (her) voice, with which she guided me to the light;

66   Indeed, at times I had the royal garment of silk before my eyes;[o]

68   And with familial love leading me and drawing me on,

69   I passed by the Labyrinth.[p]
        And leaving Babylon behind, on the left,[q]

70   I reached Meson,[r] which is a great coast,[s]

75   **112** But I could not recall my splendor;
        For, it was while I was still a boy and quite young that I had left it behind in my father's palace.

76   But when suddenly I saw my garment reflected as in a mirror,

77   I perceived in it my whole self as well,
        And through it I recognized[a] and saw myself.

78   For, though we derived from one and the same we were partially divided; and then again we were one, with a single form.

79   Nay, also the treasurers who had brought the garment

80   I saw as two beings, but there existed a single form in both,
        One single royal token consisting of two halves.[b]

81   And they had my money and wealth in their hands, and gave me my reward:

82   The fine garment of bright colors,

83   Which was embroidered with gold, precious stones, and pearls to give a suitable impression.[c]

84   It was clasped at the collar,[d]

86   And the image of the King of Kings was (woven) all through it;

87   Stones of lapis lazuli had been agreeably fixed to the collar.

88   **113** And I saw, in turn, that impulses[a] of acquaintance (*gnōsis*) were rippling throughout it,

89   And that it was ready to utter discourse.

---

i. The dragon.

j. Verse 60 is a feature only of the Syriac version.

k. Cf. verse 29.

l. Translation uncertain. The Greek MS appears to say "I straightened it (the clothing) and the road," which is illogical. The Syriac version has "And I took my way straight to come."

m. Possibly corrupt. Here the Syriac explicitly refers to the royal message personified (the word "letter" is grammatically feminine in Greek): "And my letter, my awakener, I found before me on the road."

n. Or "it" (see the preceding note).

o. Verse 67 is a feature only of the Syriac version.

p. Cf. note 109b.

q. The narration here follows the style of Hellenistic voyage stories.

r. A place name (the Syriac version has "to the great Maišān, to the haven of merchants"; cf. note 109a). In Greek the word *meson* also means "intermediate."

s. Verses 71–74 are a feature only of the Syriac version.

112 a. Or "gained acquaintance."

b. Lit. "one single royal *symbolon* in both."

c. Translation uncertain.

d. Translation uncertain. Verse 85 is a feature only of the Syriac version.

113 a. Lit. "motions" (Greek *kinēseis*).

90   Then I heard it speaking:
91   "It is I who belong to the one who is stronger than all human
          beings and for whose sake I was designed[b] by the father
          himself."
92   And for my part, I took note of my mature age.[c]
93   And all the royal impulses[d] reposed on me, as its energy
          increased:
94   Thrust out by that being's[e] hand, it[f] hastened to the one who
          was receiving it;[g]
95   And a longing aroused me to rush and meet that being and to
          receive it.[h]
96   Spread out . . . of colors . . . I was brought back,[i]
97   And I completely clothed myself in my superior royal robe.[j]

Return to the royal realm

98   Once I had put it on, I arose into the realm[k] of peace
          belonging to reverential awe.
99   And I bowed my head and prostrated myself before the
          splendor of the father who had sent it to me.
100   For, it was I who had done his commands,
          And likewise it was he who had kept the promise.[l]
101   And I mingled at the doors of his archaic royal building.
102   He took delight in me, and received me with him in the
          palace.
103   And all his subjects were singing hymns with reverent voices.
104   He suffered me also to be ushered in to the King's Court[m] in
          his company:
105   So that with my gifts and the pearl I might make an
          appearance before the king himself.

b. Lit. "written."
c. Or "stature."
d. Lit. "motions."
e. "that being's": cf. verse 80. The original reading of the text is possibly "their."
f. The garment.
g. I.e. hastened to me as I went to receive
it.
h. The garment.

i. The text of this verse in the Greek MS
is corrupt. The Syriac version has "And I
stretched forth and took it. With the beauty
of its colors I adorned myself."
j. The "robe" is the "garment" spoken
of earlier in the hymn; cf. verses 9–10.
k. Or "land."
l. Cf. verses 12–13.
m. "Court": lit. "doors."

THE GOSPEL ACCORDING
TO THOMAS

(GTh)

Contents

The Gospel According to Thomas ("The Gospel of Thomas") is an anthology of 114 "obscure sayings" of Jesus, which, according to its prologue, were collected and transmitted by St. Didymus Jude Thomas. The sayings do not appear within a biographical narrative about Jesus, although some of them individually contain elements of dialogue or an abbreviated setting. Instead, Jesus' sayings in GTh are unconnected and in no particular order. They claim to be timelessly true, like sayings of ancient sages or proverbs spoken by heavenly Wisdom; accordingly, their speaker is called "the living Jesus," i.e. the Jesus of eternity. Historical framework is irrelevant to the message of GTh, for the salvation that it proclaims is not the future reign of god on earth, to be ushered in by a messiah, but rather the recognition of one's true nature and acquaintance with oneself, leading to immediate repose and rendering "death" (i.e. the realm of human affairs) trivial. "The kingdom is inside of you. . . . When you become acquainted with yourselves . . . you will understand that it is you who are children of the living father." Jesus' suffering, death, and resurrection are not discussed in GTh; his role here is purely that of a teacher of wisdom. GTh is thus a Christian gospel in which the crucifixion of Jesus has no importance.

The opening paragraph of GTh directs the reader's attention to the need of interpreting Jesus' sayings in order for them to be effective: "Whoever finds the meaning of these sayings will not taste death." Without recognition of their hidden meaning, Jesus' sayings are merely "obscure." The interpretive clue to this hidden meaning was provided by references (especially in GTh 18, 29, 50) to a Hellenistic myth of the heavenly origin, fall, incarnation, awakening, and return of the soul. The structure of the myth was known in more coherent form in another work of Thomas scripture, HPrl. Once the myth had been recognized or reconstructed by the ancient reader it would have provided a framework within which the other, more traditional sayings could be interpreted (cf. Table 4).

Sayings attributed to Jesus, whether single or grouped in collections, written or transmitted orally, were one of the most authoritative types of literature for early Christians, especially in the eastern Mediterranean. Collected sayings of Jesus were an important source of material incorporated in written gospels of the biographical type, above all Mt and Lk. Distinct sayings collections continued to be used even after those more complex gospels came into circulation.

If one examines all the surviving sayings attributed to Jesus, no matter where, a wide range of religious perspectives can be found: wisdom sayings and proverbs reminiscent of Old Testament wisdom books; prophetic sayings pronouncing god's judgment; eschatological sayings; legal sayings regulating community life; Christological sayings, in which Jesus describes or predicts his role and position.

Against this background it is obvious that GTh is by no means a well-distributed sample of these usual saying types, but rather concentrates on particular types that are appropriate to its message of salvation—especially wisdom sayings or general truths, and prophetic sayings that emphasize the presence of god's reign ("kingdom") within Jesus and each believer. Eschatological sayings are conspicuously absent, and sayings in which Jesus describes himself stress not the future but the present.

The author of GTh has written it so as to stress the authority and authenticity of Jesus' sayings in several ways.

1. The literary genre of GTh—disconnected sayings of the wise—is traditionally reserved for authoritative wisdom attributed to eminent sages of the past or even to heavenly wisdom (Dame Wisdom). The use of this genre constitutes a claim of authority.
2. The speaker in GTh is explicitly said to be Jesus, who is "the light (that presides) over all" and the source from which the entirety comes and to which it goes. These epithets and the lack of any historical framework reinforce the implication that Jesus is heavenly Wisdom herself.
3. The attribution of the GTh sayings to Jesus is said to be authenticated by Jude (St. Thomas), Jesus' twin, as recorder of the sayings. Jude's personal authority was especially high in the regional church that used GTh.
4. As patron saint of the collection, Jude is meant to be credited not only with recording and authenticating the sayings, but also with including allusions to the myth of the soul and adding certain interpretive phrases here and there to older sayings. In this way he is made out to be the teacher of the hidden meaning (GTh 1) of Jesus' sayings, so as to make traditional sayings of Jesus effective for his community in a particular way.

Literary background

The compiler of GTh is unknown. Its date of composition must be before A.D. ca. 200, the date of the earliest manuscript (a Greek papyrus fragment); and after the foundation of Christianity. Attempts to date GTh more precisely depend on a delicate hypothetical evaluation of how the earliest Christian literature (including oral literature) evolved, especially sayings collections. One qualified expert has recently estimated that GTh was probably composed in the first century A.D.; many other scholars assign it roughly to the middle of the second. At any rate, its literary genre and some of the individual sayings are extremely ancient. The place of composition may be Edessa in northern Mesopotamia (see Map 6), or another city of the same region (see the "Historical Introduction" to Part Four). The language of composition is Greek; if a Syriac version was also published—as one might expect in Edessa—it apparently does not survive, though the use of GTh by the author of the Syriac *Acts of Thomas* and by Mani, the Babylonian founder of the Manichaean world religion, may be evidence of a sort for its onetime existence in Syriac.

Some of the sayings in GTh are closely parallel to ones in the gospels of the canonical New Testament, especially Mt and Lk. But GTh is not based on those gospels. Rather, its sources are ultimately related to the lost sayings collections from which Matthew and Luke drew the sayings of Jesus quoted in their biographical gospels, especially the so-called synoptic sayings source ("Q"). New Testament scholars have especially been interested in the sayings of GTh that have close parallels in the New Testament gospels; through the technique of form criticism, they have ascertained that in some instances GTh preserves earlier, more original forms of certain sayings than Mt or Lk do.

The claim (GTh prologue) that Jude, the twin brother of Jesus, edited the collection makes GTh an example of pseudepigraphy.

The genre of GTh is the wisdom book, i.e. anthology of wise sayings (cf. above,

"Contents"). Such sayings collections were widely used both in Greek culture and among various other peoples of the ancient Middle East. The best-known parallels are the Old Testament wisdom books of Proverbs, Sirach, Wisdom of Solomon, Ecclesiastes, and parts of Job.

The use of the term "gospel" to characterize an anthology is distinctly Christian and within Christian literature is highly unusual (although GTh is entitled "gospel" it bears no relation to the biographical genre called by this name, e.g. the Gospel of Mark). Another instance of a Christian anthology called "gospel" is the Valentinian *Gospel According to Philip,* which either was composed somewhere in Syria or Mesopotamia or, at least, used Syrian or Mesopotamian materials.

GTh is not to be confused with *The Infancy Gospel of Thomas,* a biography in which the boy Jesus performs miracles to demonstrate his divinity.

Mythic characters

I. Inhabitants of the Kingdom of Light

The LIVING FATHER
The HOLY SPIRIT
Jesus' TRUE MOTHER
The ENTIRETY
The LIVING JESUS

II. Humankind

ADAM
Twenty-four PROPHETS of Israel
A SAMARITAN
JEWS
JOHN THE BAPTIST
PHARISEES AND SCRIBES
Jesus' disciples, including:
    DIDYMUS JUDE THOMAS
    JAMES the Just
    SIMON PETER
    MATTHEW
    JESUS' MOTHER MARY
    Another MARY (?)
    SALOME
MESSENGERS and PROPHETS of the kingdom, who will come
Others, both good and bad

Text

Three papyrus manuscripts of the original Greek text survive. All three were discovered at Oxyrhynchus (Bahnasa) in Egypt (see Map 6); they are extremely fragmentary. The editors of these manuscripts estimate their dates of copying at various decades within the third century A.D.

(a) Papyrus Oxyrhynchus 1, fragments of a codex, now in the Bodleian Library in Oxford

(b) Papyrus Oxyrhynchus 654, an excerpt written on the back of a discarded document, now in the British Library in London

(c) Papyrus Oxyrhynchus 655, fragments of a scroll, now in the Harvard Houghton Library in Cambridge, Massachusetts

The full text is known only in Coptic translation, attested by a single manuscript from Nag Hammadi:

(d) MS NHC II (pp. 32–51)

The Coptic manuscript (d) was copied just before A.D. 350, and is now in the Cairo Coptic Museum.

The wording of the Greek manuscripts differs slightly from the Coptic, suggesting that there was more than one ancient edition of the work in Greek that circulated in Egypt.

In the Coptic manuscript the sayings (*logia,* plural of Greek *logion*) are not divided from one another, probably through an inadvertence, nor are they numbered. One of the fragmentary Greek manuscripts (P. Oxy. 654) has division marks in the margin and text, dividing the sayings. But this Greek manuscript contains only a very small portion of the text; most of the modern divisions and all the numbering are thus purely hypothetical, being based on the contents of the text, especially the occurrence of the phrase "Jesus said." Scholars have agreed on a standard system of division and numbering; it is given in parentheses in the translation below. In modern reference to GTh the text is almost always cited according to these standard saying or logion numbers. Readers are advised to follow this practice.

The translation below is based upon my own critical edition of the Coptic version and H. Attridge's critical edition of the three fragmentary Greek manuscripts, all found in vol. 1 of B. Layton, ed., *Nag Hammadi Codex II,2–7* (see "Select Bibliography" under Koester).

SELECT BIBLIOGRAPHY

Grant, R. M., with D. N. Freedman and W. R. Schoedel. *The Secret Sayings of Jesus.* Garden City, N.Y.: Doubleday & Company, 1960.

Koester, H. *History and Literature of Early Christianity,* 146–60 ("The Tradition of the Message of Jesus"). Vol. 2 of his *Introduction to the New Testament.* Philadelphia: Fortress Press, 1982.

——————. "Introduction [to the Gospel of Thomas]." In vol. 1 of *Nag Hammadi Codex II,2–7 Together with XIII,2*, Brit. Lib. Or.4926(1) and P. Oxy. 1, 654, 655.* Edited by B. Layton. Nag Hammadi Studies. Leiden: E. J. Brill, in press. (Authoritative for genre, background, theology, synoptic parallels.)

Ménard, J.-E. *L'Évangile selon Thomas.* Nag Hammadi Studies, vol. 5. Leiden: E. J. Brill, 1975. (Full-scale commentary.)

Quispel, G. "The Gospel of Thomas and Jewish Christianity." Chap. 3 of his *Gnostic Studies.* Vol. 2, 1–237. Uitgaven van het Nederlands historisch-archaeologisch instituut te Istanbul, no. 34. Leiden: Nederlands Historisch-Archaeologisch Instituut te Istanbul, 1975.

Puech, H.-Ch. "The Gospel of Thomas." In *New Testament Apocrypha* by E. Hennecke, edited by W. Schneemelcher. Vol. 1, 278–307. Philadelphia: The Westminster Press, 1963.

Robinson, J. M., and H. Koester. *Trajectories Through Early Christianity.* Philadelphia: Fortress Press, 1971.

THE GOSPEL ACCORDING TO THOMAS[a]

(Prologue, 1)
Importance of interpreting the obscure sayings

10 **32** THESE are the obscure[b] sayings that the living Jesus uttered and
12 which Didymus Jude Thomas[c] wrote down. •And he said, "Whoever   Jn 8:52
finds the meaning[d] of these sayings will not taste death."

(2)
Seek until you find

14 JESUS said, "Let one who seeks not stop seeking until that person   92
16,17 finds; •and upon finding, the person will be disturbed; •and being   Mt 7:7 ?
18 disturbed,[e] will be astounded; •and will reign over the entirety."[f]   Lk 11:9 ?

(3)
The kingdom is within us

19 JESUS said, "If those who lead[g] you (plur.) say to you, 'See, the   113
23 kingdom is in heaven,' then the birds of heaven will precede you. •If   Lk 17:20 ?
25 they say to you, 'It is in the sea,'[h] then the fish[i] will precede you. •But
the kingdom[j] is inside of you. And it is outside of you.
26   "When you become acquainted with yourselves,[k] then you will be
1 recognized. **33** •And you will understand that[a] it is you who are children
2 of the living father. •But if you do not become acquainted with yourselves,
then you are in poverty, and it is you who are the poverty."

(4)
The first will be last

5 JESUS said, "A person advanced in days will not hesitate to question   Mt 11:25 ?
8 a little child seven days old about the place of life. •And that person   Lk 10:21 ?
9 will live. •For many that are first will be last,[b] and they will become   Mt 19:30
one."   Mt 20:16
    Mk 10:31
    Lk 13:30

Title 32 a. In the manuscript, the title is found after the text (at 51:27f).

b. Or "hidden."

c. "Didymus" and "Thomas" mean "twin" (in Greek and Syriac or Aramaic, *didymos* and *tā'mā* etc.). The Greek fragment (P. Oxy. 654) instead has "and which Jude, who is called Thoma."

d. Or "interpretation."

e. "will be disturbed; and being disturbed": not present in the Greek fragment (P. Oxy. 654).

f. "and will reign over the entirety": the Greek fragment instead has "[and] being astounded, will reign; and [reigning], will [gain repose]." The last two words are partly preserved in the Greek.

g. The Greek fragment (P. Oxy. 654) instead has "attract."

h. "in the sea": the Greek fragment instead has "under the earth."

i. The Greek fragment instead has "the fish of the sea."

j. The Greek fragment instead has "And the kingdom [of god]."

k. Or "know yourselves."

33 a. "When you . . . understand that": the Greek fragment instead has "[Those who] become acquainted with [themselves] will find it; [and when you] become acquainted with yourselves, [you will understand that]."

b. The Greek fragment (P. Oxy. 654) next has "and the last, first."

(5)
The obscure will become disclosed

10 JESUS said, "Recognize what is before your (sing.) face and what is
13 obscure[c] to you (sing.) will become disclosed unto you. •For there is
nothing obscure that will not become shown forth."[d]

Mt 10:26
Mk 4:22
Lk 8:17
Lk 12:2

(6)
True fasting, prayer, and charity

14,15 HIS DISCIPLES questioned him and said to him, •"Do you want[e] us
to fast? And how shall we pray? Shall we[f] give alms? And what kind of
18 diet shall we follow?" •Jesus said, "Do not lie, and do not do what you
19 hate. For all things are disclosed before heaven.[g] •For there is nothing
22 obscure[h] that will not be shown forth, •and there is nothing covered that
will remain without being disclosed."[i]

Mt 6:1
Mt 6:16
v.15
14
5+

(7)
The lion and the human being

23 JESUS said, "Blessed is the lion that the human being will devour so
26 that the lion becomes human. •And cursed is the human being that the
lion devours; and the lion will become human."

(8)
A parable of an intelligent fisherman

28 AND HE said, "What human beings[j] resemble is an intelligent fisherman
who, having cast his net into the sea, pulled the net up out of the sea
32 full of little fish. •The intelligent fisherman, upon finding among them a
fine large fish, threw all the little fish back into the sea, choosing without
2 any effort the big fish. 34 •Whoever has ears to hear should listen!"

Mt 13:47

(9)
A parable of a sower

3 JESUS said, "Listen, a sower came forth, took a handful, and cast.
5 Now, some fell upon the path, and the birds came and picked them out.
6 Others fell upon rock, and they did not take root in the soil, and did
9 not send up ears. •And others fell upon the thorns, and they choked the
11 seed; and the grubs devoured them. •And others fell upon good soil,
and it sent up good crops and yielded sixty per measure and a hundred
and twenty per measure."

Mt 13:3
Mk 4:3
Lk 8:5

c. Or "hidden."
d. The Greek fragment (P. Oxy. 654) next has "and nothing buried that [will not be raised]."
e. The Greek fragment (P. Oxy. 654) instead has "How do you want."
f. The Greek fragment instead has "And how [shall we]."

g. "before heaven": the Greek fragment instead has "before truth."
h. Or "hidden."
i. "and there is nothing . . . disclosed": not present in the Greek fragment.
j. "human beings": lit. "the man."

(10)
Jesus has cast fire

14 JESUS said, "I have cast fire upon the world, and see, I am watching   Lk 12:49
over it until it blazes."

(11)
The living will not die

16 JESUS said, "This heaven will pass away, and the one above it will   Mt 24:35 ?
18 pass away. •And the dead (elements) are not alive, and the living   Mk 13:31 ?
19 (elements) will not die. •In the days when you (plur.) used to ingest   Lk 21:33 ?
21 dead (elements), you made them alive. •When you are in the light what
will you do?
22,23   "On the day that you were one, you made two. •And when you are
two, what will you do?"

(12)
The disciples will come to James

25 THE DISCIPLES said to Jesus, "We are aware that you will depart   Mt 18:1 ?
26,27 from us. •Who will be our leader?" •Jesus said to them, "No matter   Mk 9:34 ?
where you come[a] it is to James the Just[b] that you shall go, for whose   Lk 9:46 ?
sake heaven and earth have come to exist."

(13)
The disciples tell Jesus what he resembles

30 JESUS said to his disciples, "Compare me to something and tell me   Mt 16:13
what I resemble."   Mk 8:27
32   Simon Peter said to him, "A just angel is what you resemble."   Lk 9:18
34   Matthew said to him, "An intelligent philosopher is what you resemble."
2 35 Thomas said to him, "Teacher, my mouth utterly will not let me
say what you resemble."
4   Jesus said, "I am not your (sing.) teacher, for you have drunk and
become intoxicated from the bubbling wellspring that I have personally
7 measured out." •And he took him, withdrew, and said three sayings to
him.
8   Now, when Thomas came to his companions they asked him, "What
did Jesus say to you?"
10   Thomas said to them, "If I say to you (plur.) one of the sayings that
he said to me, you will take stones and stone me, and fire will come out
of the stones and burn you up."

(14)
True fasting, prayer, and charity

14 JESUS said to them, "If you (plur.) fast, you will acquire a sin, and if   6+
you pray you will be condemned, and if you give alms, it is evil that

---

34. a. Or "come from."
   b. According to early Christian tradition,
a brother of Jesus (and so of Thomas) who
was leader of the first Christian community

of Jerusalem; died A.D. 62. His name was
venerated by an Aramaic-speaking branch of
Christianity that flourished east of the Jordan
River.

19 you will do unto your spirits. •And when you go into any land and travel
in the country places,[a] when they receive you eat whatever they serve
23,24 to you. •Heal those among them who are sick. •For, nothing that enters
25 your mouth will defile you (plur.). •Rather, it is precisely what comes
out of your mouth that will defile you.''

Mt 10:8 ?
Lk 10:8
v.24
Mt 15:11
Mt 15:17
Mk 7:15

(15)
One not born of woman

27 JESUS said, ''When you (plur.) see one who has not been born of
woman, fall upon your faces and prostrate yourselves before that one:
30 it is that one who is your father.''

(16)
Jesus has come to impose divisions

31 JESUS said, ''People probably think that it is peace that I have come
33 to impose[b] upon the world. •And they do not recognize that it is divisions[c]
36 that I have come to impose upon the earth—fire, sword, battle. •Indeed,
1 there will be five in a house. **36** •There will be three over two and two
4 over three, parent over child and child over parent. •And they will stand
at rest by being solitaries.''

Mt 10:34
Lk 12:51

(17)
Jesus will bestow what has not been perceived

5 JESUS said, ''I shall give you (plur.) what eyes have not seen, what
ears have not heard, what hands have not touched, what has not come
upon the human heart.''

1Co 2:9

(18)
The end is where the beginning is

9 THE DISCIPLES said to Jesus, ''Tell us how our end will come to
11 pass.'' •Jesus said, ''Then have you laid bare the beginning,[a] so that
13 you are seeking the end? •For the end will be where the beginning is.
14,15 Blessed is the person who stands at rest in the beginning. •And that
person will be acquainted with the end and will not taste death.''

(19)
The preexistent is blessed

17 JESUS said, ''Blessed is that which[b] existed before coming into being.
19 If you exist as my disciples and listen to my sayings, these stones will
minister unto you.

Five trees in paradise

21 ''Indeed, you have five trees in paradise, which do not move in
24 summer or winter, and whose leaves do not fall. •Whoever is acquainted
with them will not taste death.''

---

35. a. Or ''travel in the places.''　　**36** a. Or ''the first principle.''
　　b. Or ''cast.''　　　　　　　　　　　b. ''that which'': or ''the person who.''
　　c. Or ''distinctions.''

(20)
A parable of a mustard seed

26 THE DISCIPLES said to Jesus, "Tell us what[c] the kingdom of heavens
28 resembles." •He said to them, "What it resembles is a grain of mustard
29 seed. •It is smaller than all other seeds, but if it falls upon plowed terrain
it puts forth an enormous foliage and is a shade for birds of heaven."

Mt 13:31
Mk 4:30
Lk 13:18

(21)
A parable of children living in a plot of land

33,35 MARY said to Jesus, "What do your disciples resemble?" •He said,
"What they resemble is children living in a plot of land that is not theirs.
2 **37** When the owners of the land come they will say, 'Surrender our
4 land to us.' •They, for their part, strip naked in their presence in order
to give it back to them, and they give them their land.

A story of a landowner and a bandit

6 "Thus I say that the owner of an estate, knowing that a bandit is
coming, will keep watch before the bandit comes and not let the bandit
10 break into the house of the estate[a] and steal the possessions.[b] •You
11 (plur.), then, be on your guard against the world. •Arm yourselves with
great power lest the brigands find a way to get to you; for the trouble
15 that you expect will come. •Let an experienced person dwell in your
midst!

103
Mt 24:43
Lk 12:39

Lk 12:35

From a parable of a harvest[c]

17 "When the crop had matured, that person came in haste, sickle in
18 hand, and harvested it. •Whoever has ears to hear should listen!"

Mk 4:29

Mt 13:9
Mk 4:9
Lk 8:8

(22)
Those who enter the kingdom resemble little ones

20,20 JESUS saw some little ones nursing. •He said to his disciples, "What
these little ones who are nursing resemble is those who enter the
23 kingdom." •They said to him, "So shall we enter the kingdom by being
24 little ones?" •Jesus said to them, "When you (plur.) make the two one
and make the inside like the outside and the outside like the inside and
the above like the below, and that you might make the male and the
female be one and the same, so that the male might not be male nor the
female be female, when you make eyes in place of an eye and a hand
in place of a hand and a foot in place of a foot, an image in place of an
image—then you will enter [the kingdom]."

Mt 18:1
Mk 10:13
Lk 18:15

(23)
Few are chosen

1 **38** JESUS said, "I shall choose you (plur.)—one out of a thousand
2 and two out of ten thousand. •And they will stand at rest by being one
and the same."

---

c. Lit. "who."

37 a. "estate"; lit. "kingdom, dominion."
b. "the house . . . the estate . . . the

possessions": lit. "his house . . . his estate
. . . his possessions."
c. A fragment of a parable. Some words
are missing before "When the crop . . ."

(24)
A person of light enlightens the whole world

3 HIS DISCIPLES said, "Show us the place where you are, for we must
6,7 seek it." •He said to them, "Whoever has ears should listen! •There is   Mt 6:22
9 light existing within a person of light. •And it enlightens the whole   Lk 11:34
world: if it[a] does not enlighten, that person[b] is darkness."

(25)
Love your sibling

10,11 JESUS said, "Love your (sing.) sibling like your own soul;[c] •look out   Mt 22:39
for that person like the apple of your eye."   Mk 12:31
                                                                                Lk 10:27

(26)
The speck and the beam

12 JESUS said, "You (sing.) see the speck in your sibling's eye, but you   Mt 7:3
14 do not see the beam in your own eye. •When you expel the beam from   Lk 6:41
your own eye then you will be able to see to expel the speck from the
eye of your sibling."

(27)
Abstinence from the world

17 ⟨JESUS said⟩,[d] "If you (plur.) do not abstain from[e] the world you will
19 not find the kingdom.[f] •If you do not make the sabbath a sabbath you
will not behold the father."

(28)
The world is intoxicated

20,22 JESUS said, "I stood at rest in the midst of the world. •And unto them
23 I was shown forth incarnate; I found them all intoxicated. •And I found
24 none of them thirsty. •And my soul was pained for the children of
25,27 humankind, •for they are blind in their hearts and cannot see. •For,
empty did they enter the world, and again empty they seek to leave the
29,29 world. •But now they are intoxicated. •When they shake off their wine
then they will have a change of heart."[g]

(29)
Independence of spirit and body

31 JESUS said, "It is amazing if it was for the spirit that flesh came into
32 existence. •And it is amazing indeed if spirit (came into existence) for
34 the sake of the body. •But as for me, I am amazed at how this great
wealth has come to dwell in this poverty."

---

38 a. "And it . . . if it": or "And he . . . if   fragment (P. Oxy. 655).
he."   e. "abstain from": lit. "fast unto."
  b. Or "it."   f. The Greek fragment instead has "the
  c. Or "your own self."   kingdom of God."
  d. These words are inadvertently omitted   g. Or "will repent."
in the Coptic MS, but present in the Greek

(30)
Jesus dwells where there are two or more

2 **39** JESUS said, "Where there are three divine beings they are divine.
4 Where there are two or one, I myself dwell with that person."[a]   Mt 18:20

(31)
Prophets and physicians are not accepted at home

5 JESUS said, "A prophet is not acceptable in that prophet's own native   Mt 13:57
6 town. •A physician does not heal people who are acquainted with that   Mk 6:4
physician."   Lk 4:24

(32)
A city on a hill cannot be hidden

7 JESUS said, "A city built upon a high hill and fortified cannot fall. Nor   Mt 5:14
can it become hidden."

(33)
No one hides a lamp

10 JESUS said, "Whatever you (sing.) hear with your ear, proclaim upon   Mt 10:27
13 your (plur.) rooftops into the other ear.[b] •Indeed, no one lights a lamp   Lk 12:3
15 and puts it under a vessel, nor puts it in a hidden place. •Rather it is   v.13
put on a lampstand so that each who enters and leaves might see its   Mt 5:15
light."   Mk 4:21
   Lk 8:16
   Lk 11:33

(34)
The blind cannot lead the blind

18 JESUS said, "If a blind person leads a blind person both will fall into   Mt 15:14
a hole."   Lk 6:39

(35)
No one robs the strong without subduing them

20 JESUS said, "No one can enter the house of the strong and wreck it   Mt 12:29
23 without first tying that person's hands. •Thereafter, one can ransack[c]   Mk 3:27
the person's house."   Lk 11:21

(36)
What we wear is unimportant

24 JESUS said, "Do not worry from dawn to dusk and from dusk to dawn   Mt 6:25
about what you (plur.) will wear."[d]   Lk 12:22

39. a. The Greek fragment (P. Oxy. 1) appears to have had (39:4f) "Where there are [three, they are] godless. And where there is [one] alone, I say that I myself am with that one. Lift a stone and you (sing.) will find me there. Split a piece of wood, and I am there." For the last two sentences, see also no. 77.

b. I.e. into someone else's ear.

c. Or "overturn."

d. The Greek fragment (P. Oxy. 655) instead has "[what food] you (plur.) [will] eat, [or] what [clothing] you will wear. [You are much] better than the [lilies], which [neither] card nor spin. And for your part, what [will you wear] when you have no clothing? Who would add to your stature? It is he who will give you your clothing."

(37)
The disciples must strip off their garments

27 HIS DISCIPLES said,[e] "When will you be shown forth to us and when
29 shall we behold you?"[f] •Jesus said,[g] "When you strip naked without
being ashamed, and take your garments and put them under your feet
like little children and tread upon them, then [you] will see the child of   Mt 16:16 ?
1 the living. 40 •And you will not be afraid."

(38)
Jesus' sayings have long been awaited

2 JESUS said, "On many occasions you (plur.) have wanted to hear these   Mt 13:16 ?
4 sayings that I am saying unto you. •And you have no one else to hear   Lk 10:23 ?
5 them from. •Days will come when you will seek me, and you will not
find me."

(39)
Pharisees and Scribes impede acquaintance

7 JESUS said, "The Pharisees and the Scribes have taken the keys to   102
9 acquaintance and hidden them. •They have neither entered nor let those   Mt 23:13
                                                                          Lk 11:52
11 who want to enter enter. •You (plur.), then, be as shrewd as snakes and   Mt 10:16
as innocent as doves."

(40)
A parable of a grapevine

13,14 JESUS said, "A grapevine has been planted outside the father. •And   Mt 15:13
because it is not sound, it will be plucked out by the root and will
perish."

(41)
The person who has will receive

16,17 JESUS said, "The person who possesses[a] will be given more. •And the   Mt 13:12
person who does not have will be deprived of even the little that that   Mk 4:25
                                                                       Lk 8:18
person has."   v.17
                                                                       Mt 25:29
                                                                       Lk 19:26

(42)
We should be passersby

19 JESUS said, "Be passersby."[b]

---

e. The Greek fragment (P. Oxy. 655) instead has "said to him."

f. The Greek fragment instead has "When will you be visible to us, and when shall we behold you?"

g. The Greek fragment instead has "He said."

40 a. Lit. "who has in his hand."

b. "passersby": participle of the Greek verb *paragein*, "to go past (something or someone)." Epitaphs on Greek tombstones of the period often salute the "stranger" or "passerby" (usually called *ksenos* or *paroditēs*), as though in the words of the corpse buried in the tomb. Cf. no. 56. The saying may also be a recommendation of the life of a wandering ascetic, like St. Thomas in *The Acts of Thomas*.

(43)
Disciples should recognize Jesus in his sayings

20 HIS DISCIPLES said to him, "Who are you, since you say these things
21 to us?" •⟨Jesus said to them⟩,ᶜ "Do you (plur.) not understand who I
23 am from the things I am saying to you? •Rather, you have come to be
24,25 like Jews. •For they love the tree, and hate its fruit. •And they love the
fruit, and hate the tree."

Mt 7:16 ?
Mt 12:33 ?
Lk 6:43 ?

(44)
On blasphemy

26 JESUS said, "Whoever utters blasphemy against the father will be
27 forgiven. •And whoever utters blasphemy against the son will be forgiven.
29 But whoever utters blasphemy against the holy spirit will not be
forgiven—neither on earth nor in heaven."

Mt 12:31
Mk 3:28
Lk 12:10

(45)
Grapes do not come from thorns

31 JESUS said, "Grapes are not harvested from thorn trees,ᵈ nor are figs
34 gathered from thorn bushes,ᵉ for these do not bear fruit. •Good people
1 produce good from their store. 41 •Evil people produce wicked things
4 from their evil store within their hearts, and say wicked things. •For out
of the heart's abundance they produce wicked things."

Mt 7:16
Lk 6:44
v.34
Mt 12:34
Lk 6:45

(46)
Little ones are more exalted than John the Baptist

6 JESUS said, "From Adam unto John the Baptist there has been none
among the offspring of women who has been more exalted than John
10 the Baptist, so that such a person's eyes might be broken.ᵃ •But I have
said that whoever among you (plur.) becomes a little one will become
acquainted with the kingdom, and will become more exalted than John."

Mt 11:11
Lk 7:28

Mt 18:3
Mk 10:15
Lk 18:17

(47)
Opposites cannot coexist

12 JESUS said, "A person cannot (at the same time) mount two horses or
14 draw two bows. •And a slave cannot serve two owners, but truly will
17 honor the one and scoff at the other. •No person drinks vintage wine
19 and immediately desires to drink new wine. •And new wine is not put
20 into old wineskins lest they burst. •And vintage wine is not put into new
22 wineskins lest it go bad. •And old patches are not sewed to new garments,
for a rip will develop."

Mt 6:24
Lk 16:13
v.17
Lk 5:39
v.19
Mt 9:16
Mk 2:21
Lk 5:36

c. These words are inadvertently omitted
in the MS.
   d. The Coptic word denotes the *acacia nilotica*.
   e. The Coptic word denotes the *leucacanthus*.

41 a. The exact meaning of this expression
is unknown.

(48)

The power of unity

24 JESUS said, "If two make peace with one another within a single house
they will say to a mountain 'go elsewhere' and it will go elsewhere."

106
Mt 17:20
Mt 21:21
Mk 11:22
Lk 17:6 ?

(49)

Solitaries have come from the kingdom

27 JESUS said, "Blessed are those who are solitary and superior,[b] for you
29 (plur.) will find the kingdom; •for since you come from it you shall
return to it."

(50)

We have come from the light

30 JESUS said, "If they say to you (plur.), 'Where are you from?' say to
them, 'It is from the light that we have come—from the place where
light, of its own accord alone, came into existence and [stood at rest].
1,1 **42** •And it has been shown forth in their image.'[a] •If they say to you,
'Is it you?'[b] say, 'We are its offspring, and we are the chosen of the
4 living father.' •If they ask you, 'What is the sign of your father within
you?' say to them, 'It is movement and repose.'"

(51)

Arrival of repose and a new world

7 HIS DISCIPLES said to him, "When will the repose of the dead come
10 to pass, and when will the new world come?" •He said to them, "That
(repose) which you (plur.) are waiting for has come, but for your part
you do not recognize it."

(52)

The twenty-four prophets of Israel

12 HIS DISCIPLES said to him, "Twenty-four prophets spoke in Israel,
15 and they all spoke by you."[c] •He said to them, "You (plur.) have
abandoned the one who is living in your presence, and you have spoken
of those who are dead."

(53)

True circumcision

18 HIS DISCIPLES said to him, "Does circumcision help or does it not?"
19 He said to them, "If it helped, people's fathers would beget them from
22 their mothers already circumcised. •But true circumcision in spirit has
become very profitable."

b. Or "Blessed are the solitaries and the
elect persons."

42 a. Or "in their images."

b. Possibly the original reading of the text
is "Who are you?"
　　c. Or "in you."

(54)

The poor

23 JESUS said, "Blessed are the poor,[d] for yours (plur.) is the kingdom of heavens."   Mt 5:3 / Lk 6:20

(55)

We should hate our family

25 JESUS said, "Those who do not hate[e] their fathers and their mothers 27 cannot be disciples of me, •and those who do not hate their brothers and their sisters and take up their cross like me will not become worthy of[f] me."   16 ?, 101 / Mt 10:37 / Lk 14:26 / Mt 16:24 / Mk 8:34 / Lk 9:23

(56)

The world is a corpse

29 JESUS said, "Whoever has become acquainted with the world has found a corpse, and the world is not worthy of the one who has found the corpse."

(57)

A parable of wheat and tares

32 JESUS said, "What the kingdom of the father resembles is a man who 35 had a [good] (kind of) seed. •His enemy came at night and scattered 2 grass seed in with the good seed. 43 •The man did not let them pluck out the grass, saying to them, 'Do not, lest you (plur.) go to pluck out 5 the grass and then pluck out the wheat along with it. •For, on the day of the harvest the grass will be obvious, and it will be plucked out and burned.'"   Mt 13:24

(58)

The laborer

7 JESUS said, "Blessed is the person who has labored and found life."

(59)

We should meditate on the one who is alive

9 JESUS said, "Consider the one who is alive[a] while you (plur.) are alive, lest you die and then seek to behold that one—and you will not be able to behold."

(60)

A parable of a Samaritan and a lamb

12 ⟨THEY SAW⟩[b] a Samaritan man carrying a lamb as he went into Judaea.

---

d. Apart from its literal meaning, "the poor" was early Christian jargon used as a self-designation by an Aramaic-speaking branch of Christianity. Cf. note 34b.

e. Lit. "He who does not hate."

f. Or "become equal to."

43 a. Or "that which is alive."

b. These words are inadvertently omitted in the Coptic MS.

13,15 He said to his disciples, "This ⟨. . .⟩ . . . the lamb."ᶜ •They said to him,
16 "So that he might slaughter it and have it to eat." •He said to them,
"He will not eat it while it (or he) is alive, but rather when he has
18 slaughtered it so it becomes a carcassᵈ." •They said, "Otherwise, he
19 cannot do it?" •He said to them, "You (plur.), too, seek for yourselves
a placeᵉ for repose, lest you become a carcass and be devoured."

(61)
Jesus on Salome's couch

23 JESUS said, "Two will repose on a couch:ᶠ one will die, one will live."   Lk 17:34
25,26 Salome said, "Who are you, O man? •Like a stranger (?)ᵍ you have   Mt 24:40 ?
28 gotten upon my couch and you have eaten from my table." •Jesus said
29 to her, "It is I who come from that which is integrated. •I was given   Mt 11:27
30 (some) of the things of my father." •⟨. . .⟩ʰ "I am your female disciple."   Lk 10:22
⟨. . .⟩ⁱ
31 "Therefore I say that such a person, once integrated,ʲ will become
33 full of light; •but such a person, once divided, will become full of
darkness."

(62)
Jesus tells his secrets to the worthy

34 JESUS said, "It is to those [worthy] of [my] secrets that I am telling   Mt 13:11
1 my secrets. 44 •Do not let your (sing.) left hand understand what your   Mk 4:11
right hand is doing."   Lk 8:10
                                                                        v.1
                                                                     Mt 6:3

(63)
A parable of a rich man who died

2,4 JESUS said, "There was a rich man who had considerable wealth. •He   Lk 12:16
said, 'I shall invest my wealth so as to sow, reap, plant, and fill my
7 barns with crops, lest I run short of something.' •These things are what
9 he was thinking in his heart, and that very night the man died. •Whoever
has ears should listen!"

(64)
A parable of a dinner for out-of-town guests

10,11 JESUS said, "A man was receivingᵃ out-of-town visitors. •And having   Mt 22:1
13 prepared the dinner, he sent a slave to invite the visitors. •The slave   Lk 14:16
15 went to the first and said to that one, 'My master invites you.' •That
person said, 'Some wholesale merchants owe me money; they are coming
to me this evening, and I shall go and give them instructions. I must
18 decline the dinner invitation.' •The slave went to another and said to
20 that one, 'My master invites you.' •That person said to the slave, 'I

---

c. The Coptic MS here erroneously has "This one is in the neighborhood of the lamb." One or more words have inadvertently been omitted, and the original reading of the text is uncertain here.
d. Or "corpse."
e. Or "an occasion."
f. Ancient Mediterranean peoples often dined in a reclining position upon a couch or bench.
g. The MS here erroneously has "As for

one." The original reading of the text is uncertain.
h. One or more words are inadvertently omitted here.
i. One or more words are inadvertently omitted here.
j. The Coptic MS here erroneously has "once having become devastated."

44 a. Or "had the habit of receiving."

have bought a building, and I am needed for a time. I am not free.'
22 The slave went to another and said to that one, 'My master invites you.'
23 That person said to the slave, 'My friend is about to get married, and it
is I who am going to give the dinner. I cannot come; I must decline the
25 dinner invitation.' •The slave went to another and said to that one, 'My
27 master invites you.' •That person said to the slave, 'I have bought a
village; I am going to collect the rents. I cannot come, I must decline.'
29 The slave came and said to its master, 'The people you have invited to
31 the dinner have declined.' •The master said to his slave, 'Go outside
34 into the streets; bring in whomever you find, to have dinner.' •Buyers
and traders [will] not enter the places of my father.''

(65)
A parable of the murder of a vineyard owner's son

1 **45** HE said, ''A kind man owned a vineyard, and put it in the hands
of cultivators for them to cultivate, so that he might get its produce
4 from them. •He sent his slave so the cultivators might give the produce
6 of the vineyard to the slave. •They seized, beat, and all but killed his
8 slave, and the slave went and spoke to its owner. •Its owner said,
10 'Perhaps they did not recognize it (the slave),'[a] •and he sent another
11 slave. The cultivators beat the other slave. •Next the owner sent his
13 son and said, 'Perhaps they will show respect for my son.' •Those
cultivators, since they recognized that it was he who was heir to the
16 vineyard, seized him and killed him. •Whoever has ears should listen!''

Mt 21:33
Mk 12:1
Lk 20:9

(66)
The rejected building stone

16 JESUS said, ''Show me the stone that the builders rejected: that is the
building stone.''[b]

Mt 21:24
Mk 12:10
Lk 20:17

(67)
Any deficiency is utter deficiency

19 JESUS said, ''If anyone should become acquainted with the entirety
and should fall short at all (?), that person falls short utterly.''[c]

Mt 16:26
Mk 8:36
Lk 9:25

(68)
The persecuted are blessed

21 JESUS said, ''Blessed are you (plur.) whenever they hate you and
23 persecute you. •And wherever they have persecuted you, they will find
no place.''

(69)
The internally persecuted and the compassionate are blessed

24 JESUS said, ''Blessed are those who have been persecuted in their
26 hearts. •It is they who have truly come to be acquainted with the father.
27 Blessed are they who hunger for the belly of the needy to be satisfied.''

Mt 5:10
Lk 6:22

Mt 5:6
Lk 6:21

---

45 a. The Coptic MS here erroneously has
"Perhaps it (the slave) did not recognize
them."

b. "building stone": or perhaps "foundation stone, cornerstone, keystone."
c. Or "falls short of the whole place."

(70)
Our salvation is within us

29 JESUS said, "If you (plur.) produce what is in you, what you have will
31 save you. •If you do not have what is in you, what you do not have
[will] kill you."

(71)
Destruction of "this building"

34 JESUS said, "I shall throw down [this] building, and no one will be   Mt 26:61
able to build it [. . .]."   Mk 14:58

(72)
Jesus is not an arbitrator of possessions

1 **46** SOME PERSON [said] to him, "Tell my siblings to share my   Lk 12:13
3 father's possessions with me." •He said to that person, "My good
4 fellow, who has made me into an arbitrator?" •He turned to his disciples
and said to them, "So am I an arbitrator?"

(73)
Workers for the harvest

6,7 JESUS said, "The harvest is plentiful but the workers are few. •So   Mt 9:37
plead with the lord[a] to dispatch workers for the harvest."   Lk 10:2

(74)
The cistern is empty

9 HE said, "O lord, there are many around the drinking trough but nothing
in the cistern."[b]

(75)
Solitaries will enter the bridal chamber

11 JESUS said, "There are many standing at the door, but it is the solitaries
who will enter the bridal chamber."[c]

(76)
A parable of a merchant and a pearl

13 JESUS said, "What the kingdom of the father resembles is a merchant   Mt 13:45
who owned some merchandise, and then learned about the existence of   HPrl 12
16 a certain pearl. •That merchant was shrewd, sold the merchandise, and
19 bought the single pearl. •You (plur.), too, seek the ceaseless and enduring   Mt 6:20
treasure, where moth does not approach to eat nor worm to destroy."   Lk 12:33

---

46 a. Or "the owner."
  b. Or "well."
  c. Or "wedding hall." For Valentinian

imagery of the "bridal chamber," see especially GPh.

(77)
Jesus is the entirety and is everywhere

22,24 JESUS said, "It is I who am the light (that presides) over all. •It is I who am the entirety: it is from me that the entirety has come, and to
26,27 me that the entirety goes. •Split a piece of wood: I am there. •Lift a stone, and you (plur.) will find me there."[d]

(78)
The goal of coming out to the countryside

28 JESUS said, "Why have you (plur.) come out into the countryside?   Mt 11:7
29 To see a reed shaken by the wind? And to see a person dressed in fine   Lk 7:24
apparel [like your] governors[e] and your members of court, who wear fine apparel and cannot recognize truth?"

(79)
Those who have kept the father's utterance are blessed

3 **47** A WOMAN in the crowd said to him, "Blessed are the womb that   Lk 11:27
6 bore you and the breasts that nourished you!" •He said to [her], "Blessed are those who have heard the father's utterance (or Word) and truly
9 kept it! •For days are coming when you (plur.) will say, 'Blessed are   Lk 23:28
the womb that has not conceived and the breasts that have not given   Mt 24:19 ?
milk!'"   Mk 13:17 ?
      Lk 21:23 ?

(80)
The world is like the body

12 JESUS said, "Whoever has become acquainted with the world has found the body, and the world is not worthy of the one who has found the body."[a]

(81)
The rich should reign and renounce

15,16 JESUS said, "The one who has become rich should reign. •And the one who has power should renounce."[b]

(82)
Fire and the kingdom are with Jesus

17 JESUS said, "Whoever is near me is near fire, and whoever is far from   Mk 12:34 ?
me is far from the kingdom."

(83)
Light is hidden by images

19,21 JESUS said, "Images are visible to human beings. •And the light within

---

d. The Greek fragment (P. Oxy. 1) gives these last two sentences as parts of no. 30.
e. Or "kings, emperors."

47 a. This saying is nearly identical with no. 56, which likens the world to a "corpse" (Greek *ptōma*) rather than the body (Greek *to sōma*).
  b. Or "deny."

these (images) is hidden by the image of the father's light: it^c will be
23 disclosed. •And his image is hidden by his light.''

(84)
Our encounter with our preexistent images

24 JESUS said, ''When you (plur.) see your resemblance you are happy.
26 But when you see your images that came into existence before you and
are neither mortal nor visible, how much you will have to bear!''

(85)
Adam was not worthy of us

29 JESUS said, ''It was from a great power and a great wealth that Adam
33 came into being: and he did not become worthy of you (plur.). •For,
had he been worthy [he would] not [have tasted] death.''

(86)
The son of man has nowhere to lay his head

34 JESUS said, ''[Foxes have] their dens and birds have their nests. Mt 8:20
2 **48** But the son of man^a has nowhere to lay his head and gain repose.'' Lk 9:58

(87)
Soul should be independent of body

4,6 JESUS said, ''Wretched is the body that depends upon a body. •And
wretched is the soul that depends upon^b these two.''

(88)
We should give to messengers and prophets

7 JESUS said, ''The messengers^c and the prophets are coming to you
9 (plur.), and they will give you the things that you possess. •And you,
too—give them the things that you have, and say among yourselves,
'When are they coming to take their own?' ''

(89)
We should wash not only the outside

13 JESUS said, ''Why are you (plur.) washing the outside of the cup? Mt 23:25
14 Don't you think that the one who made the inside is the very same one Lk 11:39
who made the outside?''

(90)
Jesus' yoke is easy

16 JESUS said, ''Come (plur.) to me, for my yoke is easy (to use) and my Mt 11:28
19 lordship^d is mild, •and you will find repose for yourselves.''

---

c. Or ''he.''

48 a. Or ''a child of humankind.''
  b. ''depends upon . . . depends upon'':

lit. ''hangs from.''
  c. Or ''angels.''
  d. Or ''ownership,'' the relation of owner
to slave.

(91)
Recognition of Jesus' presence

20 THEY said to him, "Tell us who you are, so that we might believe in
21 you." •He said to them, "You (plur.) are testing the face of heaven and
earth, and you have not recognized the one who is in your presence!
24 And you do not recognize how to test the present time."ᵉ

Mt 16:1
Lk 12:54

(92)
We do not seek what Jesus wishes to tell us

25,26 JESUS said, "Seek and you (plur.) will find. •Yet, now I am willing to
say the things which you used to ask me about and which I did not say
to you; and you are not seeking them."

2
Mt 7:7
Lk 11:9

(93)
Do not give the holy to dogs

30 ⟨JESUS said⟩,ᶠ "Do not give holy things to dogs, lest they throw them
31 upon the dunghill. •Do not throw pearls to swine lest they [. . .]."ᵍ

Mt 7:6

(94)
Seekers will enter

33,34 JESUS [said], "One who seeks will find. •The door will be opened to
one [who knocks]."

Mt 7:8

(95)
We should not lend at interest

35 [JESUS said], "If you (plur.) have money, do not lend it out at interest.
1 49 Rather, give [it] to one from whom you will not get it back."

Lk 6:34
Mt 5:42 ?

(96)
A parable of a woman baking bread

2 JESUS [said], "What the kingdom of the father resembles is [a] woman
who took a small amount of leaven, [hid] it in some dough, and produced
5 huge loaves of bread. •Whoever has ears should listen!"

Mt 13:33
Lk 13:20

(97)
A parable of a woman with a jar of meal

7 JESUS said, "[What] the kingdom of the [father] resembles [is] a woman
9 who was conveying a [jar] full of meal. •When she had traveled far
[along] the road, the handle of the jar broke and the meal spilled out
12 after her [along] the road. •She was not aware ofª the fact; she had not
13 understood how to toil. •When she reached home she put down the jar
and found it empty."

e. "the present time": or "this time of crisis," Greek *kairos*.
f. These words are inadvertently omitted in the Coptic MS.
g. Perhaps "[grind them to bits]"; the

Coptic MS is imperfect here.

49 a. Lit. "She did not have acquaintance of."

(98)

A parable of an assassination

15 JESUS said, "What the kingdom of the father resembles is a man who
17 wanted to assassinate a member of court. •At home, he drew the dagger
and stabbed it into the wall in order to know whether his hand would
20 be firm. •Next, he murdered the member of court."

(99)

Jesus' true family

21 THE DISCIPLES said to him, "Your brothers and your mother are   Mt 12:47
23 standing outside." •He said to them, "It is those who are here and who   Mk 3:32
                                                                          Lk 8:20
25 do the will of my father that are my siblings and my mother. •It is they
who will enter the kingdom of my father."

(100)

Give unto Caesar the things that are Caesar's

27 THEY showed Jesus a gold coin and said to him, "Caesar's agents are   Mt 22:16
29 exacting^b taxes from us." •He said to them, "Give unto Caesar the   Mk 12:14
                                                                         Lk 20:21
things that are Caesar's, give unto god the things that are god's, and
give unto me that which is mine."

(101)

We should hate our family and love our true family

32 ⟨JESUS said⟩,^c "Those who do not hate their [father] and their mother   55+
34 as I do cannot be [disciples] of me. •And those who [do not] love their
36 [father and] their mother as I do cannot be [disciples of] me. •For my
1 mother [. . .]. **50** •But my true [mother] gave me life."

(102)

Pharisees impede nourishment

2,2 JESUS said, "Woe unto the Pharisees. •For what they resemble is a   39+
dog sleeping in the manger of some cattle, for it neither eats nor [lets]
the cattle feed."

(103)

A parable of a landowner and brigands

5 JESUS said, "Blessed is the man who recognizes [which] district the   21+
brigands are going to enter, so as to arise, gather (the forces of) his   (37:6)
domain, and arm himself before they enter."

(104)

Do not pray or fast while the bridegroom is present

10 THEY said [to Jesus], "Come, let us pray today, and let us fast."   Mt 9:14
12 Jesus said, "What is the sin that I have committed? Or how have I been   Mk 2:18
                                                                         Lk 5:33

b. Or "extorting."
c. These words are inadvertently omitted
in the MS.

14 overcome? •Rather, when the bridegroom leaves the bridal chamber then let people fast and pray.''

(105)
Acquaintance with the father and the mother

16 JESUS said, "Whoever is acquainted with the father and the mother will be called the offspring of a prostitute.''

(106)
The power of wholeness

18 JESUS said, "When you (plur.) make the two into one you will become 48+
20 sons of man,[a] •and when you say, 'O mountain, go elsewhere!' it will go elsewhere.''

(107)
A parable of a lost sheep

22 JESUS said, "What the kingdom resembles is a shepherd who had a   Mt 18:12
24,25 hundred sheep. •One of them, the largest, strayed away. •He left the   Lk 15:4
26 ninety-nine and sought the one until he found it. •After having toiled, he said to the sheep, "I love you (sing.) more than the ninety-nine.''

(108)
Assimilation to Jesus

28 JESUS said, "Whoever drinks from my mouth will become like me;
29 I, too, will become that person, and to that person the obscure[b] things will be shown forth.''

(109)
A parable of a hidden treasure

31 JESUS said, "What the kingdom resembles is a man who possessed a   Mt 13:4
33 hidden treasure in his field without knowing it. •And [upon] dying he
35,35 left it to his [son]. •The son [was] not aware of the fact.[c] •He assumed
1 (ownership of) the field and sold it. 51 •And the person who bought it came plowing, [found] the treasure, and began to lend out money at interest to whomever he wished.''

(110)
The rich should renounce

4 JESUS said, "The one who has found the world and become rich should renounce the world.''

---

50 a. Perhaps extending to all Christians of either sex. "Son of man" or "child of the human being" was a traditional eschatological title applied to Jesus in some early Christian circles; the arrival of the heavenly "son of man" would signal the arrival of god's kingdom.

b. Or "hidden."

c. Or "did not have acquaintance of the fact."

(111)
The living will not die

6 JESUS said, "The heavens and the earth will roll up in your (plur.)
7 presence. •And the living from the living[a] will not see death."—Doesn't Jesus mean that the world is not worthy of a person who has found the self?[b]

(112)
Soul should be independent of flesh

10,11 JESUS said, "Woe to the flesh that depends upon[c] a soul. •Woe to the soul that depends upon flesh."

(113)
The kingdom is already spread over the earth

12 HIS DISCIPLES said to him, "When is the kingdom going to come?"   3
14 ⟨Jesus said⟩,[d] "It is not by being waited for that it is going to come.   Lk 17:20
15,16 They are not going to say, 'Here it is' or 'There it is.' •Rather, the kingdom of the father is spread out over the earth, and people do not see it."

(114)
The female element must make itself male

18 SIMON PETER said to them, "Mary should leave us, for females are
20 not worthy of life." •Jesus said, "See, I am going to attract her to make her male so that she too might become a living spirit that resembles you
24 males. •For every female (element) that makes itself[e] male[f] will enter the kingdom of heavens."[g]

---

51 a. Lit. "the one who is alive out of the one who is alive."

b. "Doesn't Jesus . . . the self": probably a comment added to the text by an ancient reader and later erroneously incorporated in the text.

c. Lit. "hangs from."

d. These words are inadvertently omitted in the Coptic MS.

e. Or "every woman who makes herself."

f. "female (element) . . . male": it was a philosophical cliché that the material constituent of an entity was "female," while its form (or ideal form) was "male."

g. In the Coptic manuscript, the title of this work is written after the text (at 51:27f).

THE BOOK OF THOMAS
THE CONTENDER WRITING TO
THE PERFECT

(BTh)

Contents

Like HPrl and GTh, *The Book of Thomas: The Contender Writing to the Perfect*[1] ("The Book of Thomas the Athlete," "The Book of Thomas the Contender") is composed of materials associated with the traditional teaching of wisdom. In it, Jesus ("the savior") appears as an extraordinarily wise and authoritative teacher; his message is an uncompromising proclamation of the distinction between the wise ("perfect") and the foolish, and a prediction of the punishment that awaits the fool. Jesus is not mentioned by name in BTh; he is only called "savior." The myth of the soul that is represented in HPrl and hinted at in GTh provides a framework for the savior's teaching in BTh but does not form an important part of his message. Especially noteworthy is an explicit elaboration of the model of divine twinship (138:4f) between the savior and Jude Thomas.

The conception of the human being found in BTh seems to make a threefold distinction between the flesh or body, the perceptive faculties or soul, and the intellect or faculty capable of self-acquaintance, though this distinction is never clearly stated. The first half of the work concerns acquaintance or self-knowledge (*gnōsis*) and the valuelessness of the flesh. The second half (142:21f) is harshly ascetical and sermonlike, describing in detail the punishment that awaits the foolish person in hell and condemning the fool, who is subject to the influence of flesh. Generally speaking, the first half emphasizes the nature of the saved, while the second half describes the damned. A unifying pair of themes—light (*gnōsis*, the savior) and fire (desire, lust)—runs throughout the two sections.

Literary background

The date of composition of BTh is unknown; in any case, it must be before A.D. 350, the approximate date of the manuscript, and later than that of GTh, to which (GTh prologue, 1) allusion is made in BTh 138:1f. The mythic content of the work resembles HPrl and GTh (see introduction to HPrl, "Contents"). In the opening paragraph of BTh, the author states that he is a certain Mathaias, and claims to have compiled it by editing eyewitness records of conversations between the apostle

---

[1] Or *The Book of Thomas the Contender, Writing to the Perfect.*

Jude Thomas and "the savior" (Jesus); the work is thus probably an example of pseudepigraphy. It is unclear whether "Mathaias" here means the apostle Matthew or someone else. The language of composition was Greek.

BTh has a complex mixture of genres in which various traditional materials are subordinated to others.

I. Anthology of wise sayings
    A. Revelation dialogue
        1. Treatises
            a. The nature of acquaintance (*gnōsis*)
            b. The fate of souls and bodies
            c. The wise and the fool
    B. Eschatological sermon
        1. Description of the underworld
        2. Woes and blessings
        3. Call to wakefulness

In its opening the work characterizes itself as a wisdom book or *anthology of wise* ("obscure") *sayings,* alluding to the prologue of GTh, and in effect claiming to parallel the latter's contents. However, the term "sayings" is apt only in the second half (142:21 to the end), since the body of the work opens with a *revelatory dialogue* between Jesus and his disciple Jude Thomas; for this genre, see the introduction to BJn in Part One. The incongruity of the dialogic genre with the opening characterization has led some modern critics to conclude that in its present form BTh is merely a compilation of two earlier works: one a revelation dialogue, the other a collection of sayings. The wording of the title (which can be understood as two titles conjoined) has been cited in support of this view. The opening sentence alluding to a sayings collection would then have been an original part of the sayings material now found in 142:21f.

The savior's revelation in this dialogue takes the form of a philosophical *treatise* broken up into a series of lengthy replies given by the savior. These include an explicit discussion of the mystical theology implied by the model of divine twinship; and apocalyptic descriptions of the fate of souls and bodies and of the character of the wise and the fool.

The second half, or sayings section, continues the topic of the wise and the fool, now in the form of an eschatological monologue or *sermon.* Here the savior describes the punishments of hell that await the fool in the *underworld,* comparable to traditional Greek underworld (*nekyia*) literature. The sermon concludes with traditional *woes and blessings* and an eschatological *call to wakefulness.*

The style of BTh is often obscure, perhaps in keeping with the author's characterization of the work as "obscure sayings" (138:1f).

Mythic characters

I. Inhabitants of the Kingdom or Essence of Light

The KING, who is good (God the father)
The FEMALE BEING WHO IS TRULY WISE (Wisdom)
The SAVIOR. JESUS.

II. Inhabitants of the Heavens

The (chief) RULER
The AUTHORITIES

III. Inhabitants of Earth and Hell

Humankind:
  The IGNORANT
  The PERFECT, including Jude Thomas, Mathaias, and others
Wicked DEMONS
The ANGEL who rules Tartarus

Text

The original Greek apparently does not survive. The text is known only in Coptic translation, attested by a single manuscript from Nag Hammadi, MS NHC II (pp. 138–45), which was copied just before A.D. 350 and is now in the Cairo Coptic Museum.

The translation below is based on my own critical edition of the Coptic: B. Layton, ed., "The Book of Thomas," in vol. 2 of B. Layton, ed., *Nag Hammadi Codex II, 2–7* (see "Select Bibliography" under Turner), in press.

SELECT BIBLIOGRAPHY

Turner, J. *The Book of Thomas the Contender from Codex II of the Cairo Gnostic Library from Nag Hammadi (CG II,7): The Coptic Text with Translation, Introduction, and Commentary.* Society of Biblical Literature Dissertation Series, no. 23. Missoula, Mont.: Scholars Press and the Society of Biblical Literature, 1975.

—————. "Introduction [to the Book of Thomas]." In vol. 2 of *Nag Hammadi Codex II,2–7 Together with XIII,2*, Brit. Lib. Or. 4926(1) and P.Oxy. 1, 654, 655.* Edited by B. Layton. Nag Hammadi Studies. Leiden: E. J. Brill, in press.

THE BOOK OF THOMAS
THE CONTENDER WRITING
TO THE PERFECT[a]

I. CIRCUMSTANCES OF COMPOSITION

1 **138** The obscure[b] sayings that the savior uttered to Jude Thomas, GTh prol.
2,3 and which I, Mathaias, also wrote down. •I used to travel and listen to GTh 1
them as they were talking to one another.

II. THE NATURE OF ACQUAINTANCE (GNŌSIS)

Acquaintance with the savior is acquaintance with the self

4 The savior said, "Thomas, brother, while you have time in the world,
listen to me and I shall make a disclosure to you concerning what you
have thought about in your heart.
7 "Now, since it is said that you are my double[c] and my true companion,[d]
examine yourself and understand who you are, how you exist, and how
10 you will be. •Inasmuch as you are going to be called my sibling,[e] it is
12 not fitting for you to be unacquainted with your self. •And I recognize
12 that you have understood. •For, you have already understood that it is
14 I who am acquaintance with truth. •Thus, supposing that you go about
with me, even if you are without acquaintance you have already gotten
15 acquaintance, •and you will be called the man who knows himself.

Acquaintance with the self is acquaintance with the entirety

16 "For, those who have not known themselves have not been acquainted
17 with anything. •But those who have only known themselves have also
19 received acquaintance with the depth of the entirety.[f] •So for this reason,
Thomas (my) brother, you have personally seen what is obscure to[g]
humankind and what people are impeded by when they lack acquaintance."

III. INTERPRETATION OF THE SAVIOR'S SAYINGS

21 Then Thomas said to the lord, "So I beg you, then, before your
24 ascension to tell me [about the] things I am asking you about. •[And] Ac 1:3 ?
once I have heard from you about the obscure[h] things, then I can speak
26 of them. •And it seems clear to me that it is difficult to do the truth
before humankind."
27,28 The savior answered, saying, •"If things that are visible[i] unto you
(plur.) are obscure[j] to you, how can you hear about those that are not

---

138 Title a. In the manuscript, the title is
found after the text (at 145:17f).
  b. Or "hidden."
  c. Or perhaps "twin," the meaning of the
name "Thomas" (in Aramaic and Syriac).
  d. "my true companion": some scholars
conjecture that the original reading here was
"my fellow contender"; cf. the title of the
work.
  e. According to early Christian tradition

in Syria, Mesopotamia, and India, Jude
Thomas was Jesus' twin brother.
  f. In classic gnosticism the "entirety" is
the sum total of spiritual reality deriving from
the first principle, by way of the Barbēlō
aeon.
  g. Or "hidden from."
  h. Or "hidden."
  i. Or "obvious."
  j. Or "hidden."

30 visible? •If the deeds[k] of truth that are visible in the world are difficult for you (plur.) to do, how then will you do those of exalted majesty and
34 of the fullness, which are not visible? •How then will you (plur.) be
35 called laborers? •For this reason you are learners, and have not yet received the majesty of perfection."
36,37 But Thomas answered and said to the savior, •"Tell us about the things you are saying, for they are not obvious to us, [but, rather,] obscure."

The flesh will perish

39 The savior said, "[Each] body [. . .] domestic animals, when they are born [. . .] obvious,[l] in the manner of [. . .] this, too, the things above
43 [. . .] those which are obvious; •but it is from the root of them alone
1 that [they] are obvious. **139** •And it is their fruits that nourish them.
2 These visible bodies themselves eat of the creatures that resemble them.
4,4 So for this reason bodies are mutable. •But what is mutable will perish
5 and cease to be, •and from that moment on it has no hope of living.
6,6 For the body is a domestic animal. •Indeed, just as the bodies of domestic
8 animals perish, so too these modeled forms[a] will perish. •Does it (the body) not result from sexual intercourse like that of the domestic
9 animals? •If it, too, is from that (intercourse), how can it produce
11 anything different than they do? •For this reason, then, you (plur.) are children until you become mature[b]."

Difficulty of explaining the invisible

12,12 And Thomas answered, •"For this reason I declare to you, lord, that those who speak of things that are not visible[c] and are difficult to explain
16 resemble people who shoot their arrows at a target in the night. •Of course, they shoot their arrows as people do, for it is at the target that
17,18 they shoot; •yet it is not visible. •But when the daylight comes and hides the darkness, then the accomplishment of each will be shown forth.
20 And you, O lord our light, are giving enlightenment."

The light is here for only a short time

21 Jesus said, "Where the light dwells is in the light."[d]
22 Thomas spoke, saying, "Lord, why is the visible light, which gives light for the sake of humankind, radiant and (then) it goes out?"[e]
24,25 The savior said, "Blessed Thomas! •Now, the visible light has shone for your sakes—not so that you (plur.) might remain here, but so that
28 you might depart hence. •And when all the chosen (plur.) lay down
30 bestiality, then the light will withdraw up to its essence,[f] •and its essence will receive it unto itself, for it (the light) is a good assistant."

IV. THE WISE AND THE FOOL

The wise person flees from desire

31,32 Next, the savior continued, saying, •"Oh, the unsearchable love of
33 the light! •Oh, the bitterness of the fire blazing in the bodies of humankind,

k. Or "things."
l. Or "visible."

139 a. "modeled form": Jewish and Christian jargon for the human body, based on the fact that the creator modeled Adam out of earth.
b. Or "perfect."

c. Or "obvious."
d. I.e. the essential home of a luminous element is within the realm of light.
e. The temporary manifestation of the savior within the material realm is compared to the shining of the sun from dawn to dusk.
f. The realm of light.

35 and in their marrows—•blazing within them night and [•day]! Burning
36 people's limbs! •[Making] their hearts intoxicated! And making their
souls dumbfounded [. . . ! . . .] them among males and females [. . .]
40 and which moves them [. . .] secretly and publicly [. . .]. •For the males
[. . .] and the females [. . . it is (?)] said (?) that all who seek truth from
that female being who is truly wise[g] will construct for themselves wings
3 so as to fly, **140** •fleeing the desire that burns the spirits of humankind;
4,4 and will construct for themselves wings, •when they flee any visible[a]
spirit."
5   Thomas answered, saying, "Lord, it is precisely this that I am asking
you about, inasmuch as I have understood that it is you who benefit us
by what you say."
8,9   In turn, the savior answered and said, •"This is why we must speak
10,11 to you. •For this is the teaching of those who are perfect. •So if you   GTh 1
12 (plur.) want to become perfect you will keep these (sayings); •if not, the
13 term for you is ignorant:[b] •inasmuch as an intelligent person cannot live
14 with a fool. •For the intelligent person is perfect in every (kind of)
wisdom.

The fool is deceived by the visible realm

15,16   "But to the fool good and evil are exactly the same. •For the wise
person will be nourished by truth, and will be like a tree planted by   Ps 1:3
18 streams of water. •Indeed, there are some people who have wings
20 when they flee to the visible realm[c] that is far from truth: •for, that
which leads them, namely fire, will present to them a truthlike apparition.
22 [And] it will shine upon them with [corrupting][d] beauty, will take them
captive with dark sweetness, and will catch them up with fragrant
25,26 pleasure. •And it will make them blind with insatiable desire, •roast their
28 souls, and [be] like an irremovable stake piercing their hearts. •And like
a bit in the mouth it leads them toward its own intention.
30,31   "And it has fastened them with its chains. •And it has bound all their
limbs with the bitterness of the bondage of desire for this corruptible,
34 mutable, changeable visible realm. •By attraction they have been drawn
35 downward at all times. •As they are slain, they are drawn into (the realm
of) all the domestic animals of defilement."[e]
37   Thomas answered and said, "It is obvious—indeed, it has been said—
that [many . . .] those who are not acquainted [. . .] soul(s)."

The wise person relies upon truth

40,41 [Then the savior] answered, saying, •"[Blessed (?) is] the wise person   GTh 2
who has [sought truth]; once having found it, has relied[f] upon it forever;
and has not feared those who wish to cause a disturbance."

We should associate with our own kind

2,3 **141** •Thomas answered and said, •"Lord, is it best for us to rest among[a]
our own?"
4,4   The savior said, •"Indeed, it is useful and good for you (plur.).

---

g. Wisdom (Sophia), personified.

140 a. Here and in the following passage, "visible" means "belonging to the material realm."
     b. Lit. "your name is ignorance."
     c. Translation uncertain. The text appears to say, "Inasmuch as some people have

wings, they flee to the visible realm."
     d. Or "[perishable]."
     e. I.e. are drawn into utter materiality.
     f. Or "reposed."

141 a. "rest among": or "rely upon, repose within."

Fate of the others: the body

5,6 "For, the visible parts[b] of humankind[c] will perish, •since the instru-
7 ment[d] of their flesh is going to perish. •And when it is dispersed it will
9 come to reside among visible things, among things that are seen. •And
next, because of the love of the faith, which they formerly had, the fire
11 that can be seen torments them.[e] •They will be regathered to the visible
realm.

Fate of the others: the soul

12 "On the other hand, among parts not visible, those which possess the
faculty of sight[f] will, in the absence of prior love, become corrupted by
14 concern for the present life and by the burning of the fire. •There will
15 only be a little while until the visible[g] will perish: •then misshapen[h]
16 phantoms will come to exist, •and they will dwell forever in the midst
of the tombs over the corpses, in torment and corruption of soul."

We should ignore the fool

18 And Thomas answered and said, "What can we say in the presence
20,21 of these (people)? •What shall we say to blind persons? •Which teaching
shall we utter to wretched mortals, who say, 'We have come for [doing]
good, not for reviling,' or moreover will [say], 'If we had not been born
in the flesh we would not have become acquainted with the iniquitous'?"
25 The savior said, "Truly, do not consider those people to be human
27 beings; rather, count them [as] domestic animals—•for just as animals
devour one another, so also human beings of this kind devour one
another.

Punishment of the fool

29 "But they are excluded from the [kingdom], inasmuch as they love
30 the sweetness of fire, •are servants of death, and pursue deeds of
32,32 defilement. •They perfect the desire of their ancestors. •They will be
cast down into the abyss and will be punished by the fate belonging to
35 the bitterness of their evil nature. •Indeed, they will be flogged until
36 they rush (?) whither they know not. •And they [will recede] from their
38 limbs not patiently but [in] despair. •And they rejoice at [. . .] madness
39 and dumbfoundedness. •Being [. . . , they] rush [toward] dumbfoundedness without understanding [their madness, thinking] that they are
wise. [. . .] their body [. . .], with their hearts set upon their own selves
2 and their thoughts upon their actions. 142 •But it is flame that will
consume them."
2 And Thomas answered and said, "Lord, what will that which has
4 been cast down into them do?[a] •For I am very anxious about them,
5 since many oppose them."
5 The savior answered and said, "What do you yourself think?"

---

b. I.e. the body.

c. "humankind": presumably meaning others, the ignorant. In his next intervention (141:18f), Thomas refers to them as "these (people) . . . blind persons . . ." The text of the present passage may be corrupt or incomplete; more logical would be e.g. "the visible parts of foolish humankind."

d. Or "vessel": a cliché for the material body.

e. In hell.

f. The animate faculties or soul.

g. The body.

h. Or "formless."

142 a. Or "Lord, how will the person fare who has been cast down into them?"

7 Jude, who is called Thomas, said, "It is you, lord, who should speak and I, who should listen to you."

9 The savior answered, "Listen to what I shall tell you and believe in
11 the truth. •The sower and the sown will perish in their fire, by fire and
14 water, and will hide in the tombs of the darkness. •And after a long time they will be shown forth as the fruits of the evil trees, being severely pruned[b] and killed in mouths of domestic animals and human beings—through the resources of rain, wind, air, and the light shining above."

Punishment of those who scoff at us

18,20 And Thomas answered, "Truly, you have persuaded us, lord; •we
21 have thought with our hearts, and it is obviously thus. •And your
21 utterance is free of envy.[c] •Yet, unto the world the sayings that you say to us are laughable and ridiculous, inasmuch as they are not recognized.
24 How then can we go and proclaim them, inasmuch as we are [not] esteemed [in] the world?"

26 The savior answered and said, "Truly, I say unto you (plur.), whoever hears [your] words and turns away or ridicules (them) or grimaces at
29 them—•truly, I say to you, such a person will be delivered unto the
32 ruler above, who rules all the authorities as their king; •and the ruler will turn that person away,[d] casting the person downward from on high
35 into the abyss, to be shut up in a dark, narrow place •and so be unable to turn or move because of the great depth of Tartarus and the burdensome [bitterness] of Hades, which prevails [. . .] them against that person
39 [. . .]. •They will not release[e] [. . .] pursue you (plur.), [they will] hand [. . .] over [. . .] angel who controls Tartarus [. . .] flame(s), pursue them [. . .] fiery whips showering sparks in the face of the pursued. **143**
2,3 That person, if fleeing to the west, finds fire; •if turning south, finds it
4 there as well; •if turning north, is met again by the threat of seething
5 fire; •but will not find the way to the east so as to flee that way and be
6 saved: •for, that person did not discover it while incarnate so as to find it on the day of judgment."

V. EXHORTATION

Woe to those who live for the flesh

8 Next, the savior continued, saying, "Woe unto you, O godless people without hope, who are set upon things that will not come to pass.

10 "Woe unto you (plur.), who put your hope in the flesh and the prison
11 that will perish. •How long will you forget and suppose that the
13,14 incorruptibles will perish? •Your hope is set upon the world. •And your
15 god is the present life. •What you destroy is your own souls.

15 "Woe unto you (plur.) in the fire that burns within you, for it is insatiable.

17 "Woe unto you (plur.) because of the wheel turning in your thoughts.

18 "Woe unto you (plur.) who are gripped by the burning that is [in] you, for it will plainly consume your flesh, and will secretly break your souls and prepare you ⟨. . .⟩ in one another.

21,23 "Woe unto you who are captives, for you are bound in caves. •You
24 (plur.) laugh, rejoicing in mad laughter. •You do not think about your

---

b. Or "chastized."

c. Or "your utterance is generous."

d. The chief of the demonic heavenly rulers ("authorities") will impede the soul if it tries to progress through the heavens and

escape from the material realm. The idea was commonplace; cf., for example, EpG 26.13.2.

e. Or "forgive."

24 destruction. •You neither think about where you are, nor know that you
27 dwell in darkness and [death]. •Rather, you are intoxicated with fire,
27,28 and you are [full] of bitterness. •Your hearts are dumbfounded because
29 of the burning within you. •And the poison and the blows of your
30 enemies are pleasant unto you. •And the darkness has risen upon you
31 as the light. •For, you have delivered your freedom into servitude.
32 You have made your hearts into hearts of darkness, and have delivered
34 your thoughts into foolishness. •And you have filled your thoughts with
35 the smoke of the fire that is in you. •And your light [has become hidden]
by the cloud [of . . .], and you have [. . .] the garment[a] that you wear
38,39 [. . .]. •And you have been restrained [by] groundless hope. •In whom
40 [have you] believed? •Do you [not recognize that you] all [reside] in
1 those which [. . .] you as though [. . .]. **144** •You have baptized your
souls in the water of darkness, and have progressed in your own desires.
2 "Woe unto you (plur.) who dwell in error without gazing at the light
of the sun that judges the entirety and gazes upon the entirety; for it
6 will turn unto all deeds to make those that are hostile into slaves. •And
furthermore, do you not think about how the moon gazes down by night
and by day beholding the corpses of your slaughters?
8 "Woe unto you (plur.) who love the sexual intercourse that belongs
to femininity and its foul cohabitation.
10 "And woe unto you (plur.) who are gripped by the authorities of your
bodies; for they will afflict you.
12 "Woe unto you (plur.) who are gripped by the agencies of wicked
demons.
14,15 "Woe unto you (plur.) who beguile your limbs with fire. •Who will
cause dew of rest to descend upon you, so as to extinguish the many
17 fires from within you, along with your burning? •Who will give you the
sun to radiate upon you so as to dispel the darkness within you and hide
19 the darkness and the foul water? •Will the sun and the moon bestow
good fragrance upon you (plur.), along with air, spirit, earth, and water?

A parable of a grapevine and weeds

21 "Indeed, if the sun does not radiate upon bodies, they will rot and
23 perish, like a weed or a grass: •if the sun radiates upon such, it grows
25 strong and chokes the grapevine; •while if the grapevine grows strong,
shades the weeds [and] also all the underbrush sprouting beside it,
[spreads], and broadens out, it alone will inherit the land that it is
30 growing in, •and it will have dominated every place that it has shaded.
31,32 Next, then, if it increases it will dominate the whole plot of land. •And   Mt 13:24 ?
33 it will flourish for its lord and please him greatly, •for he would have
34 had to take great pains to pluck out the weeds: •but the grapevine alone
36 has removed them and choked them; •and they have died and become
like soil."

Woe to disbelievers

36 Then Jesus continued and said to them, "Woe unto [you (plur.)], for
38 you have not accepted the teaching. •And those who are [. . .] will
40 labor, proclaiming [. . .]. •And you are fleeing into [. . .] will fetch [them]
down [. . .] kill them daily, so that they might arise from death.

---

143 a. A Platonist cliché for the material
body.

Blessings to those who persevere

1 **145** "Blessed are you (plur.) who have already understood temptations and have fled from alien things.

3 "Blessed are you (plur.) who are mocked and are not esteemed, because of the love that your lord has for you. Mt 5:11 Lk 6:22

5 "Blessed are you (plur.) who weep and who are caused distress by 7 those who have no hope: •for you will be freed from every kind of bondage. Mt 5:4 Lk 6:21

Salvation from the flesh

8 "Be wakeful and pray with entreaties that you (plur.) might not dwell in the flesh but might leave the bondage of bitterness belonging to this 10,11 life. •And if you pray with entreaties you will find repose: •for you will 12 have left behind labor and mockery. •Indeed, if you leave the labors and passions of the body, you will receive repose from him who is good. 14 And you will reign with the king, being in harmony with him as he is in 15 harmony with you, •from now unto eternity of eternities. Amen!" a

Mt 26:41 Mk 14:38 Lk 22:46 ?

Mt 11:28

145 a. In the manuscript, the title of this work is written after the text (at 145:17f).

PART FIVE

OTHER
EARLY CURRENTS

PART FIVE

HISTORICAL INTRODUCTION

Throughout this book, the term "gnostic" has been limited to its original historical sense: the name of a particular sect that considered itself to be the children of Seth (Part One). By extension, this term also applies to the reformed branch of gnostics that we know as Valentinianism (Parts Two and Three). When historians reconstruct the education that led Valentinus to undertake his brilliant reformation of gnostic Christianity, they must take into account many religious forces other than the gnostics (see Table 1). One of these was the school of St. Thomas (Part Four), which first came to power in northern Mesopotamia. The scriptures written by this school were soon transmitted to the region of Egypt, where they (or something like them) must have illuminated Valentinus along the way toward an inner, self-centered mysticism such as classic gnostic spirituality had been unable to attain (see Map 4). The mysticism of the Thomas scripture was thus a major intellectual force in Valentinus's reformation of gnostic thought.

But in gnostic Alexandria, that swelling tidal pool of esoteric religions, philosophies, and sects, other strong currents also flowed in Valentinus's direction. They are harder to trace all the way to their destination, because we have no precise record of Valentinus's intellectual development, either by himself or by an observer. Two of these currents are so tantalizingly similar to Valentinianism that they can hardly be omitted from the appendix to a collection of gnostic scripture. The writings of *Basilides* are works of a skilled, independent, and outrageously original philosopher within Christianity, who must have been Valentinus's colleague in his early days of teaching. The *Hermetic Corpus* comes from a school of pagan theosophists in Egypt, ostensibly irrelevant to gnostic thought but in fact very close in tone and rhetoric to the writings of Valentinus and his school. Hermetic treatises were popular with theologians of the ancient church; it would therefore be no surprise if Valentinus had taken note of them. The two included here must date to the second or third century A.D., but there is no means to be more definite. If Valentinus did not read precisely these Hermetic treatises, he probably knew of others like them.

The Writings of Basilides

THE WRITINGS OF BASILIDES

HISTORICAL INTRODUCTION

The life and thought of Basilides

Basilides the Christian philosopher[1] was active in Alexandria A.D. ca. 132–35, and also before those years. He must have been a convincing teacher and a successful organizer, for the Christian movement that he founded was still active in Egypt in the fourth century A.D. One of the early leaders of the Basilidean school was Basilides' son Isidore. Nothing specific is known about Basilides' own life or career, and none of his works survives extensively. His followers in Alexandria later reported that he had claimed a kind of apostolic sanction for his teaching by maintaining that he had received lessons in Christian religion from a certain Glaucias, who—they said—had been an interpreter of St. Peter. If there is any truth in this claim, his contact with Glaucias may well have occurred in Alexandria; Fragment G (BasFrG), from Basilides' *Commentaries,* Book 23, appears to be a commentary on part of 1 Peter 4:12–19. A similar claim of apostolic sanction was being made about the same time by followers of Valentinus (see Part Two, "The Writings of Valentinus").

A brief and somewhat ambiguous idea of Basilides' philosophy is conveyed by the surviving fragments and reports of his teaching. He taught a *cosmogonic myth* whose general type, to judge from St. Irenaeus's account (IrBas), was similar to that of classic gnostic scripture. The fragments of Basilides' *ethical philosophy* deal with Christian problems and use traditional Christian language and scripture. The solutions he proposes partly depend on application of categories from the ethics of Stoic philosophy (see below). To elaborate a Christian *doctrine of salvation,* Basilides depends on Platonist or Pythagorean ideas; see Fragments E–H. An eclecticism made up of just such components continues to play an important role in Alexandrian Christian philosophy up to the end of the second century, when it can still be seen in the system of St. Clement of Alexandria.

Since Valentinus began his career as a teacher within the Christian circles of Alexandria at some time between A.D. 117 and 138, he almost surely must have learned about Basilides' teaching. St. Irenaeus asserts (IrV) that Valentinus "adapted the fundamental principles of the so-called gnostic school of thought to his own kind of system"; in other words, that Valentinian mythic speculation is based upon the classic gnostic myth. But it should be noted that Basilides' mythic philosophy is also close to both the gnostics and Valentinus, and so Basilides may somehow have exerted a major influence upon the development of Valentinus's system. Indeed, St. Irenaeus himself (*Against Heresies* 1.24.1) noted the similarity of Basilides' philosophy to the teaching of Satorninos, who may have been a gnostic (cf. IrSat).

---

[1] *Not* identical with Basilides the Preacher, who was active in Persia at roughly the same time and whose description of Persian dualist theology is quoted by Hegemonius in *Acta Archelaei* 67.4–12 Beeson. In contrast, the Basilides mentioned in the appendix to the *Acta* (68 appendix, 3) is Basilides the philosopher; this fact is of little significance, since the appendix is not by Hegemonius.

The Stoic background of Basilides' ethics

In his ethical system Basilides seems to have adapted Christian problems, terminology, and scripture to categories of Stoic ethics, though the evidence for Basilides' system is so scant that only scattered resemblances can be seen; these are noted in the discussion of the individual Fragments. In his overall philosophical system, Basilides is not a Stoic but an eclectic.

Stoicism, founded ca. 300 B.C. by Zeno of Citium, continued to flourish as a philosophical school and sect in the time of Basilides. Stoics held a strongly deterministic view of fate or providence, that is, the operation of divine reason minutely controlling all events in the universe. The operation of reason, they held, is the "will of god"; it is always good. Two consequences result from this in the Stoic view. First, anything that might seem like evil within the universe, such as human suffering, must really have a rational cause, and so ultimately be good. Suffering, for example, may actually have educational value for the soul. Furthermore, suffering may be seen as falling within a category of things that are ethically "indifferent" (*ta adiaphora*), that is, neither good nor bad in themselves but only good or bad in the way they are put to use (e.g. life and death, pleasure and pain, beauty and ugliness, strength and weakness).

Second, the virtuous life, for Stoics, is a life led in agreement with reason, in agreement with "nature"—whether one's own rational nature or the rational nature of the whole universe as a system. Because of the control of providence the individual soul does not generally possess free will. But it has the choice of either assenting willingly to its fate—in which case it will be happy; or chafing at the bit—in which case it will be unhappy (but still have exactly the same fate). Virtue, in Stoic analysis, is not a kind of action but rather a kind of state of the rational soul, in which one is in perfect rational agreement with nature and is unperturbed. The virtuous or wise person is one who has attained that state; such people are rare. Once the soul's state of virtue has been achieved, the person will as a result perform virtuous deeds, make virtuous choices, and be happy. Such a person is unaffected by emotions, desires, hatred, etc., and has no need of external laws or commandments in choosing the right course of action.

The literary evidence for Basilides' teaching

Of Basilides' own writings, only scattered fragments and reports now survive, and what survives does not form an entirely coherent picture. He is one of the two earliest known authors of commentaries on Christian (New Testament) scripture, cf. BasFrG. He also wrote poetry or songs (*ōdai*), and produced his own edition of a gospel; these are now lost.

Most trustworthy of all the reports about Basilides are those by St. Clement of Alexandria, who wrote in A.D. ca. 200, within Basilides' own city. St. Clement is not entirely hostile to Basilides, and in general his conciliatory attitude toward thinkers he disagrees with adds to his trustworthiness as a reporter. But one must take care to distinguish Clement's reports about Basilides from those concerning Basilides' successors. St. Clement preserves seven fragments and reports of Basilides; an eighth is recorded by the Christian philosopher Origen of Alexandria (A.D. ca. 185–ca. 254).

In addition, a very early report of Basilides' teachings, probably by St. Justin Martyr (writing in Rome A.D. ca. 150), is adapted by St. Irenaeus of Lyon for inclusion in his monumental refutation of heresies (Justin's original work is now lost). This report fits more or less coherently with the fragments found in Clement and Origen; it is translated below (IrBas).[2]

---

[2] A second, utterly different report of Basilides' teachings is found in St. Hippolytus of Rome, who wrote A.D. ca. 222–35. St. Hippolytus's report agrees less obviously with the fragments and reports given by St.

SELECT BIBLIOGRAPHY

Grant, R. "Place de Basilide dans la théologie chrétienne ancienne." In *Revue des études augustiniennes* 25 (1979): 201–16, including a reference to recent studies.

Harnack, A. *Geschichte der altchristlichen Literatur*. Teil I, *Die Überlieferung und der Bestand;* Halbband 1, Sektion II.1(8), *Basilides*. 2d ed. Leipzig: Hinrichs, 1958 (original edition, 1893).

Hilgenfeld, A. *Die Ketzergeschichte des Urchristentums urkundlich dargestellt*, 195–230. Leipzig: Fues, 1884.

Waszink, J. "Basilides." In *Reallexikon für Antike und Christentum*. Vol. 1 (1950), with a survey of older scholarship.

Clement of Alexandria, and has little parallel connection with Valentinus or other Christian theologians in the gnostic tradition. It is possibly by a later follower of Basilides. Acceptance of the Hippolytan report as a genuine account of Basilides' own teaching would necessarily exclude Justin's report found in Irenaeus. An English translation of St. Hippolytus's report is conveniently printed in *The Ante-Nicene Fathers* (ed. A. Roberts, J. Donaldson, A. C. Coxe; Grand Rapids, Mich.: William B. Eerdmans Publishing Co., 1971 [reprint]), vol. 5, 103–9.

BASILIDES' MYTH

ACCORDING TO
ST. IRENAEUS OF LYON
AGAINST HERESIES 1.24.3–7
(IrBas)

Contents and literary background

This incomplete summary by St. Irenaeus of Lyon, written in Greek about A.D. 180, may be based upon a lost work of St. Justin Martyr (A.D. ca. 150). Although Basilides was not a gnostic in the limited, classic sense of the term, in a sketchy way this summary parallels almost the full extent of the gnostic myth, including a description of the first principle (an "unengendered parent"); the first principle's expansion into a complex spiritual universe; creation of a material universe consisting of 365 heavens at the center of which is our world; creation of the nations of humanity and of the Jewish nation in particular; and the coming of Jesus Christ. Related problems are also mentioned, including the components of the human being, the authority of the Jewish bible, Christology, and ethics. A "true history" of the crucifixion is given, according to which Simon of Cyrene was crucified in place of Jesus, who for his part ascended directly to his parent without experiencing crucifixion and resurrection.

A very important feature shared with gnostic myth is Basilides' denigration of the god of Israel, and his report of that god's self-serving preference for the Jewish nation (1.24.4). Since no details are reported about the creation of the first human being, it is difficult to assess more precisely the relationship of Basilides' myth to that of the gnostics. Basilides agrees with the school of St. Thomas (especially GTh) in a Christology that entirely does without a crucifixion and resurrection of Jesus. His "true history" about Jesus and Simon of Cyrene merely serves to contradict non-Basilidean gospel accounts of Jesus' passion (as found e.g. in the gospel of Mark), and incidentally confirms that such accounts were known and used at Alexandria in Basilides' time. Basilides published his own edition of the gospel (now lost), which must have omitted mention of a crucifixion and resurrection of Jesus.

Only the first half of the summary reports Basilides' own teachings. The second half ("Esotericism of Basilides' Followers") refers to certain ones of Basilides' successors—unidentified—and should not necessarily be used in reconstructing Basilides' own original teaching.

Mythic characters

I. The Highest Beings[1]

The UNENGENDERED PARENT
INTELLECT, the parent's first-born; Christ, Jesus (Kaulakaua[2])
The VERBAL EXPRESSION (Word)
PRUDENCE
WISDOM (Sophia)
POWER

II. The Rulers

AUTHORITIES
RULERS   } in 365 sets, one set per heaven
ANGELS
among them being
    (ABRASAKS, chief of all the heavens[3])
    The GOD of the Jews, chief of the 365th heaven (under which we live)

III. Humankind

PEOPLE on earth, including
    JESUS, an earthly manifestation of INTELLECT
    SIMON OF CYRENE

Text

St. Irenaeus wrote in Greek, but the present passage is known only in an ancient Latin version of his work, attested by a number of medieval manuscripts. A summary in Greek of Irenaeus's original Greek text is given by the fifth-century Christian historian Theodoret of Cyrrhus (*Compendium,* 4), and another summary is included in a description of Basilides by the fourth-century church father St. Epiphanius of Salamis (*Against Heresies* 24.1.1—24.10.8); they shed light upon the Greek vocabulary, wording, and text of the lost original. The translation below is based on the critical edition of the Latin text by Rousseau and Doutreleau, altered by comparison with the Greek summaries: A. Rousseau and L. Doutreleau, eds., *Irénée de Lyon, Contres les hérésies: Livre I* [Book 1] (Sources chrétiennes, no. 264; Paris: Le Cerf, 1979), vol. 2, 324–33.

[1] Cf. BasFrA.
[2] According to Basilides' successors.
[3] According to Basilides' successors.

I. BASILIDES' TEACHINGS

Production of a quintet out of the parent

1.24.3 First,[a] by the unengendered parent there was engendered
    intellect.

And from it was engendered
    verbal expression (Word).

From the verbal expression,
    prudence.

From prudence,
    wisdom (Sophia) and
    power.   BasFrA

Production of the rulers and 365 heavens

And out of power together with wisdom (there were engendered)
    authorities;[b]
    rulers;[c]
    angels.

These (authorities, rulers, and angels) he calls "first" ones. And by
them the first heaven[d] was crafted.

By an act of emission on their part, other angels came into being, and
they made another heaven closely resembling the first one. Then, in
turn, by an act of emission on the part of these, there were produced
other angels, corresponding to those that were above them, and they
stamped a corresponding third heaven. And from the third level of
descendants (was produced) a fourth, and thereafter in like manner were
made—they say—still other rulers[e] and angels, (up to a total of) 365

1.24.3 a. In the preceding sentence, St. Irenaeus attributes the teaching reported here
to Basilides himself, not to his successors.
  b. The original reading of the text is uncertain here; possibly "powers" is correct.

c. Or "realms."
  d. The summary in St. Epiphanius instead
has "the highest, or first, heaven."
  e. Or "realms."

heavens. And it is because of them that the year has that quantity of days, corresponding to the number of heavens.

Our world and the god of Israel

1.24.4 Moreover, the angels who occupy the last heaven, the one that is visible to us,[a] crafted all the things that are within the world; and among themselves they divided up the earth and the nations that are upon it. BasFrB

Now, their chief[b] is the one who is known as the god of the Jews. And since the latter wanted to subject all nations to its own, the Jews, all the rest of the rulers resisted and opposed it; and so all the other nations, too, resisted (the Jewish) god's nation.

The savior and the crucifixion

Then the unengendered, unnameable parent saw their ruin,[c] and sent its first-born, the intellect, called Christ, to save people who believed in it, from the authority of the beings that had crafted the world. And unto the nations belonging to them it (intellect) appeared on earth as a man, and he performed deeds of power. Hence he did not suffer. Rather, a certain Simon of Cyrene was forced to bear his cross for him,[d] and it was he who was ignorantly and erroneously crucified, being transformed by the other, so that he was taken for Jesus; while Jesus, for his part, assumed the form of Simon and stood by, laughing at them. For because he was an incorporeal power and was the intellect of the unengendered parent, he was transformed however he willed. And thus he ascended to the one who had sent him, mocking them.[e] For he could not be held back and was invisible to all.

Confession of Jesus but not of Jesus crucified

Therefore people who know these things have been set free from the rulers that crafted the world. One should not acknowledge the man who was crucified,[f] but rather the one who came in the form of a man, was thought to have been crucified, was named Jesus, and was sent by the parent so that by this providential arrangement of events he might destroy the works of the craftsmen of the world. Thus, he says, anyone who confesses the man who was crucified[g] is still a slave and is still under the authority of the beings that created bodies; while anyone who denies him[h] both is freed from them and has acquaintance with the unengendered parent's providential arrangement of events. BasFrE BasFrC

Salvation only of soul

1.24.5 Salvation[a] belongs only to the soul; the body is by nature corruptible.

1.24.4 a. "who occupy . . . to us," following the text of Theodoret's summary; the Latin version of St. Irenaeus instead has "who keep the last heaven and who are visible to us."

b. Or "their ruler."

c. I.e. the ruin of all nations because of their struggles, instigated by the god of the Jews.

d. Cf. Mt 27:32.

e. "them": the rulers of the 365 heavens.

f. I.e. Simon of Cyrene.

g. I.e. Simon of Cyrene.

h. "who denies him": generally, whoever denies that the crucified man was the Christ; but perhaps also specifically, whoever when challenged by persecutors denies allegiance to the crucified Simon (cf. note 1.24.6b).

1.24.5 a. Or "survival."

Source of the law and the prophets

Moreover, he says, the prophets[b] came into being through the crafts-   BasFrC
men of the world, while the law[c] came specifically through their chief,
who led the people[d] out of the land of Egypt.

Meat sacrificed to idols

He[e] enjoined[f] (his followers) not to worry about meat sacrificed to
idols,[g] to consider that it is nothing, and to use it without concern.

"Indifferent" things

Furthermore, one should consider use of the remaining kinds[h] of
behavior and all kinds of pleasure as matters of indifference.[i]   BasFrD

II. ESOTERICISM OF BASILIDES' SUCCESSORS

Sorcery

And these people[j] make use of sorcery, spells, invocations, and all
the remaining kinds of superstitious practice.

Esoteric divine names

And they also concoct certain names, as it were, of angels. They
report that some reside in the first heaven, others in the second, and
thus they strain to relate in full the names, sources,[k] angels, and
authorities of the 365 heavens that they have fabricated. And thus, they
say, the name under which[l] the savior descended and ascended was
Kaulakaua.[m]

b. I.e. the prophetic books of the Old
Testament.

c. The law of Moses as found in the first
five books of the Old Testament.

d. "the people": in the terminology of
Jewish religion, a usual way to speak of the
Jewish nation.

e. I.e. Basilides.

f. "enjoined," following the text of Theodoret's summary; the Latin version of St.
Irenaeus here omits any verb.

g. When an animal had been sacrificially
offered to a pagan deity, certain cuts of the
carcass would be ritually burned on the altar,
others consumed in a sacred meal, and the
remainder sold commercially through public
butchers. Some Christians took great care to
avoid such meat; see, for example, 1 Co 8,
Rv 2:14 and 20.

h. "the remaining kinds": a non sequitur.
Obviously St. Irenaeus or his source has
lifted this sentence unfairly out of a context
in which were listed: (a) examples of virtuous
behavior; (b) examples of vicious behavior;
(c) examples of remaining kinds of behavior.
Such lists are typical in summaries of Stoic
ethical teaching.

i. "matters of indifference": Basilides here
uses ethical vocabulary from Stoic philosophy, which taught that certain possible goals,

such as riches or poverty, pleasure or pain,
were "matters of indifference." See above,
"The Stoic background of Basilides' ethics"
in the introduction to "The Writings of Basilides."

j. Basilides' successors.

k. Or "realms."

l. The original reading of the text is uncertain here.

m. Or "Kaulakau." St. Hippolytus, writing in Rome A.D. ca. 222–35, reports in
Against Heresies 5.8.4, that a gnostic-like
sect named the Naasenes spoke of Adamas,
the prototypical human being (cf. BJn 8:28f),
as "Kaulakau"; of earthly Adam as "Sau-
lasau"; and of the river that flows from earth
back to the spiritual realm as "Zeēsar."
These three esoteric names ultimately correspond to Hebrew phrases occurring in Is
28:10: "Therefore the word of the Lord will
be to them precept upon precept (*tsau la-
tsau*), precept upon precept, line upon line
(*kau la-lau*), line upon line, here a little (*zᵃⁱr
šam*), there a little." It is not known whether
Basilides' successors took over the esoteric
name Kaulakaua from the Naasenes; but if
so, they perhaps identified the savior (Christ)
with heavenly Adamas of classic gnostic
myth.

Those with acquaintance are invisible and cannot suffer

1.24.6 So whoever learns these things and becomes acquainted with all the angels and the causes of their existence—such a person becomes invisible and incomprehensible to all angels and authorities, just as Kaulakaua was. And just as the child[a] was unrecognized by all, so too, those people shall not be recognized by any; but rather, whereas they know all and pass through all, they themselves are invisible and unrecognized by all. For, they say,

> Recognize them all,
> But let none recognize you!

For this reason, such people are prepared to deny;[b] or, rather, they are not even susceptible to suffering on behalf of the name,[c] for they are like all.[d]

And few people can know these things—only one in a thousand, and two in ten thousand.[e]

Jewish and Christian identity

On the one hand, they say, they are no longer Jews; on the other hand, they have come to be no longer Christians.[f]

Secrecy

One is wholly forbidden to reveal their mysteries; rather, one must keep them secret in silence.

Relation to astrology

1.24.7 They locate the positions of the 365 heavens just as astrologers do; for they accept the astrologers' principles, adapting them to their own kind of system.[a]

And the ruler of them[b] is named Abrasaks, and that is why this (ruler) has the number 365 within it.[c]

1.24.6 a. I.e. the intellect or first born child of the unengendered parent.

b. To deny that they are Christians, if they are challenged in a time of anti-Christian persecution.

c. "suffer on behalf of the name": a Christian cliché for voluntary suffering or death in time of persecution so as not to deny one's membership in the Christian religion.

d. "all": cf. "all angels and authorities" mentioned above.

e. GTh 23.

f. "on the other hand . . . no longer Christians," following the text of St. Epiphanius's summary; the Latin version of St. Irenaeus here erroneously has "on the other hand, (they are) not yet Christians."

1.24.7 a. Lit. "to their own character of classroom."

b. I.e. the heavens.

c. In Greek, the numerals are expressed by letters of the alphabet (A = 1, B = 2, etc.), decimally. According to this system the numerical value of the letters A-B-R-A-S-A-X (with X = Greek *Ksi*) is $1 + 2 + 100 + 1 + 200 + 1 + 60 = 365$. The name Abrasaks, along with its variant Abraksas, was widely used in Greek magic and astrology.

BASILIDES

FRAGMENTS OF LOST WORKS

(BasFrA-H)

A. The Octet of Subsistent Entities (Hypostases)
B. The Uniqueness of the World
C. Election Naturally Entails Faith and Virtue
D. The State of Virtue (Frag. 4 Vö.)
E. The Elect Transcend the World
F. Reincarnation (Frag. 3 Vö.)
G. Human Suffering and the Goodness of Providence (*Commentaries*, 23) (Frag. 2 Vö.)
H. Forgivable Sins

Only three of the Fragments appear in Völker's standard collection (W. Völker, ed., *Quellen zur Geschichte der christlichen Gnosis* [Sammlung ausgewählter kirchen- und dogmengeschichtlicher Quellenschriften, new ser., no. 5; Tübingen: Mohr (Siebeck), 1932] 38–44). Völker's other fragments are not by Basilides himself and so have been excluded.

The Cosmological Fragments

Fragment A

THE OCTET OF SUBSISTENT ENTITIES (HYPOSTASES)

(BasFrA)

Contents and literary background

Fragment A is an important supplement to St. Irenaeus's summary of Basilides' theology. Here one learns that Basilides conceived of a primary octet of constituents within the godhead; Valentinus used the same structure (IrV 1.11.1). Six constituents are mentioned by St. Irenaeus (IrBas 1.24.3); the other two are listed here. To judge from this fragment, Basilides called the constituents "subsistent entities" (*hypostases*). Valentinus may have used this technical term, though in a different application (VFrB).

Nothing is known about the work to which this fragment refers. It was composed in Alexandria. The language of composition is Greek.

Text

The source of this fragment is the late-second-century Christian intellectual St. Clement (Titus Flavius Clemens) of Alexandria. The translation below is based on Stählin's text: O. Stählin, ed., *Clemens Alexandrinus,* vol. 2: *Stromata Buch I–VI* (3d ed.; Griechische christliche Schriftsteller, vol. 15; Leipzig: Hinrichs, 1960) 4.162.1 (vol. 2, p. 320,2–4 St.-Fr.).

Fragment A

BASILIDES believes that "justice" and its offspring "peace" substan-　IrBas 1.24.3
tially exist, being arranged inside an octet,[a] where they remain.

---

a. For the other six members of the octet
(parent, intellect, verbal expression, prudence, wisdom, power) cf. IrBas 1.24.3.

THE UNIQUENESS OF THE WORLD

(BasFrB)

Contents and literary structure

Although in Basilides' model of the universe (IrBas 1.24.3) there are 365 heavens, there is but a single world, suggesting that the heavens are concentrically arranged about the earth. The doctrine that the world is unique was a philosophical commonplace, accepted by Stoics as well as other schools of thought.

The assertion, made in this report, that Basilides denied the uniqueness of god can be understood in the light of his doctrine of a primal octet (BasFrA).

Nothing is known about the work from which this fragment comes. It was composed in Alexandria. The language of composition is Greek.

Text

The source of this fragment is the late-second-century Christian intellectual St. Clement (Titus Flavius Clemens) of Alexandria. The translation below is based on Stählin's text: *Stromata* (cf. BasFrA) 5.74.3 (vol. 2, p. 376,2–5 St.-Fr.).

Fragment B

MOSES[a] *did not permit altars and sacred precincts to be constructed in many places, but therefore set up one single temple of god, and he proclaimed that*

the world is only-begotten   IrBas 1.24.4

as Basilides says, and that god is unique, at which point Basilides no longer agrees.

See also *Fragment F*

"BASILIDES . . . has related the apostle's statement (Paul, in Ro 7:9) to *irrelevant, blasphemous tales (myths)* . . ."

a. The italicized words are by St. Clement.

The Ethical Fragments[1]

Fragment C

ELECTION NATURALLY ENTAILS FAITH AND VIRTUE

(BasFrC)

Contents and literary background

A soul's virtue—its "salvation"—is its "nature" or rational state, according to Stoic ethics. This fate is dictated by providence (god) and makes the virtuous person "elect" in traditional Christian terms. Virtue does not result from the exercise of a totally free will, for the soul possesses no such thing. Though a rational soul will assent to its fated destiny, this is *"not* the rational assent of a soul possessing free will." Basilides describes the soul's assent by the Christian term "faith," and its rational state by "kingdom" (cf. GTh 3). By means of its rational nature, the soul "understands god," in a kind of superior "intellection." Because of its perfectly rational state, the wise soul unhesitatingly proceeds to correct, good actions; it has no need of external "commandments."

Nothing is known about the work from which this fragment comes. It was composed in Alexandria. The language of composition is Greek.

Text

The source of this fragment is the late-second-century Christian intellectual St. Clement (Titus Flavius Clemens) of Alexandria. The translation below is based on Stählin's text, but with alterations: *Stromata* (cf. BasFrA) 5.3.2–3 (vol. 2, p. 327,19–28 St.-Fr.).

---

[1] Cf. above, "The Stoic background of Basilides' ethics" in the introduction to "The Writings of Basilides."

Fragment C

5.3.2 FOR BASILIDES thinks that it is by nature that a person IrBas 1.24.4
understands god, explaining that the choicest kind of intellection is faith
and "kingdom," and an acquisition[a] of good things, and that it is a thing
worthy of riches, near to the creator. And if so, then—he says—faith is
riches but not authority; it is nature and source;[b] it is an undefined
beauty of an unsurpassed creation; but it is *not* the rational assent of a
soul possessing free will.

5.3.3 Therefore the commandments of both the old and the new IrBas 1.24.5
covenants[c] are superfluous if one is "saved by nature," as Valentinus
has it, or if one is "by nature faithful and elect," as Basilides thinks.

5.3 a. The MSS here erroneously have "a
creation."

  b. Or "substance" or "a subsistent entity."

c. "commandments of both the old and
the new covenants": the law of god as given
to Israel in the Old Testament, and the ethical
teaching of Jesus given to his followers.

Fragment D

THE STATE OF VIRTUE

(BasFrD)

Contents and literary background

The "will of god" is providence (fate), which according to Stoic ethics controls all events in the universe. A virtuous person assents to all ("loves all") that is and that comes to pass. Such a person is motivated not by "desire" or its opposite, but only by agreement with reason or nature and by assent to god's will.

Nothing is known about the work from which this fragment comes. It was composed in Alexandria. The language of composition is Greek.

Text

The source of this fragment is the late-second-century Christian intellectual St. Clement (Titus Flavius Clements) of Alexandria. It counts as Frag. 4 in W. Völker's enumeration. The translation below is based on Stählin's text: *Stromata* (cf. BasFrA) 4.86.1 (vol. 2, p. 286,3–6 St.-Fr.).

Fragment D

AS[a] *BASILIDES himself says,* We assume that one part of the so-called   IrBas 1.24.5
"will" of god[b] is to love all—*and[c] they[d] reserve the word "all" to refer
to the entirety;*[e] a second, is to desire nothing; and a third, is to hate
nothing.

a. The italicized remark is by St. Clement.

b. I.e. what god "wants" human beings to do.

c. The italicized remark is by St. Clement.

d. I.e. the followers of Basilides; apparently St. Clement found Basilides' statement quoted and interpreted in a work by one of his followers.

e. "the entirety": the universe as a whole. In accordance with the strong Stoic element in Basilides' ethical theory, to "love all" must mean to live in complete harmony with the rational order of the universe, accepting all of one's fate without regret or protest; accordingly there is no place for desire or revulsion, since all is dictated by providence.

THE ELECT TRANSCEND
THE WORLD

(BasFrE)

Contents and literary background

Basilides accepts the Platonist and Pythagorean doctrine of reincarnation of souls (BasFrF) and believes that each soul retains its identity from one incarnation to the next, at least to the extent that in a subsequent life it will pay for its sins of a previous one (BasFrG). Souls therefore survive (IrBas 1.24.5) the series of bodies that they inhabit and "transcend" them, being permanent and therefore "alien" to the corruptible (IrBas 1.24.5) realm of bodies and matter.

Nothing is known about the work to which this fragment refers. It was composed in Alexandria. The language of composition is Greek.

Text

The source of this fragment is the late-second-century Christian intellectual St. Clement (Titus Flavius Clemens) of Alexandria. The translation below is based on Stählin's text: *Stromata* (cf. BasFrA) 4.165.3 (vol. 2, p. 321,27–30 St.-Fr.).

Fragment E

"I AM A stranger in the land," it says, "and a sojourner among you." _{Gn 23:4}
                                                                       Ps 39:12

And thence Basilides understood[a] (the passage) to say that the elect IrBas 1.24.4
are alien to the world, as if they were transcendent by nature.

---

a. Translation slightly uncertain.

REINCARNATION

(BasFrF)

Contents and literary background

This fragment, preserved by Origen, may come from Basilides' *Commentaries,* like Fragment G.

Of particular interest is Origen's objection to Basilides' "tales" or "myths" (Greek *mythoi*), and his statement that Basilides used them to explicate the passage from Rm 7:7. Since Origen himself accepted a doctrine of reincarnation, it cannot be reincarnation that he here calls "irrelevant and blasphemous." Rather, it must be Basilides' cosmogony that he finds so distasteful, presumably the same cosmogony that is summarized in IrBas. Origen's remark lets us know that the full statement of Basilides' cosmogonic myth included an account of the origin of souls and the cause and mechanism of their reincarnation.

The work from which this fragment comes was composed in Alexandria. The language of composition was Greek.

Text

The source of this fragment is the early-third-century Christian philosopher Origen of Alexandria, *Commentary on the Epistle to the Romans.* Origen wrote this commentary in Greek about A.D. 244, but the present passage of text survives only in a translation in Latin by Rufinus of Aquileia, made in the fourth century. It counts as Frag. 3 in W. Völker's enumeration. The translation below is based on Lommatzsch's text as reprinted by Migne: J. P. Migne, genl. ed., *Patrologiae Cursus Completus: Patrologia Graeca,* vol. 14 (Origenes, *Opera Omnia,* vol. 4), col. 1015.

Fragment F

PG 1015A   *"I[a] DIED," it says.[b] For (Paul means) sin now began to be imputed to me. But Basilides, missing the fact that this passage must be understood to refer to natural law, has related the apostle's statement to irrelevant, blasphemous tales; on the basis of this saying of the apostle's, he tries to defend[c] the doctrine of reincarnation, namely the idea that souls get transferred from one body to another. He says:*

1015B   Indeed, the apostle has said, "I was once alive apart from the law,"[a] at some time or other. That is (Paul means), before I came into this body, I lived in the kind of body that is not subject to the law: the body of a domestic animal or a bird.   Rm 7:9

1015A a. The italicized remark is by Origen.

b. Cf. Rm 7:7b–10: "If it had not been for the law, I should not have known sin. I should not have known what it is to covet if the law had not said, 'You shall not covet.' (8) But sin, finding opportunity in the commandment, wrought in me all kinds of covetousness. Apart from the law sin lies dead.

(9) I was once alive apart from the law, but when the commandment came, sin revived and *I died;* (10) the very commandment which promised life proved to be death to me" (Revised Standard Version).

c. The original reading of the text is uncertain here.

1015B a. Cf. note 1015A b.

HUMAN SUFFERING AND THE GOODNESS OF PROVIDENCE

Commentaries, Book 23
(BasFrG)

Contents and literary background

It has been suggested that this passage comes from an exegetical comment on part of 1 Peter 4:12–19: "Beloved, do not be surprised at the fiery ordeal which comes upon you to prove you, as though something strange were happening to you. (13) But rejoice insofar as you share Christ's sufferings, that you may also rejoice and be glad when his glory is revealed. (14) If you are reproached for the name of Christ, you are blessed, because the spirit of glory and of God rests upon you. (15) But let none of you suffer as a murderer, or a thief, or a wrongdoer, or a mischief-maker; (16) yet if one suffers as a Christian, let him not be ashamed, but under that name let him glorify God. (17) For the time has come for judgment to begin with the household of God; and if it begins with us, what will be the end of those who do not obey the gospel of God? (18) And 'If the righteous man is scarcely saved, where will the impious and sinner appear?' (Pr 11:31) (19) Therefore let those who suffer according to God's will do right and entrust their souls to a faithful creator" (Revised Standard Version).

In this famous fragment, Basilides defends the assumption that providence (fate, the will of god) is both all-powerful and good. From this assumption he is led to conclude that all human suffering must be just punishment for sinfulness, hence suffering is not an evil but simply an aspect of god's justice and goodness, and in the long run can even have educational value (4.82.1).

As special limit cases Basilides considers: (a) the suffering of the Christian martyrs; (b) the suffering of a newborn baby; (c) the suffering of the exceptional person who has never committed sinful acts; (d) the suffering of "certain (famous) figures" meaning, so St. Clement informs us, the suffering of Jesus (4.83.1).

For these special cases, two explanations are proposed by Basilides. First, someone who did not commit sin in the present life may nevertheless have sinned in a previous one; thus justice is exercised over the long range of history. Second, suffering may be requital for what Basilides vaguely terms "sinfulness" (Greek *to harmartētikon*)—not sinful deeds, but merely sinful desires, sinful inclinations, the capacity for sin, or just sheer humanness. The suffering of Jesus' soul, which presumably became incarnate only once, must have been a requital for its "sinfulness"—in this case not sinful acts, but simply Jesus' full humanity. Since Basilides assumes that Jesus was never crucified (IrBas 1.24.4), the "suffering" in question does not refer to his passion, but to less severe kinds of suffering.

The souls that were recently incarnate as Christian martyrs, Basilides holds, had attained an especially excellent (though still imperfect) state in their former life (4.83.2); and so by the kindness of providence, in this next cycle of reincarnation they were allowed to receive their suffering in an honorable way, a way that even appears to them to be painless (4.81.2).

Basilides was sometimes criticized by later Christian writers for disparaging the martyrs or opposing martyrdom, but nothing in this Fragment supports such an interpretation, given his philosophical assumptions.

The *Commentaries,* an exposition of 1 Peter and (presumably) other books, was written in Alexandria. The language of composition was Greek.

Text

The source of this fragment is the late-second-century Christian intellectual St. Clement (Titus Flavius Clemens) of Alexandria. It counts as Frag. 2 in W. Völker's enumeration. The translation below is based on Stählin's text but with alterations: *Stromata* (cf. BasFrA) 4.81.2—4.83.2 (vol. 2, pp. 284,5—285,6 St.-Fr.).

Fragment G

4.81.1 *BASILIDES,*[a] *in Book 23 of his "Commentaries," speaks of those who suffer punishment as martyrs, with the following words.*

4.81.2 I believe that all who experience[a] the so-called "tribulations" must have committed sins other than what they realize, and so have been brought to this good end.[b] Through the kindness of that which leads each one of them about,[c] they are actually accused of an extraneous set of charges so they might not have to suffer as confessed criminals convicted of crimes, nor be reviled as adulterers or murderers, but rather might suffer because they are disposed by nature[d] to be Christian. And this[e] encourages them to think that they are not suffering.

4.81.3 But even if a person should happen to suffer without having sinned at all—which is rare—still, that person's suffering is not caused by the plotting of some power. Rather, it is analogous to the suffering of a newborn baby, who seems not to have sinned.

4.82.1 *Then,*[a] *farther along, he adds:*

A newborn baby, then, has never sinned before; or more precisely, it has not actually committed any sins, but within itself it has the activity of sinning.[b] Whenever it experiences suffering, it receives benefit, profiting by many unpleasant experiences. Just so, if by chance a grown man has not sinned by deed and yet suffers, he suffered the suffering for the same reason as the newborn baby: he has within himself sinfulness,[c] and the only reason he has not sinned (in deed) is because he has not had the occasion to do so. Thus not sinning cannot be imputed to him.

4.82.2 Indeed, someone who intends to commit adultery is an adulterer even without succeeding in the act,[a] and someone who intends to commit murder

---

4.81.1 a. The italicized remark is by St. Clement.

4.81.2 a. Or "are subjected to."
  b. " 'tribulations' . . . good end": persecution at the hands of non-Christian governmental powers. In the traditional language of eschatological Christianity, "tribulations" are sufferings associated with the persecution of the righteous, which will usher in the messianic age, and thus are "good." In this passage, Basilides dissociates himself from the eschatological presuppositions of the term.
  c. Providence.
  d. Fated.
  e. I.e. their Christian nature.

4.82.1 a. The italicized remark is by St. Clement.
  b. I.e. the potential or inclination for sin.
  c. I.e. the potential or inclination for sin.

4.82.2 a. Mt 5:27f.

is a murderer even without being able to commit the act. Just so, if I see the aforementioned sinless person suffering despite having done no wrong, I must call that person evil by intent to sin. For I will say anything rather than call providence evil.

4.83.1 *Then,[a] farther along, he speaks of the lord outright as of a human being:*

Nevertheless, let us suppose that you[b] (sing.) leave aside all these matters[c] and set out to embarrass me by referring to certain (famous) figures,[d] saying perhaps, "And consequently so-and-so must have sinned, since he suffered!" If you permit, I shall say that he did not sin, but was like the newborn baby that suffers. But if you press the argument, I shall say that any human being that you can name is human; god is righteous. For no one is "pure of uncleanness," as someone once said.[e]

4.83.2 *Actually,[a] Basilides' presupposition is that the soul previously sinned in another life and undergoes its punishment in the present one. Excellent souls are punished honorably, by martyrdom; other kinds are purified by some other appropriate punishment.*

4.83.1 a. The italicized remark is by St. Clement.

b. Basilides here addresses the reader or dedicatee of his treatise, or an imaginary interlocutor.

c. Or "arguments."

d. According to the remark (italicized above) by St. Clement, who probably knew the whole treatise from which this extract comes, Basilides is here discussing Jesus' suffering.

e. The prophet Job (Jb 14:4).

4.83.2 a. In this italicized passage St. Clement summarizes Basilides' ethical teachings in relation to his doctrine of reincarnation.

FORGIVABLE SINS

(BasFrH)

Literary background and text

Nothing is known about the work from which this fragment comes. It was composed in Alexandria. The language of composition is Greek.

The source of this fragment is the late-second-century Christian intellectual St. Clement (Titus Flavius Clemens) of Alexandria. The translation below is based on Stählin's text: *Stromata* (cf. BasFrA) 4.153.3 (vol. 2, p. 316,14–15 St.-Fr.).

Fragment H

NOT ALL sins, says Basilides, are forgiven,[a] but only those committed involuntarily and out of ignorance.

---

a. In the preceding sentence St. Clement discussed the lord's forgiveness of human sins.

The Hermetic Corpus

TRACTATES 1 AND 7

THE HERMETIC CORPUS

TRACTATES 1 AND 7

HISTORICAL INTRODUCTION

Hermes Trismegistus and the "Hermetic Corpus"

In native Egyptian religion the divine patron of literature and learning was Thoth, god of the moon and calendar and scribe of the gods. In Greece, Thoth was identified with Hermes; Greeks living in Hellenistic and Roman Egypt called him Hermes *trismegistos,* "thrice great" Hermes, using one of Thoth's native Egyptian epithets.

Around the figure of Hermes Trismegistus grew up a substantial body of Greek pseudepigraphic literature composed in Egypt, some of it attributed to Hermes and some attributed to his alleged disciples—Asclepius (Imhotep), Agathodaimon (Chnoum), Ammon, Isis, Horus, Tat; while others of these "Hermetica"—that is, works associated with Hermes Trismegistus—now bear no attribution at all (cf. CH7 below).

Manetho of Sebennytos, a Hellenistic Egyptian historian who flourished in the third century B.C., reports[1] a tradition, possibly associated with the Hermetica, that there had been a chain of authority through which Thoth-Hermes had transmitted his teachings to a succession of family members. The original Egyptian text of these teachings was said to have been engraved on tablets and left in "the land of Seiris" before "the flood," then translated into Greek by a subsequent generation, and eventually kept in Egyptian temples. In a suggestive parallel, Hellenistic Jewish tradition made a similar assertion about tablets left in Seiris, but claimed that it was Seth and his descendants who had left and transmitted the record. Classic gnostic scripture continued in the line of this Hermetic-Jewish claim: 3Tb 118:10f, RAd 85:3f, cf. RR 92:10f (with note 92b), Zs 130:1f.

The earliest Hermetica concerned astrology and the powers of gemstones and plants; these pseudo-technical works go back at least to the early second century B.C. However, the pseudo-*philosophical* Hermetica (such as Poim and CH7, below)—which include both cosmological and moral treatises—come from a later period: the earliest such works may have been written at the end of the first century B.C., and those which now survive are usually held to be from the second and third centuries A.D. The "philosophical" Hermetica are of course not real philosophy, any more than astrology is the same as astronomy, for both kinds of Hermetica claim to be based not on observation and reason but on revelation. Typically, they stress the importance of personal acquaintance (*gnōsis*) with god. The "philosophical" content of these works, such as it is, shows contact with eclectic Middle Platonism of the times, and no contact with traditional Egyptian religion or Christianity. In a few rare cases allusions to Jewish scripture or style are found, notably in Poim; it is

---

[1] *Manetho,* ed. W. G. Waddell (see "Select Bibliography"), 208–11 (Appendix I). The attribution of this passage to Manetho is in doubt, and the wording of the text is uncertain.

distinctly possible that Platonizing Jewish philosophers like Philo of Alexandria had been read by some of the authors of the Hermetica. There are also similarities between Hermetic "philosophy" and classic gnostic scripture or Valentinian gnostic writings; these have sometimes led scholars to postulate gnostic influence upon the Hermetica—though indeed nothing prevents one from assuming exactly the contrary.

Anthologies of philosophical Hermetica were gathered and published both in Late Antiquity and in the later Byzantine period. One of these anthologies survives today; it is known as the "Hermetic Corpus," *Corpus Hermeticum,* or simply "Hermes Trismegistus." The individual tractates in this collection are usually thought to have been composed between A.D. 100–300, but the anthology itself was not collected until perhaps the eleventh century A.D., at which time a Byzantine editor subjected the tractates to stylistic revision. Two tractates of the Hermetic Corpus are translated below (Poim, CH7).

Nothing specific is known about the authors or original readers of the Hermetic Corpus. But it should be noted that the Hermetic tractates do not hold together in a unified mythic cycle or symbolic system, not even a loose one like that of classic gnostic scripture (see the introduction to Part One). Although they share in a limited range of style, tone, and diction, they do not use an exclusive in-group language (jargon), and they show no other obvious signs of group solidarity or sectarian separatism. The original social context of the Hermetic Corpus therefore remains a mystery.[2]

SELECT BIBLIOGRAPHY

Dodd, C. H. *The Bible and the Greeks.* London: Hodder & Stoughton, 1935. (Jewish influence on the Hermetica.)

Festugière, A. J. *La Révélation d'Hermès Trismégiste.* Études bibliques. Paris: J. Gabalda. Vol. 1, *L'Astrologie et les sciences occultes.* 3d ed. 1950. Vol. 2, *Le Dieu cosmique.* 2d ed. 1949. Vol. 3, *Les Doctrines de l'âme.* 1950. Vol. 4, *Le Dieu inconnu et la gnose.* 1954. (Literary and philosophical background.)

Mahé, J.-P. *Hermès en Haute-Egypte.* 2 vols. Bibliothèque copte de Nag Hammadi, Section "Textes," vols. 3 and 7. Québec: Presses de l'Université Laval, 1978, 1982. (Literary development of the philosophical Hermetica.)

Manetho of Sebynnutos. *Manetho with an English Translation,* by W. G. Waddell. Loeb Classical Library. Cambridge, Mass.: Harvard University Press, 1940.

Nock, A. D., and A. J. Festugière, eds. [*Hermès Trismégiste.*] *Corpus Hermeticum.* Vol. 1, *Traités I–XII.* 2d ed. Paris: Belles Lettres, 1960. Vol. 2, *Traités XII–XVIII, Asclépius.* 2d ed. Paris: Belles Lettres, 1960. Vol. 3, *Fragments extraits de Stobée I–XXII.* Paris: Belles Lettres, 1954. Vol. 4, *Fragments extraits de Stobée XXIII–XXIX, Fragments divers.* Paris: Belles Lettres, 1954. (Best edition, detailed commentary.)

Pearson, B. "Jewish Elements in *Corpus Hermeticum* I (*Poimandres*)." In *Studies in Gnosticism and Hellenistic Religions Presented to Gilles Quispel on the Occasion of His 65th Birthday,* edited by R. van den Broek and M. J. Vermaseren, 336–48. Études préliminaires aux religions orientales dans l'empire romain, vol. 91. Leiden: E. J. Brill, 1981.

Philonenko, M. "Une Utilisation du Shema dans le *Poimandres.*" In *Revue d'histoire et de philosophie religieuses* 59 (1979): 369–72.

Yates, F. *Giordano Bruno and the Hermetic Tradition.* Chicago: University of Chicago Press, 1964. (Modern influence of the Hermetic Corpus.)

---

[2] A curious historical riddle is propounded by the claim that Valentinians, according to a sixth-century A.D. witness in Constantinople, were known as "Hermetics" (Greek *Hermaioi*): Timothy of Constantinople, *On the Reception of Heretics,* in J. P. Migne, genl. ed., *Patrologiae Cursus Completus: Patrologia Graeca,* vol. 86, part 1 (Eusebius Alexandrinus et al., *Opera,* vol. 1 = Leontius Byzantinus, *Opera,* vol. 1), col. 17B.

POIMANDRĒS

(Poim)

Contents

Ever since the Italian Renaissance, *Poimandrēs* ("Pimander") has been one of the most famous works of Hermes Trismegistus. In large part it tells of the world's creation and the origins of humankind. By a terrible misunderstanding in chronology, Renaissance Humanists of the fifteenth century thought that Plato had based his own mythic account of creation (*Timaeus*) upon this very work. In actual fact, something like the opposite is true. The cosmogony of Poim is indebted both to Plato's *Timaeus* and to Genesis, and unmistakably evokes both texts. In all likelihood the author also knew the work of Alexandrian Jewish Platonists like Philo Judaeus, whose cosmological treatise *On the Creation of the World* had already set a striking precedent for the accommodation of Platonic and Mosaic cosmogony. Other Jewish connections can be traced in the author's rhetoric and use of liturgical phraseology (Poim 31).

Readers familiar with the classic gnostic myth of origins (as in BJn) or the Valentinian myth (IrPt) have often been struck by their similarities to Hermetic cosmogony. There are four main areas in which Poim resembles these gnostic parallels:

(*a*) The plot and the structure of the myth
(*b*) Dependence on Jewish cosmogony and presence of Jewish literary characteristics in the style
(*c*) A tone of piety and a stress upon the believer's duty to be an apostle of *gnōsis*
(*d*) A strict dualist distinction between the true self (intellect) on the one hand, and body and soul on the other

In the case of the first three points of resemblance (*a*) (*b*) (*c*), there are also significant differences that separate Poim from its gnostic parallels, leaving it mostly closer to Philo or Plato than to classic gnostic scripture.

(*a*) The craftsman in Poim is neither ignorant nor malicious, unlike Ialdabaōth in gnostic myth (see, for example, BJn).
(*b*) Poim uses, paraphrases, and adapts the Jewish cosmogony of Genesis, but does not set out to show that Genesis is wrong, as gnostic myth often does; Poim is not revisionistic, it does not try to tell a "true history."
(*c*) The duty of the gnostic teacher in Poim is not related to a predestined distinction between the saved and the not-to-be-saved; there is no clear delineation of a sect in view, no grand division of humankind, no church of Hermes.

Differences such as these suggest that gnostic scripture and Poim are not directly related, but rather, that they are products of a Platonizing milieu in which the cosmogonies of both Genesis and Plato's *Timaeus* were taken very seriously.

On the other hand, the fourth point (d) was held in common by secular Platonism, Hellenistic Jewish Platonism, gnostic and Valentinian scripture, the Hermetica, Christians at large, and many ordinary educated people; it is thus a cliché.

Of special interest is the language used to describe the seer's state of mystical suspension, found in the opening of the work.

The name "Poimandrēs" is found only in this work and is thus unique. Its etymology has not been discovered, and ancient readers probably would have been as baffled by the name as moderns are. "Poimandrēs" superficially resembles three words: Greek *poimēn* "shepherd"; the Greek stem *andr-* "man"; and Coptic *p-eime nte-* "the knowledge of."

Literary background

The author of Poim is unknown; some scholars suspect that Poim and CH7 are by the same author because of their similarity in style and content. The ancient title of Poim attributes the work to the Greco-Egyptian deity Hermes Trismegistus; it is thus an example of pseudepigraphy. Accordingly, Poim may have been composed in Egypt; however, nothing in its contents is distinctively Egyptian in character. The date of composition must be before the end of the third century A.D., since the concluding prayer is excerpted in a papyrus MS from Egypt copied at that time (see "Text," below). The language of composition is Greek.

Poim has a complex mixture of genres in which various traditional materials are subordinated to others:

I. Autobiography of a seer
   A. Angelic revelation and revelation dialogue
      1. Treatise on the soul
         a. Cosmogony and uranography
         b. Anthropogony (creation of human beings)
         c. Fate of the soul
      2. Sermon
      3. Prayer

Like Zs and Fr, Poim is presented as the spiritual autobiography of a religious seer, recounting Hermes' conversion to a career of philosophical preaching after an *angelic revelation* and *angelic revelation dialogue* (for this genre see the introduction to BJn). Although the revelation opens with a *cosmogony* and *uranography* (description of the structure of the universe), explaining creation and the composition of the heavens, it should also be compared to ancient *treatises on the soul* in which the origin of the soul and body, the relation of the two, and *the soul's ultimate fate* are discussed. The *sermon,* which follows the author's reported conversion, shares some traits with the animated classroom lecture or "diatribe" (for which see the introduction to TRs); its style is comparable to that of CH7, TRs, and the conclusion of Zs. In the final *prayer* the author directly addresses the highest god in a hymn of praise.

Not only the contents of Poim but also its overall structure are thus roughly parallel to BJn: an autobiographical frame story, in which the circumstances and contents of a vision are recorded; a dialogue between the revealer and the reporter; a concluding poem (in parallel strophes).

Mythic characters

I. The Realm of Absolute Power

GOD, the parent of the entirety
The divine INTELLECT or Poimandrēs, possibly identical with god
FORETHOUGHT, god's design

Countless POWERS or existents
Luminous, holy REASON (the Word), a child of god
The SECOND INTELLECT, the craftsman
Seven CONTROLLERS, its crafted products
The archetypal HUMAN BEING

II. Humankind

SEVEN original HUMAN BEINGS
Their POSTERITY, including the author

III. Lower Spiritual Beings

Guardian DEMONS of individual human beings
An AVENGING DEMON

Text

The original Greek text is attested by a number of medieval manuscripts now in European libraries, all of them late (fourteenth to sixteenth centuries). In addition an excerpt of Poim (the concluding hymn, 31–32) is found in a papyrus from Egypt, which was copied probably at the end of the third century A.D. and is now in the papyrus collection of the East Berlin Museum (P. Berol. 9794). The wording of the excerpt differs somewhat from the original, as a result of its adaptation as a self-contained prayer. The translation below is based upon Nock's critical edition: *Corpus Hermeticum,* vol. 1 (see "Select Bibliography," above), 7–19.

POIMANDRĒS
by
THRICE-GREATEST HERMES

I. THE APPEARANCE OF THE POIMANDRĒS

1 Once upon a time, when I was occupied with thought about the existents and my mental faculty was very much uplifted, and my corporeal perceptions had been held in check, like those of people weighed down by sleep after a surfeit of food or physical labor, some immensely great being of unlimited size seemed to call my name and say to me, "What is it you want to hear and behold? And to think of, learn about, and become acquainted with?"

2 I said, "But who are you?"
"I," it said, "am the Poimandrēs, the intellect of the realm of absolute power. I know what you want. And I am with you everywhere."

3 I said, "I want to learn about the existents, to think of their nature, and to become acquainted with god. Oh," said I, "how I want to hear!"
It then said to me, "Keep in mind all that you want to learn about, and I shall teach you."

II. THE REVELATION OF THE POIMANDRĒS

4 Having said this, it changed in appearance. Immediately, all became disclosed[a] to me in a moment, and I saw an indeterminate vision.

A. THE CREATION OF THE UNIVERSE
Division of light and darkness

All turned into calm and gracious light; and seeing it, I felt a burning desire. And after a little while there was a downward-tending darkness, Gn 1:2 which had come into being in one place; it was frightful and gloomy, and was coiled like a serpent, so far as I could make out.[b]

The four elements

Then the darkness changed into a kind of moist nature, which was unspeakably jumbled and gave off smoke, as from a fire. And it produced a kind of nonverbal mournful sound. Then a cry was inarticulately emitted from it,[c] so as to seem like a voice of ⟨. . .⟩. **5** And from the light ⟨. . .⟩.[a]
Holy reason[b] descended upon the natural order.[c] And unmixed fire leaped up out of the moist nature upward into the heights. It was buoyant and bright, and at the same time, active. And air, being light in weight, followed spirit,[d] as it ascended from earth and water to the fire, so that

---

4 a. Lit. "opened."
  b. "like . . . make out": or "so that I thought it was a serpent."
  c. "it": the "moist nature."

5 a. "⟨. . .⟩ . . . ⟨. . .⟩": in each of these places one or more words are inadvertently

omitted in the MSS.
  b. Or "verbal expression" or "Word."
  c. Or "nature," i.e. the moist nature.
  d. "spirit": i.e. the upper atmosphere (ether), virtually identical with fire according to one commonly accepted view of the elements of the universe.

it seemed to hang from it. And earth and water were left by themselves, mixed together so that ⟨earth⟩[e] could not be contemplated apart from water. And they were in motion because of the spiritual reason[f] that "moved" in obedience.[g]　　Gn 1:2

The relation of reason and intellect

6　The Poimandrēs said to me, "Have you thought about what this vision means?"

"I shall become acquainted with it," said I.

"That light," it said, "is myself, intellect, your god,[a] who is prior to the moist nature that appeared out of darkness. And the luminous reason that derives from intellect is a child of god."

"What does that mean?" I said.

"Look at it this way. The element within you that sees and hears is reason, belonging to the lord; and your intellect is its parent, i.e. god.[b] Indeed, they are not separate from one another, for their union constitutes life."

"Thank you," said I.

A vision of the prior source

"Then think about the light and (you will) find out about this matter."

7　After it said this, it looked me in the face for a long time, and I trembled because of its appearance. Then it looked up, and with my intellect I contemplated the light: it consisted of countless powers, and had become an unlimited world, and the fire had been encompassed by a very great power and had become static, being held fast. These are the things I myself saw mentally, thanks to the reason belonging to the Poimandrēs. **8**　And as I was in a state of terror, it then said to me, "With your intellect you have seen the archetypal intelligible form, the prior source of the infinite beginning." That is what the Poimandrēs said to me.

Source of the physical elements

"So," I said, "where have the elements of the natural order come from?"

Then it continued: "(They have come) from god's purpose,[a] which received reason, saw the beautiful world,[b] and imitated it, creating[c] a world with its own elements and its own generated products, namely souls.　　Gn 1:4

The craftsman (second intellect), the controllers, and destiny

9　"Now, the divine intellect, being androgynous since it existed as life and light, engendered rationally[a] a second intellect as craftsman; and the latter, being god of fire and spirit, crafted seven controllers,[b] which

e. This word is inadvertently omitted in the MSS.

f. "reason": or "verbal expression" or "Word."

g. I.e. in obedience to god's directive activity in the creation of the world as recorded in Gn 1:1f.

6 a. I.e. the divine principle present within you and every intellect-endowed person.

b. Or "your intellect is god the parent."

8 a. I.e. forethought (cf. 19), here treated as a distinct personage.

b. I.e. the archetypal world.

c. Translation uncertain.

9 a. Or "by means of reason (or verbal expression or the Word)."

b. I.e. the planets, the "governors" in astrology.

encompass the perceptible world in orbits. And their control is called destiny.

Heavenly bodies and irrational animals

10 "Immediately, the reason of god leaped up out of the downward-tending elements, toward the pure crafted product, the natural order, and it united with the intellect that is a craftsman,[a] for it was of the same substance. And thus the downward-tending elements of the natural order were left behind as mere irrational matter.

11 "And the intellect that is a craftsman,[a] together with reason, which encompasses the orbits and spins them with a rush, started its crafted products[b] rotating and let them rotate from indeterminate beginning to infinite end—for they begin where they leave off. And, just as the intellect[c] willed, their revolution brought forth living animals out of the downward-tending elements—irrational ones, for they had not retained reason. And air brought forth flying things, while water brought forth swimming things. Then land and water separated from one another, just Gn 1:7, Gn 1:9 as the intellect willed. And ⟨the earth⟩[d] produced out of itself the Gn 1:24 quadruped living animals ⟨and⟩[e] creeping things that it possessed, animals wild and tame.

B. THE CREATION OF HUMAN BEINGS

The archetypal human being

12 "Then the intellect that is parent of all,[a] by being life and light, engendered a human being equal to itself; and it (intellect) had a burning desire for it, since it was its own offspring. For it (the offspring) was very beautiful, having its parent's image. For truly, even god had a burning desire for its own form. And it handed over (to its offspring) all its own crafted products.

The archetypal human being descends into the natural order

13 "But when it (the human being) saw the craftsman's creation in the fire,[a] it too wanted to act as a craftsman; and permission was granted by the parent. Situating itself in the craftsman's sphere, with access to complete authority, it looked at the crafted products[b] of its sibling.[c] They had a burning desire for it,[d] and each one shared (with it) some of its own rank. Perceiving their essence and receiving a share of their nature, it[e] wanted to break through the spherical walls of their orbits and see the might of the being that was in charge of the fire.

14 "And having complete authority over the world of mortals and of irrational living animals, it broke through the container,[a] bent down through the composite framework,[b] and showed god's beautiful form to

---

10 a. I.e. the second intellect.

11 a. I.e. the second intellect.
  b. I.e. the seven "controllers."
  c. I.e. the second intellect.
  d. These words are inadvertently omitted in the MSS.
  e. This word is inadvertently omitted in the MSS.

12 a. I.e. the first intellect, the divine intellect or Poimandrēs.

13 a. "fire": the original reading of the text

is uncertain here.
  b. I.e. the seven controllers.
  c. I.e. the first craftsman.
  d. "it": i.e. the human being.
  e. I.e. the human being.

14 a. The idea that the heavenly spheres are contained by a heavenly "container" or envelope is found in Greek astrology of the second century A.D.
  b. "composite framework": or "armature" or "framework," i.e. the structure of nested heavenly spheres surrounding earth and contained by the "container."

the downward-tending natural order. Seeing that it (the human being) possessed unsatiating beauty, all the activity of the controllers, and the form of god, it (the natural order) smiled with burning desire, for it saw something like the intelligible form of the very beautiful appearance of the human being in the water, and its shadow on the ground. For its own part, it saw within it,[c] in the water, the form like unto itself, and it loved it and wanted to reside there. This purpose was achieved the instant that it was made, and it (the human being) occupied the irrational form. Then the natural order received its beloved and wholly twined around it; and they had intercourse. For they were lovers.[d]

The duality of humankind

15 "And for this reason, unlike all other living animals on earth human beings have a twofold character—on the one hand mortal because of their body, and on the other hand immortal because of the essential[a] human being. For although they are immortal and have authority over all, they experience mortality because they are subordinate to destiny. Thus although they are superior to the composite framework, they have become slaves of the composite framework. And although androgynous[b] and springing from an androgynous parent, and sleepless because of a sleepless ⟨. . .⟩ are overcome ⟨. . .⟩."[c]

The birth of seven earthly human beings

16 And thereafter, ⟨. . . said, ". . .⟩,[a] O intellect of mine. For on my part I have a burning desire for this subject."

So the Poimandrēs said, "It is precisely this that has been a hidden mystery down to the present day. Indeed, once the natural order had united with the human being in intercourse, it wrought a very amazing miracle. For since the human being possessed the nature of the composite framework of the seven,[b] which as I told you consisted of fire and spirit, the natural order did not delay,[c] but immediately engendered seven human beings corresponding to the natures of the seven controllers; they were androgynous and upright."

And thereafter, I said, "O Poimandrēs, I am really filled with desire and longing to hear this. Don't digress!" And the Poimandrēs said, "Please be quiet, I have not yet developed my first subject." "I shall be quiet," said I.

17 "So, in line with what I said, the origination of these seven beings was as follows. Now, ⟨earth⟩[a] was feminine and water was the impregnator. Maturity came from fire. And the natural order got spirit from upper atmosphere (ether). And it brought forth the bodies according to the ideal form of the human being.[b] Now, from being life and light, the [Gn 2:7] human being became soul and intellect: soul from life, and intellect from light. And all things of the perceptible world remained thus until the end of a cycle and the beginnings of species.

c. I.e. the human being saw within the natural order.

d. The Greek word for "natural order" is grammatically feminine; that for "human being" is grammatically masculine.

15 a. I.e. archetypal.

b. Cf. 16, where the seven controllers are said to be androgynous.

c. "⟨. . .⟩ . . . ⟨. . .⟩": in each of these places one or more words are inadvertently omitted in the MSS.

16 a. "⟨. . . said, ". . .⟩": through an inadvertence, the MSS omit a few words here. In the omitted passage, the narrator now begins to speak.

b. I.e. the seven controllers.

c. There was no gestation period.

17 a. This word is inadvertently omitted in the MSS.

b. I.e. the archetypal human being.

The distinction of male and female

18 "Finally, listen to the subject you are longing to hear about. When the cycle had been completed, by god's purpose the bonding of all (creatures) was undone. For all living animals, which had been androgynous, were parted in two at the same time as human beings. And one set became in turn males, and the other accordingly females. Then immediately god said, in a holy saying,[a] 'All you creatures and crafted products, be fruitful with fruitfulness and multiply with multiplication! Gn 1:22 And let those who have intellect recognize themselves as being immortal, and recognize that the cause of death is burning desire. Let them recognize all the existents.'

19 "After god had said this, forethought, acting through destiny and the composite framework, created sexual intercourse and established origination; and all things multiplied according to their kinds.   Gn 1:11 etc.

Two kinds of people

"Furthermore, people who have recognized themselves have reached the choicest good. But those who love the body, which derives from the error of burning desire, remain wandering aimlessly in the darkness, perceptibly experiencing the realm of death."

The origins of death and life

20 "Those who lack acquaintance—" said I, "what enormous sin can they be committing to merit being deprived of immortality?"

"Fellow, it seems that you have not reflected upon the things you have heard. Didn't I tell you to think?"

"I am thinking and remembering, and of course I am grateful."

"If you have thought about it, then tell me, why are those in death worthy of death?"

"Because the prior source of each individual body is the gloomy darkness,[a] out of which came the moist nature, out of which within the perceptible world has been put together the body, by which is fostered death."

21 "Fellow, you have thought correctly. But why is it that 'those who think about themselves advance into themselves,' as the saying[a] of god has it?"

"Because," said I, "it is of light and life that the parent of the entirety is composed, and the human being comes from that parent."

"You speak well! God the parent, from whom comes the human being, is light and life. Now, if you learn that god is of life and light, and that you are too, then you will advance again into life." That is what the Poimandrès said.

The role of intellect in the pious and the impious

"But also tell me, O intellect of mine," I said, "how it is that I shall advance into life. For god says,[b] 'Let those who have intellect recognize themselves.' **22** So do not all people have an intellect?"

"Hush! Be quiet! I myself, the intellect, am present with those who

---

18 a. The "holy saying" seems to be Gn   21 a. Or "oracle."
1:22, but here paraphrased.   b. In 18.

20 a. Described in 4.

are pious, good, pure, and merciful, and who are devout. My advent becomes a help, and immediately they find out about all things; they lovingly propitiate the parent; and they give thanks, blessing and affectionately lifting up praise to the parent as ordained. And before handing over the body to its proper death they loathe the perceptions, knowing about their activities. But, what is more, I, the intellect, personally prevent the offensive activities of the body from being accomplished. As the guardian of the gates, I shall prevent the entrance of evil and shameful activities, cutting off any thoughts about them.

23 "But I am distant from those who are foolish, evil, wicked, envious, greedy, murderers, and impious. I give them over to the avenging demon,[a] who with its point of fire attacks and perceptibly pricks them: it gets them all the more ready to do their lawless deeds, so that they may receive even worse retribution. And they never stop focusing their desire on boundless yearnings, insatiably struggling in the dark; and that is what tortures them, and it increases even more the fire directed against them."

C. THE FATE OF THE SOUL

The rising of the soul

24 "You have taught me everything very well, O intellect, just as I wanted. But tell me also ⟨about⟩[a] the process of rising."

In reply the Poimandrès said, "First of all, at the moment of the material body's unloosening, you hand over this body for alteration; the intelligible form that you possessed[b] disappears; and you hand over your habits of life, henceforth inactive, to your demon.[c] And the body's perceptions return to their sources,[d] becoming distinct components and together rising back into the agencies;[e] strong emotion and desire proceed (back) into irrational nature. **25** And thus one finally starts upward through the composite framework, handing over

> in the first heavenly sphere[a] the agencies of growth and
>   waning away;
> in the second, the means of evil action—a craft henceforth
>   inactive;
> in the third, the deception of desire—henceforth inactive;
> in the fourth, eminence associated with rule—henceforth free
>   from avarice;
> in the fifth, impious arrogance and the rashness of
>   recklessness;
> in the sixth, evil pretexts for wealth;
> in the seventh heavenly sphere, plotting falsehood.

Becoming divine

26 "And next, stripped of the composite framework's effects and having only one's very own power,[a] one comes to the nature[b] of the

---

23 a. A traditional Greek theme associated with postmortal judgment in the underworld.

24 a. This word is inadvertently omitted in the MSS.
  b. I.e. the shape visibly displayed by the material body.
  c. "demon": i.e. the personal guardian angel of the individual person.
  d. Lit. "wellsprings."
  e. "agencies" (or "powers"): as a technical term in astrology, the "agencies" are

controlling forces exerted upon our world by celestial bodies.

25 a. Lit. "the first belt (or zone)."

26 a. At this point the faculties and passions of the soul have already been handed back to their various sources in or below the seven heavenly spheres. Only the intellect or true self remains.
  b. Or possibly "natural order."

eighth heaven and along with the existents lifts up praise unto the parent. And those who are present rejoice together at one's advent. So having assimilated to those who are also there, one hears also certain powers that exist superior to the nature of the eighth heaven lifting up praise unto god with a kind of sweet voice. And next, in an orderly manner they ascend to the parent and personally hand themselves over to become powers, and by becoming powers they come to be within god. Such is the good end of those who possess acquaintance: to become god.

III. THE APOSTOLIC MISSION OF THE AUTHOR

"So why wait? Since you have received all (these teachings), will you not become a guide for those who are worthy, in order that the race of humanity might be saved by god through you?"
27 Once the Poimandrēs had said this, it mingled with the powers before my very eyes.[a]

And for my part, when I had given thanks and blessed the parent of the entirety, I was released by the Poimandrēs, now endowed with power and educated in the nature of the all and the supreme vision. I began to proclaim to people the beauty of devotion and acquaintance.

The author begins to preach

"O people, inhabitants of earth! You who have given yourselves up CH7 1 to drunkenness and sleep and to unacquaintance with god! Get sober! Stop carousing, all enchanted by irrational sleep."
28 And they, when they heard me, came to me with one accord. Then I said, "Why, O inhabitants of earth, have you given yourselves up to death even though you have the ability to share in immortality? Repent, O you who have traveled with error and participated in lack of acquaintance! Depart from the darksome light,[a] share in immortality, give up corruption!"
29 And some of them went on chattering and kept aloof, for they had given themselves up to the way of death. But others earnestly asked to be taught, casting themselves at my feet. For my part, I made them stand up, and I became the guide of the people, teaching the sayings[a] about how and in what way they would be saved. I sowed in them the sayings of wisdom, which got nourished by immortal water.[b] Then when it became evening and the sun's light began to totally fade, I bade the people give thanks to god. And when they had completed the act of thanksgiving all turned, one by one, to their own beds.
30 I, then, engraved the benefaction of the Poimandrēs upon my memory,[a] and being full of what I wanted I became very happy. Indeed, the sleep of the body became soberness of soul; the closing of the eyes became true sight;[b] my silence became pregnant with the good; and the created products that my discourse brought forth were good people. This happened to me because I received discourse[c] about the realm of absolute power from my intellect, that is, from the Poimandrēs. Divinely inspired with truth, I came to my mission. Therefore I am offering a blessing from all my soul and strength unto god the parent.

---

27 a. Or "had said this to me, it mingled with the powers."

28 a. I.e. daylight and the material world on which it shines.

29 a. Or "oracles" or "discourses."

b. Lit. "ambrosial water."

30 a. Lit. "upon myself."
b. Platonist clichés expressing the advantages of the soul's disengagement from the material body.
c. Or "reasoning."

IV. THE AUTHOR'S PRAYER OF BLESSING

31   Holy is the god and parent of the entirety.

Holy is the god whose purpose has been accomplished by its own powers.

Holy is the god that wills to be known, and is known, by its own.

Holy are you, who have rationally[a] composed the existents.

Holy are you, of whom all the natural order is naturally an image.

Holy are you, whose form the natural order has not been able to represent.

Holy are you, who are mightier than all power.

Holy are you, who are greater than all preeminence.

Holy are you, who are better than praises.

Accept the hallowed, rational sacrifices of a soul and a heart stretched out to you,

O you who are beyond verbal expression, ineffable, and invoked in silence.

32   I ask that I may not fall short of acquaintance with our essence:

Grant me your approval and strengthen me,

And with this grace I shall enlighten those of the people who lack acquaintance

And who are my siblings, your children.

Thus I believe, thus I bear witness.

I am advancing into life and light.

Blessed are you, O parent.

Your human being wishes to express hymns of sanctification in your company:

To whom you have handed down complete authority.

---

31 a. Or "by reason" or "by the Word."

THAT THE GREATEST HUMAN EVIL IS UNACQUAINTANCE WITH GOD

(CH7)

Contents

That the Greatest Human Evil Is Unacquaintance with God ("Corpus Hermeticum VII," "Hermetic Tractate 7") is a short philosophical sermon on the human body as a hindrance to acquaintance (*gnōsis*) with god. The work is noteworthy for its strong negativity: if lack of acquaintance is "the greatest human evil," then its immediate cause, the body, might be considered the most evil thing in the world. A similar attitude had long before gained philosophical respectability, for example in the dialogues of Plato (e.g. *Phaedo*, written ca. 384–370 B.C.); but in CH7 pessimism about the body is especially striking because it is not substantially balanced by any other kind of material.

Like TRs, CH7 opens with a polemic against ordinary learning, here called "reasoning unaccompanied by acquaintance (with god)." Thus the speaker explicitly presupposes some intellectual training on the part of the audience, and exhorts them to rise yet higher by attempting a suprasensual ("mental") ascent toward deity (cf. Zs, Fr); deity, for its part, is accessible to those who seek it (it "wills to be known"). Though ostensibly addressing a large and diverse audience, the speaker assumes that only some listeners will be able to respond ("those who can").

Because CH7 is so brief, there is room for only one image to be developed. In the imagery of the text, our material world is inundated by a "flood" of ignorance; the human intellect is a mariner borne away toward destruction by a strong current. The mariner must make for a countercurrent that will carry the boat into a safe harbor, to be met by a "leader" and personally conducted to a temple of acquaintance, filled with sober contemplatives whose mind is fixed on god. The text gives no hint of whether the "leader" to *gnōsis* is a teacher (as in Poim), a savior, or philosophy itself. The other images of the text are clichés, well known from popular philosophy, especially in the Platonizing tradition.

Literary background

The author of CH7 and its place of composition are uncertain. Some scholars suspect that CH7 and Poim are by the same author because of their similarity in style and content. Since it was transmitted as a part of the "Hermetic Corpus,"

CH7 may be from Egypt (the text does not actually mention Hermes-Thoth, the syncretized Egyptian god of wisdom). The date of composition must be before A.D. ca. 313, since the opening sentences are paraphrased by Eusebius of Caesarea in a work finished probably in that year (*Contra Hieroclem* 42). Eusebius calls the author of the sermon "the herald (or preacher) of truth." The language of composition is Greek.

The extreme brevity of CH7 and some of its stylistic features (questions and patronizing moral exhortation addressed to the audience, shift from second person plural to second person singular) are typical of the philosophical sermon or animated classroom lecture, a style sometimes called "diatribe," though its long sentences built up from balanced antitheses are closer to public artistic oratory. Useful comparative material can be found in TRs, the concluding sermon of Zs, and most immediately in the conclusion of Poim.

Text

The original Greek text is attested by a number of manuscripts now in European libraries, all of them late (fourteenth to sixteenth centuries); and by a short paraphrase in a fourth-century author (see above, "Literary background"). The translation below is based upon Nock's critical edition: *Corpus Hermeticum,* vol. 1 (see above, "Select Bibliography") 81–82.

THAT THE GREATEST HUMAN EVIL IS UNACQUAINTANCE[a] WITH GOD

1 People, where are you rushing, so intoxicated and having so fully drunk the strong wine of reasoning unaccompanied by acquaintance?[b] You cannot hold it; already you are about to throw it up. Stop, get sober! Look up with the eyes of the mind[c]—and if you cannot all do so, at least those of you who can! For the imperfection that comes from unacquaintance[d] is flooding the entire earth, corrupting the soul along with the body that encloses it and preventing it from putting in at the havens of safety.[e] **2** So do not be swept away by the main current! Rather, you who can must avail yourselves of a countercurrent, take to the haven of safety,[a] put in there, and look for a leader to show you the way to the doors[b] of acquaintance, where there is bright light, pure from darkness; where no one is intoxicated, but all are sober, fixing their eyes on that being who wills to be seen—but mentally,[c] for that being cannot be heard or told of or seen by eyes, only by intellect and mind.

But first, you (sing.)[d] must tear off the tunic[e] that you are wearing, the robe of unacquaintance,[f] the foundation of imperfection, the bond of corruption, the dark enclosure, the living death, the perceptible corpse, the portable grave, the resident brigand, who acts in hatred through what he loves and with his instruments of hatred causes corruption.[g] **3** Such is the tunic, the enemy, that you have put on, which strangles you and pulls you down toward itself, lest by looking up and beholding the beauty of truth and the good that lies in it you should come to hate its[a] imperfection, once you know about its plot that it has plotted against you in rendering insensible the reputed[b] sensory organs by stopping them up with a mass of matter and filling them with loathsome pleasure: to keep you from hearing what you ought to hear, to keep you from seeing what you ought to see.

Title 1 a. Or "Lack of Acquaintance."

b. Lit. "drunk the unmixed reasoning of unacquaintance." The ancient Greeks mixed water with their wine; "unmixed" wine was unusually strong and intoxicating. Reasoning unaccompanied by acquaintance with god is here compared to strong wine.

c. Lit. "heart."

d. Or "lack of acquaintance."

e. Or "salvation."

2 a. Or "salvation."

b. Or "doorway."

c. Lit. "with their heart."

d. From here on only the singular form of "you" is used in the Greek original.

e. I.e. the body, which the soul "wears" like a "tunic." This and the following metaphors for the body were Platonist clichés.

f. Or "lack of acquaintance."

g. Translation uncertain.

3 a. I.e. the enemy's, the body's.

b. The original reading of the text is uncertain here.

GENERAL BIBLIOGRAPHY

(a) Bibliographical essay on the older literature

Cerfaux, L. "Gnose préchrétienne et biblique." In *Dictionnaire de la bible. Supplément*. 1938.

(b) Complete classified bibliography since 1948

Scholer, D. *Nag Hammadi Bibliography, 1948–69*. Leiden: E. J. Brill, 1971. Supplemented annually in the journal *Novum Testamentum,* beginning with vol. 13 (1971). Covers "Gnosticism"; "Gnostic Texts (Pre-Nag Hammadi), Schools, and Leaders"; "New Testament and Gnosticism"; and the "Coptic Gnostic Library."

(c) General treatments in book form (but not including collected essays, conference proceedings, or textual anthologies)

Amélineau, E. *Essai sur le gnosticisme égyptien, ses développements et son origine égyptienne*. Paris: E. Leroux, 1887.

Anrich, G. *Das antike Mysterienwesen in seinem Einfluss auf das Christentum*. Göttingen: Vandenhoeck & Ruprecht, 1894.

Anz, W. *Zur Frage nach dem Ursprung des Gnostizismus: Ein religionsgeschichtlicher Versuch*. Leipzig: Hinrichs, 1897.

Bauer, W. *Orthodoxy and Heresy in Earliest Christianity*. 2d ed. Philadelphia: Fortress Press, 1971.

Baur, F. C. *Die christliche Gnosis; oder, Die christliche Religions-Philosophie in ihrer geschichtlichen Entwicklung*. Tübingen: Osiander, 1835.

Bloom, H. *The Flight to Lucifer: A Gnostic Fantasy*. New York: Farrar, Straus, Giroux, 1979.

Bousset, W. *Hauptprobleme der Gnosis*. Göttingen: Vandenhoeck & Ruprecht, 1907.

Brox, N. *Offenbahrung, Gnosis und gnostischer Mythos bei Irenaeus von Lyon*. Salzburg: Anton Pustet, 1966.

Buonaiuti, E. *Lo gnosticismo*. Rome: Francesco Ferrari, 1907.

Burkitt, F. C. *Church and Gnosis: A Study of Christian Thought and Speculation in the Second Century*. Cambridge: Cambridge University Press, 1932.

Colpe, C. *Die religionsgeschichtliche Schule: Darstellung und Kritik ihres*

Bildes vom gnostischen Erlösermythus. Göttingen: Vandenhoeck & Ruprecht, 1961.

Doresse, J. *The Secret Books of the Egyptian Gnostics: An Introduction to the Gnostic Coptic Manuscripts Discovered at Chenoboskion*. New York: Viking Press, 1960.

Elsas, C. *Neuplatonische und gnostische Weltablehnung in der Schule Plotins*. Berlin: Walter de Gruyter, 1975.

Faye, E. de. *Gnostiques et gnosticisme: étude critique des documents du gnosticisme chrétien aux II*^e *et III*^e *siècles*. 2d ed. Paris: Paul Geuthner, 1925.

Festugière, A. J. *La Révélation d'Hermès Trismégiste*. Paris: J. Gabalda. Vol. 1, *L'Astrologie et les sciences occultes*. 3d ed. 1950. Vol. 2, *Le Dieu cosmique*. 2d ed. 1949. Vol. 3, *Les Doctrines de l'âme*. 1950. Vol. 4, *Le Dieu inconnu et la gnose*. 1954.

Friedländer, M. *Der vorchristliche jüdische Gnosticismus*. Göttingen: Vandenhoeck & Ruprecht, 1898.

García Bazán, F. *Gnosis: La esencia del dualismo gnóstico*. 2d ed. Buenos Aires: Ediciones Universitarias Argentinas, 1978.

Graetz, H. *Gnosticismus und Judenthum*. Krotoschin: B. L. Monasch & Sohn, 1846.

Grant, R. M. *Gnosticism and Early Christianity*. 2d ed. New York: Harper & Row, 1966.

Helmbold, A. K. *The Nag Hammadi Gnostic Texts and the Bible*. Grand Rapids, Mich.: Baker Book House, 1967.

Hilgenfeld, A. *Die Ketzergeschichte des Urchristentums urkundlich dargestellt*. Leipzig: Fues, 1884.

Horn, J. *Über die biblische Gnosis*. Hannover: Gebrüder Hahn, 1805.

Jonas, H. *Gnosis und spätantiker Geist*. Göttingen: Vandenhoeck & Ruprecht. Vol. 1, *Die mythologische Gnosis mit einer Einleitung zur Geschichte und Methodologie der Forschung*. 3d ed. 1964. Vol. 2/1, *Von der Mythologie zur mystischen Philosophie*. 2d ed. 1966.

—————. *The Gnostic Religion*. 3d ed. Boston: Beacon Press, 1970.

Koschorke, K. *Die Polemik der Gnostiker gegen das kirchliche Christentum*. Leiden: E. J. Brill, 1978.

Lacarrière, J. *The Gnostics*. New York: E. P. Dutton, 1977.

Langbrandtner, W. *Weltferner Gott oder Gott der Liebe: Der Ketzerstreit in der johanneischen Kirche, Eine exegetische-religionsgeschichtliche Untersuchung mit Berücksichtigung der koptisch-gnostischen Texte aus Nag Hammadi*. Frankfurt: Lang, 1977.

Leisegang, H. *Die Gnosis*. 4th ed. Stuttgart: Alfred Kröner, 1955.

Lewald, E. *Commentatio ad historiam religionum veterum illustrandam pertinens de doctrina gnostica*. Heidelberg: Mohr & Winter, 1818.

Liechtenhahn, R. *Die Offenbahrung im Gnosticismus*. Göttingen: Vandenhoeck & Ruprecht, 1901.

McGuire, A. "Valentinus and the *Gnōstikē Hairesis:* An Investigation of Valentinus's Position in the History of Gnosticism." Ph.D. diss., Yale University, 1983.

Mahé, J.-P. *Hermès en Haute-Egypte.* 2 vols. Québec: Les Presses de l'Université Laval, 1978, 1982.

Matter, J. *Histoire critique du gnosticisme, et de son influence sur les sectes religieuses et philosophiques des six premiers siècles de l'ère chrétienne.* 3 vols. Strasbourg: Levrault, 1843–44.

Möller, W. *Geschichte der Kosmologie in der griechischen Kirche bis auf Origenes, mit Specialuntersuchungen über die gnostischen Systeme.* Halle: Fricke, 1860.

Neander, A. *Genetische Entwicklung der vornehmsten gnostischen Systeme.* Berlin: Dümmler, 1818.

Pagels, E. *The Gnostic Gospels.* New York: Random House, 1979.

Perkins, P. *The Gnostic Dialogue: The Early Church and the Crisis of Gnosticism.* New York: Paulist Press, 1980.

Pétrement, S. *Le Dieu séparé: les origines du gnosticisme.* Paris: Le Cerf, 1984.

——————. *Le Dualisme chez Platon, les gnostiques et les manichéens.* Paris: Presses Universitaires de France, 1947.

Quispel, G. *Gnosis als Weltreligion.* Zürich: Origo, 1951.

Reitzenstein, R. *Hellenistic Mystery-Religions: Their Basic Ideas and Significance.* Pittsburgh: Pickwick Press, 1978.

——————. *Poimandres: Studien zur griechisch-ägyptischen und früh-christlichen Literatur.* Leipzig: B. G. Teubner, 1904.

Rudolph, K. *Gnosis: The Nature and History of Gnosticism.* San Francisco: Harper & Row, 1977.

Sagnard, F. *La Gnose valentinienne et le témoignage de saint Irénée.* Paris: J. Vrin, 1947.

Schenke, H.-M. *Der Gott "Mensch": Ein religionsgeschichtlicher Beitrag zur Diskussion über die paulinische Anschauung von der Kirche als Leib Christi.* Göttingen: Vandenhoeck & Ruprecht, 1962.

Schmithals, W. *Gnosticism in Corinth: An Investigation of the Letters to the Corinthians.* Nashville, Tenn.: Abingdon Press, 1971.

——————. *Paul and the Gnostics.* Nashville, Tenn.: Abingdon Press, 1972.

Segal, A. *Two Powers in Heaven: Early Rabbinic Reports About Christianity and Gnosticism.* Leiden: E. J. Brill, 1977.

Sevrin, J.-M. *Le Dossier baptismal séthien: études sur la sacramentaire gnostique.* Bibliothèque copte de Nag Hammadi, Section "Études," no. 2. Québec: Les Presses de l'Université Laval, 1986.

Steffes, J. P. *Das Wesen des Gnosticizmus und sein Verhältnis zum katholischen Dogma: Eine dogmengeschichtliche Untersuchung.* Paderborn: Ferdinand Schöningh, 1922.

Stroumsa, G. *Another Seed: Studies in Gnostic Mythology.* Nag Hammadi Studies, vol. 24. Leiden: E. J. Brill, 1984.

Tardieu, M., and J.-D. Dubois. *Introduction à la littérature gnostique.* Vol. 1. Initiations au christianisme ancien. Paris: Le Cerf, 1986.

Tittman, C.-C. *Tractatus de Vestigiis Gnosticorum in Novo Testamento Frustra Quaesitis.* Leipzig: Breitkopf, 1773.

Vallée, G. *A Study in Anti-Gnostic Polemics: Irenaeus, Hippolytus, and Epiphanius*. Waterloo, Ontario, Canada: Wilfrid Laurier University Press, 1981.

Widengren, G. *The Gnostic Attitude*. Santa Barbara, Calif.: University of California, Institute of Religious Studies, 1973.

Williams, M. *The Immovable Race, A Gnostic Designation and the Theme of Stability in Late Antiquity*. Nag Hammadi Studies, vol. 29. Leiden: E. J. Brill, 1985.

Wilson, R. McL. *The Gnostic Problem: A Study of the Relations Between Hellenistic Judaism and the Gnostic Heresy*. 2d ed. London: A. R. Mowbray, 1964.

—————. *Gnosis and the New Testament*. Philadelphia: Fortress Press, 1968.

Yamauchi, E. M. *Pre-Christian Gnosticism: A Survey of the Proposed Evidences*. London: Tyndale Press, 1973.

INDEX OF
NAMES AND SUBJECTS

The page references listed in the Index are not exhaustive, but often the reader is taken to a page where additional cross-references will be found.

INDEX OF
SCRIPTURE REFERENCES

SCRIPTURES
AND
TESTIMONIA

The Revelation of Adam
Satorninos (According to St. Irenaeus)
The Secret Book According to John
The Sethians (According to St. Epiphanius)
The Three Tablets of Seth
The Thunder—Perfect Intellect
Treatise on Resurrection (Epistle to Rheginus)
Valentinus: Fragments of Lost Works
    The Divine Word Present in the Infant
    On the Three Natures
    Adam's Faculty of Speech
    Adam's Name
    Jesus' Digestive System (Epistle to Agathopous)
    Annihilation of the Realm of Death
    The Source of Common Wisdom (On Friends)
    The Vision of God (Epistle On Attachments)
Valentinus, The Gospel of Truth
Valentinus, Summer Harvest
Valentinus's Myth (According to St. Irenaeus)
Zōstrianos (Excerpts)